American Architectural History

The study of American architectural and urban history has undergone substantial growth and change during the past two decades. *American Architectural History: A Contemporary Reader* provides a critical introduction to this development. It features twenty-four illustrated selections drawn from the past twenty years of publishing in the field, arranged chronologically from colonial to contemporary subjects. The editor provides a comprehensive introductory essay and sets the book's major themes in context.

The chapters examine American architecture through a diverse range of sites, objects, issues, events, and scholarly methods. They are organized into six broad themes pertinent to particular eras. The first section considers European-American and Native-American approaches to shaping architectural and community space before the American Revolution. The second looks at some of the builders and building forms of a nation newly independent and then undergoing processes of cultural consolidation. The third examines architecture and urbanism as related to the changing social and economic circumstances accompanying America's rapid post-Civil War expansion. In the fourth section, architecture is studied in relation to the country's rising power and international contact in the late nineteenth and early twentieth centuries. The essays in the fifth section discuss the dissemination of, and eventual movement away from, modernism in the post-World War II period. In the sixth and final section, recent concerns about urban form and public space are represented.

The readings chosen for this volume represent significant recent scholarship on key topics in American architectural history and urban history; each is concise, lively, accessible, and engaging. In terms of content and scope, there is no collection, in or out of print, directly comparable to this one.

Keith L. Eggener teaches American art and architectural history at the University of Missouri-Columbia. He is the author of *Luis Barragán's Gardens of El Pedregal* (Princeton Architectural Press) and is associate editor of the *Buildings of the United States* series (Oxford University Press/Society of Architectural Historians).

American Architectural History

A Contemporary Reader

Edited by

Keith L. Eggener

Routledge
Taylor & Francis Group

LONDON AND NEW YORK

Publication of this book has been supported by a grant from the Graham
Foundation for Advanced Studies in Fine Arts.

First published 2004
by Routledge
29 West 35th Street, New York, NY 10001

Simultaneously published in the UK
by Routledge
11 New Fetter Lane, London EC4P 4EE

Routledge is an imprint of the Taylor & Francis Group

© 2004 Keith L. Eggener for selection and editorial matter

Typeset in Sabon and Akzidenz Grotesk by
Florence Production Ltd, Stoodleigh, Devon
Printed and bound in Great Britain by
TJ International Ltd, Padstow, Cornwall

Library of Congress Cataloging in Publication Data
American architectural history: a contemporary reader/edited by
Keith L. Eggener.
    p. cm.
Includes bibliographical references and index.
1. Architecture–United States–History.   I. Eggener, Keith.
NA705.A483 2004
720′.973–dc22   2003020543

British Library Cataloguing in Publication Data
A catalogue record for this book is available from the British Library

ISBN 0–415–30694–9 (hbk)
ISBN 0–415–30695–7 (pbk)

For Irina Hans
(1976–2002)

"Some shape of beauty moves away the pall
From our dark spirits."
                    John Keats, "Endymion"

Contents

Acknowledgments

For responding to my inquiries about bibliography and pedagogy, or for other assistance, information, advice, encouragement, or support, I thank the following individuals: Anthony Alofsin, Barry Bergdoll, Carla Yanni, Anna Andrzejewski, Richard Longstreth, Marc Treib, Neil Levine, Dell Upton, Carma Gorman, Carol Krinsky, David Cateforis, Eric Mumford, Hannah Johnson, Kristin Schwain, Howard Marshall, James Housefield, Joan Draper, Julie Nicoletta, Katherine Solomonson, Kim Hoagland, Lauren Soth, Marianne Doezema, Mark Gelernter, Mary McLeod, Meredith Clausen, Michael Rabens, Osmund Overby, Paul Turner, Ted Wolner, Timothy Parker, and Tod Marder. For taking on this project and helping it assume its finished form, my appreciation goes to Caroline Mallinder, Michelle Green, and the Routledge staff.

Financial support for this project was generously provided by the Graham Foundation and the Research Council of the University of Missouri-Columbia. Administrative, production, and research assistance came from Daffany Hood, Beth Kopine, Rebecca Roe, and Irina Hans. Without their participation this book would not have been possible—or at least not nearly so much fun. As always, Susan Toth Eggener and our children, Gus and Rosalind, provided moral support and a life apart from work. My gratitude is the very least that they deserve.

For several months during 2002 Irina Hans worked with me on this book as a research and production assistant. In that role, as in almost everything she did, Irina exhibited levels of enthusiasm and vitality that I found alternately invigorating and exhausting, and almost always astonishing. Irina completed her master's degree in art history (with a fine thesis on the religious imagery of Andres Serrano) at the University of Missouri-Columbia in the spring of 2002. That fall she was in Washington, DC, where she had been awarded the Harry and Beverly Mandil Internship at the Smithsonian American Art Museum. With excitement and a great deal of promise, she was beginning to make applications to PhD programs in art history. Irina was shot and killed one night in October, 2002, while making her way home in DC, the target of a random and utterly senseless act of violence. She is missed and mourned by many, myself included. This book is dedicated to her memory.

ILLUSTRATION ACKNOWLEDGMENTS

The author and publisher would like to thank these individuals and organizations for permission to reproduce material. We have made every effort to contact and acknowledge copyright holders, but if any errors have been made we would be happy to correct them at a later printing.

Avery Architectural and Fine Arts Library, Columbia University in the City of
    New York 10.7
Bernard Hoffman/Time Life Pictures/Getty Images 18.2
Brown University Library 8.2
Courtesy *Chicago Tribune* 16.1, 16.2, 16.3
Courtesy Winterthur Museum 8.1
Courtesy The Winterthur Library: Joseph Downs Collection of Manuscripts and
    Printed Ephemera 9.6, 9.7
Dell Upton 4.1, 4.4, 4.5, 4.7, 4.8, 4.9, 4.10
Digital image © The Museum of Modern Art/Licensed by SCALA/Art Resource,
    NY 20.2
Edward S. Curtis Collection, Library of Congress 2.1, 2.4
Ezra Stoller © Esto, all rights reserved 17.2, 17.3
Farm Security Administration, Office of War Information Photograph Collection,
    Library of Congress 2.3, 5.4
Frances Benjamin Johnston Collection, Library of Congress 12.3
Frank and Frances Carpenter Collection, Library of Congress 2.2
Historic American Buildings Survey, Library of Congress 2.6, 2.7, 2.8, 3.3, 4.3, 4.6,
    4.11, 5.1, 5.2, 6.1, 6.2, 6.3, 7.1, 7.3, 10.5, 10.6, 12.2, 14.2, 14.4, 14.5, 17.1
Library of Congress 1.2, 2.5, 7.2, 9.1, 9.4, 9.5, 10.1, 10.2, 10.3, 10.4, 13.1, 14.3
Keith Eggener 12.4, 18.1, 21.1, 21.2, 22.1, 22.2, 23.1, 23.2, 24.1, 24.2, 24.3
Marc Treib 3.1, 3.2, 3.4, 3.5, 3.6
Missouri Historical Society, St Louis 19.2
Neil Levine 20.1, 20.3, 20.4, 20.5, 20.6
Osmund Overby 14.6
St Louis Post Dispatch 19.1
Utah State Historical Society, all rights reserved 9.3

WRITTEN MATERIAL

The editor and the publisher gratefully acknowledge the authors whose works are reprinted here and the publications in which these essays originally appeared. For the most part the texts appear in their original form; some reductions or slight modifications have been made, mainly to the notes (and all are indicated by ellipses [. . .]). In several cases, the number of illustrations has been reduced, sometimes substantially, and substitutions for original illustrations have been made.

John R. Stilgoe, *Common Landscape of America, 1580–1845* (Yale, 1982), pp. 87–107. Reprinted by permission of John Stilgoe and Yale University Press. Copyright © 1982 by Yale University.

Peter Nabokov and Robert Easton, *Native American Architecture* (Oxford, 1989), pp. 16–50. Reproduced by permission of Oxford University Press. Copyright © 1989 by Peter Nabokov and Robert Easton.

Marc Treib, *Sanctuaries of Spanish New Mexico* (California, 1993), pp. 24–45. Reprinted by permission of Marc Treib and the University of California Press. Copyright © 1993 by Marc Treib.

Dell Upton, *Holy Things and Profane: Anglican Parish Churches in Colonial Virginia* (MIT, 1986), pp. 199–218. Reprinted by permission of Dell Upton and The MIT Press. Copyright © 1986 by the Architectural History Foundation.

John Michael Vlach, *Back of the Big House: The Architecture of Plantation Slavery* (North Carolina, 1993), pp. 1–17. Copyright © 1993 by the University of North Carolina Press. Used by permission of the publisher and John Michael Vlach.

Mary N. Woods, *From Craft to Profession: The Practice of Architecture in Nineteenth-Century America* (California, 1999), pp. 9–26. Reprinted by permission of the University of California Press. Copyright © 1999 by Mary N. Woods.

W. Barksdale Maynard, *Architecture in the United States, 1800–1850* (Yale, 2002), pp. 244–255. Reprinted by permission of W. Barksdale Maynard and Yale University Press. Copyright © 2002 by W. Barksdale Maynard.

Gwendolyn Wright, *Building the Dream: A Social History of American Housing* (MIT, 1981), pp. 73–89. Reprinted by permission of Gwendolyn Wright and Pantheon Books, a division of Random House, Inc. Copyright © 1981 by Gwendolyn Wright.

Kenneth L. Ames, "First Impressions," *Death in the Dining Room, and Other Tales of Victorian Culture* (Temple, 1992), pp. 7–43. Reprinted by permission of Temple University Press. Copyright © 1992 by Temple University. All rights reserved.

Daniel Bluestone, *Constructing Chicago* (Yale, 1991), pp. 105–151. Reprinted by permission of Yale University Press. Copyright © 1991 by Yale University.

Mona Domosh, *Invented Cities: The Creation of Landscape in Nineteenth-Century New York and Boston* (Yale, 1996), pp. 35–64. Reprinted by permission of Mona Domosh and Yale University Press. Copyright © 1996 by Yale University.

Richard Guy Wilson, "Architecture and the Reinterpretation of the Past in the American Renaissance," *Winterthur Portfolio*, Spring 1983, pp. 69–87. Reprinted by permission of Richard Guy Wilson and the University of Chicago Press. Copyright © 1983 by the Henry Francis du Pont Winterthur Museum.

Robert W. Rydell, "A Cultural Frankenstein? The Chicago World's Columbian Exposition of 1893," in Neil Harris *et al.*, *Grand Illusions: Chicago World's Fair of 1893* (Chicago Historical Society, 1993), pp. 142–170. Reproduced by permission of Robert W. Rydell and the Chicago Historical Society.

James F. O'Gorman, *Three American Architects: Richardson, Sullivan, Wright* (Chicago, 1991), pp. 133–154. Reprinted by permission of James F. O'Gorman and the University of Chicago Press. Copyright © 1991 by the University of Chicago.

Anthony Alofsin, "Wright, Influence, and the World at Large," in Anthony Alofsin (ed.), *Frank Lloyd Wright: Europe and Beyond* (California, 1999), pp. 1–18. Reprinted by permission of Anthony Alofsin and the University of California Press. Copyright © 1999 by the Regents of the University of California.

Margaret Kentgens-Craig, *The Bauhaus and America: First Contacts: 1919–1936* (MIT, 1999), pp. 18–33, 158–166. Reprinted by permission of The MIT Press. Copyright © 1999 by the Massachusetts Institute of Technology.

Alice T. Friedman, *Women and the Making of the Modern House: A Social and Architectural History* (Abrams, 1998), pp. 127–159. Copyright © 1998 by Alice T. Friedman. Reprinted by permission of Alice T. Friedman and Harry N. Abrams, Inc. Published by Harry N. Abrams, Inc., New York. All rights reserved.

Joan Ockman, "Mirror Images: Technology, Consumption, and the Representation of Gender in American Architecture Since World War II," in Diana Agrest *et al.* (eds), *The Sex of Architecture* (Abrams, 1996), pp. 191–210. Copyright © 1996 by Harry N. Abrams, Inc. Reprinted by permission of Joan Ockman and Harry N. Abrams, Inc. Published by Harry N. Abrams, Inc., New York. All rights reserved.

Katharine G. Bristol, "The Pruitt-Igoe Myth," *Journal of Architectural Education*, May 1992, pp. 163–171. Reprinted by permission of MIT Press Journals. Copyright © 1991 by the Association of Collegiate Schools of Architecture, Inc. (ACSA).

Neil Levine, "Robert Venturi and 'The Return of Historicism'," in Christopher Mead (ed.), *The Architecture of Robert Venturi* (New Mexico, 1989), pp. 45–67. Reproduced by permission of Neil Levine and the University of New Mexico Press. Copyright © 1989 by the University of New Mexico Press.

Mary McLeod, "The Battle for the Monument: The Vietnam Veterans' Memorial," in Helene Lipstadt (ed.), *The Experimental Tradition: Essays on Competitions in Architecture* (Princeton Architectural Press, 1989), pp. 115–137. Reprinted by permission of Mary McLeod and the Architectural League of New York. Copyright © 1989 by the Architectural League of New York.

Michael Sorkin, "Introduction: Variations on a Theme Park," in Michael Sorkin (ed.), *Variations on a Theme Park: The New American City and the End of Public Space* (Hill and Wang, 1992), pp. xi–xv. Compilation copyright © 1992 by Michael Sorkin. Reprinted by permission of Hill and Wang, a division of Farrar, Straus and Giroux, LLC.

Mike Davis, *City of Quartz, Excavating the Future in Los Angeles* (Vintage, 1992), pp. 223–240. Reprinted by permission of Verso, the imprint of New Left Books, Ltd. Copyright © 1990 by Verso.

Marc Spiegler, "Planes of Existence," *Metropolis*, July/Aug. 1997, pp. 33–38. Copyright © 1997 by Bellerophon Publications, Inc. Permission to reprint granted by *Metropolis*.

Keith L. Eggener

Introduction

> There is a new architectural history to be written, and there is an old
> architectural history to be rewritten.
>
> John Coolidge, 1942[1]

As if in renewed response to Coolidge's words, a new history of American architecture
has emerged during the past two and a half decades. This collection of twenty-four previously published writings, with subjects ranging from colonial to contemporary times and
representing a diverse group of individuals, sites, objects, issues, events, and scholarly
viewpoints, provides an introduction to this development. Directed toward students and
teachers of American architecture and cultural history, it surveys the evolving state of the
field and aims to facilitate the formation of informed, critical perspectives on it.

    American, architecture: these two words are so widely and variously used as to
require regular redefinition. During the 1940s Nikolaus Pevsner said that "the term architecture applies only to buildings designed with a view to aesthetic appeal." In the famous
opening line of his book, *An Outline of European Architecture*, Pevsner declared that
"A bicycle shed is a building; Lincoln Cathedral is a piece of architecture."[2] Forty years
later, Spiro Kostof began his more inclusive *A History of Architecture* (1985) by stating
that "all past buildings, regardless of size, status, or consequence," should now be
studied."[3] If anything, the boundaries of architecture have only continued to expand and
blur in recent years. The essays featured here speak of a variety buildings, from unique
examples of "high art" to prefabricated multiples, from the mundane to the monumental,
from objects fashioned by professional designers to spaces created by their own
unschooled inhabitants. Beyond buildings, however, these writings consider many other
things as within the realm of architecture. Included here are examinations of building
furnishings and associated artifacts, the rituals contained in and the social structures reinforced by particular built spaces, the modifications made to buildings and landscapes by
their users (as opposed to their initial designers), the professional and cultural discourses
and the urban and rural landscapes within which buildings are situated. Many of the
writers talk "around" architecture, using buildings and design as launching points for
wide-ranging discussions of culture and society. For many contemporary scholars the
preferred terms for this extraordinarily complex physical, experiential, and imaginative
terrain are the *built environment* or the *cultural landscape*.[4] We might still identify all of

this as architecture, but only with the understanding that we have moved well beyond Pevsner's definition of the word.

If *architecture* stands as an increasingly nebulous term, *American* architecture is no less so. A flood of questions arises. What does it mean today—in an era of multinational corporations and porous national borders, instantaneous global media coverage and globetrotting citizens (architects included), mounting cultural homogeneity and frequently divisive identity politics, resurgent nationalism and conjoined fears of terrorism and imperialism—to speak of an American architecture? What are the roles that architecture plays with regard to local, regional, national, or international politics, economy, and cultural definition? Just how do we go about determining an architecture's nationality? More specifically, through what processes and under what conditions do a colonial mission church at the northern limits of New Spain, or a seventeenth-century English planter's house in Virginia, become American? Is a government center in Dacca, designed by an architect based in the US but built and occupied by Bangladeshis, more properly called American or Bangladeshi? What of a museum built in St Louis according to designs by an architect from Osaka, the foreign pavilions at a world's fair in Chicago, a MacDonald's restaurant in Moscow, or the constructions of American contractors in a post-war Iraq? When and how, if at all, do such projects come to be called American? Is architecture's nationality at all dependent on its makers' or users' awareness of, or desire to comment on, their own national identities? Or is it, instead, a relatively simple function of politics and geography? As a cultural, geo-political, or even ideological designator, how clear or useful anymore is the word *American*, even when qualified by such terms as North, South, Central, or Latin?

Among other things, the essays in this volume should cause readers to reflect critically on these questions, on the varied meanings and implications of American identity and on architecture's historical relations to these. The only part of these questions that I will deal with here has to do with geographical limitations and terminology. First, the essays gathered here stick mainly to the convention—found in popular contemporary textbooks by Leland Roth, Dell Upton, David Handlin, Mark Gelernter, and others—which defines as American that architecture located within the present-day boundaries of the United States of America.[5] This geographical bracketing results from the intellectual and editorial need to give shape to an otherwise impossibly broad and inchoate field of study, and from the recognition of a discursive tradition going back to the first half of the nineteenth century. Even so, there will be exceptions to this rule, particularly in those works by scholars such as Anthony Alofsin or Margaret Kentgens-Craig, who consider American architecture in broadly international terms. Second, mindful of the fact that *American* is an imprecise term, and one on which the US has no exclusive claim, I will throughout this introductory essay use the word to refer to historical artifacts and discourses located primarily within the present-day boundaries of the US.[6]

There is, of course, a long and rich tradition of historical scholarship on American architecture predating 1980. While some of the essays reprinted here chart new territory, others build on or overturn aspects of this earlier scholarship. To understand the state of recent American architectural history then, it helps to recognize what it is evolving from. The remainder of this introduction consists of three sections. First is an historiographical outline of the period before 1980 (divided into three chronologically ordered subsections). Following this, some of the key developments and intellectual tendencies appearing in the years since 1980 are discussed. In neither case have I aimed for comprehensiveness; rather, I have focused on major themes and pointed to authors, works, and events that support or represent these themes. Finally, a brief concluding section describes the selection process and organization of this volume and offers suggestions for its use.

WRITING ON AMERICAN HISTORICAL ARCHITECTURE BEFORE 1865

Judged by current standards, the writing on American architecture and its history produced before the Civil War is romantic, anecdotal, and unsystematic. Its primary elements were lists and description, biography, and moralizing. Descriptions of buildings typically were vague, random, and incomplete. Architects' biographies, usually based on little more than oral history, were celebratory, even heroic, in tone.[7] Authors were sometimes critical when discussing the state of contemporary American architecture, and they presented the past as a model for current builders, yet they offered little or no discussion of the causes of stylistic change or regional difference. Occasionally they did make note of such perceived qualities in American architecture and architectural practice as equality, individuality, and independence; English architects, by contrast, were represented as subject to the tastes and whims of their aristocratic patrons. Most crucially, these early discussions were related to the growth, maturation, and cultural definition of post-Revolutionary American society. Well-placed Americans such as Thomas Jefferson and Yale University president Timothy Dwight saw a correlation between architecture, behavior, and belief. Architecture—the term's use then limited mainly to religious, domestic, funerary, and public buildings of a certain grandeur and permanence—was understood as "a symbolic expression of a culture's ideals and achievements and as an instrument for intellectual and moral improvement."[8] According to Dwight, "The perception of beauty and deformity, of refinement and grossness, of decency and vulgarity, of propriety and indecorum, is the first thing which influences man to escape from a groveling, brutish character. . . . In most persons, this perception is awakened by what may be called the exterior of society, particularly by the mode of building."[9]

While the first book-length histories of American art and architecture were not published until the 1830s and 1840s, scattered comments on American cities and buildings did appear in many earlier sources. Jefferson's derisive remarks on the buildings of Williamsburg, from his *Notes on the State of Virginia* (1782–1784), are well known. "It is impossible to devise things more ugly, uncomfortable, and happily more perishable," he wrote. "The genius of architecture seems to have shed its maledictions over this land."[10] Other eighteenth-century observers, including some Europeans, took a more positive view. Writing in 1760, the English clergyman Andrew Burnaby spoke of the "many fair houses and public buildings" and "handsomely built" streets of Philadelphia. Similarly pleased by Boston, he reported that "the whole has much the air of some of the best country towns in England."[11] Pastor William Bentley's diaries, written in New England in the 1790s, included sympathetic descriptions of some seventeenth-century American buildings.[12] By the first decades of the nineteenth century, the carpenters' guides of Asher Benjamin and Owen Biddle pointed to earlier American buildings, such as Philadelphia's Christ Church (1753) and Boston's Hancock House (1737), as valuable examples for contemporary builders.[13]

During the early to mid-nineteenth century many noted architects produced sporadic written comments on historic architecture, typically in letters and other documents not intended for publication. Among these were Benjamin Latrobe, William Strickland, Thomas Tefft, and Richard Upjohn.[14] More accessible discussions of architecture and architects were published in the earliest general surveys of American fine arts. The first of these was William Dunlap's *A History of the Rise and Progress of the Arts of Design in the United State*s (1834). Dunlap's second of three volumes began with a brief essay describing the various architectural styles, from ancient Egyptian to contemporary American neo-classicism. He made special note here of Washington, DC, pointing to its major monuments and to the architects and builders involved with these. Elsewhere in the book he provided notes of varying lengths on the lives and works of prominent American architects. Short entries were included for William and George Strickland, Maximilian Godefroi (*sic*), and John Dorsey, longer ones for Pierre Charles L'Enfant, Latrobe, Robert Mills, and Alexander Jackson Davis. Depending on their length—none were more than a couple of pages, some only a line or two—these entries included anecdotes, biographical information, building lists, and brief building descriptions.[15] A characteristic discussion is Dunlap's one-paragraph entry on the Philadelphia-based architect William Strickland (1787–1854):

> I think I remember Mr. William Strickland when in the scene shop of the Park Theatre, a companion of Hugh Reinagle and a pupil of John Joseph Holland. When Holland rebuilt the theatre, Strickland's father was the carpenter. If I err, it is because Mr. Strickland is among the very modest artists, who do not choose to answer my inquiries, or assist my efforts to be accurate in the history of the Arts of Design. He has studied diligently—been to Europe to see the work of art, and stands high as an architect. He built the Bank of the United States, Philadelphia, after the model of the antique, the only model we have.[16]

The first book produced in the US to be devoted exclusively to architectural history was Louisa Tuthill's *The History of Architecture from the Earliest Times; Its Present Condition in Europe and the United States*, published in Philadelphia in 1848. Among other features, Tuthill included: a chapter on the "principles of architecture"; another on the qualifications necessary to practice architecture; a discussion of the "causes which retarded the progress of the art in the United States"; a section on "materials for building in the United States"; lists and some descriptions of important buildings in major American cities, many of these illustrated by engravings or woodcuts; discussions of historic and contemporary American urban forms, domestic architecture, cemeteries, and other building types; and a glossary of architectural terms. Dedicated "to the Ladies of the United States of America, the Acknowledged Arbiters of Taste," Tuthill's book emphasized the links between moral development and architectural design. The exercise of good

taste in building, she believed, would ultimately result in personal and societal improvement. Moreover, "a taste for Architecture [adds] to the innocent pleasures of life as much
as a taste for flowers, or furniture, and [is] as suitable for women as a knowledge of
Chemistry or Astronomy."[17] The book met with a lukewarm reception, due perhaps to its
unusual topic, its lack of any evident practical application, and the fact that it was
addressed to women—the "arbiters of taste" perhaps, but neither architects nor the principal patrons of architecture in that era.

Following Tuthill, the next treatments of architectural history published in the US
came in works like John Bullock's *The History and Rudiments of Architecture* (1853) and
Minard Lafever's *The Architectural Instructor* (1856). Directed specifically toward architects, engineers, mechanics, and builders, these volumes, unlike Tuthill's, were more
professionally specialized and practical in tone, less historically comprehensive and moral-
istic.[18] Historical discussions were limited mainly to matters of style.

THE PROFESSIONALIZATION OF AMERICAN ARCHITECTURAL HISTORY

A fledgling field before 1865, American architectural history began to mature once
American architects recognized it as something worth knowing about. Although architectural practice in the US had become increasingly professionalized between 1820
and 1860, the first schools of architecture appeared only after the Civil War.[19] As architectural education became more sophisticated and systematic, so too did architectural
history.[20]

The US' first professional school of architecture was established at the
Massachusetts Institute of Technology (MIT) in 1865 and, from the beginning, courses in
art and architectural history were offered there and at other new programs in the
Northeast and Midwest.[21] Modeled on the European academies where some of their
faculty had studied—particularly the Parisian École des Beaux-Arts—the new American
architectural schools also drew on the lessons of prominent European critics and historians such as Gottfried Semper, Eugène Viollet-le-Duc, John Ruskin, Jacob Burckhardt,
Hippolyte Taine, and Auguste Choisy.[22] Historical study, it was believed, would teach
American students the principles of cultural hierarchy (e.g., in terms of aesthetic achievement), with Greek and Roman classicism in the paramount position. Such study would
emphasize their professionalism by distinguishing them from the "mere" builders, carpenters, and mechanics who lacked such formal training. Most importantly, the knowledge
gained would provide them with a lexicon of appropriate, historically sanctioned forms
and design solutions. Architectural history was, thus, intimately bound to contemporary
practice. When taught and written by such academically affiliated architects as William
Robert Ware (MIT, Columbia), Henry Van Brunt (MIT), and, later, Ralph Adams Cram
(MIT), it was in large part a handmaiden to, or an instrument of, design.[23]

Although American architects and educators of the late-nineteenth century privileged
European exemplars, there was also mounting interest about this time in native builders
and buildings. New biographies of American designers past and present appeared. Friends

or relatives of the architects, often women, wrote many of these; such works included Ellen Susan Bulfinch's volume on her grandfather, Boston architect Charles Bulfinch, and Harriet Monroe's book on her brother-in-law, Chicago architect John Wellborn Root. While these books typically retained the celebratory tone of earlier artists' biographies, some, such as Mariana Griswold van Rensselaer's *Henry Hobson Richardson and His Works* (1888), were substantial and well-researched—if still hagiographic—volumes. Providing ample historical documentation, numerous illustrations, and thoughtful critical analysis of individual works, van Rensselaer made a reasoned case for Richardson as "not only the greatest American artist but the greatest benefactor of American art who has yet been born . . . so thoroughly modern, so thoroughly American . . . ."[24]

As it had been a generation earlier for those like the poet Walt Whitman, cultural definition, the meaning of Americanness, now became a preoccupation of many. Interest in the American scene was widespread around the time of the nation's Centennial celebrations in 1876, as indicated by a surge in publications on American colonial architecture.[25] Authors and architects such as Charles Follen McKim and Robert Swain Peabody pointed to the charm and picturesque qualities of seventeenth-century English and Dutch colonial houses and called for their preservation. Such buildings were said to have inestimable value as models for contemporary practice. "Our colonial work is our only native source of antiquarian study and inspiration," Peabody wrote in 1878. "Whatever the attractions of other sources, from no field can suggestions be drawn by an artist more charming and more fitted to our usages, than from the Georgian mansions of New England."[26] Colonial architecture, moreover, provided material evidence of a national history and a developing cultural consciousness. Calls for more thoroughgoing study of it ensued. "We submit," McKim wrote:

> if it is worth while to write the genealogies of generations of men, the roofs that have faithfully sheltered them come in for a greater tribute of respect than mere occasional magazine or newspaper articles can furnish, since these must be necessarily imperfect and incomplete. Hitherto they have been brought before the public either as curious objects, or as haunted houses, or as the scene of some story or other, mentioned as shadows, and admired for their ivy. Now let somebody write about them as *Architecture*.[27]

McKim's call was soon answered. By the 1890s, a new body of scholarship in American colonial architecture emerged. More rigorous, thorough, complex, and inclusive than any before it, this new work was grounded in exacting archaeological fieldwork and archival research—as opposed to the earlier habits of generalized observations, assumptions, and oral history. The authors responsible considered not just how buildings looked, but *why* certain forms arose when and where they did. Their explanations referred not only to structure, materials, technology, or biography, but to social, intellectual, and environmental conditions. Montgomery Schuyler, in a lengthy *Architectural Record* article of 1895, examined colonial buildings in light of their chronology, authorship, quality of workmanship, materials and design, their use of classical orders, and the rise of the architectural profession.[28] Norman Isham, in his books *Early Rhode Island Houses* (1895) and *Early Connecticut Houses* (1900), both written with Albert Brown, gave close attention to building technology and to broader social and economic contexts. Comparable to Isham's works in their "scientific" approach—involving careful fieldwork, the study of primary documents, and the production of measured drawings—were the writings of Glenn Brown, particularly his work on the US Capitol, originally published in *American Architect and Building News* in 1896. In 1914, Fiske Kimball called Brown's Capitol studies "almost the only worthy monument of our architectural history."[29] More recently, Dell Upton has written that the "most significant intellectual legacy" of this generation of scholars was the "organizing assumption that architecture is an expression of social practice," which resulted in an "emphasis on spatial type over visual style, use over design."[30] This is a legacy that continues to inform the writing of American architectural history today.

THE TWENTIETH CENTURY

The expansion of American architectural history that began in the late-nineteenth century continued apace during the first decades of the twentieth. By 1913, Schuyler had published several important articles on topics ranging from the evolution of the skyscraper, to the architecture of American college campuses, to the work of such figures as Richard Morris Hunt and Leopold Eidlitz.[31] In 1915, the first PhD dissertations in the history of American architecture were completed; these were Fiske Kimball's study of Jefferson and the Classical Revival (University of Michigan), and Frederick Sterns' examination of ancient earth lodges in eastern Nebraska (Harvard).[32] During the 1920s and 1930s, a flurry of new surveys and monographs appeared. Among these were: Talbot Hamlin's *The Trend of American Architecture* (1921) and *The American Spirit in Architecture* (1926); Kimball's *Domestic Architecture in the American Colonies and the Early Republic* (1922) and *American Architecture* (1928); George Edgell's *The American Architecture of Today*; Lewis Mumford's *Sticks and Stones* (1924) and *The Brown Decades, A Study of the Architecture of America, 1865–1895* (1931); Philip Youtz's *American Life in Architecture* (1932); Hugh Morrison's *Louis Sullivan: Prophet of Modern Architecture* (1935); Henry-Russell Hitchcock's French-language monograph on Frank Lloyd Wright, for the "Maitres de l'architecture contemporaine" series (published in Paris by *Cahiers d'arts*, 1928),[33] and his *Architecture of Henry Hobson Richardson and His Times* (1936). Contemporary with these publications was the founding, in 1933, of the Historic American Buildings Survey, a division of the US Department of the Interior. Local inventories and field guides also proliferated at this time. These various projects studied architectural examples past and present, vernacular and academic. They catalogued and analyzed colonial-era houses and churches, nineteenth-century farm and factory buildings, modern skyscrapers and bridges, and the work of such by-now canonical masters as Peter Harrison, Bulfinch, Jefferson, Latrobe, Mills, Davis, Richardson, the Roeblings, Frederick Law Olmsted, Sullivan, Wright, and McKim, Mead, and White. Writers pointed to these buildings and designers as the basis of present-day American achievement, often using nationalistically charged terms. According to Thomas Tallmadge's *The Story of Architecture in America*, published in 1927, the US now stood in a position of "leadership of the world in architecture."

Tallmadge predicted that the quality of American architecture would soon surpass that of Periclean Athens or thirteenth-century France.[34]

While Tallmadge's recklessly chauvanistic pronouncements and colloquial tone[35] have not aged well, others in this era produced works of more rigorously analytical, intellectually sophisticated scholarship. This is particularly true of Kimball, Hitchcock, Morrison, and Mumford. Of all these, Mumford is the one whose work has most in common with the essays collected in this anthology. Eschewing stylistic analysis as an end in itself, he studied American architecture in relation to the broad social, economic, and intellectual currents underlying and informing style. There is, moreover, an instrumental quality, a spirit of political activism, in his writing that finds much resonance today.[36] Following the lead of literary critic Van Wyck Brooks, Mumford sought to uncover a "usable past." As Brooks wrote in 1918:

> The spiritual welfare of this country depends altogether upon the fate of its creative minds. If they cannot grow and ripen, where are we going to get the new ideals, the finer attitudes, that we must get if we are ever to emerge from our existing travesty of a civilization? . . . The present is a void. . . . The past is an inexhaustible storehouse of apt attitudes and adaptable ideals.[37]

With this in mind, Mumford probed the past, not as an antiquarian exercise, but for its potential solutions to current social, cultural, and environmental problems.[38]

For Mumford's generation, American architectural history was not simply a minor chapter or provincial offshoot of a greater European history, but a vital cultural tradition of its own, one to be studied on its own terms. Related to this was the element of nationalism already mentioned. As indicated by the titles of their books, Hamlin, Edgells, Youtz, and the others partook of a fascination widespread, during the inter-war period, with the question of Americanness. This interest was due in part to recognition of the US' new and not yet fully defined international status in the wake of World War I. Not just architects or architectural historians, but artists, critics, political and cultural historians, novelists, composers, and many others now plumbed the character and significance of American culture and spoke of American exceptionalism—that configuration of characteristics and attitudes that made the US a distinct and cohesive entity. Wanda Corn has studied this tendency with regard to the development of American art historical studies during these and subsequent years. "By focusing on uniqueness and exclusivity," she writes,

> one could explain the visual and intellectual appeal of American art without having to apologize for the fact that it did not measure up to the innovation and originality of its European peers. . . . The Americanness issue enabled scholars to turn what had commonly been assumed to be a provincial and marginal body of work into a complex and intellectually exciting project.[39]

Applying Corn's terms to architecture is complicated by the fact that, as early as the mid-nineteenth century, Europeans had openly admired American engineering and planning (e.g., prisons, bridges, and skyscrapers) and the innovative work of figures such as

Richardson, Sullivan, and Wright.[40] Yet, for many early twentieth-century American architects and architectural writers there remained a nagging sense of cultural inferiority. This helps to explain why so many earlier scholars of American art and architecture—and here Mumford is exemplary—favored sociological and cultural studies approaches over connoisseurship.

Providing an important counterweight to this fascination with Americanness was a body of work produced by Hitchcock and a few others during the late 1920s and early 1930s. While his book on Richardson showed that Hitchcock, too, could be an American exceptionalist, his writings on contemporary European architecture took a different turn—critical and international, instead of historical and nativist. Most important among these were *Modern Architecture: Romanticism and Reintegration* (1929), *The International Style: Architecture Since 1922* (1932), co-written with Philip Johnson and featuring a preface by Alfred H. Barr, Jr, and *Modern Architects* (1932), done in collaboration with Johnson, Barr, and Mumford. One key assumption of these publications was that the most significant *contemporary* architecture was coming not from the US but from Europe—from Le Corbusier, Walter Gropius, Ludwig Mies van der Rohe, J. J. P. Oud, and others. What Hitchcock and his co-authors (particularly Johnson and Barr) christened the International Style, was characterized in almost exclusively formal and spatial— that is connoisseurial—terms. They pointed to the new architecture's emphasis on spatial volumes over solid masses, regularity as opposed to symmetry, and on proportions, technical perfection, and the intrinsic qualities of materials over applied ornament. Sociological or technical considerations barely entered into these discussions. American architecture had a place here, but mainly as a precursor or a provincial offshoot. Wright's work was understood as an important formal influence on architects like Gropius and Oud, but he was clearly of a different generation. His work's romantic individualism stood in stark contrast to the rational, functional, standardizing, technological orientation of the younger Europeans that Hitchcock and Johnson championed. The new architecture of this sort that had appeared in the US was for the most part the work of émigrés like Richard Neutra and William Lescase.[41]

"American nationalists," Barr predicted in his preface to *The International Style*, "will oppose the Style as another European invasion."[42] Indeed, the "invaders" were fought by some, but others, soon and with greater effect, absorbed them into discussions of a new American architecture with deep native roots. Architect and curator John McAndrew, in his *Guide to Modern Architecture, Northeastern States* (1940) and in other publications for the Museum of Modern Art, gave renewed attention to American historical architecture. Of particular interest were his observations on the value of historic and vernacular building for contemporary American architects aiming to domesticate the International Style. "In the last few years," McAndrew wrote, "modern architects, less self-conscious about showing off their modernity than before, have seen the economical and comfortable virtues of our folk-architecture, and also its beauty."[43] James and Katherine Morrow Ford took a similar line in *The Modern House in America* (1940). Within a few years, Hitchcock, in his *In the Nature of Materials, 1887–1941: The Buildings of Frank Lloyd Wright* (1942), reevaluated the American master on his own terms, now finding in his work a continued vitality, creativity, and relevance both regional and universal. In a time of international political and military crisis—the rise of Fascism, the outbreak of World War II—Mumford deepened his long-running exploration of American architectural history and regional traditions. "When a nation has hard days ahead of it," he wrote in *The South in Architecture* (1941), ". . . it is well for that nation to turn back for a moment to its sources. . . ." In the work of Jefferson and Richardson he found deep and abiding American values that could succor the nation through troubled and uncertain times.[44]

The crisis in world affairs during these years was accompanied by a crisis in architectural history. Scholars now questioned the relevance of the field during times of war and considered what new directions it should take. As Eve Blau recently argued, the notion of crisis is intrinsic to historical thinking—which is always provisional, unstable, self-critical, and dynamic—and this crisis bears both negative and positive aspects. During the early 1940s American architectural historians positively embraced the idea of disciplinary crisis, involving themselves in "an ongoing engagement with the critical methods, historiography, institutional structures, and ideological and philosophical frameworks of the discipline itself."[45] This engagement was carried out, among other places, in the earliest issues of *The Journal of the American Society of Architectural Historians*.[46] Talbot Hamlin, Carroll Meeks, John Coolidge, and others, outlined proposals there for a "New History of Architecture," one that would constructively inform contemporary architectural education and practice. If this new history was instrumental in its relation to practice, it was also, according to Meeks,

> a frankly subjective, analytic system based on scholarship and brought to life by creative imagination. It demonstrates how buildings and cities are conditioned by a series of specific milieus, each with it own moral, social, and technical values, each different from every other. . . . At the same time, it traces the status of the builder—his duties, education, obstacles and opportunities, and the degree to which he is a free agent.[47]

Coolidge, meanwhile, insisted that the new history did not aim to "jettison" the work of past historians but, rather, to address that work's inadequacies, to reconsider its objectives and revise and supplement its methods. Essential to the task were a new rigor and specificity, and an approach that, like Mumford's best work, exchanged style as a guiding principle for close considerations of social and intellectual contexts. "Glib generalizations" would not do. "If, then, in rewriting architectural history today," Coolidge said, "the most widespread demand is for a grand demonstration of the relation of architecture to social life, equally pressing is the need for a series of trial studies tracing the specific connections between single groups of buildings and the intellectual currents surrounding them."[48]

A new generation of scholars rose to meet Coolidge's challenge. During the 1940s, dissertations were produced on the religious architecture of Spanish-colonial New Mexico, the early work of Frank Lloyd Wright, American collegiate architecture, Jamestown, Rockefeller Center, the architecture of the Connecticut river valley, American railroad stations, and industrial architecture. George Kubler, Grant Carpenter Mason, Carroll Meeks, John Kouwenhoven, William Pierson, Vincent Scully, Anthony Garvan, Walter Creese, Alan Gowans, Abbott Lowell Cummings, and Bainbridge Bunting are among the best known of those who completed doctoral dissertations in American architectural history between 1940 and 1952.[49] These figures would come to dominate the field until well into the 1970s and 1980s. They would produce such landmarks of scholarship as Scully's *The Shingle Style: Architectural Theory and Design from Richardson to the Origins of Wright* (1955), Kubler's *Art and Architecture in Spain and Portugal and Their American Dominions, 1500 to 1800* (1959), Gowans' *Images of American Living: Four Centuries of Architecture and Furniture as Cultural Expression* (1964), Carl Condit's *The Chicago School of Architecture: A History of Commercial and Public Building in the Chicago Area* (1964), Bunting's *Houses of Boston's Back Bay: An Architectural History, 1840–1917* (1967), Cummings's *The Framed Houses of Massachusetts Bay, 1625–1725* (1979), and Pierson's multi-volume series, with William Jordy, *American Buildings and Their Architects* (1970–1978). Though these men were, for the most part, professional historians rather than architects, their influence on design was, in some cases, profound. Scully, for one, would become an early and important champion of such major architects as Louis Kahn and Robert Venturi, a prime influence on generations of younger architects, a key interrogator of modernism, and an early advocate of postmodernism.[50]

The 1940s and 1950s saw other important developments in the field. European scholars such as Sigfried Giedion, Christopher Tunnard, Bruno Zevi, and Reyner Banham, now gave serious and sustained attention to the history of American architecture.[51] The Swiss-born Giedion was especially important, not only for the ample inclusion of American buildings in his widely read book *Space, Time and Architecture* (1941), but for his influential emphasis on such themes as urbanism, technology, and the links between architecture and fine art.[52] In 1947–1948 James Marston Fitch published his *American Building: The Forces That Shape It*, which emphasized environmental factors and anticipated the ecologically based concerns shared by many architects and architectural historians during the 1960s and 1970s. As a teacher at Columbia University and an advocate of historic preservation, Fitch went on to organize the first professional academic program in that field. Ordinary, non-architect-designed buildings and vernacular landscapes were studied, with extraordinary intelligence and sensitivity, by John Brinckerhoff Jackson. In the pages of his magazine *Landscape*, and in courses taught at Harvard and Berkeley, he presented farms and highways, barns and billboards, as emblematic of collective American values and attitudes. The current state of American vernacular architectural studies is unimaginable without his example.[53]

During the 1960s and 1970s, the study of architectural history developed with impressive vigor and range at American universities. New PhD programs were established, in both fine arts departments and schools of architecture. Survey courses in American architectural history became standard fare at both. Such courses also began to appear at foreign universities, in Mexico, England, and elsewhere. New American studies and folklore programs were established—in the US, but also in France, Germany, Italy, and England—and within these many studied built environments. Dramatically increased numbers of dissertations in architectural history were produced. In 1971, for instance, more dissertations were completed in the field than in all the years between 1898 and 1940 combined.[54]

American architectural history came to incorporate a widely expanded range of topics, methods, objects, and ideas. With the perceived end of modernism—marked by the publication of such landmark books as Jane Jacobs' *Death and Life of Great American Cities* (1961), Bernard Rudofsky's *Architecture Without Architects* (1964), and Robert Venturi's *Complexity and Contradiction in Architecture* (1966)—many neglected topics were revisited, or examined for the first time. Interest in classicism was renewed, most spectacularly in *The Architecture of The École Des Beaux-Arts* (1977), edited by Arthur Drexler (and catalog for a major exhibition at the Museum of Modern Art), and more modestly with the republication of writings by the nineteenth-century American Beaux-arts architect Henry Van Brunt.[55] Other previously overlooked topics studied in these years included the Gothic Revival Style, African-American architects and architecture, the history of architectural education and practice, and architecture's manifold relations to popular culture. In books such as *The Making Of Urban America; A History of City Planning In The United States* (1965), John Reps considered the historical development and formal variations of America's small towns, cities, and suburbs. Reyner Banham historicized the impact of environmental engineering on modern building in *The Architecture of the Well-Tempered Environment* (1969), while in *Los Angeles: The Architecture of Four Ecologies* (1971) he explored such unconventional subjects as Disneyland and the Los Angeles Freeway system. As John Michael Vlach studied the African sources of the shotgun house, Jeffrey Meikle explored the phenomenon of streamlining in architecture and industrial design during the 1930s and 1940s. Lizabeth Cohen looked at the material culture of turn-of-the-century working-class houses, while Betsy Blackmar analyzed property relations and housing in late eighteenth-/early nineteenth-century New York.[56] Informed by recent feminist writing, Gwendolyn Wright, Dolores Hayden, Susana Torré, and others began to consider the roles of women in American architecture past and present. In books like Hayden's *The Grand Domestic Revolution* (1981), these authors shed new light on the politics of architecture, on the work of neglected thinkers and designers like Julia Morgan and Catherine Beecher, and on such issues as gendered space and professional practice.[57]

Architectural historians, along with others in the humanities and social sciences, grew increasingly self-reflexive in these years, questioning the nature, limits, and possibilities of their discipline and their own roles as practitioners of it. The intra-disciplinary debates of the 1940s were renewed. John Maass, for example, in an article published in the *Journal of the Society of Architectural Historians* in 1969, critiqued the current state of the field and pointed to what he saw as a continuing "bourgeois standard," which kept the focus on stylistic issues and prevented architectural historians from studying buildings of the lower classes.[58] Yet, even as he wrote, art and architectural historians were exercising a new interdisciplinarity, exploring a new range of topics, and drawing on the latest research and methods from history, sociology, anthropology, psychology, and economics. At the same time, scholars from these and other disciplines were coming to the study of American built environments, bringing significant insights and new energy to the field. Important work was produced in these years by sociologists Richard Sennett and William H. Whyte, folklorist Henry Glassie, cultural geographers Peirce Lewis and D. W. Meinig, and social, cultural, literary, and labor historians such as William H. Wilson, Clifford Clark, Neil Harris, Thomas Bender, Gary Kulik, John Kasson, Ruth Schwartz Cowan, and Alan Trachtenberg.[59]

During the 1970s, the influence of literary and cultural theorists was also entering into the study of American material culture, architecture included. Many names new to the field of architectural history became familiar to readers: Michel Foucault, Roland Barthes, Jacques Lacan, Julia Kristeva, Henri Lefebvre, Georges Bataille, Pierre Bourdieu, Gilles Deleuze, Michel de Certeau, Pierre Nora, Walter Benjamin, Jürgen Habermas, Eric Hobsbawm, David Harvey, Raymond Williams, Laura Mulvey, Fredric Jameson, Edward Said, Clifford Geertz, and others. In journals like *Perspecta* and *Oppositions*—the latter launched in 1973 by Kenneth Frampton, Peter Eisenman, Mario Gandelsonas, Anthony Vidler, and Kurt Forster—architectural writing was now inextricably bound to theoretical concerns. The new, theoretically informed writing was far removed from the instrumental, practice-oriented work of earlier periods. It was, according to Eve Blau, "a practice of mediation with a continuously critical function," yet it "resist[ed] instrumentality in design," and "until very recently evinced little interest in historical thinking."[60] Focused on contemporary intellectual currents and broad ideological terrain, this writing often ignored specific objects. At the same time, however, particularly within the burgeoning realm of American material culture studies, efforts were being made to establish close contact with history and objects. In his book *In Small Things Forgotten: An Archaeology of Early American Life* (1977)—a seminal study whose methods and assumptions underlie many of the essays included here—historical archaeologist, James Deetz, showed how American architecture and its associated artifacts could be understood as material culture, as physical evidence of mind, of community values, beliefs, and aspirations. He asked his readers to concentrate on the materiality of architecture and other objects, and to treat these as primary historical evidence. "Don't read what we have written," he concluded, "look at what we have done."[61]

AMERICAN ARCHITECTURAL HISTORY SINCE 1980

A distinct set of characteristics is apparent in the writing on architectural history, American and otherwise, produced during the past two and a half decades.[62] First, building on a substantial intradisciplinary history, notably the developments of the 1960s and 1970s, recent architectural history demonstrates an intensified interdisciplinarity; this is apparent in both the topics authors choose to work on and the methods they use to study them. Second, as opposed to the more expansive themes and surveys favored by many earlier writers, it is now more common for authors to focus on carefully circumscribed topics—specific sites, objects, ideas, organizations, or events—with the understanding that a close focus offers the richest interpretative possibilities. Finally, while most contemporary architectural historians utilize a close focus, they also view their subjects as engaged in broader discourses; in other words, they see architecture as culturally embedded and active. The essays gathered here may be taken as representative of these three tendencies.

The interdisciplinarity—the "fluid and permeable" nature—of contemporary architectural history has been noted by many authors.[63] Recent scholars of American architecture have found ideas and inspiration in cultural and intellectual history, literary

Robert Rydell's impassioned critique of the racist and sexist implications of the 1893 World's Columbian Exposition. Authorial self-consciousness also accounts for the markedly presentist vantage point on the part of many contemporary writers, who see their task as one of reanimating past works by viewing them through contemporary lenses. If such reanimation also tells us something about ourselves, then so much the better. As Kenneth Ames writes in *Death in the Dining Room*:

> How odd once ordinary things have become. This transformation of the ordinary into the odd is an illusion, however, an illusion made possible by our own ethnocentrism and limited perspective. In fact, the goods were always odd. The beliefs were always odd. And for that matter, the goods of today are odd. The beliefs of today are odd. Like the Victorians, we too live in the fantasy world of culture. Our fantasies are different from theirs, but they remain fantasies, attempts to build convincing and durable bridges across the great darkness, attempts to craft convincing and lasting answers to the great questions, attempts to provide convincing and effective solutions to the great persisting problems of humankind. Looking at Victorian America revealed through the goods in this book brings us to the sobering realization that one society's truths usually become another society's authentic fictions.[75]

SELECTION, ORGANIZATION, AND USE OF THIS BOOK

The selections for this volume were made in consultation with art, architectural, and urban historians, historic preservationists, American studies scholars, and cultural historians currently teaching at colleges and universities across the US. From a long list of excellent possibilities, I have chosen readings produced since 1980 that not only represent significant scholarship on important topics, but that are concise, lively, accessible, and engaging. Editing has been kept to a minimum throughout (and is in all cases marked in the text by ellipses [. . .]). Many of these essays appear regularly on college course reading lists; others are less well known but nonetheless valuable. Collected here, they may be taken as an alternative to photocopied course readers, unwieldy or unfamiliar electronic reserve systems, and the time and tedium involved in producing these and in securing the permissions often necessary for their use. Inevitably, exclusions far outnumber inclusions in a book such as this one and, although diversity of subject matter, method, and authorial voice was a primary concern, comprehensiveness was not.

As Foucault demonstrated, all systems of organization are more or less contrived.[76] With regard to historical materials, chronology is no more arbitrary a means of organization than any other, and rather less so than most. Because chronology still provides the most common structure for courses and textbooks on American architecture, the essays in this book have been organized along chronological lines—albeit by broad themes pertinent to particular eras. There are six of these thematic subsets. The first considers European-American and Native-American approaches to shaping architectural and community space before the American Revolution—or, in the case of Native American cultures, before relocation and other effects of the Indian Removal Bill signed by

President Andrew Jackson in 1830. The second part looks at some of the builders and building forms of a nation newly independent and then undergoing processes of cultural consolidation and self-definition. The third examines architecture and urbanism as related to the changing social and economic circumstances accompanying America's rapid post-Civil War urban and industrial growth. In the fourth part, architecture is studied in relation to the country's rising power and international contact in the late nineteenth and early twentieth centuries. The essays in the fifth part discuss the dissemination of, and eventual aversion to, modernism in the post-World War II period, while also making reference to modernism's relations to history and convention. In the sixth and final part, recent concerns about urban form and public space are represented. Each part is introduced by a note on the individual essays therein and by a brief bibliography pointing to related readings.[77]

People wishing to use the readings in ways other than those just outlined should have no trouble identifying alternative groupings. For example, the selections by Mary N. Woods, Anthony Alofsin, and Neil Levine each offer analyses of particular aspects of a single designer's career. Dell Upton, W. Barksdale Maynard, Kenneth L. Ames, and Richard Guy Wilson discuss the social and cultural implications of space and style. Margaret Kentgens-Craig and Mary McLeod consider professional discourse and public reception (with specific reference to architectural competitions), while Mona Domosh and Peter Nabokov and Robert Easton emphasize environmental and economic settings. Marc Treib, Daniel Bluestone, James F. O'Gorman, and Marc Spiegler concentrate on specific building types. John R. Stilgoe and Michael Sorkin address broad issues of urbanism and planning. John Michael Vlach, Robert W. Rydell, Katharine G. Bristol, and Mike Davis discuss race and class. Gwendolyn Wright, Joan Ockman, and Alice T. Friedman consider evolving notions of home, family, morality, and gender. There are numerous other ways in which the readings might be productively combined, and each stands well on its own.

Notes

1   J. Coolidge, "Preliminary Steps Towards 'The New History of Architecture'," *Journal of the American Society of Architectural Historians* 2, April 1942, 3. Unless they are directly quoted or paraphrased, book and journal titles given in full in the text are not included in the notes.

2   N. Pevsner, *An Outline of European Architecture*, New York: Charles Scribner's Sons, 1948, p. xix.

3   S. Kostof, *A History of Architecture: Settings and Rituals*, New York: Oxford University Press, 1985, p. 12.

4   See, for example, D. Upton, "Architectural History or Landscape History?," *Journal of Architectural Education* 44, August 1991, 195–199.

5   L. M. Roth, *American Architecture: A History*, Boulder, CO: Icon Editions/Westview Press, 2001; M. Gelernter, *A History of American Architecture: Buildings in Their Cultural and Technological Context*, Hanover, NH: University Press of New England, 1999; D. Upton, *Architecture in the United States*, Oxford: Oxford University Press, 1998; D. Handler, *American Architecture*, London: Thames and Hudson, 1985.

6   I do this for the simple reason that it is a convention, and because "American" is a less ungainly adjective than "United States."

7   On this early period see E. B. MacDougall (ed.), *The Architectural Historian in America: Studies in the History of Art* 35, Washington, DC: National Gallery of Art, 1990, particularly the

essays by MacDougall ("Before 1870: Founding Fathers and Amateur Historians," pp. 15–20), and L. Koenigsburg ("'Lifewriting': First American Biographers of Architects and Their Works," pp. 41–58). See also J. Schimmelman, *Architectural Books in Early America*, 2nd edn, New Castle, DE: Oak Knoll Press, 1999.

8   MacDougall, "Before 1870," p. 15.

9   Quoted in C. E. Clark, Jr, "Domestic Architecture as an Index to Social History: The Romantic Revival and the Cult of Domesticity in America, 1840–1870," in R. B. St George (ed.), *Material Life in America, 1600–1860*, Boston: Northeastern University Press, 1988, p. 539.

10   Quoted in L. M. Roth (ed.), *America Builds: Source Documents in American Architecture and Planning*, New York: Harper and Row, 1983, p. 23.

11   Quoted in C. N. Glaab (ed.), *The American City, A Documentary History*, Homewood, IL: Dorsey Press, 1963, pp. 20–22.

12   W. B. Rhoads, "The Discovery of America's Architectural Past," 1874–1914, in MacDougall (ed.), *Architectural Historian in America*, p. 23.

13   For recent discussions of Benjamin and Biddle, see K. Hafertepe and J. F. O'Gorman (eds), *American Architects and Their Books to 1848*, Amherst, MA: University of Massachusetts Press, 2001, especially the essays by Hafertepe ("*The Country Builder's Assistant*: Text and Context," pp. 129–148), and M. J. Lewis ("Owen Biddle and *The Young Carpenter's Assistant*," pp. 149–162).

14   Rhoads, "The Discovery of America's Architectural Past," p. 23.

15   W. Dunlap, *A History of the Rise and Progress of the Arts of Design in the United States* (1834), Boston: C. E. Goodspeed and Co., 1918 reprint edn, 3 vols. Another early, comparable text is B. Lossing's, *Outline History of the Fine Arts Embracing a View of the Rise, Progress, and Influence of the Arts among Different Nations, Ancient and Modern*, New York: Harper and Brothers, 1840.

16   Dunlap, *Rise and Progress*, 2: 173.

17   L. Tuthill, *The History of Architecture from the Earliest Times; Its Present Condition in Europe and the United States*, Philadelphia: Lindsay and Blakiston, 1848, "Dedication," and p. viii. For a recent discussion of Tuthill and her work see S. Allaback, "Louisa Tuthill, Ithiel Town, and the Beginnings of Architectural History Writing in America," in Hafertepe and O'Gorman (eds), *American Architects and Their Books*, pp. 199–215.

18   Another volume worth mentioning, particularly for its publication date—in the midst of the Civil War—is J. J. Jarves, *The Art Idea: Sculpture, Painting and Architecture in the United States*, Boston: Houghton Mifflin, 1864.

19   The short-lived American Institution of Architects was founded in New York in 1836. The 23 original members included Thomas U. Walter, Asher Benjamin, Minard Lafever, Alexander Parris, Alexander Jackson Davis, and Ithiel Town. Far more successful was the American Institute of Architects, founded in 1857 by Richard Upjohn and active to this day. See M. N. Woods, *From Craft to Profession: The Practice of Architecture in Nineteenth-Century America*, Berkeley, CA: University of California Press, 1999, pp. 28–38.

20   MacDougall, "Before 1870," p. 15. It should be noted that the professionalization of architecture and architectural history occurred alongside a general rise in disciplinary formation and specialization, and professionalization in many fields. See K. S. Lynn, *The Professions in America*, Boston: Houghton Mifflin, 1965. See also S. Burns, *Inventing the Modern Artist, Art and Culture in Gilded Age America*, New Haven, CT: Yale University Press, 1996.

21   See G. Wright, "History for Architects," in G. Wright and J. Parks (eds), *The History of History in American Schools of Architecture, 1865–1975*, New York: The Temple Hoyne Buell Center for the Study of American Architecture, 1990, p. 16.

22   For more on these figures see B. Bergdoll, *European Architecture, 1750–1890*, Oxford: Oxford University Press, 2000.

23   See Wright, "History for Architects," pp. 16–23; R. Plunz, "Reflections on Ware, Hamlin, McKim, and the Politics of History on the Cusp of Historicism," in Wright and Parks (eds), *History of History*, pp. 53–72; and K. N. Morgan and R. Cheek, "History in the Service of Design:

American Architect-Historians, 1870–1940," in MacDougall (ed.), *Architectural Historian in America*, pp. 61–73.24 Quoted in Koenigsberg, "Lifewriting," p. 49.

25   As Maynard has shown, numerous writers earlier in the nineteenth century had discussed American colonial architecture, though mainly in literary or philosophical contexts, rather than historical or design-related ones. See B. Maynard, "'Best, Lowliest Style!' The Early-Nineteenth Century Rediscovery of American Colonial Architecture," *Journal of the Society of Architectural Historians* 59, September 2000, 338–359.

26   Quoted in Roth (ed.), *America Builds*, pp. 238, 242.

27   Ibid., p. 233. See also M. Bacon, "Toward a National Style of Architecture: The Beaux-Arts Interpretation of the Colonial Revival," in A. Axelrod (ed.), *The Colonial Revival in America*, New York: W. W. Norton and Co., 1985, pp. 91–121.

28   M. Schuyler, "A History of Old Colonial Architecture," *Architectural Record* 4, January–March 1895, 312–366.

29   Rhoads, "America's Architectural Past," p. 32.

30   D. Upton, "Outside the Academy: A Century of Vernacular Architecture Studies, 1890–1990," in MacDougall (ed.), *Architectural Historian in America*, p. 204.

31   See M. Schuyler, *American Architecture and Other Writings*, W. H. Jordy and R. Coe (eds), Cambridge, MA: Belknap Press of Harvard University Press, 1961.

32   See P. Kaufman and P. Gabbard, "Appendix: American Doctoral Dissertations in Architectural and Planning History, 1898–1972," in MacDougall (ed.), *Architectural Historian in America*, pp. 288–313. According to Corn, the first dissertations in American *art* history did not appear until the 1940s. See W. M. Corn, "Coming of Age: Historical Scholarship in American Art," in M. A. Calo (ed.), *Critical Issues in American Art: A Book of Readings*, Boulder, CO: Icon Editions/Westview Press, 1998, p. 29, n. 23.

33   For discussion of the early European response to Wright's work see the essay by Anthony Alofsin in this volume.

34   T. Tallmadge, *The Story of Architecture in America*, New York: W. W. Norton and Co., 1927, pp. 5, 303.

35   Tallmadge, for instance, subtitled his book's introduction "In Which the Reader is Given His Stool by the Fireside," thus inadvertently (one assumes) calling to mind Christopher Robin and Pooh.

36   In this volume see, for example, the essays by Katharine G. Bristol, Mike Davis, and Michael Sorkin.

37   V. W. Brooks, "On Creating a Usable Past," *The Dial* 64, 1919, 339.

38   On Mumford, see R. Wojtowicz, *Lewis Mumford and American Modernism: Utopian Theories for Architecture and Urban Planning*, Cambridge: Cambridge University Press, 1996.

39   Corn, "Coming of Age," p. 6. For further discussion of the Americanness issue see Corn's *The Great American Thing: Modern Art and National Identity, 1915–1935*, Berkeley, CA: University of California Press, 1999.

40   For more on the early European response to American architecture, see: J.-L. Cohen, *Scenes of the World to Come: European Architecture and the American Challenge, 1893–1960*, Paris: Flammarion, 1995; and A. Lewis, *An Early Encounter With Tomorrow: Europeans, Chicago's Loop, and the World's Columbian Exposition*, Urbana, IL: University of Illinois Press, 1997.

41   See H. R. Hitchcock, Jr and P. Johnson, *The International Style: Architecture Since 1922*, New York: W. W. Norton and Co., 1932, and A. H. Barr, Jr *et al.*, *Modern Architects*, New York: Museum of Modern Art, 1932. For more on Hitchcock see H. Searing, "Henry-Russell Hitchcock: The Architectural Historian as Critic and Connoisseur," in MacDougall (ed.), *Architectural Historian in America*, pp. 251–263. For an historical perspective on the MOMA exhibition see T. Riley, *The International Style: Exhibition 15 and the Museum of Modern Art*, New York: Rizzoli/CBA, 1992.

42   Barr, "Preface," in Hitchcock and Johnson, *International Style*, p. 15.

43   J. McAndrew, *Guide to Modern Architecture, Northeast States*, New York: Museum of Modern Architecture, 1940, p. 14. See also his "Architecture in the United States," *Bulletin of the Museum of Modern Art*, vol. 6, nos. 1–2, February 1939, 2–12.

44   Our problem is one of life and death: on our success in facing it our very survival as a democratic people may depend. We must give form and order to a democratic civilization: we must create houses, schools, factories, farmsteads, villages, and cities that are fit to be called the home of a democratic people. . . . We must treat architecture, not as the luxurious art of the rich and powerful, but the fundamental expression of a democratic society.

                                     (L. Mumford, *The South in Architecture*, New York: Harcourt, Brace, and Co., pp. 8–9, 144–145)

45   E. Blau, "A Question of Discipline," *Journal of the Society of Architectural Historians* 62, March 2003, 125–127.

46   The Society was founded in 1940; the word "American" was later dropped from the Society's name and the journal's title.

47   C. L. V. Meeks, "The New History of Architecture, *Journal of the American Society of Architectural Historians* 2, January 1942, 5.

48   Coolidge, "Preliminary Steps," pp. 6, 10–11. Coolidge, Meeks and other Americans of this generation were certainly affected by the sophisticated, recent work of émigré art and architectural historians such as Erwin Panofsky and Richard Krautheimer. See, for example, E. Panofsky, *Studies in Iconology, Humanistic Themes in the Art of the Renaissance*, New York: Oxford University Press, 1939, and R. Krautheimer, "Introduction to an 'Iconography of Medieval Architecture'," *Journal of Warburg and Courtauld Institutes* 5, 1942, 1–33.

49   See Kaufman and Gabbard, "American Doctoral Dissertations," pp. 292–294. William Jordy and Carl Condit, two other key figures of this generation, wrote their dissertations during these years in history and English, respectively.

50   See the essays, and the introduction by N. Levine, in V. Scully, *Modern Architecture and Other Essays*, Princeton, NJ: Princeton University Press, 2003.

51   See, for example, C. Tunnard and H. H. Reed, *American Skyline: The Growth and Form of Our Cities and Towns*, New York: New American Library, 1956, and Bruno Zevi, *Frank Lloyd Wright*, Milan: Il Balcone, 1954. Several of Banham's early essays are reproduced in M. Banham *et al.* (eds), *A Critic Writes: Essays by Reynar Banham*, Berkeley, CA: University of California Press, 1996.

52   On Giedion see S. Georgiadis, *Sigfried Giedion: An Intellectual Biography*, trans. C. Hall, Edinburgh: Edinburgh University Press, 1993. See also E. Sekler, "Sigfried Giedion at Harvard University," in MacDougall (ed.), *Architectural Historian in America*, pp. 265–273.

53   For a good selection of Jackson's *Landscape* essays of the 1950s see E. H. Zube (ed.), *Landscapes: Selected Writings of J. B. Jackson*, Amherst, MA: University of Massachusetts Press, 1970.

54   Kaufman and Gabbard, "American Doctoral Dissertations," pp. 291–292, 303–304. For more on this period see Wright, "History for Architects," pp. 36–46.

55   W. A. Coles (ed.), *Architecture And Society: Selected Essays Of Henry Van Brunt*, Cambridge, MA: Belknap Press of Harvard University Press, 1969.

56   J. M. Vlach, "The Shotgun House: An African Architectural Legacy," *Pioneer America: Journal of Historic American Material Culture* 8, January–July 1976, 47–70. J. Meikle, *Twentieth-Century Limited: Industrial Design in America, 1925–1939*, Philadelphia, PA: Temple University Press, 1979. R. S. Cowan, "The Industrial Revolution in the Home: Household Technology and Social Change in the Twentieth Century," *Technology and Culture* 17, January 1976, 1–23. B. Blackmar, "Re-walking in the 'Walking City': Housing and Property Relation in New York City, 1780–1840," *Radical History Review* 21, Fall 1979, 131–148.

57   See also D. Hayden, *Seven American Utopias: The Architecture of Communitarian Socialism, 1790–1975*, Cambridge, MA: MIT Press, 1976; Susana Torré, *Women in Architecture: A Historic and Contemporary Perspective*, New York: Whitney Library of Design, 1977; and G. Wright, *Moralism and the Modern Home: Domestic Architecture and Cultural Conflict in Chicago, 1873–1913*, Chicago, IL: University of Chicago Press, 1980.

58   John Maass, "Where Architectural Historians Fear to Tread, *American Society of Architectural Historians Journal* 28, March 1969, 3–8.

59   See, for example, R. Sennett, *The Fall of Public Man*, New York: Knopf, 1976; W. H. Whyte, *The Last Landscape*, Garden City, NY: Doubleday, 1968; H. Glassie, *Folk Housing in Middle Virginia*, Knoxville, TN: University of Tennessee Press, 1975; P. Lewis, *New Orleans, The Making of an Urban Landscape*, Cambridge, MA: Ballinger Pub. Co., 1976; D. W. Meinig (ed.), *The Interpretation of Ordinary Landscapes*, New York: Oxford University Press, 1979; W. H. Wilson, *Coming of Age: Urban America, 1915–1945*, New York: Wiley, 1974; J. Kasson, *Civilizing the Machine: Technology and Republican Values in America, 1776–1900*, New York: Grossman Pubs., 1976; and A. Trachtenberg, *Brooklyn Bridge: Fact and Symbol*, New York: Oxford University Press, 1965.

60   Blau, "A Question of Discipline," 128. See also M. Schwarzer, "History and Theory in Architectural Periodicals: Assembling Oppositions," *Journal of the Society of Architectural Historians* 58, September 1999, 342–348. For a representative collection of recent, theoretically informed architectural writing see K. M. Hays (ed.), *Architecture Theory Since 1968*, Cambridge, MA: MIT Press/Columbia Books of Architecture, 1998.

61   J. Deetz, *In Small Things Forgotten: An Archaeology of Early American Life*, Garden City, NY: Anchor Press/Doubleday, 1977, p. 161. For more on material culture scholarship see: T. J. Schlereth (ed.), *Material Culture Studies in America*, Walnut Creek, CA: AltaMira Press, 1999; and S. Lubar and W. D. Kingery (eds), *History From Things: Essays on Material Culture*, Washington, DC: Smithsonian Institution Press, 1993 (see particularly the essay by J. D. Prown, "The Truth of Material Culture: History or Fiction?," pp. 1–19).

62   For a wide-ranging overview of architectural history activity in this period, conducted by several well-informed authors, see E. Blau (ed.), "Architectural History 1999/2000: A Special Issue of *JSAH*," *Journal of the Society of Architectural Historians* 58, September 1999. See also M. Trachtenberg, "Some Observations on Recent Architectural History," *Art Bulletin* 70, June 1988, 208–241.

63   See, for example, A. Friedman, "The Way You Do the Things You Do: Writing the History of Houses and Housing," *Journal of the Society of Architectural Historians* 58, September 1999, 407.

64   Dell Upton, for example, was trained in an American studies program; John Michael Vlach studied folklore; Mona Domosh is a cultural geographer.

65   See A. Friedman, "The Way You Do the Things You Do."

66   Ibid.

67   S. Lavin, "Theory Into History, or, the Will to Anthologize," *Journal of the Society of Architectural Historians* 58, September 1999, 497.

68   C. Gallagher and S. Greenblaat, *Practicing New Historicism*, Chicago, IL: University of Chicago Press, 2000, p. 20. See also H. A. Veeser (ed.), *The New Historicism*, New York: Routledge, 1989.

69   For a succinct discussion of discourse analysis, see M. Leja, *Reframing Abstract Expressionism: Subjectivity and Painting in the 1940s*, New Haven, CT: Yale University Press, 1993, pp. 10–12.

70   N. Stieber, "Editorial: Architecture Between Disciplines," *Journal of the Society of Architectural Historians* 62, June 2003, 176.

71   See, for example, Foucault's *The Order of Things: An Archaeology of the Human Sciences*, New York: Pantheon Books, 1970, and *Discipline and Punish: The Birth of the Prison*, trans. A. Sheridan, New York: Pantheon Books, 1977.

72   In this volume see, for example, the essays by Kenneth L. Ames, Anthony Alofsin, Joan Ockman, and Katharine G. Bristol.

73   Corn, "Coming of Age," p. 17.

74   See M. Fried, *Realism, Writing, Disfiguration: On Thomas Eakins and Stephen Crane*, Chicago, IL: University of Chicago Press, 1987; D. Lubin, *Act of Portrayal: Eakins, Sargent, James*, New Haven, CT: Yale University Press, 1985; and A. Nemerov, *Frederic Remington and Turn-of-the-Century America*, New Haven, CT: Yale University Press, 1995.

75   K. L. Ames, *Death in the Dining Room and Other Tales of Victorian Culture*, Philadelphia, PA: Temple University Press, 1992, p. 6.

76   See Foucault, *Order of Things*.

77   In keeping with this book's concentration on relatively recent scholarship, most items in these bibliographies post-date 1970. For more comprehensive bibliographies see those in Roth, *American Architecture*; Upton, *Architecture in the United States*; and Gelernter, *A History of American Architecture*.

Part 1 |

Staking claim, shaping space

The first European settlers in what is now the US saw the American landscape as virgin territory, raw and undeveloped. They brought with them tools and memories, patterns and conventions, which they used to shape their new homes. The tools and memories they retained for some time; the patterns and conventions, however, needed to be adapted to the new environments—quite different from those left behind in Europe—if people were to survive and prosper. The land shaped the people as they shaped it.

Never again would the American continent seem so utterly and frighteningly void of design as it did to these first settlers, so in need of ordering systems for its habitation and successful exploitation. As environmental historian John R. Stilgoe demonstrates, the grid provided Europeans with one of their first and most successful tools for ordering this space. Focusing in this excerpt on the grid's practical and economic advantages, Stilgoe shows how the design of a mercantile city like Philadelphia became a template for shaping other towns and territories across the American continent.

While European settlers did not always recognize or appreciate their efforts, Native American groups had long preceded them in shaping the land for human habitation. Peter Nabokov and Robert Easton provide a broad introduction to Native-American architecture, one that extends across time, region, and culture. They consider technology, climate, economics, social organization, religion, and history as the major "modifying factors" in traditional Native-American building; meanwhile, they see buildings themselves as indicative of the elements dominating the lives of particular groups. A brief discussion of the architectural and cultural effects of contact with Europeans concludes their essay and points to two important, related themes: cultural borrowing, hybridity, and translation in architecture, and architecture's role in the expression of cultural continuity and identity.

Seeking a foothold in the harsh, remote northern limits of New Spain, while dependent on Indian labor and restricted to the same limited range of materials available to local native groups, European settlers in what is, today, New Mexico, were likewise confronted by these issues. In establishing missions and "rationalizing" existing Indian construction techniques as they did, the Spanish aimed to assert a European presence in the "wilderness." Marc Treib, an architect by training, offers here a detailed examination of the design, construction, and form of Spanish-colonial-era sacred spaces in New Mexico. Following this, Dell Upton, a former student of historical archaeologist James Deetz and folklorist Henry Glassie, looks at other spaces, both sacred and secular, through a different lens: as the material signs of culture. Upton considers the hierarchical ordering of spaces and the patterns of use and ritual found in certain English-colonial Virginia churches, courthouses, and dwellings. In these he finds evidence of deep social structures and of shifting conceptions of time, memory, and nature.

Further reading

Carson, C., R. Hoffman, and P. J. Albert (eds), *Of Consuming Interests: The Style of Life in the Eighteenth Century*, Charlottesville, VA: University of Virginia Press, 1994.

Cooke, J. E. (ed.), *Encyclopedia of the North American Colonies*, 3 vols, New York: C. Scribner's Sons, 1993.

Cronan, W., *Changes in the Land: Indians, Colonists, and the Ecology of New England*, New York: Hill and Wang, 1983.

Cummings, A. L., *The Framed Houses of Massachusetts Bay, 1625–1725*, Cambridge, MA: Belknap Press of Harvard University Press, 1979.

De Cunzo, L. A. and B. L. Herman (eds), *Historical Archaeology and the Study of American Culture*, Winterthur, DE: Henry Francis Dupont Winterthur Museum, 1996.

Deetz, J., *In Small Things Forgotten: An Archaeology of Early American Life*, New York: Anchor Books, Doubleday, 1996 expanded and revised edn.

Edgerton, S. Y., *Theaters of Conversion: Religious Architecture and Indian Artisans in Colonial Mexico*, Albuquerque, NM: University of New Mexico Press, 2001.

Garrett, W., *American Colonial: Puritan Simplicity to Georgian Grace*, New York: The Monacelli Press, 1995.

Pierson, W. H. Jr, *American Buildings and Their Architects, Vol. 1: The Colonial and Neoclassical Styles*, New York: Oxford University Press, 1970.

Reps, J. W., *The Making of Urban America: A History of City Planning in the United States*, Princeton, NJ: Princeton University Press, 1965.

Scully, V., *Pueblo: Mountain, Village, Dance*, New York: Viking Press, 1975.

St George, R. B. (ed.), *Material Life in America, 1600–1860*, Boston, MA: Northeastern University Press, 1988.

Sweeney, K. M., "Meeting Houses, Town Houses, and Churches: Changing Perceptions of Sacred and Secular Space in Southern New England, 1720–1850," *Winterthur Portfolio* 28: 1 (1993): 59–93.

Upton, D. (ed.), *America's Architectural Roots: Ethnic Groups That Built America*, New York: Preservation Press and John Wiley and Sons, 1986.

Upton, D. and J. M. Vlach (eds), *Common Places: Readings in American Vernacular Architecture*, Athens and London: University of Georgia Press, 1986.

Wenger, M. R., "The Central Passage in Virginia: Evolution of an Eighteenth-Century Living Space," *Perspectives in Vernacular Architecture* 2 (1986): 137–149.

Chapter 1

John R. Stilgoe

National design
Mercantile cities and the grid

Everyone recognizes checkerboard America. Like a great geometrical carpet, like a Mondrian painting, the United States west of the Appalachians is ordered in a vast grid. Nothing strikes an airborne European as more typically American than the great squares of farms reaching from horizon to horizon.

Only the fields are noticeable from 20,000 feet. At lower altitudes flyers discern among them the scattered farmsteads connected by ruler-straight gravel and blacktop roads. They marvel at the pattern and scrutinize the fields and farmsteads, wondering what crops show up so yellow at midsummer and worrying that the farmers might be lonely. Few look closely at the lines that hatch the countryside below; the lines seem accidental, the result of pastures abutting wheat fields and the building of roads. Almost no one perceives the regular spacing of the lines or guesses that the lines predate the fields and structures.

Section lines, like lines on graph paper, made the grid and make it still. They objectify the Enlightenment in America. Late in the eighteenth century they existed only in surveyors' notebooks and on the rough maps carefully stored in federal land office drawers. Here and there a blazed tree or pile of stones marked an intersection, but otherwise the lines existed only as invisible guides. Not until farmers settled the great rectangles platted by the surveyors and began shaping the land did the lines become more than legal abstractions of boundaries. Along them farmers built fences to mark their property limits and to divide livestock from corn, and along many they built roads too. Now and then a historically minded flyer, often a foreigner intrigued by the geometric regularity of the countryside below, swoops down and hedgehops above a section line, following it as Wolfgang Langewiesche did in 1939. "First it was a dirt road, narrow between two hedges, with a car crawling along it dragging a tail of dust. Then the road turned off, but the line went straight ahead, now as a barbed wire fence through a large pasture, with a thin footpath trod out on each side by each neighbor as he went, week after week, year after year, to inspect his fence. Then the fence stopped, but now there was corn on one side of the line and something green on the other."[1] On and on Langewiesche flew, following the half-abstract, half-physical line across pasture land and arable, through a small town, and on into farms again. "When I climbed away and resumed my course," he remarked half-wonderingly, "I left it as a fence which has cows on one side and no cows on the other. That's a section line."[2] Like many amateur pilots, Langewiesche appreciated section lines because they run rigidly north-south, east-west; despite being an eighteenth-century creation, they are a superb navigational aid. Nothing man has built into the American wilderness is more orderly.

On the ground, only the most perceptive travelers consciously recognize section lines. Here and there a hilltop offers a view of lines and right-angle intersections, but elsewhere the grid is masked by the slightly rolling topography that characterizes most of the Middle West. Farmers and other inhabitants of the grid country think nothing of the straight roads and property lines they have inherited from their forebears. Not until they drive east, into the coastal states and Kentucky, Vermont, and Tennessee, are they suddenly aware that behind them lies a landscape of more obvious order. All at once they recognize the absence of the geometrical structure that shapes their space, colors their speech, and subtly influences their lives, and they perceive the dominance of older, distinctly regional landscape skeletons.

MERCANTILE CITIES

William Penn introduced the grid to the English colonies in 1681, when he directed his agents and surveyors to lay out a city in Pennsylvania (Figure 1.1). Philadelphia was a city by intention, not accident, and it was markedly different from the few other large towns along the coast. Penn did not invent the urban grid—the towns of northern New Spain

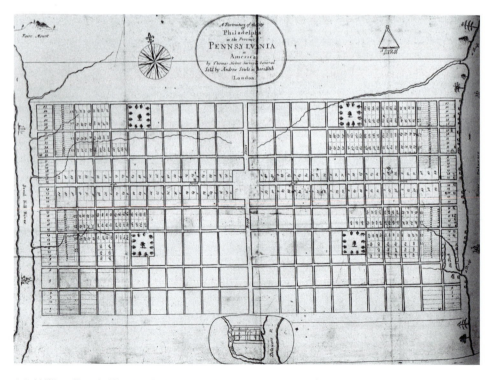

1.1 William Penn's Plan for Philadelphia, Pennsylvania, 1682 (from John C. Lowber, *Ordinances of the Corporation of the City of Philadelphia*, Philadelphia: Moses Thomas, 1812)

1.2 *The City of Boston,* Parsons and Atwater delineators, published by Currier and Ives, New York, 1873

were ordered about a plaza and streets intersecting at right angles, and nine years before Philadelphia, Charleston in South Carolina was laid out "into regular streets"—but he emphasized the grid above walls, meetinghouses, and public squares. From the beginning, its streets defined and distinguished Philadelphia.

Until the 1740s colonial space struck visitors as simply rural. Only Boston (Figure 1.2), Newport, New York, Charleston, and above all Philadelphia broke the uniformity of farming settlements. As late as the 1690s, even Boston scarcely impressed visiting Europeans, although it was the center of most New England shipping, the seat of the Bay Colony government, and frequently compared by its inhabitants to the "city of London."[3] But at the close of the seventeenth century, Philadelphia promised only an imminent urbanity; Boston seemed certain to retain its place as the foremost English "merchandise" town.

The city upon a hill envisioned by John Winthrop began as an agricultural settlement on a peninsula. Like all other New Englanders, its inhabitants occupied themselves with allocating house lots and planting land, and with regulating the use of common pasture, meadow, and woods. Two years after its founding, approximately forty houses, each surrounded by a vegetable garden and some already dignified by sapling fruit trees, clustered haphazardly about a meetinghouse. Bostonians worried about growing enough food for themselves and focused their attention on the poor soil and the daily adventure of agriculture in a new place and a new climate.[4] Even as more and more immigrants landed at Town Cove and sought food, shelter, and seed, Bostonians behaved as did most other New Englanders, shaping the land and ordering society.

Seventeen years later 315 houses and 45 additional buildings bespoke Boston's new role. England's Civil War reduced immigration to a trickle after 1642 and deprived Bostonians of their entrepôt livings. All at once citizens discovered the necessity of locating new markets, and they directed their attention to the West Indies and Europe. At first Bostonians captured only the coasting trade, bringing lumber and cattle and cod from New Hampshire and the Grand Banks to the hungry plantations of the southern colonies and the West Indies, and carrying home molasses.[5] The trade prospered as New England's agricultural settlements produced larger and larger surpluses, and the Bostonians built larger ships and sailed for the Portuguese Islands, England, and the European continent in what became known as the triangular trade. Within two decades of the closing of immigration, Boston was something that other New England settlements except Newport were not, although exactly what puzzled visitors and natives alike. It was easy enough to see the physical differences, however, and traveler after traveler remarked on them.

Commerce weaned Bostonians from agriculture, and soon they jammed houses and other structures so closely together that houselot gardening almost vanished, at least near the waterfront. Craftsmen worked frantically erecting houses for newcomers like William Rix, who commissioned a one-room house, sixteen feet long and fourteen wide, with a cellar and loft, clapboarded walls and roof, and a timber chimney. It was an impossibly small house for a family man who made his living by weaving, and Rix requested a second structure to house his loom and other tools. Compared with Governor Winthrop's "mansion," Rix's house was simple indeed, a clear objectification of Puritan hierarchical society. But the loom-shed acquired a special significance because it revealed that Rix did not farm full time and that his specialized occupation kept him busy enough to require and support a specialized structure.[6] Craftsmen like Rix understood the necessity for specialized workspace, and Boston's carpenters, brickmakers, limeworkers, masons, sawyers, brewers, bakers, coopers, tanners, butchers, smiths, shipwrights, sailmakers, ropemakers, joiners soon produced structures of every sort, each type adapted to a particular calling.

Weavers and other craftsmen bought most of their food and raw materials from husbandmen who lived in outlying agricultural settlements and who walked to Boston filled with anticipation not only of profits but of excitement. In Boston they exchanged their produce for cash or services or else bartered it for imported or manufactured items impossible to obtain in their home settlements. Retail shops blossomed along the narrow, twisting streets, catering mostly to Bostonians but also to countrymen. "The town is full of good shops well furnished with all kinds of merchandise," remarked one inhabitant, and it was filled with shoppers too. By 1680 Boston supported twenty-four silversmiths, a sure sign of growing prosperity.

Six years after the founding of Boston the selectmen ordered that two "street ways" be laid out to accommodate the townspeople. Never again, however, did the town pay much attention to its growing traffic problem. More and more frequently it temporarily solved access problems by empowering individuals to open streets at their own cost; at the time the policy seemed sound. Boston received a new street or two, and the undertakers realized a profit by selling the abutting lots. Not surprisingly, such streets were narrow and crooked, but their very irregularity produced a wealth of changing views and surprises.[7]

That Bostonians thought in terms of streets rather than roads or ways is significant because in the late sixteenth century *street* had already acquired richly evocative connotations. The word no longer meant merely a road or cartway but a passage in a city or town, a pathway through the verticality made by houses and other structures, and often bordered with pedestrian sidewalks. Even more than the king's highway, a street promised excitement and activity, and particularly the likelihood of meeting strangers, because *street* connoted above all else half-controlled urban chaos. Seventeenth-century Bostonians understood the connotation very well indeed, for as early as the 1650s their streets, in the words of one observer, were "full of girls and boys sporting up and down, with a continued concourse of people." Strangers of every sort thronged the streets: newly arrived immigrants waiting while their representatives selected fertile sites for settlements, seamen from English ships, merchants from other colonies, and countrymen from nearby towns. Whether the strangers tarried for only several days or decided to settle permanently in the port, Bostonians usually made them welcome because almost always they paid in cash for whatever goods and services they obtained. Unlike the ideal space specified in [Winthrop's 1635 essay on] "The Ordering of Towns," the town's built environment quickly adapted to a continuous concourse of strangers. Boston was a place of exciting streets, not of roads and lanes.

Unlike most other New England settlements, Boston—and later Newport—acquired two spatial foci, and then several more. In its earliest years Boston focused on its meetinghouse, and because of its almost island-like site, no settlement more closely resembled the concentric utopia described in "The Ordering of Towns." Within one or two years, however, a second focus challenged the meetinghouse hierophany. Town Cove made a natural landing place, where deep water closely abutted the shore and where islands and headlands sheltered anchored ships from storms. William Wood foresaw that its deep harbor would make Boston the "chief place for shipping and merchandise" in New England, and other seventeenth-century visitors agreed.[8] Bostonians proved Wood correct. They built their first wharf at Town Cove, and then another, and then several more, until by 1645 fifteen wharves jutted into the harbor. Waterfront matters preoccupied the town elders, who ordered that piers be kept clear of buildings, that "no annoying things be left or laid about the sea shore" to decay and smell, and that two privies be erected at the wharves for the convenience of strangers. Bostonians rapidly grew too numerous for a single meetinghouse, and their clergy determined to split into separate "churches" or congregations, each of which erected its own meetinghouse. By 1680 Boston lacked the single religious hierophany that characterized almost all other New England settlements. Its jammed streets converged on an ever more congested—and ever more exciting—waterfront. Ministers warned of the evils of greed but their sermons failed to distract the people's attention from worldly matters.

New Amsterdam, Newport, and later Charleston struggled to emulate successful Boston, but not for decades did they achieve even a measure of Boston's prosperity or a semblance of Boston's excitement. Nevertheless, in each town wise men insisted that waterfronts receive increasing capital investment and scrutiny; shortly after 1680, for example, a group of Newport men built Long Wharf, a structure that surpassed even Boston's most handsome piers. In each town the public treasury supplemented private investment in anything that quickened commerce—bridges, ship channels, drainage ditches, and even

It was a Dutch engineer and city planner, Simon Stevin of The Hague, who deciphered the contradictions in seventeenth-century town-planning theory. Like so many of his countrymen, Stevin immersed himself in mercantile economics (he popularized double-entry bookkeeping in Western Europe) but his business sense clashed with his training in military engineering. Eventually he devised a compromise solution to design problems bedeviling city fathers intent on military protection and economic growth. He discarded the old notions of circles and other ideal forms and substituted for them the concept of symmetry. Stevin's ideal city is a rectangle, walled to be sure, but ordered by a grid of streets intersecting at right angles. Instead of one, it has several foci: a cathedral square, a palace for its prince, several small squares intended as neighborhood marketplaces, and a waterfront devoted to commerce.[12] Little of Stevin's ideal design was new in 1630; it synthesized plans and designs known, although only theoretically, since 1500. Stevin's insight lay first in his understanding that a grid of streets might be extended in any direction with little modification of the encompassing walls, and that a grid allowed for major changes anywhere within the walls. Stevin's ideal city is not, therefore, a static form like the ideal Spanish *estensión* or ideal New England town focused on a single central plaza or meetinghouse. Rather it is engineered to accept and order change, and especially to order growth. Far more importantly, however, Stevin explicitly recognized the evolving nature of society, not only in the Netherlands but elsewhere. Mercantile capitalism was slowly destroying the old order of hierarchy and eunomy objectified in so many *landschappen*, and the grid town seemed to him—and to many successors—perfectly adapted to a new way of life.

Penn probably knew nothing of Stevin's essays and designs, but there is no dismissing the striking similarity between his plan of Philadelphia and the Dutch engineer's plans for an ideal city. Like Stevin, Penn seems to have understood the changing nature of society, and for all that the proprietor of Pennsylvania may have learned from the grid-street plans submitted in the competition to rebuild London after the Great Fire of 1666, Philadelphia's pattern derived in large measure from the spirit of an era of change.[13]

In the beginning Penn intended to lay out Philadelphia as an agricultural village in which every purchaser of 500 acres of planting land would be entitled to a houselot of 10 acres. Almost immediately, however, Penn abandoned the scheme and determined to build a mercantile, not an agricultural, town. He instructed his surveyors to find a site "where most ships may best ride, of deepest draught of water, if possible to load or unload at the bank or key side," and only afterward noted that the site ought to be healthy and fertile too. Philadelphia's waterfront preoccupied Penn. He ordered that no house be located closer to the shore than a quarter mile in order that streets and warehouses might be built without hindrance, and he stressed that each waterfront lot have at least 800 feet of shore. When Penn arrived at Philadelphia in 1682 he immediately extended the grid of streets to the bank of the Schuylkill, so that the city had *two* waterfronts. He concerned himself less with the inland or "backward" part of the city, although he specified that every house be seated in the middle of its lot, so that the city "may be a green country town, which will never be burnt, and always be wholesome," and he located a great square of ten acres at the center (for a meetinghouse, government hall, markethouse, and schoolhouse—and perhaps for his own residence) and a lesser square of eight acres in each of the four quarters of the city (for marketplaces). Between the waterfronts, however, Philadelphia's most striking feature was its grid of streets.[14] Nine great streets ran from "front to front," all crossed at right angles by twenty-one others. All were fifty feet wide, except for High and Broad streets, whose hundred-foot widths convinced newcomers that Philadelphia seemed destined for an urban greatness far beyond that of Boston or, indeed, most European cities.

Penn's surveyors platted only 1,280 acres, and at first the city's straggling appearance disappointed visitors. Within three years, however, 600 houses lined the streets nearest the city axis, and the waterfronts, particularly the Delaware one, flourished. A new dock 300 feet square jutted into the river, and near it stood the shops and houses of all manner of craftsmen from shoemakers and glaziers to brickmakers and woodturners. By 1685 men thought nothing of building in brick and had begun work on a great brick meetinghouse. Such furious activity resulted in part from steady immigration; Pennsylvania attracted settlers from England and its colonies as well as from elsewhere in Europe. The newcomers often discovered a place for themselves in Philadelphia especially if they knew a useful trade, and never began farming. But much of the growth came from Penn's understanding of the city's mercantile function; twice a week great markets convened at the central square, and twice each year a great fair attracted husbandmen and traders from across the growing colony.[15] Penn's emerging road system brought more and more produce to Philadelphia for sale and trans-shipment to Europe or other colonies and offered quick access to the interior for imported goods. Like Stevin's ideal city, Philadelphia reached both to a developing backcountry and to the world of ocean commerce. Soon traffic jammed its great straight streets.

For fifteen years Penn's original plans directed the city's growth. Vine Street, Chestnut Street, Strawberry Street, and the other two-mile-long streets that linked the two waterfronts ordered visitors' impressions of the city while channeling traffic and real estate development. But around the turn of the century several canny inhabitants exploited the potential for common development implicit in Penn's grand design. They subdivided the great houselots and snaked narrow alleys down the middle of blocks; the modifications provided landowners with addition access and the possibility of selling or renting "streetfront" property. Gabriel Thomas, who had arrived in Philadelphia in 1681, described the subdivision process in 1698. He found "very many lanes and alleys" between Front Street and Second Street on the Delaware waterfront and decided that the narrow ways represented Philadelphia industry as much as the great streets. Thomas was no doubt pleased with the 2,000 brick houses he saw about him, most "three stories high, after the mode in London," and with the many warehouses and shops, and like most other commentators on the city's appearance and character emphasized the citizens' accomplishments rather than such serious shortcomings as unpaved and miry streets. Penn's great grid guided the growth of the city well into the eighteenth century but within its framework landowners experimented with other designs.

Benjamin Franklin encountered the grid on his arrival in Philadelphia in 1721, when he walked away from the dock in search of a meal and bought the famous three pennyworth of bread, which he carried under his arms. "Thus I went up Market Street as far as

Colonial cities remained small, in both size and population, and even Philadelphia seemed only a tiny interruption in land shaped for agriculture. Away from the crowded waterfront, where scarcity of building land made every foot of dry soil extremely expensive, city dwellers enjoyed (sometimes) a small yard graced with a fruit tree, and many continued to keep a stall-fed cow or two, along with poultry. Despite the best efforts of city fathers to protect children and property, hogs wandered along the streets, eating whatever offal they discovered and now and then interfering with pedestrian movement. Beyond the high-priced land, householders enjoyed even larger lots and planted gardens in order to enjoy fresh vegetables in summer. Now and then a traveler wondered where landscape ended and cityscape began because some of the houses in the vague interface sheltered men who worked part-time at agriculture, and part-time at urban crafts like boatbuilding. Somewhere along the road from "the country," travelers entered "the city," but only where the city boasted a grid of straight streets did travelers see anything like a clear edge. Otherwise they drifted through the zone no one called suburban but in which builders combined the agriculture-based shapes and structures with the spaces and buildings derived from commerce. No fortifications and gates marked the division between rural and urban space.

GRID

May 20, 1785, is a momentous date in United States history. On that day Congress authorized the surveying of the western territories (the "backland," as the Congressmen called them during the lengthy debates) into six-mile-square townships. Each township, Congress directed, would be bounded by lines running due north-south and east-west; other parallel lines would divide each township into thirty-six square sections of 640 acres each. The Land Ordinance of 1785 began in compromises that truly satisfied no one, but with minor revisions it determined the spatial organization of two-thirds of the present United States.[19] The Ohio farmer of 1820—and much later the Wyoming rancher and the California fruit grower—settled and shaped wilderness surveyed according to the traditional and Enlightenment optimism that translated the *urban* grid of Philadelphia onto land destined for agriculture. [. . .]

For all its shortcomings, the grid proved reasonably effective in ordering the land for sale and settlement. People grew accustomed to it, so accustomed in fact that even had the federal government wished to alter it or to discard it for some better form, public opposition would have proved too strong. Phrases such as "a square deal" and "he's a foursquare man" entered the national vocabulary as expressions of righteousness and fairness. By the 1860s the grid objectified national, not regional, order, and no one wondered at rural space marked by urban rectilinearity. [. . .]

Notes

1   Wolfgang Langewiesche, *I'll Take the Highroad* (New York: Harcourt, 1930), pp. 126–27; *A Flier's World* (New York: McGraw-Hill, 1951); "The USA From the Air," *Harpers* 21 (October 1950): 176–88. Foreigners are especially intrigued by the grid (Harold Haefner,

Höhenstufen, offentliche Ländereien und private Landnutzung auf der Ostseite der Sierra Nevada (Zurich: Juris, 1970), and Arthur Glikson, *The Ecological Basis of Planning* (The Hague: Nijhoff, 1972), esp. p. 57.

2   Langewiesche, *Highroad*, p. 127.

3   Carl Bridenbaugh, *Cities in the Wilderness* (New York: Ronald, 1938); Robert Albion, *The Rise of New York Port* (London, 1939); Blaine Brownell and David Goldfield, *The City in Southern History*, (Port Washington, NY, 1977). Most United States scholars totally ignore the cities of New Spain. For the early modern European background to New World urbanization, see Karl Huellmann, *Städtewesen des Mittelalters* (Bonn: Marcus, 1826).

4   Walter Muir Whitehill, *Boston: A Topographical History* (Cambridge: Harvard University Press, 1968), esp. pp. 1–21.

5   William B. Weeden, *Economic and Social History at New England, 1620–1789* (Boston: Houghton, 1891).

6   On Rix, see Darrett Rutman, *Winthrop's Boston: Portrait of a Puritan Town, 1630–1649* (1965) (New York: Norton, 1972 reprint ed.), pp. 192–94.

7   Rutman, *Winthrop's Boston*; Edward Johnson, *Wonder-Working Providence* (New York, 1910), p. 71.

8   William Wood, *New England's Prospect* (1654), ed. J. F. Jameson (New York: Scribner's, 1910), p. 59; on wharves, see Rutman, *Winthrop's Boston*, pp. 40, 83, 193, 207, 247–48; on churches, pp. 95–251.

9   On Charleston, see Howard Nelson, "Walled Cities of the United States," *AAG Journals* 51 (March 1961), esp. 254; on "forts and half moons," see *Statutes at Large of South Carolina, 1662–1838*, ed. Thomas Cooper and David J. McCord (Columbia, SC: Johnston, 1836–41), VII: pp. 28–30.

10 Bridenbaugh, *Cities in the Wilderness*, p. 66; Henry Smith, "Charleston: The Original Plan and the Earliest Settlers," *South Carolina Historical and Genealogical Magazine* 9 (January 1908): 12–27; John Reps, *The Making of Urban America* (Princeton, NJ: Princeton University Press, 1965), pp. 174–77.

11 Robert Beverly, *The History and Present State of Virginia* (1705), ed. Louis B. Wright (Charlottesville: University of Virginia Press, 1968), p. 105; Hugh Jones, *The Present State of Virginia* (1753), ed. Richard L. Morton (Chapel Hill: University of North Carolina Press, 1956), pp. 25, 28; on Annapolis and Williamsburg, see also Reps, *Making of Urban America*, pp. 108–14.

12 Simon Stevin, *Materiae Politica: Burgherliche Stoffen* (Leyden: Iustus Livias, 1649), esp. "Van de ordening der Steden" [pagination is missing or erratic].

13 On Penn's possible drawing from the London fire plans, see Reps, *Making of Urban America*, p. 163.

14 Samuel Hazard, *Annals of Pennsylvania from the Discovery of the Delaware* (Philadelphia: Hazard, 1850), pp. 505–13.

15 William Penn, "Instructions" [1681], Historical Society of Pennsylvania, *Memoirs* 2 (1827): 213–21; Rowland Ellis, "Philadelphia in 1698," *Pennsylvania Magazine of History and Biography* 18 (July 1894): 245–48; Stephanie Grauman Wolf, *Urban Village: Community and Family in Germantown, Pennsylvania* (Princeton, NJ: Princeton University Press, 1976).

16 Benjamin Franklin, *Autobiography* (1789), ed. Russell B. Nye (Boston: Houghton, 1958 reprint ed.), pp. 22, 23, 25.

17 On taverns, see Bridenbaugh, *Cities in the Wilderness*, pp. 106–10, and Franklin, *Autobiography*, pp. 22–23, 25.

18 Joshua Gilpin, "Journal of a Tour from Philadelphia through the Western Counties of Pennsylvania in the Months of September and October, 1809," *Pennsylvania Magazine of History and Biography* 50 (1926): 64–78, 163–78, 380–82; John Pearson, "Description of Lancaster and Columbia in 1801," *Lancaster County Historical Society Journal* 61 (1957): 49–61; John Penn, "Journal of a Visit to Reading, Harrisburg, Carlisle, and Lancaster in 1788," *Pennsylvania*

Magazine of History and Biography 3 (1879): 284–95; John C. Ogden, *An Excursion into Bethelem and Nazareth in Pennsylvania in the Year 1799* (Philadelphia: Grist, 1800); see also Richard C. Wade, *The Urban Frontier: The Rise of Western Cities, 1790–1830* (Cambridge: Harvard University Press, 1959) (the Drake quotation is on p. 29). See also Reps, *Making of Urban America*, pp. 204–39, and Pierce Lewis, "Small Town in Pennsylvania," *AAG Journals* 62 (1972): 323–51.

19 For an introduction to the evolution of the grid, see Hildegard Johnson, *Order Upon the Land: The United States Rectangular Land Survey and the Upper Mississippi Valley* (New York: Oxford University Press, 1976), "Rational and Ecological Aspects of the Quarter Section: An Example from Minnesota", and "The Orderly Landscape: Landscape Tastes and the United States Survey"; see also Jackson, "The Order of a Landscape: Reason and Religion in Newtonian America," in D. W. Meinig, ed., *The Interpretation of Ordinary Landscapes* (New York: Oxford University Press, 1979), pp. 153–63, and Charles Whittlesey, "Origins of the American System of Land Surveys," *Association of Engineering Societies Journal* 3 (September 1884): 275–80.

Chapter 2

Peter Nabokov and Robert Easton

"Modifying factors" in Native American architecture

It is impossible to single out why any Indian dwelling looked and worked the way it did. To be sure, Indians were responding to the climate around them and making the most of natural building materials at hand. But the evolution of a particular habitation also was affected by social organization, patterns of gathering food, religious life, and history. To understand the factors that form Indian architecture, one must look for what environment and culture made possible, not inevitable. Before proposing a major determinant for the design of a tribal building, one must undertake the "long and painstaking accumulation of recalcitrant detail," in the words of architectural scholar P.G. Anson, to clarify how the structure functioned in every aspect of life.

Amos Rapoport, the leading proponent of a multidisciplinary analysis of vernacular architecture, writes in *House Form and Culture*: "Materials, construction and technology are best treated as modifying factors, rather than form determinants, because they decide neither what is to be built nor its form." Our chapters interweave these "modifying factors" into a full-bodied narrative, but we consider six of them paramount: technology, climate, economics, social organization, religion, and history. Moreover, we are interested as much in how these factors help to interpret an Indian dwelling as in what the dwelling can tell us about Indian life. For one tribe, social factors may play a major role in determining building size; for another, the demands of gathering food might have a greater impact. For a third, the importance of a structure to religious beliefs might have the strongest consequences, and a fourth might manifest a struggle for dominance between Indian and non-Indian building traditions.

TECHNOLOGY

Indians had no choice but to build with raw materials from the land around them. They fashioned their dwellings from wood, bark, leaves, grass, reeds, earth, snow, stone, skin, and bones. Their principal types of construction were (1) tensile or bent frame with covering, (2) compression shell, and (3) post and beam (joined) wood frame with various walling materials.

The wigwam style of framing exemplified tensile construction (Figure 2.1). The dome-shaped frame gained enough springy strength from its bent saplings to support bark, mat, or thatch covers. In the compression shell, illustrated by the snow block iglu of the

2.1
Wichita Grass
House,
Southern
Plains, probably
Oklahoma or
Texas

2.2
Eskimo Iglu,
Alaska

Arctic or the stone-and-adobe walls of the Southwestern Pueblo, the building material served both as structural support and wall covering (Figures 2.2 and 2.3). The joined-frame type was used for a variety of conical, rectilinear, or gabled structures found across North America. Their superstructure was made of straight poles or timbers which were tied together or otherwise joined and covered with planks, skins, or earth (Figure 2.4). Few, however, of the Indian house types conformed exactly to these methods. Both the pueblo (compression shell) and the Plains earthlodge (joined frame) were roofed with wooden beams covered by smaller poles and completed with a padding of fine twigs and grass and a layer of earth. Where joining required cordage, the means of preparing lengths of inner bark, slender withe, or root fibers was a basic craft that often escaped the scrutiny of early ethnographers. To a considerable extent, Indian architecture was tied, wrapped, and knotted together.

Although important to Indians in profound ways, houses were not usually conceived as articles of permanent craftsmanship. Much of their building technology had an improvisational and practical flavor. This is not to say that building methods were arbitrary. Construction techniques followed time-honored rules, but little attempt was made to preserve materials. On the Northwest Coast the woodwork in large family houses was painted or sculpted only where it was meant to impress onlookers. Even at the Pueblo Bonito ruins in western New Mexico, walls of elaborately patterned stonework were

2.3
Taos Pueblo, New
Mexico, sixteenth
century and after

2.4
Apsaroke (Crow) Tipi,
Montana, 1908

plastered over, and, by historic times, pueblo walls were hastily manufactured and rarely bonded.

Constructing each house type called for special skills and tools. To bend a sapling into a smooth arch might call for debarking, trimming, aging, prebending, or steaming so that weak points would not splinter and crack. Felling trees, peeling bark, splitting boards, cutting and rainproofing hides, and making fiber ties were skills that were transmitted from the old to the young, often through prescribed interpersonal relationships and at appropriate moments in the tribal calendar.

Materials and construction techniques contributed to the appearance of Indian buildings, but did not restrict the ideas of their builders, who often pushed materials to their limits as they made structures in all shapes and sizes. We must stress again that the question of Indian architecture is less what they could build than what they wanted to build. Expanding a building to accommodate new family members, for example, could most easily be accomplished by rectilinear structures. In nearly every geographical area Indians built houses of extended length to meet social requirements. Early Eskimo structures of the late Dorset Period could be more than 150 feet long with stone sidewalls and, probably, a series of connected tent roofs. In the eastern woodlands, the Iroquois lashed together pole and bark longhouses exceeding 300 feet in length. The Coast Salish people of the Northwest put up shed-roofed plank buildings that were more than 600 feet in length, sheltering an entire tribe under one roof. The modular plan of both the Iroquois and Coast Salish structures allowed sections to be added or removed as new individuals married into the family.

It was difficult to enlarge circular structures, but they could be joined. When Eskimo families wanted more space, they clustered their winter snow houses, or joined two tents with an inner passageway in summertime. The Mandan of North Dakota, preferring smaller earthlodges during the winter, sometimes added sleeping chambers connected to the main lodge by a short tunnel.

CLIMATE

Indian builders developed ways to keep the cold, rain, wind, and heat at bay. Techniques for warming or cooling were sometimes part of the hidden engineering of a dwelling and might have little effect on its outward appearance. The smaller and more subterranean the building, the easier it was to heat, but in chilly climates, dwellings often were built at ground level and were large and drafty.

Indians had other means of adapting to the weather besides designing their houses for protection. Partitions of hanging mats broke up drafts in large structures, and split-plank, adobe, or snow-block windbreaks frequently were built against doorways. Some Subarctic tribes relayered their floors with fresh, fragrant pine boughs every week. During the worst of a winter season some tribes migrated to warmer or more sheltered environs. They might wear heavy clothing indoors, and they were trained from childhood to tolerate variations in temperature. They also built a variety of structures and spaces in which to spend time during the different "seasons" of a single day.

Indian dwellings were generally heated from centrally located hearths, or separate family fires in large structures (Figure 2.5). A wide range of insulating methods was devised. The earth surrounding pit houses retained heat and was an effective barrier against wind chill. Southwestern Pueblos built above ground level used the same heat-retention principle. Their thick adobe walls soaked up heat from the sun during the day, and at night, radiated warmth into the rooms.

Indian builders employed a range of double-shelled walls. On the Plains, tipis had an inner liner that created an insulating air pocket. When temperatures dropped, this space could be filled with dry grass, and snow could be piled around the outside. In the Aleutian Islands, the natives built double walls of planks, stuffing moss or grass in between for insulation, and stacking sod against the outside walls and roof.

2.5 Karl Bodmer, *The Interior of the Hut of a Mandan Chief*

Relief from the heat was also important. Nearly everywhere Indian encampments included arbors. In the Southwest they were simple post and beam structures, shaded with leafy boughs, split cactus trunks, or cornstalks. In the southern Plains, the Kiowa and Wichita devised large bowed frames that they thatched with willow boughs to within a few feet of the ground. In scorching weather they frequently splashed the cover with water; evaporation lowered the shaded area's temperature by ten degrees or more. A long, running arbor shading an entire village was built by the Yokuts of the Central Valley in California.

In the Southeast, where humidity as well as heat was a problem, houses needed as much air flow as possible. The Seminole of the Florida swamps achieved this by constructing thatch-roofed, open-sided buildings with deep eaves and raised floors so that air circulated above and below. The raised floor also protected the occupants from the fluctuating ground water, insects, and snakes.

SOCIAL

Social organization significantly influenced the size of Indian dwellings and living arrangements. Local resources and methods of food gathering might restrict the size of a

2.6 Taos Pueblo, plan of the central portion

community, but social rules usually governed who lived with whom and who slept beside whom, where one moved after marrying, the size of dwellings, and their spatial relationships. The way in which tribal people arranged their spaces and used their dwellings reflected the way they organized their society as a whole. Architecture, then, was a principal tool for socialization—a means by which members of a tribe learned rules of behavior and a particular worldview.

Social customs also dictated who worked on the erection of the building, who owned it, and where it should be positioned in a village complex. Tribes such as the Siouan speakers of the Plains, and some Pueblo villages along the Rio Grande, split their societies into halves, social divisions known to anthropologists as "moieties." In some villages the residences of the two groups were placed on opposite sides of a stream or valley (Figure 2.6). During their summer gatherings, the Siouans pitched their tipis in a circle with an invisible line running north-south—dividing "Sky" clans from "Earth" clans. Many different housing patterns were found across Native America, from single dwellings for extended families, to grouped dwellings for single patrilineal families, to areas within large villages where clan members clustered together.

Men and women's roles in the construction and ownership of dwellings were sharply defined. Over most of central North America, women held sway over home and hearth, either building or supervising construction of their houses. Along the West Coast from Alaska to Southern California and on the eastern seaboard, however, men were largely responsible for building. In parts of the Southwest, and in pockets of the Great Basin, men and women shared the labor equally. Among the Mandan Hidatsa of the upper Missouri River, women held the right to erect earthlodges, but men cut and erected the frame.

Cheyenne women had a "guild" which convened with feasting and prayer whenever they gathered to cut and sew covers and make porcupine quill ornaments for their tipis. Where kinship was traced through the female line and children automatically became members of the mother's clan, the house and its property were generally considered hers. Thus, among the Navajo, a divorce usually forced the husband to leave his wife's dwelling and return to his parents' home.

Sometimes house-building was a ritualized means of cementing relations among tribes, or between clans, moieties, and important families. Among the Hisanai of the southern Plains and the Kwakiutl of the Northwest Coast, kin or clan groups, each supplying specific materials and each with a different construction assignment, worked together, as in a barn raising. Such collaborative efforts often tightened kinship bonds and raised the status of the new occupants.

Within the confines of the house, rules concerning the use of space could be quite strict. Even for hunting people frequently on the move, such as the Cree of central Canada, temporary quarters and sleeping assignments were in traditional places determined by sex, family, marital status, and age. The Cree told of a supernatural woman who traveled ahead of the hunters to set up their tents and prepare camp—so that no matter where they moved, it was as if they were staying in the same place. Cree youngsters were warned not to count the tent poles in their lodges or her magic would fail. The Cree, Eskimo, Pawnee, and many other groups also recreated that "same place" by carefully observing rules of domestic etiquette. In that way role relationships among tribal members were preserved and people found a measure of privacy and peace within spaces that most Europeans and Americans today would find too exposed and too cramped.

ECONOMICS

No Indian group had a single dwelling suited to all seasons; even Pueblo people were semi-nomadic, moving into summer quarters near their cornfields. Most tribes relied on different food sources at least for summer and winter, and occupied different camps in fall and spring. Each location commonly had its characteristic house type. Modern archeology refers to a hunting and gathering society's base camp as their "central place." Even if a band traveled widely, they often had one such location which was to them "home." Indians on the Northwest Coast considered themselves more "at home" in winter, when they occupied the family plank houses built on coastal sites that families had owned for years. Their summer fishing and berry-gathering camps were inland, up the rivers. When some tribes departed for the summer spots, they untied the wallboards of their winter houses, lashed them between canoes, and used them as siding for the more makeshift summer quarters. In the fall they returned to the bare frames of their winter homes and walled them up again with the same boards.

The opposite seasonal pattern was customary for the earthlodge dwellers of the northern Plains. They were more "at home" during the summer in large, cool, earth-roofed buildings, which were framed with heavy cottonwood timbers and situated on high river terraces. They left these structures to occupy portable tipis during their autumn hunts, moving into smaller earthlodges in protected, wooded areas along the Missouri River floodplain when winter came.

For more sedentary people such as the woodland dwellers of upper New York state, intense occupation of a single village site often exhausted both local building supplies and garden soil. Every ten or fifteen years, when the saplings they used as their primary building material became sparse, the Iroquois would resettle the entire community, often downhill from the original site. Insect infestation, overcrowding, and a pile-up of garbage could also cause a village to move on.

Fluctuations in supplies of food or water quickly affected population size, which in turn had an impact upon architecture. In Chaco Canyon in New Mexico, North America's most advanced expression of public architecture was achieved because Indians were able to divert rainwater that fell on surrounding mesas for agricultural use. But an apparent decrease in the amount of summer rain in the thirteenth century probably upset this fragile dependence, and the tribes could no longer support themselves nor their high-density apartment-house complexes.

Highly mobile native bands such as the Eskimo of the Arctic or the Paiute of the Great Basin stayed "at home" only when the weather forced them to. For the Eskimo in their turf or snow houses, winter was a time of seclusion; for the Paiute in their brush- or tule-covered shelters, the only time spent indoors was in January and February when the Nevada desert was frozen. For both groups winter was a period of family gatherings and storytelling, but afterwards they were anxious to be on the move again. The literature on Indian settlement patterns usually ignores the fact that a seminomadic existence not only made good sense, but that Indians deeply enjoyed it. Apparently some tribes followed a food-seeking, nomadic way of life because they had little other choice, but they also relished the sense of freedom, the reunions with distant kin, and the activity and change of scenery.

RELIGION

The buildings of Native Americans encoded not only their social order but often their tribal view of the cosmos. Many Indian narratives tell of a "Distant Time" or a "Myth Age" when a "First House" was bestowed upon a tribe as a container for their emerging culture. Some tribes likened the creation of the world itself to the creation of a house, strengthening the metaphoric correspondence between dwelling and cosmos. Thereafter Indian peoples held the ritual power to renew their cosmos through rebuilding, remodeling, or reconsecrating their architecture.

The idea that houses served as models of the universe is suggested by the folklore and architectural terms of native groups as distant from one another as the Eskimo, the Mohave, the Navajo, the Hopi, the Delaware, and the Blackfeet. To the Navajo, mountains were models for the first house, its four principal posts symbolically equated with the four cardinal directions, and its floor space divided into day and night domains.

The Hidatsa of North Dakota believed the universe was a mammoth earthlodge, its sky dome held up by four enormous pillars just like those of their own four-post lodges.

The mythological house and the buildings consecrated as their replicas could represent the four quarters of the sky, zenith and nadir, and the "skydome," which shamans could enter through a "sky door" or "sun hole," in order to obtain special powers. The "earth-navel" and cosmic tree, or center-of-the-world pole, were two other important cosmological concepts (which the historian of religions Mircea Eliade has named the "umbilicus mundi" and "axis mundi") that were often represented architecturally.

The tribal cosmos might also be multilayered. Usually there were three tiers, with the present world situated on the middle plane. The Delaware, though, envisioned their universe as twelve houses, one on top of another, which they symbolically entered during their annual Big House ceremony.

Origin myths also helped to teach tribal members the proper way to collect building materials, good construction techniques, and how to bless the finished building. Sometimes a myth was recited before construction began. The tale of the first Wichita grass house prescribed which materials should be harvested by women and which by men. It also regulated each phase of construction, described the prayers to be uttered, and dictated how the building, its doors and four cedar ribs jutting from the top, was to be aligned with the cardinal directions.

Symbolic correspondence between building and body was also common. Among the Tolowa of Northern California, a special sweathouse was dedicated to the spirit of an ancient supernatural salmon just before the annual spawn. As the hopeful fishermen entered to pray for a healthy catch, they believed they were entering the salmon's body; the ridgepole had become its backbone and the roof boards its ribs. On the Plains, the "Hugging Bear" design, found on both Blackfeet and Kiowa tipis, produced the effect of a giant furry creature embracing its occupants. For tribes as distant from one another as the Sanpoil of the Plateau and the Winnebago of the Great Lakes, the sweat bath was envisaged as the body of a sacred being which people entered to be purified or cured.

Houses and the materials that went into them were often considered alive. "Your house is a person," said an Achumawi Indian from Northern California during a visit to the linguist Jaime de Angulo. "It knows very well that I am a stranger here. That's why I sent it tobacco smoke, to make friends with it. I said 'House, you are the house of my friend. You shouldn't do me harm. House, I want you to protect me.'" During the years of European domination such attention to the inner, sacred life of architecture focused upon ceremonial structures such as the Delaware Big House, the Apache puberty tipi, the Papago Rain House, and the Plains Sun Dance lodge. Among the Kickapoo of Oklahoma and Mexico, and certain tribes of the Southwest, however, the ritual renovation of domestic space is still observed.

Village plans also reflected tribal mythology. The Creek of the Southeast constructed their ceremonial "square grounds" to reflect the directional order in the universe and to signify the progression of a man's life through it. Four arbors, which were aligned with the cardinal directions, surrounded a four-log fire around which boys, middle-aged warriors, and aged men were assigned seating according to age. In the center of the circular plazas of the Mandan villages on the Missouri River, a shrine protected an effigy of their culture hero, Lone Man. He had instructed the Mandan in how to marry, hunt, and build houses, and had saved them from the Great Flood by placing them inside an enclosure symbolized by the shrine. The temple lodge on the innermost circle of buildings around the plaza always faced the direction where Lone Man disappeared after saying good-bye to his people. Everyday Mandan life revolved around these affirmations of their divine origins.

HISTORY

Modifications in Indian architecture did not begin with the arrival of Europeans. Change had been under way for at least nine and a half thousand years—roughly the date of the oldest North American Indian house thus far identified, a 12-foot-long oval-shaped dwelling which stood near the Stanislaus River in eastern California. In pre-Columbian times numerous Native American societies flourished, and a succession of architectural ideas evolved. Some building forms developed rapidly, some gradually, and their rates of change can only be plotted in areas where archeological remains reveal considerable depth of time.

Scholarly interest in the pedigree of Indian buildings has been limited largely to one house type: the pit house. Indians burrowed into the ground to sink the floors for many different forms of dwellings, and tracing the distribution of semisubterranean houses has produced a kind of architectural family tree. The superstructure of the Kamchadal pit house in Siberia is similar to that of an early Pueblo kiva (Figure 2.7), which in turn was a survivor of an older domestic pit house form in the Southwest. Across the Arctic the semisubterranean winter house—commonly rectangular—is found everywhere. To the south are the pit houses of British Columbia's interior with their unique, slanting inside supports. In California, valley bands lived in dug-out dwellings that bore a remarkable resemblance to the Plateau pit houses. It has been argued that upper Missouri River earth-lodges extended this tradition into the Great Plains, and that it continued into the partly excavated town houses of the Southeast.

The problem with such hypotheses of direct architectural influence is that there is usually a dearth of minute data, a wide range of time periods, and too variable a range of terrains and climates to make them convincing. It might be more profitable to develop small-scale architectural sequences in limited geographical regions and time periods. What is probable, however, is that tribes retained outdated house types for other uses, either as ritual structures or for storage. Because of the gradual nature of architectural change in pre-Columbian Native America, tribal areas often became a sort of architectural memory bank.

With the arrival of Europeans, architectural change in Indian settlements accelerated. Disease, resettlement, and warfare forced the coalescence of some villages and building traditions (Figure 2.8), and the virtual abandonment of others. As metal tools and nails, then paints and cloth, and finally milled lumber and molded bricks became available, traditional materials such as buffalo hide, elm bark, and other natural supplies became harder to get. Reservation life also restricted the Indians' freedom of movement

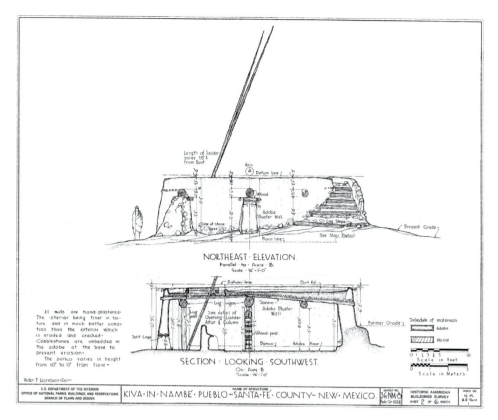

2.7 Kiva, Nambé Pueblo, Santa Fe Co., New Mexico

to obtain building materials. Indian agents and missionaries frowned on all "primitive" and "pagan" expressions of traditional Indian cultures, often singling out for disapproval old forms of house-life. Social reformers and East Coast "friends of the Indian" reproduced in their publications photographs of tipis and bark houses with captions decrying the "old, unhealthy, disease-breeding mode of existence" that they represented.

Despite strong pressure to forsake their architectural heritage, some Indian groups were reluctant to give up the buildings and the way of life they represented. They had already retained outmoded house types out of nostalgia for a golden age; the Hopi Kisi, a brush shelter used during the Snake ceremony, or the Mandan Okipa (temple lodge) both were probably descendants of domestic structures. Instructed to behave like Europeans, a number of Indian groups clung to their traditional architecture even more tenaciously. Others viewed the structures blending European and Indian elements as the foundation of a new "traditional" identity. Many of the stories in this book describe a historical struggle between cultures waged on an architectural front.

It is tempting to make comparisons between Indian architecture and that of contemporary America, to forget that these traditional dwellings arose out of specific historical, demographic, ecological, and cultural circumstances. These buildings seem to offer what we miss so much. Their architectural imprint, often ephemeral, blends harmoniously with

2.8 Karl Bodmer, *Encampment of Piekann Indians, near Fort McKenzie, Muscleshell River, Montana*, c.1842

the land, and the ebb and flow between residents and surroundings is smooth. They are places where people can live together in comfort and tranquillity.

These buildings often resist description because there is so little to them in material terms; in large measure, they must be experienced to be fully understood. Yet many of their secrets will remain forever with the builders. A number of house types were never recorded, and most of those included in this book have been eclipsed. Like the oral tradition which passed them along, the intimate knowledge of their construction materials and building skills was always a few generations away from disappearance. The aesthetics and proportions which determined the right "look and feel" for many of these buildings, and their criteria for selecting the best natural materials for them are often irretrievable.

Chapter 3

Marc Treib

Church design and construction in Spanish New Mexico

CHURCH PATTERNS

When the missionaries began evangelical work in Mexico in the early 1500s, they carried with them the architectural prototypes of the churches of Spain. The centuries of Moorish occupation had precipitated there the development of fortified religious architecture, particularly in those areas of southern Spain in proximity to the lands of the "infidels." Even though the traditions of Spanish Romanesque and Gothic architecture continued in the New World, military uncertainty caused their modification. Walls were thick, penetrated by few openings, and buttressed by masonry piers. According to George Kubler and Martin Soria:

> The massing of mid-century [sixteenth] churches suggests military architecture. The bare surfaces of massive walls were a necessary result of untrained labor and of amateur design. Furthermore the friars needed a refuge, both for themselves, as outnumbered strangers surrounded by potentially hostile Indians, and for their villagers, who were exposed, especially on the western and northern frontiers, to the attacks of nomad Chichimec tribes after 1550.[1]

In their simplicity, their single nave, and the relation of the *convento* to the church, the monastic churches neatly presaged the later religious sanctuaries erected in New Mexico.

Vestiges of these prior concerns remained in Mexican church architecture into the seventeenth century, but their prominence was undermined by an expenditure of accumulating wealth and the exuberance of the baroque attitude toward form and space that countered the Protestant Reformation. Splendor and light became the foremost vehicles for reasserting the power of the church, and an enthusiasm for architecture paralleled religious ecstasy. The single-naved church, perhaps extended by transepts, served as the basic form in Andalusia and later in the New World; but with the development of a facility in central Mexico for working stone, an elaboration in both size and complexity followed suit.

Early builders restricted areas of ornamentation to the facade, doors, and window surrounds. With the ultrabaroque, however, the ornamental field exploded.[2] Decoration focused the celebrants' attention on the facade and the altar. At the extreme, the building's mass merged with its ornamentation and virtually dissolved in luminous illusion. The physical limits of the space admitted no visual bounds, and the light that flooded through cupolas and lanterns dramatically illuminated the theater of belief. In some New World colonies, this extremity of architectural expression waited for decades, if not centuries, to achieve a near parity with the churches of the homeland. In certain Mexican churches, in contrast, the architectural exuberance at times surpassed that of contemporary Spain. In New Mexico, to the contrary, exuberance never really arrived.

The native building technology of the sixteenth century was limited primarily to stone implements; the vast majority of tools and ironware needed to construct the new churches was imported by Europeans. At first churches were small, particularly the rural missions set in the mountain country or jungles of Mexico.[3]

As late as the close of the sixteenth century, decades after the Conquest of Mexico, these outlying churches remained simple affairs: single rectangular halls with neither the transepts nor side aisles common to the Romanesque or Gothic religious architecture of Spain. Built of stone, mud, or a combination of the two, the churches employed wooden beams, rather than masonry vaults, to support the roof.

Even in the most isolated areas the church grew correspondingly with the size of the community, and for these rural missions the church and the village were nearly synonymous. Building came under the priest's supervision, and he no doubt based his plans on memories of Spanish or central Mexican ecclesiastical prototypes. Military engineers or civilian builders probably contributed critical construction expertise. In one documented instance, Padre Nicolás Durán brought to Lima a scale architectural model of the Casa Professa in Rome to serve as an object lesson for Peruvian religious architecture.[4] Few records of such formalized transmission of architectural ideas as this one remain, however, and by the mid-sixteenth century Mexico was producing noteworthy architecture by resident designers.[5] The sophistication of an architectural idea and its methods of realization varied with the period and the place in which the church was built.

In Peruvian towns, architecture developed from the beamed, single-nave structure of the vaulted form more reminiscent of the Iberian Peninsula. At times the vaults were more ornamental than structural, built of plaster over wooden lath rather than carefully fitted stone. In the hinterland, however, in mountain districts such as those around Lake Titicaca, vestiges of the primitive church remained, the closest parallel forms to those of the religious architecture of early New Mexico. And like the New Mexican churches, these buildings were tempered by necessity in their isolated locations; their fabrics avoided the elaborate formal play of urban religious architecture and more directly addressed the exigencies of their sites and religious programs.

The combination of the *reducción* and the tremendous number of rapid conversions exerted insistent pressures on both the clergy and the physical fabric of their churches. As a result, hundreds or perhaps even thousands of new or would-be Christians waiting to receive conversion required religious accommodation. Because the diminutive church structures allowed by rural construction methods could not embrace all these converts, a new form of open-air chapel known as the *atrio* was developed to serve this purpose.

Even though it was common practice to enter the Hispanic church through a walled burial ground called the *campo santo*, the conversion of this enclosed but unroofed space to ceremonial use was a Mexican contribution. This development was not wholly without precedent, however. Faced with similar programmatic demands, the churches of early

Christiandom and many of the great pilgrimage churches of Europe had included an outdoor altar from which mass could be celebrated. But the adaptation of the sanctuary's form to strengthen the prominence of the entry and the slight reorientation of the focus of the church toward the atrio represented a development of historical precedent.

Although permitted to enter the cemetery, Indians were forbidden to enter the church until they had successfully completed catechism. Certain devotions were performed by the priests on the front steps of the church, however, the congregation having gathered within the walled enclosure of the campo santo. In time a rudimentary chapel directed toward the exterior was integrated into the front or side of the church to accommodate these new uses.[6]

CHURCH TYPES

In seventeenth-century New Mexico the mission answered both liturgical and propagandistic callings. The building served as a sanctified house that signified the Christian presence in the "wilderness." At the same time, architecture itself served as an instrument of conversion, a structure of scale and splendor sufficient to create an appropriate sense of awe and respect for Catholic doctrine.

While bound to pledges of poverty for themselves, the mendicant orders were relatively unrestrained in their creation of places of worship. In Mexico the Dominicans, the Augustinians, and even the Jesuits were criticized for the lavishness of their constructions, which were at times drastically overbuilt for the small hamlets in which they were located. By the beginning of the 1700s baroque architecture had penetrated Mexico with concepts of free space and undulating form, the exuberant curve, planes of elaborate decoration, and, perhaps most important, a sense of light. The missionaries who served in New Mexico, however, were unable to implement the elaborate styles of the already widespread Mexican baroque, hampered as they were by two mitigating factors. As Franciscans, they were bound to vows of poverty, chastity, and obedience, the inherent simplicity of which extended to expressions in architecture. More important, much of the new architecture of central Mexico was simply impossible to duplicate concurrently in New Mexico given the state of the building technology in the colony, the building skills of the native laborers, and the local materials. Nevertheless, the churches of the early seventeenth century were the largest ever to be built in New Mexico. They were erected when religious fervor ran high and the Pueblo peoples had not yet been decimated by famine, raids by Plains Indians, or European diseases; and they expressed a religious institution that intended to remain.

The first church type constructed for the specific purpose of Catholic religious services was a relatively modest, single-nave structure measuring about twenty-five by seventy-five feet, its apse articulated as a smaller rectangle. Representative of this early type is the chapel at Gran Quivira dedicated to San Ysidro (1629–1632?), the patron saint of agriculture. Built of a gray-yellow limestone, the chapel's walls were mud plastered inside and out according to the normal Indian and European practice. The roof, of wooden beams on which were laid smaller ceiling pieces and a thick layer of earth,

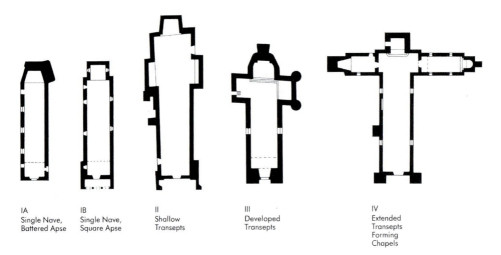

IA
Single Nave,
Battered Apse

IB
Single Nave,
Square Apse

II
Shallow
Transepts

III
Developed
Transepts

IV
Extended
Transepts
Forming
Chapels

3.1 Churches of Spanish New Mexico. Generic plan types

suggested Indian methods dating from Anasazi times. The Europeans provided the architectural design for the church, but the Indians provided the physical labor and practical building knowledge derived from centuries of construction experience. If San Ysidro was ever completed, it was soon outgrown or found wanting, and its stones were probably reused in the more ambitious structure, San Buenaventura, that succeeded it.

A church consisted primarily of a nave to shelter the congregation and an altar at which the priest could celebrate the mass (Figures 3.1 and 3.2). The scale of the church was circumscribed by need. Walls of mud could only be practically piled to a height of about thirty feet, stone to perhaps fifteen feet higher. The width of the nave was fixed by the length of the beams available in the relative vicinity. There were no aisles to widen the nave, and thus the length of the church was the principal variable. Modifications to the archetypal building plan developed as a response to the particularities of the site, the availability of building material, and the desired height of the walls. The altarpiece, usually a later addition to church furnishings and often imported, typically reflected contemporary Mexican taste far better than did the church structure itself, which remained a relatively consistent form for nearly three centuries. Thus, the Indian mission and the Spanish colonial church employed the same basic architectural competence—that is, the same vocabulary of building form—up to the Anglo influx of the mid-nineteenth century.[7] The Santuario at Chimayo, built as late as 1816, used roughly the same construction and architectural form as had churches from the early sixteenth century, and the same building techniques continue in use even today.

Larger or more complex church structures sometimes extended their naves with partially or fully stated transepts, and in some instances, such as San José de Giusewa or Quarai, these churches also had secondary altars for devotions other than the high mass. The main altar occupied the sanctuary (chancel or choir). This part of the structure, particularly in early-seventeenth-century churches such as Abo and Quarai, was battered in plan to a considerable degree, perhaps nostalgically recalling the true hemispherical apse of the

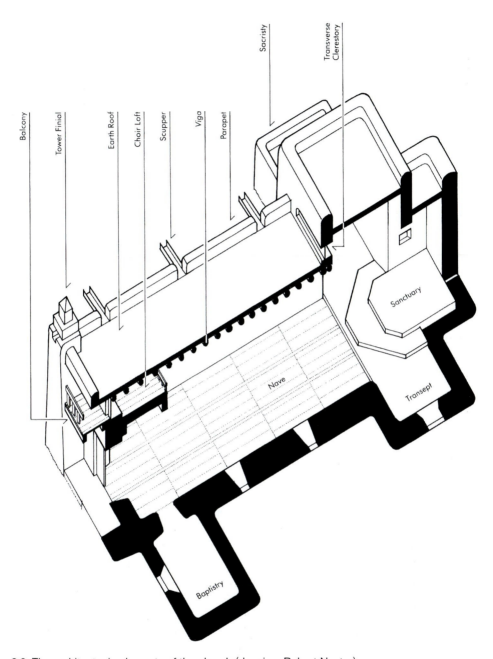

3.2 The architectonic elements of the church (drawing, Robert Nestor)

Balcony

Tower Finial

Earth Roof

Choir Loft

Scupper

Viga

Parapet

Sacristy

Transverse Clerestory

Sanctuary

Nave

Transept

Baptistry

Continental prototypes. The pronounced form of the angled apse became a prominent feature of New Mexican mission architecture and is well represented by San Miguel in Santa Fe. These almost prosaic features—the thick-walled nave, the flat roof, the articulated apse, and the basic long and low profile wedded to the ground—combined to create the distinctive form of the Spanish sanctuaries of the colonial period.

SITING

Just as there were good reasons for founding villages in certain locations, so there were good reasons for siting churches in particular places. In the latter case, however, the logic of the choice was quite simple: parish churches were established as the centers of their communities; mission churches were built where conditions allowed. Site selection was always a compromise, the missionary trying to balance his hope for an imposing site against the realities of the topography and the pueblo's values.

Once the missionary had secured a foothold in the community, he usually tried to acquire permission to build the church and convento on a physically suitable and prestigious site. A central location was conceptually ideal, but acceptable sites were difficult to locate. For pueblos located along the Rio Grande, flat land in proximity to the community was relatively easy to find. This was less the case, however, in villages located on rising land or in the mountains. Where suitably level terrain was in limited supply, friars were forced to accept sites that were far less than ideal. The series of churches built at Pecos, for example, occupied a narrow slice of the *mesilla* remaining after the construction of the two segments of the pueblo itself.[8] The first church at Pecos was erected well outside the pueblo proper, and all four churches built there had to add fill to the ridge so as to level

3.3 San Esteban del Rey Mission, Acoma Pueblo, New Mexico, 1629 and after

the floor of the nave. Concepción at Quarai rose on the ruins of a prior pueblo. More spectacular was the case of Acoma, where the inhospitability of the rock necessitated the importation of thousands of baskets of earth to level the site and fill the campo santo held within its stone retaining walls, a process that took several decades to complete (Figure 3.3).

In the Spanish villages the church's position on the (often fortified) plaza was nearly standard; but most missions evidenced little consistency in their placement. In the pueblos several factors mitigated against a single, idealized siting or orientation that would guarantee prominence to the religious edifice. For one, the church arrived in the pueblo long after the physical structure of the village had been determined, and the Indian dance plaza hardly matched the more regularized architectural statement of its Spanish counterpart. The native space represented or suggested instead a locus, rather than an absolute center, and was rarely constructed as a clearly defined architectural entity. Typically, it was already surrounded, however irregularly, with dwellings and kivas by the time the Franciscans arrived. In truth, the native populations probably had little desire to admit the church, which would become the largest structure in the village, into the center of its community. Thus, most churches remained resolutely on the periphery of the pueblo.

Basically, the church occupied whatever site its builder could find where land was sufficient and where the missionary was allowed to build. Although sufficiently elevated to become a focal point for the community when seen from a distance, San José at Laguna stands on a site well behind the plaza. Zia turns its low, massive back on the pueblo and becomes a quiet neighbor. San Esteban at Acoma dominates the village's architecture; its height and mass are almost antagonistic to the adjacent rows of dwellings. Only at Tesuque, Isleta, and the rebuilt San Jerónimo at Taos pueblo do the churches rest squarely on the plaza; and even in these instances, they lack the same sense of conviction about siting displayed by a church in a Spanish town. Kubler offered four possible reasons the separation of church and pueblo might have been desirable: the pueblos' hostility to friars, the friars' mistrust of the pueblo, the function of churches as forts, and the need for ample land for mission buildings, fields, and corrals.[9] Of these, only the last seems plausible because the "separation" of these churches from the pueblo rarely exceeded fifty yards and because settlers on occasion took refuge within the pueblo from Apache or Comanche attacks. The relegation of the religious sanctuary to land beyond the pueblo and the chronic problems it might occasion were well illustrated by the situation at Picuris. During the late eighteenth century Comanche raids wreaked havoc on the church, ultimately necessitating its removal and reconstruction within the pueblo walls, with Spanish and Pueblo brought together against a common enemy.[10]

In theory, churches would have followed an east-west orientation, with the principal facade facing west. But the realities of frontier construction mitigated against a consistent orientation, and New Mexican churches faced in virtually all directions, thereby confounding attempts to utilize the transverse clerestory to its best advantage. Even in Mexico City by the turn of the nineteenth century, the religious reasons for an east-west orientation had been for the most part lost to the building tradesmen. "I have heard it said," the anonymous author of a treatise roughly translated as *Architectural*

Practice in Mexico City confessed, "that a church should be oriented in such a way that the principal door looks toward the west, to satisfy some rite of the church that I do not understand. Where there are no other buildings to obstruct the site one should orient it as prescribed, but if buildings prohibit this, one builds where he can."[11] Although written fully two centuries after the founding of the Catholic enterprise in New Mexico, this admission of relativity applied almost universally to religious construction in the northern province.

LAYOUT

How much of the building project was designed prior to its realization is not precisely known, although the complex spatial programs of the church and convento, compounded by the particularities of each site, suggest that considerable deliberation preceded construction. Possibly the friar used a charcoal stick or ink to mark design studies on a board, hide, or paper, if supplies of the latter were still available.[12] The definitive layout, with adjustments for the site constraints, was necessarily made directly on the ground.

To lay out the church, the friar had several options, all of them quite basic measuring techniques. In Mexico proper, lime was used to mark out the plan of the building on the site.[13] A free expenditure of valuable lime in such a manner would have been wasteful in the frontier conditions of New Mexico, so colored soils or sands could have served as worthy substitutes. A simple lightweight cord—easy to use and revise and easy to transport—was probably the principal means for marking the plan of the building on the ground. In conjunction with stakes for locating the corners, wall intersections, and principal building points, this medium was typically used in surveying and was readily applied to building construction.[14]

Most useful to the religious builder would have been an understanding of geometry, in particular the three/four/five relationship of the right, or Pythagorean, triangle. Measurement was based on the *vara*, roughly thirty-three inches, although minor variations did exist. Using strings as measuring tapes, the builder could lay out with relative precision the edifice and its rooms. Alignment was ascertained with the compass and solar or celestial sightings, all of which were known to the military and presumably to the educated Franciscans. These instruments could have been employed in combination, with one used as a means to confirm the other. While relative accuracy could be attained, construction with massive stone or mud walls allowed for relative imprecision, as the thicknesses varied depending on the moisture in the adobe and the wall's state of preservation.

Each friar brought tools to found the church, including shovels and hoes for digging foundations and mixing adobe; axes, adzes, saws, chisels, and augers for working the timber; and nails, tacks, and hinges for fitting the pieces together.[15] Given that construction was undertaken by a sizable team of native labor organized in gangs under the supervision of a foreman, these tools would have been the minimum needed unless some domestic means was used to reproduce them. Fortunately, making adobe blocks required little formwork; and stone was used as it was found in situ.

SITEWORK

With the plan of the church laid out on the ground, excavation for the stone foundation began. Whether the church was built of masonry or adobe, the first step in construction was to secure a solid foundation. Large stones were placed in foundation trenches excavated along the perimeter of the building to provide a structurally stable base for the mud or stone walls. The stones also retarded capillary action and provided better drainage than the earth alone would have allowed. Drainage was a critical factor in earthen construction. (The present-day use of cement stucco instead of mud plaster has interrupted the natural evaporation patterns from the ground through the wall to the air, thereby undermining more than one church.) If the site was neither level nor gently sloping upward toward the altar, earth removal or terracing was necessary. The nave of the church at Jemez Springs was cut into the steep hillside, and the excavated material was used to fill the downhill side until a relatively level floor was finally devised. Even the altar was stepped up several feet to take advantage of the topography—a sensible strategy given that bedrock could not be reformed. The slope and the interruption of the natural drainage pattern are the probable reasons for the church's double floor: two layers of earth separated by a layer of burnt wood or charcoal, the latter intended to absorb the ground seepage and desiccate the upper earthen layer.

Jemez Springs was an instance of extremely inhospitable topographic conditions, but it was certainly not the only instance. Consider the uneven surface of the Acoma mesa, where even the land for the campo santo was imported in baskets, or the limited strip of buildable land at Pecos, or the contoured hilltop at Laguna. All these sites required goodly amounts of labor just to establish workable footings and erect a suitable platform for construction. At Acoma, about eighteen inches of earth were used to fill and level the surface of the mesa to create a suitable floor.

The floors were finished as tamped, compacted earth, packed to almost rock hardness over the years. In residential construction animal blood was sometimes used as a sealant, and the practice may also have been used in the churches. Women swept floors weekly and in some churches repacked the surface each year with new mud and straw.[16] In the case of Abo, stone flags completed the interior floor surface, but this was common practice only at the Salinas missions.

Allowing the floor to remain earthen also served a practical need because the more noted personages of the parish would be buried inside the church as space allowed. Presumably for health reasons, a royal decree banning burials within the church was issued in 1748, although it took more than a year to reach Santa Fe. The practice remained desirable, however, in light of frontier conditions, fear of native deprecations, and the pious impulse to lay at rest near the altar. Higher fees for interment within the nave made the custom more attractive for the clergy as well as the congregation. In 1822, 1826, and again in 1833, the Mexican government renewed the proscription, probably with the same ineffectual result.[17]

A masonry wall, deriving its strength from mass, was piled to nearly six feet in thickness (a rubble core filled with a more finished surface) to attain the height of fifty feet the early church builders sought. There was a pronounced battering to the walls, reducing their thickness as the walls rose and producing a section resembling an elongated version of a truncated pyramid. At Quarai the walls of the nave were considerably splayed in plan, adding some stability to the basic quadrilateral form, although its effect must have been minimal in comparison to the dead weight of the wall itself. In sum, these stone churches derived their structural capacity from the straightforward laying of stone on stone, which thickened the wall as required to allow it to reach the level of the roof beams.

Abo was one exception to this general pattern; there the thickness of the walls was reduced, and the walls were stiffened instead by buttresses—extra masses, like columns, attached or "engaged" to the walls themselves. This practice, which may have had its origins in the fortress churches of Spain, provided additional bearing surface just below the beams where the weight was concentrated, thereby helping transmit the load to the ground. At the crossing—the intersection of the nave and transepts—the wall was considerably thickened to accommodate the sizably increased load and to support the bell tower. In comparison to Quarai or Gran Quivira, Abo's walls were light and elegant, although hardly thin when compared with modern construction in wood or steel. Nevertheless, neighboring churches in the Salinas area avoided the risk the builders at Abo took when contriving its more sophisticated structural system.

The Spanish did not introduce mud construction into New Mexico; they merely rationalized its production. Although stone was a building material at Mesa Verde and Chaco Canyon, it was used in conjunction with mud, which functioned as a mortar and finishing material. Exactly when the transition to a mostly mud or purely mud wall construction took place has not been ascertained, but the transference of the mesa top or cave villages to the river valleys made obvious the superseding of stone construction.

Continuing an attitude that perhaps derived from ceramic production, New Mexican builders did not use mud as a unit material, although blocks shaped like loaves of bread and called turtle backs were used to build the Casa Grande in Arizona.[19] The Indians built their pueblos on the basis of puddled construction: with or without a form, they piled up heaps of mud in layers to make walls. Piled up one or two feet at a time, walls were raised in a manner that paralleled the construction of pottery using rolled coils of clay. From a central point, these coils spiraled outward and upward and were ultimately smoothed over inside and out to remove traces of rough construction and lend unity to the surfaces. This technique enabled construction to proceed without formwork and with no time spent in the production of units. But extensive time was needed for each layer of the walls to season properly, drying slowly to retard cracking.

Mud bricks had existed in New Mexico prior to European contact, but their use was not widespread. The Spanish introduced the idea of unit construction in large numbers—in this case the manufacture of the basic mud brick and its use in a manner similar to stone. This common unfired mud brick was called adobe.

The word adobe derives from the Arabic *atob*, which suggests a Moorish, rather than a Spanish, origin.[20] Indeed, the earthen constructions of North Africa provided a centuries-old proving ground for this remarkably practical building system. Adobe is also related to the English daub, which formed one part of the wattle and daub construction of medieval England: applying (daubing) mud over a wooden framework.

Therefore, use of the word mud in this context is an oversimplification. Mud for adobe is not *any* form of wet earth; it is a carefully balanced product of clay, soil, and a binder such as straw, all blended in proper proportion. Although the straw does not increase the tensile properties of the brick, during drying it helps modulate evaporation in different parts of the block. Too much clay in the mix causes the bricks to shrink and crack while drying; too much sand causes them to become brittle and fall apart. An ideal composition is required, a balanced mixture derived in any locality only through a process of trial and error.

Wooden frames, with neither tops nor bottoms, form a number of bricks at a time. The mud is mixed in batches, and the form is filled while lying flat on the ground. A short time later, after the mud has set, the mold is lifted off, leaving a neat field of wet adobes each measuring roughly ten by fourteen by four inches. When the bricks are sufficiently dry, they are turned over and eventually stacked diagonally or on edge to complete the drying process. Unlike brick, adobe is not fired to high temperature in a kiln; being non-vitrified, the blocks are always susceptible to deterioration by moisture and wind. Traditionally, a layer of mud plaster applied over the adobe wall has been its primary means of protection against the elements. The absorption of moisture from the ground or the air or evaporation can cause a marked change in the size of the bricks, a movement that renders the use of the more stable cement plaster coatings impractical.

When the adobe matured, construction could begin. The builders laid up each course of blocks in an adobe mortar that rendered the construction homogeneous. Timbers imbedded horizontally within the wall at vertical intervals of up to four feet served to lessen cracking between bricks as the adobe or mortar dried or settled, or could be used to reinforce the joint between new walls and old construction. After a few vertical feet of construction, the entirety was left to dry. Moisture permanently trapped in the walls could ultimately lead to the structural failure of that section, or of the entire church, so judiciousness was the rule. Obviously this concern for moisture restricted construction to those periods of the year when rain was not a threat, a practice that compounded the extensive time periods required to build a church, often at least five to six years during the early periods. At difficult sites such as Acoma the construction activity extended over decades.

Adobe provides excellent bearing strength in compression and, in sufficient thickness, thermal mass. The unbaked brick, however, is quite vulnerable to erosion by water and wind. During normal exposure certain portions of the external surface of a wall abrade, while other sections dissolve in rain, contributing to the subtly curving contour of an adobe structure. Wind erodes the top parapet, tapering the upper wall backward, while eroded earth is deposited at the base of the wall, giving it a pronounced bulge. Although in most cases walls are constructed as truly vertical or cleanly slanting, they acquire a sculptured profile that is never quite the same in any two places.

Erosion is both a natural and an unforgiving process, and church builders were forced to consider its effects when devising construction techniques. If the buildings are not replastered at regular intervals, weathering will eventually deteriorate the structural portions of adobe walls. One problem is known as coving. As water drains off the wall, or pours from the drains, it splashes on the ground and decays the base of the wall. Poor drainage compounds the effects of the problem, although a stone foundation can lessen it. Unless the water sources are checked, however, the wall will become seriously undermined, or coved, which can ultimately lead to the collapse of the structure.

The parapet remained another chronic problem area. Because this section of the wall extends past the roof level, it is exposed to weathering on three surfaces and is thus three times as susceptible to erosion. In many instances the parapet is the first part of the wall to deteriorate, furthering pronounced dissipation on the tops of the walls, destroying the roof and beams, and eventually leading to ruin. Perhaps in no other method of construction is the adage that an ounce of prevention is worth a pound of cure so true. And even though there have been many attempts to eliminate the required upkeep, such as a pitched roof to cover the tops of walls, bricks or concrete blocks used for the parapets (now a common practice), a hybrid adobe made of mud mixed with cement or oil, and the more usual—although technically unsuccessful—application of cement stucco, nothing is as technologically and aesthetically triumphant as the time-consuming application of mud plaster.

The walls of stone or adobe were plastered on both inside and outside to appear monolithic and to suggest the more finished wall surfaces of the advanced religious architecture of Mexico or Spain. On the exterior the mud plaster served not only to integrate the separate bricks (because a chemical bond was formed) but also to add an inch or more of protective surface as a first line of defense against the elements. At Quarai and Jemez Springs traces of plastering and even painted decoration were discovered during excavation, indicating that the *perceived* surface was ultimately the architectural concern and that the vehicle of construction, stone or mud brick, was only the means to that end.

Building and plastering the walls of the church were women's work performed during the initial construction and then every second year for maintenance. As in ceramic production, the final coat of mud plaster was smoothed or burnished with sheepskin, deerskin, or small, round stones.[21] The technique was most often employed when interiors were plastered with *yeso* (or *yesso*), a baked gypsum mixed with wheat flour and water to form a thick paste. Yeso walls were typical of Moorish interiors and created a surface much harder and more durable than mud, but this technique was less widespread than coating a wall with whitewash.[22]

ROOFS

The builders constructed the corners of the church first; the intersection of the walls helped stiffen the structure as it rose. The remainder of each wall was then laid between the corners until it reached to the height of the plate line of the roof. Large beams, called *vigas*, provided the standard roof structure (the vault was not used in New Mexican church architecture). The beams were cut during the winter months from the extensive conifer forests that blanketed the mountains. Winter was the desirable time for forestry both for the internal consistency of the wood and the relative ease with which the logs could be hauled the ten to thirty miles to the building site. In addition, agricultural fields were dormant and required less care, thus allowing time to work on building projects. Although the wheel and the cart were available, their use in construction was probably limited. It is conceivable, of course, that wheels from supply wagons could have been used to haul vigas if conditions allowed. During the winter, logs were either dragged on the ground or carried on sledges if snow was sufficient.

Although the Spanish brought iron axes, saws, and adzes with them as part of their basic church building supplies, the task of cutting the required timber remained formidable. As in Indian construction, beams were cut over the required length; the excess increment was accepted and allowed to extend through the completed adobe or stone wall. Cutting the beams too short was regarded as a minor disaster. For example, when the beams at Zia were found to be of insufficient length, the builders constructed a second wall inside the first rather than wait a year to recut the timber. Most commonly, the beams were left round, with only the bark and branches removed. Rotting continually plagued roof construction because the beams were packed in the adobe wall, which freely conducted moisture and ensured its continued contact with the wood beams. Deterioration of this sort seems to have been regarded as a normal part of the construction process; only in the twentieth century were alternate methods used in restoration work. During the 1923 rebuilding of the church roof at Zia, for example, the ends of the beams were surrounded by stones to prevent their coming into direct contact with the adobe while allowing a freer passage of air.[23] Today beams are dipped in creosote or some other wood preservative to forestall deterioration.

At times vigas in churches sat directly on the stone or adobe walls, but more commonly they were set on corbels, wooden support pads, or cushions between the viga and the wall material, which in turn was supported by a wooden plate. This practice produced a minimal support benefit, however, and the use of corbels was primarily a decorative practice. Indeed, the rows of corbels in some churches are the principal ornamentation. Isleta, San Miguel, and Laguna all feature splendidly carved wood corbel blocks, their decorative effect heightened by the contrast of their intricate designs to the rudely shaped vigas above them. In some instances a wooden molding ran continuously around the interior of the nave just below the level of the corbels, a purely aesthetic practice said to have been the architectural rendering of the Franciscan waist cord.

An average viga measured about fifteen inches in diameter and spanned just under thirty feet, limits fixed by the maximum height and caliper of the available trees. In response to the length of the span and the weight of the roof above, the beams were spaced quite closely. If a large congregation required a sizable church, the length of the nave was elongated to provide the necessary volume. At its extreme this practice produced tubelike spaces almost 130 feet long as, for example, at San Felipe. Except in the earlier Salinas churches, heights, like widths, rarely exceeded thirty feet and were often less than the width of the nave. Fray Domínguez, visiting the old Santa Clara church, commented that its interior reminded him of nothing so much as the inside of a cannon.[24] Kubler also noted that in many churches one longitudinal wall was noticeably thicker than the other,[25] suggesting that the thicker wall served as a working platform when the vigas were raised into place. This remark was only speculative, however, because James Ivey noted that hoisting tackle was used on Spanish ships and, presumably, for building and military purposes as well. Church builders should have had access to this equipment when lifting the vigas into place either from the roof or from the ground with wooden tripods.

Not all roof beams were left round, however. In the early Salinas missions it was not uncommon for builders to saw or adze the beams into a square section and stack them together in bundles of six. Not only did grouping the finished timber contribute to an overall level of craft rare in the province, but also the additional depth provided by the composite stack augmented the carrying capacity of each individual beam. Square and bundled beams, however, died out rather early, supplanted by the round viga as the common form. Of pine or spruce, the round vigas were mounted so that their undersides and the plane of the ceiling were horizontal, thereby utilizing the natural tapering of the tree trunks to slope the roof for drainage.

Although the vigas provided the primary structure, they were too widely spaced to support the roofing materials directly. A secondary layer of smaller poles of peeled juniper, cottonwood, or aspen, perhaps four inches in diameter and known as *latillas*, were positioned perpendicularly across the beams or set obliquely in a herringbone pattern, a design best represented by the underside of the choir loft at Laguna. An alternate system used split cedar logs called *rajas* or *savinos*—if riven from native juniper—installed with their flat side down to form a roughly textured ceiling. A third, more polite alternative was the adzed board, or *tabla*, usually reserved for the finest room of the home. The choice of one system over another was decided on the basis of availability of wood types, tools and skilled labor, and the aesthetic preferences of the makers.[26]

A layer of cedar twigs, grass, plant fibers, reed, or even fabric was placed on the latillas, and on top of that a foot or more of earth and adobe was packed. Builders hoped that in times of rain, water would seep and diffuse within the thick earthen mat before it penetrated to the interior of the nave—a hope that could only be called naive when measured against experience. A flat roof and parapet, even if minimally sloped to drain through holes in the parapet provided with scuppers called *canales*, was a poor system at best. The expansion and contraction of the roof's structure caused fissures between roof and walls, and once water gained entrance, the situation deteriorated at an ever-increasing rate. Only vigilance and continual maintenance could turn the tables on the elements and postpone the inevitable collapse of the walls.

And even in the face of these constant efforts, roofs leaked continuously: reports of ceilings dripping, floors eroding, and inside walls washing away were numerous. As late as the beginning of the twentieth century priests bemoaned the lack of waterfastness of the nave of the Cochiti church and rationalized the need for a metal roof to combat the elements.[27] In spite of the radical aesthetic consequences, the pitched metal roof gained widespread popularity in the nineteenth century because it covered the parapet and protected the upper part of the wall, sealing it off from the intrusion of water and wind. For the late-eighteenth-century missions along the more humid coast of California broad tile roofs were ubiquitous, extending outward to form arcades that sheltered both the wall and the strolling friar. Nevertheless, the New Mexican church, like the Pueblo Indian dwellings before it, relied on the flat earthen roof, although it was a far from perfect solution.

APERTURES

Openings in masonry structures have always presented a challenge because stone, brick, and especially mud are weak in relation to tensile forces. In more advanced structural applications the arch was used to support the section of the wall above the aperture; in New Mexico this role was assigned to a lintel. Wooden pieces, usually squared, although sometimes left round, were placed one against another above an opening throughout the entire thickness of the wall. Where the wall continued over the top of a window or door, the wooden lintel was embedded in the adobe or stone and subsequently carried the weight of the wall above it. In some churches these lintels have been plastered over; in others they remain in view. At Ranchos de Taos, for example, the timbers that span the openings above the arched windows are painted white, clearly visible against the adobe into which they have been set.

Although the Franciscans brought iron hinges to the colony along with tools and locks, such as those noted by Joseph Toulouse at Abo, most doors were made to pivot on wooden pins.[28] Chimayo clearly illustrates this technique and demonstrates that the practice continued well into the nineteenth century. The doors themselves were assembled of multiple pieces of wood joined, nailed, or fastened together with metal brought by the missionaries. Wherever possible, the doors were fitted with locks. Domínguez was careful to comment on the existence not only of locks on the main doors to the church but also of locks on various chests and furnishings. A somewhat typical note was found in the description of Zuni: "At the head there is a beautiful wooden table which the priest uses for vesting. It has two drawers, one above the other, *with a key to the top one*. . . . The following are in the drawer *which has a lock*" (italics added).[29]

ILLUMINATION

New Mexican architecture is an architecture of both mass and light: the structure itself is little without the radiance that imparts visual life to the inert soil. As Charles Lummis wrote of New Mexico's light, "One cannot focus upon sunlight and silence; and yet without them adobe is a clod."[30]

Today we find beauty in these structures' simple volumes, striking profiles, soft textures, and vital, if rudimentary, ornamentation. But in the creation of a sense of sanctity and significance within the church, light was the critical ingredient. If the vault and the dome were nonexistent in New Mexico, and if elaborate, gilded decoration was impossible to procure, then brilliance and sparkle had to be created by other means. Pueblo rooms were dark. Lacking glass, the Indians made small eyelike windows of flaked mica stone called selenite, at least one example of which still remains at Acoma. The Spanish brought glass in small pieces into the province, but glass was a precious commodity because it had to be transported overland from Durango or Chihuahua. Hence its use was not widespread. More commonly Spanish church builders used oiled hides or adapted the native practice, creating windows of translucent selenite set in wooden grills that admitted a soft and diffused light.[31] The individual units rarely exceeded five inches square, however. Even with the opening of trade in American goods during the Mexican period, the size of the panes remained limited. Shipping invoices that served as customs declarations for a shipment of products from St. Louis in 1854 listed glass of only eight by ten inches and ten by twelve inches. Presumably, only smaller panes could be economically produced and transported by wagon.[32]

George Kubler, in his pioneering work *The Religious Architecture of Early New Mexico*, asserted that the transverse clerestory was the most characteristic invention of the New Mexican church (Figure 3.5).[33] He suggested that the clerestory was a vestige of the Mexican cupola, a form unattainable with New Mexico's limited technology and materials. The light quality and configuration of the church's cross-section, however, recalled more closely the stepped roofs of Moorish construction, such as the mosque at Córdoba, Spain, begun in 785 and converted into a Catholic church in the thirteenth century at the time of the Reconquest. The mosque's space comprised a seemingly infinite number of bays spanned by horseshoe arches that disappeared into the murky distance. A series of linear clerestories provided strips of diffused illumination running nearly the full length of the mosque. Its soft and indistinct lighting and the strength of its structure were recalled in the New Mexican nave.

Raising the ceiling height between the nave and the choir area in the New Mexican church introduced a slit of light that, with care and luck, would fall directly on the altar. The effect of this device can be stunning and is best witnessed today at San Agustín at Isleta and San Ildefonso (Figure 3.6). Unfortunately, other factors governed the selection of church sites within the pueblo so that the nave was not consistently oriented toward

3.5 San José, Las Trampas, New Mexico. The longitudinal profile of the church reveals the raised chancel roof necessary to create a transverse clerestory

3.6 Interior of San
Agustín, Isleta Pueblo,
New Mexico

3.6 Interior of San Agustín, Isleta Pueblo, New Mexico

the south, which would have guaranteed continued light throughout the day, or the east, which would have secured light during the morning mass. Santo Domingo, for example, faces roughly west, while the sequence of Pecos churches actually reversed orientation in subsequent reconstructions.

The theatrical impact of the clerestory doubles when one enters the church after crossing a bright, sandy plaza, as the eyes require some minutes to accustom to the darkness. Then at the end of the nave is revealed the striking presence of light flung across the crucifix and altar, a radiance enhanced by the basic darkness of the interior.

Windows in the early churches were precious commodities, and Domínguez provided detailed descriptions of them in his report. But at that time windows were fewer than those seen in churches today and were almost certainly of smaller dimensions. Often restricted to a single side of the nave, such as the south at Acoma or the west at Isleta, these apertures high in the wall provided accents of light rather than a principal source of illumination—that role was granted to the transverse clerestory. Only with the large-scale importation of glass made possible by the railroads in the late nineteenth century could the size of windows be feasibly increased or new ones cut. With their enlargement came a rather significant modification in the quality of light within the church. Even more severe was the effect of changes wrought by the pitched metal roof that accompanied American jurisdiction. While protecting the adobe walls from deterioration by water, the roof completely sealed off the clerestory, making the windows the sole source of light. Only at Santa Cruz, where a southfacing window lights the *reredos* (altarpiece) and altar, has a qualitative equal to the clerestory been found. [. . .]

Notes

1   George Kubler and Martin Soria, *Art and Architecture in Spain and Portugal and Their American Dominions, 1500–1800*, (Baltimore: Penguin Books, 1959), p. 71.

2   Manuel Toussaint, *Colonial Art in Mexico*, trans. and ed. by Elizabeth Wilder Weismann (Austin: University of Texas Press, 1967), pp. 275–277.

3   The full story of Hispanic-American architecture lies beyond the scope of this book; what concerns us, however, are those church structures built specifically for other remote native populations in the Americas that provide parallels with the churches built later in New Mexico.

4   Harold Wethey, *Colonial Architecture and Sculpture in Peru*, (Cambridge: Harvard University Press, 1940), p. 18. The churches that were supposedly built on the model of the Gesú in Rome actually displayed a greater affinity for Gothic and Renaissance prototypes. "The truth is that the Jesuit order never officially adopted a specific type of floorplan in Peru or anywhere else" (p. 18).

5   George Kubler, *Mexican Architecture in the Sixteenth Century*, (New Haven: Yale University Press, 1948), pp. 105–106. Kubler confirmed that "the vast official documentation for the colony contains almost no reference to drawings prepared in Spain for American use" (p. 105).

6   For the definitive presentation and analysis of the atrio and the development of related Mexican religious architecture, see John McAndrew, *The Open-Air Churches of Sixteenth-Century Mexico* (Cambridge: Harvard University Press, 1969); and Toussaint, *Colonial Art*, pp. 25–31, 57.

7   This term *architectural competence* is borrowed from Henry Glassie, *Folk Housing in Middle Virginia* (Knoxville: University of Tennessee Press, 1975), pp. 19–40. [. . .]

8   See Stanley Stubbs, Bruce T. Ellis, and Alfred E. Dittert, Jr., " 'Lost' Pecos Church," *El Palacio* 64 (1957): 67–92.

9   Kubler, *The Religious Architecture of New Mexico in the Colonial Period and Since the American Occupation* (1940) (Albuquerque: University of New Mexico Press, 1972 reprint ed.), p. 19.

10 While visiting Picuris in 1776, Domínguez recorded the uncertainty of existence on the frontier. The new church would be built, he assured the reader, but its site was to be adjusted to take defense into account. The Comanche raids "are so daring that this father I have mentioned [Don Pedro Fermin de Mendinueta] assures me that he escaped by a miracle in the year '69, for they sacked the convent and destroyed his meager supplies; yet he considered them well spent in exchange for his life and freedom from captivity . . . Orders were issued for the erection of a new building [church] in a safe place. This is near one block of, but outside, one plaza of the pueblo, with the intention that the convent should be in that block. But according to the plan, all is to be defensible as a unit, for the present space between the church and the block where the convent is to be built will be a cloister." Fray Francisco Atanasio Domínguez, *The Missions of New Mexico*, trans. and ed. by Eleanor B. Adams and Fray Angelico Chavez (Albuquerque: University of New Mexico Press, 1956), p. 92.

11 Mardith K. Schuetz, trans., *Architectural Practice in Mexico City: A Manual for Journeyman Architects of the Eighteenth Century* (Tucson: University of Arizona Press, 1987), p. 43.

12 The supplies for each friar establishing a mission included "one ream of paper." France V. Scholes, "The Supply Service in New Mexico Missions of the Seventeenth Century," *New Mexico Historical Review* 5 (1930): 100.

13 "After outlining the foundation with powdered lime, the trench is opened, leveled, and straightened with a mason's square and lines." Schuetz, *Architectural Practice*, p. 21.

14 Kubler cited the surveying practice of "setting ords for a new town," illustrated in *Pintura del Gobernador*, circa 1566. Kubler, *Mexican Architecture*, p. 159.

15 Scholes, "The Supply Service," pp. 103–104.

16 E. Boyd, *Popular Arts of Spanish New Mexico* (Santa Fe: Museum of New Mexico Press, 1974), p. 48.

17 Ibid., p. 446.

18 Cited in Paul A. F. Walter, "Mission Churches in New Mexico," *El Palacio* 5 (1918): 116.

19 The Casa Grande was built by the Hohokam people between A.D. 1300 and 1400. Hand-formed lumps of soil (called "turtle backs" because of their rounded forms) patted into place are believed to be the principal elements of construction. See David R. Wilcox and Lynette O. Shenk, *The Architecture of the Casa Grande and Its Interpretation* (Arizona State Museum Archaeological Series no. 115, Tucson, Arizona, 1977).

20 William Lumpkins, "A Distinguished Architect Writes on Adobe," *El Palacio* 77 (1972): 3.

21 Lee H. Nelson, ed., *Preservation of Historic Adobe Buildings*, Preservation Briefs 5 (Washington, DC: Technical Preservation Services Division, Department of the Interior, 1978). The process of burnishing, more effective when the device is slightly wet, is actually a process of sealing and polishing by gradually redistributing surface particles through continued rubbing. This technique is used to great aesthetic effect in the making of unglazed ceramics as the burnished areas— whether reduced or oxidized—acquire a brilliant shine without glazes.

22 Ronald F. Dickey, *New Mexico Village Arts* (1949) (Albuquerque: University of New Mexico Press, 1970 reprint ed.), p. 51.

23 Note the resemblance between this technique and the function of foundation stones. Odd S. Halseth, "Report of Repairs on Zia Mission: October 29 to December 8, 1923," *El Palacio* 16 (1924): 10–12.

24 "There is no heading for the nave of this church, because its adornment is so soulless that I consider it unnecessary to describe anything so dead. Nevertheless, although its chief resemblance is to a culverin because of its length and narrowness, it also resembles a wine cellar, and it contains two poor benches provided by Father Fray Sebastian Fernandez." Domínguez, *The Missions*, p. 115.

25 Kubler, *The Religious Architecture*, p. 34. Ivey, however, stressed the importance of block and tackle in church construction: "It is frequently forgotten that such equipment was known to virtually every Spaniard in the New World, since all had arrived there on board ships with innumerable pulleys, winches, and other lifting devices in constant use." He dismissed Kubler's interpretation that one nave wall's greater thickness was due to its use as a lifting surface: "Shear legs or some similar system of lifting had to have been used in the construction of the Salinas missions, contrary to the statements of George Kubler." Most of the beams had intricate carvings and were finished before they were installed. "If finished beams had been rolled to a wall top and then dragged into position, as depicted by Kubler, they would have been extensively damaged on the finished surfaces and edges. Instead they had to be lifted clear of the walls and lowered into position." James E. Ivey, *In the Midst of Loneliness, The Architectural History of the Salinas Missions* (Santa Fe: Southwest Cultural Resources Center Professional Papers, no. 15, 1988).

26 Bainbridge Bunting and John P. Conron, "The Architecture of Northern New Mexico," *New Mexico Architect* 8 nos. 9–10 (1966): 27.

27 Fray Jerome Hesse, "The Missions of Cochití and Santo Domingo, N.M.," *Franciscan Missions of the Southwest* (1913): 27.

28 See Joseph H. Toulouse, Jr., *The Mission of San Gregorio de Abo: A Report on the Excavation and Repair of a Seventeenth-Century New Mexico Mission* (Santa Fe: School of American Research, 1949). It was more common for doors to be mounted on wooden pivots than on metal hinges. "A pintle hinge would be fashioned from a stile extended beyond the top and

bottom rails of the door, and allowed to rotate in a socket carved from the door frame. Such a pintle pivot door is known in New Mexico as a *zambullo*." Viviana Nigro Holmes, "Architectural Woodwork of Spanish Colonial New Mexico," *New Mexico Studies in the Fine Arts* 10 (1985): 18.

29   Domínguez, *The Missions*, pp. 198–199.
30   Charles F. Lummis, *The Land of Poco Tiempo* (1893) (Albuquerque: University of New Mexico Press, 1952 reprint ed.), p. 6.
31   "Like the alabaster window panes of Ravenna's Byzantine churches, selenite is not transparent but is translucent, giving a subdued bath of light to the interior. Electric bulbs dangling from a cord, fluorescent tubes and plastic shades that have been installed in several chapels to replace obstructed clerestory windows give, in comparison, sorry lighting." Boyd, *Popular Arts*, p. 48.
32   Inventory of goods from Glascow and Brother, St. Louis, which consisted mostly of clothing and food stuffs: "3 half boxes window glass 8 × 10. 3 half boxes window glass 10 × 12." Ibid., p. 325.
33   Kubler, *The Religious Architecture*, p. 67.

Chapter 4

Dell Upton

Space
Parish churches, courthouses, and dwellings in
colonial Virginia

The social space of the Virginia church and the landscape of which it was a part was a dynamic one. It was most effective when people moved from one space to another. The continual reassembly of the community and the constant visible construction and destruction of the social order were the deepest experience the Anglican parish church had to offer Virginians. [. . .] The church was intended as a self-contained fusion of the divine and social worlds. The artificial insularity of ritual space created by the architecture implied that the world of the church was opposed to the world outside. In fact, the church was part of a network of dynamic spaces, each of which used similar means to create differing, but complementary symbolic environments.

Every church was surrounded by a churchyard. Seventeenth-century law required "That there be a certayne portion of ground appoynted out, and impaled or fenced in (upon the penalty of twenty Marques) to be for the buriall of the dead." A yard was created at the same time as the church itself. The sexton or another member of the parish was employed to "grub" and clean the space around the building, removing most of the trees along with the construction debris, and creating a dirt area surrounding the new building. On exceptionally barren lots sycamores and other trees might be planted for shade. The bounds were then defined. The yards made in 1719 at St. Peter's Parish church and St. Paul's Parish upper church were 100 feet square, while the one built by John Moore at the upper church of Christ Church Parish, Middlesex County, in 1733 was 134 feet by 110 feet. Most ranged from 100 to 150 feet on a side. The newly designated churchyard was then enclosed. In the wealthiest parishes, 4½- to 5-foot-high English-bond brick walls with ogival or semicircular copings were built. A good example survives at Blandford church, Petersburg (Figure 4.1). Although much of the wall has been rebuilt, the 163-by-143-foot enclosure is substantially the one called for as part of Colonel Richard Bland's contract to enlarge the church in 1752. It has semicircular coping bricks; gates, marked by sandstone finials, aligned with the south and west doors; and a large unrepointed section at the north. Such a wall was handsome but expensive, and might cost as much as sixteen thousand pounds of tobacco, or the equivalent of a year's salary for the minister. Consequently, most parishes, even those that built elaborate churches, elected to build wooden post-and-rail or pale (picket) fences. Truro Parish's vestry reconsidered its order to build a brick wall around the new Pohick church in 1774, "having just finished two expensive Churches, and a Glebe not yet purchased," and settled for a post-and-rail fence instead. Cedar, locust, chestnut, and white oak were preferred for the posts, with these woods plus yellow pine, poplar, and lightwood employed for pickets and rails. Like other exposed wooden structures, the fence was then tarred. Sometimes a ditch around the outside reinforced the wooden structure. A fence of this sort was much less costly than a brick wall, and might be built for fifteen hundred to fifty-five hundred pounds of tobacco, although the Westover Parish vestry once paid eight thousand for a pale fence.[1]

Whatever the structure of the fence, an elaborate gate, aligned with the doorway of the church building, usually marked the division between the churchyard and the outside. [. . .] The fence built in 1719 at St. Peter's Parish church, New Kent County, was to have "Wide Handsom Gates made after the fform of Iron Gates. wth: Handsom Square Peares (or Posts) for the Gates. with a hollow Spire a Top." The brick wall would be "Genteely Rompt [ramped] at each Side of the Gates," and have "a handsome Coopin Brick" on top. The wall and gates were in all other respects to be "as well Done as the Capitol wall in Williams:Burgh." The post-and-rail fence at Pohick church was similarly provided with "three handsome Palisade Gates" and a palisade gate appears in a nineteenth-century illustration of Bruton Parish church (Figure 4.2).[2]

Although Bruton Parish churchyard in the colonial capital contains handsome eighteenth-century monuments, most churchyards were little used as burial places. Those members of the gentry who deigned to be interred at church often demanded separate accommodations, giving a similar effect to that created by the private pew enclosures inside. Colonel William Poythress, for example, was given permission in 1754 "to Inclose a piece of Ground for a Burying place for his Family tho' the Same should be within the

4.1 Blandford Church, Petersburg, Virginia, 1734–37 (Col. Thomas Ravenscroft undertaker); addition and wall, 1752–70 (Col. Richard Bland undertaker)

4.2 Bruton Parish
Church, Williamsburg,
Virginia, 1711–12
(James Morris
undertaker). A mid-
nineteenth-century
view showing the
church with its wall
(c.1754, Samuel
Spurr) and palisaded
gate (from William
Meade, *Old Churches,
Ministers and Families
of Virginia*,
Philadelphia:
Lippincott, 1857)

Walls of the Church Yard, provided that he inlarge the same" to make up for the space
lost to public use. Even burial inside the church was losing favor among the gentry.
Longstanding custom gave burial inside the building an honorific connotation, but it made
more impression in the seventeenth and early eighteenth centuries, when parishes established regular fee schedules for burial inside the building. The keepers of the register of
Christ Church Parish, Middlesex County, for example, were careful to note which parishioners had been interred inside. As late as the second quarter of the eighteenth century,
Robert Carter of Corotoman directed in his will that the chancel of the new Christ church,
Lancaster County, "be preserved as a burial place for my family as the present chancel
is." When a grandson of Carter died a few years later, his father brought the corpse to
Lancaster County "to be buried at our Church." But Robert and Charles Carter's actions
were out of touch with their peers' habits. Increasingly, eighteenth-century commentators
noted, planters preferred to hold funerals and to be buried at home, and the churchyards,
in which everyone had a right to be interred, were abandoned to the poor. One Sunday at
Nomini church, Philip Fithian overheard an "impious expression" uttered by a fellow-
tutor employed by the Washington family. The man remarked that "if I was buried here
it would grieve me to look up and see *Swine* feeding over me," since the yard was
unfenced. Fithian's own employer, Robert Carter, later echoed the tutor's remark in
observing that "he dislikes much the Common method of making Burying Yards round.
Churches, & having them almost open to every Beast." The unease caused Fithian by such
comments was soothed when he learned that "only the lower sort of People are buried at

the Church; for the Gentlemen have private burying-Yards." Even strangers, if they were members of the elite, were interred in private burying grounds when they died far from home. John Harrower, a tutor in Spotsylvania County, recorded the death of a woman traveling with her daughter and slave. The woman was buried in the graveyard at Snow Creek plantation, and her funeral service was attended by local grandee Mann Page and several other gentlemen.[3]

If the churchyard had little significance as holy ground, it was nevertheless an indispensable part of the church's space and was fitted up for intensive use. In addition to the church, the churchyard might contain a variety of other structures. Most common was a vestry house, a small building used for meetings of the parish's governing body. It was a minimal building, usually wooden, and ranged in size from twelve-by-sixteen to sixteen-by-twenty feet. A door, a window, and a chimney were all the accommodations needed, and some buildings skimped even on those. At the predecessor of the present Pohick church, for example, the Truro Parish vestry constructed a sixteen-foot-square vestry house "framed work & Clapboarded the Covering boards to be Sapt & an Inside wooden Chimney a plank floor & to be lofted with Clapboards & raised on Blocks." When the parish built its brick churches in the 1760s and 1770s, the quality of the vestry houses was improved as well. The new vestry house at Falls church (soon to become part of newly created Fairfax Parish) was a sixteen-by-twenty-foot brick building with a brick or tile floor, shingles, and a "large inside Chimney." Like most such buildings, it was provided with a table and three benches. Those rare churches with towers used the second stories as vestry rooms (Figure 4.3). Vestry houses and vestry rooms were used so rarely they were often rented out as schools or residences, and sometimes taken over by squatters between vestry meetings. The Blisland Parish vestry ordered its church wardens to "turn Wm: Broadway & his Family out of the Vestry House" and rent it out for the benefit of the poor relief fund, and the Truro Parish vestry allowed William Weston to use its vestry house at Pohick in return for his covering it.[4]

Of equal importance were the more ephemeral structures that equipped the churchyard as a gathering place for the parishioners before the service commenced. Here each member of the community arrived, some inconspicuously, some with great pomp, to join the assembling congregation. For the gentry, arrival on horseback was an important show of social standing. Hugh Jones claimed to "have known some spend the morning in ranging several miles in the woods to find and catch their horses only to ride two or three miles to church," a tale repeated by many other writers in the eighteenth century. Horseblocks in the churchyard fixed the ceremony of mounting and dismounting, and helped focus attention on the arrivals and departures of the parish elite. Horses were fastened to a hitching rail, which was sometimes covered, and occasionally a stable was provided. For those few with vehicles, some parishes provided a "Shelter house for the Reception of Chairs & Horses." The church site was chosen for its access to water, and a well head was built or a spring enclosed in palings. A sundial marked the time, and now and then bells futilely summoned the congregation of large rural parishes.[5]

Colonial church contracts specified that shutters and locks be provided so that churches could be secured when not in use, especially when they were located in a town or near a population center. Churchyards retained their customary uses as everyday public

4.3 St. Peter's Parish Church, New Kent Co., Virginia, 1701–3, tower and vestry, 1739–40 (William Walker undertaker)

gathering places, despite nearly two hundred years of Anglican efforts to extinguish the secular use of churches and a Virginia law forbidding it. On several occasions, William Byrd observed drinking parties in churchyards. When officers of the militia were being feted at the governor's house in Williamsburg, the men were treated with a hogshead set up in Bruton Parish churchyard. In the evening, the officers took a walk about the town and "found a comic freak of a man that was drunk that hung on the pales."[6]

It was on Sunday morning, of course, that the churchyard really came to life. At midmorning, the parishioners began to gather in groups, standing or sitting on benches scattered under the trees "for the People to sitt on before Divine Service." Notices were tacked to the church door, as they had been on medieval parish churches. Fithian recorded one "dated Sunday Decemr 12th Pork to be sold to-morrow at 20/. per Hundred." Church-door notices were used to "outlaw" slaves, the Virginia term for legal declarations that a slave had run away and that anyone who killed him or her might claim a reward. Gentlemen discussed business, and "rings of Beaux" chatted before and after the service. While they were waiting, the parishioners might witness the punishment of an unruly resident of the parish. St. Peter's Parish ordered the construction of a pair of stocks outside the churchyard wall in 1704. They were rebuilt in 1735 when the vestry ordered "That the Church Wardens cause a good and substantial Pair of Stocks to be forthwith erected near the Church-Yard Wall, for the Restraint of licentious and disorderly Persons several such having lately appeared in the Church, to the great Disturbance of the Minister and Congregation, during divine service."[7]

At Jamestown in the early years of settlement, the governor made a formal processional entry, accompanied by a guard of fifty liveried halberdiers. The tradition of the ranked procession was maintained throughout the colonial period. It marked formal occasions like the 1770 funeral of Lord Botetourt reported in the *Virginia Gazette*. It also was repeated less formally in the entry of the parish gentlemen into the church on a Sunday. At a signal, the parishioners entered the building, but the elite males hung back until the rest of the parish was in place, sometimes until the commencement of the sermon. In churches where men and women sat separately, the absence of the local gentlemen was particularly conspicuous. When they finally entered as a group, moving along the long axial route from the west door, and possibly using the cross aisle at the chancel door, they caught everyone's attention. Aware of the gaze of their inferiors, they did not acknowledge it. Bowing briefly, gravely, almost imperceptibly, to the parson as they passed the desk, they finally made their way to their seats in the chancel, or ascended private stairs to galleries or hanging pews.[8]

The services were often as offhand as the attendance. Landon Carter reported several instances in which the minister did not show up, or came early and rushed through the service before anyone had arrived. However long the service lasted, at the end, the gentlemen waited again, and exited en masse, the group movement and fragmented seating arrangements together demonstrating to all who cared to notice the structure of local society in pre-Revolutionary Virginia.[9]

The religious ritual had spiritual value to some Virginians, but the activity of churchgoing was predominantly secular. The constant assemblings and reassemblings, the array, dissolution, and reformation of the social body as the parishioners moved from home to churchyard, into church and back home again, were what attracted Virginians on Sundays. Similar principles of movement, of dissolution and regrouping, were evident throughout the formal landscape created by the gentry. Two other elements of that landscape will help put the church's role into sharper focus.

The courthouse complemented the church as a place where public rituals reaffirmed and made visible the character of Virginia society. As with the church, its design embodied the principle of movement. The courthouse was an axial building. Most courthouses were rectangles, with jury rooms at one end or in a loft over the courtroom. After 1730, some were T-shaped, with a courtroom stretching the full length of the building, and jury rooms flanking it at the entrance end. The courtroom was entered axially or from the sides at one end of the room. At the far end, under the Royal Arms, sat the county justices, who were often the same men who sat as vestrymen in parish affairs. They occupied a long, raised bench that might be "divided Wainscot fashion above & below into twelve seats," like the one James Jones built for Lancaster County in 1740 (Figure 4.4). Among the justices there were distinctions. All had attained their offices by virtue of their rank in the county hierarchy, but some were recognized as wiser and more skillful than their peers. The senior magistrates, or justices of the quorum, sat in the center, the most senior of all often provided with a chair. The end of the courthouse was sometimes curved: the compass shape as a marker of importance here makes a rare secular appearance. The specific architectural reference in these courthouses was to the Capitol in Williamsburg, an allusion made more explicit when the courthouse incorporated an oval window in the

4.4 Lancaster Co. Courthouse, Virginia, 1740 (James Jones undertaker). Reconstructed plan. Key: cj = chief justice's seat; j = justices' benches; jb = jury bench; b = bars, with benches attached

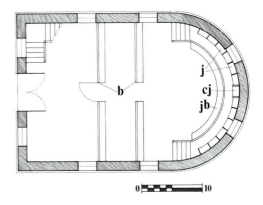

apse, as did the one built in 1726 in Norfolk County. The ultimate reference was to the tribunes of Roman basilicas. In addition to their associative value, the apses of county courthouses added a further note of differentiation to the bench, for the senior justices were not only central, they were farther away from the entrance. The judges were raised two or three feet from the floor and beneath them, seated on a lower platform or at floor level, facing the "congregation" (as the King and Queen County records called the audience), were the jury. Between the congregation and the jury were a table for the clerk, a chair for the king's attorney, and chairs or elevated boxes for the sheriff and crier. The participants were separated from the public by a bar, or balustrade. Like the aisles of churches, the public area was frequently paved with brick or stone, but, unlike the churches, the courthouse had no seats. This congregation had to stand. The hierarchy of the court was displayed visually along a longitudinal and gradually ascending axis, and was reinforced by distinctions such as seats for the justices and none for the public. A few courthouses even had a door near the judges' end corresponding to the south door of the church.[10]

Occasionally the entry of an eighteenth-century courthouse was sheltered by a long, low arcade, which was also paved and was frequently furnished with benches. In the walled yard enclosing the building the congregation gathered and conducted business much as they did at church, awaiting the signal to enter the courtroom, where they found the justices in place.[11]

The processional use of space extended to the great plantation house. The return of so much of eastern Virginia to woodland disguises the fact that the large planter liked to be dimly visible, but aloof from traffic, when in his house. The greatest planters were seated above the rivers, and visible from them. They were equally visible from the roads. According to Philip Fithian, Nomini Hall could be seen from as far away as six miles. It was linked to the road by a three-hundred-yard poplar avenue. Its domestic outbuildings defined a court on either side, in the center of which stood the house. One was thus led from the road along an avenue to the house, which was set off in a series of terraced increments and ultimately by a high basement.[12]

A similar route was incorporated into Mount Airy, Richmond County (Figure 4.5). The visitor to Mount Airy passed a series of physical barriers that were also social barriers.

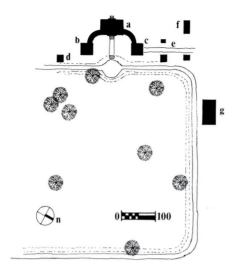

4.5 Mount Airy, Richmond Co., Virginia, c.1760. Site plan. Key: a = main house; b = family wing; c = kitchen and working wing; d = schoolhouse; e = domestic outbuildings, eighteenth and nineteenth centuries, arranged along a street; f = orangerie; g = stable, early nineteenth century

The house sat on a terraced site above the Rappahannock River, its site a formalized version of the planter's habit of placing the main house on a hill with its subsidiary buildings around it. Mount Airy was tantalizingly visible from afar, but it disappeared into the hill top as one approached it. To reach the mansion, one traveled around to the rear, then approached along a path that skirted a sunken park. The informal park was in contrast to the formal layout of the house on its terraces, and it also served to make the terraces appear higher than they were. The curved drive showed the visitor the house from a variety of prospects analogous to those experienced when approaching from afar. It ended with the arrival on the lower of two terraces. A low flight of steps led to an upper terrace forming a forecourt defined by two advance buildings. These were originally freestanding, but were connected to the house sometime later in the eighteenth century. The connection served to heighten the constriction of space that accompanied the passing of social barriers and the ascent of terraces and steps, and thus to focus one's gaze in a manner similar to that effected by the apse of the county courthouse. Having crossed the upper terrace, one approached the looming house by way of a much higher flight of stairs. This led not into the house, but into a recessed loggia, a shorter version of that in the courthouse (Figures 4.6 and 4.7). At last the front door gave entrance to a large reception hall. More exclusive, but still public rooms opened off this. A visitor to the owner, John Tayloe, passed a series of five barriers—two terraces, a flight of steps, a loggia, and an entrance hall—before being admitted to the dining table, the ritual center of the planter's hospitality. Each barrier served to reinforce, architecturally and psychologically, John Tayloe's centrality, affirming the visitor's status as he or she was allowed to pass through it. At the same time, the layout of Mount Airy set Tayloe off from his surroundings. It functioned analogously to the private pews in church, but the complete separation provided by his plantation house would have defeated the purpose of the church gathering.

For the large plantation house, movement is again the key. More important than being in a certain room was the route taken to get there, or how far along the formal route one progressed. George Washington met his neighbors and conversed with them at the

4.6 Mount Airy, north facade

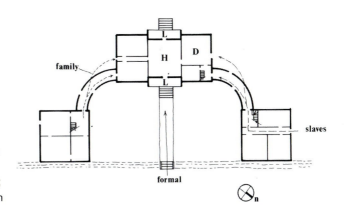

4.7 Mount Airy. Sketch plan showing formal, family, and slaves' routes. Key: H = hall; L = loggias; D = dining room

land door of Mount Vernon, but he met Benjamin Henry Latrobe, his nephew's friend, in the east river portico and led the architect by stages through several rooms of the house in the course of several days' visit. John Harrower's employer received business visitors, including the tutor and his charges, in the passage of his house, and Robert Carter heard a slave's plea for better treatment in his. And while Eliza Custis's family and friends visited in the parlor, the slaves waited in the passage, though they listened to and participated in the merriment taking place inside.[13]

Latrobe's experience at Mount Vernon reminds us that the formal route was not the only way to reach the heart of the house. Just as the clergyman and the justice had separate doors, so did those who were exempt from the intentions of the formal route. Mount Vernon and Mount Airy both had secondary entrances for intimates. At Mount Airy the

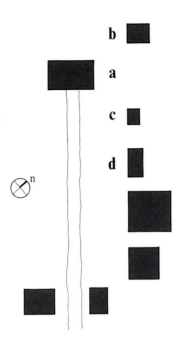

4.8 Joseph Jordan Farmstead, Isle of Wight Co., Virginia, 1795 and after. Sketch site plan. The original and nineteenth-century outbuildings that survived in 1975 defined an approach to the house (a). The parlor door and the entrance to the cellar faced the kitchen (b) and smokehouses (c, d). The other buildings were farm structures. All the buildings except the house were demolished in 1979

east block was a private building. The route from it to the main house was through a doorway marked by an elaborate Palladian opening, into a small side passage. After the hyphens [curved passageways linking the main house to the dependencies] were built, they connected the dependency directly with the northeast room of the main house.

The competitiveness and communal display of church and courthouse were thus given a new form in the great plantation. The single planter argued for his own standing in a setting in which there were no rivals. The architectural devices were the same, however, and as in the church and the courthouse, the meaning of the experience was grasped by moving through space. It was a kind of experience, moreover, that was not confined to the great plantation. The lesser county elite used it in their much more modest houses. Houses as small as one and two rooms were tied to their landscapes in similar ways. Front and rear doors in the house provided public access, and access to the farm buildings, which in some parts of Virginia in the eighteenth century were set in an axial street of two parallel rows stretching from the house to the main road (Figure 4.8).[14]

The use of vernacular structures to achieve similar architectural effects to those attained in churches and great plantations is evident. The small house lacked the formalized unity of Mount Airy but was organized along similar principles. Indeed, the high-style exterior at Mount Airy can be thought of as a fashionable new guise for a longstanding Virginia practice. The small house shared with the mansion the tradition of breaking up household functions into a main building and a series of domestic outbuildings. The one- or two-room house typically was furnished with a separate kitchen, a dairy for cool storage of milk and milk products, and a smokehouse for the preservation and storage of meat. These were integrated with the main house in straightforward ways. The kitchen

4.9 Second Edwards House, Isle of Wight Co., Virginia, early nineteenth century

normally stood near one end of the house and was accessible from a secondary entry, placed, in a two-room house, in the end of the smaller parlor or chamber. Near it stood the auxiliary smokehouse and dairy. Often there was a cellar under the house, accessible from outside at the parlor end, but not from inside the house (Figure 4.9). The cellar was another of the outbuildings, but by locating it under the house the planter achieved the same kind of raising that the terraces and high basement accomplished at Mount Airy, and that the magistrates' bench, the chancel, and the pulpit did in other settings.[15]

In the smallest houses the domestic outbuildings were usually set beside or behind the main house, but they were sometimes used to define a ceremonial route for the visitor. The route carried the outsider past the sources of the planter's wealth directly into the hall, or main room, the most elaborately decorated space of the house. In some examples, the stair was moved from its customary position on the wall between hall and chamber to the far rear corner, by the fireplace (Figure 4.10). This resulted in reduced accessibility of stair to the visitor, terminating the processional route in the hall. At the same time the stair could be a decorative feature, an opportunity that was taken in all the surviving houses with chimney-wall stairs. The hall provided controlled access, through a door, to

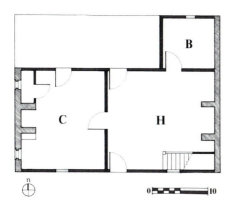

4.10 King House, Suffolk, Virginia, late-eighteenth century. Plan. Key: H = hall; C = chamber or parlor; B = back room or chamber

Sudden all are out, so that we seem like a Town; but most of the Inhabitants are black." Repeatedly in the seventeenth and eighteenth centuries, travelers characterized the appearance of plantations as resembling villages. Durand de Dauphiné, a visitor in the 1680s, thought that "when you come to the home of a person of some means, you think you are entering a fairly large village." William Hugh Grove in 1732 described the York River as lined with "pleasant Seats on the Bank which Shew Like little villages, for having Kitchins, Dayry houses, Barns, Stables, Store houses, and some of them 2 or 3 Negro Quarters all Seperate from Each other but near the mansion houses which make a shew to the river of 7 or 8 distinct Tenements, tho all belong to one family." A century after Durand's initial use of the metaphor, the German traveler Johann David Schoepf noted that a Virginia plantation "has often more the appearance of a small Village."[19]

Schoepf's village was meant to be seen and to command the surrounding landscape. Whether rising above its surroundings on terraces, as at Mount Airy, or on a basement, as in the home of Captain B.H., whom Schoepf visited, the planter's house "stood out well by contrast" with the slave houses and outbuildings around it. Benjamin Latrobe noted that Mount Vernon could be seen from a mile away, and Luigi Castiglioni offered the complementary observation that the view it commanded was equally pleasing. "The view of the Potomac River and of the boats that go up and down it to Alexandria, the spectacle of a broad expanse of cultivated terrain contrasting with the adjacent hills still clad in ancient oaks and lofty pines, contribute to render the site varied and charming." Philip Fithian caught the spirit when he wrote in his *Journal* in August 1774, of a family walk from Nomini Hall. "Then we stroll'd down the Pasture quite to the River, admiring the Pleasantness of the evening, & the delightsome Prospect of the River, Hills, Huts on the Summits, low Bottoms, Trees Of various Kinds, and Sizes, Cattle & Sheep feeding some near us, & others at a great distance on the green sides of the Hills, People, some fishing, others working, & others in the Pasture among the Horses;—The Country emphatically in her goodly Variety! I love to walk on these high Hills where I Can see the Tops of tall Trees lower than my Feet, at not half a Miles Distance—Where I can have a long View of many Miles & see on the Summits of the Hills Clusters of Savin Trees, through these often a little Farm-House, or Quarter for Negroes; these airy Situations seem to me to be the Habitations of Health, and Vigor."[20]

The culmination of this kind of planning, and of the intentions behind it, was Thomas Jefferson's Monticello (Figure 4.11). Situated on the flank of its little mountain, Monticello, like Mount Airy, was approached by a circuitous route that concealed it until one was very near. Though Monticello could not be seen, its builder commanded a prospect of a vast territory around it. The "Blue Mountains," the lowlands, other planters' houses—all were part of a prospect Isaac Weld thought stretched forty miles in each direction. Weld noted approvingly that "The mists and vapours arising from the low grounds give a continual variety to the scene." Although the mountain rose above Monticello, it, too, was turned to visual advantage. Gardens, vineyards, and orchards lined it, picturesque garden walks were threaded through it, and Jefferson originally intended to place striking pavilions on it that could be seen from his house.[21]

The entire landscape of Piedmont Virginia was thus focused on Thomas Jefferson at Monticello. The house was filled with revolving desks, dumb waiters, two-faced clocks,

4.11 Thomas Jefferson, Monticello, Charlottesville, Virginia, 1796–1809

devices to open doors in unison. It was the articulated landscape in its most hopeful form—the natural and human world refashioned to converge on the individual at its center. The architectural techniques were the same as those found in the pre-Revolutionary church, courthouse, and plantation. Emphasis by height and distance was there, on a grander scale than any attempted before the Revolution. Yet there was a critical difference—a dislocation, a disengagement at Monticello. Jefferson could see, but not be seen. The relationship was one-sided. The complementary quality of the older landscape was gone. The processional aspect is also missing from Jefferson's landscape; everything can be absorbed from a single point by the central actor. The dome, which might provide the focal point, leading the visitor to the building and providing a vantage point for its occupants, is at the rear of the house. It might be a centralizing dome of heaven, but it is not visible from the state rooms of the building. Its presence must be imagined, rather than perceived, at the heart of the scheme.[22]

At Jefferson's Monticello, the landscape of the plantation was entirely disengaged from the landscapes of the courthouse and church. The collapse of the Anglican parish and the diminution of court day's importance during the Revolution were complemented by the ascendancy of the plantation. The centrality of the individual planter was established. For pre-Revolutionary Virginians, however, this reorganization was not clear. The gentry used the church, the courthouse, the plantation complexes, and the connective tissue of the landscape all equally as important tools of social assertion.

However, the landscape was not exclusively the gentry's. It incorporated elements created by slaves and dispossessed whites, whose contradiction of the gentry's social vison became more evident as the eighteenth century passed. But while the landscape asserted the gentry's aims imperfectly, it worked *well enough* during most of the eighteenth century. Moreover, there are signs that the gentry system was beginning to accommodate the social changes of the eighteenth century, and might have made the transition to the nineteenth century without serious disruption in many areas. The disintegration recorded in Samuel Mordecai's letter and enshrined at Jefferson's Monticello was not inevitable. Nevertheless, the gentry synthesis of church, courthouse, and plantation house was an unstable one.

The power of the gentry landscape was undermined by inconsistencies within it and by systematic exclusions from it. Just as family members and other intimates were exempted from the formal route through the plantation house, so were slaves. At Mount Airy their route began in the street of outbuildings that stretched west from the west dependency, passed through that dependency, which contained the kitchen and other work rooms, and into the main house through a small pedimented doorway in the dining room. Like the east wing, this was later connected directly to the house by the hyphen. The slave's route thus mirrored the private routes that led from the east wing. But the slave was exempted for a different reason. Eighteenth-century Virginians did not imagine that their slaves would be susceptible to the same kinds of displays at church, home, or court that were intended to bind the white community together, and to rationalize its hierarchical form. Rather, they assumed only force could bind slaves.

Because the planters did not expect slaves to be drawn into assenting to Virginia's social structure through public ceremonies, they exempted slaves from their formalities. In the planter's landscape, blacks could pass almost at will, even to places where whites from outside were forbidden. The traveler Alexander Macaulay was annoyed to be reminded of this in 1783 when he visited Christiana Campbell's house in Williamsburg, thinking that it was still a tavern. In "a large cold room on the left hand," the parlor, Macaulay observed several slaves lounging about. Macaulay, however, was left in the passage, until he marched indignantly into the parlor. This remarkable absence of clear barriers also characterized the slave's sojourn in public, once he or she had passed the all-important barrier of obtaining permission to leave the master's property. Slaves mixed with court-day crowds. At church, if they went, there was no definite seating arrangement reserved to them. The "slave gallery" of the nineteenth century was a rarity in the eighteenth century. Slaves might share a section set aside for them, but as often as not they would sit in, or adjacent to, their masters' pews.[23]

In the end, the gentry landscape was meant to have an integrating function, to make a place for everyone. While it incorporated new conceptions about the nature of the world, about time and memory, its explicit intention was to manifest old hierarchical and patriarchal values, to demonstrate the planter's superior claims. It served equally importantly as a device to help the gentry understand and adjust to the changes that were transforming eighteenth-century Virginia.

Notes

VSL = Virginia State Library, Richmond.
VB = Vestry Book (unless otherwise noted, all of these are located in the VSL).

1   William W. Hening, ed., *The Statutes at Large* (1819–23), 10 vols. (Charlottesville: University of Virginia Press, 1969 reprint ed.), 1: 160–61; Petsworth VB, pp. 167, 120; Kingston VB, p. 2; St. Andrew's VB, fol. 63; Cumberland VB, p. 433; Upper VB, p. 220; Blisland VB, pp. 69, 85; St. Peters VB, pp. 174–75, 56; St. Paul's VB, p. 86; Christ, Middlesex VB, pp. 234, 37, 161, 165;

Bristol VB, p. 128; Truro VB, pp. 135–36, 127; Lynnhaven VB, p. 45; William Byrd, *The Secret Diary of William Byrd of Westover, 1709–1712*, ed. Louis B. Wright and Marion Tinling (Richmond: Dietz Press, 1941), p. 138. A set of specifications in the St. George's, Spots., vestry book gives a good idea of the appearance and construction of one of these fences. The vestry agreed "to Rail in the Churches at Rappahannock and Mattapony [with] Ten feet pannels five Rails to each to be done with white oak Posts and Poplar rails without any Sap the Posts to be burnt all under ground and six Inches above . . ., the Tenents of rails to be Tar'd before fixed in the Mortice." (St. George's, Spots. VB, 1: 55.)

2   St. Peter's VB, p. 174; *Virginia Gazette* (Purdie and Dixon) March 31, 1774.

3   Bristol VB, p. 136; Christ, Middlesex VB, pp. 18–19; W.A.R. Goodwin, *Historical Sketch of Bruton Church, Williamsburg, Virginia* (Petersburg: Franklin Press, 1903), pp. 42–43; "Carter Papers," *Virginia Magazine of History and Biography* 6, no. 1 (July 1898): 3; John Carter to William Dawkins, September 11, 1733, John, Landon, and Charles Carter Letter Book, 1732–1781, microfilm, Colonial Williamsburg Foundation, p. 18; Hugh Jones, *The Present State of Virginia*, ed. Richard L. Morton (1724; reprint ed., Chapel Hill: University of North Carolina Press, 1956), p. 97; Fraser D. Neiman, *The "Manner House" Before Stratford (Discovering the Clifts Plantation)* (Stratford, Va.: Robert E. Lee Memorial Association, 1980), pp. 28–29; Médéric-Louis-Élie Moreau de Saint-Mèry, *Moreau de St. Mèry's American Journey [1793–1798]*, trans. and ed. Kenneth Roberts and Anna M. Roberts (Garden City, N.Y.: Doubleday, 1947), p. 53; Philip V. Fithian, *Journals and Letters of Philip Vickers Fithian, A Plantation Tutor of the Old Dominion, 1773–1774*, ed. Hunter Dickinson (Charlottesville: Dominion Books, 1969), pp. 41, 61; *The Journal of John Harrower, An Indentured Servant in the Colony of Virginia 1775–1776*, ed. Edward Miles Riley (Williamsburg: Colonial Williamsburg Foundation, 1963), pp. 87–88. Most of the elaborate 18th-century tombs now standing in colonial churchyards, it might be mentioned, were moved there in the 20th century from their original plantation locations.

4   St. Paul's VB, p. 196; Christ, Lancaster VB, p. 16; Truro VB, pp. 58, 102–3; Blisand VB, p. 175.

5   Jones, *Present State*, p. 84; Alexander MacSpaman, *America Dissected* (1752), reprint in Wilkins Updike, *A History of the Episcopal Church in Narragansett Rhode Island*, ed. Daniel Goodwin (2d ed.; Boston: Merrymount Press, 1907), 3: 12; T.H. Breen, "Horses and Gentlemen: The Cultural Significance of Gambling Among the Gentry of Virginia," *William and Mary Quarterly* 3d ser. 34, no. 2 (April 1977): 248–49; St. Mark's VB, pp. 26, 65; Petsworth VB, p. 89; Elizabeth City VB, pp. 67, 85, 126, 55–56, 88; Christ, Middlesex VB, pp. 18, 78, 81, 321; Truro VB, p. 48; Upper VB, pp. 19–20, 220; St. Peter's VB, p. 217, 108, 224; Wicomico VB. fols, 47, 10, 36, 96; Byrd, *Diary*, p. 470.

6   Wicomico, VB, fols. 60–61, 75, 91; Bristol VB, p. 51; Truro VB, pp. 88, 91; Byrd, *Diary*, pp. 174, 233. In an attempt to eliminate the nonliturgical uses of parish churches that were common in the Middle Ages, Anglican authorities between 1550 and 1640 issued 200 separate articles and injunctions prohibiting them. (Marcus Binney and Peter Burman, *Chapels and Churches: Who Cares?* (London: British Tourist Authority, 1979), p. 111.

7   Albemarle VB, p. 44; Wicomico VB, fol. 53; Newport VB, p. 84; Bristol VB, p. 184; Truro VB, p. 132; Gerald Randall, *Church Furnishing and Decoration in England and Wales* (London: B.T. Batsford, 1980), p. 31; Fithian, p. 29; Gerald W. Mullin, *Flight and Rebellion: Slave Resistance in Eighteenth-Century Virginia* (New York: Oxford University Press, 1972), pp. 56–58; Landon Carter, *The Diary of Colonel Landon Carter of Sabine Hill, 1752–1778*, ed. Jack P. Greene (Charlottesville: University of Virginia Press, 1965), p. 289; St. Peter's VB, pp. 104, 240–41.

8   William Strachey, *A True Reportory of the Wreck and Redemption of Sir Thomas Gates, Knight* (1625), in *A Voyage to Virginia in 1609*, ed. Louis B. Wright (Charlottesville: University Press of Virginia, 1964), pp. 80–81; Rhys Isaac, *The Transformation Of Virginia, 1740–1790* (Chapel Hill: University of North Carolina Press, 1982), pp. 326–28; Fithian, pp. 29, 100, 137; Carter, p. 536.

9   Carter, p. 743.

10 A.G. Roeber, "Authority, Law and Custom: The Rituals of Court Day in Tidewater Virginia, 1720 to 1750," *WMQ* 3d ser. 37, no. 1 (January 1980): 29–33, 36–37; Wesley Frank Craven, *The Southern Colonies in the Seventeenth Century, 1607–1689* (Baton Rouge: Louisiana State University Press, 1949), p. 274; William H. Seiler, "The Anglican Parish in Virginia," in *Seventeenth-Century America: Essays an Colonial History*, ed. James Morton Smith (Chapel Hill: University of North Carolina Press, 1959), pp. 139, 141–42; Richard R. Beeman, "Social Change and Cultural Conflict in Virginia: Lunenburg County, 1746 to 1774," *William and Mary Quarterly* 3d ser. 35, no. 3 (July 1978): 467; Lancaster County Order Book No. 8, 1729–1743, MS., VSL, pp. 286–87; Norfolk County Orden, 1724–1734, MS., VSL, p. 60; Essex County Wills and Deeds No. 10, MS., VSL, fol. 109; A.G. Roeber, *Faithful Magistrates and Republican Lawyers: Creators of Virginia Legal Culture, 1680–1810* (Chapel Hill: University of North Carolina Press, 1981), pp. 78–80; Marcus Whiffen, "The Early County Courthouses of Virginia," *Journal of the Society of Architectural Historians* 18, no. 1 (March 1959): 2–10. James Jones, builder of the Lancaster County courthouse, also built St. Mary's White Chapel Parish church at the same time, while Peter Malbone, who undertook the 1726 Norfolk County courthouse, was also responsible for the 1734–36 Lynnhaven Parish church. This discussion of courthouses and the reconstructed plans that accompanied it has benefited from a careful criticism by Carl Lounsbury, who is preparing a book on Virginia courthouses.

11 Roeber, "Authority, Law and Custom," pp. 48, 35. It is unlikely that the use of benches in the arcade had anything to do with concern for the common people as Roeber suggests.

12 Harrower, *Journal*, p. 37; Fithian, pp. 79–82, 95, 178; Benjamin Henry Latrobe, *The Virginia Journals of Benjamin Henry Latrobe, 1795–1798*, ed. Edward C. Carter and Angeline Potts (New Haven: Yale University Press for the Maryland Historical Society, 1977), p. 163; Dell Upton, "The Origins of Chesapeake Architecture," in *Three Centuries of Maryland Architecture* (Annapolis: Maryland Historical Trust, 1982), pp. 44–57; Dell Upton, "White and Black Landscapes in Eighteenth-Century Virginia," *Places* 2, no. 2 (winter 1985): 59–72.

13 Latrobe, pp. 163–70; Harrower, *Journal*, p. 104; Fithian, pp. 129–30; Daniel Blake Smith, *Inside the Great House: Planter Family Life in Eighteenth-Century Chesapeake Society* (Ithaca: Cornell University Press, 1980), p. 43.

14 The following discussion of small houses is derived from Dell Upton, "Vernacular Domestic Architecture in Eighteenth-Century Virginia," *Winterthur Portfolio* 17, nos. 2–3 (summer–autumn 1982): 95–119; and Dell Upton, "The Virginia Parlor, National Museum of American History, Smithsonian Institution: A Report on the Henry Saunders Howe and Its Occupants," MS., National Museum of American History, 1981.

15 Upton, "Origins," pp. 44–57.

16 Aubrey C. Land, "Economic Base and Social Structure: The Northern Chesapeake in the Eighteenth Century," *Journal of Economic History* 25, no. 4 (December 1965): 639–54; Upton, "Virginia Parlor," pp. 20–34.

17 Thomas Anburey, *Travels Through the Interior Parts of North America* (1789; reprint ed., Boston: Houghton, Mifflin, 1923), 2: 196; William Meade, *Old Churches, Ministers and Families of Virginia* (1857), 2 vols. (Baltimore: Genealogical Publishing Co., 1966 reprint ed.), 2: 45.

18 For discussions of changing concepts of time, see E.P. Thompson, "Time, Work Discipline, and Industrial Capitalism," *Past and Present* no. 38 (December 1967): 56–97; on the orrery and its place in 18th-century thought, see Daniel J. Boorstin, *The Last World of Thomas Jefferson* (Boston: Beacon Press, 1948), p. 13 and passim.

19 Land, "Economic Base," p. 649; Edmund S. Morgan, *Virginians at Home: Family Life in the Eighteenth Century* (Williamsburg: Colonial Williamsburg, 1952), chapters 1, 4; Harrower, *Journal*, p. 83; Isaac, *Transformation*, pp. 70–79; Upton, "Origins," pp. 48–57; Upton, "Vernacular Domestic Architecture," p. 102; Joseph A. Ernst and H. Roy Merrens, "'Camden's Turrets Pierce the Skies!': The Urban Process in the Southern Colonies During the Eighteenth Century," *William and Mary Quarterly* 3d ser. 30, no. 4 (October 1973): 554, 568–73; John C. Rambolt, "The Absence of Towns in Seventeenth-Century Virginia," *Journal of Southern*

History, 35, no. 3 (August 1969): 343–60; Carville Earle and Ronald Hoffman, "Staple Crops and Urban Development in the Eighteenth-Century South," *Perspectives in American History* 10 (1976): 7–78; Fithian, p. 73; Durand de Dauphiné, *A Huguenot Exile in Virginia, or Voyages of a Frenchman Exiled for his Religion*, trans. and ed. Gilbert Chistard (New York: Press of the Pioneers, 1934), p. 120; "Virginia in 1732: The Travel Journal of William Hugh Grove," ed. Gregory A. Stiverson and Patrick H. Butler III, *Virginia Magazine of History and Biography* 85, no. 1 (January 1977): 26; Johann David Schoepf, *Travels in the Confederation [1783–1784]*, trans. and ed. Alfred J. Morrison (Cleveland: Arthur H. Clark Co., 1911), 2: 32.

20 Latrobe, p. 163; Luigi Castiglioni, *Luigi Castiglioni's Viaggio: Travels in the United States of North America, 1785–87*, trans. and ed. Antonio Pace (Syracuse: Syracuse University Press, 1983), p. 112; Fithian, p. 178.

21 Frederick Doveton Nichols and Ralph E. Griswold, *Thomas Jefferson, Landscape Architect* (Charlottesville: University Press of Virginia, 1978), pp. 90–116; Castiglioni, *Viaggio*, pp. 185–86; Isaac Weld, Jr., *Travels Through the States of North America . . . During the Years 1795, 1796, and 1797* (London: John Stockdale, 1799), p. 119.

22 For a description of Monticello and some of its contents, see Frederick D. Nichols and James A. Bear, Jr., *Monticello: A Guidebook* (Monticello: Thomas Jefferson Memorial Foundation, 1967).

23 "Journal of Alexander Macaulay," *William and Mary Quarterly* 1st ser. 11, no. 3 (January 1903): 187; Duke de La Rochefoucault Liancourt, *Travels Through the United States of North America, the Country of the Iroquois, and Upper Canada, in the Years 1795, 1796, and 1797* (London: T. Davison for R. Phillips, 1799), 2: 5; *Colonial Churches in the Original Colony of Virginia* (2d ed.; Richmond: Southern Churchman, 1908), p. 183 Moreau de Saint-Mèry, *American Journey*, p. 64.

bound up with ideals of self-sufficiency and Christian virtue. These pattern books codified and disseminated architectural style and theory, while also contributing through their widespread influence to national cultural consolidation. Moreover, as Gwendolyn Wright shows in this excerpt from her larger social history of American housing, during the mid-nineteenth century, single-family American houses, whatever their style, were idealized as temples of virtue, essential to child-rearing and the production of a virtuous, independent citizenry—to the creation and maintenance, in effect, of the democratic republic.

Further reading

Bender, T., *Toward an Urban Vision: Ideas and Institutions in Nineteenth-Century America*, Lexington, KY: University Press of Kentucky, 1975.

Carter, T. (ed.), *Images of an American Land: Vernacular Architecture in the Western United States*, Albuquerque, NM: University of New Mexico Press, 1997.

Clark, C. E. Jr, *The American Family Home, 1800–1960*, Chapel Hill, NC: University of North Carolina Press, 1986.

Fryd, V. G., *Art and Empire: The Politics of Ethnicity in the United States Capitol, 1815–1860*, New Haven, CT: Yale University Press, 1992.

Hafertepe, K. and J. F. O'Gorman (eds), *American Architects and Their Books to 1848*, Amherst, MA: University of Massachusetts Press, 2001.

Hayden, D., *The Grand Domestic Revolution: A History of Feminist Designs for American Homes, Neighborhoods, and Cities*, Cambridge, MA: MIT Press, 1981.

Jackson, K. T., *Crabgrass Frontier: The Suburbanization of the United States*, New York: Oxford University Press, 1985.

Kasson, J. F., *Civilizing the Machine: Technology and Republican Values in America, 1776–1900*, New York: Penguin Books, 1977.

Kennedy, R. G., *Greek Revival America*, New York: Stewart, Tabori & Chang, 1989.

Pierson, W. H. Jr, *American Buildings and Their Architects, Vol. 2: Technology and the Picturesque, The Corporate and Early Gothic Styles*, New York: Oxford University Press, 1978.

Rigal, L., *The American Manufactory: Art, Labor, and the World of Things in the Early Republic*, Princeton, NJ: Princeton University Press, 1998.

Ryan, M. P., "'A Laudable Pride in the Whole of Us': City Halls and Civic Materialism," *The American Historical Review* 105: 4 (2000): 1131–1170.

Turner, P. V., *Campus: An American Planning Tradition*, Cambridge and New York: MIT Press and The Architectural History Foundation, 1984.

Upton, D., "Pattern Books and Professionalism: Aspects of the Transformation of Domestic Architecture in America, 1800–1860," *Winterthur Portfolio* 19: 2–3 (1984): 107–150.

Vale, L., *Architecture, Power, and National Identity*, New Haven, CT: Yale University Press, 1992.

Chapter 5

John Michael Vlach

The plantation landscape

Beyond the white master's residence, back of and beyond the Big House, was a world of work dominated by black people. The inhabitants of this world knew it intimately, and they gave to it, by thought and deed, their own definition of place. Slaveowners set up the contexts of servitude, but they did not control those contexts absolutely. There were many chinks in the armor of the "peculiar institution." Taking advantage of numerous opportunities to assert counterclaims over the spaces and buildings to which they were confined, slaves found that they could blunt some of the harsh edges of slavery's brutality. The creation of slave landscapes was one of the strategies employed by blacks to make slavery survivable. It is now widely accepted that blacks and whites both played important roles in shaping everyday life in the South. Many expressions of southern folklore—tales, proverbs, sayings, dance steps, tunes, recipes, beliefs, quilt patterns, house types, and the like—are known equally well by both races. Consequently, we can expect to accurately understand southern plantation landscapes only if the contributions of slaves are acknowledged and included. To study these places without including the slaves' perspectives would not only be inadequate, it would be futile.

The creation of a slaves' landscape was a reactive expression, a response to the plans enacted by white landowners. To mark their dominance over both nature and other men, planters acquired acreage, set out the boundaries of their holdings, had their fields cleared, selected building sites, and supervised the construction of dwellings and other structures. The design of a plantation estate was an expression of the owner's tastes, values, and attitudes. To appreciate what slaves eventually did with the realms fashioned by planters and to more fully understand the choices available to them, it is necessary first to consider the world the slaveholders made. The achievements of the planter class provided the social context that slaves would manipulate for their own ends. Ultimately, the slaveholders' world would become the raw material with which slaves would attempt to satisfy some of their own social aspirations.

THE PLANTER'S LANDSCAPE

A plantation was not always understood to be a large agricultural estate. Indeed, in its earliest usage, the word *plantation* referred simply to an "act of planting." Any farm, even a garden or a clump of trees, might be called a plantation. It was only after England's conquest of Ireland in the sixteenth century that the meaning of the word was expanded to signify a large holding, namely "a settlement in a new or conquered country," like the newly formed Plantation of Ulster and later the Plimoth Plantation in Massachusetts. Not until 1706, according to the *Oxford English Dictionary*, was there written evidence that the word indicated "an estate or farm producing a crop with servile labor," the connotation generally intended by contemporary usage.

For most of the seventeenth century, a southern planter was a poor farmer who held claim to about a hundred acres and owned no slaves.[1] His house was, according to British traveler J. F. D. Smyth, likely to be a tumbledown dwelling built "almost all of wood, covered with the same; the roof with shingles, the sides and ends with thin boards, and not always lathed and plastered within; only those of the better sort are finished in that manner, and painted on the outside. The chimneys are sometimes of brick, but more commonly of wood, coated on the inside with clay. The windows of the best sort have glass in them; the rest have none, and only wooden shutters."[2] English revenue agent Edward Randolph reported in 1696 that when Virginia planters laid claim to new lands, they would merely "clear one Acre of that land, and . . . plant and tend it one year . . . but take no care of their Crop, nor make any further use of their land."[3] Generally, a common planter's fields were haphazardly tended; crops were raised in odd-shaped plots scattered about his holdings. Hills of tobacco and corn were scratched up with hoes between dead trees and the remnants of charred stumps, while livestock foraged freely, without supervision, across unfenced woodlands, marshes, and pastures. Ground that was worn out by too many seasons of planting a single crop was allowed to grow up in briars and bushes. These scraggly holdings, although productive enough to support their owners, were denounced by many visitors, who saw in the increasingly gullied and eroded farms only ruin and waste.[4]

By the last quarter of the seventeenth century, this apparent disregard for the look of the land was effectively countered by a small group of well-off planters, those who were able to assemble large holdings extending over thousands of acres.[5] Among this rising group of fashion-conscious social elites, which included no more than two dozen family lines, neatness and order were considered important attributes of landscape management. According to the new dictates of the Georgian mode, a proper gentleman's house was not only substantially constructed but was, in plan, symmetrically balanced. The predictable order of a house's facade and of its spatial arrangement was extended to the surrounding gardens and, as far as was reasonable, to the layout of the entire estate.

Bacon's Castle in Surry County, Virginia, built about 1665, was among the earliest of these new, imposing estates (Figure 5.1). Although the house was modest in size, it was constructed in brick at a time when almost all of the houses in Virginia were wooden frames sheathed with thin skins of riven boards, and therefore it was no doubt seen as a mansion. Standing two-and-a-half stories high, Bacon's Castle was also distinguished from the houses of the common folk by its fashionable curved gables, triple diamond-set chimney stacks, and full-height porch and stair towers. Another expression of status was the large, formal pleasure garden, enclosed by walls and hedges, that stretched out in front of the building. Divided into eight rectangular units by graveled paths, the garden

5.1 Bacon's Castle, Surry Co., Virginia, begun 1665

also contained several secluded nooks equipped with built-in benches where visitors might take their ease.[6]

The inspiration for estates like Bacon's Castle and the others that followed it was provided by English manorial estates, which usually consisted of a "smaller Georgian house set in a park of modest proportions—a warmth of red brick, a flash of stucco, among luxuriant trees." The parklands surrounding these manor houses were, writes landscape historian W. G. Hoskins, their most impressive feature: "Parks grew yet more extensive during the eighteenth century, in the age of the territorial aristocracy. Building themselves magnificent houses, they needed (or thought they needed) more square miles of conspicuous waste to set them off."[7] It was quite understandable, then, that the estates developed by the Virginia gentry would remind British visitor William Hugh Grove of the pleasant parks and manor houses of the English midlands.[8] The members of this upper class, too, had made themselves into a "territorial aristocracy," and they, too, quickly put as much distance as possible between themselves and the rest of the population.

The resemblances between the aristocratic estates of England and the American colonies were more than coincidental. Frances Carter, wife of Robert Carter of Nomini Hall, informed her husband that she would not feel comfortable in Virginia until he had "made her a park and stock'd it."[9] Some Virginia planters either patterned their houses upon specific English country houses or availed themselves of architectural guidebooks published in London to ensure that their homes would conform to the latest British fashions. William Byrd II, for example, is believed to have based the design of Westover, the great house overlooking the James [river] that he built in 1735, on Drayton Court, the Northamptonshire seat of the Earl of Peterborough.[10] Almost a decade earlier, Mann Page had fashioned his mansion at Rosewell after Cound Hall in Shropshire.[11] English influences were also conveyed by such books as William Lawson's *A New Orchard and Garden* (1618), which contained detailed diagrams and instructions for laying out formal gardens, or Walter Blith's *English Improver; or, a New Survey of Husbandry* (1649). The new Virginia plantations were so thoroughly linked to British antecedents that, even two decades after the American Revolution, a Polish visitor to Washington's Mount Vernon would remark: "The General has never left America, but when one sees his house and his garden it seems as if he had copied the best samples of the grand old homesteads of England."[12]

Similar developments were also visible during the early eighteenth century in the Carolina lowcountry. In the hinterlands of Charleston, for example, members of the Middleton family established two impressive estates. The house at Crowfield, the plantation built by William Middleton in 1730, was approached by a long, ramrod-straight avenue, and its grounds were ornamented with numerous "garden contrivances" including basins, fishponds, canals, elegant parterres, and a bowling green. The whole estate was laid out symmetrically along a north-south axis extending from the road through the house and gardens to the rice fields beyond. Ten years later, Henry Middleton acquired a large plantation tract along the Ashley River, one of twenty he was to own in his lifetime. By 1755 his Middleton Place was as sumptuous as his brother William's plantation. Both were thoroughly British in character; Crowfield was, in fact, named for an English holding belonging to the family. The gardens on the two plantations are readily compared with the detailed views of the landscaping of English country estates found in J. Kip's *Britannia Illustrata* (1709), a book that may have guided the Middleton brothers.[13]

These grand estates in the Carolinas and the Chesapeake region were extraordinary places. Vast beyond comprehension in size and elaborately designed and decorated, they were atypical, showplace plantations. Yet, their very exceptionalism made them so impressive that, by the middle of the eighteenth century, the definition of *plantation* would change once more. No longer just a large farm run with supervised captive labor, from the middle of the eighteenth century onward the ideal plantation was a large, tastefully appointed country estate belonging to a prominent gentleman.

The tangible glory of manorial estates served as the most persuasive propaganda for the celebration of the plantation ideal. Implicit in the structured layout of Georgian houses, formal gardens, and extensive stretches of fenced and cultivated fields was a strong sense of the planter's dominance over both nature and society. The wide gap between the material condition of a great planter and that of even his closest local rival was underscored by the way in which his house was approached. Access was achieved by moving along a route marked by a series of threshold devices—gates, drives, forecourts, steps, terraces, porches, passageways, doors—all of which were intended to make the house, and its owner, appear more impressive.[14] At Thomas Lee's Stratford Hall, for example, a low wall stretched across the forecourt of the building, effectively stopping visitors from riding their horses up to the steps. Only a "humbling pedestrian access" to the house was allowed.[15]

Guiding these planters in setting up their estates was a highly rational formalism. The world was, in their view, suitably improved only after it was transformed from its

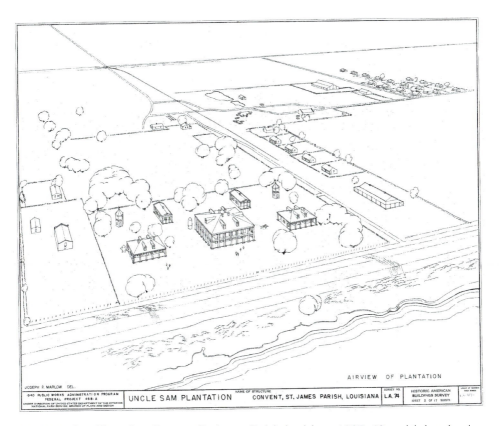

AIRVIEW OF PLANTATION

JOSEPH P. MARLOW DEL. /940 PUBLIC WORKS ADMINISTRATION PROGRAM FEDERAL PROJECT 49-B-A UNDER DIRECTION OF UNITED STATES DEPARTMENT OF THE INTERIOR NATIONAL PARK SERVICE, BRANCH OF PLANS AND DESIGN NAME OF STRUCTURE UNCLE SAM PLANTATION CONVENT, ST. JAMES PARISH, LOUISIANA SURVEY NO. LA. 74 HISTORIC AMERICAN BUILDINGS SURVEY SHEET 2 OF 17 SHEETS

5.2 Uncle Sam Plantation, Convent, St. James Parish, Louisiana, 1837–49; aerial view drawing

chaotic natural condition into a scene marked by a strict, hierarchical order. The planters' landscapes were laid out with straight lines, right-angle corners, and axes of symmetry, their mathematical precision being considered as a proof of individual superiority (Figures 5.2 and 5.3).

Although the aloofness and reserve signaled by this rigid imposition of order was intended chiefly to ensure that the plantation owner received the respect he felt was his due, ironically such expressions of social hierarchy actually made the new plantation ideal appealing to "middlin'" yeomen. The commoners who were effectively put in their place upon visiting a Westover or a Stratford Hall were anxious to have their own turn to exercise a similar social authority. It is not too surprising, then, that when new plantations were created in interior portions of the South during the nineteenth century, the old manorial model served as their inspiration. This new generation of planters, often young Virginians or Carolinians gone west to seek their fortunes, hoped to attain at last the prominent social rank that their foreparents had sought. As they moved first to the frontiers of Georgia and Kentucky and later as far west as Texas, they carried an eighteenth-century idea with them as an important item of cultural baggage. Architectural historian Roger G. Kennedy aptly observes that this "New South was the Old Tidewater South transported across the Piedmont."[16]

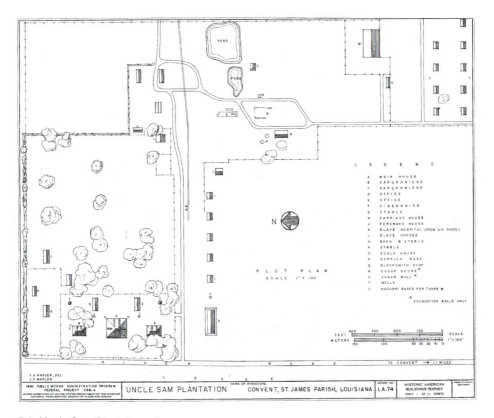

5.3 Uncle Sam Plantation, plan

Certainly the plantation established by Benjamin Grey in central Kentucky was as impressive as any back in old Virginia. A journalist visiting Grey's estate in 1843 wrote that his house "stands near the centre of the domain on rising ground, and commands a fine view of the country around. ... A pretty yard of smooth greensward, decked with shrubbery and evergreens, is enclosed around with pointed white palings, and adjoining this is a noble park." Grey's neighbor Nicholas Hart, in an attempt to imitate the ancient ways of the English nobility, stocked his own park with a herd of elk.[17] The conspicuous grandeur of Oak Valley, a plantation located in Yazoo County, Mississippi, as described by private tutor DePuy Van Buren, once again suggests manorial aspirations: "In the front ground, you see magnificent China-trees. The orange myrtle, with its glossy green foliage, trimmed in the shape of a huge strawberry; the crape myrtle with its top hanging thick with long cone shaped flowers of a peach-blow color; the cape jasmine, with its rich polished foliage spangled all over with white starry blossoms ... and that richest and sweetest blossom of tropical shrubs—the japonica."[18]

Further evidence of the westward diffusion of the Tidewater plantation form is provided by some of the sugar plantations in southern Louisiana. Along the shores of Bayou Teche, plantations developed by Anglo-Americans were laid out in what geographer John B. Rehder calls a "block plan." On these estates, the planter's mansion, farm buildings, and slave houses were all clustered closely together in a gridlike pattern. Plantations of this type were easily distinguished from the estates of French planters, who employed a linear format. While the block plan probably stems from the formal geometry first used in the design of gentry estates in Virginia and Carolina, mid-nineteenth-century visitor Thomas Bangs Thorpe thought he recognized along the shores of the Teche "expressions so often witnessed in the lordly parks of England."[19]

Although plantations were established all over the South, by 1860 the largest, and therefore the most lavishly developed, estates tended to be concentrated in three distinct areas. The oldest and generally most prominent plantations were located in a coastal region extending from the Chesapeake Bay to northern Florida and not more than a hundred miles inland from the Atlantic. A second concentration of large plantation estates occupied a fifty-mile-wide area of cotton lands running through the middle portions of South Carolina, Georgia, and Alabama, terminating in eastern Mississippi. A third plantation zone consisted of the fertile bottomlands of the lower Mississippi Valley, from just above Memphis to below New Orleans. There were also noteworthy plantation zones in the Florida Panhandle, northwestern Alabama, and along the Gulf Coast of Texas, but these were smaller enclaves rather than major regions.

Large plantations dotted the southern countryside fairly evenly from Maryland to Texas, signaling to all passersby the financial and social rewards of the plantation system. However, well into the nineteenth century, those benefits were still only realized by a few families. Historians have usually granted planter status to those men and women who owned at least twenty slaves. Thus in 1860, when plantation agriculture had reached its furthest extent, there were only 46,274 plantations in the entire South. Though this figure may seem large, it represents only 12 percent of all slaveholding families, who in turn made up only 24 percent of all white southerners.[20] The greatest proportion of these estates—some 20,789—were run with between twenty and thirty slaves and though considered small plantations, they were, in fact, only slightly larger than slaveholding farms and not very different in character. Only the plantations that were run with large numbers of slaves, a hundred or more, approached the manorial ideal. By this measure, there were in 1860 only about 2,300 truly large-scale plantations, and perhaps only half of those were developed to the state of elegance promoted by the widespread southern mythology.[21] By the middle of the nineteenth century, less than 1 percent of all slave-holding families fit the plantation stereotype, a percentage that had remained constant since the middle of the eighteenth century.[22]

How such an unrepresentative place as the great plantation estate came to dominate the self-perception of the South is a matter about which there has been considerable discussion. It is enough to say here that both those farmers who owned only a few slaves and those who owned none were impressed by the lavish plantations inhabited by the gentry, and they looked upon them with a mixture of admiration and envy. The deference with which the few great planters in any county were regarded is related no doubt to the messages that were visually conveyed by the design of their estates, crystal-clear indica-tions of a landlord's dominance that required the submission of black laborer and white visitor alike.

According to architectural historian Dell Upton, the highly formalized layout of showplace plantations constituted an "articulated processional landscape," a spatial system designed to indicate the centrality of the planters and to keep them aloof from any visitors behind a series of physical barriers that simultaneously functioned as social buffers.[23] A yeoman farmer entering a planter's estate would follow a prescribed, formal route that led to the planter's parlor or office. Although the intricate sequence of gates, terraces, pathways, and other threshold markers was intended to emphasize the yeoman's lack of standing in relation to the planter, it could just as easily have indicated whether the yeoman's social position was improving. In other words, a visitor's status was measured by how far into the planter's world he or she was allowed. The plantation ideal remained pervasive in the South for more than a century because the will of the elite was matched by the acquiescence of those who could only dream of owning such a grand place.

Even though ownership of a lavish plantation estate was beyond the reach of most southerners, planters of more modest means still tried to make their homes and gardens fashionable by incorporating some formal qualities of design or decoration. A Greek Revival porch, for example, complete with columns and entablature, might be grafted awkwardly onto a humble log cabin as a statement of presumed sophistication. Self-proclaimed arbiters of taste promoted the formal plantation style, usually by berating struggling would-be planters for their failures. In 1857 a Georgia newspaper editor wrote that, on plantations in his locale, there was "the singular want of elegance and comfort about the domestic arrangements of those who are able to provide them. . . . A log house half decayed with age, or a frame house without paint, and . . . a yard without a shrub or a flower . . . are too frequently the insignia of a planter's premises."[24] Even more shrill was the attack launched by John Forsyth in an address to an Alabama horticultural society in 1851. He directed his listeners to "Go to the homestead of a Southern farmer and tell me what you see." Making no pause for an answer, he thundered, "The planter's home is generally a rude ungainly structure, made of logs, rough hewn from the forest; rail fences and rickety gates guard its enclosures. And why? . . . We murder our soil with wasteful culture because there is plenty of fresh land West—and we live in tents and huts when we might live in rural palaces."[25] The plantation ideal established such high architectural expectations that most planters were doomed to fail; the only acceptable level of success was great success.

In the second quarter of the nineteenth century, the most representative planters owned between twenty and thirty slaves and devoted the larger portion of their four or five hundred acres to cotton, probably on recently cleared "newgrounds." In 1853 Frederick Law Olmsted visited just such a plantation in northern Louisiana. He found that the owner's house was but a "small square log cabin, with a broad open shed or piazza in front, and a chimney, made of sticks and mud, leaning against one end." Nearby was "a smaller detached cabin, twenty feet in the rear . . . used for a kitchen." The spaces surrounding this cabin suggested an obvious concern with workaday routine that was relieved only slightly by a few ornamental shrubs:

> About the house was a large yard, in which were two or three China trees, and two fine Cherokee roses; half a dozen hounds; several negro babies; turkeys and chickens, and a pet sow, teaching a fine litter of pigs how to root and wallow. Three hundred yards from

the house was a gin-house and stable, and in the interval between were two rows of comfortable negro cabins. Between the house and the cabins was a large post, on which was a bell to call the negroes. A rack for fastening horses stood near it. On the bell-post and on each of the rack-posts were nailed the antlers of a buck, as well as on a large oak-tree near by. On the logs of the kitchen a fresh deer skin was drying. On the railing of the piazza lay a saddle. The house had but one door and no window, nor was there a pane of glass on the plantation.[26]

Plantation life, particularly in the western portion of the cotton belt, was essentially a Spartan pioneer experience on the edge of a constantly advancing frontier.[27] Settlements like the one visited by Olmsted were carved out of the wilderness in the optimistic hope that a substantial upgrading would follow after a few harvests. More often, however, these temporary homes were abandoned altogether as the cycle of planting was started again on a new, more promising tract of land. The common planter might follow the model of a large plantation estate and create an ensemble of buildings including a separate kitchen, a string of slave houses, and several barns and storage cribs, but these were, as Forsyth had complained, only "rude ungainly structures," and no one would ever have mistaken such a house for a "rural palace."

That plantations existed along a spectrum ranging from superbly appointed mansions set amidst well-tilled fields to expedient shelters thrown together in slash-and-burn clearings is certainly borne out by the testimony of former slaves. Martha Colquitt from Lexington, Georgia, recalled: "Our Big House sure was one grand fine place. Why, it must have been as big as de Mill Stone Baptist Church. It was all painted white with green blinds and had a big old high porch dat went nigh all 'round de house." This dwelling presents a marked contrast to the house of Mary Ella Grandberry's master in Barton, Alabama, which she described in the 1930s as "a li'l old frame building like a ordinary house is now. He was a single man and didn't have so terrible much, it seem ... just to look at him you'd think he was a poor white man."[28]

The appearance of a plantation certainly varied with the crop that its owner attempted to grow. The cultivation of tobacco, cotton, rice, and sugar, the primary staples of the plantation economy, each followed different schedules and work routines and used different equipment and storage structures. One type of plantation could be distinguished from another by its barns, mills, and other gear. The identity of a tobacco plantation was marked by the distinctive tobacco barns used to cure the leaves before they were packed into huge barrels. Standing in the yards of most cotton plantations were both a gin house and a press for compacting processed lint into bales. By the second quarter of the nineteenth century, rice plantations often had large steam-powered mills to complement the older threshing platforms and winnowing houses where slaves had previously refined the rice by hand. The mills located on Louisiana's sugar plantations were large sheds, sometimes as much as three hundred feet long, containing boilers, engines, conveyor belts, rollers, and evaporators. Because these mills spewed clouds of smoke and steam as the cane juice was transformed first into syrup and then into raw sugar, it is not surprising that sugar plantations were said to resemble New England factory towns.[29]

The appearances of plantation fields also varied with the crop that was grown. The rice fields of South Carolina and Georgia, for example, stood out prominently because they were developed on reclaimed wetlands. Rice paddies were diked off from the surrounding marshes, leveled, and then irrigated ingeniously by means of a system of sluice gates and canals. The landscape resulting from these efforts was, according to Olmsted, "Holland-like."[30] The sugar fields of Louisiana, laid out in rectangular units marked off by ditches and cross-drains, also had an engineered appearance. British observer William H. Russel thought John Burnside's sugar plantation was impressive in part because his fields were judged to be "as level as a billiard-table."[31] Because the crop did not require any specialized techniques of cultivation, a cotton planter's acres did not look very different from any other farm. And because cotton planters tended to specialize only in their single cash crop, their fields showed the viewer little more than continuous furrows pushing up the same plant, often right up to the door of the planter's house. Contemporary visitors, hoping for more diversity, denounced the monotonous rows of cotton as drab.[32]

Other variables affecting the visual appearance of a plantation included the size and organization of the available work force, the condition of the soil, and the willingness of its owner to embrace up-to-date methods of cultivation, harvest, and processing. There were also inevitable subregional differences within an area as large as the South, a geographic zone reaching from the Atlantic Ocean to the prairies of central Texas and from the Gulf of Mexico to the Ohio River Valley.

Any plantation reflected not only the local ecology and climate, but the consequences of a particular settlement history as well. Finding it difficult, if not impractical, to ignore the customs of the cultural region in which their estates were located, planters frequently used the same designs for houses, barns, and outbuildings as yeoman neighbors. In the Tidewater South, where single-pen barns were favored, for example, planters also used single-crib barns. Similarly, the planters in the Piedmont and upland South showed their regional allegiances by selecting double-crib barns over other possible barn types. Maryland plantation estates closely resembled mid-Atlantic farmsteads both in their layout and in their selection of buildings. It is apparent that so-called plantation architecture was often nothing more than a particular expression of whatever vernacular tradition happened to be dominant in a given region. It is difficult, then, to refer with confidence to a single "plantation style" of architecture, for these regional variations in building customs affected the design of houses as well as service structures.

THE AFRICAN AMERICAN PLANTATION LANDSCAPE

The experiences of plantation slaves were quite different from those of plantation owners, not only because of their status as captive laborers, but because so many of them were held on the larger and therefore less typical plantations. Historian John B. Boles demonstrates how so many slaves came to live on large-scale manorial holdings.

> Imagine a universe of ten slaveholders, eight owning two slaves apiece, one owning twenty-four, and the tenth possessing sixty. Obviously most slaveholders (80 percent) would own

5.4 Slave houses, Hermitage Plantation, Savannah, Georgia, nineteenth century

fewer than five slaves, but most slaves (84 out of 100) would reside in units of more than twenty. Such an imaginary model suggests what the numbers reveal. In 1850 . . . over half [of the slaves], 51.6 percent, resided on plantations of more than twenty bondsmen. The figures were more pronounced in the Deep South, and still more so in 1860, when fully 62 percent of the slaves in the Deep South lived in plantation units.[33]

Plantations, albeit unintentionally, served as the primary sites at which a distinctive black American culture matured. By 1860 over 800,000 slaves were living mostly in the company of other slaves, in groups of fifty or more. On almost 11,000 plantations, consequently, slave settlements were big enough to resemble, in the words of former slave occupants, "little towns."[34] No doubt their quarters did resemble villages (Figure 5.4). A group of fifty slaves probably contained about ten families housed in as many as ten but no fewer than five cabins, depending on the type of buildings used as quarters. Slave settlements containing larger populations obviously required more houses and thus were even more townlike. Bill Homer, a former slave from Shreveport, Louisiana, described a large grid pattern of slave houses when he recalled that the quarters on his plantation "was fifty one-room cabins and dey was ten in a row and dere was five rows."[35] A map of the Stapleton plantation on St. Helena Island, South Carolina, drawn up in 1789, shows that the slave quarter, containing eighteen cabins, was set out in a block pattern three rows deep and six rows wide.[36]

Although slaves had no legal power, they were often able nonetheless to use their marginal status to their advantage. Kept for the most part in small frame or log houses, slaves knew that they were being humbled by their master, who owned a big mansion—or at least a bigger house—that often was located on the highest ground available.

However, because their more modestly constructed slave quarters frequently were located some considerable distance from the planter's residence, slaves also had ample opportunity to take control of many domestic concerns. Beyond their master's immediate scrutiny, beyond its boundary lines, slaves created their own landscape. This was a domain that generally escaped much notice, mainly because it was marked in ways that planters either considered insignificant or could not recognize.

Rhys Isaac has suggested that paths and trails into the countryside were the central elements of the slave landscape in Virginia. Some of these secret tracks led to clandestine meeting places in the woods, used sometimes for ritual purposes and at other times for festive parties at which fiddles were played and stolen pigs barbecued. Paths also led from the slave quarters across the fields to a particular corn house or to some other food store that was known to have a conveniently loose board in its gable. A shortcut through the woods or marshlands that surrounded the fields may have allowed slaves from different plantations to rendezvous more conveniently and to return to their assigned tasks with less chance of detection. On those plantations located near navigable streams and rivers, the waterways were yet another domain over which slaves exercised particular control by means of their boating skills.[37] The whole ensemble of sites and pathways constituted, in Isaac's terms, "an alternative territorial system."[38]

This system, used wherever large groups of African Americans were gathered together, encouraged racial solidarity and provided slaves with a means to escape, at least temporarily, from their masters' control. Moreover, the informal qualities of this type of landscape, specific material indications, may also have reflected an ethnic choice. The loose, ad hoc scheme of preferred paths and gathering places was created incrementally by a series of improvisational responses to the given landscape rules of white masters. Because similar improvisational responses by black people to Anglo-American culture are known to have resulted in the creation of distinctive African American forms of speech, music, and dance, it is not too farfetched to suggest a parallel development in their responses to their assigned environments.[39]

Some slaves are known to have countered the geometrically circumscribed order imposed by their masters' logic with what seemed like chaos. For example, the forty-one slaves at Mount Vernon who were assigned to the so-called Muddy Hole Farm, where they worked under the supervision of a black overseer, located their cabins randomly among the trees at the edge of the cleared fields. Those slaves living on the plantation's other "farms," where they were supervised by white overseers, had their cabins set in straight lines at regular intervals along the edge of a road.[40] One observer of Georgia rice plantations similarly noted that when slaves were given the chance to build their own houses, "they wanted their cabins in some secluded place, down in the hollow, or amid the trees, with only a path to their abode."[41] In one of the slave villages at J. J. Smith's cotton plantation near Beaufort, South Carolina—apparently located far away from his central processing area—although the cabins consisted of a row of boxy frame buildings, all were set at odd, irregular angles to one another.[42]

If the black system of place definition positively embraced the random and meandering givens of the natural world, their spaces would naturally strike white observers as sloppy and poorly maintained. British visitor Edward Kimber, in fact, went so far as to certify that slave settlements located on the backlands of plantations (those fields beyond their owners' immediate scrutiny) produced "Indolence and Nastiness."[43] What white people were prone to criticize as sloppy (or worse, as "nasty") was the slave preference for a landscape marked by few overt boundaries and fixed sites, an environment open to and characterized by movement. Planters who wanted their places clearly and certainly defined could only be annoyed at the way slaves acted. In an 1833 issue of the *Southern Agriculturist*, a South Carolina planter wrote: "A plantation might be considered as a piece of machinery; to operate successfully all of its parts should be uniform and exact and the impelling force regular and steady."[44] Clearly slave actions went against this advice, countering its suggestions with behavior that seemed deliberately careless. In the light of what is known about life within various slave communities, the inhabitants' actions were indeed deliberate, for they hoped thereby to carve out a domain of their own and thus improve, however slightly, the conditions of their captivity.

Within their settlements, slaves established strong family identities, created distinctive art forms, and developed meaningful religious rituals.[45] To the furthest degree possible, they took charge of their lives. Among the many tangible signs of black initiative and autonomy, the foremost spatial statements were the extensive vegetable gardens, sometimes as big as half an acre per person, in which slaves raised much of their own food. Such self-sufficiency was undergirded by other demonstrations of slave skill. Frances Anne Kemble, who in the late 1830s lived on a plantation in coastal Georgia with a slave population approaching five hundred, observed that slaves who had woodworking abilities built furniture and boats, which they sold for considerable sums in the nearby town of Darien.[46] On other plantations, slaves developed similar entrepreneurial enterprises, selling chickens, ducks, and pigs that they raised, and even a horse or two. Others were able to improve their material conditions by offering their blacksmithing, tailoring, or coopering skills for hire.[47] Frederick Law Olmsted noted that in one particularly large slave village, again in Georgia, the slaves daily secured their homes and possessions under lock and key, asserting their right to personal space and property.[48] By acting as if they owned the quarters, these slaves had overturned the declared order of the plantation. Although everything they had could be taken away in a moment if the master so desired, few planters wanted to disturb the inner workings of large slave villages. As long as the slaves performed their assigned tasks with reasonable efficiency, planters concerned themselves neither with the routines of the slave quarters nor the domestic claims being exercised there.

Once they were able to establish a level of proprietorship in the quarters, some slaves felt emboldened enough to exert a claim over their work spaces as well. Philip Fithian, a tutor in Westmoreland County, Virginia, during the late eighteenth century, found that the slaves at Nomini Hall regularly took over the stables as a place in which to hold their private entertainments. From his frequent complaints that his pupil, Henry Carter, spent too much time in the kitchen or in the various craft shops, we can infer that these buildings, too, were regarded as black spaces and therefore off limits to white boys who hoped to become well schooled in the refined ways of gentlemen.[49] The cook at the Merrick plantation in Louisiana not only ran the kitchen but determined who could have access to it. Caroline Merrick, at one time the plantation's Young Miss, remembered being driven out of the room by the cook's stern rebuke: "*Go* inter de *house*, Miss Carrie! Yer ain't no manner er use heah only ter git yer face red wid de heat."[50]

After years of toil in the fields, slaves sometimes began to feel that the harvest was their achievement rather than their master's. He may have owned the crop, but they had created it. There is no more eloquent expression of a slave's identification with the soil he worked than the claim made by a former South Carolina slave named Morris. Early in the twentieth century, when he was about to be thrown off the plantation where he had lived all his life, he went to the landlord to state his case.

> I was born on dis place before Freedom. My Mammy and Daddy worked de rice fields. Dey's buried here. De fust ting I remember are dose rice banks. I growed up in dem from dat high. . . . De strength of dese arms and dese legs and of dis old back . . . is in your rice banks. It won't be long before de good Lord take de rest of pore old Morris away too. An' de rest of dis body want to be with de strength of de arms and de legs and de back dat is already buried in your rice banks. No . . . you ain't agoin' to run old Morris off dis place.[51]

The ironies of plantation slavery were many and profound, for although the plantation system was the very reason people of African descent were enslaved, it also provided them with an arena in which they could begin to piece back together their shattered lives. While ownership of a plantation clearly divided whites into distinct have and have-not classes, blacks generally found themselves drawn together in sufficient numbers to constitute coherent social groups. Comforted by the fellowship of the quarters, they were able to confront the injustice of their captivity in ways both subtle and obvious; among their various strategies of accommodation and resistance was the creation of their own version of the plantation. Recognizing that they could define a space for themselves, they took back the quarters, fields, gardens, barns, and outbuildings, claiming them as parts of a black landscape. Empowered by this territorial gesture, they were able to forge an even stronger sense of community, which few planters would ever recognize or acknowledge.

Even when slaves were most persistent in establishing their own landscapes, they attempted few bold gestures. Instead, they prudently relied on subtle adjustments to their dwellings, or they sought out spaces where their masters were unlikely to intrude. Their domains, consisting mainly of rough and ungainly dwellings together with their cluttered yards, reflected not a lack of ability but their material poverty. Denied the time and resources needed to design and build as they might have wanted, they simply appropriated, as marginalized peoples often do, the environments to which they were assigned.

The slaves' agenda is the hidden dimension of a southern plantation. Looking over these places, one sees most clearly the pattern of well-known, European-derived fashions. The ordered surfaces of building facades and well-tended grounds, however, were underpinned by a slave community whose labor provided the wealth with which planters created their impressive estates. The more than two-and-a-half-million slaves held on plantations in 1860 clearly dominated the southern countryside. It was, finally, their formidable demographic presence that transformed plantations into undeniably black places. This circumstance fostered such a self-reliant attitude among slaves that they were inspired to think about their captivity and its various physical contexts in ways that they found most reassuring. Just as slaves usually did not consider it a crime to take extra rations from the master's storehouse in order to satisfy their hunger, neither did they consider the buildings and spaces in which they were forced to work to be solely his property.[52] Thus the kitchen might be claimed by the slave cook, the dining room by the house servant, the loom house by the weaver, the barn by the field hand.

Acts of appropriation leave few physical marks, and therefore they must be consciously recalled in order to be factored into our interpretation of surviving slave buildings and spaces. Consequently, southern plantations can only be described accurately and analyzed fully if we remember the territorial prerogatives claimed and exercised repeatedly by slaves.

Notes

1   Edmund S. Morgan, *American Slavery, American Freedom: The Ordeal of Colonial Virginia* (New York: W. W. Norton, 1975), p. 94.

2   Quoted in Rhys Isaac, *The Transformation of Virginia, 1740–1790* (Chapel Hill: University of North Carolina Press, 1982), p. 33.

3   Quoted in Morgan, *American Slavery*, American Freedom, p. 220.

4   John R. Stilgoe, *Common Landscape of America, 1580 to 1845* (New Haven, Conn.: Yale University Press, 1982), pp. 75–76.

5   Louis B. Wright, *The First Gentlemen of Virginia: Intellectual Qualities of the Early Colonial Ruling Class* (San Marino, Calif.: The Huntington Library, 1940), pp. 158, 190, 286, 346.

6   Thomas Tileston Waterman, *The Mansions of Virginia, 1706–1776* (Chapel Hill: University of North Carolina Press, 1946), pp. 22–25; Nicholas Luccketti, "Archaeological Excavations at Bacon's Castle, Surry County, Virginia," in William M. Kelso and Rachel Most, eds., *Earth Patterns: Essays in Landscape Archaeology* (Charlottesville: University Press of Virginia, 1990), pp. 24, 27, 32, 35.

7   W. G. Hoskins, *The Making of the English Landscape* (London: Pelican, 1970), pp. 167, 170.

8   Gregory A. Stiverson and Patrick H. Butler III, eds., "Virginia in 1732: The Travel Journal of William Hugh Grove," *Virginia Magazine of History and Biography* 85 (1977): 26.

9   Louis Morton, *Robert Carter of Nomini Hall: A Virginia Tobacco Planter of the Eighteenth Century* (Williamsburg, Va.: Colonial Williamsburg, Inc., 1941), p. 207, n. 4.

10   Wright, *First Gentlemen of Virginia*, p. 330.

11   Waterman, *Mansions of Virginia*, pp. 108–9.

12   Quoted in Anne Leighton, *"For Use or for Delight": American Gardens in the Eighteenth Century* (Boston: Houghton Mifflin, 1976), p. 269; see also Clement Eaton, *The Growth of Southern Civilization, 1790–1860* (New York: Harper and Row, 1966), pp. 3–4.

13   Samuel Gaillard Stoney, *Plantations of the Carolina Low Country* (Charleston: South Carolina Art Association, 1955), pp. 59, 61–62, 119, 170–75.

14   Dell Upton, "White and Black Landscapes in Eighteenth-Century Virginia," *Places* 2, no. 2 (1985): 66.

15   Fraser D. Neiman, "Domestic Architecture at the Clifts Plantation: The Social Context of Early Virginia Building," in Dell Upton and John Michael Vlach, eds., *Common Places: Readings in American Vernacular Architecture* (Athens: University of Georgia Press, 1986), p. 311.

16   Roger G. Kennedy, *Greek Revival America* (New York: Stewart, Tabori, and Chang, 1989), p. 286.

17   Eugene L. Schwaab, ed., *Travels in the Old South Selected from Periodicals of the Times* (Lexington: University Press of Kentucky, 1973), 2: 292, 295.

18   Quoted in Eaton, *Growth of South Civilization*, pp. 122–23.

19   John Burkhardt Rehder, "Sugar Plantation Settlements of Southern Louisiana: A Cultural Geography," Ph.D. diss., Louisiana State University, 1971, pp. 84–86, 100–3, 109; Schwaab, *Travels in the Old South*, 2: 495.

20   Ulrich B. Phillips, *Life and Labor in the Old South* (Boston: Little, Brown, 1929), p. 339; John B. Boles, *Black Southerners, 1619–1869* (Lexington: University Press of Kentucky, 1983), p. 75.

21   Harold D. Woodman, ed., *Slavery and the Southern Economy: Sources and Readings* (New York: Harcourt, Brace and World, 1966), p. 15.

22   See Isaac, *Transformation of Virginia*, p. 21, for a discussion of figures on mid-eighteenth-century plantation ownership.

23   Upton, "White and Black Landscapes," p. 66.

24   Quoted in James C. Bonner, "Plantation Architecture of the Lower South on the Eve of the Civil War," *Journal of Southern History* 11 (1945): 372.

25   Ibid., p. 374.

26   Frederick Law Olmsted, *The Cotton Kingdom: A Traveller's Observations an Cotton and Slavery in the American Slave States*, ed. by Arthur M. Schlesinger (New York: Alfred A. Knopf, 1953), p. 280.

27   The small plantation in northern Louisiana described by Olmsted can profitably be compared to the profile of a slaveowning farm in Yell County, Arkansas, detailed by John Solomon Otto in "Slaveholding General Farmers in a Cotton County," *Agricultural History* 55 (1981): 167–78.

28   Norman R. Yetman, ed., *Life Under the "Peculiar Institution": Selections from the Slave Narrative Collection* (New York: Holt, Rinehart, and Winston, 1970), pp. 61, 144.

29   Olmsted, *Cotton Kingdom*, p. 249. See also John Michael Vlach, "Plantation Landscapes of the Antebellum South," in Edward D. C. Campbell, Jr., and Kyrn S. Rice, eds., *Before Freedom Came: African-American Life in the Antebellum South* (Charlottesville: University Press of Virginia, 1991), p. 41, Figure 43.

30   Olmsted, *Cotton Kingdom*, p. 181.

31   Quoted in J. Carlyle Sitterson, *Sugar Country: The Cane Sugar Industry in the South, 1753–1950* (Lexington: University Press of Kentucky, 1953), p. 47.

32   Bonner, "Plantation Architecture of the Lower South," p. 375.

33   Bales, *Black Southerners*, p. 107.

34   George P. Rawick, ed., *The American Slave: A Composite Autobiography* (Westport, Conn.: Greenwood Press, 1972), 3 (pt. 4): 177, 15 (pt. 2): 364.

35   Yetman, *Life Under the "Peculiar Institution,"* p. 168.

36   See Vlach, "Plantation Landscapes of the Antebellum South," p. 28, Figure 30.

37   Dell Upton, "Imagining the Early Virginia Landscape," in Kelso and Most, *Earth Patterns*, p. 74.

38   Issac, *Transformation of Virginia*, pp. 52–53.

39   J. L. Dillard, *Black English: Its History and Usage in the United States* (New York: Vintage, 1972); Eileen Southern, The Music of Black Americans (New York: W. W. Norton, 1971); Lynne Fauley Emery, *Black Dance in the United States from 1619 to 1970* (Palo Alto, Calif.: National Press Books, 1972).

40   See Mechal Sobel, *The World They Made Together: Black and White Values in Eighteenth-Century Virginia* (Princeton, N.J.: Princeton University Press, 1987), pp. 105, 109.

41   Quoted in Eugene D. Genovese, *Roll, Jordan, Roll: The World the Slaves Made* (New York: Random House, 1972), p. 534.

42   Charles Joyner, "The World of the Plantation Slaves," in Campbell and Rice, *Before Freedom Came*, p. 79, Figure 70.

43   Edward Kimber, "Observations in Several Voyages and Travels in America," *William and Mary Quarterly*, lst ser., vol. 15 (1906–7): 148.

44   James O. Breeden, ed., *Advice among Masters: The Ideal of Slave Management in the Old South* (Westport, Conn.: Greenwood Press, 1980), p. 31.

45   See Herbert G. Gutman, *The Black Family in Slavery and Freedom, 1750–1925* (New York: Vintage, 1976); John Michael Vlach, *The Afro-American Tradition in Decorative Arts* (Cleveland, Ohio: Cleveland Museum of Art, 1978); Lawrence W. Levine, *Black Culture and Black Consciousness: Afro-American Folk Thought from Slavery to Freedom* (New York: Oxford University Press, 1977).

46   Frances Anne Kemble, *Journal of a Residence on a Georgian Plantation in 1838–39* [1863], ed. by John A. Scott (Athens: University of Georgia Press, 1984), p. 63.

47   Philip D. Morgan, "The Ownership of Property by Slaves in the Mid-Nineteenth-Century Low Country," *Journal of Southern History* 49 (1983): 399–420.

48   Olmsted, *Cotton Kingdom*, p. 185.

49   Upton, "White and Black Landscapes," p. 70.

50   Elizabeth Fox-Genovese, *Within the Plantation Household: Black and White Women of the Old South* (Chapel Hill: University of North Carolina Press, 1988), p. 142 (emphasis in original).

51   Charles Joyner, *Down by the Riverside: A South Carolina Slave Community* (Urbana: University of Illinois Press, 1984), pp. 42–43.

52   Genovese, *Roll, Jordan, Roll*, pp. 602–3.

Chapter 6

Mary N. Woods

The first professional
Benjamin Henry Latrobe

Benjamin Henry Latrobe, a young English architect and engineer, immigrated to the United States in 1796. After working in this country for ten years, he wrote to a former student:

> The profession of Architecture has been hitherto in the hands of two sets of Men. The first of those [gentlemen] who from travelling or from books have acquired some knowledge of the theory of Art, know nothing of its practice, the second of those [mechanics] who know nothing but the practice, and whose early life being spent in labor, and in the habits of a laborious life, have had no opportunity to acquire the theory. The complaisance of these two sets of Men to each other, renders it difficult for the Architect to get in between them, for the Building Mechanic finds his account in the ignorance of the *Gentleman-Architect*, as the latter does in the Submissive deportment which interest dictates to the former.[1]

Latrobe expected deference, not competition, from the gentlemen and building mechanics he encountered in the United States. He introduced and championed English ideas of professionalism and often claimed the distinction of being the first professional architect and engineer to practice in the United States. Only a professional architect's design, Latrobe explained to Thomas Jefferson, was a "simultaneous consideration of the purpose, the connection and the construction of his work."[2] The professional alone combined theoretical knowledge with a practical understanding of building.

From the outset Latrobe and other early professional architects found themselves embroiled in controversies over duties, authority, and compensation. Latrobe's twenty-four years in the United States were difficult and frustrating. Although proud that he could claim to be the first professional architect, he admitted that he had

> not so far succeeded as to make it [architecture] an eligible profession for one who has the education and the feelings of a Gentleman, and I regret exceedingly that my own Son . . . has determined to make it his own. The business in all our great cities is in the hands of mechanics who disgrace the Art but possess the public confidence, and under the false appearance of Oeconomy have infinitely the advantage in degrading the competition. With them the struggle will be long and harassing.[3]

Building craftsmen (usually called building mechanics in the eighteenth and early nineteenth centuries) and clients undoubtedly found Latrobe's claims for the professional architect's superiority ludicrous. Master builders had controlled the design and construction of public and private works since the earliest days of European settlement along the East Coast. To them, Latrobe was a prickly and arrogant interloper. Planters and merchants, the American elite, were equally unimpressed with his claims of gentility. They regarded him as a skilled surveyor and mechanic, but not their peer.[4]

MASTER BUILDERS IN THE COLONIAL AND FEDERAL PERIODS

The trading companies and religious groups that settled North America in the seventeenth century encouraged skilled builders—known variously as mechanics, artisans, artificers, tradesmen, and craftsmen—to immigrate to the New World. Because these men possessed the skills needed to construct new settlements, they were promised passage, land, and exemption from taxes and military service. After London was rebuilt in the wake of the great fire of 1666, there was little work for either established masters or journeymen. Many building craftsmen decided to immigrate to the colonies.[5]

Carpenters were the preeminent building artisans in the colonies because of the abundance of wood for construction. One historian estimates that they outnumbered all other building artisans by four to one. There were, for example, about 13 carpenters in Philadelphia by 1690; a century later there were 450 carpenters in the city. Other building artisans—joiners, bricklayers, masons, glaziers, painters, and plasterers—joined carpenters in the major colonial centers of Boston, New York, and Philadelphia by the early eighteenth century.[6]

Master carpenters possessed both technical and supervisory skills. Timber frames were complicated assemblages of heavy, hand-cut members joined by mortise and tenon. Raising a frame for even a simple one- or two-room house required a crew of several men. Because carpentry was not only skilled but also dangerous and seasonal work, it commanded high wages in the colonies, where there was a chronic dearth of skilled labor. A carpenter in seventeenth-century Massachusetts earned more than twice as much as his counterpart in England. In 1663 Massachusetts Bay Colony judges established a ceiling of two shillings a day on carpenters' wages because of price gouging.[7]

The first building trade organizations in the colonies were associations of master carpenters. The Carpenters' Company of Philadelphia, the earliest organization, may date from the 1720s. It was exceptionally powerful because its members controlled the measurement and valuing of all building work through a secret price book. Thomas Jefferson so respected the Carpenters' Company that he insisted its price book be used for estimating construction costs at the United States Capitol.[8]

Other building associations, usually formed by carpenters, appeared elsewhere in late eighteenth-century America. There are references to a Society of House Carpenters in New York by the early 1770s, and Boston carpenters agreed on a price list and rules of work in 1774. Philadelphia bricklayers, by contrast, did not organize a guild until 1790. Apart from guilds organized around a specific craft, there were more inclusive organizations. New York City artisans, manufacturers, and tradesmen formed the General Society of Mechanics and Tradesmen in 1785, and ten years later the Associated

Mechanics of Boston and the Massachusetts Charitable Mechanics Association were established. But southern craftsmen, both white and African American, were dispersed and relatively few in number. Moreover, white southerners would not have permitted African Americans to organize for any purpose. There were no craft guilds south of Baltimore and Washington, D.C.[9]

Early craft organizations were select associations of master artisans, men with workshops, apprentices, and journeymen. They were successful employers and businessmen who could afford the steep membership fees. The artisans, tradesmen, and manufacturers who composed the Massachusetts Charitable Mechanics Association organized around the issue of runaway apprentices. The twenty-five carpenters who became members represented only 15 percent of all master carpenters in Boston. The eighty members of the Carpenters' Company in Philadelphia in 1787 represented only one out of every six master carpenters in the city.[10]

Some master carpenters were also builders. Called "undertakers" for most of the colonial period, they were entrepreneurs as well as craftsmen. These men were the general contractors of their day, acquiring materials and labor and then directing work on the site. If they drafted basic architectural drawings and supervised, they were known as architects. The majority of master craftsmen, however, were not even employers, much less entrepreneurs. They worked alone, but they worked for themselves.[11]

Robert Smith (1722–77) was perhaps the most renowned master carpenter and master builder of the late eighteenth century. Apprenticed to a builder in his native Scotland, Smith was working in Philadelphia by 1749, remodeling Governor James Hamilton's residence, Bush Hill. He was responsible for Carpenters' Hall and the Walnut Street Prison in Philadelphia—the former the headquarters of the Carpenters' Company and the latter one of the first brick vaulted structures in the English-speaking colonies. Smith's practice as a designer extended from Rhode Island to Virginia. He specialized in institutional buildings: Nassau Hall at Princeton University, the College of Rhode Island (now Brown University), New College at the University of Pennsylvania, and the insane asylum in Williamsburg, Virginia. Yet Smith was also the undertaker for Benjamin Franklin's house and the Philadelphia Almshouse, and he invested heavily in local real estate. A member of both the Carpenters' Company and the American Philosophical Society, he designed fortifications for the Revolutionary Army at no cost. Nearly twenty years after his death Smith was honored with an exhibition of his architectural drawings at the Columbianum, an academy of fine arts in Philadelphia.[12]

During his lifetime Smith was described as a carpenter, house carpenter, and builder. But his design and construction of imposing public and private buildings set him apart from the typical master builder, and he was also called an architect. He was not, however, what an Englishman meant by a gentleman in spite of his standing and wealth. Bridging the divide between manual and intellectual vocations, Smith blurred the distinctions between gentleman and artisan, artist and tradesman. Philadelphia master carpenters like Smith synthesized design with supervision and execution with investment to a remarkable degree. No single artisan or group of masters elsewhere in the colonies could match their prominence, power, or wealth.[13]

6.1 William Buckland, Hammond-Harwood House, Annapolis, Maryland, 1774

Robert Smith was an unusual figure in early American architecture. In colonial Boston no master craftsman attained Smith's prominence as a designer and builder. Thomas Dawes (1731–1811) prospered as a master mason and builder, but he had only a modest career as a designer.[14] John Hawks (1731–90) was one of the first Americans referred to as an architect. Trained originally as a carpenter and builder in England, Hawks prepared the most extensive set of architectural drawings—for the governor's palace in Tryon, North Carolina—to survive from the colonial period. But he drifted away from architectural work in North Carolina, a relatively poor and thinly populated colony with limited opportunities for architecture.[15]

William Buckland (1734–74) and Samuel McIntire (1757–1811) were the only other master craftsmen who attained substantial architectural reputations in early America. Their careers, however, were not as wide-ranging as Robert Smith's. While the Philadelphia master received commissions along the eastern seaboard, Buckland worked in northern Virginia and Maryland (Figure 6.1), and McIntire was based in Salem, Massachusetts. But Buckland and McIntire surpassed Smith in the variety and inventiveness of their designs. Trained as wood-carvers and joiners, Buckland and McIntire were specialists who created and assembled paneling, furniture, and architectural ornament. The drafting skills and knowledge of materials and styles necessary for joiners served them well as architects.

Apprenticed in London, Buckland immigrated as an indentured servant, engaged to finish George Mason's Gunston Hall in northern Virginia. After his servitude ended, he found clients among the planters, merchants, lawyers, and clergy scattered across

PARADOXES OF PRACTICE

But Latrobe confused clients and artisans because his actions often contradicted his professional claims. He did not always exercise what he defined as his professional rights of supervision. After winning a bitter fight to supervise the penitentiary work in Richmond, he left the city in late 1798 to devote himself to the Bank of Pennsylvania, promising the governor he would return to supervise completion of the penitentiary. But he never did, sending only some written instructions for the workmen. Latrobe's abandonment of the very responsibilities he had fought for so fiercely surely puzzled and exasperated the penitentiary client, superintendent, and workmen. It also further confused the professional architect's role in supervision. In this light, Latrobe's complaints about subsequent alterations to the penitentiary seem disingenuous.[39]

The Richmond penitentiary work certainly paled by comparison with the Philadelphia bank and waterworks commissions he had in hand by the spring of 1798. Philadelphia, with a population of fifty thousand, was then the largest city in the United States; its wealth and sophistication clearly suited Latrobe's ambition.[40] The Bank of Pennsylvania was a fireproof building constructed of masonry vaults. The facade, sheathed in marble, used the first example of the Greek orders to be built in the United States. It was, along with Bulfinch's Massachusetts Statehouse, the first complex vaulted structure east of the Mississippi River.[41] The waterworks were the most extensive and ambitious municipal system then designed in the United States, with innovative steam engines pumping water from the Schuylkill River through a brick vaulted conduit to the city (Figure 6.3).[42]

Important private commissions like William Cramond's Sedgeley (the first Gothic Revival villa in the United States) and speculative row houses on Walnut Street followed in 1799. These works established Latrobe as the leading designer of architectural and engineering works in Philadelphia and the United States. His comment that "for my professional reputation I should have done enough had I only built the Bank of Pennsylvania and supplied the city with Water" suggests how much he had accomplished in only a few years.[43] But, ironically, he was soon to despair of his career. He complained to his father-in-law in 1803: "But as it is I have absolutely nothing to do there [Philadelphia]. . . . Of other public works, even on a moderate scale, there is no prospect; and since the Cramond house I have not even had a transitory application to design a private building."[44] His plight was so desperate that James Traquair, who had worked as stonemason on the bank commission, asked Thomas Jefferson if he had any work for Latrobe. With no commissions in sight, Traquair explained, the architect was planning retirement to a farm.[45]

Latrobe's troubles were a result of the expense of his high-profile commissions. The final costs for both the Bank of Pennsylvania and the Philadelphia waterworks far exceeded his original estimates. Sedgeley's bloated budget of forty thousand dollars made prospective home owners wary of Latrobe,[46] and this reputation for financial extravagance followed him to Washington. When some fifty-one thousand dollars in unauthorized expenditures for the Capitol came to light in 1807–8, a congressional committee investigated and considered dismissing Latrobe for professional misconduct.

6.3 Benjamin Henry Latrobe, Fairmount Waterworks, Philadelphia, Pennsylvania, begun 1814

He was ultimately exonerated but only because the legislators concluded artists like Latrobe "were not very nice about calculations in money matters."[47] Although he supported Latrobe publicly, Jefferson chastised him privately for his faulty cost estimates and chronic inattention to the building accounts. This mismanagement, he wrote Latrobe, "has done you great injury, and has been much felt by myself."[48]

Latrobe had only a limited understanding of the American building economy. Both private and public sector works were severely undercapitalized. Banking reserves were small, and the financial system was local and fragmented. Public revenues were limited, consisting only of customs duties. The government preferred to raise funds from private sources for many public works. Private investors were adamant about short-term gains whether they financed public projects like canals and waterworks or private undertakings like speculative housing. They wanted to limit costs rather than build the impressive but expensive structures that Latrobe advocated. Public officials faced the wrath of both political opponents and the electorate if building projects proved more expensive than the original estimates.[49]

Latrobe had to become a peripatetic architect and engineer because the American building market was so localized and thinly capitalized. During the remaining seventeen years of his career, he traveled throughout the country in search of enough challenging and lucrative work to sustain his professional practice and genteel life. In Delaware he laid out the Chesapeake and Delaware Canal and surveyed the town of Newcastle during the early 1800s. He also became the chief architect for the federal government in Washington, D.C., and then an engineer for the navy in 1803–4. His federal salary was apparently insufficient because he also undertook private and commercial work in both Philadelphia and Washington, D.C. When he received a commission for the customhouse and waterworks in New Orleans, he spread his attentions over an even greater geographic area. Congress suspended work on the Capitol in 1811 as the threat of war with Britain grew. Latrobe shifted his focus to the New Orleans work, but the war eventually suspended building operations there as well. A year later Latrobe was on the move again, resettling in Pittsburgh to design steamboats for Robert Fulton. But this enterprise collapsed, too, and he returned to Washington, where friends secured his reappointment as architect to rebuild the burned Capitol in 1815. After bitter quarrels with the supervising commissioner, Latrobe resigned this position in 1817. He moved to Baltimore, where he oversaw work on the cathedral and the exchange, the latter designed with the cantankerous Maximilian Godefroy, with whom he quarreled. In 1818 he resumed work on the New Orleans water system. The constant search for work ended when he succumbed to yellow fever there in 1820.

Latrobe's far-flung practice made it necessary, he wrote in 1803, to "act on many occasions by proxy."[50] John Lenthall, an experienced English mechanic, became the clerk of the works (building superintendent) at the Capitol. He was, in Latrobe's opinion, a good assistant. A clerk like Lenthall, Latrobe wrote, directed and combined the work of all the mechanics so that they worked "without loss of time or waste of material or dispute among themselves." He also made working drawings and, in Latrobe's absence, determined whether contracts for labor and materials were being faithfully fulfilled.[51] Because of Lenthall, Latrobe wrote that he could work on the Capitol with "only an occasional personal attendance." Consequently, the architect did not move his family to Washington for several years after accepting the federal appointment in 1803.[52]

But Latrobe's confidence in Lenthall was ultimately too great. In 1808 his clerk was killed when the vault covering the Supreme Court in the Capitol collapsed and fell down on him. The fatality occurred as Lenthall and his workers took down the temporary supports for the vault. Although Latrobe accepted responsibility, in public statements he did allude to Lenthall's premature and clumsy removal of the wooden centering.[53] In a private letter to Jefferson, Latrobe's explanation of the events leading up to the collapse was more candid than his public accounts. Lenthall had redesigned the vault to use less material and centering in order to economize, and Latrobe had consented to these "bolder and more dangerous vaults" against, he confessed to Jefferson, his better judgment.[54] Jefferson must have wondered why Latrobe, given his doubts about the vault's structural integrity, was not there to supervise the removal of the centering. This was a serious dereliction of his often vaunted professional responsibilities, which proved fatal to Lenthall. As with the Virginia penitentiary commission, Latrobe seemed far more zealous in asserting his supervisory rights than in actually attending to them.

As Latrobe's practice spread beyond Philadelphia, he needed assistants in his office as well as clerks on the scattered building sites. Frederick Graff, the son of a bricklayer and a carpenter's apprentice, began working for him in 1799. William Strickland and Adam Traquair, whose fathers had worked on Latrobe's Bank of Pennsylvania, were sent to his office in the early 1800s. Lewis DeMun, a former French military officer, came around 1802, followed by Robert Mills, previously a student of James Hoban and draftsman for Jefferson, in 1803.[55]

Latrobe's assistants helped to prepare the extraordinary number of detailed working drawings and written instructions required to execute his innovative structural and architectural designs. These documents were especially necessary because Latrobe was so often absent from the building site. Scaled plans, elevations, sections, and details in building had become more common with the advent of costlier structures designed with vaulted spaces and in new styles like neoclassicism during the second half of the eighteenth century. Drawings for engineering projects, by contrast, were still rather primitive. Master mechanics on engineering projects rarely used scaled drawings and often simply chalked full-size details on boards. Thus, either Latrobe or his assistants had to teach them how to decipher and use scaled engineering drawings. "I must indeed work hard," Latrobe wrote his brother, "having to make the Men who are to execute, as well as the designs of my work."[56]

As Latrobe juggled commissions, he sent his assistants to construction sites with drawings, documents, and contractors' payments. DeMun, Mills, and Strickland also helped Lenthall prepare working drawings for the Capitol. As they grew more experienced, they assisted in surveying the site and executing feeder lines for the Delaware Canal project. Mills supervised work on the Bank of Philadelphia and the William Waln house when Latrobe finally moved to Washington, D.C., in 1807.[57] But managing a staff was time-consuming and frustrating. John Barber, a chief clerk, and Thomas Breillat, a draftsman, absconded with office papers, books, and monies in the summer of 1800. Strickland, only an adolescent when he entered Latrobe's office, sometimes disappeared for days without a word.[58]

Furthermore, some clients objected to Latrobe's staff arrangements. Accustomed to a master builder who charged a single fee for design, contracting, craftsmanship, and supervision, they especially balked at hiring a superintendent like Lenthall and then paying Latrobe too. The architect often found it necessary to explain just what he did and did not do. "To execute the work either by myself or by proxy, is wholly out of my profession," he wrote to William Waln. "It is not necessary that I should oversee or superintend the workmen as they are at labor." Even if he were willing to supervise the construction of Waln's house, Latrobe continued, no one could afford such a costly use of his time.[59]

Latrobe's fees were indeed high, and he found it difficult to collect them. Although he tried to charge 5 percent of the building budget, the standard professional fee in his view, he rarely got it. This was not surprising when one considers that his better-established professional mentors in England had trouble receiving this amount.[60]

LATROBE'S LEGACY

Latrobe was not stoic about his professional difficulties. He complained regularly about "the indignities ... which I must suffer in the prosecution of my profession" and about his "great misfortune to be born and educated a *Gentleman*, at least on this side of the

Atlantic."[61] Since the nineteenth century, critics and historians have generally accepted Latrobe's own interpretation of these events. In 1834 William Dunlap described Latrobe's career as proud but painful because of Americans' ignorance of art and science. Talbot Hamlin, who won a Pulitzer Prize for his 1955 biography of Latrobe, saw the architect as a tragic figure. He died destitute and nearly forgotten, Hamlin wrote, because of the national suspicion of artists and experts.

Today architectural historians routinely acclaim Latrobe as the father of the architectural profession in the United States. During the last twenty years, he has received what in the academic community passes for canonization: an exhaustive and expensive project devoted to the publication of his correspondence, journals, travel sketches, and architectural and engineering drawings.[62] Yet his legacy to the architectural profession is far more problematic than such assessments suggest. Latrobe was imperious, temperamental, inconsistent, and improvident—qualities the public still associates with the professional architect. Other architects like L'Enfant, Hallet, and Godefroy exhibited these same traits, but they never identified themselves as fully and vociferously as Latrobe did with professionalism. Nor were they as successful as Latrobe.

In a letter to Jefferson, Latrobe stated that his task was "to dictate in matters of taste" to the president, Congress, and the public. He clearly had little patience or respect for the leaders of the new Republic when they became involved with artistic or architectural issues. Congress was an assembly of clowns and buffoons, he wrote, who could appreciate only the architectural literalism of his corncob capitals in the Capitol.[63] Jefferson advised him to moderate his tone and his designs if he wished to practice in a republic—"The object of the artist is lost if he fails to please the general eye." But Latrobe seemed to relish his own arrogance: "There is perhaps among all the *persons* holding employment under government, not one, so unpopular as myself . . . I believe that I have the despotism of manner which belongs to all artists, and appears to be inseparable from some degree of reputation."[64]

Although Latrobe asserted that he was a "man of business and account," he was clearly out of his depth in financial matters. All his major commissions—the Bank of Pennsylvania, the Philadelphia waterworks, Sedgeley, and the Capitol—cost far more than the original estimates he gave the clients. But he transformed this reputation for extravagance, as he did his arrogance, into a point of pride, writing that "the fault which the public have found with my professional character, is that my ideas and projects are too extended to be practicable for some centuries to come."[65]

He managed his personal finances as poorly as he did his building budgets. In pursuit of wealth he repeatedly made highly speculative and ultimately disastrous investments: in land, a steel mill, a gold mine, power looms, and steamboats. His canal commissions were also risky; like other early engineers, he gambled and took his salary in stock shares. If the canal company failed, as the Chesapeake and Delaware did in 1805, Latrobe received nothing. He often had to borrow from family and friends. Ever the gentleman, he also signed notes guaranteeing others' debts. In 1817 he finally had to declare personal bankruptcy. Risky investments and imprudent loans surely had as much to do with his precarious finances as American philistinism.[66]

Although Latrobe's professional difficulties were partly of his own making, they were also the result of basic economic realities of early nineteenth-century America.[67] There was simply not enough capital to underwrite the ambitious private and public projects that Latrobe and other immigrant architects like L'Enfant, Hallet, Godefroy, and Hadfield considered worthy of their training and talent. Even Bulfinch, a well-connected Bostonian, could not make a living from his architectural practice. Although Latrobe was quick to proclaim himself the first professional architect, he had little insight into what that meant in harsh economic terms. Architectural scholars simultaneously gloss over Latrobe's responsibility for his own financial predicament and obscure its systemic causes.

On only one occasion did Latrobe cease his railings about persecution of the professional architect and reflect more dispassionately on his American career: "Had I, in England, executed what I have done here, I should now be able to sit down quietly and enjoy *otium cum dignitate* [leisure with dignity]. But in England the croud [*sic*] of those whose talents are superior to mine is so great, that I should perhaps never have elbowed through them. Here I am the only successful Architect and Engineer."[68]

Latrobe's legacy to the next generation of professional architects was not just a corpus of buildings. He had identified the professional architect with public buildings of artistic and structural excellence. Less positively, he had associated the architect with arrogance, temperament, and fiscal imprudence. Unlike Latrobe, L'Enfant, Hallet, Godefroy, and Hadfield, antebellum architects worked during an unprecedented period of opportunity and economic expansion in the four decades before the Civil War. Growth and prosperity made cooperation and organization, the next phase of professional development, possible for them.

Notes

1   Letter of July 12, 1806 to Robert Mills, in John Van Horne, ed., *Correspondence and Miscellaneous Papers of Benjamin Henry Latrobe* (New Haven, Conn.: Yale University Press, 1986), vol. 2, 239.
2   Letter of March 29, 1804 to Jefferson, in John Van Horne and Lee Formwalt, eds., *Correspondence and Miscellaneous Papers of Benjamin Henry Latrobe* (New Haven, Conn.: University Press, 1984), vol. 1, 472.
3   Letter to Henry Ormond of November 20, 1808, *Correspondence of Latrobe*, 2: 680.
4   Letter of May 25, 1817 to Richard Caton in John Van Horne, ed., *Correspondence and Miscellaneous Papers of Benjamin Henry Latrobe* (New Haven, Conn.: Yale University Press, 1988), vol. 3, 882.
5   Howard Rock, *Artisans of the New Republic* (New York: New York University Press, 1984), 15 n. 5; and Roger W. Moss Jr., "Origins of the Carpenters' Company," in *Building Early America*, ed. Charles Peterson (Radnor, Pa.: Chilton Book Company, 1976), 36–37.
6   W. J. Rorabaugh, *The Craft Apprentice* (New York: Oxford University Press, 1986), 6; Hannah Benner Roach, "Thomas Nevell," *Journal of the Society of Architectural Historians* 24 (May 1965): 153; and Louise Hall, "Artificer to Architect in America," typescript, The American Institute of Architects Archives, Washington, D.C., 1954, 12.
7   Rorabaugh, *The Craft Apprentice*, 6; and Mark Erlich, *Working with Our Hands: The Story of Carpenters in Massachusetts* (Philadelphia: Temple University Press, 1986), 21.
8   The earliest surviving records of the Carpenters' Company are from the 1760s. When legislature incorporated the company in 1740, the date of organization given was 1724. Benjamin Loxley,

an early member, noted that the company began in the winter of 1726 or 1727. See Charles Peterson, "Benjamin Loxley and Carpenters' Hall," *Journal of the Society of Architectural Historians* 15 (December 1956): 24–25, 26–27; and Moss, "Origins of the Carpenters' Company," 43–45. For the Capitol, see Letter of July 17, 1793 from Jefferson to George Washington, in Saul K. Padover, ed., *Thomas Jefferson and the National Capitol* (Washington, D.C.: Government Printing Office, 1946), 186.

9   Rita S. Gottesman, *Arts and Crafts in New York, 1726–1776* (New York: Historical Society, 1938), 50, 53, 193; *Constitution of the Associated Mechanics of Boston* (1795), in Charles Evans, ed., *The Early American Imprint Series No. 1*, ed. Charles Evans, no. 28315; and Joseph T. Buckingham, comp., *Annals of the Massachusetts Charitable Mechanics Association* (Boston: Press of Crocker and Brewster, 1853), 3–5; title page to *Charter, Articles, Supplement and By-Laws of the Bricklayers' Company* (Philadelphia, 1888); and Catherine Bishir, "A Proper Good Nice and Workmanlike Manner," in Catherine Bishir, Carl Lounsbury, Charlotte Brown, and Ernest Wood, *Architects and Builders in North Carolina* (Chapel Hill: University of North Carolina Press, 1990), 95, 99–100.

10   Gary Kornblith, "From Artisan to Businessman: Master Mechanics in New England, 1789–1850" (Ph.D. diss., Princeton University, 1983), 87, 96–97; and Charles Peterson, introduction to *The Rules of Work of the Carpenters' Company of the City and County of Philadelphia* (1786; reprint, Princeton, N.J.: Pyne Press, 1971), xvi–xvii.

11   Carl Lounsbury, *An Illustrated Glossary of Early Southern Architecture*, (New York: Oxford University Press, 1994), s.v. "architect," "contractor," "master," and "undertaker."

12   Roger Moss and Sandra Tatman, *Biographical Dictionary of Philadelphia Architects* (Boston: G. K. Hall, 1985), s.v. "Robert Smith." and Charles Peterson, "Carpenters' Hall," *Transactions of the American Philosophical Society* 43 (March 1953): 121–123.

13   Moss and Tatman, *Biographical Dictionary of Philadelphia Architects*, s.v. "Robert Smith."

14   Frederic Detwiller, "Thomas Dawes: Boston's Patriot Architect," *Old-Time New England* 68 (summer–fall 1977): 1–18.

15   Bishir, *Architects and Builders in North Carolina*, 43–44.

16   Rosamund Beirne and John Scarff, *William Buckland, 1734–1774: Architect of Virginia and Maryland* (Baltimore: Maryland Historical Society, 1958), 6–16, 34–48, 67.

17   Quotation from the *The Diary of William Bentley* (1905–1914) in Wayne Andrews, *Architecture, Ambition, and Americans* (New York: Free Press, 1964), 96.

18   Moss and Tatman, *Biographical Dictionary of Philadelphia Architects*, s.v. "Samuel Rhoads," "Samuel Powell," and "Robert Smith." Rhoads and Powell, like Smith, were master carpenters and builders prominent in Philadelphia's political, cultural, and economic life.

19   Lounsbury, *Illustrated Glossary of Early Southern Architecture*, s.v. "architect," "builder," and "contractor." The term "contractor" did not come into general use until the late eighteenth century in America.

20   Carl Bridenbaugh, *Peter Harrison* (Chapel Hill: University of North Carolina Press, 1949); Fiske Kimball, *Thomas Jefferson, Architect* (1916; reprint, New York: Da Capo Press, 1968); Elinor Stearns and David N. Yerkes, *William Thornton: A Renaissance Man in the Federal City* (Washington, D.C.: American Institute of Architects Foundation, 1976); and Harold Kirker, *Architecture of Charles Bulfinch* (Cambridge, Mass.: Harvard University Press, 1969).

21   Christopher Misner, "Management: Architect-Developers," *Progressive Architecture* 69 (January 1988): 61–62.

22   H. Paul Caemmerer, *The Life of Pierre Charles L'Enfant* (Washington, D.C.: National Republic, 1950), 1–9, 43, 95; Robert Alexander, *The Architecture of Maximilian Godefroy* (Baltimore: Johns Hopkins University Press, 1974); Pamela Scott, "Stephen Hallet's Designs for the United States Capitol," *Winterthur Portfolio* 27 (summer/autumn 1992): 146–147; Michael Richman, "George Hadfield," *Journal of the Society of Architectural Historians* 33 (October 1974): 234–235; and for the Trumbull quotation, see Andrews, *Architecture, Ambition, and Americans*, 73.

23   Letter of April 8, 1798 to Henry Antes, in Edward C. Carter II, ed., *The Virginia Journals of Benjamin Henry Latrobe, 1795–1798* (New Haven, Conn.: Yale University Press, 1977), vol. 2, 367–368; and Letter of February 14, 1798 to James Wood, *Correspondence of Latrobe*, 1: 40, 78.

24   Editorial Note, *Correspondence of Latrobe*, 1: 6; and letter of December 31, 1814 to Henry Latrobe, *Correspondence of Latrobe*, 3: 608.

25   Frank Jenkins, *Architect and Patron* (London: Oxford University Press, 1961), 108–109, 112–115; and Adolf K. Placzek, ed., *Macmillan Encyclopedia of Architects* (New York: Free Press, 1982), s.vv. "Samuel Cockerell" and "John Smeaton."

26   John Soane, *Plans, Elevations, and Sections of Buildings* (London: I. Taylor, 1788), 7. See Talbot Hamlin, *Benjamin Henry Latrobe* (New York: Oxford University Press, 1955), 36–40, for a discussion of Soane's architectural influence on Latrobe.

27   Letter of May 21, 1807 from Latrobe to Jefferson; August 18, 1807 Letter from Latrobe to Jefferson; and Letter of April 27, 1807 from Jefferson to Latrobe, all in Padover, *Thomas Jefferson and the National Capitol*, 390, 394–396, 386–387. Paul Norton, who described the contretemps as the first serious rift between Latrobe and Jefferson, studied it in "Latrobe's Ceiling for the Hall of Representatives," *Journal of the Society of Architectural Historians* 10 (May 1951): 5–10.

28   Letter of January 16, 1809 to Isaac Hazelhurst, *Correspondence of Latrobe*, 2: 693.

29   For Latrobe's private and public references to the architect as an artist, see the following: Letter of March 29, 1804 to Jefferson, *Correspondence of Latrobe*, 1: 472; and Anniversary Oration, Society of Artists of the United States, May 8, 1811, *Correspondence of Latrobe*, 3: 65–69. Latrobe, an early member of this society of professional and amateur artists, served as vice president from 1811 until 1814. See William Dunlap, *A History of the Rise and Progress of the Arts of Design in the United States* (1834; reprint, Boston: C. E. Goodspeed, 1918), vol. 2, 234, for the remark about Latrobe's sketchbook.

30   Latrobe made this statement in the context of a lawsuit against Thornton for defamation of character. See "Memoranda of Facts Relating to the Causes of Difference between Dr. William Thornton and B. Henry Latrobe" to Walter Jones and John Law, June 26, 1808?, in *The Papers of Benjamin Henry Latrobe*, microfiche edition, ed. Edward Carter II (Clifton, N.J.: James T. White, 1976).

31   Letter of March 26, 1806 from Latrobe to Bishop John Carroll, *Correspondence of Latrobe*, 2: 210–214, 24 n. 1.

32   Ibid.

33   Darwin Stapleton, "Engineering Practice of Latrobe," in *The Engineering Drawings of Benjamin Henry Latrobe*, ed. Darwin Stapleton (New Haven, Conn.: Yale University Press, 1988), 67.

34   Editorial Note and Letter of December 13, 1806 from Latrobe to Bishop Carroll, *Correspondence of Latrobe*, 2: 51–52, 324–325.

35   Letter of January 14, 1820 from the Trustees of the Baltimore Cathedral to Latrobe, *Correspondence of Latrobe*, 3: 1040.

36   Letter of August 31, 1797 to Governor James Wood and the Council of the State of Virginia, *Correspondence of Latrobe*, 1: 61–63; Letter of July 12, 1806 to Mills, *Correspondence of Latrobe*, 2: 243; and Jeffrey Cohen and Charles Brownell, "Virginia State Penitentiary," in *The Architectural Drawings of Benjamin Henry Latrobe*, ed. Jeffrey Cohen and Charles Brownell (New Haven, Conn.: Yale University Press, 1994), part 1, 101.

37   Editorial Note and "Agreement for Executing the Marble Work of the Bank Pennsylvania," February 26, 1799, *Correspondence of Latrobe*, 1: 128–129, 129–136. See Letter of February 23, 1799 from Latrobe to Wood, *Correspondence of Latrobe*, 1: 125, 129, 136 n. 4, for references to the bank as his masterpiece.

38   Letter of January 22, 1807 to William Waln, *Correspondence of Latrobe*, 2: 368–369.

39   Subsequent letters detailing Latrobe's inspection of work and joint reports that he and Thomas Callis, the building superintendent, issued indicate that the dispute was resolved by 1798. See,

for example, Letter of July 9, 1798 from Latrobe to Governor Wood, a report on the architect's inspection of a stone arch in the penitentiary cellar, *Correspondence of Latrobe*, 1: 87–89; and Letter of February 23, 1799 to Governor Wood, *Correspondence of Latrobe*, 1: 125–128.

40 Stapleton, "Engineering Practice of Latrobe," 28.

41 The Spanish missions in the Southwest and California, like San José y San Miguel de Aguayo (1768–1777) in San Antonio, Texas; San Xavier del Bac (1784–1797) near Tucson, Arizona; and San Carlos Borromeo (1793–1797) in Carmel, California, were domed and vaulted structures.

42 Letter of February 23, 1799, *Correspondence of Latrobe*, and Stapleton, "Engineering Practice of Latrobe," 28–30.

43 Letter of 1812, quoted in Cohen and Brownell, "Virginia State Penitentiary," 180.

44 Letter of October 11, 1803 to Isaac Hazelhurst, *Correspondence of Latrobe*, 1: 341.

45 Letter of May 30, 1801, Jefferson Papers, Massachusetts Historical Society, Boston, Massachusetts.

46 Editorial Note, *Correspondence of Latrobe*, 2: 128–129; Cohen and Brownell, in *Architectural Drawings of Latrobe*, part 1, 199; Stapleton, "Engineering Practice of Latrobe," 70; Letter of January 22, 1807 from Latrobe to William Waln, *Correspondence of Latrobe*, 2: 368.

47 *Annals of the Tenth Congress, Second Session* (1808), 1870, 1973–1976. Representative Richard Stanton, chair of the investigating committee, made the comment about artists and money. See Letter of April 8, 1808 from Latrobe to Stanton, *Correspondence of Latrobe*, 2: 584–591, and 590 n. 2.

48 Letter of April 26, 1808 from Jefferson to Latrobe, *Correspondence of Latrobe*, 2: 612–613.

49 Lee Formwalt, *Benjamin Henry Latrobe and the Development of Internal Improvements in the New Republic, 1796–1820* (New York: Arno Press, 1982), 123–124.

50 Letter of October 11, 1803 to Hazelhurst, *Correspondence of Latrobe*, 1: 341.

51 Letter of May 18, 1803 from Latrobe to Hugh Brackenbridge, *Correspondence of Latrobe*, 1: 300. See Padover, *Thomas Jefferson and the National Capitol*, 520 for a summary of Lenthall's duties at the Capitol.

52 While he worked on the Capitol, Latrobe had commissions for the Delaware canal, Nassau Hall at Princeton University, and Dickinson College in Carlisle, Pennsylvania. See Letter of October 11, 1803 to Hazelhurst.

53 Latrobe, "Report on the Public Buildings" (November 18, 1808), *Correspondence of Latrobe*, 2: 671; and Letter of November 20, 1808 from Latrobe to Samuel Smith, editor of *National Intelligencer*, *Correspondence of Latrobe*, 2: 662–664.

54 Letter of September 23, 1808 from Latrobe to Jefferson quoted in Padover, *Thomas Jefferson and the National Capital*, 436–439.

55 Cohen and Brownell, *Architectural Drawings of Latrobe*, 184; and Stapleton, "Engineering Practice of Latrobe," 30. Some were Latrobe's pupils as well as his assistants.

56 Jeffrey Cohen, "Early American Architectural Drawing in Philadelphia," in *Drawing toward Building*, ed. James O'Gorman (Philadelphia: University of Pennsylvania Press, 1986), 15–16; Stapleton, "Engineering Practice of Latrobe," 63; and Letter of November 4, 1804, *Papers of Latrobe*, microfiche edition.

57 Letter of September 5, 1807 from Latrobe to Jefferson; Letter of April 25, 1807 to John Spear Smith; Letter of May 25, 1807 to President and Directors of Bank of Philadelphia; and Letter of May 3, 1807 to William Waln. All in Pamela Scott, ed., *The Papers of Robert Mills* (Wilmington, Del.: Scholarly Film Resources, 1990).

58 Cohen and Brownell, *Architectural Drawings of Latrobe*, 184.

59 Letter of January 22, 1807 to William Waln, *Correspondence of Latrobe*, 2: 367–369.

60 Letter of February 14, 1798 from Latrobe to Governor Wood, *Correspondence of Latrobe*, 1: 77–78; Letter of November 4, 1804 from Latrobe to Christian Latrobe, *Papers of Latrobe*, microfiche edition.

61 Letter of July 21, 1806 to Isaac Hazelhurst and Letter of October 22, 1807 to Lewis DeMun, *Correspondence of Latrobe*, 2: 265, 359.

62   Dunlap, *Rise and Progress of the Arts of Design*, 2: 233–234; Hamlin, *Benjamin Henry Latrobe*, 562–565; and Edward Carter, introduction to *Papers of Latrobe*.

For references to Latrobe as father of the profession, see also Leland Roth, *A Concise History of American Architecture* (New York: Harper and Row, 1979), 67; and Bishir, "Traditional Building Practice," in Bishir *et al.*, *Architects and Builders in North Carolina*, 125. J. Meredith Neil was the first exception to architectural writers' chorus of praise for Latrobe. See Neil, "Benjamin H. Latrobe's Precarious Professionalism," *Journal of the AIA* 53 (May 1970): 67–71.

63   Letters of May 21, 1807 and August 28, 1809 from Latrobe to Jefferson, quoted in Padover, *Thomas Jefferson and the National Capitol*, 392, 462.

64   Letter of April 27, 1807 from Jefferson to Latrobe quoted in Padover, *Thomas Jefferson and the National Capitol*, 386; and Letter of April 21, 1813 from Latrobe to William Jones, Secretary of the Navy quoted in Formwalt, *Latrobe and Internal Improvements*, 184.

65   For Latrobe's reference to being a "man of business," see Letter of April 13, 1803 to John Randolph, *Correspondence of Latrobe*, 2: 591. See Letter of January 20, 1812 to Dewitt Clinton, quoted in Stapleton, "Engineering Practice of Latrobe," 68, on building for posterity.

66   Formwalt, *Latrobe and Internal Improvements*, 117–124, 291. It was not unusual for engineers in early America to be compensated with stock. Far from being seen as a conflict of interest, such an arrangement supposedly guaranteed that an engineer did his best. See Daniel Calhoun, *The American Engineer: Origins and Conflict* (Cambridge, Mass.: MIT Press, 1960), 16.

67   Formwalt makes this point with regard to Latrobe's engineering practice, but it applies, I believe, to his architectural career as well. See Formwalt, *Latrobe and Internal Improvements*, vi, 123–124, 290–294.

68   Letter of November 4, 1804 to Christian Latrobe, *Correspondence of Latrobe*, 1: 563.

Chapter 7

W. Barksdale Maynard

The Greek Revival
Americanness, politics and economics

AMERICANNESS

When twentieth-century historians sought to demonstrate that American architecture had always been boldly independent and innovative—worthy of the greatness of the world-straddling nation of their day—their favorite example was the Greek Revival. They argued that this nineteenth-century movement was unique to America and expressed peculiarly democratic meanings. These ideas do not seem to have obtained in the 1890s, when the revival was still understood to have been an English import. But by 1926, when American art and antiques suddenly seemed valuable, Howard Major would call the revival "An American Style for Americans. . . . It is the only thoroughly American architecture" and was our "national style, our independent creation." The temple-form house, in particular, "was independent of contemporaneous European influence." Lewis E. Crook agreed: such a house "had no counterpart in Europe. The direct classicism of the revivalist in the temple form of architecture first gained a foothold in the South and produced our own great national style in architecture—America's independent contribution to the art." Joseph Jackson titled his 1926 chapter on the Greek Revival, "Beginnings of a National Architecture," and promoted the Americanness theme: Strickland's Second Bank (Figure 7.1) "certainly . . . was not flavored with any British influence," and his Merchants' Exchange showed how "American Architecture had released itself from British tradition." Leopold Arnaud, introducing Hamlin's *Greek Revival Architecture*, wrote, "The word 'Revival' is an unfortunate misnomer, for this style was only a revival in that its decorative vocabulary was based upon classic Greek detail. In all other respects it was typically of America. Never before or since has there been less influence from Europe." Arnaud's comments show the cast of the times; when he writes of "a conscious separation from Europe and a fierce will to be American," he refers to the 1830s but could easily be describing the 1930s, years of crisis and intense patriotism in which interest in Greek Revival architecture surged. Hamlin's book, born at the very moment of U.S. world ascendancy, made the architectural-Americanness idea gospel for the rest of the century. In vain did Nikolaus Pevsner protest against his "contention . . . that the Greek Revival is the first national American style. I fail to see that."[1]

As Pevsner knew, the Greek Revival was really an international phenomenon, with many of its greatest American monuments inspired by British examples. As for the temple-form house, abundant wood allowed Grecian porticos to multiply here, but they were far

7.1 William Strickland, Second Bank of the United States, Philadelphia, Pennsylvania, 1824

from uncommon in England. Among public buildings, the Patent Office at Washington (Figure 7.2) owed much to Smirke's General Post Office in London but was even closer kin to the Doric monuments of Edinburgh by William Burn, Thomas Hamilton, and Playfair, and would actually seem to be derived from Burn's John Watson's School. The Treasury Department (Figure 7.3) has been called "distinctively American" but actually shows close affinities to Nash's stylophilic redevelopment of the western districts of London. An obvious parallel in his Carlton House Terrace (begun 1827), which has thirty-two columns in a row, all topped by a balustrade; twenty columns form a freestanding screen like the thirty-column one at the Treasury. And, appropriately enough, Mills's building is exceedingly similar to London's "New Treasury," Soane's Board of Trade, Whitehall. This last comparison underscores the generally retardataire character of American architecture; the Greek Revival had crested in London in the late 1820s and was fast transforming into the Italianate by the mid-1830s, yet American architects in appropriating Nash and Soane's grandiose urbanism largely persisted in clothing it in Greek, not Roman, garb. Mills used Erechtheum Ionic on the Treasury in a recollection of the lessons he had learned from his master Latrobe and the Bank of Pennsylvania of thirty-seven years before. When called upon to defend his design to a congressional committee, however (political enemies charged him with construction delays and design flaws), he mentioned only French buildings as precedents for a long colonnade—the Louvre and Alexandre Theodore Brongniart's Bourse, Paris (1808–13), the Bourse being "the most magnificent of modern structures." Perhaps it would have been foolhardy to talk of England to already irate American politicians.[2]

   Political conditions unique to America are one thing, but architectural taste is another entirely. Taste during these years was a truly international language, and the

7.2 Robert Mills, following Ithiel Town and William P. Elliot, Patent Office, Washington, DC, 1836–40, enlarged 1847–67

Greek Revival, far from being an American revolt against British cultural hegemony, was if anything an eager—one could almost say servile—acquiescence to foreign preferences. As we saw earlier, Americans were almost desperate in their desire to be considered tasteful by English standards, recoiling in anguish at the "spleen . . . sneers and self-complacency" of Mrs. Trollope and others and redoubling their efforts to conform. Margaret Hall wrote of the Americans, "Their desire for our approbation exceeds anything I could have conceived . . . their whole minds seem to be bent in seeming quite English in their manners and customs, but a lurking suspicion that they are not quite what they ought to be makes them seek to have their opinion confirmed by those who they think qualified to judge." Political rivalries aside, in aesthetic matters England was not considered a foreign culture, but nurturing parent to America's. Architect William H. Ranlett wrote in the 1840s, "It has often been made a reproach to our national character that we imitate all other people in our architecture, while we have nothing that we can claim as our own. But so far from this being a reproach, it is rather a credit, that having a knowledge of the old world's experience we have the intelligence to avail ourselves of the wisdom of our ancestors."[3]

An English writer on the Picturesque once expected that a gentleman landscaper "will be checked from exceeding the boundaries which good sense prescribes, by that powerful species of restraint, the fear of ridicule"—and this fear was a powerful motivator driving the improvement of American architecture and pushing it in the direction of archaeological correctness. Restraint and discipline lay at the heart of the ancient Greek achievement, as the marquis de Chastellux wrote James Madison in 1783: "The remedy against the caprices of the fashion is the study of the arts, the knowledge of abstract beauty, the perfection of taste ... do you not see that the Greeks, who had some how acquired very early, such just notions of the arts and taste; do you not see, I say, that they never varied in their modes?"[4]

The only way to avoid architectural solecisms was to obey classical taste rigidly. Accordingly, Americans became more than ordinarily obsessed with the rules and with building by the book, which helped give the U.S. Greek Revival its frequently literal and temple-form cast. Virginia lawyer and man of letters George Tucker, writing in the *Port Folio*, understood that Americans, like all moderns, would inevitably "remain slavish imitators in architecture" even though "national vanity may spurn at a perpetual servitude of imagination" to the precedent of Greece. In his pioneering *History of the Rise and Progress of the Arts of Design in the United States* (1834), William Dunlap acknowledged that his compatriots, as with the English, "have no standard of beauty, but that which is derived from the country of Homer and Phidias," and Tucker had agreed that "all the most civilized nations of the earth unite in considering the Grecian architecture as the standard of excellence." Massachusetts architect Edward Shaw, who once asked a traveling friend to measure the Parthenon for him—a modest request!—wrote of architecture, "If this science were more generally studied throughout the United States, we should be exempt from those architectural abortions which now so often disgrace our cities and villages." The writer N. P. Willis quoted a commentator on the Albany State House who stressed its failure to obey the norms: "The rules of architecture, whether Egyptian, Hindoo,

7.3 Robert Mills, Treasury Department, Washington, DC, 1836–42

message of [Greek Revival] plantation architecture"; the revival "flourished especially in the Deep South of the slaveowners." But there is in fact little evidence that links southern attitudes on slavery with architectural tastes; and if the Greek Revival justified slavery so effectively, one might wonder why the style waned in the South (as elsewhere) in the 1860s just as the slavery issue became most urgent and, as Robert Gamble writes, "at the very time when Southern nationalism was gaining momentum." That slavery and architectural taste had little real connection is suggested by the remarks of a Georgia writer who urged new obedience to the dictates of the *northern* architect Downing so that "the prevailing style of building with massy Doric columns and Corinthian capitals, to private residences, will rapidly disappear." This was in 1853, in a Deep South inflamed by *Uncle Tom's Cabin* and with slavery on everyone's mind. During this same period, master builder Abner Cook designed temple-form Greek Revival mansions for wealthy citizens of Austin, Texas. As historian Kenneth Hafertepe has shown, however, many of the owners were born outside the South, owned few slaves, and opposed secession; only one went on to fight for the Confederacy. He concludes, "The association of white-columned mansions with Southern secession or Southern nationalism does not hold up."[11]

In accounting for the southerner's choice of Greek Revival as a domestic style, one historian finds that "aesthetic erudition was far less important than the heroic ideals of democratic Athens and Republican Rome, whose venerable political systems had been based on slave labor"; but in fact the opposite was probably true—the display of proper taste was much more significant than political associations. If insecurity about taste accounts for the literalism of the Greek Revival in America at large, the situation must have been especially acute in the South, which has always fretted about its backwardness. Lamenting that "the South is far behind the North," John Forsyth called upon the people of the Ridge of Chunnenugge to reform their architecture and thereby "rescue your Alabama, a part of our loved sunny South, from the reproach now cast upon it by every traveller, of being behind the civilization of the age in the refinements and elegancies of rural life."[12]

The South is a land of legends, and historical commentary on its Greek Revival architecture has frequently been marked by creative speculation. Over the years, however, some have worked to disentangle the web of "pallid myth" that has grown up around the subject. In 1945, James C. Bonner first tried to overturn the white-column notion of "the Greek Revival as the traditional rural house of the plantation South." He identified Greek Revival homes as primarily an urbane phenomenon of "towns and villages. . . . It is too often forgotten that before 1860 it was there, and not on the plantation, that they achieved their highest perfection in the Lower South." In the 1970s, Gamble made a bold assertion: "There seems to be little evidence that Southerners on the eve of the Civil War associated neoclassical architecture and the classic-style portico with the viruses of a peculiarly Southern way of life." And Mills Lane has more recently reminded us "The Greek Revival was neither particularly American nor particularly Southern."[13]

If politics is an imperfect and limited explanation for the Greek Revival, economics may be a better one. From its first application in America, the Grecian was considered a frugal means of building, as it had been in Britain; J. C. Loudon held that the best new houses were Greek "from its greater compactness, and from its having comparatively few ornaments." Strickland's Second Bank exemplified economy-minded planning, having been designed in response to an advertisement that read, "In this edifice, the Directors are desirous of exhibiting a chaste imitation of Grecian Architecture, in its simplest and least expensive form." The Greek Revival accommodated the financial constraints of the homebuilder, Mills wrote: "The natural good taste and the unprejudiced eye of our citizens required only a few examples of the Greek style to convince them of its superiority over the Roman for public structures, and its simplicity recommended its introduction into their private dwellings."[14]

Advertising his services as an architect in a New York newspaper in 1825, Ithiel Town stressed the Grecian's universality, chasteness, and economy:

> It will be the subscriber's endeavour, to introduce, generally, the taste which from its simplicity, elegance, and grandeur, is evidently gaining the confidence and admiration of all who possess a true and classic taste, throughout the civilized world; and while the Grecian Architecture or even the general spirit and taste of it possesses this important advantage over the trifling, unmeaning innumerable little parts, in the prevailing modern taste in building, it is, *very fortunately* at the same time, a much more permanent and economical style for general use, both in public and private buildings.

One will notice the absence of any reference to politics, republicanism, or uniquely American conditions; on the contrary, Greek is appropriate "throughout the civilized world." Later Louisa Tuthill, too, equated Greek with economy, not political circumstances: "It is as easy to plan a city, a village, or a building, in good taste, as in bad taste, and *as cheap too*, since that is an all important consideration. Simplicity of style in architecture is in itself a beauty. A Doric temple is perfectly simple, yet what object of art is more imposing and beautiful?"[15]

The word constantly applied to the Greek Revival was *chaste*, which at once connoted beauty achieved with economy. As Tucker wrote, the greatness of Greek lay in "*utility* and convenience," "*utility*" and "*beauty*," as ancient architects "seem always to have hit the happy mean between too much and too little variety." Chasteness went hand in hand with the middle-state ethos that perfectly suited antebellum America—a strong economic rationale for the Greek Revival."[16] [. . .]

Notes

1   William Rotch Ware, *Georgian Period*, 3 vols. 1898–1901 (New York: U.P.C. Books, 1923 reprint ed.), 1: 255. Howard Major, *The Domestic Architecture of the Early American Republic: The Greek Revival* (Philadelphia: J.B. Lippincott, 1926), 11–14. Lewis E. Crook, Jr., "Foreword," in Ernest Ray Denmark, *Architecture of the Old South* (Atlanta: Southern Architect and Building News, 1926), n.p. Joseph Jackson, *Development of American Architecture* (Philadelphia: David McKay, 1926), 196, 204, 208. Leopold Arnaud, in Talbot Hamlin, *Greek Revival Architecture in America* (New York: Oxford University Press, 1944), xvii, xv. Nikolaus Pevsner, *An Outline of European Architecture* (New York: Charles Scribner's Sons, 1948), 229.

2   "Distinctively" in Rhodri Windsor Liscombe, *Altogether American: Robert Mills, Architect and Engineer, 1781–1855* (New York: Oxford University Press, 1994), 192. Helen Gallagher, *Robert Mills* (New York: Columbia University Press, 1935), 59. Mills to the committee, February 10,

1838, in "New Treasury and Post Office Buildings," *House Report* 737, 25th Congress, 2nd Session (March 29, 1838), ser. no. 335: 26.

3   John Fanning Watson, *Annals of Philadelphia, and Pennsylvania, in the Olden Time*, 2 vols. (1842) (Philadelphia: J.B. Lippincott, 1870 reprint ed.), 1: 244. Margaret Hall, *The Aristocratic Journey: Being the Outspoken Letters of Mrs. Basil Hall Written During a Fourteen Months' Sojourn in America, 1827–1828*, ed. by Una Pope-Hennessey (New York: G.P. Putnam's Sons, 1931), 70. William H. Ranlett, *The Architect, A Series of Original Designs, for Domestic and Ornamental Cottages and Villas*, 2 vols., 1847–49 (New York: Dewitt and Davenport, 1851–53 reprint ed.), 2: 71.

4   T. Hornor, *Description of an Improved Method of Delineating Estates* (London: J. Harding, 1813), 57. To James Madison, January 12, 1783, in Marquis de Chastellux, *Travels in North America in the Years 1780–81–82* (1786) (New York: White, Gallaher, and White, 1827 reprint ed.), 378.

5   [George Tucker], "Thoughts of a Hermit," *Portfolio* 4, no. 6 (December 1814): 569, 560. See also Hamlin, *Greek Revival*, 377. William Dunlap, *History of the Rise and Progress of the Arts of Design in the United States*, ed. by Alexander Wyckoff, 3 vols. (1834) (New York: Benjamin Blom, 1965 reprint ed.), 1: 2. [Tucker], "Thoughts," 559. Edward Shaw, *The Modern Architect* (Boston: Dayton and Wentworth, 1854), n.p. N.P. Willis, *American Scenery*, 7 vols. (London: George Virtue, 1840), 1: 23–24. James Fenimore Cooper, *Home as Found* (1838) (New York: G.P. Putnam's Sons, 1913), 113. [Tucker], "Thoughts," 568. J. Meredith Neil, *Toward a National Taste: America's Quest for Aesthetic Independence* (Honolulu: University Press of Hawaii, 1975), 144.

6   [Anne Newport Royall], *Sketches of History, Life, and Manners, in the United States* (New Haven: for the author, 1826), 274. [Freeman Hunt], *Letters About the Hudson River and its Vicinity* (New York: Freeman Hunt, 1836), 141–44.

7   W.H. Eliot, *A Description of Tremont House* (Boston: Gray and Bowen, 1830).

8   Arnaud, in Hamlin, *Greek Revival*, xvi–xvii. G.E. Kidder Smith, *The Architecture of the United States*, Vol. 2: *The South and Midwest* (Garden City, NY: Anchor Books, 1981), xx. Marian Scott Moffett, "Foreword," in Henry Wiencek, *Plantations of the Old South* (Birmingham, AL: Oxmoor House, 1988), 4. Alan Gowans, *Styles and Types of North American Architecture* (New York: Icon Editions, 1992). Liscombe, *Altogether American*, 192. Roger G. Kennedy, *Greek Revival America* (New York: Stewart, Tabori, and Chang, 1989), 270.

9   Benjamin Henry Latrobe, "Anniversary Oration to the Society of Artists," in *The Correspondence and Miscelleneous Papers of Benjamin Henry Latrobe*, ed. by John C. Van Horne, 3 vols. (New Haven: Yale University Press, 1984–88), 3: 81, 76. Robert Mills, "The Architectural Works of Robert Mills," in Don Gifford, ed., *The Literature of Architecture* (New York: E.P. Dutton, 1966), 88.

10   "Greek Fever," in Stephen Larrabee, *Hellas Observed: The American Experience of Greece, 1775–1865* (New York: New York University Press, 1957), ch. 3. "Corner Stone."

11   James Patrick, *Architecture in Tennessee, 1768–1897* (Knoxville: University of Tennessee Press, 1981), 118. Kenneth Severens, *Southern Architecture* (New York: E.P. Dutton, 1981), 45. Wendell Garrett, *Classic America: The Federal Style and Beyond* (New York: Rizzoli, 1992), 292. Robert Gamble, "White-Column Tradition: Classical Architecture and the Southern Mystique," in Susan Ford Wiltshire, ed., *The Classical Tradition in the South: A Special Issue, Southern Humanities Review* (1977): 53–55. Rusticus, "Fruits, Flowers, &c," *Soil of the South* [Columbus, Georgia] 3, no. 1 (January 1853): 404. Kenneth Hafertepe, *Abner Cook, Master Builder on the Texas Frontier* (Austin: Texas State Historical Association, 1992), 142.

12   Severens, *Southern Architecture*, 44–45. John Forsyth, "Address . . . Before the Chunnenuggee Horticultural Society," May 1, 1851, *Soil of the South* [Columbus, Georgia] 1, no. 8 (August 1851): 125.

13   Michael W. Fazio and Patrick A. Snadon, s.v. "Greek Revival architecture," in Charles Reagan Wilson and William Ferris, eds., *Encyclopedia of Southern Culture* (Chapel Hill: University of

North Carolina Press, 1989), 18. James C. Bonner, "Plantation Architecture of the Lower South on the Eve of the Civil War," *Journal of Southern History* 11, no. 3 (August 1945): 380–81. Gamble, "White-Column Tradition," 55. Mills Lane, *Architecture of the Old South* (New York: Abbeville Press, 1993), 177.

14   J.C. Loudon, *The Suburban Gardener, and Villa Companion* (London: Longman *et al.*, 1838), 120. *Philadelphia Gazette and Daily Advertiser*, May 13, 1818, in Marcus Whiffen, *American Architecture Since 1780* (Cambridge: MIT Press, 1969), 153. Robert Mills, "The Architectural Works of Robert Mills," reprinted in Gifford, ed., *Literature of Architecture*, 89.

15   Town, advertisement, *New York Evening Post* (November 1, 1825), 4. Louisa C. Tuthill, *History of Architecture From the Earliest Times* (Philadelphia: Lindsay and Blakiston, 1848), 327.

16   [Tucker], "Thoughts," 560–63.

Chapter 8

Gwendolyn Wright

Independence and the rural cottage

To the majority of citizens in the early republic, the ideal American home was an independent homestead, attractive enough to encourage family pride yet unpretentious and economical. Itinerant artists, traveling across the countryside on horseback, specialized in paintings that portrayed these very qualities. Such artists decorated the interiors of homes with bright geometric patterns and naïve murals, and often did a painting of the family dwelling or a portrait of the family members. Rural women and young schoolgirls took the home as a favorite subject for their needlework samplers, surrounding the image of the simple, productive house and garden with virtuous proverbs or biblical quotations.

The country's leaders were surprisingly attentive to American predilections in domestic architecture. A few, such as Thomas Jefferson, were distressed about the aesthetic disarray that could result from thousands of quickly built, untutored dwellings, occupied for only a short time by restless homesteaders. For those who feared attacks on private property, even the forms seemed an invitation to anarchy. Jefferson was troubled by the impermanent look of most of the simple wooden houses in his native state of Virginia. He wanted to see an end to these "ugly, uncomfortable, and—happily—more perishable" dwellings.[1] A stable agrarian citizenry in substantial brick or stone houses would form a solid basis for the young nation's strength.

For Jefferson, and for many other civic leaders, there was a problem of guiding, but not regulating, domestic settings. How could Americans create an environment that protected the respect for order, self-sufficiency, and spirituality they held in common, without imposing on the freedom of each individual and each family to live as they pleased? The answer was the concept of the model home. Some prototypes could be small and inexpensive; each would be ornamented, so that the family would recognize their home as a place of beauty, repose, and Christian virtue. There was also a mechanical image at work here, a notion of continuous improvements on a templet to make the product better and cheaper. Optimistic belief in inevitable progress encouraged the assumption that aesthetic, technological, and social breakthroughs would keep occurring. This would not be a legislated model, based on regulations or laws everyone had to follow. Instead, it would be a guide, an inspiration that each builder and each family would adapt to the circumstances at hand. Several kinds of dwellings were publicized as model homes during these years, but the greatest attention was bestowed on the detached cottage for the independent farmer and his family. This rural home, like the family for whom it was designed, was considered the basis for America's strength and progress.

By 1830, ministers, schoolteachers, physicians, poets, and jurists all over the country were instructing their fellow citizens about good homes. Writers noted the trappings of an interior and the style of a façade as indications of the character of residents. The popular lady novelists Lydia Sigourney and "Fanny Fern" often relied on architectural description to enliven their stories and their moral advice to readers. So, too, did Henry David Thoreau, Washington Irving, and James Fenimore Cooper, who was especially vehement against the "mushroom" appearance of Greek Revival cottages, which seemed to spring up out of nowhere, unplanned, like an infestation.[2] Soon Henry Ward Beecher and Horace Bushnell were preaching to their congregations about an ideal home on earth, for which they gave occasional detailed specifications. Beecher even advertised household products and later wrote a sentimental novel, *Norwood* (1867). Bushnell's *Christian Nurture* (1847) described how the home and family life could foster virtuous "habits," thereby encouraging the development of gentle Christian children. Regulation and love would build "domesticity of character."[3] The right home environments could help assure the blessed eternal peace of "home comforts" in heaven. These writers all wanted Americans to become more aware of the power of "influence" they attributed to the domestic setting. They hoped families would create better homes and thereby strengthen the bonds of family life.

The task of defining the American home was a national mission. The goal was a general idea of the optimum setting for "the typical American family"—still depicted as an independent yeoman farmer and his hardworking immediate kin. This representative national home would not be the stately mansion of the wealthy, as if the grandest structure stood for the aspirations of the entire population. It was an average house for a family "of the middling sort."

There was, as yet, relatively little emphasis on the home as a unique statement, an individualized setting for a particular family. Increasingly, though, home and "outside world" came to be posed as separate spheres. True, the familiar communal festivities of the barn-raising, the quilting bee, and other less formal gatherings took place in the homes of any small village. At the same time, the private home was becoming the locus of a sentimental search for meaning and security. Authors of domestic guides spread this concept. According to Lydia Sigourney, one of the best-known writers of the early nineteenth century, the woman was responsible for perfecting an alternative to the commercial world where her husband and sons had to work:

> For she, with harmonizing will,
> Her pleasures in her duties found,
> And strove, with still advancing skill
> To make her home's secluded bound
> An Eden refuge, sweet and blest,
> When weary, he returned for rest.[4]

Duty to husband involved adorning the home in the image of a private haven, rich in simple beauty and her own homemade ornament.

Even more consummate was the woman's power as a mother. Around 1820, childhood suddenly became the focus of numerous books, sermons, and meetings. It was presented as a distinct period of development, quite separate from adult life yet critically determinant of later adult character. The Calvinist doctrine of the infant's inherent sinfulness gave way to a focus on the child's social nature and individual conscience, both of which were supposedly molded during the first few years of life. The family, in effect, created the child's personality and character. By 1830 child-rearing was seen as indisputably a female task, though not an innate skill. If a woman lived in a city, she might attend a maternal association, where women exchanged information. But for the most part, she had to rely on recently published books and magazines for advice. These described the awesome power of the mother and the home, and then intimated the course the mother should pursue in teaching her children values.

Increased attention to the individual, especially the individual child, and to the home as a place for moral education, encouraged a focus on private spaces within the home. Children who had misbehaved had to be isolated from their siblings for self-examination, Bushnell and other ministers explained. They should not be forced into a dark closet but into a small room for solitary reflection. A vigorous campaign against corporal punishment stressed the superior effect of the good home environment in the development of a strong personal conscience. While there was no thought given to the idea of private bedrooms for every child, the emphasis on increased privacy and greater specialization of rooms was evident.

Both Lydia Sigourney and Catharine Beecher, author of a *Treatise on Domestic Economy* (1843), insisted that each house needed separate areas for family social life, personal privacy, and household production. The kitchen and pantry were usually set off from the main body of the house in a rear wing. The frequent use of the phrase "work room" in guides and floor plans indicates that in most rural families, the wife and daughters spent much of their time here, making butter churns and curtains, soap and brooms, as well as preserving food, cooking, and washing clothes. In *Walden*, Thoreau lamented the tendency to isolate these activities architecturally, complaining that "there is as much secrecy about the cooking as if he [the host] had a desire to poison you"; but his protest went against the grain.[5]

Nomenclature announced the higher level of specialization in other areas as well. The "parlor" was the room where the family entertained visitors. The "sitting room" was for more intimate family gatherings in the evenings. A few larger houses contained both, but most designers had to choose the appropriate word, and they stressed its connection to a sociable or a family-centered domesticity.

Whichever word was used, the formal front room contained a great variety of pieces and styles, creating a rather festive air. In rural areas, it was common to paint stenciled decorations on the walls and to marbelize furniture in imitation of exotic woods. Machine-made rugs, geometric floor mosaics, and carefully swept arrangements of sand created a variety of patterns underfoot. Birdcages were common. With relatively little space allocated to storage in most houses, the walls were covered with hooks bearing hats, coats, framed pictures, farming and cooking utensils, and high shelves, where plates and platters were kept (Figure 8.1). By 1840, almost all New England women could read, and interest in education abounded throughout the country. Consequently, a bookshelf stood in most parlors. Since this room was the repository for "art," it usually contained family-made paper lace, landscape paintings, embroidery, and shadow boxes, together with the revered activity of such work in progress. This was the room for social events and daily family gatherings. The cover for the sheet music of an 1841 ballad entitled "My Mother's Bible" depicted a family gathered around the parlor table, while the father read by a kerosene light (Figure 8.2). A line from the song brought the setting and the sentiments together: "Again that little group is met within the halls of home." However, the idealized image has done away with the disarray and flamboyant decoration that would have been found in most homes.

In the 1840s, builders began to publish architectural books that brought together floor plans, details, perspective drawings, and empassioned texts, assuring readers that these house plans would enable them to create perfect homes (Figure 8.3). Many such "pattern books" contained specifications for all the buildings needed for a small town: a church, a school, a store, and a variety of houses, ranging from estimates of $200 to $20,000. In the titles of the books—Edward Shaw's *Rural Architecture* (1843), Alexander Jackson Davis's *Rural Residences* (1842), Andrew Jackson Downing's *Cottage Residences* (1842), or Calvert Vaux's *Villas and Cottages* (1854)—authors emphasized their variations of the authentic American rural cottage or farmhouse.

8.1 John Lewis Krimmel, *Quilting Frolic*, 1813

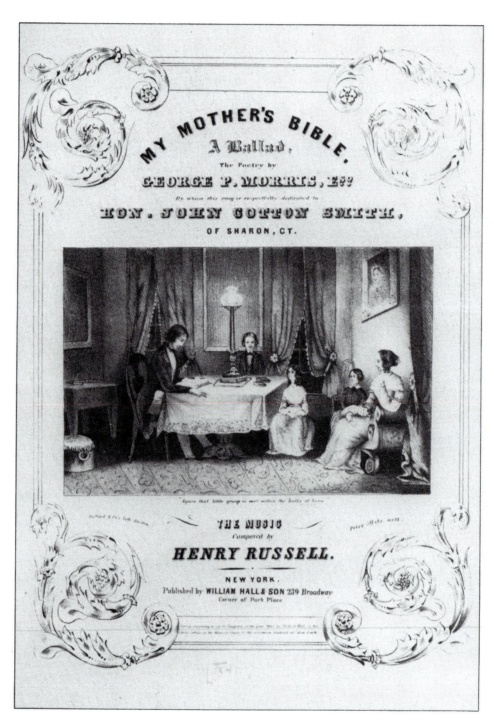

8.2 "My Mother's Bible: A Ballad," New York, 1841

8.3 Andrew Jackson Downing, Design for a Cottage (from his *The Architecture of Country Houses*, New York: D. Appleton and Co., 1850)

A typical proposal for a farmer's cottage showed four rooms—a parlor, family sitting room, workroom, and bedroom—as well as a hall, a porch, a pantry, and two closets, all squeezed into 525 square feet. In such a small area, rooms had to serve several functions. The sitting room doubled as a dining room and a children's bedroom. For larger houses, some designers included explanations of the newly defined spaces, proposing that an extra downstairs room could be used for an elderly relative's bedroom or for a sick child. Others suggested that a separate dining room would enhance domesticity. With this attention to use, the symmetrical placing of rooms was abandoned, even in the smallest cottage. The dwelling was evolving into a more intricate, specialized setting, with each room having a distinct shape.

Within the national prototype, builders presented ingenious variations of their model cottages. In *The Immigrant Builder* (1859), Charles Dwyer described inexpensive dwellings of sod blocks, rammed earth, adobe, and lightweight wood frame, so that a homesteader could use the cheapest materials of the region where he settled. Other authors showed more artistic variations, with the façades based on the myriad revival styles of nineteenth-century Europe. Each style corresponded to a particular terrain: a wooded hillside, a rocky seacoast, a plain, a town. There were still a number of Greek-style dwellings in these pattern books, but they seemed controlled and severe alongside the florid examples of Byzantine, Italianate, Gothic, Norman, Lombard, and Tudor styles. Davis boasted fourteen distinct styles in his book of house designs. Diversity had become fashionable.

Nineteenth-century builders actually spoke of "styles," not revivals, the term we use today for historical references in architecture. They were interested in evoking a mood, using certain architectural motifs to set the stage, rather than in presenting a clear portrait of a particular historical period. The effect of the new range of styles was an informality, a license to play with composition and ornament. The box shape of the house was broken; bay windows and porches formed a more complex outline. Medieval-inspired ornament and a pointed gable roof were evidence of the Gothic style; square bays, a heavy extending roof supported by brackets, and a campanile-like tower were the basis of the Italianate. Soon the creative possibilities open to the carpenter expanded these definitions. The rich, flat carving under roof barge boards, over doors and windows, dripping from shutters and porch supports—described then and now as "gingerbread"—was, in general, impossible to classify.

As pattern-book images germinated, they spread to other forms of literature. A Philadelphia publisher, Louis Antoine Godey, and his editor, Sarah Josepha Hale, decided to promote an "own-your-own-home" movement by featuring American villa and cottage designs in their monthly women's fashion journal. Between 1846 and 1898, *Godey's Lady's Book* published some 450 model house designs—the basis, according to one report, for over four thousand houses built in a single decade.[6] Readers who wrote to the journal's office received a complete set of drawings for any model house. The marriage in *Godey's* of sentimental poetry and prose, delicate feminine fashions, and idealized American homes brought together several kinds of specialized literature into a new discourse on domesticity.

The pattern books of Andrew Jackson Downing, a widely respected Hudson River Valley landscape gardener, offer a systematic presentation of this period's code of domesticity. Like other ante-bellum home designers, Downing foresaw a far-reaching, pastoral landscape, dotted with pleasant houses, varied but always orderly, each one set in its own extensive, well-tended garden. In his books on rural and suburban residential design, and in his editorials for *The Horticulturist*, Downing outlined his rules and categories for all American homes. First, houses should fit with their surroundings, for only certain styles appeared appropriate in particular settings. Second, houses should look like houses and not like other structures. Here Downing relied on the theory of associations developed by eighteenth-century English aesthetic philosophers. The value of an object or a view depended on deeply rooted symbolic associations it evoked. However, Downing and other American pattern-book writers challenged the idea that all associations were based on highly educated perceptions, for this had decidedly elitist overtones; instead, they asserted that many architectural forms—and particularly those of domestic buildings—elicited universal responses. Therefore, all houses needed certain domestic symbols to articulate the feelings AngloAmerican culture connected with the home. Downing called this "expression of purpose." Chimneys and overhanging roofs with high gables and deep eaves evoked home, as did the welcoming entry porch and the comfortable side piazza. Delicate ornament, such as Gothic trefoil tracery over a window or a carved Italianate bracket under the roof, reminded a viewer of the elegance and handiwork within. Gothic details also reinforced the religious ties of a Christian home.

According to Downing, who cited the English art critic John Ruskin, domestic architecture should express the owner's "condition" or class, his occupations, and background. (The man of the household was specifically the reference in this iconography.) Downing catalogued three kinds of houses for three groups in the society: villas for "persons of competence," cottages for mechanics or working men, and farmhouses for farmers. He felt that distinctions were necessary and that no one should try to present a grander image than was appropriate. "But *unless there is something of the castle in the man*," he wrote, "it is very likely, if it be like a real castle, to dwarf him to the stature of a mouse."[7] Every American deserved a good house, from the working man's undecorated cottage of rough wood to the wealthy man's Italian campanile tower. All the same, since no pattern-book designer could believe that anyone in America would remain either poor, a worker, or a servant for very long, they paid relatively little attention to the quality of housing for these classes.

Pattern-book designers considered themselves a critical component in the creation of a democratic republic. Their publications, which explained how to build good homes in the country, supposedly provided every citizen with the opportunity for independence. If all Americans had access to plans for orderly dwellings, adapted to every budget and region, then those who continued to live in rural hovels or crowded into unkempt urban tenements did so because they were less civilized, instinctively less drawn to the good models than were their neighbors. Henry Cleaveland, Charles Dwyer, and others considered this argument in some detail, positing a hierarchy that ran from animals to less-than-human savages (including poor whites) to a pinnacle of a virtuous, average American family living by Christian values in their own small cottage. Each included in his argument several examples of one-room and two-room cottages in rammed earth or rough logs to support the claim that a decent home was available to any American at almost no expense. There was no excuse for poverty.

Morality was central to Downing's vision and to that of most ante-bellum domestic designers. He called for "republican homes," comfortable and beautiful yet never so ostentatious as to belittle the neighbors or aggrandize the children's manners. Every American dwelling, he insisted, could be "a home of the virtuous citizen," if it were thoughtfully planned.[8] Downing posed domestic architecture as a counterforce to the "spirit of unrest" and the feverish pace of American life.[9] Yale theologian Timothy Dwight, writing of his travels through New England, had also worried about the power of the disorderly, unpleasant setting. "The habitation has not a little influence on the mode of living," he wrote, "and the mode of living sensibly affects the taste, manners, and even the morals, of the inhabitants. If a poor man builds a poor house, without any design or hope of possessing better, he will . . . conform his aims and expectations to the style of his house. His dress, his food, his manners, his taste, his sentiments, his education of his children, and their character as well as his own, will all be seriously affected by this ugly circumstance."[10] Downing's friend Nathaniel Willis (the brother of the novelist "Fanny Fern") wrote about the powerful symbolism of domesticity in his magazine, the *Home Monthly*. For Willis, too, morality was closely tied to control. He looked to "home associations" in architecture, landscaping, and literature to balance the franticness of "our plastic and rapidly maturing country."[11]

The cottages in pattern books were meant as family farmhouses, although many were erected in the small frontier towns that speculators built in promising locations. Despite the growing urban population, the nation was still overwhelmingly rural. Every writer on domestic life and architecture and every communitarian "social architect" insisted that true men and women could be raised only in the country. Nathaniel Willis was one of many who connected rural virtues to republican values: "[W]hile a family *in town* may be governed and held together mainly by money, there is a republic within the ring fence of a *country residence*."[12] Anti-urban sentiment was widespread, and it extended beyond a fear of the poor. A book describing the homes of famous national authors captured the mood with its passing references to urban habitations, with their "dreary monotony of front. . . . houses which are mere parallelograms of air."[13] Rural Americans wanted diversity and symbolism, an Eden of interest and delights away from the city.

Given these sentiments, builders were quick to play up natural materials in domestic construction. Pattern books praised unpainted wood siding. Vertical board-and-batten was favored because it represented the simple wood studs of the structure beneath the sheathing. If paint were used, it was to be of a hue that would harmonize with the natural surroundings: russets, lichen greens, and grays replaced the white of Greek temples. Every pattern-book writer agreed that a house looked best when it was made of timber, stone, or clay found in the surrounding area rather than more expensive, fashionable materials transported from afar.

Insistence on local materials often translated into an attack on aristocratic luxury and a sentimental celebration of the homes of the rural poor. Writers warbled that the most beautiful paintings, which evoked the noblest sentiments in the observer, portrayed the humble farm rather than the mansion. In *Walden*, Thoreau called upon all suburbanites to remember this fact when choosing a house design, and to opt for the least pretentious style. (He went so far as to champion the model of the Indian community in which, he claimed, every family had a shelter as good as the best; simplicity was thus the key to equality as well as the mark of goodness and beauty.) Not even the impermanence and coarseness of the crudest frontier house could quell pride in American design. As one pattern-book author claimed: "[W]e are proud of the flimsy, unsubstantial structures, so sneered at by foreigners, which dot the whole face of the country. They are the homes of the people, who will by-and-by build and own better ones."[14] Homespun rusticity was an admirable aesthetic to these builders, who carefully cultivated the primitive in their drawings and in their rhetoric.

The cult of the ordinary and commonplace—what Emerson exalted in *The American Scholar* as "the common . . . the familiar, the low"—extended to a romance with the log cabin.[15] Such a construction type was actually a Scandinavian model, comparatively rare on the frontier; but by the late 1830s, writers of all national backgrounds claimed the rugged American log cabin as a common cultural heritage. The fad reached new proportions with the studied populism of Jacksonian Democrats. Supporters of Harrison's 1840 presidential campaign then took it up, passing out pamphlets and hard cider from makeshift log cabins, and proclaiming the cabin as a symbol of solid American frontier vigor. Catching the enthusiasm, pattern-book designers included idealized drawings of log cabins among their model houses, praising the supposedly indigenous forms and the visibly hardy strength of the materials.

Celebration of the natural and the ordinary was not particular to America, of course. Throughout Europe, the rise of romanticism brought a widespread fascination with the natural and the unspoiled, whether magnificent or commonplace. Appeals that the builder take the surrounding landscape into account—a general formula by 1840—cited eighteenth-century English theorists of the picturesque. American styles were also derivative. Even the Greek Revival, the symbol of national independence, took place after a classical revival in England and on the continent. The Gothic Revival, which followed, combined a glorification of the American landscape with architectural reminders of European history.

While acknowledging these influences, American builders, unlike most professionally trained architects, saw it as their duty to introduce originality. The theme of national unity through intense individualism and artistic creation ran through every pattern book. Stylistic inventiveness was lauded as a way to be fashionable and to assert cultural independence. By the 1850s, builders were mixing styles and playing with decorative motifs quite freely. They introduced daring "inventions"—hexagonal or circular dwellings, with rooms cut into unusual elliptical shapes or curious wedges. By far the most popular of these eccentricities was the octagon house. In *A Home for All* (1848), the phrenologist and spiritualist Orson Fowler claimed that the octagon was a 20 percent more efficient use of a given square-foot area, and intimated that it possessed certain mystical powers. For a decade, octagonal dwellings, schoolhouses, and other structures were erected from Natchez to San Francisco.

Fowler's functionalist argument echoed the self-praise of other builders who claimed that their housing models were "built to live in," based on "common sense," while those in rival books were too expensive and elitist, preoccupied with aesthetics at the expense of practicalities. The desire to use science and technology—or sometimes pseudo-science and gadgetry—for the common good of the society was another distinguishing feature of American romanticism.

In building, the most important technological innovation of the ante-bellum years was the balloon frame. This type of construction, first used in Chicago in 1839, radically transformed the work of building a house. The earlier method had relied on heavy pieces of lumber, connected by hand-cut pegs and mortise-and-tenon joints; an entire frame wall was fitted on the ground and lifted into place by a crew of men. The balloon frame, as its name implies, was based on much lighter, pre-cut pieces of lumber, held together with nails. It required fewer workers, and much less time and expense. The factory production of nails and the mill cutting of standardized sizes of lumber made the balloon frame available to carpenters and self-sufficient individual builders along any well traveled route.

A keen interest in applied science and innovative home technology spurred the patenting of countless household conveniences at mid-century, including ice cutters, pie sectioners, cherry pitters, and lawn mowers. The word "gadget" (from the French *gachette*, a piece of machinery) entered the national vocabulary. Builders had at least one chapter on domestic technology in their guides, including instructions for an open wooden drainpipe to carry off waste water from the kitchen, a concrete cesspool, or a fresh-water cistern, with its charcoal and ash filter beneath a false floor. Because almost every household had to rely on its own system of water supply and its own provisions for waste disposal, these were also carefully described. Even in the large cities, except for Philadelphia, the provision of municipal reservoirs and waterworks was relatively recent, and there were no controls over the delivery of services by private companies. Household technology showed the need to ensure health on a private basis, as well as Yankee ingenuity.

Despite the interest in technological innovations and the homogenizing influence of pattern-book designs, the late colonial styles remained the basis for much of the construction that took place west of the Alleghenies throughout the first half of the century. American romanticism in architecture had a distinctly conservative side. Families from England brought with them the knowledge of how to construct a simple foursquare frame dwelling, its façade unadorned, save for symmetrically placed windows and doors. Dutch, Germans, or Scandinavians, who began to immigrate in large numbers after 1830, reproduced approximations of the houses they had known, with high brick or stone corbels on the side, plastered masonry, and small, asymmetrically placed windows. Dwellings of the western cities and rural areas were generally simpler than those in or near the established cities of the eastern seaboard. The nationally popular styles such as the Greek or Gothic appeared much later in the West. This was due in part to the hold of the immigrants' diverse cultural traditions and in part to a shortage of time and skilled labor. Yet Lexington or Cincinnati or Cleveland could boast merchants' houses as fashionable as any in Philadelphia or Boston. Stylistic constraint and simplicity of forms, especially in the early houses of frontier towns, was also an expression of many settlers' belief that they would soon be moving to a better house. A definite pattern was established early on. Seeking to escape the pressures of a limited land supply, Americans tied social mobility, as well as economic security, to property ownership.

The most conspicuous theme in American model cottages, as in actual homes of the mid-nineteenth century, was privatism. Each pattern-book drawing showed a single, isolated dwelling surrounded by a carefully tended garden. Occasional double houses appeared, but designers stressed separate entrances for each family and thick party walls. They also declared that these were transitional dwellings for families who would surely go on to their own private dwelling. As one commentator explained, Americans tended to enjoy associations with others in their politics but not in their homes.[16] The suspicion of urban row houses, communitarian settlements, and industrial boardinghouses was both political and architectural. In builders' guides and in other forms of popular literature, detached dwellings in the countryside were taken as the symbol of certain key national virtues. On an individual level, they represented personal independence. On a social level, they showed family pride and self-sufficiency. Politically, the architecture seemed an expression of democratic freedom of choice. And economically, it mirrored the pattern of private enterprise, rather than planning for the overall public good, which characterized American society.

Notes

1   Thomas Jefferson, *Notes on the State of Virginia* (1785; reprint ed., New York: W. W. Norton & Co., 1972), p. 418.
2   James Fenimore Cooper, *Home as Found* (1838; reprint ed., New York: D. Appleton, 1902), pp. 125–30.
3   See Bernard Wishy, *The Child and the Republic* (Philadelphia: University of Pennsylvania Press, 1968); Anne L. Kuhn, *The Mother's Role in Childhood Education: New England Concepts, 1830–1860* (New Haven: Yale University Press, 1947); Daniel Calhoun, *The Intelligence of a People* (Princeton: Princeton University Press, 1974), pp. 132–305; Philip J. Greven, Jr., *The Protestant Temperament: Patterns of Child-Rearing, Religious Experience and the Self in Early America* (New York: Alfred A. Knopf, 1977); and Barbara M. Cross, *Horace Bushnell: Minister to a Changing America* (Chicago: University of Chicago Press, 1958).
4   Lydia Sigourney, *The Western Home and Other Poems* (Philadelphia: Parry & MacMillan, 1854), p. 31.
5   Henry David Thoreau, *Walden: or, Life in the Woods* (1854; reprint ed., Garden City, N.Y.: Doubleday & Co., 1960), p. 207.
6   George L. Hersey, "Godey's Choice," *Journal of the Society of Architectural Historians* 18 (October 1959): 104. Also see Ruth E. Findley *The Lady of Godey's: Sarah Josepha Hale* (Philadelphia: J. P. Lippincott, 1931) and Isabelle Webb Entrekin, *Sarah Josepha Hale and Godey's Lady's Magazine* (Philadelphia: J. P. Lippincott, 1946).
7   Andrew Jackson Downing, *The Architecture of Country Houses* (1850: reprint ed., New York: Dover Publications, 1969), p. 262.
8   Ibid., pp. xix–xx, 269–70.
9   Andrew Jackson Downing, *Rural Essays* (1854; reprint ed., New York: Da Capo Press, 1974), pp. 13, 202.
10 Timothy Dwight, *Travels in New-England and New York*, 4 vols. (1821–22; reprint ed., Cambridge: Harvard University Press, 1969), 4: 73.
11 Nathaniel Willis, *The Rag-Bag, A Collection of Ephemera* (New York: Charles Scribner, 1855), p. 36.

12   Nathaniel Willis, *Out-Doors at Idlewild, or, the Shaping of a Home on the Banks of the Hudson* (New York: Charles Scribner, 1855), p. 447.

13   *Homes of American Authors* (1853), p. 124, cited in Kirk Jeffrey, Jr., "Family History: The Middle-Class American Family in the Urban Context, 1830–1870" (Ph.D. diss., Stanford University, 1971), p. 72.

14   Daniel Harrison Jacques, *The House: A Pocket-Manual of Rural Architecture* (New York: Fowler & Wells, 1859), p. 29.

15   Ralph Waldo Emerson, *The American Scholar* (1837), in *Selections from Ralph Waldo Emerson*, ed. Stephen E. Whicher (Boston: Houghton Mifflin, 1957), p. 78.

16   Gervase Wheeler, *Homes for the People in Suburb and Country* (New York: Charles Scribner, 1855), pp. 25–26.

Part 3 |

Materialism and mediation in the Gilded Age

During the last three decades of the nineteenth century, the US experienced explosive economic and urban growth. The post-Civil War period was a great age of optimism for much of the country, an age of enterprise and of great appetites. It was also an era of pervasive anxiety over those very appetites, of economic instability and terrible poverty for many, and of widespread efforts—often profound—to reconcile materialism with "high" culture, religion, and traditional values. Architecture in this climate became an important vehicle for legitimizing the new corporate and commercial culture, a means of mediating between base materialism and higher, less tangible goals and values.

The first essay in this section, by material culture historian Kenneth L. Ames, analyzes the domestic space and furnishings of the Victorian-era, middle-class front hall. Alluding to the contemporary field of "impression management," Ames presents these spaces and artifacts as part of a highly self-conscious effort to structure and manage the increasingly complex and unstable social relations and perceptions emerging in the period. As Ames shows, if hall furnishings displayed the social and economic status of their owners, they also served to stimulate memory and sentiment, and to support social bonding.

Moving from the domestic to the public realm, Daniel Bluestone offers a revisionist reading of the first great wave of Chicago skyscrapers. Undoubtedly, late nineteenth-century Chicago was—as it is usually described—a brash, raw, aggressively competitive, commercial city; yet it was also a city whose leading citizens harbored significant cultural aspirations. Unlike mid-twentieth-century observers, who emphasized the proto-modernist minimalism and structural rationalism of the city's early skyscrapers, the people who built and first used these structures valued their material comfort and convenience, their luxurious materials and refined, artful ornamentation and interior design. According to Bluestone, these buildings "made a greater effort to transcend commercial utility than to express it symbolically." They operated to legitimize the new corporations they housed and to ennoble the new forms of white-collar, middle-class work they enabled. Ultimately, "skyscrapers helped to redefine downtown as an acceptable arena for both respectable gentlemen and ladies."

Cultural geographer Mona Domosh, likewise, studies architecture's role in legitimizing new forms of commercial activity and social behavior. Domosh examines the evolving culture of shopping, including department store architecture and the larger commercial districts of which they were a part—particularly along New York's so-called

"Ladies Mile." For production to expand, it was necessary that consumption expand along with it. Retail shopping thus became a daily ritual for many middle- and upper-class women, a preeminent form of women's work. Accommodating these women involved the creation of new, "feminized" urban environments—safe, respectable, elegant theaters of display and consumption, where commerce and culture, fashion and religion were artfully combined.

By the century's end, an exuberant and often grandiose classicism, inspired by the architecture of the Italian Renaissance, became the dominant mode of "high-style" design. While serving the forces of commerce and industry—in the form of railroad stations, bank buildings, corporate headquarters, world's fair pavilions, and dwellings for the most rapacious capitalists—classical architecture and related City Beautiful planning schemes also embodied a widespread belief in America's role as the rightful heir to the great themes and achievements of Western Civilization. Richard Guy Wilson closes this section by investigating the "special relationship" many turn-of-the-century Americans felt they had with the Italian Renaissance—"a philosophical and moral force" they pondered as their own country rose to previously unimaginable levels of wealth and power.

Further reading

Bradley, B. H., *The Works: The Industrial Architecture of the United States*, New York: Oxford University Press, 1999.

Cronen, W., *Nature's Metropolis: Chicago and the Great West*, New York: W. W. Norton and Co., 1991.

Giberti, B., *Designing the Centennial: A History of the 1876 International Exhibition in Philadelphia*, Lexington, KY: University Press of Kentucky, 2002.

Harris, N., *Cultural Excursions: Marketing Appetites and Cultural Tastes in Modern America*, Chicago, IL: University of Chicago Press, 1990.

Jackson, J. B., *American Space: The Centennial Years, 1865–1976*, New York: W. W. Norton, 1972.

Landau, S. B. and C. W. Condit, *The Rise of the New York Skyscraper, 1865–1913*, New Haven, CT: Yale University Press, 1996.

Ryan, M. P., *Civic Wars, Democracy and Public Life in the American City in the Nineteenth Century*, Berkeley, CA: University of California Press, 1997.

Schuyler, D., *The New Urban Landscape: The Redefinition of City Form in Nineteenth-Century America*, Baltimore, MD: The Johns Hopkins University Press, 1986.

Siry, J., *Carson Pirie Scott: Louis Sullivan and the Chicago Department Store*, Chicago, IL: University of Chicago Press, 1988.

Siry, J., *The Chicago Auditorium Building: Adler and Sullivan's Architecture and the City*, Chicago, IL: University of Chicago Press, 2002.

Trachtenberg, A., *The Incorporation of America: Culture and Society in the Gilded Age*, New York: Hill and Wang, 1982.

Van Slyck, A., *Free To All: Carnegie Libraries and American Culture, 1890–1920*, Chicago, IL: University of Chicago Press, 1995.

Weingarden, L. S., "Naturalized Nationalism: A Ruskinian Discourse on the Search for an American Style of Architecture," *Winterthur Portfolio* 24: 1 (1989): 43–68.

Wilson, W. H., *The City Beautiful Movement*, Baltimore, MD: The Johns Hopkins University Press, 1989.

Wright, G., *Moralism and the Model Home: Domestic Architecture and Cultural Conflict in Chicago, 1873–1913*, Chicago, IL: University of Chicago Press, 1980.

Chapter 9

Kenneth L. Ames

First impressions
Front halls and hall furnishings in Victorian America

First impressions. You can make them only once. An accurate observation, but hardly new. Victorian Americans were acutely aware of the power of first impressions. They knew that what people saw first had a disproportionate impact on the formation of opinions and judgments. It was because they understood so well the importance of first impressions that the Victorians created distinctive forms of material culture to mold and manipulate them.

The modern term for this behavior is *impression management*.[1] When we hear people speak of impression management today, it is usually in the context of the corporate world. The ability to manage people's perceptions can put someone on the road to success in human relations generally and in business in particular. The Victorians had a somewhat different orientation, for while they shared today's commercial values, the current high status accorded to corporate life was only beginning to emerge in the second half of the nineteenth century.[2] In Victorian America the domestic realm was still the major arena for acting out social strategies. The furnishings people put in the hallways of their houses, the first interior spaces visitors saw, played important roles in shaping first impressions and in framing and manipulating Victorians' perceptions of themselves and their relationships to others (Figure 9.1). Hall furnishings were widespread and prominent components of the Victorian system of impression management.

It may seem a bit peculiar to speak of hallways and first impressions. Obviously, before visitors even entered a house, they acquired data they could evaluate from the city, the neighborhood, and the exterior of that house. All this information, however, was external to the house and was understood to be superficial, potentially misleading, even suspect. The interiors of people's houses provided more accurate, more authentic information about them. Moving inside a house brought someone into a more intimate association with its inhabitants. Knowing the inner house was something like knowing the inner person. Exteriors of houses and houses unfurnished spoke of architects and builders. But the insides of houses and houses furnished spoke of the life that went on within and the character of those who lived it.

This chapter is about hall furnishings, the first clues of that inner domestic life in Victorian America. My argument is that these objects, little appreciated today, were once significant parts of a deliberate and pervasive strategy to ceremonialize and ritualize the commonplace activities of everyday life. They played important roles in a style of life that was highly self-conscious and tightly scripted. They were critical components of an

9.1 Charles Parsons and Lyman Atwater, *The Four Seasons of Life: Middle Age*, James Merritt Ives delineator, published by Currier and Ives, New York, 1868

elaborate artifactual system that was central to the Victorians' understanding of themselves and their place in the world. They were tools for managing not only impressions but comprehensions, cosmologies.

To understand hall furnishings we need to know something about halls, for these spaces and their relationship to other spaces in houses had some influence on the objects placed within them. I say "some" because I do not want to suggest that architectural or spatial determinism was at work here. Architecture and space enabled a certain mode of furnishing but did not dictate it. Cultural factors were far more important. This becomes clear when we recognize that halls in many nineteenth-century houses were often nearly identical in plan, proportion, and scale to those in eighteenth-century houses. What differentiated the later buildings from the earlier were cultural conventions of use and meaning—and thus of furnishing. One of these was the premise of specialization, a cornerstone of capitalism and a pervasive characteristic of Victorian material culture.[3] In Victorian America, each room of a house was understood to perform a distinctive set of functions. These functions were revealed, served, and advanced by an equally distinctive set of artifacts. Specialization was more frequently demonstrated through furnishings than through any intrinsic properties of the rooms themselves. In other words, unfurnished, eighteenth- and nineteenth-century halls looked pretty much the same; furnished, they looked dramatically different. The movable material culture—that is, culture in visible, tangible, and portable form—made all the difference.[4]

As these comments may suggest, middle- and upper-middle-class domestic building in America has been more notable for continuity than lack of it. A few basic ideas, altered occasionally by ideological, economic, or other factors, underlie the spatial organization of most single-family, free-standing houses.[5] It is possible to assign most middle- and upper-middle-class houses of the nineteenth century to one of two classes on the basis of hall type. The first type of hall, popular into the fourth quarter of the century, was a relatively narrow passage that connected the outside of the house to its interior spaces. This type was based on late Renaissance ideas introduced to this country in the eighteenth century with the Georgian style. Although frequently obscured by an overlay of complicated ornament or lively asymmetry, Georgian concepts of spatial organization were perpetuated in Victorian houses; many nineteenth-century plans closely resemble eighteenth-century examples. A characteristic feature of these houses of the Georgian-Victorian continuum was the conceptualization of the hall as a passage. Until about 1880, this was the dominant mode.[6]

In the second and later type of hall, the passage was expanded into a large living space. Derived from medieval great halls and the multifunction rooms of pre-Georgian dwellings in colonial America and associated with the English reform movement, this type was widely published and illustrated in the last quarter of the century and became a prominent feature of many architect-designed houses.[7]

These two hall alternatives can be related to two different conceptual models for domestic structures and domestic life in the nineteenth century. The first was the courtly

9.2 John Riddell, Plan for Cottage No. 12 (from his *Architectural Designs for Model Country Residences*, Philadelphia: John Riddle, Lindsay and Blakiston, 1861)

vision of the house as villa or palace. The second was a more consciously domestic notion of the house as hereditary estate or old homestead.[8] My emphasis here is on the pre-reform model of the house as palace and the hall as passage. It was for this physical and cultural setting that Victorian America created its most innovative and distinctive hall furnishings.

A typical upper-middle-class house plan illustrates the characteristics of this concept of hall (Figure 9.2). The space was usually 6 to 8 feet wide and 12 to 20 feet long, or considerably longer if it ran all the way from the front of the house to the back, as it does here. Its chief architectural embellishments were the framed doorways to parlor, drawing room, library, dining room, or the outside, and the stair and its ornamented newel post (Figure 9.3). Little or no communal activity took place in this form of hall. Its shape, dimensions, and placement emphasized its primary functions as connector and separator of rooms. In most houses of this class, people did not enter directly from the outside into one of the living spaces but rather into the hall (or into the hall through a vestibule).[9] Although it was possible to move from some rooms to others without entering the hall, it was also possible to enter each room from the hall without passing through any other, thus preserving privacy and the specialized function of each space. With this arrangement, social peers of the homeowners could visit in the formal spaces of the house,

9.3 Front hall of Joseph R. Walker House, Salt Lake City, Utah, *c.*1900

while social inferiors remained in the hall or were directed elsewhere and kept from intruding on the family or its guests. In other words, this form of hall emphasized control and hierarchy.

The hall just described might be identified more precisely as a front hall. Many houses with a front hall also had a back hall, which was sometimes an extension of the front hall, sometimes another, smaller corridor adjacent to it. A back hall was not necessarily a discrete space; in some cases, its function was incorporated within another room. [. . .] To divide the front hall from the back, and formal space from utilitarian, there was usually some real or symbolic barrier—a door, lower ceiling, narrower passage, or change in wall or floor materials or finish. There was also a rear stair, usually narrower and steeper than the front stair and free of architectural pretense. This creation of separate and unequal halls and stairs mirrored the segregation of ceremonial and utilitarian functions within houses and the division of nineteenth-century society into two broad classes: served and servant.

Similar stratification was seen in the way the plans of upper-middle-class houses were conceptually divisible into two units. The first, larger than the other, was the formal or ceremonial portion of the house. Behind it, performing the mundane duties that sustained the former, was the service section, consisting of kitchen, pantry, and laundry room. The significant difference in the way the two areas were conceived was reflected in their decorative treatment. The front section was architecture as John Ruskin understood it; the rear was only building. Designs for facades of houses appeared in architectural books in great numbers, but backs were rarely shown, for the front belonged to ceremony and first impressions, but the rear only to utility. The front stair was for dramatic and gracious descent to meet family and guests; the back stair was for servants carrying slop buckets and dirty laundry. This spatial arrangement of Victorian homes documents social realities and distinctions that have largely disappeared in the northern parts of the United States.[10]

HALLSTANDS

Although they were formal and ceremonial spaces, front halls were usually too small for much furniture. Very large front halls sometimes contained a table, stand, or pedestal, and two chairs or a settee or both. Most halls, regardless of size, contained at least a hallstand. Unlike most furniture of its era, the hallstand has no obvious historical antecedents. It is a nineteenth-century invention, a Victorian original. Appearing around the time of Victoria's accession, the life cycle of the hallstand parallels the course of Victorian America. After the middle of the century, the hallstand became more popular and the focus of considerable design attention. It attained its greatest elaboration and monumentality in the 1860s and 1870s, was rethought and reformed in the 1880s, then gradually declined in scale and importance. By 1920, the hallstand was largely extinct.[11] And so was Victorian culture.

Examples of typical hallstands of the late 1870s are illustrated [here] (Figure 9.4). Some were manufactured in Grand Rapids, Michigan, noted for quality furniture for the

Plate 22.

J.W. KIMBALL, DESIGNER & PUBLISHER, HOTEL BRUNSWICK, BOSTON.

9.4 Hallstands and hall chairs, manufactured by Conrad Edkhardt, New York, New York (from J. Wayland Kimball, *Kimball's Book of Designs: Furniture and Drapery*, Boston: J. Wayland Kimball, 1876)

middle-and upper-middle-class markets.[12] Others were made in New York City. They show that although the decorative details varied considerably, a high degree of consistency prevailed in the overall concept of the form. Four functional components were generally incorporated: provisions for umbrellas, hooks or pegs for hats and coats, a looking glass, and a small table, often with a drawer and a marble top. Each of these components was conceptually separable from the others, but the synthesis of the four, or sometimes only the first three, into an architecturally conceived whole constituted a hallstand.

Provisions for umbrellas normally followed the arrangement shown here. Crook-shaped or armlike devices mounted on each side of the stand at a height of about 25 to 30 inches above the floor supported the upper ends of the umbrellas. In the base of the hallstand, one or two dished receptacles caught and held whatever water might drip from them. Cast-iron pans were the most common. Inexpensive hallstands had thin sheet-metal boxes, but expensive hallstands, particularly those built in as part of the woodwork, had marble dishes. Regardless of the material, all served to protect the floor or carpet and keep the umbrella accessible.[13]

That such an impressive piece of furniture should be designed for such an apparently mundane purpose indicates something about the status of umbrellas. From a twentieth-century perspective, the umbrella might be called the insigne of the Victorian age. The umbrella's long and eventful history has been recorded by several artifact historians.[14] The umbrella was well known in antiquity in both Europe and Asia, but its modern history stems from contacts between the East and West during the Renaissance. It came from Asia by sea to Portugal and by land to Italy, spreading from these places to others. At the outset, the umbrella was associated with high status; slaves or servants held umbrellas over their owners or employers when they walked in public. By the eighteenth century, the umbrella and a related form, the parasol, had become relatively common. They were depicted frequently in paintings and prints of that period and were mentioned in written documents. The parasol served largely a cosmetic purpose, protecting women's skin from the rays of the sun. Although its use spread through many levels of society, the parasol remained a mark of women of leisure. The umbrella performed a more utilitarian function. It was commonly carried by men after the middle of the eighteenth century. Perhaps because the wealthy owned carriages that protected them from the weather, carrying an umbrella became associated with lesser affluence and, sometimes, republican sentiments. In the nineteenth century, the umbrella became a bourgeois attribute, a portable emblem of respectability. Its prominence reflects a culture pervaded by middle-class values.

The hallstand's provisions for hats and coats underline the nineteenth-century emphasis on attire and appearance. The popularity of the hallstand coincides with that of the top hat, which in its most extreme form became the "stovepipe" hat of Abraham Lincoln and his generation. James Laver has argued that the top hat was what we would call *macho* today. He further argues that such assertions of masculinity are most extreme at the time of greatest role differentiation between the sexes. He associates the gradual decline of the top hat with that of male-dominated society.[15]

Hats and coats were usually hung on turned wooden pegs on moderately priced hall-stands and on small bronzed or gilt metal hooks on more costly pieces. Regardless of material, they rarely projected more than 6 inches or so from the surface of the hallstand. There were generally only six or eight pegs or hooks arranged symmetrically around the mirror. The relatively few attachments for hats, coats, cloaks, or other outer garments make it clear that the hallstand was not intended as open storage. Only a limited number of objects could be placed on it. An analysis of period photographs may help determine what, if any, rules governed the selection. Some homes had storage closets near the hall. Others had closets behind the stair, easily accessible from the hall, yet they still had a hallstand in the front hall.[16] When large numbers of people came to a party, coats were apparently placed on beds in the bedrooms, as they are today. Therefore, there were reasons other than storage for placing garments on the hallstand. I suggest what these reasons might have been after discussing the two remaining components.

The hallstand's third component, the mirror, underlined again the Victorian fixation with personal appearance, but had additional ramifications. Mirrors were a Victorian convention. They appeared where they still do in twentieth-century interiors—on walls in bedrooms and dressing rooms; on chests of drawers, dressing tables, and wardrobes; and

For the most part, cards were supposed to be left in person. Some etiquette books suggested that cards could be sent with a messenger or by mail. Others took a less flexible stance and maintained that it was a breach of etiquette to do anything but deliver them oneself. Certainly not to do so violated the concept of conspicuous leisure and the idea that the relationship was meaningful, for to mail cards or send them with a servant suggested that a woman had household responsibilities or some other activity she valued more highly. Related to the emphasis on leisure was the requirement that cards be left between noon and five o'clock in the afternoon. Since these were normal business hours, it is clear that most men could not be expected to leave cards. They were at work,

9.7 Silver and gold-plated card receivers (from the trade catalog of Reed & Barton, Taunton, Massachusetts, 1885)

conforming to the ideology of separate spheres, while their wives engaged in the parallel work of creating and sustaining social bonds.[32]

Cards were critical components of ceremonial calling. This ritual encompassed what we might call primary calling and secondary calling, human interaction and artifact interaction. When individuals were not present, cards sometimes became their surrogates. Since husbands did not normally accompany their wives when they paid calls, the wife could leave her husband's card where she visited. If the lady of the house being visited was at home, the lady visitor could leave two of her husband's cards, one for the lady and the other for her husband. To leave her own card would have been redundant, since she had already seen the lady of the house in person.

If the same woman were paying calls and the woman she intended to visit was not at home, she might leave three cards, one of her own and two of her husband's. The latter two were to be distributed as before, but her card would be left for the mistress of the house; "a lady leaves a card for a lady only." This cult of protecting the virtue of matrons extended to that of maidens as well, for in some circles it was not considered appropriate for a young lady to have visiting cards of her own. Her name was printed beneath that of her mother on the latter's card. The use of *Miss* on a card was often reserved for older unmarried women.[33]

The card ritual associated with ceremonial calling was in many ways a social perpetual-motion machine that, once set going among equals, could not with propriety be stopped unless one party died or moved away.[34] Among social unequals, it could be halted when the superior ignored the inferior. When there was no intention to visit but only to maintain contact, to sustain a bond, a woman merely handed three cards to a servant, who presumably placed them in the card receiver, the contents of which were later sorted and evaluated.[35] Whatever the intention of the individual—to pay a visit or only a surrogate visit by way of a card—a kind of social code of Hammurabi prevailed: a card for a card, a call for a call. A person of equal or lower social status, visited or called on, was obliged to reciprocate.

Rules governed how and when people of different social status might interact. Calling or only leaving a card could signal differing degrees of intimacy. Among social equals, the law cited here was normally in operation. In cases of obvious social distinction, the situation was different. If a woman of higher social position returned a card with a call, it was considered a compliment. If the roles were reversed and a woman of lower social status returned a card with the more intimate, more familiar call instead of just a card, the gesture could be interpreted as brash or presumptuous.

The use of cards and servants as barriers was extensive in the last century. For example, a man wishing to meet a young woman could arrange to have his card left at her home by a female friend. If the young woman had no interest in meeting him, the solution was simple: His card was not noticed. Similarly, an intended visit could be reduced to the level of a call through the expedient of having the servant announce that someone was "not at home." This fiction observed the letter of the social law of calling while acknowledging that other needs might occasionally take precedence over this ritual.[36]

Today, much of the activity associated with calling, with impression management and contact maintenance, takes place in business rather than private life. Telephone calls are our cards, and secretaries—or answering machines—the servants who announce that the important person is at a meeting or cannot be reached. Yet even if some aspects of these rituals survive, contemporary American society no longer cherishes the same set of values the Victorians did or expresses itself in the same ways. The Victorians believed in the ceremonies of daily life as ways to attain elegance and personal nobility, as ways to demonstrate to themselves and others their high level of civilization and their exceptional control over themselves and their world. These self-consciously civilized people embraced social competition while they endorsed social bonding. Yet there was clearly more behind hall furnishings of the nineteenth century than conspicuous consumption, invidious comparison, and self-congratulation. These elaborated objects emphasized and enshrined personal possessions. Hats, coats, umbrellas, and cards were social tools, but they were also tangible pieces of human lives. As such, they touched the emotional, sentimental side of a culture also fascinated by memory and connectedness. Behind these hall furnishings, partly concealed by their courtly, formal facades, were cultural impulses much like those we locate more easily in souvenirs, albums, and popular songs like "The Old Arm Chair," "The Old Oaken Bucket," and "Home, Sweet Home."

If the people who owned the objects we have been discussing could vigorously defend social station and privilege, they could also be moved by associations and relationships with their friends and relatives. The objects they placed in their halls revealed not only these competing facets of the Victorian personality but the very nature of the hall. For it was a space that was neither wholly interior nor exterior but a sheltered, social testing zone that some moved through with ease and familiarity and others never passed beyond. For the latter, first impressions were often final impressions.

Notes

1   On the so-called primacy effect, see David I. Kertzer, *Ritual, Politics, and Power* (New Haven: Yale University Press, 1988), 83; and Richard Nisbett and Lee Ross, *Human Inference: Strategies and Shortcomings of Social Judgment* (Englewood Cliffs, N.J.: Prentice-Hall, 1980). On impression management, see James T. Tedeschi, ed., *Impression Management Theory and Social Psychological Research* (New York: Academic Press, 1981). See also Dale Carnegie, *How to Win Friends and Influence People* (New York: Simon & Schuster, 1964). First impressions are also directly related to cognitive development. A typical nineteenth-century statement of this understanding is found in Jean Paul Richter, "Thoughts," *The Diadem* (Philadelphia: Carey & Hart, 1846): "In advanced age the grandest moral examples pass by us, and our life-course is no more altered by them than the earth is by a flitting comet; but in childhood the first object that excites the sentiment of love or of injustice flings broad and deep its light or shadow over the coming years" (p. 71).

2   For various perspectives on this issue, see Alan Trachtenberg, *The Incorporation of America* (New York: Hill and Wang, 1982); T. J. Jackson Lears, *No Place of Grace: Anti-Modernism and the Transformation of American Culture* (New York: Pantheon, 1981); Mark Twain and Charles Dudley Warner, *The Gilded Age: A Tale of To-Day* (Hartford: American Publishing Co., 1874); and the observations of various foreign visitors to this country during the nineteenth century.

3   In the most general terms, American middle-class housing can be said to shift from few multi-functional rooms in the seventeenth century to many specialized rooms in the nineteenth century. For extensive commentary on specialization in nineteenth-century material culture, see Siegfried Giedion, *Mechanization Takes Command* (New York: Norton, 1969).

4   The literature on reality as constructed socially through culture is enormous. The seminal text is Peter L. Berger and Thomas Luckmann, *The Social Construction of Reality* (New York: Doubleday, 1966). Two titles particularly relevant here are Grant McCracken, *Culture and Consumption* (Bloomington: Indiana University Press, 1988); and Kertzer, *Ritual, Politics, and Power*.

5   For an overview of domestic building and an annotated listing of key titles, see David Schuyler, "Domestic Architecture," in *Decorative Arts and Household Furnishings in America*, ed. Kenneth L. Ames and Gerald W. R. Ward (Winterthur: Winterthur Museum, 1989), 61–75.

6   On eighteenth-century house plans, see George B. Tatum, *Philadelphia Georgian* (Middletown: Wesleyan University Press, 1976); and Bernard L. Herman, *Architecture and Rural Life in Central Delaware* (Knoxville: University of Tennessee Press, 1987).

7   Vincent J. Scully, Jr., *The Shingle Style and the Stick Style* (New Haven: Yale University Press, 1971). Thousands of house plans appear in the numerous nineteenth-century architectural manuals published for the lay public. For an extensive listing of these, see Henry-Russell Hitchcock, *American Architectural Books* (New York: Da Capo Press, 1976). Models for "living halls" are illustrated in Joseph Nash, *The Mansions of England in the Olden Time* (New York: Bounty Books, 1970; originally published 1839–1849).

8   For discussion of competing models for middle-class domesticity, see Wendy Kaplan, *"The Art That Is Life": The Arts and Crafts Movement in America* (Boston: Little, Brown, for the Museum of Fine Arts, 1987); and Rosalind H. Williams, *Dream Worlds: Mass Consumption in Late Nineteenth Century France* (Berkeley: University of California Press, 1982).

9   In some more costly homes, the hall was separated from the outside by a vestibule. On one level, the vestibule served further to insulate the interior of the house from the outside by keeping out wind and weather. On another, it heightened the sense of drama associated with entering or leaving the house by adding another stage to the process.

10   A seminal discussion of front and back zones appears in Erving Goffman, *The Presentation of Self in Everyday Life* (Garden City, N.Y.: Doubleday, 1959). Benjamin Disraeli, *Sybil; or The Two Nations* (London: H. Colburn, 1845). Explicit acceptance of stratification is found in Andrew Jackson Downing, *The Architecture of Country Houses* (New York: D. Appleton, 1850). Downing argues that a cottage is appropriate for a family with no more than two servants, but three or more servants entitle one to a villa. Much of Downing's approach can be traced to John Claudius Loudon, *Encyclopædia of Cottage, Farm, and Villa Architecture and Furniture* (London: Longman, Rees, Orme, Brown, Green, & Longman, 1833). Recent research on Downing is summarized in George B. Tatum and Elisabeth MacDougall, eds., *Prophet with Honor. The Career of Andrew Jackson Downing* (Washington D.C.: Dumbarton Oaks, 1989). John Ruskin, *The Seven Lamps of Architecture* (New York: Wiley, 1866).

11   The hallstand is atypical in that, unlike most genteel middle-class furnishings of the nineteenth century, it has no obvious courtly antecedents. Hallstands are an international phenomenon, found throughout the Western and Westernized world in the last century. Comments on the history of the form can be found in Christopher Gilbert, *Loudon Furniture Designs* (East Ardsley, England: S. R. Publishers, 1970), 56–57; Thomas Webster and Mrs. Parkes, *An Encyclopædia of Domestic Economy* (New York: Harper & Brothers, 1845), 287–288; Rudolph Ackermann, ed., *The Repository of Arts, Literature, Commerce, Manufacture, Fashions, and Politics* (London: R. Ackermann, 1809–1828); Charles F. Montgomery, *American Furniture: The Federal Period* (New York: Viking, 1966), 435; Henry Havard, *Dictionnaire de l'Ameublement et de la Décoration* (Paris: Maison Quantin, 1887–1890), 4: 512–514, 516–517. Despite its prominence and extensive production, the hallstand has not held much appeal for twentieth-century enthusiasts of elegant furniture: "As a piece of furniture, it was seldom designed; it merely occurred." John Gloag, *A Short Dictionary of Furniture* (New York: Holt, Rinehart and Winston, 1965), 282. To contextualize Gloag's condescending comment, see Kenneth L. Ames, "The Stuff of Everyday Life," in Schlereth, *Material Culture: A Research Guide*, 79–112. On the 1870s as the visual high point of Victorian style (and the high point of Victorian culture?), see Carroll L. V.

Meeks, *The Railroad Station* (New Haven: Yale University Press, 1964), 1–25. The story of the decline of the hallstand is capably told in Leslie A. Greene, "The Late Victorian Hallstand: A Social History," *Nineteenth Century* 6, no. 4 (Winter 1980): 51–53.

12 For more on Grand Rapids furniture of the 1870s, see Kenneth L. Ames, "Grand Rapids Furniture at the Time of the Centennial," in *Winterthur Portfolio* 10, ed. Ian M. G. Quimby (Charlottesville: University Press of Virginia, 1975), 23–50.

13 For documentation and analysis of an expensive example, see Elizabeth Agee Cogswell, "The Henry Lippitt House of Providence, Rhode Island," *Winterthur Portfolio* 17, no. 4 (Winter 1982): 203–242.

14 On umbrellas, see William Sangster, *Umbrellas and Their History* (London: Cassell, Petter, and Galpin, c. 1870); Louis Octave Uzanne, *Les Ornements de la Femme* (Paris: Librairies-imprimeries reunies, 1892); A. Varron, "The Umbrella," *Ciba Review* 42 (1942): 1510–1548; T. S. Crawford, *A History of the Umbrella* (Newton Abbot, England: David and Charles, 1970). Canes were also placed on hallstands. For a classic analysis of this object in nineteenth-century society, see Thorstein Veblen, *The Theory of the Leisure Class* (New York: Macmillan, 1912), 265. The connotations of the umbrella and the cane or walking stick differed significantly. While both were widely used by males, as images amply record, the umbrella was often associated with the parson, the cane with the dandy or rake.

15 James Laver, *Modesty in Dress* (Boston: Houghton Mifflin, 1969), 121–123. Today Laver's point seems debatable. Top hats are gone and American society is still male dominated. It might be more accurate to say that such explicit signs of male domination subside at times when expression of male domination must be muted. For more on the dynamic relationship of male and female attire, see Grant McCracken, "The Voice of Gender in the World of Goods: Beau Brummell and the Cunning of Present Gender Symbolism," a paper delivered at the Winterthur conference on material culture and gender, November 1989.

16 For closets in eighteenth-century houses, see Tatum, *Philadelphia Georgian*; and Herman, *Architecture and Rural Life in Central Delaware*.

17 On grooming rituals, see McCracken, *Culture and Consumption*, 86–87. On appearances in nineteenth-century America, see Karen Halttunen, *Confidence Men and Painted Women* (New Haven: Yale University Press, 1983). On glass and mirrors, see *Glass: History, Manufacture and Its Universal Application* (Pittsburgh: Pittsburgh Plate Glass Co., 1923); and Serge Roche, Germain Courage, and Pierre Devinoy, *Mirrors* (New York: Rizzoli, 1985). Trade catalogs document the full range of mirrors and mirror-bearing goods available in the nineteenth century. A helpful guide to one major collection is E. Richard McKinstry, *Trade Catalogues at Winterthur. A Guide to the Literature of Merchandising* (New York: Garland, 1984). The modern use of the mirror in the fine arts occurs in the work of Michelangelo Pistoletto, among others. See Edward Lucie-Smith, *Late Modern, The Visual Arts Since 1945* (New York: Praeger, 1969).

18 Giedion, *Mechanization Takes Command*, 329–332.

19 People with less space or money could purchase the components of the hallstand as separate artifacts. Metal umbrella stands and wooden, wall-mounted hat and coat racks, usually with small mirrors, were the most common.

20 Ray Faulkner and Edwin Ziegfield, *Art Today* (New York: Holt, Rinehart and Winston, 1969); Henry Glassie, *Folk Housing in Middle Virginia* (Knoxville: University of Tennessee Press, 1975), 170–175; Glassie, "Folk Art," in *Folklore and Folklife, an Introduction*, ed. Richard M. Dorson (Chicago: University of Chicago Press, 1972), 272–279. It is not symmetry, however, that distinguishes Victorian artifacts and design from those that precede or follow them but profusion, elaboration, complexity. The latter traits are simultaneously self-conscious expressions of affluence, knowledge, and a high level of civilization. When symmetry is added, the whole becomes a demonstration of order and of control of self, materials, techniques, machinery, natural substances and laws, and the culture of other people, past and present. In short, in the Victorian world, complex symmetry demonstrated mastery in the broadest sense.

21 For comments on issues of style and symbol, see Dell Upton, "The Power of Things: Recent Studies in American Vernacular Architecture," in Schlereth, *Material Culture: A Research Guide*, 57–78; Karl Lehmann, "The Dome of Heaven," in *Modern Perspectives in Western Art History*, ed. W. Eugene Kleinbauer (New York: Holt, Rinehart and Winston, 1971), 227–270; Earl Baldwin Smith, *The Dome, a Study in the History of Ideas* (Princeton: Princeton University Press, 1950); John Summerson, *Heavenly Mansions* (New York: Norton, 1963), 1–28. Most of the hall-stands illustrated here are examples of what was known as the néo-grec style in the 1870s (although explicit naming of styles of household goods in mainstream culture was no more prevalent than it is today). For comments on the néo-grec, see Kenneth L. Ames, "What Is the Néo-Grec?" *Nineteenth Century* 2, no. 2 (Summer 1976): 12–21; and Ames, "Sitting in (Néo-Grec) Style," *Nineteenth Century* 2, nos. 3–4 (Fall 1976): 50–58.

22 Todd S. Goodholme, ed., *A Domestic Cyclopedia of Practical Information* (New York: H. Holt & Co., 1877), 223.

23 Clarence Cook, *The House Beautiful* (New York: Scribner, Armstrong & Co., 1878), 31. A similar sentiment appears in Goodholme, *Domestic Cyclopedia*: "Probably the worst possible step is to buy the stereotyped hat and umbrella rack. No matter how elaborate, they are always the same thing over again, and generally very ugly" (p. 223). Both texts were part of what has been called the household art movement; see Martha Crabill McClaugherty, "Household Art: Creating the Artistic Home, 1868–1893," *WintherthurPortfolio* 18, no. 1 (Spring 1983): 1–26.

24 If anything, the reformers were more self-conscious. For design reform in this country in the 1870s, see Doreen Bolger Burke *et al.*, *In Pursuit of Beauty: Americans and the Aesthetic Movement* (New York: Rizzoli with the Metropolitan Museum of Art, 1986).

25 Self-consciousness in the nineteenth century takes many forms. It can be seen in the establishment of what would become state historical societies in the Midwest with the first wave of Yankee immigration: Wisconsin in 1846 and Minnesota in 1849. It can also be seen in the widespread popularity of diaries. See Gayle R. Davis, "Women's Frontier Diaries: Writing for Good Reason," *Women's Studies* 14 (1987): 5–14; Elizabeth Hampsten, *Read This Only to Yourself, the Private Writings of Midwestern Women* (Bloomington: Indiana University Press, 1982); Thomas Mallon, *A Book of One's Own: People and Their Diaries* (New York: Ticknor, 1984); and Lillian Schlissel, *Women's Diaries of the Westward Journey* (New York: Schocken, 1982).

26 As at the Lippitt house in Providence. See Cogswell, "Henry Lippitt House."

27 Plank-seat chairs were inexpensive but durable forms of seating, normally used by the poor or in utilitarian contexts where upholstery was not necessary or appropriate. Unlike hallstands, hall chairs can be readily traced to antecedents in eighteenth-century Britain and Europe. They were, for example, found in great Palladian houses of eighteenth-century England, occasionally adorned with a family crest. Hall chairs are additional instances of the devaluation of aristocratic symbols. The quotation is from Cook, *House Beautiful*, 33. Psychological manipulation in a particularly bald form can be seen at the Lippitt House, where the hall chairs are so overscaled that they dwarf normal-sized people who try to sit on them. See Cogswell, "Henry Lippitt House."

28 Esther B. Aresty, *The Best Behavior* (New York: Simon & Schuster, 1970); Norbert Elias, *The Civilizing Process* (New York: Urizen Books, 1978); Arthur M. Schlesinger, *Learning How to Behave* (New York: Macmillan, 1946).

29 Continuities and changes in the prescriptive literature of calling and cards can be traced through the following volumes: *Etiquette for Gentlemen* (Philadelphia: Lindsay & Blakiston, 1845); George Winfred Hervey, *The Principles of Courtesy* (New York: Harper & Brothers, 1852); Emily Thornwell, *The Lady's Guide to Perfect Gentility* (New York: Derby & Jackson, 1856); Henry Lunettes (Margaret Cockburn Conkling), *The American Gentleman's Guide to Politeness and Fashion* (New York: Derby & Jackson, 1857); Henry P. Willis, *Etiquette and the Usages of Society* (New York: Dick & Fitzgerald, 1860); *The Bazar Book of Decorum* (New York: Harper & Brothers, 1871); Florence Hartley, *The Ladies' Book of Etiquette* (Boston: J. S. Locke & Co., 1876); *Decorum* (New York: Union Publishing House, 1880); and George D. Carroll, *Diamonds*

10.1 Downtown skyline, Chicago, Illinois, c.1900. The tall buildings include (from left to right): in the distance, the Ashland Block; in the middle ground, the rear wall of the Title and Trust Building; in the background, the top of Unity Building, the Masonic Temple; in the foreground, the rear wall of the Hartford Building

expression of science, technology, mechanized industry, and modern urban life."[4] Here Condit wove together two premises, one about the nature of architecture, the other about the nature of nineteenth-century urban society and culture. Both Giedion and Condit sought in the past and proposed for the present a unified art and culture, and there-fore a style of building that would be the physical representation of Zeitgeist. Identifying the *spirit* of the nineteenth century as industry, technology, and commerce, they reasoned that these forces required symbolic codification. The challenge was for the architect to realize a new style based on the new materials, technologies, and forms of modern building.

More critical than historical, these analyses of Chicago skyscrapers were not entirely lucid about the factors that prevented designers from easily meeting that challenge. As Giedion formulated the historical process, an inherent logic unfolded within *architecture* and *construction* such that these abstractions acted nearly as historical agents, with lives or motivations of their own. "For a hundred years architecture lay smothered in a dead, eclectic atmosphere in spite of its continual attempts to escape. All that while construction played the part of architecture's subconsciousness, contained things which it prophesied and half revealed long before they could become realities."[5] With architecture pressing forward, what held architects back was a fatal ambivalence. *Cultural schizophrenia* or a *split personality* beset nineteenth-century Americans, and a *split civilization* compromised nineteenth-century art and architecture. A *schism* or gap existed between architecture and engineering, design and construction, art and industry, feeling and rationality.[6]

Deliverance from dead eclecticism, so the account goes, came when architects began to draw stylistic inspiration from the new building techniques—and in particular from the steel-frame structural system. Chicago's 1880s commercial architecture succeeded in bridging the gap between "bare construction" and "architecture in the grand manner." Giedion concludes: "With surprising boldness, the Chicago School strove to break through to pure forms, which would unite construction and architecture in an identical expression."[7] Thus skyscraper architects confronted the "technical and aesthetic problem of creating in masonry a form appropriate to the needs and the spirit of the new commercial and industrial culture." They created a stylistic "revolution." They fostered an aesthetic "emancipated from the last vestige of dependence on the past."[8] In short, early skyscraper designs created by Chicago architects prefigured important elements of twentieth-century modern style and form.

Seen from modernism back, then, Chicago skyscrapers might be celebrated as unalloyed expressions of modern, commercial life. Neither Condit nor Giedion detected reservations about capitalist society in Chicago's tall buildings. Framed in this manner, Chicago's spectacular skyscrapers would seem to provide evidence that whatever concerns about commerce had earlier informed designs for Gothic revival churches and the movement for public parks, these had been resolved by the 1880s—if not by city builders as a whole, then at least by those individuals who built skyscrapers. Skyscrapers might establish the maturity of bourgeois culture in the last decades of the century—the culture's reconciliation with material striving and the healing of the schizophrenia of the times.

There is little doubt that skyscraper clients and architects accepted—and, indeed, centrally participated in—commercial and industrial capital. Like Giedion and Condit, late nineteenth-century architects, builders, and critics of Chicago's skyscrapers felt that commerce, industry, and technology largely defined the spirit of the city. Nonetheless, both in word and in stone, the Chicagoans of the era demonstrated social and cultural ideals distinct from those attributed to them by their historians.

This analysis of Chicago skyscrapers draws on but modifies Giedion's and Condit's view. It does not begin with the rise of the skyscrapers' enabling technology—steel-frame construction, elevators, terracotta fireproofing, or novel foundation techniques—or with the aesthetic challenge presented by unprecedented building heights. It begins with aspects of the skyscraper that impressed contemporaries rather than what impressed modernist architects and critics of a later era. From this view, it appears that Chicago architects made a greater effort to transcend commercial utility than to express it symbolically. The reconciliation of city builders with commerce did not lead them to eschew pretensions to beauty through ornament. They considered ornament and refinement to be justifications for, rather than antitheses of, material striving. Prizing material comfort and consumption, late nineteenth-century middle- and upper-class Chicagoans rationalized materialism by equating taste with culture. Not surprisingly, the buildings they produced did a great deal more than express their structural basis. Skyscrapers, then, are best understood

10.3 Randolph Street, looking east from La Salle Street, Chicago, Illinois, 1900. With the City Hall and Courthouse at the right, this section of Randolph Street included three prominent skyscrapers: in the foreground, Ashland Block, Burnham and Root, 1891–92; middle ground, the Schiller Building, Adler and Sullivan, 1891–92; and in the background, the Masonic Temple, Burnham and Root, 1891–92

real estate investor Malhon D. Ogden described the dramatic change that followed the fire: "That part of the burnt district north of Van Buren street, and between La Salle street and the South Branch of the River, before the fire, was covered with countless old rookeries and miserable shanties, occupied, for the past twenty years, as dens of infamy and low gambling dives, the resort and rendezvous of thieves, burglars, robbers, and murderers of all grades and colors, to the exclusion of all decency, or business purposes." The neighborhood had proved difficult to change because land owners allegedly received high rents from the "cutthroat class" for the "pestilent neighborhood [which] vouchsafed them from detection and arrest for crimes committed." The fire cleared the ground; it "destroyed the rookeries, drove the thieves away," and, with a not fully consonant conclusion, "large numbers of our heaviest wholesale and retail houses have located west of La Salle Street and north of Adams street."[16] The fire made way for a refined world of business, increasingly housed in skyscrapers and spatially and conceptually dissociated from other, less acceptable ways of making a living. The result was not merely a rebuilt, but a transformed, downtown.

Indeed, the creation of office buildings in downtown Chicago was linked to the creation of new forms of work established at a social and cultural distance from productive labor. The McCormick reaper works provides a good example of the evolving office activity that filled and shaped downtown skyscrapers. During the 1850s, McCormick's only two office clerks worked part time in the factory to fill their ten-hour days. [...] By the late 1870s, the McCormick company had grown to the extent that it employed sixteen full-time clerks just to handle correspondence and accounts.[17] "The work is more and more complicated every year," wrote one manager in 1879, and office workers maintained "4 sets of regular books now besides all the auxiliary books." With the expansion of office work and office personnel came a distinct office culture within the company. [...] A growing distinctness of office and plant operations [...] led the company to join other Chicago manufacturers who, forced by competition for centrally located land and rising prices, moved their offices downtown and their sprawling manufacturing plants to outlying areas.[18] The office corps moved downtown into the McCormick block on Dearborn Street and kept in contact with the factory using telegraphs, telephones, and express wagons. [...]

As they joined financial, legal, and administrative businesses downtown, manufacturers devised images of their enterprises distinct from factory, foundry, and warehouse. In the 1880s, during a period of abrasive labor strife at the McCormick company and across the nation, McCormick changed its stationery letterhead. In the place of a bird's-eye-view etching of its manufacturing plant, complete with billowing smokestacks, the company substituted a bucolic image of a horse-drawn McCormick reaper. As police and striking workers battled in Chicago streets, McCormick's suppression of the factory suggested its discomfort in the face of the powers of production. New letterhead was a small token of a larger tendency in which businesses downplayed productive labor and the people who performed it.

The role of skyscrapers in the reformulation of business imagery is clear from contemporary guidebook descriptions. Earlier in the century, tourists routinely visited the extensive stockyards, lumberyards, and factories that made the city famous. Tourist guidebooks published in the late nineteenth century reflected and encouraged a realignment of the public's image of Chicago commerce. Skyscrapers received extended review in the tour itinerary, while factories receded into the background, into the guides' "general information" sections. One of the most thorough Chicago guidebooks of the 1890s, John J. Flinn's *Standard Guide of Chicago*, for example, passed over the major north-side manufacturing and warehouse district, commenting, "I will not ask you to penetrate this section now, but you can do so at your leisure."[19] In rather sharp contrast, Flinn recommended that city visitors devote at least a half day to the "study of" the Masonic Temple building, which at 22 stories and 302 feet was the world's tallest building. From the Masonic Temple's roof garden and observatory Flinn encouraged tourists to survey the stockyards, the Grant locomotive works, and the city's steel works, distilleries, breweries, and grain elevators.[20] This view of industry was distant, detached, and sanitized. The skyscraper, with its "comprehensive view," obviated much of the need to "penetrate" the city's industrial districts. In the context of many guidebooks, at least, the skyscraper took over as the representative expression of Chicago commerce.

Skyscraper designers accommodated their buildings to this role, shaping them as new workplaces and new symbols of a refined form of work. The specialized office building permitted architects, designers, and investors to devote money and imagination to the distinct needs and desires of the office tenant. Offices no longer simply occupied the left-over space above the storefront, in the corner of warehouses, or in the factory buildings. For discriminating tenants, the new office buildings combined office space with service, convenience, comfort, and even luxury. Building advertisements, rental agents' rhetoric, and architectural criticism all suggested that good commerce called for skyscraper designs with applied art and beauty.[21] If they omitted some of the intricate facade designs found in smaller, earlier, masonry and cast-iron-fronted commercial buildings, many architects who designed brick skyscrapers sought a balanced exterior massiveness, at times quiet and at times picturesque. Architect John Root felt that a profusion of exterior ornament was a "subtle means of architectural expression" that might go unheeded in "the midst of hurrying busy thousands of men."[22] In many buildings by Root and his contemporaries, starting with the entrance, energetic and artful interior design compensated for the occasional austere exterior.[23] Here, then, was not hostility to ornament but a judgment about where it would prove effective. Slighted by historians but notable to contemporaries, the entrances, lobbies, and elevators of Chicago skyscrapers were crucial to the ways that *clients*—building tenants and the business associates who visited them—experienced the buildings.

A host of examples establishes that architects thought artful embellishment was crucial to the clients' experience. Designs for skyscraper entrances differed substantially from those of earlier office blocks. The entrances to Chicago's preelevator office blocks were frequently unembellished. They occupied breaks between retail stores fronting the sidewalk. Some specialized office blocks built in the 1860s and 1870s did have more ornate entrances that were framed with porticoes and emphasized in the composition of the upper facade. The window bays immediately over these entries and the gables, finials, and cornice crowns at the roof ennobled both the entrances and the buildings. Truncated corners in such early office buildings as Van Osdel's McCormick and Reaper blocks, Jenney's Portland block, Burling and Whitehouse's First National Bank block, Frederick and Edward Baumann's Bryan and Metropolitan blocks, Willett's Times building, and the Union building added grandeur to the entries while providing an unusual focal point for building designs constrained by the formal regularity of lots in the street grid. Yet many buildings lacked grand or even distinctive main entrances.

In contrast, the plan, form, and image of skyscrapers fostered a more emphatically monumental aesthetic for their entrances. More highly ornamented entries were encouraged by skyscraper plans: earlier office blocks often supplemented front entrances with inconspicuous side entries, which provided stairs to the offices opening on the landings above the first floor. Multiple stairways and landings obviated the need for space-consuming systems of interior corridors. In skyscrapers, banks of elevators concentrated circulation within the building and thus favored a single entrance. Skyscraper form piled up hundreds and thousands of tenants who generated traffic that required larger entrances. Finally, monumental entries seemed appropriate to the ennobled and perhaps ennobling symbols of commerce.

Many skyscraper architects adapted the technique of emphasizing entrances by articulating facade bays rising over them, even though the extraordinary height of many late nineteenth-century office buildings made this a less impressive compositional gesture than in lowrises. In the Chamber of Commerce building [Baumann and Huehl, 1888–90], for example, the modest projection of the three windows above the Washington Street entrance portico was seen as an important part of the building's "claims to beauty."[24] Burnham and Root similarly composed many of their office buildings with an entrance pavilion established through a unified composition of the entrance with the bays and cornice above. In addition to adapting aspects of earlier office block design, many architects gave skyscraper entrances formal compositional autonomy. The monumental entrance on Solon S. Beman's nine-story Pullman building (1882–84) exemplified this approach. The main Adams Street entrance took the form of a triumphal arch, twenty-two feet wide at the sidewalk, elliptical in shape, and supported by massive columns with rectangular bases, polished red granite shafts, and foliated capitals. Connecting the two wings of the U-shaped building, the arch gave access to an eighty-foot-long court leading to an inside entrance and the building's elevators. Beman distinguished the Pullman's grand entry arch further by terminating it two and one-half stories above the ground, in marked disharmony with the building's dominant string courses.

Like the Pullman, Burnham and Root's Woman's Temple (1890–92) had an exterior light court and a massive, arched entrance. In Jenney's Home Insurance building (1883–85) the "grand entrance on La Salle Street [was] one of peerless beauty—a veritable marble hall, and a portal such as no palace in Europe can boast of."[25] A massive portico supported by four Corinthian columns projected from the arched entrance. [Owner Perry] Hannah's Chamber of Commerce building had a similar entrance, a remnant of the 1872 building used by Chicago's Board of Trade. The architects, Baumann and Huehl, had successfully appropriated the board's quasi-civic architecture for their building's owners and white-collar tenants. Buildings ranging from Burnham and Root's Phenix, Rookery

(Figure 10.4), and Masonic Temple buildings to Sullivan's Stock Exchange to Boyington's Columbus Memorial to Holabird and Roche's Old Colony provided the grand entrance, an architectural gesture characteristic of leading civic and cultural buildings.

The palatial images established by grand entrances were heightened by skyscraper lobbies. Here tenants and visitors waited for the elevators in highly embellished spaces. The lobby of the sixteen-story Unity building, designed by Clinton J. Warren in 1891, seemed like a "Fairyland" to one city guide:

> Entering through the great arch of the portal, rising to the height of a story and a half, the walls of the outer vestibule are composed of Numidian, Alps, Green and Sienna marbles. Over the inner door is an artistic screen of glass and bronze. Passing through the rotunda the eye is dazzled by its surprisingly brilliant beauty, designed in the style of the Italian renaissance. From the floor of the marble mosaic whose graceful design and harmonious color combinations are taken from the best example of the renaissance in the Old World, rises the first story by a marble balcony with marble balusters and balustrades.[26]

Corinthian columns with finely carved capitals, gold-leaf and silver chandeliers, and the silver-plated latticework of the elevators added to the grandeur. George H. Nesbot and Company of Chicago designed and fitted the Unity building lobby. Nesbot, A. H. Andrews, Henry Dibblee, the Winslow Brothers, and other designers and companies created a series of impressive lobbies in Chicago.

After passing through the columned portico of the Chamber of Commerce, visitors and tenants entered a vestibule with a mosaic floor and ceiling. Each of the thirteen floors had a different mosaic pattern. By the time they had finished the building, Burke and Company of Chicago had laid thirty-five thousand square feet of mosaic. The marble wainscoting quarried from the Italian Apennines and finished in Belgium was put in place so that the grain would run continuously from one slab to the next.[27]

For all the impressiveness of its marble and mosaic work, it was ornamental iron that made the Chamber of Commerce building's interior stand out most notably. Intricately detailed cantilevered balconies ran around each of the building's thirteen floors, overlooking the enclosed light court. Winslow Brothers manufactured the balcony guards and rails using a lively foliated design that was adapted with some variations for elevator screens, columns, fascias, and stairways. Sun flooded in from the rooftop skylight and highlighted the bronze work. Winslow Brothers' interior metalwork, with complex patterns drawn from natural foliage and geometric shapes, embellished the lobbies of numerous Chicago skyscrapers, including the Auditorium (Figure 10.5), Caxton, Columbus Memorial, Home Insurance, Manhattan, Monadnock, Old Colony, Phenix, Pontiac, Rand McNally, Rookery, Stock Exchange, Tacoma, and Woman's Temple build-ings.[28] Much like appropriated nature in city parks, the natural forms of foliated building ornament could evoke a consciousness of matters beyond the commerce of the urban market.

Essential to the skyscraper were elevators, first encountered by visitors and tenants as part of an embellished lobby. Nineteenth-century Americans commonly saw utilitar-ian machinery and technology as fit objects for aesthetic appreciation and hence for

10.4 Burnham and Root, Rookery Building, Chicago, Illinois, 1885–88

10.5 Adler and Sullivan, Auditorium Building, Chicago, Illinois, 1886–89. Marble and ornamental iron stairway

ornamentation.[29] Designers of skyscrapers gave elevators extensive artistic treatment. Winslow Brothers and other companies provided elevator enclosures and guards that flowed with lively floral and geometrical patterns in bronze and wrought iron. Chicago's Hale Elevator Company offered more than one hundred designs for its elevator cars, ranging in price from $200 to $2,000. Despite this variety, the manager of the Reaper office building, which had just installed Hale elevators, advised Mrs. Cyrus McCormick to engage her New York furniture designer to design the car for the elevator in her home. "It is so prominent an article that most everybody sees and so much a matter of taste that I should think you need to give considerable time and attention to it yourself."[30] Although they enjoyed less choice than Mrs. McCormick, white-collar workers in the Reaper building and elsewhere might enjoy beautiful elevators. For manufacturers such as the Hale Elevator Company and their clients, elevators were not merely an important and convenient technology, they presented an opportunity to display taste and were ornamented accordingly.

Such ornament was simply essential to builders interested in winning tenants for offices, commanding high rents, and advertising themselves through skyscrapers. A skyscraper could vouch for the substance and good character of the company associated with the building either by name or by tenantry. In skyscraper lobbies, the Roman and Florentine mosaics and Halian, St. Sylvester, Italian, and other marbles covering floors, ceilings, walls, and staircases all alluded to such substance.[31] Contemporary descriptions of skyscrapers make clear the utility of such materials and workmanship as character reference; take, for example, this view of the Chamber of Commerce building: "From foundation to roof every inch of the building bears the impress of superb workmanship. There is not a trace of shoddyism about the structure. There is no veneering. There is no paint. Everything from the mosaic ceiling of the first floor to the Italian marble wainscoting of the thirteenth is real—not an imitation. No cheap substitutes have found their way into this work."[32] No doubt many business concerns were happy to associate themselves with such a building. [. . .]

Architectural refinement reflected upon the work taking place in skyscraper offices and on the workers who performed it. Chicago businesses faced the world less at the factory and more in the office place, presenting themselves in sales and advertising through a middle-class, white-collar workforce that was more presentable than the working class. For professionals, managers, and lowly clerks, removal from industrial work entailed a social dignity that was enhanced by the offices themselves.[33] Beyond the elevators, these office tenants found a variety of modern technological systems combining artistic appearance and mechanical precision—gas and electric light fixtures, steam radiators, air vents, bathroom fixtures, and door hardware.

The skyscraper's supporting technologies and architectural embellishments promoted the light, ventilation, cleanliness, comfort, healthfulness, and beauty of office accommodations. In the early 1890s, new skyscrapers such as the Monadnock, Unity, Woman's Temple, Masonic Temple, and Ashland filled their offices with tenants anxious to move out of "old, second, third, and fourth class office buildings."[34] Tenants indifferently cast aside old workplaces, and like urban flat dwellers took leave of a place on May 1st moving days with only the "slightest encouragement" and few regrets.[35] In 1886, for example, the publishers of *Railway Age* moved their offices into the recently completed Home Insurance building. They had considered their old building first class when they occupied it a few years earlier. The six-story office block at 103 Adams Street had a modern elevator and a small light well for light and ventilation, but it suffered "greatly by comparison" with the new skyscrapers. Although the structural system supporting the Home Insurance building has stirred great debate among historians, it made no impression at all on the magazine's publishers.[36] They were impressed with the marble used for floors, ceilings, stairs, and wainscoting, with the hardwood office interiors, the rapid elevators, and the provision of natural light, gas and electrical illumination, steam heating, and fire and burglar protection. These fine features and the "high character of its tenantry" made the Home Insurance the "finest and most complete office building in America . . . supplied with every convenience that modern skill and lavish expenditure of money could command . . . a model of beauty, convenience, and comfort."[37]

In spite of some highly decorative exteriors, the interiors of the office blocks of the 1860s and 1870s appeared crude by skyscraper standards.[38] In the "first class" office blocks of the 1860s, such as the Larmon and McCormick blocks, physicians, lawyers, real estate agents, jewelers, and bankers occupied offices located above assorted storefront businesses. The offices depended on fireplaces and stoves for heat, gas jets for light, and open windows for ventilation. Dark corridors, long flights of stairs and, eventually, rather slow elevators provided access to offices. City water was available but in the 1860s, the Larmon and McCormick blocks continued to rely on privy toilets, with lime added for sanitation. Tenants cleaned their own offices. Starting in 1867, the Pinkerton detective service included the Larmon and McCormick blocks on its nightly rounds, but no special watchman or guard and only one part-time janitor worked inside the buildings.[39]

By contrast, skyscrapers of the 1880s and 1890s furnished tenants with a wide variety of modern technologies well in advance of their availability to other city buildings and neighborhoods. In the early 1880s, electric lights replaced gas illumination in office buildings, long before the transition took place in other parts of the city. Skyscrapers centralized systems of steam heating and mechanical ventilation, removing from the tenant the responsibility for heating and ventilating offices. Extensive water and sewerage systems won suitable architectural expression in large, elegant toilet rooms and eventually furnished water and toilets on every office floor. Hot and cold running water became a standard feature of many office suites in the 1880s. A succession of electric bell signal systems, pneumatic message tubes, and office building telephone exchanges helped tenants to communicate with other parts of the building and the city. While urban residents struggled with the vagaries of intraurban transportation, elevator technology moved ever greater numbers of people more quickly through increasingly tall buildings. Letter chutes moved mail from nearby each office to a central collection box almost effortlessly. Throughout the skyscraper boom, the fittings of a *modern* and *complete* building changed as higher levels of artistic finish and mechanical services were offered in the competition for tenants.

In the design and promise of the skyscraper, nothing proved more fundamental than the provision of higher quality natural light for offices. Investors, architects, tenants, and architectural critics carefully scrutinized these provisions.[40] Architects expanded office block light shafts into tremendous skyscraper light courts. Skyscraper architects and investors sacrificed large amounts of interior space to provide for natural light, and the desire for greater light helped determine not only the floor plan of the skyscraper but also the building site selected. [. . .] Galleries and open courts dramatized the entire matter of natural light, which served as the cornerstone of attempts to "secure the best tenants." In Burnham and Root's Rookery building, the ground story lobby and shops were lighted by an impressive skylight, and glazed bricks lining the interior walls helped reflect natural light into offices on the upper floors (Figure 10.6).

An 1888 *Tribune* article, "The Sacrifice of Space for Light," reported: "Dark rooms will not rent, and it therefore does not pay to construct them. The question is how to get the greatest amount of rentable space with the smallest cubic contents, and each lot presents its own peculiar problem. The old practice was to cover the entire lot, and the consequence was dark rooms in a considerable proportion of the space." Dark offices

10.6 Burnham and Root, Rookery Building, Chicago, Illinois, 1885–88. Lobby looking toward balcony. This view shows the interior prior to Frank Lloyd Wright's remodeling, 1905

rented only at very low rates, and "buildings constructed according to the latest ideas have readily taken tenants away." Thus, experts criticized the narrow light shaft initially planned for the Chamber of Commerce building as insufficient. The *Tribune* sympathized with Hannah, Lay and Company which, having purchased the lot for $625,000, understandably balked at throwing large areas into light courts. Yet the paper predicted that "careful figuring on rent is apt to lead to the conclusion to leave 'a little more' out of doors."[41]

In its final design, the Chamber of Commerce's 35 foot by 108 foot light court turned the ideals of light and ventilation into a grand architectural gesture. Tenants and visitors passed through the columned portico and the mosaic and marble vestibule, past the ornate elevator enclosure and into a two-hundred-foot-high light court. Here "a perfect flood of light penetrates the central court, so that the interior of the building is almost as brightly illuminated as the exterior during the day."[42] The design had powerfully captured and framed the sky, enhancing both the aesthetic and practical qualities of the architecture. Few buildings contained such a prospect. In 1892, Burnham and Root's Masonic Temple building opened with an interior light court that rose through ornate balconies and by office windows twenty-two stories—more than 302 feet—to a glass skylight on the roof (Figure 10.7). In these skyscrapers, interiors now competed with

refreshments—and during the summertime—concert music or vaudeville theater. One guide reported, "on the warmest evenings these open air amusement houses are delightfully cool, and swept by the lake breezes."[50] The middle- and upper-class tenants of the skyscraper achieved an alliance of these seemingly opposite landscapes—skyscrapers and parks, offices and suburbs, work and leisure. These same people who responded enthusiastically to well-lighted skyscraper offices proposed, built, and used urban parks, and embellished residential districts and suburban communities.

Finally, human services as well as technology and aesthetic design made the skyscraper attractive to white-collar office workers. Without leaving the building, tenants had access to a variety of stores, restaurants, and professional services such as barbers, cigar and newspaper stands, tailors, doctors, dentists, lawyers, and bankers. Owners of the Columbus Memorial and the Ashland buildings appealed to particular constituencies by providing specialized medical and legal libraries. Aside from the convenience of doing business with the building's other tenants, building managements offered a vast array of personal services. Doormen, elevator operators, messenger boys, and building detectives were the most visible representatives of these services. Janitorial staffs cleaned the public areas of skyscraper buildings and for an additional fee cleaned tenant offices. Engineers, electricians, and mechanics worked to keep the buildings' mechanical systems functioning properly. Building managers coordinated and oversaw the entire operation, while rental agents attracted and helped accommodate tenants. The use of nonstructural wall partitions in many new buildings permitted tenants to obtain office space that met their particular requirements. Human or mechanical failure, such as slow elevator service, cold offices, lighting failures, broken promises concerning prospective tenants or impertinence on the part of doormen or elevator operators, all provoked loud protests from tenants.[51]

Even those employees primarily committed to the successful operation of a skyscraper's technology could contribute to an atmosphere of efficient and personalized service for tenants. Earlier office blocks had generally employed only a rental agent, a janitor, and occasional outside help to perform needed repairs. In the Larmon and McCormick blocks, less than 5 percent of rental revenue was spent on service employment during the 1860s. By contrast, at the Board of Trade building, over 20 percent of office rental revenue went to pay building employees. In 1886, for example, the Board of Trade employed 37 men and 4 women—including 7 elevator operators, a chief engineer, electrician, steamfitter, machinist, blacksmith, carpenter, 3 firemen, a coal passer, a laborer, and 4 day janitors who washed windows, light globes, and lamps, wound the clock, and cleaned both ironwork and sidewalks. At night, 9 men and 3 women spent 12 hours cleaning 81 rooms, 9 water closets with 64 flush toilets, the halls and the corridors. The nighttime crew scrubbed water closets every day, the corridors twice a week, and—for an additional $7 to $14 monthly—offices once a week. Watchmen guarded the building twenty-four hours a day. Some skyscrapers even provided janitor quarters on the roof of the building. At the Board of Trade, a manager had general charge of all the employees and of rental, bond, and insurance accounts.[52] Middle-class tenants could be secure in their status; they were members of a class that was served.

Distinguishing even lowly clerks from blue collars, scholars have noted, was part of a rationalizing effort, a means of controlling the new workforce.[53] For example, contemporary reviewers of the Pullman building noted that it was much more extensive and elaborate than required for the purposes of office accommodations. The building's "palatial" character reflected the "same spirit" evident in the model company town at Pullman.[54] In both venues, Pullman revealed a belief that clean and pleasant surroundings would promote worker productivity. In 1873, the company built an office building with a restaurant, library, and sitting rooms for employees and their families. By "cultivat[ing] society, as it were, among the employees" and by making company headquarters "attractive," Pullman hoped that the building would be "productive of harmony and good feelings, while it will interest them more in the work for which they are employed . . . [and] make them more useful."[55] Perhaps an embellished office building with a grand, ennobling entrance might do more than indicate the presence of refined workers; it might actually cultivate them. Ever more difficult to achieve at the factory, harmony could be sought at the office.

Skyscrapers thus codified a more benign image of modern commerce, narrowing, focusing, and purifying images of work. They were refinements of the downtown area, all the more powerfully so given the general clearing of downtown blocks accomplished by developers both before and after the fire of 1871. Skyscrapers helped redefine downtown as an acceptable arena for both respectable gentlemen and ladies. They achieved monumental status, calling for special homage and awed respect transcending their workplace character. Skyscrapers became the object of special pilgrimages to ornate lobbies, sumptuous restaurants, and rooftop gardens.[56] As a center of administration and coordination, the office building contained little visible production. Flinn's guide observed, "What all the people who occupy the offices do will be a source of wonder to the visitor . . . but as they are all compelled to pay high rentals it is presumed that they are doing something to coax the almighty dollar in their direction."[57] Work itself could seem comfortably abstract within skyscrapers.

In fact, tall buildings stood among the late nineteenth century's most dramatic and expensive custom-built products, assembling parts from literally hundreds of subsidiary manufacturers. Like a plethora of new mass-produced consumer products, skyscrapers were promoted as a means to foster human efficiency, comfort, and pleasure and to buttress a rising standard of living. As a new organizing form for business life, as an eager patron of diverse mechanical innovations, as a competitive, custom-made, revenue-producing structure, the skyscraper compelled architects to consider judiciously their complex designs, combining elements of both beauty and utility.

Architects' awareness of the complex nature of tall office buildings appeared both in their skyscraper designs and in their writings about them. Emphasizing cultural and aesthetic simplicity over complexity, Condit and Giedion focused narrowly on a handful of interesting, somewhat austere, structurally expressive commercial buildings. By designating their architects as a *school* and giving these buildings status as a *style*, they obscured important aspects of skyscraper history and the history of urban culture. In the nineteenth century, even architectural critics who lauded the relative plainness and simplicity in Chicago skyscrapers questioned the need for structural expressionism: "There is no greater folly than to maintain that Chicago architects have not found a suitable means of architecturally expressing modern steel construction," said one writer in the *Tribune*.

"The steel skeletons of the office buildings need be no more expressed than the bones of the critics rash enough to father this statement."[58] Even if architects considered the expression of skeleton construction to be essential, distinct styles could have developed. For example, depending on the placement of spandrel and pier panels, a skyscraper's steel skeleton could express itself as vertical, horizontal, or in balance. These diverse solutions, all of which appeared in Chicago, could only questionably represent a single style or school. In fact, many Chicago architects and critics spoke as if a new style had emerged; yet simple massive scale defined it more closely than any narrowly conceived aesthetic treatment. In 1886, the *Tribune* reported that "when Chicago takes old Rome's arches and sticks on top of them a skyscraper block containing 5,000 rooms, a cafe, an opera-house, a barbershop, and a billiard saloon, the whole thing is an architectural triumph and justly belongs to the new school of Chicagoesque."[59] A few years later another commentator declared, "The title, commercial style . . . may be said to embrace, generally, all modern houses over seven stories in height."[60]

As commerce provided a foundation for the development of Chicago architecture and culture, it was rarely conceptualized as an end in itself. The city building elite hoped that a refined, civilized life and art would emerge from modern commercial society and remained dissatisfied with forms that seemed to express only Mammon. Louis Sullivan probed this aspect of the skyscraper concisely when he wrote, "Problem: How shall we impart to this sterile pile, this crude, harsh brutal agglomeration, this stark, staring exclamation of external strife, the graciousness of those higher forms of sensibility and culture that rest on the lower and fiercer passions?"[61] Modern twentieth-century architects and their critical champions traced the lineage of their designs back to Sullivan, but they overlooked or condemned Sullivan's exuberant ornament and the transcendent aspirations of his proposals for commercial architecture. In writing on the design of the tall office building, "artistically considered," Sullivan echoed a familiar theme from cultural commentaries of the time; he equated commerce in its utilitarian aspects with a certain crudity. Art and beauty were intended to refine commerce's utility. Of the skyscraper, Sullivan wondered, "How shall we proclaim from the dizzy height this strange, weird, modern housetop the peaceful evangel of sentiment, of beauty, the cult of a higher life?"[62]

Part of the answer was the continuing and conscious association between cultivation and ornament: a skyscraper should be "every inch a proud and soaring thing," expressive of sentiment by means of embellishment. For example, the first floor and the entrance, where public attention centered, should be designed "in a more or less liberal, expansive, sumptuous way—a way based exactly on the practical necessities, but expressed with a sentiment of largeness and freedom."[63] In skyscrapers designed by Sullivan and his contemporaries, "sumptuous" ornament, found especially at the top and bottom of the building, and in grand entrances and embellished lobbies helped mediate the distance between commerce and culture, function and form. Structural expressionism informed only certain aspects of certain buildings because commerce and utility formed only a part of the urban culture they expressed.[64]

William Le Baron Jenney, the architect of the Home Insurance building and other notable Chicago skyscrapers, shared something of Sullivan's cultural outlook and idealism. Initially he had balked at the idea of settling in the unrefined Midwest. Seeking employment in the east, he wrote to Frederick Law Olmsted after the Civil War. "Art & Construction have been my serious study since '58, and it is my wish to continue it. In the West there [is] little knowledge and little desire for Art: besides one here must live within themselves without the means of profiting by the works of others."[65] When Jenney took up permanent residence in Chicago, he did not resign himself to an artless, commercialized world but rather promoted beauty and refinement in art and construction. Despite zones of structural expression in some of his buildings, Jenney did not think that the mere expression of technology or utility was sufficient. He adhered to "an old and well-established principle in architecture, to ornament construction, never to construct for the sake of ornament." Styling himself an arbiter of artistic taste, Jenney crusaded for art education, galleries, and intelligent art criticism that would in turn give art "a place in the thoughts of the people as a co-laborer and equal with her sisters, Agriculture, Commerce, and Manufacture."[66]

Jenney's interest in the cultural associations of his design work as well as his own understanding of visual perception as it related to architecture influenced his ornamental treatment of the skyscraper. As he saw it, a tall building "presents to the distant observer, its skyline and broad masses of light and shade; as he approaches nearer, the large details are made out, and add to the interest of the design. The details are further enriched by details within details, the interest increasing as the observer advances." Applied to skyscrapers, this design theory explains a more sumptuous treatment of the more visible lower parts of the building and a corresponding simplicity in the removed sections of the upper facade.

At first view, John W. Root's philosophy of commercial design stands at odds with the attitudes of Sullivan and Jenney. Root forcefully advocated adapting designs to the commercial requirements of the client, the exigencies of modern technology, and the "deeper spirit of the age." He called for the "frankest possible acceptance of the commercial conditions underlying the office building"; he sought an architecture adjusted to the "age of steam, of electricity, of gas, of plumbing and sanitation."[67] Significantly, in most of Root's own buildings, attention to commercial conditions did not preclude artistically arranged and ornamented exteriors and lavishly appointed interiors. *Commercial* did not imply mean.

Root departed from Sullivan in condemning the "profusion of delicate ornament" in commercial architecture, which could only be lost "in the midst of hurrying, busy thousands of men." Such intricate delicate ornament, perhaps like some of Sullivan's patterns, was more appropriate "for the place and hour of contemplation and repose." The majority of Root's designs concentrated strong, massive, historically derived ornament in a manner that would capture the attention of hurrying crowds. At street level, at entrances, at corners and at roofs, ornament helped give the overall mass of the building, rather than individual parts, a distinctive definition; it gave the building, in Root's words, "simplicity, stability, breadth, dignity."[68]

Root's concentrated fields of ornament, his monumental entrances, and his embellished ground-story walls and lobbies clearly grappled with the skyscraper's urban street setting, a significant gesture. Photographic views presented by many critics and historians often distort this context by focusing greatest attention on the upper facades of buildings, the parts farthest removed from sidewalk encounter. Like other architects, Root designed his buildings to stand on busy downtown streets. Contemporary journalist Julian Ralph appreciated the difficulty of experiencing Chicago's skyscrapers, for in its rushing, bustling street life, all three hundred acres of downtown could be compared to the New York Stock Exchange. On streets where it seemed that "men would run over horses if the drivers were not careful," Ralph recommended hiring a cab and lying down, with face pointed upwards, to look at the great business buildings.[69] Responsiveness to the street context, to the massive presence on the skyline, and to human perception helped determine the concentrated ornamentation of entrances and lobbies as well as the overall aesthetic development of the skyscraper.

In building after building, then, Root joined other Chicago architects who opted for cultural association over structural expression. These architects showed an enduring fondness for ornamentation and a general reluctance to give architectural expression to the steelcage structure.[70] Architects who drew on traditional forms did not foster an arid design formalism. With historicist designs, they sought to suggest continuity with past cultures that served the late nineteenth century as a familiar repository of civilized art and beauty. With patterns of foliated ornament, they sought associations of nature, a source of sensibility, refinement, and beauty counterpoised to commerce. Design for a hurrying culture was less attuned to the more abstract, subtle aesthetics of bare, structurally expressive forms, which were so often dismissed as "hitching post" or dry goods box architecture.[71]

Ornament linked skyscrapers not only to the past but to other contemporary and related structures. The tall office building did not redefine downtown alone nor develop its elaborate system of human and mechanical services in isolation. Department stores, hotels, and theaters incorporated, and in some cases established, the forms of service found in skyscrapers. Luxury hotels built in the 1820s and 1830s led the way in introducing Americans to new mechanical systems of lighting, heating, and plumbing. In their emphasis on rising standards of domestic convenience, comfort, and human services, hotels set a pattern that skyscrapers followed.[72] Hotels, theaters, and various cultural institutions in the second half of the nineteenth century shared with new office buildings sumptuous and rather elegantly appointed interiors. Moreover, downtown department stores shared many elements with city skyscrapers. Women's parlors, libraries, and lunch clubs introduced into some office buildings in the 1890s followed department store precedents.[73] Like skyscrapers, too, department stores finally employed embellished entrances and interiors that gestured to taste and culture.

Even with their similarities, important distinctions existed between these related buildings and the skyscraper. The skyscraper functioned above all as a place of work. Most of the time, one entered to earn a living rather than spend leisure time or money. For members of the middle class, stores, theaters, and hotels were the site of relatively fleeting visits; office buildings became a mainstay in the daily lives of large and growing numbers of city residents.[74] Skyscrapers, then, belong within a larger ordering of the nineteenth-century city. From the middle-class view, by the close of the century Chicago comprised a variety of linked and gendered realms of life, including: first, residential enclaves, reserved for sensibility and culture and increasingly identified with consumption; second, department stores, public initiators of private consumption that facilitated respectable female presence in downtown; third, downtown skyscrapers, workplaces for white-collars and professionals, arenas for sales, advertising, and marketing; fourth, factories, warehouses, lumberyards and other sites of productive labor—a blue-collar world located along the riverbanks and rail lines and, increasingly, on city outskirts, and surrounded by working-class residences. In this context, skyscrapers were a particular piece of the city; they mediated between production and consumption, work and leisure, commerce and culture.

Yet a fair number of late nineteenth-century Americans played with the notion that a skyscraper might stand for the whole of their metropolis. Contemporaries spoke of tall office buildings as "cities unto themselves" or "a city under one roof."[75] Observers viewed the Chamber of Commerce as "a city within itself." In part, this characterization spoke to the building's impressive size and its resulting capacity to house people and activity: "There are more people doing business inside its walls than you will find in many prosperous towns, and the amount of business transacted here daily equals that done in some of the most pretentious communities in the country. Every branch of commerce and nearly every profession is represented here."[76] Size alone clearly made the skyscraper a source of pride and wonder.

Equally significant, however, these common characterizations of the skyscraper as city expressed a desire for the whole of urban life to resemble the rationalized realm of the tall building. Chicago's "famous tall buildings" embodied the city's characteristic "roar and bustle and energy," while at the same time excluding many of the city's notorious sources of physical discomfort.[77] In 1888, one observer noted that business in a high building "is remote from the noises of the street, and business may be transacted within its door without interruption from such external annoyances."[78] In 1891, *Industrial Chicago*, a chronicle of Chicago development, declared that the skyscraper's "empire is the air. Creeping heavenward, it seems to reach beyond the smoke and noise of the city and beg for a place above the clouds. Comfort, cleanliness and light are within it."[79]

Distance from the street brought social comfort as well. As one Chicagoan wrote in 1892, the city was notable not only for "daring structures . . . which court the clouds" but also for the "varied life that pulsates along the thronged arteries."[80] Profiled in Sigmund Krausz's *Street Types of Chicago*, newsboys, shoe shines, ditch diggers, street preachers, street toughs, and a host of peddlers regularly plied their trades on downtown streets. Just as these street types became subjects of scrutiny and middle-class reform campaigns, the skyscraper helped separate white-collar workers from them and from lower-class street commerce in general. Viewed from skyscraper windows, in fact, people in the street seemed "like pigmies"—comfortably small, they could be rendered exotic for Krausz's book and for office tenants.[81]

The power of the skyscraper derived in part from its supposed embodiment of the progressive promise of the commercial city. Accordingly, building owners sometimes emphasized the metaphor of skyscraper as *city*. In 1892, the Masonic Temple building, the tallest office building in the world, opened with six of its twenty-two floors devoted to stores and shops, grouped around an open atrium court. The building management considered giving these floors street names instead of numbers.[82] Internalizing street and shopping activity, investors in the building sought to provide a commercial setting superior to any in the city. Admiring this "ideal plan," the *Economist* reported that it "would avoid the inconveniences of having to pass along the crowded streets by slow and uncertain means of locomotion in heat, or wet, or cold, and would present . . . attractions which could not be reached even on the street level in the magnificence of the ensemble and the grandeur of the architectural effect."[83] Limited in scale, closely controlled in design, housing a willing, paying, and largely middle-class tenantry, the skyscraper more readily approximated the supposed advantages of the city than the city did. The skyscraper appeared to be a smoothly functioning system, a city that worked.

As such, skyscrapers embodied important ideals of the nascent American city planning movement. Before Daniel H. Burnham laid out the Columbia Exposition or undertook his various urban planning projects, he spent years involved in the design and planning of skyscrapers.[84] In their combination of art, technology, human organization, beauty, cleanliness, and public amenity, Chicago's skyscrapers both anticipated and partially fulfilled the promise of the Columbian Exposition's model urban plan.[85] [. . .]

Mitigating the tension between commerce and culture, skyscrapers might transcend some of the cosmopolitanism of downtown. The Pullman building was "centrally located . . . and yet sufficiently retired to escape much of the noise and confusion of a downtown site." It was "particularly adapted to the higher grades of office building."[86] Burnham and Root's Woman's Temple building managed to be both a "quiet retired holy place" and a "humming hive of business."[87] As tenants and visitors sought out office building restaurants, observatories, stores and offices on light courts and upper floors, they were promised seclusion and insulation not unlike the retreat of suburban residences—quiet, clean, protected, removed.[88]

Building management carefully controlled access to the building, promised discretion in the selection of tenants, and made an effort to mix tenants in an economically beneficial manner. To those unsettled by "intrusions" upon their residential and religious precincts, promoters offered reassurance. Said one: "Particular care will be taken in renting this building, and all objectionable occupations and persons will be rigidly excluded."[89] These assurances enjoyed some basis in skyscraper economics: elevators made all floors easily accessible and diminished the social heterogeneity among tenants that existed in earlier walk-up buildings. A skyscraper might present a more stable restricted enclave than many other urban settings.

This aspect of the skyscraper sparked enthusiasm but also stirred debate, for even while they fostered images of an ideal city, skyscrapers compounded urban problems. From within, the tall building's advantages seemed undeniable; from outside, a less optimistic view arose. In the 1890s, criticism of the skyscraper coalesced in restrictive legislation. The economic depression of the 1890s stopped most skyscraper development in Chicago, but an 1892 ordinance that limited building heights to 150 feet had already inhibited it. The ordinance limited heights to 125 feet on streets less than 80 feet wide and to 100 feet on streets less than 40 feet wide.

The city council, local press, and various professional and civic associations provided the forum for lengthy debate about the height of buildings. Businessmen, sanitarians, architects, engineers, realtors, builders, physicians, art critics, and numerous urban reformers all took positions on the proper form and height of downtown build-ings.[90] The debate revealed cultural ambivalence about new building technologies and about the city's physical and social ability to accommodate the skyscraper. Critics insisted that investors, in their close attention to winning tenants and seizing profits, should not be permitted to ignore the surrounding city or the need for orderly development. A model of internal coordination, the skyscraper manifested a disturbing degree of design anarchy in relation to the city plan and streetscape.

The debate over skyscrapers revolved around a series of apparent contradictions.[91] With their metal frames, large windows, huge light courts, and careful planning, sky-scrapers promised light, airy, and healthy office accommodations. Critics attacked them for casting the city street into shadow, making the air stagnant and thus threatening public health. Furthermore, the burning of 1 million tons of soft coal annually for office building heating, elevator, and lighting plants produced large clouds of dark soot over downtown, belying the promise of light and clean air made in skyscraper rental brochures. Skyscrapers promised an efficient concentration of business; critics attacked them for congesting streets and making downtown a less efficient place for business. Skyscrapers incorporated a number of innovations in fireproofing; critics attacked them because their height and elevator shafts made traditional fire-fighting methods ineffective and increased the hazard of fires spreading to other parts of the city. Skyscrapers, their apologists insisted, repre-sented a legitimate exercise of property rights; critics attacked them for inflicting damage on the property of their neighbors.

Architectural efforts to transcend the dry goods box style of Chicago commercial building undoubtedly tempered contemporary critiques of skyscrapers. By self-consciously setting out to ennoble commerce with monumental forms, using rich materials, traditional architectural motifs, and expressions of white-collar cultivation, skyscraper architects facilitated their clients' relatively unfettered exercise of private property rights. They enjoyed substantial success at reformulating the nineteenth-century's view of commerce, casting material striving as the necessary basis of civility and creating a symbol that linked business with refinement and integrity. That success appears, perhaps, in the comfort with which some twentieth-century architects and critics contemplated buildings that allegedly expressed purely the spirit of modern commerce and industry.

Yet in the late nineteenth century, some critics continued to view skyscrapers as emblems of greed rather than of culture. No amount of tasteful embellishment could convince everyone that commercial striving yielded only benign results. Moreover, that attitudes toward skyscrapers revolved around mutually exclusive views that depended on whether one was inside the skyscraper or outside in the street highlights the limited nature of the conception of the skyscraper as an enclave. Elite landscape gardens had expanded into large public parks, but the reformed, white-collar workplaces provided by the skyscraper did not spur a broader movement for reform of the factory and other work-places of Chicago's poorer citizens.

As it narrowed the architectural images of nineteenth-century commerce, the sky-scraper did nothing to redress increasingly contentious relations between factory workers on the industrial periphery and white-collar workers and managers in the specialized and monumental center. Members of Chicago's civic and economic elite interested in the amelioration of social strife looked increasingly to public interests and public landscapes rather than to private property reforms. In the 1890s and 1900s, they turned to "City Beautiful" plans for monumental city halls, courts, municipal offices, libraries, museums, schools, and adjacent plazas. These public structures, which people theoretically shared in common, might stimulate pride in and civic identification with some broad conception of community, thus reducing the tensions of the commercial realm. This effort to establish a monumental civic landscape confronted the fact that, through their sheer size and novelty, skyscrapers had overwhelmed religious, civic, and cultural buildings once central to the city's public landscape and skyline. [. . .] Skyscrapers challenged attempts by the builders of Chicago's parks, churches, cultural and civic institutions, and even suburbs to monumentalize a life apart from Mammon. For all the power with which they suggested cultivation, skyscrapers monumentalized Mammon as never before.

Notes

1   The quotation is in the Minutes of the National Women's Christian Temperance Union, 1887, cclxxiv; for a discussion of the skyscraper's dominance of American urban form, see Spiro Kostof, "The Skyscraper City," *Design Quarterly* 140 (1988): 33–35.

2   Robert Bruegmann, "The Marquette Building and the Myth of the 'Chicago School'," *Threshold: Journal of the School of Architecture* 5–6 (fall 1991): 6–23 (Chicago: University of Illinois). See also Thomas A. P. van Leeuwen, *The Skyward Trend of Thought* (Cambridge: MIT Press, 1988), 20–29.

3   Sigfried Giedion, *Space, Time and Architecture: The Growth of a New Tradition* (Cambridge: Harvard University Press, 1941); Carl W. Condit, *The Rise of the Skyscraper* (Chicago: University of Chicago Press, 1952).

4   Condit, *Skyscraper*, 2. The most recent elaboration of this concept comes in Ross Miller's *American Apocalypse: The Great Fire and the Myth of Chicago* (Chicago: University of Chicago Press, 1990), 149–60. Miller argues that American nineteenth-century architects had "two insecure identities": that of the professional and that of the romantic, inventive designer; he concludes, "By incorporating style, American architects might have temporarily solved their identity crises, but there was something absurd about it all. Images that comforted the architect bore no relation to the job at hand of permanently rebuilding a city like Chicago" (p. 160).

5   Giedion, *Space, Time and Architecture*, 24.

6   Ibid.

7   Giedion, *Space, Time and Architecture*, 303–4.

8   Condit, *Skyscraper*, 16.

9   United States Census Office, *The Statistics of the Population of the United States, 9th Census, 1870* (Washington, D.C.: GPO, 1872), vol. 1; idem, *Statistics of the Population of the United States at the Tenth Census* (Washington, D.C.: GPO, 1883), 870, table 36; Department of Commerce and Labor, Bureau of the Census, *Special Reports, Occupations at the Twelfth Census* (Washington, D.C.: GPO, 1904).

10   Alfred D. Chandler, Jr., *The Visible Hand: The Managerial Revolution in American Business* (Cambridge: Harvard University Press, 1977); Olivier Zunz, *Making America Corporate, 1870–1920* (Chicago: University of Chicago Press, 1990), 103–48.

11   *Chicago Tribune*, October 28, 1888; see also Perry R. Duis, *Chicago Creating New Traditions* (Chicago: Chicago Historical Society, 1976), 21, 29.

12   In the 1880s and 1890s, buildings of ten stories were considered skyscrapers; see *Call Board Bulletin*, October 11, 1888; *Industrial Chicago*, 4 vols. (Chicago: Goodspeed Publishing, 1891), vol. 1, 168. The term *commercial style*, used interchangeably with *skyscraper*, is said to apply to

buildings of seven stories and over in *Morris' Dictionary of Chicago and Vicinity* (Chicago: Frank M. Morris, 1891), 28–29.

13   Gerald R. Larson and Roula Mouroudellis Geraniotis, "Toward a Better Understanding of the Evolution of the Iron Skeleton Frame in Chicago," *Journal of the Society of Architectural Historians* 46 (March 1987): 40–41; Rosemarie Haag Bletter, "The Invention of the Skyscraper: Notes on Its Diverse Histories," *Assemblage* 2 (February 1987): 110–11. For a somewhat different view on this subject, see, Cesar Pelli, "Skyscrapers," *Perspecta* 18 (1982): 134–51; Robert A. M. Stern, Gregory Gilmartin, and John Montague Massengale, *New York 1900* (New York: Rizzoli, 1983), 147–52, 455n19.

14   *Chicago Tribune*, February 16, 1890, quoted in *The Architecture of John Wellborn Root*, by Donald Hoffmann (Baltimore: Johns Hopkins University Press, 1973), 85.

15   Morris, *Dictionary of Chicago*, 29.

16   Ogden to George S. Boutwell, January 27, 1872, Public Building Service Records, record group 121, entry 26, box 8, National Archives, Washington, D.C.

17   McCormick Company to A. W. Nichols, January 23, 1883. This letter and all other McCormick business and real estate materials are, unless otherwise specified, located in the McCormick Papers, Manuscript Division, State Historical Society of Wisconsin, Madison.

18   *Chicago Tribune*, March 9, 1884.

19   John J. Flinn, *The Standard Guide of Chicago* (Chicago: Standard Guide Company, 1893), 47.

20   Flinn, *Standard Guide*, 55.

21   Newspaper descriptions are the single most important source of information on nineteenth-century public views of the skyscraper. There are both feature articles and notices of building plans in the real estate sections of the papers. Other important sources are building rental brochures. The Chicago Historical Society has the best collection of these, including brochures for the Board of Trade, Masonic Temple, Continental Woman's Temple, Venetian, Counselman, Isabella, Columbus Memorial, and Chicago, Burlington, and Quincy Railroad buildings.

22   John W. Root, "A Great Architectural Problem," *Inland Architect* 15 (June 1890): 71.

23   William H. Jordy, *American Buildings and Their Architects: Progressive and Academic Ideals at the Turn of the Twentieth Century* (Garden City, N.Y.: Doubleday, 1972), 73.

24   *Chicago Tribune*, October 28, 1888.

25   Flinn, *Chicago, The Marvelous City of the West: A History, an Encyclopedia and a Guide* (Chicago: Standard Guide, 1892), 574.

26   Flinn, *Standard Guide*, 197.

27   "The Chamber of Commerce Building," *Economist* 3 (March 8, 1890): 266; Flinn, *Chicago*, 570–71.

28   See *Collection of Photographs of "Ornamental Iron" Executed by the Winslow Bros., Co., Chicago* (Chicago: Winslow Bros., 1893).

29   John F. Kasson, "The Aesthetics of Machinery," in his *Civilizing the Machine* (New York: Grossman Publishers, 1976), 137–80.

30   Charles S. Spring, Jr., to Mrs. Cyrus Hall McCormick, November 13, 1879.

31   "Mosaic Floors," *Inland Architect* 17 (July 1891): 71.

32   *Industrial Chicago*, vol. 1, 197.

33   Eric J. Hobsbawn, *The Age of Empire, 1875–1914* (New York: Pantheon, 1987), 172.

34   *Chicago Tribune*, April 24, 1892.

35   *Chicago Tribune*, April 24, 1892, May 1, 1892, and May 8, 1892.

36   For a recent review of the debate, see Larson and Geraniotis, "The Iron Skeleton Frame in Chicago"; Condit, *Skyscraper*, 114; Jordy, *American Buildings*, 20–22; Theodore Turak, *William Le Baron Jenney: A Pioneer of Modern Architecture* (Ann Arbor: UMI Research Publications, 1986), 237–63.

37   "Removal of the Railway Age Offices," *Railway Age* 11 (April 8, 1886): 185–86.

38   *Chicago Tribune*, October 30, 1892.

39   McCormick Real Estate Ledgers, 1863–70.

Chapter 11

Mona Domosh

Creating New York's nineteenth-century retail district

> The admiration excited by the imposing exterior of this vast block of building—the largest in this continent, we believe, devoted to the business of a single mercantile firm—is greatly intensified by an examination of its interior. . . . The whole building, indeed, is thoroughly and unmistakably characteristic of Mr. Stewart. Constructed of iron and plenty of glass—fire-proof, with abundant light and ventilation—perfectly adapted to all its purposes, and securing the comfort of all within—it betrays the thoughtfulness of a merchant intent upon business, but not so intent as to be unmindful of the physical necessities of those in his employ.
>
> ("Stewart's Store," *Appleton's Journal of Popular Literature, Science, and Art* (1870))

The reactions to Stewart's department store on Broadway between 9th and 10th streets that had opened in 1862 were indeed filled with admiration, not only at its size—an entire block—but at its construction and design (Figure 11.1). Alexander T. Stewart spared no expense in building his new cast-iron palace, using the latest construction materials (glass and iron) and the most fashionable architectural design. That this was thought characteristic of Stewart is not surprising—the building that had previously housed his store was in its time as innovative in design and in location as his new store. In his life as well as his business practices, Stewart characterized the bourgeois spirit of New York until his death in 1876 and the subsequent foundering of his store in the 1880s. He came to epitomize the dry goods "princes" of mid-century New York—men who expanded their stores and decorated them with the latest architectural styles, and who, though probably unconsciously and indirectly, were responsible for reshaping New York's commercial district.

With the overwhelming primacy of the port of New York as an import-export center by 1830, the dry goods sector of New York's economy was set for explosive growth. As warehousing activities expanded away from the docks and wharves, the city's retailers began a spatial movement as well. Throughout the last half of the nineteenth century, New York's retailers continued to locate their stores further up Broadway, not far behind the northward movement of their best customers, the upper and middle classes. In addition, the buildings they had constructed, particularly the department stores, became larger and more ornate and began to incorporate aspects of what has been called the domestic sphere—lounges, art galleries, restaurants, and meeting spots for women. In essence, this new retailing area was a different type of urban environment, one that brought style and

few standardized prices or goods, a purchase involved a personal encounter with the owner of the shop and discussion of the quality of the item and the price. In addition, goods were not usually displayed in the shop; given the limited space, most items were stored in back rooms or on different floors and were brought out only when requested by a customer. Generally, a customer asked to see a particular item, haggled over the cost, and, if satisfied, bought the item. The shop, therefore, was little more than a backdrop for the drama of the personal encounter and act of purchase. For mid-century New Yorkers, buying an item at a dry goods store was no different from any other personal business transaction. But that process was soon to change.

Mid-nineteenth-century industrialization, particularly in textiles and in boots and shoes, led to the standardization of goods and the concurrent standardization of prices. For example, a yard of calico fabric manufactured at the Lowell textile mills would be sold at one price to wholesalers, who would then offer it to retailers. If retailers purchased large amounts of that cloth, they would pay a lower price per yard. With such savings, the retailer could make more profit by selling that item at the standard price, or pass on the savings to the customer, assuming that selling large amounts of the cloth would lead to additional profits. Either way, standardization of goods and prices meant that dealing in bulk became profitable for retailers, who needed more room to store and sell these items. In this way, industrialization and standardization directly led to the development of the department store. In addition, industrialization made affordable a larger array of goods. Mass production lowered the cost of many dry goods, making it possible for the middle classes to own a vast array of personal and household material possessions.[8] To be competitive, then, retailers needed more space to house the new variety and quantity of offerings.

Yet it was not just the size of stores that needed adjustment, but also the design. First, the large variety of goods made it increasingly difficult for customers to be familiar with the range of wares available. The goods needed to be displayed so that customers could assess the offerings and decide what to buy. Retail stores needed space to display those wares and had to create an environment where customers were encouraged to view the goods. Second, standardization of goods and prices had eliminated the need for direct dealings with an owner. Indeed, with larger stores and more variety of goods, it was no longer even possible for customers to speak with the owner. Instead, customers were helped by a salesclerk—an employee whose job did not involve price-setting but, instead, helped to display goods and assisted customers in their comparative shopping.

The act of purchasing, therefore, had become inconsequential. But in these large emporiums, the act of purchasing was more than compensated for by the activity of shopping. In these new palaces of consumption, shopping became an event in and of itself. Since standardization and mass production meant that goods were, at least in theory, equally accessible to the middle and upper classes, status was accorded not only by the possession of particular commodities, but by the means through which "the commodities become accessible and are acquired." As the goods themselves were increasingly standardized, and as the act of consumption became more impersonal, it was almost as if "the stage on which it took place became correspondingly more important."[9] Thus, the need for retailers to display a large variety of goods and encourage people to buy them, combined with the way the activity of shopping indicated and maintained social status, led to large, ornate, stylish, and leisured spaces for shopping—to what Rosalind Williams calls dream worlds of mass consumption.[10]

Women were intricately involved in the department store, not only in their role as customers, but also as store employees. Although department stores originally hired men to be the salesclerks, increasingly throughout the latter half of the nineteenth century women entered those jobs. And women also provided much of the labor in the textile and garment industries, industries that were reliant on the department store and vice versa. Because women constituted the major class of consumers, the retail environment was designed for them, embodying the bourgeois notions of respectability considered necessary for the middle- and upper-class woman. New York's consumer spaces were feminized—they were meant to appeal to late nineteenth-century bourgeois women—and therefore they had to integrate culture with commerce, the domestic with the public, the feminine with the masculine.

From the beginning, women were targeted as the major class of consumers. As early as 1846, accounts of the opening of Stewart's [first major] department store mentioned women as an established consumer class. The *New York Herald* stated that, inside the store, "we found the ladies, as usual, busy pricing goods and feasting their eyes on the profusion of gorgeous articles for sale."[11] The opening of the store prompted another commentator to suggest that at least half of women's time was spent shopping: "Half the time of the fashionable ladies of New York, at the lowest calculation, is spent in the dry goods store, in laying out plans for personal decoration. Dress forms a subject of the most grave and serious contemplation. It may be said to be the first thing they think of in the morning, and the last at night—nay, it is not the subject of the dream."[12]

According to Elaine Abelson, shopping became almost a daily ritual for middle-class women, taking up an overwhelming share of their time and becoming a major form of women's work. Throughout the nineteenth century, a new ideology of middle-class life dictated that home production was no longer acceptable.[13] America's industrial powers needed new markets and new products to keep their ever-expanding factories running profitably, and commodification of the home provided seemingly endless possibilities. The Civil War fueled increasing industrial production in the north, and, when the war ended, those industries sought new outlets to keep their factories running at capacity.[14] By the end of the nineteenth century, food, shelter, clothing, and home furnishings had all become commodities, and women's work shifted from domestic production to public consumption.

The development of the ready-to-wear clothing industry, and with it the introduction of fashionableness to the middle class, had a sweeping impact on industrial growth and the retailing trade. Although fully finished clothing was not available until the 1870s, merchants had spent years paving the way for women to believe that factory-produced clothing was better, cheaper, and simply more modern than homemade clothing. Advertisements and household advice dispensed through ladies' magazines appealed to a woman's sense of duty to provide the best up-to-date care for her family and reminded her of status that was associated with the most stylish clothing. Yet this fundamental change in how people led their lives, a change that convinced most middle-class women that ready-to-wear clothes were better than those made at home, was not sufficient to maintain the continual increase in sales demanded by dry goods manufacturers and merchants. Sales were kept high by creating a situation of open-ended demand, in other words, by introducing fashion to middle-class life. The dictates of fashion—characterized by perpetual changes in style and therefore built-in obsolescence—were conveyed in a rhetoric stating that women needed, at a minimum, a new wardrobe each season, and, to be truly fashionable, the wardrobe had to include an outfit appropriate for every distinctive occasion. By the late 1870s, a woman could find advertisements in such magazines as *Harper's Weekly* and *Harper's Bazar* for clothing appropriate for every occasion: for going for promenades, carriage rides, and walks; for staying in the house, receiving guests, and having dinner; for going out in the evening; for riding, skating, visiting the seaside; and for traveling and getting married. And, for children, each age group had appropriate garb. To give some sense of what sort of production this demand fueled, it is estimated that one elegant evening dress in the 1860s required approximately 1,100 yards of fabric.[15] An 1872 guide to New York estimated that it was not unusual for fashionable women to have wardrobes worth more than $20,000.[16] [. . .]

These extreme examples from the very wealthy of New York set the tone and style for the middle-class woman to emulate. She might not be able to afford gold jewelry or an overskirt of lace, but a middle-class woman could have touches of lace on her dress, and at least a small piece of appropriate jewelry. The point was to maintain vigilance and be aware of all fashion changes. Constant consumption, therefore, was required of the middle-class woman, not only because her appearance and that of her family were important indicators of social status, but also because correct consumption reflected on her role as mother and wife. Shopping had become such an onerous occupation for some women that New Yorker Clara Pardee wrote in her diary in 1893: "I am so sick of the stores and clothes . . . would rather the clothes grew on like feathers!"[17]

Department stores' needs for high volume sales reinforced the new consumerism associated with the fashion industry—perpetual changes in style required constant consumption. Department stores became active participants in the fashion world as they fueled demand by displaying fashion alternatives in a setting that imbued those commodities with social meaning. At the same time, department stores, because they sold mass-produced and therefore less expensive items, made available to more women the possibility of being fashionable. This further stimulated production, which led to new demands for consumption and vice versa.

In New York, where social status was, for most people, always subject to negotiation, the culture of consumerism was of critical interest. And for women, fashion was of particular interest, because fashion allowed one to display status independent of occupation or position. A man's status could be conveyed by his job, or membership in a club, or his relative position in a particular segment of society. A woman's status was dependent on a man's, as his wife or child or mother. Fashion, however, was a status indicator that was specific to the woman. Her choice of styles, fabrics, and colors were her own decisions and therefore indicative of her "good" taste, and hence of her social status. But in what ways did associating shopping with women serve the emerging bourgeois society?

Feminist historians, among others, have shown the importance of the separation of spheres to the reigning ideology of late nineteenth-century middle-class life.[18] In addition to the male-female, culture-commerce divide, production and consumption were ideologically kept separated. In reality, of course, these two different aspects of industrialization were completely interrelated: production was completely reliant on consumption, and vice versa. The values of production—self-denial, hard work, utilitarianism—were distinct from those of consumption, because successful consumption required self-indulgence, leisure time, and playfulness. How, then, could these two value systems be maintained and encouraged without undermining each other? How could hard work be encouraged at the same time as self-indulgence? The values of production could be maintained in the face of a growing need for consumption by aligning production with the world of men, and consumption with the world of women. Women could be self-indulgent, while men worked hard to support them. In addition, since women were thought to represent "naturally" moral characteristics, they could consume without fear of overindulgence. Women's moral character would keep their materialism in check, thereby protecting the family's moral status.

In her analysis of Victorian Britain, Sally Shuttleworth argues that the distinction between consumption and production was symbolically played out in a variety of cultural discourses. In particular, she suggests that discussions of diseases concerning men's and women's bodies in contemporary medical literature reveal cultural anxieties concerning the separate economic and social spheres. Many "women's" diseases of the era were thought to be caused by women inhibiting their natural bodily flows, while for men, the problems were thought to be caused by not controlling their bodies. Thus, cultural anxiety focused around the issues of desire and self-control; women were meant to give in to their natural desires, men to resist them. This anxiety, Shuttleworth argues, was a result of the uncertainties the new bourgeois class was facing—an economic system that required constant and continual consumption to fuel its productive sector, and a social system where conspicuous displays of wealth could not assure social legitimacy.[19]

Relegating the sphere of consumption to women eased some of those tensions. Women could be consumers and visible symbols of material wealth without undermining their social standing because, it was thought, women's virtue would keep their materialism from contaminating the family's moral character. As long as women's acquisitiveness did not get out of control, their role as consumers served the needs of bourgeois society and economy. In fact, contemporary commentators attributed the success of the department store to women's consumer desires. The opening of Stewart's 1846 "marble palace" elicited the following remark in the *New York Herald*: "As long as the ladies continue to constitute an important feature in the community, the dry goods business must be in a flourishing condition. . . . In fact, dry goods are a passion with the ladies, and whilst they continue to remain so the business must flourish; for woe to the luckless husband who refuses his wife money for shopping."[20]

Women's passion for fashion was good for business and did not threaten the established values of productivity. E. L. Godkin's analysis of the success of the dry goods trade led him to the needs of American women: "The pre-eminence and attractiveness of the dry-goods trade in this country is due mainly to the great purchasing power and varied requirements of American women. . . . The consequence is that the dry-goods man has a sphere of activity opened to him such as is presented to no other trader—women are his principal customers, and their wants are innumerable, whether for use or ornament, and their fancy is a harp of a thousand strings, on which a skillful salesman may play an endless variety of tunes."[21] Thus the gender hierarchy helped maintain the distinction between consumption and production, a distinction necessary in a system that required indulging one's desires through consumption and, at the same time, controlling desire through self-discipline in order to increase production. Thus, with women as the major class of consumers, the new culture of consumption was not disruptive. Department stores incorporated women and the feminine into their landscape: the domestic was brought into the public arena.

HOUSING THE RETAILERS

As department stores moved north into residential areas, they created new landscapes, districts that spatially and socially were associated with the domestic enclaves they were striving to be near. This movement also disassociated them from the financial, wholesale, and office districts to the south, that is, from the male-defined workplaces of the city. When Alexander Stewart opened his department store on Broadway at Chambers Street, just north of City Hall, in 1846, it was heralded by some as foolhardy (Figure 11.2). It was considered uptown and on the wrong side of the street—the west side was considered more fashionable, as it was more removed from the docks along the East River, closer to the elite residential area, and supposedly more sunny. Yet Stewart's emporium was a huge economic success, making him a millionaire and allowing him to expand his store within several years of its opening. The store was the first retail establishment to move out of the more generalized wholesaling area further south and east, and its success brought many followers. By the early 1850s, Lord and Taylor had moved from Catherine Street to the corner of Grand and Chrystie streets, and Arnold and Hearn on Canal Street had split into two companies, with Hearn Brothers moving to 425 Broadway and Arnold Constable to Canal Street. Seamon and Muir was on Worth Street, with the store of Strong and Adriance next door.[22]

By 1862, however, Stewart needed more space for his growing business and moved the retailing portion of his store uptown following his customers (the upper middle class of New York was now living as far north as Union and Washington squares), to Broadway between 9th and 10th streets, leaving his downtown store to serve as a warehouse. And, as was the case after Stewart's bold move several years earlier, other stores followed. James McCutcheon and Company opened its store just to the south of Stewart's, at 748 Broadway, B. Altman moved to Third Avenue, two blocks west, and R. H. Macy's moved to Sixth Avenue, several blocks east and north.[23]

Throughout the 1870s and 1880s, department stores continued to move north up Broadway, and, particularly in the 1890s, onto Sixth Avenue.[24] In 1875, the retailing focus was on Broadway between 10th and 23rd streets. [. . .] By the mid-1880s an entire

11.2 Joseph Trench and John Snook (?), A. T. Stewart's department store, Broadway at Chambers Street, New York, New York, 1846, enlarged 1850 (from James D. McCabe, Jr., *Lights and Shadows of New York Life; or, The Sights and Sensations of the Great City*, Philadelphia, Chicago: National Book Publishing Co., 1872)

district—from 10th Street up to 23rd Street, and from Sixth Avenue east to Broadway—was dedicated to retail and entertainment. Previously this area had been residential, but, with the encroachment of commercial activities, the middle and upper classes of New York continued their flight northward, moving up Fifth Avenue toward Central Park. As Christine Boyer has documented, New York's elite residential district moved northward throughout the nineteenth century, moving first out of lower Broadway to the area around Union Square and then even further north to 23rd Street and Madison Square in the 1850s.[25] Philip Hone reported in his diary the rapid transformation of Broadway into a commercial street that precipitated residential movement north: "The mania for converting Broadway into a street of shops is greater than ever. There is scarcely a block in the whole extent of this fine street of which some part is not in a state of transmutation. Three or four good brick houses on the corner of Broadway and Spring Street have been leveled. I know not for what purpose, shops no doubt. The houses, fine costly edifices to me, are to make way for a grand concert establishment."[26]

Throughout the last half of the nineteenth century New York's upper and middle classes moved more than forty blocks north. And following behind them was the emergent retail district, as it expanded north. Instead of gradually expanding block by block, the district passed over intervening blocks and relocated in a totally new area, reflecting both rapid and intense spatial expansion. [. . .]

By the turn of the century, the new retailing focus for New York City was a district centered on Fifth Avenue between Union and Madison squares, extending east to Sixth Avenue and west to Broadway. It was an area of ornamental architecture and grand boulevards, of restaurants and bars, and of small boutiques and large department stores. It was, above all, an urban landscape designed specifically for consumption. Urban dwellers had certainly purchased goods before, but in areas not devoted strictly to consumption. This new retailing district differed from its predecessors in that it catered solely to consumers. Its three-dimensional form also differed dramatically from its predecessors. While the new department stores were dramatically larger than earlier dry goods stores, they also broke new ground in the degree of ornamentation, the attention to decorative detail and display of goods, the concern with internal organization of departments, and the catering to the personal needs of the shoppers, who, in most cases, were women.

STEWART'S PALACES

The story of the most influential retailer in nineteenth-century New York—Alexander T. Stewart—and the two department stores he had constructed illustrates this process. One of New York's most successful merchant princes, Stewart was an innovator in retailing and a keen observer of and active participant in the New York real estate market. Stewart himself characterized New York's commercial spirit in many ways. He came to New York from Ireland in 1820, and in 1876 he died the second richest man in New York, much of his fortune made in real estate speculation.[27] Little interested in local political or social issues, except when they had a direct effect on his businesses, Stewart came to dominate the commercial scene of New York. Both of the commercial palaces he had built to house his stores spearheaded the northward march of retailing in the middle part of the nineteenth century.

The marble palace he had constructed in 1846 on Broadway at Chambers Street represented a bold move for several reasons—it was the largest store meant solely for retail, it was located away from the generalized commercial areas of the city, and it was designed to be an ornamental structure for the display of wares. To appreciate the boldness of this move, one has only to compare the world of Stewart's new store with its predecessors. First, its location was ideal for shopping—it was removed from the narrow streets and noise and congestion of lower Manhattan. In contrast, the wide expanse of Broadway was perfect for carriages, and women could be dropped off at the door of the store without venturing into the narrow side streets. The particular block that Stewart chose was also significant. The portion of the block that bordered Reade Street had been the site of the Washington Hotel, once a famous meeting spot of the city, and considered a handsome building and worthy of note along that stretch of Broadway. But, more important, the location bordered City Hall Park, a central area of the city that witnessed large amounts of pedestrian activity, and from which a handsome building could be displayed without interference from other structures. Stewart's store had occupied three other locations on Broadway, but now, with a well-established and expanding business and plenty of money, he decided to build a structure meant strictly for his own store.

It was clear to observers that these amenities were meant to appeal to women: "New York can now boast of the most splendid dry goods store in the world. . . . Mr. Stewart has paid the ladies of this city a high compliment in giving them such a beautiful resort in which to while away their leisure hours of the morning."[39] As historian William Leach suggests, it was women who were identified with small, ornamental items, with "fancy goods," and these were the enticements of the department store. For a man to set foot in a department store for his own pleasure was seen as a symbolic act of emasculation.[40] The desire to while away leisure hours in such an ornamental setting was a decidedly feminine attribute.

Based on this appeal to women and other of Stewart's clever business practices, his store was a huge success.[41] The impact of the store on subsequent commercial construction in New York was significant, starting a vogue for this new style up and down Broadway. An 1854 editorial in *Harper's* conveys its influence:

> A few years ago when a man returned from Europe, his eye full of the lofty buildings of the Continent, our cities seemed insignificant and mean. . . . He felt that the city had no character, but he could not see what was wanting. But the moment Stewart's fine building was erected, the difficulty appeared. . . . [It] was a key-note, a model. There had been other high buildings, but none so stately and simple. And even now there is, in its way no finer street effect than the view of Stewart's buildings seen on a clear blue brilliant day, from a point low in Broadway. . . . It rises out of the sea of green foliage in the park, a white marble cliff, sharply drawn against the sky.[42]

That the building was impressive when it opened in 1846 cannot be denied, and the "white marble cliff" did indeed become a "key-note" of New York's emerging landscape. It was a fine display of the best that New York could offer—plenty of merchandise for any who could afford it, presented in a dramatic manner. The description of opening day activities in the *New York Herald* points to the atmosphere of spectacle: "When we visited the store, about 12 o'clock, we found a line of carriages drawn up in front reaching from Chambers to Reade streets. Crowds of fashionable people were passing in and out, and all were warm in their expressions of gratification of all the beautiful and tasteful arrangements and architecture of this whole building. . . . The sales at the store yesterday were very brisk and the clerks were kept busy throughout the day."[43]

Less than fourteen years after his Chambers Street store opened, Stewart decided his prospering business needed to move further uptown, in order to capitalize on the movement of the upper middle class. He bought what had been an old farm on Broadway between 9th and 10th streets, and had constructed on the site a grand architectural display that became known as Stewart's Cast-Iron Palace.[44] Although many contemporaries considered such a move uptown foolhardy because the area was not thought convenient to its upper-class clientele, Stewart's new store was a huge and immediate success.[45] Keenly aware of real estate trends, Stewart knew quite well that the elite were moving into the area near Washington and Union squares and that his customers would certainly be attracted to such opulent architecture.

Stewart used the very latest in construction techniques and spared no expense on décor—apparently the building cost $2,755,000.[46] The new department store, designed by

John Kellum (a popular New York architect, who was also responsible for Stewart's home on Fifth Avenue), was considered an architectural marvel. Stewart surprised his contemporaries with his choice of building material for the façade, selecting cast iron instead of marble. Stewart himself had begun the vogue for marble façades with his earlier store on Broadway. But again Stewart set the trend, and, by choosing iron, Stewart allied himself with the latest in industrial technology, particularly as the Civil War brought to the public's awareness the increasing use of iron for new engineering and transportation projects.[47] The use of iron also allowed for greater window space and therefore permitted more natural light to enter the store on all stories. The six-story building, designed in the palazzo style and constructed of iron and glass, was not to be missed by visitors to the city. Like Stewart's marble palace, his new cast-iron palace became a landmark.

In this new location, Stewart was able to put into practice what he had learned during the years of business at his old store, and continued the idea of the department store as a stage of consumption designed to fit the prevailing gender ideology. The interior space was designed to contrast with the chaos of the surrounding urban form. The highly structured and symmetrically arranged aisles and counters contributed to a sense of the orderliness of the store, of, as historian Gunther Barth describes it, "a utopian order that was a relief after the disorderly anarchy of modern city life that engulfed the building."[48] Stewart maintained the civic allusions of his earlier store, centering his new building around a large rotunda (eighty feet by forty-eight feet) and at the same time magnifying the display aspects of the interior.[49] The entire store was dominated by a skylight that provided direct light to the large main floor. The five upper stories were arranged as encircling balconies, thus providing natural light to all floors and enabling shoppers to observe one another as they strolled through the enormous building. This design contributed to the atmosphere of spectacle in the store, with shoppers able to view all the activities at the main gallery, while seeing across and up and down to the various departments that surrounded them. This presented women customers with a fairly limitless visual experience, as they watched not only each other, but also the range of wares for consumption.

CREATING THE FEMININE LANDSCAPE

Yet despite all this commercialism, the presence of women ensured that the forces of consumption would not disrupt the values of productivity. In other words, women as the main class of consumers allowed the new culture of consumption to flourish without seriously disturbing the economic order. In its appeal to women and its incorporation of aspects of the domestic, Stewart's store also made the consumption necessary to support industrialization ideologically more acceptable. Yet gender also helped mediate another set of tensions—that between the commercial and the cultural. Stewart's store was attacked by New York's culture critics because it was designed as a civic structure—with dome, rotunda, and Italianate style—yet was the quintessential commercial enterprise. By so doing, it risked blurring the distinction between commerce and culture—an ideological tenet that was important to New York's middle and upper classes.

Stewart's first store met with much approval, due as much to its novelty as its actual design, but his second store sounded the warning signs for contemporary critics. Many found cast-iron architecture to be cheap and not worthy of much attention. P. B. Wight's comments on Stewart's store show the degree of disdain:

> It bears all over it an evidence of cheapness, especially when we observe it is of iron . . . a cheapness which comes from the desire to save pattern-making. In all probability, not more than six patterns were required to cast the several thousand tons which are put in this great iron wall. There is nothing inside of this store except iron columns, all cast from one pattern and no end of plaster-corniced girders, save the great cast-iron well-hole over the glove counter with its bull's eye skylight above. This is a perfect mine of wasted iron, which, if properly used, would construct several respectable buildings. It is safe to say that this building has done more to retard architectural progress in New York than any other dozen buildings of the worst possible designs. It overawes the thoughtless by its sheer size and seizes the sympathy of the sentimental by the purity of its white paint,—when it is fresh.[50]

That the commercial style of architecture was becoming unacceptable to the arbiters of good taste is not surprising; distinctions in class were often based on taste, and here we see the put-down both of Stewart himself—for mixing commerce with culture and producing cheap architecture—and of his customers who are taken in by the size and seized by "the sympathy of the sentimental." Epitomizing the bourgeois spirit, Stewart's department store is seen as a threat to that spirit in blurring the distinctions on which the bourgeois class is legitimizing itself, between the world of money and production and the world of culture and leisure. On the one hand, New York's middle and upper classes looked to the world of culture to provide a mantle of moral authority for their commercial successes. It was therefore incumbent upon them to maintain a cultural world untainted by the commercial impulse. Hence, the disdain over the "cheap" architecture of the new Stewart's store—a commercial enterprise could never hope to acquire any cultural propriety. On the other hand, the two worlds were in fact dependent on each other. By using an architectural style to associate the store with a known past, Stewart invoked the predominant logic of Victorian architecture.[51] Most of New York's prominent commercial buildings were designed with the idea of providing a known and legitimized history to these commercial enterprises. This cloak of an idealized past was not meant to hide commerce, which did not need to be hidden; instead, it associated the commercial with the cultural. A marble store with a rotunda indicated in architectural language that the commercial prince who owned the store was indeed of the ruling class, and the customers who shopped there could acquire for themselves such legitimacy by buying the appropriate items.

An apparent contradiction begins to emerge, however. On the one hand, middle-class life needed to separate the cultural and the commercial so that this class could feel culturally legitimate and therefore superior to others, those without "taste." And yet the middle and upper classes also needed the economic support of those without taste, and so offered them a chance to acquire taste by shopping in appropriately ornamented stores and buying the correct items. This led to a mixing of the categories of culture and commerce. This contradiction was inherent to the functionings of a bourgeois class in a democratic political system—a class dependent on economic wealth, and yet seeking cultural legitimacy. To maintain that wealth, they had to sell their culture to those who increasingly could afford it. Yet to distinguish themselves from those same people, the elite needed to separate the cultural realm from the mere commercial.

One can understand why the design of the new Stewart building provoked strong reactions among the tastemakers of New York. As with the city's first skyscrapers, many commercial buildings were perceived by the city's cultural elite, a fairly small subset of the economic elite, as architectural aberrations. They appealed to the wrong type of people, those who had not acquired the "correct" taste and were being sold a cheap reproduction. This blurring of the commercial and the cultural that the store represented not only created "bad" architecture, it attracted people who were taken in by the sheer delight of the spectacle. The architecture did not fulfill the pure goals of art—the building could not be read for its historical and moral codes because these styles were considered mere disguises of unbridled commercialism. This threatened those concerned with maintaining aesthetic standards.

The use of cast iron as a significant ornamental element in New York's retail structures also called into question the distinction between craftsmanship and mechanics. Cast iron and these patterns were simply affixed to steel or masonry framing. The use of cast iron, therefore, precluded the need for bricklayers or stonemasons; in fact, no traditional craft-related work was required. Cast-iron architecture, then, presaged the use of the steel frame and the rise of modernist architecture. Yet in its time it was disdained by cultural authorities for its cheapness and lack of aesthetic qualities. Many commentators wondered why cast iron continued to be used even after the fires in Boston and Chicago in the 1870s had shown the material's susceptibility to fire. Architect Leopold Eidlitz indirectly responded to that question in his attack on the use of cast iron: "Iron never can, and never will be, a suitable material for forming the main walls of architectural monuments. The only material for that purpose always has been, and now is, stone. . . . A building bedizened with cast-iron ornamentation would give to the question, for what purpose the building is erected, would be plain to me as though it was written upon it with large cast-iron letters: 'FOR SHOW MORE THAN FOR ANY OTHER PURPOSE.'"[52] Eidlitz was, of course, correct—cast iron was indeed for show, since it was the most stylish and up-to-date building material of the time, and it allowed much larger windows for display, exactly what commercial entrepreneurs wanted in the design of their new buildings. Stewart's cast-iron palace set the tone for New York's commercial enterprises, and much of the architecture of what has come to be known as the Ladies' Mile is of this cast-iron palace style, loosely based on the Italianate style. The arbiters of good taste could do little except complain.

Yet for most middle-class New Yorkers, the department store seemed not a threat at all, but rather a mediation between commerce and culture. One could now shop in the most ornamented of locations, surrounded by beautiful architecture, and often the sounds of the symphony. With the main shoppers being women, that "timid, non-commercial class," how could the department store be seen as threatening?[53] Historian William Leach has shown how religion was figured into the equation of women and fashion, thereby making less threatening these palaces of consumption. The association of religion with fashion had already become familiar to most Americans by mid-century—as a commentator noted in 1856, "real ladies and gentlemen are those who belong both to the Church and to fashion."[54] Department store owners built on this association, calling their stores cathedrals and their goods objects of devotion. A commentator compared Stewart's new store with Grace Church, and spoke of the store as dedicated to the worship of dry goods: "In walking up Broadway on the west side of that most magnificent of thoroughfares, a person must naturally find two striking objects to contemplate at that point where the street makes a bend. One is the graceful, slender, gray spire of Grace Church, piercing the blue atmosphere; the other is the gigantic mass of iron, painted of a white color, erected by Alexander T. Stewart to the worship of dry-goods, covering two acres of ground, and Theban in its Old World massiveness."[55]

Department stores learned to schedule the openings of their collections at Christmas and Easter, thus further aligning religion and fashion, and institutionalizing the commercialization of religious holidays. As William Leach suggests, "The department stores, and the fashion industry that underlay them, penetrated into and contaminated the life of established religion, creating a paradoxical marriage between commodity capitalism and religious life that has persisted into our own time."[56] Department stores, then, were central to both the commercialization of religion and association of religion with consumption. And, since religion formed an integral part of the women's sphere, the department store served to reinforce the alignment of the feminine with consumption. By turning shoppers into "worshipers" in "cathedrals" of commerce, the store owners hoped to portray consumption as a moral act, a kind of religious duty of women.

The department store solidified this association among women, femininity, and consumption. And because department stores were by far the most influential forces in the late nineteenth-century retail market, they were also the most powerful shapers of the urban environment. The use of glass in department stores was of particular importance in the display of the private world of the public spaces of the city. Plate-glass windows were originally adopted in department stores in order to bring in more natural light, but it did not take long for entrepreneurs to recognize their potential use for the display of goods. By the 1870s, plate-glass windows on the ground floor of most retail stores allowed women to shop without ever stepping off the sidewalk. And behind those windows were displayed household items from bedroom sets to crystal, garments from corsets to evening gowns. The private world was put on public display in the heart of the city.

At the same time as public spaces were becoming arenas for private consumption, the private, domestic space was becoming commercialized. The domestic sphere of home and family was meant to be untainted by commercial concerns; the home was to be a haven from the economic world. But again, the very circumstances of bourgeois life undermined this separation. Style as well as keeping up with fashion for themselves and their family required bourgeois women to spend ever-increasing sums of money on their homes. Not only was the location and external appearance of the home important for status, but throughout the last half of the nineteenth century; home decoration and design became symbols of wealth and taste. By the end of the century, department stores had expanded into the home decoration business, supplying not only the commodities but also the experts who carefully designed rooms and even complete homes that could be viewed within department stores. These settings provided models of appropriate household fashions for women to emulate in their own homes. Home was not the refuge from the economic world that the ideology of separate spheres ordained; rather, the domestic sphere had become completely commercialized, with most of its furnishings bought at the department store to express the economic status of the occupant.

The department store, then, helped to turn the private domestic world into a realm of publicly purchased and appraised commodities; it was integral in the association of women with consumerism, thus making continuous consumption ideologically acceptable; and it was by and large responsible for feminizing the downtown. Department stores were privately owned and catered to people's private, domestic needs, yet they provided forums for public exchange and created new public spaces; they were the palaces of consumption par excellence, yet that consumption was fueled by mass production; and though owned and managed by men, they were staffed by women, and catered to women and women's "sphere." The department store, in both form and function, then, fulfilled many of the contradictory demands of America's economic system in the mid- to late nineteenth century, and it, and the downtown area that it helped to fashion, need to be understood in that light.

Outside the stores, wide sidewalks enabled women's fashionable dresses to stay clean, while paved, and increasingly gas and electrically illuminated streets added to the propriety of the area for women. Rapid transit networks enabled women to come downtown to shop in the morning, return to their middle-class enclaves further uptown for lunch, and return to shop that same afternoon. When the first elevated train opened on Sixth Avenue in 1878, crowds of women used it to flock to the new stores. New Yorker Clara Pardee wrote in her diary in May 1893 that she went downtown to shop in the morning and in the afternoon, returning home for lunch.[57] But shopping experience was not limited to the interiors of the stores. Plate-glass windows allowed New York's public streets, Sixth Avenue and Broadway, to become arenas for the display of private goods. And as the public spaces became more and more dedicated to consumption and display, they became increasingly feminized—New Yorkers literally had created a Ladies' Mile. Although some scholars have argued that the participation of women in the creation of this new urban environment was somewhat emancipatory, it is difficult to suggest that this was its guiding principle.[58] Women's participation in the public life of the city was integral to maintaining the existing social and economic order. Nonetheless, as the largest class of consumers in the city, women, and the qualities ascribed to them by nineteenth-century society, played significant roles in the shaping of New York's landscape in the second half of the nineteenth century. The presence of women and the domestic sphere in department stores provided the cultural legitimacy sought after by the bourgeois owners, who were continually looking for ways of affirming and displaying their wealth and power in the city.

Notes

1   Gunther Barth, *City People* (New York: Oxford University Press, 1980), 146.
2   M. Christine Boyer, *Manhattan Manners: Architecture and Style, 1850–1900* (New York: Rizzoli, 1985), 43.

51 For a discussion of the Victorian idea that architecture could be used to stimulate particular conceptions in people's minds through association with certain laudable elements of the past, see James A. Schmiechen, "The Victorians, the Historians, and the Idea of Modernism," *American History Review* 93 (1988): 287–316.

52 Quoted in Boyer, *Manhattan Manners*, 94.

53 Godkin, *Nation*, 259.

54 *Sibyl*, November 1, 1856, quoted in Leach, "Culture of Consumption," 232.

55 D. J. K. "Shopping at Stewart's," *Hearth and Home* (January 9, 1869): 43.

56 Leach, *True Love and Perfect Union*, 232.

57 Abelson, *Ladies Thieving*, 21.

58 Leach, *True Love and Perfect Union*, 232.

Chapter 12

Richard Guy Wilson

Architecture and the reinterpretation of the past in the American renaissance

In 1894 Bernard Berenson prefaced his book *The Venetian Painters* with the observation, "Every generation has an innate sympathy with some epoch of the past wherein it seems to find itself foreshadowed. . . . We ourselves, because of our faith in science and the power of work, are instinctively in sympathy with the Renaissance . . . our tasks are more diffi- cult because our vision is wider, but the spirit which animates us was anticipated by the spirit of the Renaissance, and more than anticipated. That spirit seems like the small rough model after which ours is being fashioned." Berenson's identification of the importance of the Italian Renaissance for Americans reflects not only his own academic interests but also an acute observation of recent events in Boston and Chicago. Across the landscape in expositions, monuments, public and private buildings, and City Beautiful campaigns American architects, landscape architects, painters, sculptors, and craftsmen joined together to create an iconography that would represent their nation as the rightful heir to the great themes of civilization.[1]

The belief that the United States had a special relationship with the Renaissance was a product of a rediscovery and reinterpretation of the past. Expressions of this relation- ship can be found beginning in the 1870s and continuing until well past the turn of the century. They range from the 1879 observation of architect A. J. Bloor, "our merchant princes, our large manufacturers, our money coining miners . . . are more disposed to emulate the expenditures of the Medici . . . than to conform to the habits of their thrifty forefathers," to the statement of Henry Adams, "there is always an odor of spice and brown sugar about the Medicis. They patronized art as Mr. Rockefeller or Mr. Havemeyer does." To others the relationship did not simply rely on an analogy of wealth; rather, the Renaissance spirit was reborn. The remark made by Augustus Saint-Gaudens to Daniel Burnham in 1891 at a planning session for the World's Columbian Exposition is typical: "Look here old fellow, do you realize that this is the greatest meeting of artists since the fifteenth century!" Artist Will Low reported that many of his comrades "persuaded them- selves for a year or so that the days of the Italian Renaissance were revived on Manhattan Island." Some critics felt, as Berenson implied, that the present civilization of the United States was really a continuation of the Italian Renaissance. Harry Desmond and Herbert Croly, writing about the work of the architectural firm of McKim, Mead, and White, asked: "Can we not claim with the Renaissance an intimate intellectual kinship?" They identified the term *Renaissance* as a group of "political, social, and educational ideas" based on a "renewed faith in mankind," a humanism rooted in classical antiquity.

For them "the Renaissance as a philosophical and moral force" was "receiving its most sincere and thorough-going expression in the United States." Finally Desmond and Croly claimed, "Of all modern peoples we are most completely the children of the Renaissance; and it would be fatal for us to deny our patronage." For some the Renaissance became a vital force; Kenyon Cox, for example, stated, "Since the wave of the Renaissance first started from Italy, the country last reached by it has been the country that at any time has produced the best art." Not surprisingly, Cox felt the United States would produce the best art in the twentieth century.[2]

Another indication of the affinity Americans felt for the Renaissance can be seen in the artifacts they created. Buildings, such as the U-shaped block of houses built for financier Henry G. Villard in New York City and the Cannon House Office Building in Washington, D.C., are creative replays of the paradigms of Italian and French palaces. The redecoration in the mid 1880s of the chancel of Church of the Ascension in New York City, with the surrounds by Stanford White, the sculpture by Louis Saint-Gaudens, the mosaics by David Maitland Armstrong, and the mural by John La Farge, offers a parallel of not only Renaissance sources but also Renaissance unity. Testimony can also be sought from the participants themselves as to their intentions. The Boston Public Library, 1887–95 (Figure 12.1), has been viewed as a series of "steals" from Labrouste's Bibliothèque Sainte-Geneviève in Paris and Alberti's San Francesco in Rimini. More was intended, however, than mere quotation. In the fall of 1889 Samuel A. B. Abbott, president of the library trustees, toured Europe and wrote to his architect, Charles F. McKim: "I think if you could go over the same ground you would be satisfied with your work on the Library, for if I am not mistaken it will hold its own beside any of the great works of great architects of the Renaissance. . . . I paid particular attention to the Cancelleria, the Farnese, and the Strozzi Palaces, because you have talked so much of them, and I feel that your work will rank with them."[3]

The transliterate view of the Renaissance period became increasingly common to middle- and upper-class society and to the artistic community during the period 1876 to 1917. While there are many points of entry to an understanding of the mentality of the American renaissance, architecture provides one of the clearest, since it was the controlling art form of the period. Many artists saw as their highest duty the production of murals and sculpture to adorn public buildings.[4] Through architecture the operative myth of the American renaissance can be grasped.

THREE PHASES OF THE AMERICAN RENAISSANCE

To provide some organization for the period of the American renaissance three major chronological phases are proposed: a prelude period from the mid 1870s to 1887, a high period from 1887 to 1917, and a late period from 1917 to 1938. Prior to the early period there had been the brief appearance of the Renaissance palazzo formula during the 1840s and 1850s in the work of architects such as Ammi B. Young and John Notman. There is no evidence that these buildings had any influence on the later work under consideration or that the style chosen held any special identification for the designers or the public.[5]

12.1 McKim, Mead, and White, Boston Public Library, Boston, Massachusetts, 1887–95, Copley Square façade (from *A Monograph of the Work of McKim, Mead & White*, New York: Architectural Book Publishing Co., 1915)

Early in the prelude period, the artistic collaboration that became identified with the American renaissance makes an appearance, such as that of La Farge with H. H. Richardson on Trinity Church or Augustus Saint-Gaudens with White on the ill-fated project of Governor Morgan's tomb. Stylistically, the architecture is diffuse, a reflection of the architect's uncertainty about the images presented and their appropriateness for America. Yet, there can be seen both a nascent colonial revival and the predecessors of imperial public buildings such as Richard Morris Hunt's Lenox Library, built in New York between 1870 and 1874. During the late 1870s more direct quotations of Renaissance precedent make an appearance, especially in commissions for private houses for the wealthy. The W. K. and Cornelius Vanderbilt mansions on Fifth Avenue in New York were designed by Hunt and George Post in French Renaissance idioms and were filled with collaborative works by several artists; the windows, for example, were by La Farge and the sculpture by Karl Bitter and Saint-Gaudens. More directly related to the Italian Renaissance are the Villard houses (1882–86) in New York, designed by McKim, Mead, and White (Figure 12.2). The architecture of the block is derived from the Cancelleria in Rome, but the interiors of the houses are again a collaborative work by many artists drawn from numerous sources and still highly eclectic. In both the popular and the professional press an increased interest is evident in the period of the Renaissance, and as early as 1880 "American renaissance" is used to describe recent art.[6]

The high, or mature, period of the American renaissance was inaugurated in 1887 with the decision to commission McKim, Mead, and White to design the Boston Public Library. Both the building and its associated decoration give an indication of a changing emphasis in patronage relative to the earlier period. Although private commissions not only continued but also increased in number between 1887 and 1917, the library and the buildings designed for the World's Columbian Exposition in Chicago (Figure 12.3) made it evident that the reinterpretation of the Renaissance had an application far beyond homes for the wealthy. The compass of vision took in the entire landscape; cities were replanned, and great public monuments were created. Most of the identification with and the interpretation of the Renaissance as a historical occurrence with special significance for America came during this period. Stylistically, no single idiom dominated, although some version of the classical was the norm. Styles were arranged in a hierarchy according to their appropriateness, function, location, history, and desired image. The high Georgian could be effective for some college buildings and homes but seldom for large railroad stations, for which Roman thermae supplied both spatial organization and image. The seductiveness of this comprehensive solution can be seen in the work of most architects of the period, even that of the youthful Frank Lloyd Wright.[7]

The late period, from 1917 to 1938, is characterized by the loss of America's identification with the Renaissance. Arguments for the use of Renaissance precedents and images become flaccid and, finally, nonexistent. Frankly conservative, the American renaissance stood against the tide of artistic and social change. Until well into the 1930s it continued as the official style, as can be seen in the Federal Triangle and the National Gallery of Art in Washington, D.C. With the appointments in 1938 of Walter Gropius and Mies van der Rohe to head, respectively, the schools of architecture at Harvard

12.2 McKim, Mead, and White, Villard houses, New York, New York, 1882–87

12.3 Lagoon, World's Columbian Exposition, Chicago, Illinois, 1891–93. Left foreground, Peabody and Stearns, Mechanic Arts Building; left background, Van Brunt and Howe, Electricity Building

and the Illinois Institute of Technology, and the decision in 1939 to limit the competition for the Smithsonian Gallery of Art to a modern idiom, the American renaissance ceased to exist.

CULTURAL BACKGROUND

The lens through which Americans viewed history and reinterpreted the Italian Renaissance was colored first by the discovery of the Renaissance itself and then by three aspects of American culture: the genteel tradition, the cosmopolitan view, and the search for a national cultural identity. Interrelated and mutually dependent, they need to be discussed briefly in order to comprehend American interpretation of the Renaissance period.

Discovery of the concept of the Renaissance as a unique cultural phenomenon is the product of the mid and late nineteenth century. The first appearance of the word *Renaissance*, meaning the revival based upon antique sources of art, architecture, and letters in Italy during the fourteenth through the sixteenth centuries, did not emerge until the 1840s.[8] Initially, the Renaissance was viewed as a revival of paganism, at least for those who followed John Ruskin. In America, James Jackson Jarves provided a generally negative view in *Art Studies: The "Old Masters" of Italy* (1860). An important shift in the 1870s appeared with three books that reached American shores: Walter Pater's *The Renaissance: Studies in Art and Poetry* (1873), John Addington Symonds's *The Renaissance in Italy* (1877, especially volume 3, *The Fine Arts*), and Jacob Burckhardt's *The Civilization of the Renaissance in Italy* (1878). Differences in interpretation by these authors are not of immediate concern; more important is their sympathetic view of the period as a high point of Western civilization and the unity of art and culture. American reaction was, in general, positive. A reviewer of Symonds wrote that "the artistic force" of the Renaissance was still continuing, while a reviewer of Burckhardt claimed that it was "no exaggeration to say that our connection with the age of the Renaissance is at once immediate and genetic."[9]

To most educated Americans of the late nineteenth and early twentieth centuries, the word *renaissance* had a generalized meaning that referred to a host of associations—artistic, cultural, and historical—related to the Italy of the fourteenth through the sixteenth centuries. This was renaissance with a capital *R*, although it was recognized by the mid 1880s that manifestations of the Renaissance impulse could be found in other countries in the sixteenth through the eighteenth centuries, especially in France, England, and the American colonies.

The associations that many cultivated Americans formed in regard to the earlier culture were greatly affected by their exposure to their country's "genteel tradition." This term is not used in a pejorative sense, but rather to refer to the complex of ideas that placed great emphasis on craftsmanship, a search for the ideal, and a belief in beauty and the ideal of striving to create a high culture that would keep the forces of barbarism at bay.[10] At the core of genteel thought was a worry over the level of civilization in the United States. The genteel tradition was essentially didactic by nature, and its advocates, who included Richard Watson Gilder of *Century Magazine* and Charles Eliot Norton of Harvard, perceived themselves to be the "saving remnant," interpreters of culture for Americans. A sanctified view of art and a hazy idealism of beauty pervade much of the discussion on genteelism. Harry Desmond of *Architectural Record* asserted that it was art and not the railroad that was the culmination of civilization. Art, he claimed, had true "divinity." Desmond argued that art was not a commodity for sale; what Americans "must learn is, not that beauty pays, but that it is and for itself a worthy and delightful thing." Equally reverential was McKim's observation to this Columbia University atelier: "Young men, the thing of first importance in architecture—is beauty." Appealing for funds to complete the decorations at the Boston Public Library, McKim wrote to Maj. Henry L. Higginson, "It is not us or me that I am asking you to assist, but the cause of art for *ART*, and the accomplishment of a purpose that would be a source of civic pride not only to Boston but the whole country."[11]

The "cosmopolitan view" was another important determinant of the manner in which Americans interpreted the meaning of the Renaissance. Cosmopolitanism as a cultural force certainly grew out of the genteel outlook, but where the latter was essentially moral with a didactic intent, cosmopolitanism was amoral with a sensuous love of the exotic and foreign. The difference can be perceived in the personalities of two architects, McKim and White. McKim was the genteel personality. Known as the Bramante of his firm, he promoted architecture as the art of high civilization. To this end he founded the American Academy in Rome. His partner, White, is better known for other activities. Equally at home in the cafés of Paris or in the tower of his Madison Square Garden, White was the cosmopolitan, the Cellini, the designer of picture frames, magazine covers, and party decorations. From the 1880s on, Americans grew covetous of Europe, not only in its manifestations of high culture but in all aspects. Edith Wharton noticed the change between the earlier "chocolate-coloured" decades when wealthy Americans traveling in Europe avoided the natives for fear of moral contamination and the 1890s when Europeans were actively sought as status symbols.[12] The earlier "American scholar" attitude of Ralph Waldo Emerson, the cosmic vision of Frederic Church, and the Yankee "show me" posture of Mark Twain was replaced by an apprehension about American provincialism, typified in Henry James's *Roderick Hudson* by the hero's awkward flounderings in the Alps.

One aspect of cosmopolitanism was the increased prestige of foreign academies, especially the Ecole des Beaux-Arts in Paris. Initially, at least, it was among those Americans who had studied at the Ecole that the concept of the American renaissance took hold. For the beaux arts tradition, Italy was the fountainhead—the French Academy in Rome and the Prix de Rome are ample evidence. The lavish architectural drawings made in Rome by French students and later published and the monumental tomes of Paul Marie Letarouilly's *Edifices de Rome moderne* (1840–57) and Grandjean de Montigny's *Architecture Toscaine* (1815) project this vision.

The third aspect of American culture that affected the interpretation of the Renaissance in the United States was the search for a national identity. This search can be traced as a cultural and artistic interest to the founding of the Republic and perhaps even earlier.[13] During the nineteenth century, with the growth of historiography and nationalism, there developed throughout the Western world a preoccupation with identifying symbols or images that best expressed the political-cultural ideals of the different nations. In architecture this took the form of stylistic associationism and the belief that particular styles were an index to a nation's (or a people's) morality and historical significance.[14] Arguments over the appropriate national style can be found in the writings of major figures from the middle of the century, including Owen Jones, August W. N. Pugin, and John Ruskin. In *The Seven Lamps of Architecture* (1849), Ruskin claimed that "every form of noble architecture is in some sort of the embodiment of Polity, Life, History, and the Religious Faith of the nations." Although Ruskin was the most popular writer on architecture with the public, Eugène Emmanuel Viollet-le-Duc became more important to architects—especially Americans attending the Ecole des Beaux-Arts—because he spoke their language more directly. He claimed that "each nation, or to speak more correctly, each center of civilization . . . has . . . a genius of its own which must not be disregarded; and it is because during the last three centuries we have too often failed to appreciate our own genius, that our arts . . . have become hybrid."[15] To Viollet-le-Duc the true genius of

French architecture was the structural expression of the high Gothic; the nadir was the importation of the classic Renaissance. Viollet-le-Duc's concept of the inspired role of race or nation was derived from the ideas of his friend Hippolyte Taine, who taught history at the école in the 1860s and 1870s.

The belief that art and architecture indicated the level of civilization found a natural home in America. This belief was summed up by a reviewer of Jarves's *Art Hints*: "In other words, the history of art is the history of nations." In a later book, Jarves observed: "Each civilized race, ancient or modern, has incarnated its own aesthetic life and character in definite forms of architecture . . . To get at the prevailing life-motive of any epoch, we must read its architecture, as well as its literature."[16]

Among the many who wrote on the problems of an American national style, Henry Van Brunt is one of the most important. An architect practicing first in Boston and later in Kansas City, Van Brunt was trained in the New York atelier of Hunt. During the 1860s and 1870s he publicized Viollet-le-Duc in articles and finally in a translation of *Discourses on Architecture* (1875). Van Brunt wrote in the introduction to *Discourses*, "As all history may be read by an intelligent observation of the monuments of the past . . . it is certainly important for us to see to it that our civilization is having a proper exponent in our monuments." The "essential distinction between the arts of primitive barbarism and those of civilization," he continued, "is that, while the former are original and independent and consequently simple, the latter must be retrospective, naturally turning to tradition and precedent, and are therefore complex." Eclecticism was the solution: "We Americans occupy a new country, having no inheritance of ruins. . . . All the past is ours."[17] The complexities of putting such ideas into practice can be seen in Van Brunt's work (first in partnership with William Robert Ware, 1863–81, then with Frank Howe, 1881–1903), as he changed from the wild pyrotechnics of the 1870s, exemplified by his Memorial Hall at Harvard, to the more settled classicism of the 1890s, exemplified by his Union Station at Omaha.

For other American architects a firmer direction became obvious in the mid 1870s. The search by contemporary English architects through their own ruins for a national style, with the choice falling on the Queen Anne, and the interest in the past aroused by the Philadelphia centennial suggested a source closer to home.[18] Robert S. Peabody and McKim led the way to the colonial revival with their writings and work. Peabody began his career as a Gothic revivalist, but in an address to the American Institute of Architects in 1877 he posed the rhetorical question, "With our Centennial year have we not discovered that we have a past worthy of study?" McKim also promoted the study of American colonial remains through the publication of photographs in *New York Sketch Book of Architecture*.[19] The architecture of the wooden resort houses of the late 1870s and 1880s that has been inaccurately christened "shingle style" was viewed by contemporaries as an example of "modern colonial." A critic for *American Architect and Building News* claimed that the house in Lenox that McKim designed for Samuel Gray Ward in 1879 would "but for a few Queen Anne fantasies . . . pass for an old Puritan's homestead."[20]

REINTERPRETING THE PAST

The American renaissance appeared out of a background of the genteel cultural tradition, cosmopolitanism, a nationalistic search for identity, and, finally, the formation of a concept of the Renaissance. It was the product of a creative reinterpretation of the past, not only of the Renaissance but also of American history. From the body of work and the writing that accompanied the American renaissance, four strong influences on the task of reinterpreting the past can be identified, although they tend to coalesce: the rejection of the immediate past; the nationalistic fervor that generated a search for an appropriate national image; the view of America as the appropriate homeland for a continuation of Renaissance art and culture; and the tendency to apply scientific study to the eclectic sources of the past.

It is an axiom of history that each generation tends to disown the immediate past and discover new virtues in that of its grandfathers. To the proponents of the American renaissance the nightmare had come in the years surrounding the Civil War. The search for an American style in the 1870s and the associated trend to turn to the older simplicities of New England seaports and countryside were a reaction to the excesses of the Gilded Age and to the bloated high Victorian architecture associated with the corruption of Ulysses S. Grant and Boss Tweed. In the end it was not just this architecture that was rejected, but also most architecture dating between the 1840s and the 1880s that was unschooled, highly agitated, and indiscriminant in copying. For critics, "strong expletives" could not condemn the architecture of the immediate past too much. According to Montgomery Schuyler, it was "vulgar," while Herbert Croly claimed, "If there was any style of building which the American architect of that period missed, its omission was assuredly due to ignorance rather than to intention."[21]

Even [Henry Hobson] Richardson's work finally became the object of scorn. In 1885, a year before his death, a poll of American architects had placed five of Richardson's buildings in the top ten. A poll taken in 1899 still gave a high place to his [Romanesque revival] Trinity Church—third instead of first—but first place was given to the United States Capitol and second to the Boston Public Library, designed by Richardson's former students McKim, Mead, and White, which confronted Trinity Church across Copley Square. Seldom was Richardson attacked directly. Rather, his influence became suspect, or, as Glenn Brown, an architect in Washington, D.C., and for years the secretary of the American Institute of Architects, recalled, "He set a fashion in architecture that produced monstrosities throughout the Country."[22] Even Schuyler, who had been the most vocal in supporting Richardson and in damning the American renaissance, changed in his later years and admitted admiration for Post's New York Stock Exchange, McKim, Mead, and White's Cullum Memorial Hall at West Point, and the 1902 McMillan plan for Washington, D.C.[23] The failure of Richardson's direction can also be seen in his own office, where his successors—the firm of Shepley, Rutan, and Coolidge—followed his lead for only a short time; by 1891, their [neo-classical] design for the Chicago Art Institute had acknowledged the light of the future.

In disowning the immediate past, the major figures of the American renaissance found one basis for architecture in the more distant past—the eighteenth and early nineteenth centuries. McKim in the 1880s moved from the seventeenth-century vernacular that had been the germination of his early work to a transcription of the American Georgian and early federal styles of architecture. The famous H. A. C. Taylor house in Newport and the Alexander Cochrane house in Boston's Back Bay owe their origins to a more formalized vision of American history. A study of the past could reveal traditions evocative of location or family history. For Thomas Jefferson Coolidge, Jr., a distant relative of President Jefferson, McKim designed a house built on the north shore at Magnolia, Massachusetts, between 1902 and 1904, which he described as a "perfectly plain rectangular building, with [lower] semi-detached wings, of a type common in Maryland, Virginia and the South. The character of the main building is intended to resemble more nearly the old brick houses of Portsmouth, Newburyport and Salem."[24]

The strong strain of nationalism that can be perceived in the colonial revival gives a clue to the nationalistic aspirations of the other choices of style available to the American renaissance. Versions of classicism came to be accepted as a means by which national ideals could be expressed in public monuments, such as the Washington Arch in New York or the Lincoln Memorial in Washington. Beginning in the 1880s and continuing until World War I, the Civil War loomed as a spector to be monumentalized. In a sense the Civil War was a fortunate incident for the American renaissance mentality; it secured the admission of the United States into the pantheon of nations possessing a stock of noble themes and provided not only a storehouse of motifs but also a source of commissions. Style as an exponent of civilization and nationality continued to be a major theme, and architectural periodicals were filled with articles bearing titles such as "Style," "The Fundamentals of the Development of Style," and "A National Style of Architecture." The quest for a national style in architecture had several dimensions, one of which was the issue of continuity, which will be discussed later, and the other of which was the question of a unified style or a common basis for a style. While there were some naysayers who claimed the United States was too vast and too varied to achieve a unity of expression, most of the supporters of the American renaissance felt that some comprehensive stylistic development could be achieved.[25]

If one assumed that American architecture had to be rescued from the Victorian quagmire, then he was almost certain to conclude that a recognized tradition should be accepted and extended. Ernest Flagg is an example of an architect who shared this assumption and conclusion. Trained at the Ecole des Beaux-Arts, a designer of buildings such as Corcoran Gallery of Art in Washington, D.C., and Scribner's Store in New York, Flagg claimed that there was no American architectural style but only American techniques, such as using iron fronts on buildings or erecting high-rise structures. For Flagg, the beaux arts style offered the best promise of creating a basis of taste and common sense. At the present there was "[no] such thing as American architecture in the hodgepodge," but by following the French lead architects would begin to work and think in a common style. He concluded, "Thus we are about to enter upon a course which will make possible the evolution of a national style of our own, or perhaps enable us to set the fashion for the world."[26]

The choice of Renaissance precedent to provide national architectural unity is dramatically evident in the work of Van Brunt, who, as already noted, in the 1890s accepted a version of Renaissance classicism for his own architecture. In his writings he claimed that Renaissance architecture, "the chosen language in which the greatest architects and most advanced societies of the human race have expressed themselves," should be the basis for an American style instead of an all-embracing, "all the past is ours" eclecticism. "It is," he asserted, "our duty to express with our art the civilization of our time." A member of one of the six architectural firms represented at the Court of Honor at the World's Columbian Exposition, Van Brunt wrote extensively on what he felt were the lessons of the exposition. It was, he believed, a deliberate and orderly attempt "to present to the world . . . our civilization in its best estate." The choice of architectural style at the Court of Honor was determined by "the entire absence of any distinctively American style capable of giving adequate expression of our history." The solution was to select the "style most associated with modern civilization, a style so organized and accepted that personal fancy or caprice should have the smallest possible scope in it." He continued, "By this decision, it was not proposed that the architects of our country were to pose before the world as conservators of traditions, but to show that the youngest of nations respects and understands the past and acknowledges its fundamental indebtedness to classic art; in a wider sense, perhaps, that the grandeur of the work which America is now doing in the world is in reality based upon a wise conservatism, and that our civilization does not affect to be independent of the experience of mankind in history."[27]

Van Brunt had lived through too many changes not to be wary of absolutes, and his essays, in addition to promoting the Renaissance style as the proper solution, left open the possibility of a national style based on the vernacular, one without precedent. Yet he was still a member of the genteel generation and in a late essay asserted that freedom from tradition and custom was an earmark of "primitive or barbarous nations." The classical system of order, as it had evolved from Greece to Rome and thence to the Renaissance and on to the culture of Van Brunt's time, had, he claimed, "been respected in exact accordance with the degree of culture and artistic feeling existing among the people using it. Wherever these formulas have been disregarded, this system has been debased or travestied, and every such debasement is a sure indication of a corresponding debasement in civilization."[28]

The third influence on the reinterpretation of the past, the concept of the United States as a continuation of the civilization of the Italian Renaissance, assumed that either a genetic or generic connection existed between the two cultures. Thomas Hastings of the firm of Carrère and Hastings, architects of New York Public Library, Carnegie Institution, and Senate and House office buildings in Washington held that "a universal law of development" existed in regard to style. Art and life, he felt, were always very close in correspondence. Applying a neo-Darwinian "natural selection" interpretation, he concluded that medieval or Gothic styles were "an anachronism" for the present day. It was out of the changed necessities of the fifteenth and sixteenth centuries, which had inaugurated the modern age, that the Renaissance style had "evolved." Hastings believed that American architecture of the future would be that of "modern Renaissance." For the present, "We should study and develop the Renaissance and adapt it to our modern conditions and wants, so that future generations can see that it has truly interpreted our life."[29]

Responding to the charges that the American renaissance was too "Frenchified" or "beaux arts" oriented, Hastings claimed a line of succession with early American Classicists Charles Bulfinch, William Thornton, Benjamin Latrobe, Pierre L'Enfant. Observing that styles become nationalized, he explained: "When future generations look back on the work influenced by the Beaux-Arts in this country, they will find as great a difference of expression and of national character, as that which existed in the sixteenth century between France and Italy. . . . This difference will be the natural and the necessary outcome of the difference of our ways of living as well as of the difference of our national character."[30]

In his book *American Renaissance* (1904) Joy Wheeler Dow argued much the same, that local conditions provided national characteristics. "We want to belong somewhere and to something, not to be entirely cut off by ourselves as stray atoms." The linkage was early American architecture; the colonial, the Georgian, the Greek Revival were all manifestations to him of the Renaissance style. With Hunt's Biltmore (Figure 12.4) he summed up the argument: "We call Biltmore French Renaissance now; it will be American Renaissance later on."[31]

America's continuity in architectural design with the classical lineage of the Renaissance could be claimed for many types of buildings; however, the stranglehold of medieval association created some problems for ecclesiastical architecture. McKim, Mead, and White's work provides an example, for their churches built during the 1880s conformed to the prevailing prototypes of Gothic or Romanesque design. But with the full bloom of the American renaissance, these designs became classical in derivation, as with

12.4 Richard Morris Hunt, Biltmore, Asheville, North Carolina, 1893–95

Madison Square Presbyterian Church (1904–6) in New York. Highly colored with yellow glazed brick, green and white terra-cotta, polished green marble columns, and a Della Robbia pediment by H. Siddons Mowbray and A. A. Weinman, the church was criticized as a "heathen" departure from convention. White, the designer of the church, answered the detractors by asserting that the early Christian Byzantine style "was a protest against the idea so prevalent among laymen that a building to be church-like must be built in the Medieval Style. The style of architecture known as Gothic had nothing to do with the simple forms of early Christian religion, or with that of the Reformation, or with the style of architecture which prevailed in our own country when it had its birth as a nation. All these which belong to the Protestant religion and to us, have no affiliations whatsoever with the Gothic, but with the classic style." Essentially he reversed the old argument of the ecclesiologists. The design was, he noted, "in a style natural to and belonging to the religion which it represents and to the country in which it is built."[32]

A fourth influence on the manner in which history was reinterpreted by the American renaissance, "scientific eclecticism," recognizes both the continuing element of choice and the scientific (or pseudoscientific) language and attitude of some of the participants.[33] The architects of the American renaissance were not concerned with the exact duplication of European buildings, but rather with combining motifs drawn from different sources to create a new entity, such as the Boston Public Library. The ability to choose such motifs came from a scholarly knowledge of the past. The acquisition of this knowledge was the reason for the American Academy in Rome, for as McKim told Mowbray: "As Rome went to Greece, and later France, Spain and other countries had gone to Rome, for their own reactions to the splendid standards of Classic and Renaissance Art, so must we become students, and delve, bring back and adapt to conditions here, a groundwork on which to build." The eclectic element of the past was still operable. "We were," McKim claimed, "starving for standards within reach to stimulate our taste and inspire emulation." But "too slavish ... adherence to the letter of tradition" was not the solution, as McKim once told Wharton. By study "of the best examples" of the classic period, architects could produce designs that would suggest image sought.[34]

The development of standards, taste, or, perhaps, the keyword, *authority*, was the product of a semiscientific inquiry. Scientific methodology had applications for all aspects of nineteenth-century thought, from biology to history. In architecture, the classifying, cataloguing, filing, and recording of styles, motifs, and details became a central activity.[35] Certainly some of the emphasis on knowledge of architectural history can be related to the growing professionalism of the period, but it was also part of the contemporary aesthetic.[36] Out of the mass of documentation could key principles be discovered to give guidance to architecture?

The choice of the classical Renaissance style, according to Van Brunt, gave to "the modern architect ... all the majesty of authority and all the imposing beauty of a perfected language of form." Abstract, but with a carefully defined dogma of perfection of proportions, known details, and strict limits, classical architecture did not leave room for lawless invention and spontaneous intuition. Croly, soon to be the major philosopher of progressivism, claimed that the "increasing authority" of Renaissance architecture for Americans was a sign of "progress."[37]

Significantly, Van Brunt's first partner, Ware, founded the schools of architecture at Massachusetts Institute of Technology and later Columbia and wrote *The American Vignola* (1902, 1906). American education in architecture developed along the lines of the Ecole des Beaux-Arts but included a more scientific study of ornament and composition. From a study of the elements of the classical past and their composition into a unified whole, the student *analytique* or the building design would evolve.[38]

While the buildings of the American renaissance are never direct copies of European sources, one can observe two basic approaches to the composition of form. The first is a reliance on prototypes, such as the Italian Renaissance palazzo that in America came to house a variety of building functions—houses, banks, clubs, offices, and museums. The origins of the specific prototypes of the Boston Public Library and the Villard houses are obvious, as has been noted, and yet neither is an exact duplicate of a particular Italian Renaissance building. Changes in details, combinations of motifs from different buildings, adjustments of scale and proportion, insertion of modern functions, and different spatial arrangements make them American buildings. The second approach to form can be called elemental and involved the creation of entirely new forms out of the basic elements of architecture rather than from prototypes. Pilaster, column, arch, arcade, wall, window, frame, atrium, cornice, attic—all were elements that could be composed to create a new building form. The Corcoran Gallery is an example; architect Flagg astutely studied both the confined site and the requirements of the museum—large areas of wall surface, organized sequence of galleries, and atriums—and produced a design original from that of any previous building and yet still partaking of the air of the Renaissance. Both the elemental and the prototypical approaches toward form had their origin in French beaux arts theory, but in the architect's wider eclecticism or greater acquisitiveness of elements and forms and the intensity of his details, they became typically American.

The consequence of scientific eclecticism would be the perfection of buildings and especially of details far beyond that of any European prototypes. Observers have noted in American renaissance buildings a reproduction of ornamental details that becomes almost mechanical in regularity and fidelity.[39] The industrialized production of ornament certainly allowed such accuracy, but the aesthetic resulted in equal part from a systematic study of original details. The attitude of scientific experiment pervades the erection of full-scale models of bays and cornices by McKim, Mead, and White and by Carrère and Hastings in order to check projections, shadows, and general effect before proceeding with construction.

CONCLUSION

In attempting to be scientific and scholarly yet eclectic and artistic, disowning the immediate past for a more distant history, emphasizing nationality while still seeking to establish a continuity with the great themes of Western civilization, the American renaissance was contradictory and ambiguous. The lines of reasoning and arguments used for different choices are complex, and certainly other aspects of the reinterpretation will be suggested as the period comes more into focus. The historiography was at once astute and fallacious, profound and superficial.

Ultimately, the American renaissance reinterpretation of the past projected a compelling vision. Ideas were not left in the abstract or as ethereal concepts but were projected in reality as space, form, and materials. The reality of the image connects with the American tradition of making and not merely intellectualizing. The power of the reinterpretation can only be suggested by the energy and venom needed to overthrow it. The success of the palpable reality of the American renaissance can be seen in two concluding observations. Charles H. Reilly, an eminent British architect and educator, toured the United States in 1909 and wrote that "America has seized the lead, and . . . has established an architecture which, while satisfying the most exigent of modern requirements, is yet the conscious heir . . . of those forms and thoughts which, born in Greece more than 2,000 years ago, have been for the last four centuries, and must always be, with negligible deviations, the spring and motive of our life and art." Twenty-six years later French modernist Le Corbusier visited the United States. After viewing buildings such as Grand Central Station, he wrote: "In New York, then, I learn to appreciate the Italian Renaissance. It is so well done that you could believe it to be genuine. It even has a strange, new firmness which is not Italian but American!"[40]

Notes

1   Bernard Berenson, *The Venetian Painters* (reprinted in *The Italian Painters of the Renaissance* [New York: Phaidon Publishers, 1952], p. iii). One of many such observations, "The work will go on and on until the whole land is transformed and the walls of the buildings, from ocean to ocean, are adorned with paintings as in beautiful Italy," is in Pauline King, *American Mural Painting* (Boston: Noyes, Platt, 1902), p. 14.

2   Bloor quoted in Harry W. Desmond and Herbert Croly, *Stately Homes in America* (New York: D. Appleton, 1903), p. 251; Adams quoted in Harold D. Cater, *Henry Adams and His Friends* (Boston, 1947), p. 404; Saint-Gaudens quoted in Charles Moore, *Daniel H. Burnham, Architect, Planner of Cities*, 2 vols. (Boston: Houghton Mifflin Co., 1921), 1: 47; Will H. Low, *A Chronicle of Friendships, 1873–1900* (New York: C. Scribner's Sons, 1908), p. 285; Harry Desmond and Herbert Croly, "The Work of Messrs. McKim, Mead & White," *Architectural Record* 20, no. 3 (September 1906): 225, 226; Kenyon Cox, "Painting in the Nineteenth Century," *The Nineteenth Century: A Review of Progress* (New York, 1901), p. 281.

3   William Jordy, *American Buildings and Their Architects*, vol. 3, *Progressive and Academic Ideals at the Turn of the Twentieth Century* (New York: Doubleday, 1972), chap. 7; Samuel Abbott to Charles McKim, November 28, 1889, McKim Collection, Box 7, Library of Congress.

4   The goals of the National Sculpture Society, founded 1893, were "to spread the knowledge of good sculpture, foster the taste for, and encourage the production of, ideal sculpture for the household, promote the decoration of public buildings" (quoted in Wayne Craven, *Sculpture in America* [New York: Thomas Y. Crowell Co., 1968], p. 478). The National Society of Mural Painters stated that its goals "shall be to promote the delineation of the human figure in its relation to architecture" (reprinted in King, *American Mural Painting*, p. 152). Henry Van Brunt advised, "To decorate architecture has ever been, and must ever be, the highest function of sculptor or painter," in Henry Van Brunt, "The Columbian Exposition and American Civilization" (1893), in William A. Coles, ed., *Architecture and Society, Selected Essays of Henry Van Brunt* (Cambridge, Mass.: Harvard University Press, 1969), p. 313. In 1929 Eugene Savage, a member of the National Academy of Design, reported, "This great modern value is the recognition of architecture as the mother of the arts" (quoted in Lois Marie Fink and Joshua C. Taylor,

Academy: The Academic Tradition in American Art [Washington D.C.: Smithsonian Institution Press, 1975], p. 97).

5   Most of the American renaissance palazzi of this period were faddish copies of British clubs in Pall Mall. While the American palazzi had no effect on later work, it is certainly possible that the British clubs influenced American club design (including the designs of the Century, Metropolitan, and University clubs in New York) during the 1880s and 1890s.

6   The phrase appeared in *Californian* 1 (June 1880): 1–2. The use of renaissance to describe recent art first appeared in William C. Brownell, "The Young Painters of America," *Scribner's Monthly* 20 (May 1880): 2. Previously, Clarence Cook, "Recent Church Decoration," *Scribner's Monthly* 15 (February 1878): 569–77, noted the special relevance of Italian Renaissance art to Americans. Other expressions of an American renaissance appear in "Art and Art Life in New York City," *Lippincott's* 29 (June 1882): 597–605; J. William Benn, "Studies in the Renaissance," *American Architect and Building News* 18 (November 14, 1885): 231–33; 19 (January 16 and March 27, 1866): 27–29, 152–54; George William Sheldon, *Artistic Country Seats*, vol. 1 (New York: D. Appleton, 1886–87), preface, pp. 65, 88, 153, and passim; and Kenyon Cox, "Augustus Saint-Gaudens," *Century* 35, no. 13 (November 1887): 28–37. I am indebted to Richard Murray for some of these references.

7   See, for example, Wright's Milwaukee library and museum project in Mark L. Peisch, *The Chicago School of Architecture: Early Followers of Sullivan and Wright* (New York: Random House, 1964), Figure 1.

8   For the most provocative discussion of this theme, and one to which I owe a great debt, see Howard Mumford Jones, "The Renaissance and American Origins," in *Ideas in America* (Cambridge, Mass.: Harvard University Press, 1945), pp. 140–51.

9   Pater's book appeared under a New York imprint in 1877. Symonds's Fine Arts appeared with a New York imprint in 1879. Burckhardt's *Die Kultur der Renaissance in Italien* originally appeared in German in 1860. The first English translation appeared in London in 1878 and under a New York imprint in 1879. Review of *Renaissance in Italy, Art Interchange* 2 (May 14, 1879): 81. "The very birthmark of our civilization declares the intellectual pedigree from which we are sprung. We are children of the Renaissance. Not only are we children of the Renaissance, but as Burckhardt truly says, the influence of that mother age is still at work among us" (*New York Herald* [October 18, 1880]), p. 9.

10   "Genteel tradition" is originally from George Santayana, "The Genteel Tradition in American Philosophy," in George Santayana, *Winds of Doctrine* (London, 1913), pp. 186–215. Most of my discussion is taken from John Tomsich, *The Genteel Endeavor: American Culture and Politics in the Gilded Age* (Stanford: Stanford University Press, 1971); and Howard Mumford Jones, *The Age of Energy: Varieties of American Experience* (New York: Viking Press, 1971), chap. 6.

11   Matthew Arnold, *Culture and Anarchy* (1869; reprint ed., Cambridge: At the University Press, 1960), p. 6; Matthew Arnold, "Numbers; of the Majority and the Remnant" (1884), reprinted in *The Complete Prose Works of Matthew Arnold*, vol. 10, ed. R. H. Super (Ann Arbor: University of Michigan Press, 1974), p. 163; Harry Desmond, "By Way of Introduction," *Architectural Record* 1, no. 1 (July–September 1891): 1–4. Desmond was reacting to George William Curtis's observation that the railroad was the culmination of civilization. Harry Desmond, "Over the Draughting Board," *Architectural Record* 12, no. 5 (May 1902): 113–14. McKim quoted in Charles Moore, *The Life and Times of Charles Follen McKim* (Boston: Houghton Mifflin Co., 1929), pp. 59, 82.

12   For an illuminating discussion of cosmopolitanism, see Jones, *Age of Energy*, chap. 7; the nicknames for McKim and White were used by William A. Boring in Moore, *McKim*, p. 57; Edith Wharton, *A Backward Glance* (New York, 1934), pp. 55, 62. Any of Wharton's novels, such as *The House of Mirth* (1905) or *The Age of Innocence* (1920), indicate the changes.

13   Joshua C. Taylor, *America as Art* (Washington, D.C.: Smithsonian Institution Press, 1976), esp. chap. 1.

14   There is no good study of this aspect; George C. Hersey, *High Victorian Gothic: A Study in Associationism* (Baltimore: Johns Hopkins University Press, 1972), mentioned it only in passing, and the information is flawed. For a more complete discussion of this section, see Richard Guy Wilson, "Charles F. McKim and the Development of the American Renaissance: A study in Architecture and Culture" (Ph.D. diss., University of Michigan, 1972); and Richard Guy Wilson, "American Architecture and the Search for a National Style in the 1870s," *Nineteenth Century* 3, no. 3 (Autumn 1977): 74–80.

15   Owen Jones, *The Grammar of Ornament* (London: Day and Son, 1858), p. 5; Augustus W. N. Pugin, *The True Principles of Pointed or Christian Architecture* (London: John Weale, 1841), pp. 56–57. M. H. Port, ed., *The Houses of Parliament* (New Haven: Yale University Press, 1976), pp. 30, 32, 43, 82, and passim, covers a contemporary debate on the national style issue. John Ruskin, *The Seven Lamps of Architecture* (London, 1849), p. 183; Roger B. Stein, *John Ruskin and Aesthetic Thought in America, 1840–1900* (Cambridge, Mass.: Harvard University Press, 1967), pp. 203–5; Eugène Emmanuel Viollet-le-Duc, *Discourses on Architecture*, trans. Benjamin Bucknall, vol. 2 (1889; reprint ed., New York: Grove Press, 1959), p. 244.

16   John Neal, *North American Review* 71 (October 1855): 440; James Jackson Jarves, *The Art Idea* (New York: Hurd & Houghton, 1864), pp. 95, 286.

17   Henry Van Brunt, "Architectural Reform," in Coles, *Architecture and Society*, pp. 89–96; Henry Van Brunt, "Translator's Introduction," in Coles, *Architecture and Society*, pp. 103, 106.

18   See Wilson, "American Architecture," for a full discussion of the search for a national style. See also Mark Girouard, *Sweetness and Light: The "Queen Anne" Movement, 1860–1900* (New York: Oxford University Press, 1977), chap. 9; and Vincent J. Scully, Jr., *The Shingle Style* (New Haven: Yale University Press, 1955), which covers much of the subject, but with different emphasis.

19   Robert S. Peabody, "Colonial Architecture," in *Proceedings of the Eleventh and Twelfth Annual Conventions of the American Institute of Architects* (Boston: Alfred Muge & Sons, 1879), p. 17. This address also appeared as an article under the pseudonym Georgian, "Georgian House of New England," *American Architect and Building News* 2, no. 95 (October 20, 1877): 338–39; no. 112 (February 16, 1878): 54–55; McKim commissioned a series of photographs of Newport antiquities in 1874 and had them bound as *Old Newport Houses* (1875). One of the plates, of the Bishop Berkeley house, appeared in *New York Sketch Book of Architecture* 1, no. 12 (December 1874): pl. 45. Of interest is a photograph of the New York City Hall, by Mangin and McComb, 1811, with an exhortation by McKim, "It is a very fair specimen of the Renaissance of the time, and, on the whole, is the most admirable public building in the city," which appeared in *New York Sketch Book of Architecture* 3, no. 6 (July 1876): pl. 25.

20   Sheldon, *Artistic Country Seats*, p. 23; "Correspondence," *American Architect and Building News* 2 (December 8, 1877): 394.

21   Desmond and Croly, *Stately Homes*, p. 102; Montgomery Schuyler, "Concerning Queen Anne" (1883) (reprinted in Montgomery Schuyler, *American Architecture and Other Writings*, ed. W. H. Jordy and R. T. Coe, 2 vols. [Cambridge, Mass.: Harvard University Press, 1961], 2: 459). William Herbert [Herbert Croly], *Houses for Town or Country* (New York: Duffield, 1907), p. 10.

22   "The Ten Best Buildings in the United States," *American Architect and Building News* 17 (June 13, 1885): 282–83; "The Ten Most Beautiful Buildings in the United States," *Brochure Series* 1 (January 1900): 2–4. "When I started in practice, my designs, with the majority of other young architects in the early eighties, was Romanesque, in our ambition to follow in the steps of Richardson. The results were most disappointing. . . . Not a single one of his followers produced an example worthy of notice" (Glenn Brown, *1860–1930 Memories* [Washington, D.C., 1931], p. 27). See also pp. 341–42, where McKim, Mead, and White are praised for breaking away. Substantially the same view can be found in Thomas Hastings, "Evolution of Style in Modern Architecture," *North American Review* 191 (February 1910): 203; and Joy Wheeler Dow, *American Renaissance* (New York: William T. Comstock, 1904), p. 27.

23 Montgomery Schuyler, "The Romanesque Revival in New York" (1891), "The Romanesque Revival in America" (1891), and "A Modern Classic" (1904) (reprinted in Schuyler, *American Architecture* 1: 191–225; 2: 588–97). On the Washington plan, see Montgomery Schuyler, "The Art of City Making," *Architectural Record* 12, no. 5 (May 1902): 1–26.

24 McKim to T. J. Coolidge, January 1, 1903, McKim Collection, L.B. 11, p. 230, Library of Congress.

25 Peter B. Wight, "The Fundamentals of the Development of Style," *Inland Architect* 24 (May 1897): 33; "A National Style of Architecture," *Building* 6 (January 1, 1887): 2. Typical is Leon Labrouste, who argued that "national genius may be said to have engendered art, of which style ... constitutes the first division ... style rises and falls with the intellectual and moral levels of a people, and consequently, with its degree of civilization" ("Style," *American Architect and Building News* 44 [April 28, 1894]: 39–40). Barr Ferree, "An 'American Style' of Architecture," *Architectural Record* 1, no. 1 (July–September 1891): 39–45. R. H. Vickers, "Development of American Architecture," *Inland Architect* 3 (May 1884): 50. Frank Millet felt a comprehensive "American" art an impossibility; see Frank Millet, "What are Americans Doing in Art?" *Century* 43 (November–April 1891–92): 43.

26 Ernest Flagg, "American Architecture as Opposed to Architecture in America," *Architectural Record* 10 (October 1901): 178–80.

27 Henry Van Brunt, "The Historic Styles and Modern Architecture" (1892–93), in Coles, *Architecture and Society*, p. 302; Henry Van Brunt, "The Growth of Characteristic Architectural Style in the United States" (1893), in Coles, *Architecture and Society*, pp. 319–20; Van Brunt, "Historic Styles," p. 300.

28 Van Brunt, "Growth of Style," pp. 319–27; and Henry Van Brunt, "Two Interpreters of National Architecture" (1897), in Coles, *Architecture and Society*, p. 360; Henry Van Brunt, "Classic Architecture" (1895), in Coles, *Architecture and Society*, pp. 342, 356.

29 Thomas Hastings, "The Evolution of Style in Modern Architecture," *North American Review* 191 (February 1910): 197–99 (reprinted as "Modern Architecture" in *Journal of the Royal Institute of British Architects*, 3d ser., 20 [May 31, 1913]: 501–13; and excerpted as "The Influence of Life in the Development of an Architectural Style" in *American Architect and Building News* 104 [July 16, 1913]: 29–30).

30 Thomas Hastings, "The Influence of the Ecole des Beaux-Arts upon American Architecture," *Architectural Record* 9, no. 3 (January 1901): 83.

31 Dow, *American Renaissance*, pp. 19, 167.

32 Quoted in Charles Baldwin, *Stanford White* (New York: Dodd, Mead, 1931), p. 236. A group of clippings and letters that White or the office was responding to can be found in the McKim, Mead, and White Collection, Box 20, New York Historical Society. McKim used similar arguments in the controversy over the National Cathedral, Washington, D.C., which he lost; see Moore, *Burnham*, 2: chap. 21. An example of the Gothic rationale can be found in Ralph Adams Cram, "Architecture in America," in Ralph Adams Cram, *The Gothic Quest* (New York, 1907), pp. 139–64.

33 Eclecticism as a governing theory of design has generally been avoided by architectural historians. The only person to begin to approach it was Carroll L. V. Meeks in "Creative Eclecticism," *Journal of the Society of Architectural Historians* 12 (December 1953): 15–18. Carroll L. V. Meeks, "Wright's Eastern Seaboard Contemporaries: Creative Eclecticism in the United States around 1900," in *Acts of the Twentieth International Congress of the History of Choice: Eclecticism in America, 1800–1930* (New York: George Braziller, 1974), is largely descriptive and does not deal with the issues.

34 Quoted in Moore, *McKim*, p. 260; McKim to Edith Wharton, memo, ca. 1895, McKim Collection, L.B. 5, p. 343, Library of Congress.

35 Some of these ideas were suggested by Edgar Kaufmann, Jr., "Nineteenth Century Design," *Perspecta* 6 (1960): 56–67. At least one contemporary noted "the scientific element" in McKim, Mead, and White's work; see F. S. Swales, "Charles Follen McKim, 1847–1909," *Architectural Review* 26 (October 1909): 184.

36 The growth of professionalism in the period is traced in Robert H. Wiebe, *The Search for Order, 1877–1920* (New York: Hill & Wang, 1967).

37 Van Brunt, "Historic Styles," p. 302; see also Van Brunt, "Classic Architecture," pp. 342–58; Croly, *Houses for Town or Country*, pp. 30–31. Croly's major "progressive" work was *The Promise of American Life* (New York, 1909); he was also editor of *New Republic* from 1914 to 1930.

38 James P. Noffsinger, *The Influence of the Ecole des Beaux-Arts on the Architects of the United States* (Washington, D.C.: Catholic University Press, 1955), covers the influence on education; Fink and Taylor, *Academy*, p. 128, noted a similar effect in painting.

39 Peter Smithson, "The Fine and Folk: An Essay on McKim, Mead & White and the American Tradition," *Architectural Review* 35 (August 1965): 394–97 (reprinted in Alison and Peter Smithson, *Without Rhetoric* [Cambridge, Mass.: Harvard University Press, 1973], pp. 23–25); see also Jordy, *American Buildings*, p. 348.

40 Charles H. Reilly, "The Modern Renaissance in American Architecture," *Journal of the Royal Institute of British Architects* 17 (June 25, 1910): 635. He later wrote *McKim, Mead & White* (London, 1924). Le Corbusier, *When the Cathedrals Were White*, trans. F. E. Hyslop (1937; reprint ed., New York: McGraw-Hill Book Co., 1964), p. 60.

Part 4 |

Visions of a new era: seeing self, seeing others, being seen

By the 1890s the US had begun to emerge as a world power. With this new role came increased self-scrutiny, as well as heightened attention to, and from, others outside the country. The essays in this section deal with issues of representation and seeing in an increasingly internationalized architectural environment.

The World's Columbian Exposition in Chicago, 1892–1893, was a pivotal event on many levels, not least in these terms of international contact. The sophisticated planning, elaborate neo-classical architecture, international pavilions, and ethnological exhibits of what came to be called the White City dazzled the millions of people who poured into Chicago from around the country and around the world (and in the process also confronted the new skyscrapers of the Loop). Yet, as historian Robert W. Rydell illustrates, in an essay influenced by post-colonialist scholarship, there was a dark side to the White City. Juxtaposed with the glistening white classical temples celebrating American and European achievements in science, industry, agriculture, and the arts, were living displays—located on the Midway Plaisance, the fair's entertainment zone—of Native Americans standing beside tipis, Dahomeyan tribesmen before mud huts, Arabs riding camels down "Cairo Street," and other such "exotic amusements." While the fair's architecture and planning provided a setting for white Americans and "others" of all varieties to see more of one another than most previously had, it also served to reinforce and even dramatize existing attitudes about racial and gender hierarchy.

The next two essays in this section provide complementary views of Frank Lloyd Wright, America's most famous architect, both nationally and internationally. James F. O'Gorman concentrates on Wright's seminal prairie house designs, analyzing the forms and sources of this distinctly regionalized modern house type. Celebrating the idea and image of American place, deeply rooted in American cultural and natural history, the prairie house looked back to colonial and federal architecture, and to the work of Richardson and Sullivan, while it also referenced American literary sources and regional botanical and topographical elements. At the same time, the prairie house also expressed Wright's awareness of more far-flung sources, such as the Japanese Ho-o-den pavilion that he saw at the World's Colombian Exposition in 1893. Published in Berlin in 1910–1911, Wright's prairie style American architecture soon came to the attention of a host of architects working in Germany, Holland, Austria, Switzerland, Czechoslovakia, and elsewhere. Looking closely at the early foreign dissemination and reception of Wright's work, Anthony Alofsin demonstrates that Wright's influence outside the US, and his relationship to an emerging international modernism, was far more complex and wide-ranging than previously suspected.

While Alofsin looks outward from the US, the German architectural historian Margaret Kentgens-Craig, in this excerpt from her book on early contacts between the Bauhaus and America, turns the lens around. Viewing such seminal events as the Chicago Tribune Tower competition (1922) and the Museum of Modern Art's "International Style" exhibition (1932), Kentgens-Craig assesses what "modernism" and "Americanism" in architecture meant to Americans living in the 1920s and 1930s. In so doing, she considers how European modern architecture was received in the US, and how Americans' understanding of this architecture compared to that of Europeans.

Further reading

Alofsin, A., *Frank Lloyd Wright—the Lost Years, 1910–1922: A Study of Influence*, Chicago, IL: University of Chicago Press, 1993.

Bacon, M., *Le Corbusier in America: Travels in the Land of the Timid*, Cambridge, MA: MIT Press, 2001.

Cohen, J.-L., *Scenes of the World to Come: European Architecture and the American Challenge, 1893–1960*, Paris and Montreal: Flammarion and the Canadian Centre for Architecture, 1995.

Eaton, L. K., *Architecture Comes of Age: European Reaction to H. H. Richardson and Louis Sullivan*, Cambridge, MA: MIT Press, 1972.

Jordy, W. H., *American Buildings and Their Architects, Vol. 4, Progressive and Academic Ideals at the Turn of the Twentieth Century*, New York: Oxford University Press, 1972.

King, A. D., *The Bungalow: The Production of a Global Culture*, New York: Oxford University Press, 1995.

Lewis, A. D., *An Early Encounter With Tomorrow: Europeans, Chicago's Loop, and the World's Columbian Exposition*, Urbana, IL: University of Illinois Press, 1997.

Riley, T. (ed.), *The International Style: Exhibition 15 and the Museum of Modern Art*, New York: Rizzoli/CBA, 1992.

Riley, T. (ed.), *Frank Lloyd Wright, Architect*, New York: Museum of Modern Art, 1994.

Robertson, C., "Male and Female Agendas for Domestic Reform: The Middle-Class Bungalow in Gendered Perspective," *Winterthur Portfolio* 26: 2–3 (1991): 123–141.

Robin, R., *Enclaves of America: The Rhetoric of American Political Architecture Abroad, 1900–1965*, Princeton, NJ: Princeton University Press, 1992.

Rydell, R., *All the World's a Fair: Visions of Empire at American International Expositions, 1876–1916*, Chicago, IL: University of Chicago Press, 1984.

Schleier, M., *The Skyscraper in American Art, 1890–1931*, New York: Da Capo Press, 1986.

Solomonson, K., *The Chicago Tribune Tower Competition*, Cambridge and New York: Cambridge University Press, 2001.

Ward, D. and O. Zunz (eds), *The Landscape of Modernity: New York City, 1900–1940*, Baltimore, MD: The Johns Hopkins University Press, 1997.

Chapter 13

Robert W. Rydell

A cultural Frankenstein? The Chicago World's Columbian Exposition of 1893

Thirty years after more than a half-million Americans died in a bloody civil war, five years after a terrorist threw a bomb in Chicago's Haymarket Square, one year before massive strikes in Pullman's company town outside of the city, and three short years after the U.S. Army's assault on Native Americans at Wounded Knee, South Dakota, the Chicago World's Columbian Exposition opened to commemorate the four-hundredth anniversary of Columbus's arrival in the New World (Figure 13.1). As contemporaries noted and recent scholarship has confirmed, the fair was a landmark event in American history. Its neoclassical White City reshaped the public architecture of the nation; its World's Congresses gathered intellectuals, labor leaders, and social reformers to debate significant political and philosophical issues of the age; and its Midway Plaisance bestowed the stamp of legitimacy on mass entertainment as a vital component of American culture.[1]

13.1 *Grand Bird's-Eye View of the Grounds and Buildings of the Great Columbian Exposition at Chicago, Illinois, 1892–3*, published by Currier and Ives, New York, 1892

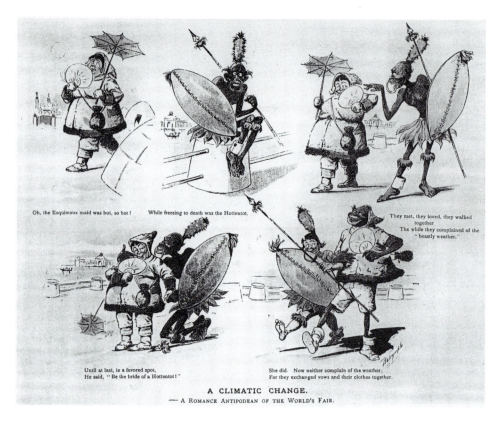

Oh, the Esquimaux maid was hot, so hot !   While freezing to death was the Hottentot.

They met, they loved, they walked together
The while they complained of the "beastly weather."

Until at last, in a favored spot,
He said, " Be the bride of a Hottentot ! "

She did.   Now neither complain of the weather;
For they exchanged vows and their clothes together.

A CLIMATIC CHANGE.
— A Romance Antipodean of the World's Fair.

13.2 "A Climatic Change—A Romance Antipodean of the World's Fair" (from *World's Fair Puck*, Chicago: Keppler and Schwarzmann, 1893)

While the fair influenced American life in fundamental ways, it did not give all Americans equal cause for celebration. African-Americans and Native Americans were denied the opportunity to participate on equal terms with whites, while women were refused the opportunity to participate on equal terms with men. Precisely because they saw the fair for what it was—a powerful instrument for reaffirming existing attitudes regarding race and gender (Figure 13.2)—Americans in positions of relative powerlessness debated the fair among themselves and adopted various strategies of accommodation and resistance to meet the challenge of the future as projected at the exposition.

These concerns about representation were not limited to Americans. To reinforce exposition promoters' visions of America's national progress and ambitions to compete with European powers for an overseas empire, the Chicago fair, like contemporary European world's fairs, also featured displays of people from Africa, Asia, the Dutch East Indies, and the Middle East. Read from the vantage point of people typed as "exotic" or "savage" and displayed, for the most part, as living ethnological exhibits along the Midway or ghettoized in the fair's Anthropology Department, the exposition stood as an artifact—an ideological construct of the age of Western imperialism. The fair posed many questions about who would be included—and on what terms—in the march of civilization towards the utopia forecast by the fair's promoters. From the perspective of nonwhites represented at the fair, especially in light of the smallpox epidemic precipitated by the exposition, the Chicago fair seemed less like a dream city than a nightmare come true.

As soon as plans for the Chicago fair were announced in 1890, African-Americans began planning for their participation in the hope that Chicago's exposition authorities would agree to exhibits that would highlight African-American achievements since emancipation. But, on the basis of their experience with America's earlier international expositions, there were not many reasons for optimism. The 1876 Philadelphia Centennial Exhibition had generally excluded African-American exhibits, and police had prevented former slave and abolitionist Frederick Douglass from sitting on the platform with opening-day speakers. At the 1884–85 New Orleans World's Industrial and Cotton Exposition, the situation was not much better. Even with the help of the federal government, African-Americans succeeded only in establishing a small exhibit devoted to advances in industrial education since emancipation. Clearly, since the decision-making power at the World's Columbian Exposition remained in the hands of whites, creating African-American exhibits at the Chicago fair would require a struggle.[2]

That African-Americans had reason to be concerned became apparent when the exposition's directors decided that all proposed exhibits for state buildings would have to be approved by committees made up of whites. This decision effectively meant that most of the exhibits that African-Americans had been organizing through their own network of county and state fairs would be excluded from the World's Columbian Exposition, especially from buildings organized to represent southern states. When the exposition's Board of Lady Managers, the administrative unit responsible for selecting exhibits for the Woman's Building, refused to allow a black woman to serve as a member, the black press exploded with rage. "We object," the *New York Age* declared. "We carry our objection so far that if the matter was left to our determination we would advise the race to have nothing whatever to do with the Columbian Exposition or the management of it." The situation was only marginally better with the national commission created by Congress to oversee the organization of the fair. After a year of bitter disappointment, African-Americans scored a minor victory when Hale G. Parker, a black school principal from St. Louis, was finally appointed as an alternate commissioner. But this appointment smacked of tokenism and did nothing to mollify the growing concern among African-Americans that their contributions to building the American republic would be ignored, if not ridiculed, at the fair.[3]

How should African-Americans respond to the overt racism manifested by exposition authorities? This question became particularly acute when world's fair organizers yielded to the demands by some black musicians, artists, and writers, including violinist Will Marion Cook and poet Paul Lawrence Dunbar, that there be a special day at the fair that would, in their opinion, resemble special days set aside at the fair to honor white ethnic groups. Variously called Jubilee or Colored People's Day, this event sharply divided African-Americans. Some, led by Ida B. Wells, the famous antilynching crusader and editor of the *Memphis Free Speech*, urged African-Americans to boycott the fair. Others, led by Frederick Douglass, who served as Haiti's representative at the fair, saw in the occasion an opportunity to condemn white supremacy and to showcase black accomplishments.[4]

The debate between Wells and Douglass struck nerves already rubbed raw by months of frustration about the fair. The nation's most widely circulated black newspaper, the *Indianapolis Freeman*, railed against Jubilee Day: "The Board of Directors have furnished the day, some members of the race have pledged to furnish the 'niggers,' (in our presence Negroes), and if some thoughtful and philanthropic white man is willing to furnish watermelons, why should he be gibbeted?"[5]

On August 25, the day set aside for Colored People's Day, Douglass arrived at the fairgrounds only to find that watermelon stands had been set up in an effort to trivialize the occasion. For an instant, it appeared that Douglass's critics had been right. But Douglass was determined to proceed with the speech he had planned to deliver, "The Race Problem in America," despite the catcalls of white hecklers. As Paul Dunbar later recalled, Douglass sounded like the abolitionist orator of old. "Men talk of the Negro problem," Douglass intoned. "There is no Negro problem. The problem is whether the American people have loyalty enough, honor enough, patriotism enough, to live up to their own Constitution." Barely pausing for breath, Douglass added: "We fought for your country, we ask that we be treated as well as those who fought against your country. We love your country. We ask that you treat us as well as you do those who only love a part of it."[6]

The audience was small, but at least one person, Ida Wells, was deeply impressed by Douglass's impassioned remarks. She apologized to Douglass for having questioned the wisdom of participating in the fair and declared that his speech "had done more to bring our cause to the attention of the American people than anything else which had happened during the fair."[7]

Wells and Douglass did more than mend fences. They agreed to collaborate with Chicago newspaper editor Ferdinand L. Barnett, Wells's future husband, and several other prominent African-Americans. Together they issued a pamphlet entitled *The Reason Why. The Colored American is not in the World's Columbian Exposition*. This pamphlet remains a noteworthy, if largely forgotten, historical document. The authors detailed the horrors confronting African-Americans in post-Reconstruction America and sharply criticized the moral turpitude of Chicago's world's fair organizers. Douglass wrote the introduction, addressing it to "the good opinion of the world." The absence of exhibits by African-Americans, Douglass emphasized, was not due to "indifference and indolence" on the part of former slaves and their children, but to the hypocrisy of exposition organizers whose values stood "in flagrant contradiction to boasted American Republican liberty and civilization." "There are many good things concerning our country and countrymen of which we would be glad to tell in this pamphlet, if we could do so," Douglass insisted:

> We would like for instance to tell our visitors that the moral progress of the American people has kept even pace with their enterprise and their material civilization; that practices by the ruling class has gone on hand in hand with American professions, that two hundred and sixty years of progress and enlightenment have banished barbarism and hate from the United States; ... that American liberty is now the undisputed possession of all the

American people; that American law is now the shield alike of black and white; that the spirit of slavery and class domination has no longer any lurking place in any part of this country; . . . that here Negroes are not tortured, shot, hanged or burned to death, merely on suspicion of crime and without ever seeing a judge, a jury or advocate; . . . and that the World's Fair now in progress, is not a whited sepulcher.

"But," Douglass concluded, "nothing of all this can be said, without qualification and without flagrant disregard of the truth."[8]

In their contribution to *The Reason Why*, Wells and Barnett called attention to the social and legal conditions confronting African-Americans in the late nineteenth century and to the World's Columbian Exposition as a monument to white supremacist values. Wells recited with grim preciseness the series of "political massacres" that occurred in the South following emancipation—the "midnight outrages of the Ku Klux Klans," discriminatory legislation that prevented African-Americans from voting, and the convict-lease system that reinstituted conditions similar to slavery. Barnett detailed the efforts African-Americans had made to obtain exhibit space at the fair and equitable representation on various administrative boards and how these efforts came to naught. Exposition managers, Barnett ruefully observed, spent over ninety thousand dollars for floats that were never used for the exposition's dedication exercises, but they refused to appropriate two thousand dollars for transporting African-American exhibits. "Theoretically open to all Americans," Barnett observed, the fair was "literally and figuratively, a 'White City' in the building of which the Colored American was allowed no helping hand, and in its glorious success he has no share."[9]

Barnett was right. Exposition directors systematically excluded African-Americans from positions of responsibility (even from positions on the fair's police force) and turned the exposition into a cultural machine that reinforced prevailing racist stereotypes. But a handful of African-Americans exhibited at the fair, and some prominent African-American leaders appeared at fair-sponsored events. For instance, New York's J. Imogen Howard, the only African-American to serve on a state world's fair commission for the Chicago fair, received display space in the Woman's Building for her *New York Statistics*, a compendium of various literary and textile products by African-Americans, while George Washington Carver, then a college student in Iowa, won space among the Iowa exhibits for his painting *Yucca Glorioso*, which received honorable mention from the judges. And several black industrial colleges set up exhibits in the Liberal Arts Building.[10]

One black college exhibit, the display established by Atlanta University describing its educational mission, inspired a revealing poem in that university's official bulletin. The poem, written in 1893 by A. T. Worden, framed a line drawing of a young African-American woman:

> Behold in this calm face
> The modern sphinx, with such a thoughtful mien
> As bids us pause, when like a Frankenstein,
> A nation dares create another race.[11]

From the perspective of many African-Americans, this is precisely what the World's Columbian Exposition signified—a veritable cultural Frankenstein.

During the Labor Congress, one of many conferences of authorities in different fields held in conjunction with the fair, several influential black leaders hammered this point home. Ida Wells and Frederick Douglass issued stinging critiques of black working conditions in the South. They were joined by the little-known principal of Tuskegee Institute, Booker T. Washington, who similarly condemned the crop-lien system as "another form of slavery." But Washington insisted that this system "could not exist but for the ignorance of the negro." Where Douglass and Wells bored deeply into the ideological bedrock of the White City, questioning assumptions of white supremacy, Washington adopted a different strategy that placed blame on the victims.[12]

Two years later, Douglass would be dead, and Booker T. Washington would be in charge of the Negro Building at the 1895 Atlanta Cotton States and International Exposition. There Washington would deliver his famous accommodationist speech, endorsing the principle of separate-but-equal. The 1893 Chicago World's Columbian Exposition marked the rise of a new generation of black leaders, some of whom determined that it would be in the best interests of African-Americans to appease the monster so clearly in view at the White City of 1893.[13]

African-Americans were not alone in trying to resolve how best to convert the Chicago fair to their own purposes. Influential upper- and middle-class white women saw in the fair an opportunity to advance the causes of voting rights, domestic reform, and greater economic opportunity for women. Unlike African-Americans, white women, by virtue of prevailing Victorian beliefs, possessed moral, if not political, authority and were successful in achieving a measure of representation at the fair. But just as the issue of representation at the fair polarized African-Americans, plans for women's representation crystallized differences among white women over strategies for redressing gender inequality in American society.[14]

Building on their earlier experiences, women regarded the 1893 fair as an appropriate vehicle for advancing their political and social reform agendas. Beginning with the Civil War Sanitary Fairs and continuing through the world's fairs in Philadelphia and New Orleans, prominent reformers had relied on the exposition medium to build popular support for a variety of causes. What was unusual in the case of the World's Columbian Exposition was that the bill authorizing congressional support for the fair included a provision for the creation of a Board of Lady Managers.

The provision was the subject of disagreement among women. Supporters of the provision, including the wealthy women who served on the fair's powerful Auxiliary Executive Committee, saw the exposition as a primary site for advancing women's charity activities and domestic reform ideas. Critics, among them women professionals and suffragists, questioned the wisdom of a separate board of women fair managers and set up a rival Queen Isabella Society. As suffragist Susan B. Anthony argued the Isabellas' case in a petition presented to Congress, their goal was to include women in regular positions of world's fair management to assure that "there will be in the exhibition a presentation of the share taken by women in the industrial, artistic, intellectual, and religious progress of the nation." When Congress rejected Anthony's petition and instead established a separate Board of Lady Managers whose members would be selected by the male exposition directorate, the stage was set for a conflict.[15]

That women succeeded in organizing exhibits was due largely to Bertha Palmer, wife of Chicago mercantilist Potter Palmer. Bertha Palmer had strongly supported the creation of the Board of Lady Managers and, after being appointed to head the board, took steps to isolate the more extreme supporters of the Isabella Society and to win others over through her insistence on integrating women's exhibits with men's exhibits in appropriate exhibition buildings. A masterful politician, she did not try to silence her critics; rather she sought to control the arena in which they voiced their concerns. To accomplish this goal, she helped organize a World's Congress of Representative Women that featured speakers presenting a variety of viewpoints on women's issues.[16]

While she was taking steps to neutralize her critics, Palmer endeavored, with less success, to win the support of the exposition's bosses. The men who ran the fair, the elite of Chicago's established mercantilist and emergent corporate leadership, while not hostile in principle to women's involvement in the fair, sought to restrict their activities to fund-raising and, when that became impossible, to subordinate women's voices to their own. For instance, exposition directors rejected out of hand Palmer's argument that men's and women's inventions should be integrated in appropriate exposition palaces and that women's exhibits should be explicitly labeled as such. Then, when, exposition directors refused to help finance the transportation of women's exhibits, Palmer reconciled herself to the same separate-but-equal rationalizations that African-Americans resorted to and agreed to concentrate the bulk of women's exhibits in a separate Woman's Building (Figure 13.3).[17]

That decision carried profound consequences. There can be no doubt that Palmer won inclusion for women in the exposition. But Palmer's accommodationist strategy had another side. It endorsed the exposition's racial calculus—a calculus that divided humanity into categories of civilization and savagery.[18]

For the white women who either supported Palmer from the start or who were won over to her position, their pride in the Woman's Building outweighed other concerns. After all, the building was designed by Sophia Hayden, the first woman to graduate from the Massachusetts Institute of Technology's program in architectural design. Its interior and exterior exhibition spaces presented a formidable assortment of displays that gave women exhibitors an opportunity to advance a broad agenda of social reform. But, if, as Bertha Palmer claimed, the Board of Lady Managers' goal was to present "a complete picture" of the social condition of women, they fell short of the mark. As historian Frances K. Pohl explains, because the board insisted on applying "elite standards of quality to the work of all races and classes" and on displaying "products rather than processes," the Woman's Building included exhibits that "conformed to the Board's well-defined aesthetic, intellectual, and moral standards."[19]

Hayden's building design was itself a monument to the efforts by some women to feminize American culture. Her "Palace of the Fair Sex," as it was dubbed by one souvenir publication, emulated Italian Renaissance designs and fit perfectly into the broader beaux-arts patterns of the White City. The building's imposing exterior ornamentation, sculpted by Alice Rideout, projected a vision of women's occupations, with figures representing

13.3 Sophia Hayden, The Woman's Building, World's Columbia Exposition, Chicago, Illinois. Note Ferris wheel and Midway in background, far right (from John McGovern, (ed.), *A Portfolio of Photographic Views of the World's Columbian Exposition*, London: The Jewell N. Halligan Co., 1894)

"Charity, Beneficence, Literature, Art, and Home Life" dominating the bas-relief over the main entrance. The overall effect was decidedly "feminine," possessing, in the words of architect Henry Van Brunt, "a certain quality of sentiment, which might be designated as . . . graceful timidity or gentleness, combined, however, with evident technical knowledge, which at once reveals the sex of its author." Or as one of the women managers described it: "Our building is essentially feminine in character: it has the qualities of reserve, delicacy and refinement. . . . Its strength is veiled in grace; its beauty is gently impressive."[20]

Within and beyond the building, as historian Mary Cordato has recently noted, exhibits organized by women expanded the constraints of prevailing Victorian attitudes to embrace a broad range of social reform issues, including public health care, public housing, and education. Visitors could examine model hospital wards, walk through a model home for a working-class family, and study the latest advances in elementary and secondary education. In addition to the Woman's Building, the Board of Lady Managers sponsored a women's dormitory building near the exposition grounds to protect visiting women from the violence of the city and a Children's Building on the fairgrounds to demonstrate the latest theories about raising the nation's young. Other exhibits, including displays devoted to women inventors and artists, bore witness to the message that the ideology of domesticity could fuel reforms that would improve women's economic and social opportunities.[21]

The ideology of domesticity gained visual representation in Mary Cassatt's mural, entitled *Modern Woman*, which decorated the south wall of the main hall in the Woman's Building. Cassatt divided her painting into three panels, with *The Arts, Music, and Dancing* and *Young Girls Pursuing Fame* framing the centerpiece: *Young Women Plucking the Fruits of Knowledge and Science*. As summarized by one historian, Cassatt's mural reflected her "commitment to see in women's everyday activities humanity's highest aspirations." Put in slightly different terms, women's domestic sphere contained the seeds of "civilization."[22]

The importance of the domestic sphere for advancing civilization was also the message of Mary Fairchild MacMonnies's heroic narrative mural, which was located directly across the main hall from Cassatt's work. Entitled *Primitive Woman*, the mural had been commissioned by Bertha Palmer to complement *Modern Woman*. Historian Jeanne Weimann aptly describes the murals: Primitive woman "crushed grapes and carried water, burdened by a babe in arms. Modern woman picked fruit, plucked a lyre, and gracefully pursued an Ideal." In the Woman's Building as in the exposition as a whole, pursuit of the civilized ideal required the representation of its counterpoint—savagery.[23]

As if to underscore that message, the Woman's Building was located in the northwest corner of the White City, at the gateway to the Midway Plaisance, the mile-long avenue that combined amusement with ethnological instruction about people who were typed as exotic or savage. The effect of crossing from the Midway to the White City was captured by novelist Clara Louisa Burnham in *Sweet Clover*: "You know that in what seemed like one step, you've passed out o' darkness and into light." Looking up at the angels on the Woman's Building, Burnham's fictional fairgoers could feel elevated by the progress they had made from the chaos associated with the Midway to the order symbolized by the White City.[24]

There was, of course, another message in this ideologically laden mapping of the exposition grounds. If the position of the Woman's Building right at the doorstep of the Midway was any indication, women, in the eyes of the exposition's male sponsors, came close to slipping into the category of "otherness" reserved for "savages" and "exotics." They were redeemed only by their capacity to serve as mothers of civilization—a stereotype that some upper- and middle-class white women were only too happy to embrace to advance their own reform agenda. As a result, women's representation at the World's Columbian Exposition recapitulated and reinforced prevailing sentiments of white supremacy.

As enraged as African-Americans may have been over their treatment by exposition authorities and as compromised as many women may have felt by the concessions they were forced to make to secure representation in the fair, these groups had a measure of political and moral standing in American society and could make themselves heard. That task was more difficult for Native Americans and nonwhites from other cultures who were put on display in what the official exhibit classification referred to as "Department M," but what was better known as the Midway Plaisance.

With its towering, revolving wheel, designed by engineer George Ferris, lifting visitors 260 feet above the exposition grounds, the Midway has been remembered as an entertainment strip. But, in addition to its amusements, the Midway also boasted so-called ethnological villages, modeled after similar displays at the 1889 Paris Exposition Universelle, which had been located near the base of the Eiffel Tower. Chicago's exposition directors knew that French colonial villages had been enormously profitable. Given the precarious financial condition of the World's Columbian Exposition, these shows gained added appeal for exposition organizers. But how could such shows be included without detracting from the refinements of the White City? The Paris example showed the way. At the 1889 fair, leading anthropologists had given their blessing to the colonial villages as authentic replications of native life and treated them as ethnological field camps. Chicago's exposition builders went one better. They placed one of America's leading ethnologists, Frederic Ward Putnam of Harvard, in charge of Department M, home of the fair's anthropology displays as well as its Midway amusements. Fair planners used these ethnological villages to support one of the central messages of the fair, namely, that the progress of Western civilization could be measured by comparing "less civilized" people to white Americans.[25]

In recent years, much has been written about the Midway Plaisance: how it "commodified the exotic"; how its ethnological intentions were subverted by its commercial prospects; and how it helped sow the seeds for popular support for American imperial adventures later in the decade.[26] But the motives and reactions of the people put on display are less clear. The people who endured exploitive conditions were not just passive victims of world's fair authorities, entrepreneurial anthropologists, and mercenary concessionaires. Some of the people put on display knowingly complied with the strategies of exposition sponsors; others contested their representation as bottom rungs on a living ladder of humanity.

The Esquimaux village was one case in point. Situated in the extreme northwest corner of the exposition grounds, several hundred yards from the Midway, the village consisted of about sixty Innuits. It was one of the first ethnological exhibits established at the exposition. Before the Innuits arrived in Chicago, the entrepreneur responsible for organizing the show had promised them "$100.00, 200 lbs. salt, 30 lbs. rice, 20 gallons of molasses, 10 lbs. tea, 200 cartridges, a Winchester rifle, one reloading outfit, 20 lbs. powder, 20 lbs. shot, 80 lbs. lead, 1000 explosive caps, one barrel of pork, 3 barrels of flour, one barrel of pilot bread, and numerous other smaller articles" in exchange for their participation. The Innuits were to arrive in Chicago in the autumn of 1892, long before the official opening of the fair, to give them a chance to adjust to the climate. But the Innuits—including a newborn baby named Christopher Columbus—were immediately put on display before crowds that paid to see them perform with their huskies and kayaks and live out their daily lives in overcrowded cabins and bark huts.[27]

Conditions for the Innuits grew worse. In February, poor food—whether it was spoiled or lacking in quantity is unclear—and the absence of fresh water, together with cramped living quarters, led one of the Innuits to seize the concessionaire's interpreter and give him "a good shaking." Police restored order, and the manager of the village told the Innuits they were his "chattels." In April, when one of the villagers refused to wear a fur coat because it made him too hot, the concessionaire ordered exposition police to arrest him. According to press reports, the concessionaire told the villager: "Wear fur clothes or you get no food." Five Innuit families immediately hired an attorney and sued the concessionaire. They complained of being held "practically as prisoners." Convinced of the legitimacy of their case, the court released the complainants from their contract. The Innuit who had earlier assaulted the interpreter found employment as a carpenter for $350 a year—a substantial increase over the $50 he would have earned for performing at the fair—while several others set up their own show amidst the honky-tonk concessions that had sprung up outside the exposition grounds.[28]

The efforts by some Innuits to control their working conditions were not unique. When the fair was in its early planning stages, several Native Americans wrote the U.S. commissioner of Indian affairs: "We, American citizens of Indian blood, most earnestly and respectfully petition you to grant us through the forthcoming World's Fair and anniversary of the discovery of America, some recognition as a race; some acknowledgement that we are still a part, however inferior, of America and the Great American Republic." Specifically, the Native Americans asked for the opportunity to develop their own exhibits. "With a Native American, or Indian exhibit in the hands of capable men of our own blood . . .," the petitioners insisted, "a most interesting and instructive and surely successful feature will be added . . . [that] will show to both and all races alike, that our own advancement has been much greater than is usually supposed." The petitioners added: "Give us . . . some reason to be glad with you that [America] was so discovered."[29]

United States government officials and world's fair authorities were only too happy to include representations of Native Americans—especially since the popular Buffalo Bill's Wild West Show, located outside the fairgrounds, would compete with Midway shows—but not on terms set by the petitioners. World's fair managers awarded an American Indian village concession to showmen Thomas Roddy and Henry "Buckskin Joe" De Ford, who proceeded to organize sixty Native Americans drawn from different tribal groups into a Midway display. Exposition directors also awarded another Native American show to Wild West entrepreneur, P. B. Wickham. Called "Sitting Bull's Cabin," this exhibit featured nine Sioux, including Chief Rain-in-the-Face, one of the original petitioners to the government for control of Native American representations.[30]

Instead of dignified representation, Native Americans experienced degrading exploitation. In one memorable performance in the Indian village, Chief Twobites and Joe Strongback removed their shirts while the interpreter for the concession "produced a keen knife and two pieces of rope and cut four deep gashes in the back of each Indian between the shoulder blades. Then raising the quivering flesh he passed the ends of the rope beneath the skin and tied them in hard."[31]

Regarded and treated as subhuman, some Native Americans on display turned to alcohol and violence, fighting with each other and show managers. Others probably contented themselves with the money they earned. If historian of anthropology Lester George Moses is right, Native Americans may have made some contractual gains by forcing showmen to negotiate with performers as individuals. But the overall response of Native Americans to the fair was anticipated by the signators of the original petition to the United States government for control over their representation at the fair. "The people[?] are almost despairing," the petitioners wrote, "and it is inevitable that our people trace the causes of that despairing and consequently desperate condition to the very event which, with such large expenditures of wealth, you are about to celebrate."[32]

The responses of another group displayed on the Midway, the Dahomeyans, are even more difficult to reconstruct. Inspired by the tremendous success of French colonial shows at the 1889 fair, Chicago's exposition builders created a Dahomeyan village under the control of Xavier Pené, an intrepid African explorer and a labor contractor who had supplied workers for the construction of the Pan-American Railroad in the 1880s. This imperial conqueror-turned-showman brought about seventy Africans to the fair, where they lived in habitat dwellings that had been constructed by local laborers before the Dahomeyans arrived. They performed an assortment of dances that generally reinforced the negative opinion given by one guidebook: "The habits of these people are repulsive; they eat like animals and have all the characteristics of the very lowest order of the human family. Nearly all the women are battle-scarred; most of them are captives."[33]

The lives of the Dahomeyans at the fair were no better than those of the Innuits. One newspaper noted that "the Dahomeyans were practically slaves. They got nothing but their board, the consideration of their services being paid to their chief at home." When his wards gave him trouble, Pené plied them with "lavish use of beer" and encouraged them to dance with pint bottles. But, as did the Innuits and Native Americans, Dahomeyans resisted their exposition masters. In her pioneering study of various Midway village performances, Gertrude M. Scott quotes the Austrian village manager's observations of the Dahomeyan women, who were forced to parade through the Midway along with other Midway performers.

> A good many people imagine, I suppose, [that the African women] are sounding the praises of the Exposition or at least voicing their wonder at the marvels they have seen since coming to this country. But the fact is that if the words of their chants were translated into English they would read something like this: "We have come from a far country to a land where all men are white. If you will come to our country we will take pleasure in cutting your white throats."

This tale, as Scott points out, may well have been apocryphal, but, given the actions of other Midway performers to take control over the conditions of their representation, it could easily contain a kernel of truth.[34]

Many people featured as Midway specimens manifested various strategies of resistance to preserve their dignity. The conditions that necessitated that resistance were not simply material, but ideological, following a system of beliefs embedded in the exposition that typed some people as "other." This "orientalist" structure of thought that pervaded the Midway crystallized in a cluster of exhibits—the Street in Cairo (Figure 13.4), the Algerian Village, the Persian Palace, the Wild East Show, the Moorish Palace, and the Turkish Theater—that were among the most popular attractions along the Midway.

Modeled on similar shows at previous European fairs that were intended to reinforce the imperial designs of European countries, these displays at the Chicago fair gave the Midway its distinctive, "exotic" look. As one journalist described the scene:

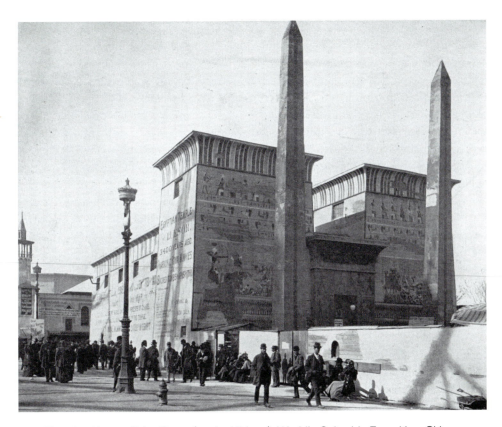

13.4 Temple of Luxor, Cairo Street (on the Midway), World's Columbia Exposition, Chicago, Illinois, 1893 (from John McGovern, (ed.), *A Portfolio of Photographic Views of the World's Columbian Exposition*, London: The Jewell N. Halligan Co., 1894)

Everybody went first to the Midway Plaisance. And what a picture that road down the center presented. Sunday or no Sunday, you met people of all nations, all stations, all classes and all dressed in holiday attire. There were Turks in European costume, with red fez, and Turks in all the glory of rich silk turbans, purple silk mantles and yellow silk trousers; Arabs in long, pale, tan-colored robes, embroidered in gold, and in long silk robes, covered with gold lace.

Together with camels, donkeys, and distinctive architectural designs, the "oriental" displays seemed authentic. But, as architectural historians Zeynep Çelik and Leila Kinney have argued, these villages played a specific purpose. "The fabricated streets, shops, artisans, and merchants," they write, "created a visible difference from the industrialized nations." The overall effect was not simply to amuse, but to perpetuate an image of under-development—an image perfectly suited to nurturing the imperial ambitions of exposition sponsors on both sides of the Atlantic.[35]

Vital to this strategy, as Çelik and Kinney argue, was the representation of Middle Eastern women. At the 1893 fair, concessionaires, who included prominent Chicago businessmen and their Middle Eastern counterparts, replicated one of the most popular attractions from the 1889 Paris exposition—the belly dance. Generally referred to as the "danse du ventre" because, as one journalist noted, the translation would "sound ill in American ears," it was performed in four theaters on the Midway by a variety of performers, but apparently not, as it has been commonly assumed, by anyone known as "Little Egypt." One account captured the lure of the dance: the dancer "revels in all the glory of oriental colors and barbaric jewelry and there it is she displays her charms, dimly hidden by a gauze nothing; a narrow zone of gauze silk though which the warm flesh tints are distinctly visible." In at least one theater, the Persian Palace of Eros, the audience was exclusively male and routinely made lewd comments about the dancers, who concluded their performance by doing the splits. Evocative of erotic fantasies, the dances, as Çelik and Kinney suggest, constituted "models of possession" that "anchor[ed] colonial power at the individual level."[36]

But this was not their sole effect. At the same time that these dances supported the Midway's exotic qualities, they had a contradictory subversive effect on prudish Victorian sexual attitudes. It was precisely this realization that led the clergy and the Board of Lady Managers to launch a crusade to close the theaters—a crusade that, given the profitability of the shows, exposition authorities were reluctant to support. In the battle for the soul of American culture, as historian James Gilbert has noted, the erotically charged commercialism of the Midway constantly threatened the overcivilized values of the White City. At every turn, it seemed, the energies unleashed by the Palace of Eros threatened to overwhelm the plaster-of-paris palaces of the White City.[37]

But those commercial and erotic energies were constrained by an iron cage of race. The presentation of white European ethnic groups stood in sharp contrast to the "exotic" cultures of the Orient. The Irish village, for instance, demonstrated that "Irish poverty will be cured by Irish industry," while the German village, operated by the immigration agent for the Atchison, Topeka, and Santa Fe Railroad, seemed bent on creating the impression that German immigrants were wholly capable of assimilating into American society. Threatened as it may have been by the raw energies of the Midway, the White City was not without its defenses, chief of which was its insistence on *herrenvolk* values of racial exclusivity.[38]

Politically and culturally correct by the standards of an age characterized by the relentless search for overseas empire, the Chicago World's Columbian Exposition manifested another characteristic of imperialism—disease. The exposition's most immediate bequest to the city of Chicago was not its architecture, mass entertainment, or insistence upon civic reform, but a smallpox epidemic that added another layer of despair to the panic caused by the economic depression that hit in the summer of 1893. As Chicago's commissioner of public health noted: "It is fair to assume that smallpox was one of the things the fair brought to Chicago." Before it ran its course in 1894, the epidemic claimed 1,213 lives.[39]

How exactly did the fair precipitate an epidemic? Historian of medicine Thomas Neville Bonner describes the general social conditions prevalent in Chicago at the time of the fair: "At the time Chicago was receiving the world's plaudits at the Columbian Exposition in 1893, it had already outdistanced other cities in the misery and degradation of its citizens." More specifically, health conditions at the fairgrounds and living conditions for workers—many of them European immigrants—employed to construct the exposition's buildings were deplorable. During the construction period, there were 5,919 medical and surgical cases reported by the exposition's medical department. Over thirty workers died building the fair; of these many died of fractured skulls. No less dramatic were the outbreaks of typhoid fever, diarrhea, and bronchitis that raged during the construction of the fair. One former worker, who later became a professor at Princeton and had largely positive recollections of his life as a laborer at the fair, let slip that more than four hundred workers were forced to live and eat together in one building where they were guarded by sentries evidently to keep them from contact with union organizers. Given that Chicago had not had a smallpox vaccination program for nearly a decade, what were intended as model dormitories for workers quickly became microbial compression chambers. Then, once the fair was built, thousands of immigrant workers remained in Chicago, often unemployed and living in circumstances that worsened with the onset of the depression. Conditions quickly ripened for a catastrophic outbreak of disease.[40]

The state of the ethnological villages during the fair compounded the already virulent situation of the period preceding the exposition. On the eve of the fair's opening, an attorney for the management of the Turkish village, in a revealing use of language, told the press that the "inmates of the Turkish village are in a wretched condition." He complained that "the sanitary arrangements are something horrible," noting that there was not one public toilet on the entire Midway. There should have been additional cause for concern when it took public health officials nearly seven weeks to quarantine the Innuits after an outbreak of measles.[41]

The consequences of neglect hit towards the end of the world's fair season. Between August and November 1893, smallpox cases reached epidemic proportions. The effects were immediately felt in the city's Emergency Isolation Hospital, more popularly known as the "pesthouse." As the *Chicago Tribune* later recalled:

> In that winter [of 1893–94] following the world's fair the Chicago pesthouse was a hideous structure, in itself, through which 3,500 cases passed. Far into the summer the epidemic ran and the buildings back of bridewell were so filled with the afflicted that ropes were stretched, soldiers established a "dead" line, and tents were set up to accommodate those crowded out of the building.

Linked causally with the exposition, the epidemic took an extraordinary toll among the powerless, especially among children, foreign workers, and Midway villagers who had been left to fend for themselves once the exposition closed.[42]

In this tragedy there was no small measure of irony. For more surely than any exhibit at the fair, the epidemic occasioned by the World's Columbian Exposition confirmed the claims by exposition builders that they stood on Columbus's shoulders. Marked by the pox that Columbus and his voyagers introduced to the New World, the World's Columbian Exposition was more true to its distant origins than its organizers had ever dreamed possible.[43]

Commenting several decades later on the architectural legacy of the World's Columbian Exposition, architect Louis Sullivan, who designed the Transportation Building, observed that the fair had "penetrated deep into the constitution of the American mind, effecting there lesions significant of dementia." Lesions there may have been, but the architecture was only symptomatic of deeper flaws in the guiding vision that directed the fair. Deeply inscribed with prevailing beliefs about race and gender, the exposition posited a common culture for some Americans at the expense of others. Consequently, it occasioned great skepticism and outrage from people who were either excluded from the fair or included only to be treated as subordinates. As a cultural and political battleground over the future direction of American society, the World's Columbian Exposition revealed tensions that would continue to haunt the United States far into the next century.[44]

Notes

1   Much has been written about the 1893 Chicago World's Columbian Exposition. Interested readers should start with: R. Reid Badger, *The Great American Fair: The World's Columbian Exposition and American Culture* (Chicago: Nelson-Hall, 1979); David F. Burg, *Chicago's White City of 1893* (Lexington, KY: University of Kentucky Press, 1976); James Gilbert, *Perfect Cities: Chicago's Utopias of 1893* (Chicago: University of Chicago Press, 1991); Neil Harris, *Cultural Excursions: Marketing Appetites and Cultural Tastes in Modern America* (Chicago: University of Chicago Press, 1990); Thomas S. Hines, *Burnham of Chicago: Architect and Planner* (New York: Oxford University Press, 1974); Helen Lefkowitz Horowitz, *Culture and the City: Cultural Philanthrophy in Chicago from the 1880s to 1917* (Lexington, KY: University of Kentucky Press, 1976), and Robert Rydell, *All the World's a Fair: Visions of Empire at American International Expositions, 1876–1916* (Chicago: University of Chicago Press, 1984), ch. 2.

2   Rydell, ch. 2.

3   Ann Massa, "Black Women in the 'White City,'" *Journal of American Studies* 8 (1974): 319–37; "The Women and the World's Fair," *New York Age*, October 24, 1891; Elliot M. Rudwick and August Meier, "Black Man in the 'White City,'" *Phylon* 26 (1965): 358. See also Dreck Spurlock Wilson, "Black involvement in Chicago's Previous World's Fairs," unpublished paper, 1984, Chicago Historical Society Library, vertical files (cited hereafter as CHS).

4   Details of this controversy are presented by Rydell, 52–53; Rudwick and Meier, 359–61; Wilson, 12–14; and Alfreda M. Duster, ed., *Crusade for Justice: The Autobiography of Ida B. Wells* (Chicago: University of Chicago Press, 1970), 118–19.

5   "The Jubilee Day Folly," *Indianapolis Freeman*, September 2, 1893.

6   William McFeely, *Frederick Douglass* (New York: W. W. Norton, 1991), 370–72, provides a fine description of the day's events. Douglass quoted in "The World in Miniature," *Indianapolis Freeman*, September 2, 1893; and, "Appeal of Douglass," *Chicago Tribune*, August 26, 1893.

7   Wells quoted in McFeely, 371.

8   Frederick Douglass, Ida Wells, and Ferdinand Barnett, *The Reason Why. The Colored American Is Not in the World's Columbian Exposition* (no imprint, 1893), 2–3.

9   Douglass, Wells, and Barnett, 13, 75, 79.

10 Wilson, 11.

11 *The Bulletin of Atlanta University* 48 (July 1893): 1, 8. CHS clipping file.

12 "An Account of a Speech before the Labor Congress, Chicago," September 2, 1893, *Booker T. Washington Papers*, ed. Louis R. Harlan, vol. 3 (Urbana, IL: University of Illinois Press, 1974), 364–65.

13 Regarding Washington's involvement with the 1895 fair, see Rydell, 82–85.

14 The role of women at the 1893 fair has attracted growing attention. In addition to Jeanne Madeline Weimann's *The Fair Women* (Chicago: Academy Chicago, 1981), readers should

consult: Frances K. Pohl, "Historical Reality of Utopian Ideal?" *International Journal of Women's Studies* 5 (1982): 289–311; Virginia Grant Darney, "Women and World's Fairs: American International Expositions, 1876–1904," Ph.D. diss. (Emory University, 1982); and Mary Frances Cordato, "Representing the Expansion of Woman's Sphere: Women's Work and Culture at the World's Fairs of 1876, 1893, and 1904," Ph.D. diss. (New York University, 1989).

15   Anthony quoted in Weimann, 36. Details concerning the controversy besetting the Board of Lady Managers and its creation are provided by Weimann, Pohl, and Cordato, passim.

16   Cordato, 216–24; Weimann, 73–101.

17   *Addresses and Reports of Mrs. Potter Palmer* (Chicago: Rand McNally, 1894), 125. See also Cordato, 228–33.

18   Pohl, 296–97, lays the basis for this claim.

19   Pohl, 298.

20   Judith Paine, "Sophia Hayden and the Woman's Building," *Helicon Nine* 1 (Fall/Winter 1979), 28–37. The Columbian Gallery and Henry Van Brunt quoted in ibid., 32, 34, 36. See also Maud Howe Elliott, ed., *Art and Handicraft in the Woman's Building of the World's Columbian Exposition* (Paris: Goupil and Co., 1893), 25.

21   See Cordato, passim.

22   Sally Webster, "Mary Cassatt's Allegory of Modern Woman," *Helicon Nine* 1 (Fall/Winter 1979), 38–47.

23   Weimann, 214.

24   Clara Louisa Burnham, *Sweet Clover* (Chicago: Laird and Lee, 1893), 201.

25   Rydell, 60–68.

26   Curtis M. Hinsley, "The World as Marketplace: Commodification of the Exotic at the World's Columbian Exposition, Chicago, 1893," in *Exhibiting Cultures: The Poetics and Politics of Museum Display*, Ivan Karp and Steven D. Lavine, eds. (Washington, D.C.: Smithsonian Institution Press, 1991), 363.

27   "Esquimaux Must Not Be Detained," *Chicago Mail*, April 3, 1893; Gertrude M. Scott, "Village Performance: Villages of the Chicago World's Columbian Exposition of 1893," Ph.D. diss. (New York University, 1990), 312–26; *Chicago Times Portfolio of Midway Types*, part 2 (Chicago: American Eng. Co. Publishers and Printers, 1893), n.p.

28   "The Fighting Esquimau," *Illustrated World's Fair* 4 (February 1893): 443; "Javanese are Bowed with Grief," *Chicago Mail*, April 21, 1893; "The Eskimos are Out," *The Bee*, April 29, 1893.

29   "To the Commissioners of the Columbian Exposition," 1891[?], Frederic Ward Putnam Papers, Box 34, Harvard University Archives.

30   L. G. Moses, "Indians on the Midway: Wild West Shows and the Indian Bureau at World's Fairs, 1893–1904," *South Dakota History* 21 (1991): 220; Scott, 326–34.

31   Moses writes on p. 217: "Indians may also have been abused and ridiculed, but neither the newspaper accounts nor the agency records that contain comments by and about Indians bears this out. Finally, how is one to judge whether or not Indians benefited from participation in the exhibition? Some may just have had a good time. It would be better to examine that topic from the perspective of the Indians themselves." Cf. "Stop the Horrid Torture Dances," *Chicago Tribune*, August 20, 1893, 12; and "Return as Freaks: Descendants of Chicago's Original Settlers Come to Town," *Chicago Tribune*, July 1, 1893, 1.

32   Scott, 328–29; Moses, 219–20; "To the Commissioners of the Columbian Exposition," op. cit.

33   Rydell, 145–46; Scott, 283–303, John J. Flinn, comp., *Official Guide to Midway Plaisance* (Chicago: The Columbian Guide Company, [1893]), 30.

34   [Unidentified newspaper clipping], Charles Harpel Scrapbooks, Manuscripts Division, CHS; Scott, 297–98.

35   Teresa Dean, *White City Chips* (Chicago: Warren Publishing Co., 1895), 15; Zeynep Çelik and Leila Kinney, "Ethnography and Exhibitionism at the Expositions Universelles," *Assemblage* 13 (1986): 39. See also, Edward Said, *Orientalism* (New York: Random House, 1979); and Timothy

Mitchell, "The World as Exhibition," *Comparative Studies in Society and History* 31 (1989): 217–36.

36   Çelik and Kinney, passim, 46; "Danse De [*sic*] Ventre on the Plaisance," *Chicago Mail*, June 3, 1893. On the controversy over "Little Egypt," see Scott, 195–213.

37   Gilbert, 130.

38   Frank H. Smith, *Art History, Midway Plaisance and World's Fair* (Chicago: Foster Press, 1893), n.p. On the centrality of *herrenvolk* concepts of race to late nineteenth-century America, see George Frederickson, *Black Image in the White Mind: The Debate on Afro-American Character and Destiny, 1817–1914* (New York: Harper Torchbooks, 1971).

39   Arthur R. Reynolds, "History of the Chicago Smallpox Epidemic of 1893, 1894, and 1895 . . . ," in *The Rise and Fall of Disease in Illinois*, ed. Isaac R. Rawlings (Springfield, IL: n.p., 1927), 313. Additional information about the epidemic can be found in *Annual Report of the Department of Health of the City of Chicago for the Year Ended December 31, 1894* (Chicago: n.p., 1895).

40   Thomas Neville Bonner, *Medicine in Chicago, 1850–1950: A Chapter in the Social and Scientific Development of a City* (Urbana, IL: University of Illinois Press, 1991), 20; "Report of the Medical Department. World's Columbian Exposition," n.d., Chicago Public Library; Walter A. Wyckoff, *The Workers: An Experiment in Reality* (New York: Charles Scribner and Sons, 1917), 248.

41   "May Breed Disease at the Fair," *Chicago Mail*, May 25, 1893; Dean, 7.

42   "No Epidemic of Smallpox," *Chicago Tribune*, February 3, 1901, 43, clipping, CHS, vertical files, f. "Smallpox."

43   Alfred A. Crosby, *The Columbian Exchange: Biological and Cultural Consequences of 1492* (Westport, CT: Greenwood Press, 1972).

44   Louis Sullivan, *The Autobiography of an Idea* (New York: W. W. Norton, 1926), 325.

Chapter 14

James F. O'Gorman

The prairie house

Frank Lloyd Wright unveiled his prairie house in the February 1901 issue of Edward Bok's *Ladies' Home Journal*, a Philadelphia-based, general circulation magazine (Figure 14.1). This "city man's country house on the prairie" (in fact a repeatable cluster of four houses arranged in a "quadruple block plan") has been recognized as the first complete realization of his suburban domestic ideal. Including porch and porte cochere, the "Home in a Prairie Town" was to rise from a hearth-centered, cruciform plan with library, living room, and dining room widely opening into one another along an axis perpendicular to the street, and with porch, living room, fireplace, entry, and porte cochere stretched along offset axes parallel to the street. Above this "footprint," the house in Wright's drawings stretched broadly in repeated tripartite Richardsonian layers, all grouped around the central masonry mass. The entrance hall was to be reached through a Richardsonian archway. Within, furniture and furnishings were all designed by the architect in the spirit of the domestic Arts and Crafts movement and the contemporary trend toward simplicity. In its essential *parti*, with spaces radiating outwardly from closed core through wings to transitional areas of porch or covered carriageway to open yard (a centrifugal sweep reinforced by banks of out-swinging French doors and double casement windows), the house was a logical step beyond the McAfee and Husser houses of the previous decade. While it was heir to a domestic planning process as old as American architecture, and though it was rooted in a profound understanding of [Henry Hobson] Richardson's work (Figure 14.2), it was also a completely Wrightian design.[1]

The project unveiled in the *Ladies' Home Journal* was the first of a series of built and unbuilt prairie houses Wright designed in the next decade and a half that mark the culmination of his earlier efforts. Many are variations of the *Ladies' Home Journal* model: the Bradley House at Kankakee, Illinois (1900), the Henderson House in Elmhurst (1901), and even, greatly expanded, the justly famous Darwin Martin House in Buffalo. In the Ward Willits House in Highland Park, Illinois (1901), Wright first built the fully articulated cruciform plan (Figure 14.3), with entry in one wing, living room in a second, dining room occupying a third, and utility spaces in a fourth, all grouped around a central masonry stack of fireplaces. Subsequent houses, ranging from square to cruciform plans, almost all have a masonry core, and most develop three-dimensionally into spreading masses through the use of pronounced horizontal lines. Some major examples, other than the Martin and Willits houses, include the Gilmore House in Madison, Wisconsin (1908), and in Illinois, the Cheney House, Oak Park, and Francis Little House, Peoria (both 1904),

A Home in a Prairie Town

By FRANK LLOYD WRIGHT

This is the Fifth Design in the Journal's New Series of Model Suburban Houses Which Can be Built at Moderate Cost

A CITY man going to the country puts too much in his house and too little in his ground. He drags after him the fifty-foot lot, soon the twenty-five-foot lot, finally the party wall; and the home-maker who fully appreciates the advantages which he came to the country to secure feels himself impelled to move on.

It seems a waste of energy to plan a house hap-hazard, to hit or miss an already distorted condition, so this partial solution of a city man's country home on the prairie begins at the beginning and assumes four houses to the block of four hundred feet square as the minimum of ground for the basis of his prairie community.

The block plan to the left, at the top of the page, shows an arrangement of the four houses that secures breadth and prospect to the community as a whole, and absolute privacy both as regards each to the community, and each to each of the four.

THE perspective view shows the handling of the group at the centre of the block, with its foil of simple lawn, omitting the foliage of curb parkways to better show the scheme, retaining the same house in the four locations merely to afford an idea of the unity of the various elevations. In practice the houses would differ distinctly, though based upon a similar plan.

The ground plan, which is intended to explain itself, is arranged to offer the least resistance to a simple mode of living, in keeping with a high ideal of the family life together. It is arranged, too, with a certain well-established order that enables free use without the sense of confusion felt in five out of seven houses which people really use.

The exterior recognizes the influence of the prairie, is firmly and broadly associated with the site, and makes a feature of its quiet level. The low terraces

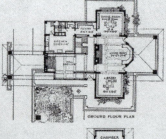

GROUND FLOOR PLAN

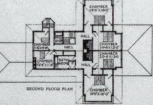

SECOND FLOOR PLAN

and broad eaves are designed to accentuate that quiet level and complete the harmonious relationship. The curbs of the terraces and formal inclosures for extremely informal masses of foliage and bloom should be worked in cement with the walks and drives.

Cement on metal lath is suggested for the exterior covering throughout, because it is simple, and, as now understood, durable and cheap.

The cost of this house with interior as specified and cement construction would be seven thousand dollars:

Masonry, Cement and Plaster	$2800.00
Carpentry	3100.00
Plumbing	400.00
Painting and Glass	325.00
Heating — combination (hot water)	345.00
Total	$6970.00

IN A HOUSE of this character the upper reach and gallery of the central living-room is decidedly a luxury. Two bedrooms may take its place, as suggested by the second-floor plan. The gallery feature is, nevertheless, a temptation because of the happy sense of variety and depth it tends to the composition of the interior, and the sunlight it gains from above to relieve the shadow of the porch. The details are better grasped by a study of the drawings. The interior section in perspective shows the gallery as indicated by dotted lines on the floor plan of the living-room.

The second-floor plan disregards this feature and is arranged for a larger family. Where three bedrooms would suffice the gallery would be practicable, and two large and two small bedrooms with the gallery might be had by rearranging servants' rooms and baths.

The interior is plastered throughout with sand finish and trimmed all through with flat bands of Georgia pine, smaller back bands following the base and casings. This Georgia pine should be selected from straight grain for stiles, rails and running members, and from figured grain for panels and wide surfaces.

All the wood should be shellacked once and waxed, and the plaster should be stained with thin, pure color in water and glue.

EDITOR'S NOTE — As a guarantee that the plan of this house is practicable, and that the estimates for cost are conservative, the architect is ready to accept the commission of preparing the working plans and specifications for this house to cost Seven Thousand Dollars, providing that the building site selected is within reasonable distance of a base of supplies where material and labor may be had at the standard market rates.

THE LIBRARY   LIVING-ROOM AND GALLERY   THE DINING-ROOM

HALL, LOOKING TOWARD ENTRANCE

INTERIOR VIEW OF THE FIRST FLOOR OF THIS HOUSE

14.1 Frank Lloyd Wright, "Home in a Prairie Town" (from *Ladies' Home Journal* 18, Feb. 1901)

14.2 Henry Hobson Richardson, Glessner House, Chicago, Illinois, 1886

the Robie House, Chicago (1906), the Coonley House in Riverside (1907), and the Roberts House, River Forest (1908).

Just as Richardson had his "lengthened shadow," his followers turned his beloved Romanesque forms into a source for repeated Richardsonian designs from Massachusetts to Texas and beyond, so Wright, too, was surrounded by a group of designers now known as the Prairie school. These architects, many of whom Wright had employed in his Oak Park studio, spread the prairie house from the shores at Wood's Hole, Massachusetts, to the hills of Oregon in a series of works, some rivaling those of the man who had himself now become master, some merely aping them. The best of these were Walter Burley Griffin, William Purcell, George Elmslie, and George Maher. As Wright was never generous in recognizing his antecedents, so he never gracefully accepted his followers. His second *Architectural Record* article, "In the Cause of Architecture" (1914), lashed out against the lot of them. They were nonetheless, like Wright himself, creative heirs to Richardson's legacy and more.

As Norris Kelly Smith has emphasized, Wright, when he introduced his mature work to the professional readership in his first *Architectural Record* article, "In the Cause of Architecture" (1908), described it as both radical and dedicated to the "cause conserva-tive." The conservative element in Wright's mature early work had an almost endless variety of strands, from the domestic to the exotic, from the recent to the distant. During

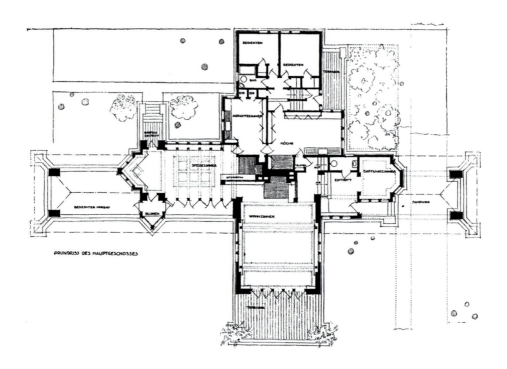

GRUNDRISS DES HAUPTGESCHOSSES

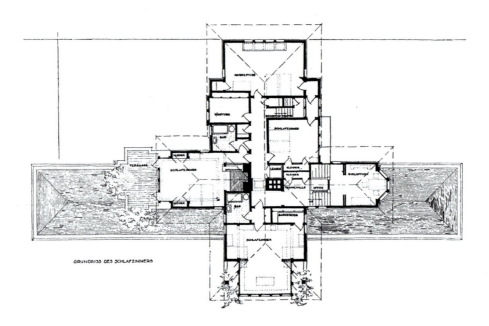

GRUNDRISS DES SCHLAFZIMMERS

14.3 Frank Lloyd Wright, Ward Willits House, Highland Park, Illinois, 1901, plan (from *Ausgeführte Bauten*, Berlin: E. Wasmuth, 1911)

the course of his extraordinarily long career, Wright was to draw upon a bewildering variety of sources for his ideas, sources European, Oriental, and native American from both above and below the border. Most of these exotic elements became important after the period of his career that captures our attention here, but one interest was to parallel his tutelage under Richardson and [Louis] Sullivan. Wright was already aware in the mid-1890s of the non-western sources that were to become increasingly important in his work. The Ho-o-den at the World's Columbian Exposition in Chicago in 1893 has frequently been mentioned as his introduction to Japanese architecture. Traces of its influence can be found in works from about 1900, as in the Foster House in Chicago, and, perhaps, the Bradley and Hickox houses in Kankakee, Illinois. In 1905 he visited Japan, and thereafter an Oriental sense invades some of the presentation drawings prepared for Wright by his assistant, Marion Mahony. Wright always insisted that it was the lesson of elimination in the Japanese woodblock print, of which he was to become a busy collector and dealer, that caught his attention, not Japanese architecture. This lesson is perhaps most apparent in the broad stucco planes and flat detailing of his houses after 1900 (although these may owe as much to the influence of the Viennese Joseph M. Olbrich, whose work Wright drew upon for aspects of his design of the Larkin Building in Buffalo and elsewhere, and certainly find their parallels in some aspects of contemporary Craftsman work). In 1916, beyond the period of our concern, Wright left for an extended stay in Japan.

Wright's intense investigation of Richardson's achievement and his courting of more exotic muses did not blind him to other traditional American sources of inspiration. The hearth-centered, centrifugal domestic plan that he used embryonically in his own house of 1889, in the Winslow House in 1893, and characteristically in his residential designs of the next decade, owes little to Richardson, although some of its elements, such as the open plan and the focal fireplace, were available in the shingle-style houses of Richardson, Silsbee, and others. Rather, it springs from deep in the nineteenth century. While we think of the characteristic eighteenth-century Georgian or Federal house plan as centered upon a void, the ceremonial stair hall that axially divides one side of a square or rectangular house from the other, an alternate domestic planning tradition placed the masonry stack at the center of the composition. Among Thomas Jefferson's surviving sketches for Monticello and other domestic designs, for example, are cruciform and hearth-centered residential plans. This type surfaces over and over again in the suburban and rural house pattern books of the nineteenth century. Quick grazing through this literature finds the cruciform in one or more examples in A. J. Davis's *Rural Residences* (1837), W. H. Ranlett's *Architect* (1847–49), A. J. Downing's *Architecture of Country Houses* (1850), Gervaise Wheeler's *Homes for the People* (1855), G. E. Woodward's *Cottages and Farmhouses* (1867), and I. H. Hobbs's *Architecture* (1873). A central masonry stack or group of stacks is common to most of these cruciform examples, and the description in the Hobbs publication of the plan of the suburban Jackson House erected near Pittsburgh, for example, includes this prescription for a proto-Wrightian, centrifugal, open interior: "the hall, dining-room, sittingroom, and parlor, can be thrown into one grand room . . . connected with back and front porches by windows running to the floor." A host of parallel designs could be cited. We should not picture Wright at any time rifling through these books in search of an appropriate geometric shape, and in any event the three-dimensional realization of any of them would have caused him to shudder. The type reached him as a common and traditional one; to know it he had no need to ransack the architectural libraries of his day.

In any event, the focal fire as symbol of home is ages old, and this symbol was reinvigorated during the nineteenth century. The sources for the spreading, hearth-centered, suburban or rural domestic ideal extend beyond architectural publications into the realm of nineteenth-century literature. Henry Wadsworth Longfellow, Charles Dudley Warner, and many others found it a symbolic focus for literary works. In his *Autobiography* Wright listed Herman Melville, for example, as among a motley (and grossly incomplete) assortment of writers whose work he "long ago consulted and occasionally remembered." Only one story by Melville could have remotely influenced Wright, "I and My Chimney" published in *Putnam's Monthly Magazine* for March 1856. How Wright might have come across this piece, if indeed he did, is anyone's guess (since scarcely anyone read Melville until his "rediscovery" in the 1920s), but the proto-Thurberesque battle of the sexes that constitutes the action of Melville's paper is cast in architecturally symbolic terms that are also proto-Wrightian.

The narrator lives in an old farmhouse (based on Melville's Arrowhead at Pittsfield, Massachusetts) whose rooms on each level group themselves around a vast masonry mass riddled with fireplaces. His wife and daughters want to improve the place by ripping out this monster and creating an open hall. Melville goes beyond this Freudian conflict, however, to describe the house as not merely rural but anti-urban. In the cities the houses are tall and thin; they are confining. This house is, in contrast, wide, having been built where there is plenty of room, and it is set amid scenic richness. The chimney "a free citizen of this free land," is the center of domestic life, and in fact it assumes for Melville here an almost sacral significance as a "grand high altar." The oversized fireplace stack in the prairie house was not only the age-old symbol of domesticity. It assumed for Wright something of the same character—Norris Kelly Smith has called it "sacramental"—that Melville gave to his narrator's chimney. With neither Melville nor Wright is there anything new here, of course, as they both reflect the nineteenth-century cult of domesticity which reemphasized the hearth-centered suburban focus of family life in contrast to the commercial world of the downtown office blocks.

Whatever the deep and broad historical and cultural sources that enter into the makeup of the prairie house (Melville's story being but one example of the kind of literary source available), Wright did not forsake the lessons of his Richardsonian apprenticeship. Any study of the plans Wright designed in these early years of the twentieth century demonstrates that they are for the most part variations on two themes. The one is an implacably symmetrical *parti*, such as we find it in the River Forest Golf Club (1901) and other public works. The other is used for most of the residential designs and consists of an axial alignment, usually of library, living room, and dining room, as in the *Ladies' Home Journal* project, plus, commonly, utility areas more loosely arranged. A variation of the latter type aligns spaces along offset axes, as in the relationship of porch and dining room in the Ward Willits House in Highland Park, which generates in two dimensions an interplay of symmetry and asymmetry that is picked up in three dimensions by the interplay of one- and two-story wings. In almost any of these mature prairie houses a balanced element has been set within an unbalanced whole. Thus the forward projecting, living room wing of the Willits House is almost classical in its balanced composition, but it fronts an unbalanced perpendicular wing that pierces it horizontally. Here we see Wright building creatively upon the symmetrical-asymmetrical interplay characteristic of Richardson's work.

As with Sullivan's Wainwright Building, which not surprisingly shows traces of the architect's concurrent study of Richardson's work, so the prairie house shows Wright's prolonged investigation of Richardsonian design. And like the Wainwright, the prairie house is profoundly different from anything Richardson achieved because it was designed in an era in which new materials and constructional technology permitted a fresh attitude toward structure, resulting in an opening of form never contemplated by the older architect. Wright's emphatic horizontals—the long spans, pronounced cantilevers, cruciform plans, open interiors, and dynamic three dimensional forms of the characteristic prairie house—owe nothing to the closed, conventionally load-bearing blocks typical of Richardson. Wright's daring exploitation of the cantilever, as in the extraordinary over-hangs of the Mrs. Thomas Gale House in Oak Park, Illinois (1904–9), or the Robie House (Figure 14.4), was made possible largely because of the availability of steel, the structural use of which, as we have seen, postdated the work of his predecessor. Where Richardson had occasionally produced a broadly continuous interior room, as in the Paine House livinghall (by supporting the main beam from the roof structure by means of an iron tension rod), Wright now habitually created coherently expansive interiors extending

14.4 Frank Lloyd Wright, Robie House, Chicago, Illinois, 1906–9

through the outer walls by means of casements, floor-to-soffit doors, porches, and over-hangs to embrace the great outdoors.

While it is essential to mark the similarities between Richardson and Wright, it is equally essential to recognize the historically profound differences that exist between the two. While both architects must be discussed against the backdrop of the English and American Arts and Crafts movement, for example, Richardson, as we can judge from his library and his work (especially his decorative designs ranging from furniture to appoint-ments, as in the New York State Court of Appeals in Albany, 1876–81), was at home in the preindustrial ideology of John Ruskin and William Morris (whose books he owned). Wright, while his connection to C. R. Ashbee and other Arts-and-Craftsmen is firmly documented, eschewed neither the machine nor its structural products. His talk at Hull-House in 1901 on "The Art and Craft of the Machine" may be cited as key testimony to Wright's Janus-headed position at the turn of the century. On one side, he looked deeply if selectively into the nineteenth century, in part through Sullivan's and Richardson's eyes; and on the other, he regarded quite receptively the mechanical and structural transform-ations provided by burgeoning American industry. In architectural terms, the result was the opening up (or as he was later to say, "destruction") of the Richardsonian box in the prairie house.

In his *Architectural Record* article of 1908, his definitive statement of intention from this period, Wright rooted architecture in nature and pronounced "a sense of the organic" as "indispensable to an architect." In this he was again an heir to the nineteenth century in general and Sullivan in particular, and through Sullivan, to the tradition of conven-tionalized ornamental design exemplified by nineteenth-century theorists. (According to his own later testimony, Wright in these years was familiar with Owen Jones's *Grammar of Ornament*.) In the first important notice of Wright's career, a 1900 article by his colleague Robert Spencer in the *Architectural Review*, this source of Wright's ornament is made evident. "It is certainly true that the highly conventionalized, the quiet, consistent structural element, is always present in his compositions, modifying and quieting the most naturalistic motives," Spencer wrote. "Nature, who knows the most rigid and subtle geometry, as well as the most voluptuous freedom of . . . form, is the source to which he has always gone for inspiration." And, Spencer notes, it was Sullivan who drew Wright's attention to this design process. Where [Frank] Furness had once filled his sketch-books with graphite studies of the lilies of his garden, searching for this organizational geometry, and Sullivan had probed a specimen lotus for its structural principles, Wright employed photographic studies of wildflowers to the same ends. As we have seen, [John] Ruskin called this process "gathering" and "governing," and examples by Wright of each of these stages are found in William C. Gannett's *House Beautiful* (1896–97), a work published by the architect and his client William Winslow. The book contains photographs taken by Wright that show him "gathering" among the wildflowers, and it contains decorative borders and other devices that are line drawings by Wright composed in part of "governed" or geometrically altered natural forms. Here are the lineal descen-dants of conventionalized floral designs by Furness and Sullivan. By means of this process, the designer put his natural source through what Wright called, in a lecture at the Art institute of Chicago in 1900, "a rare and difficult process" in which the "life principle of the flower is translated to terms of building stone," and this is "conventionalization, and it is poetry."

In his prairie houses and other works of the first decade and a half of the twentieth century, Wright sought to extend this geometrical-poetical principle from the individual flower as source for ornamental embellishment to the total environment as inspiration for the complete architectural organism. The prairie house was filled almost from the beginning with accents—"art glass" windows, ornamental friezes, decorative panels—that contain forms derived from the conventionalization of botanical specimens. Mature examples of these are usually angular analogies, exemplifying Wright's tendency "to draw away from . . . [Sullivan's] efflorescence toward the straight line and rectangular pattern" generated by the use of T-square and triangle, as he was to write in *Genius and the Mobocracy*. In its original condition, the Dana House in Springfield, Illinois, was, as were most of the prairie houses, richly provided inside and out with planters and urns filled with vegetation having its artistic analogy on the exterior frieze and in leaded glass embellished with conventionalized patterns of sumac, as well as in windows and lamps bedecked with geometric butterflies. The colorful exterior frieze of plaster and tile of the Avery Coonley House of 1907 in Riverside, Illinois, sports a repetitive pattern of conventionalized tulips. Each "tulip" is composed of a vertical "stem" forming a central axis to each side of which rectangular "flowers" and "leafs" are balanced. However much it seems to anticipate the neoplasticism of twentieth-century Dutch artists like Piet Mondrian or Theo van Doesburg, it is a direct if evolved, straight-lined, and rectangular descendant of the curvilinear floral patterns of the window tympani flanking the central *pavilion* of Furness's Pennsylvania Academy in Philadelphia.

In Wright's mind, the prairie house seemed a visual fugue in which these ornamental incidents were minor echoes of the major theme of the house. For Wright, conventionalization was an idea applicable not just to ornamental details. It embodied the complete architectural environment. In a speech to the Architectural League at the Chicago Art Institute as early as 1900, he adapted the specific process of conventionalization to the totality of architectural design. "Architecture is the most complete of conventionalizations," he wrote in the *Architectural Record* article of 1908. What he meant by this is perhaps best exemplified among his early works by the windmill he erected for his aunts at Spring Green, Wisconsin, in 1897. In Wright's mind, architecture and technology were congruent in this design and conventionalized from nature, although in this case the primary analogy is with animal rather than vegetable forms. Wright, who was frequently to provide romantic names for his designs, called his tower Romeo and Juliet, because, as he explained in his *Autobiography*, he thought of its interlocking shapes as an entwined, mutually supportive couple. Romeo is the lozenge-shaped spine that surrounds and stiffens an internal shaft that carries the rotating blades; Juliet is the octagonal stairtower that receives the thrust of and in turn strengthens the spine. To this primary anthropomorphic analogy Wright added a secondary botanical one, for he likened the floors to horizontal membranes that strengthen a hollow plant stem from within. Whether or not the structure as built works this way is immaterial; it was Wright's designing intention that it should. He was later, in skyscraper projects of the 1920s and in the Johnson Wax Tower in Racine, Wisconsin (1944), the Price Tower in Bartlesville, Oklahoma (1952), and "The Illinois," the projected mile-high publicity stunt of his last years, to exploit fully the analogy of the tree with its continuous structure of taproot, central trunk, and cantilevered limbs, abandoning completely the "inorganic" metal frame composed of additive, riveted pieces. These were the ultimate developments of the conventionalization of nature that had reached Wright from the nineteenth century through Sullivan.

The emphatic horizontal look of the houses of Wright's early maturity (or of the Prairie school in general) displays a debt to Richardson, and more. Both architects equated the level line with quietude. But the degree to which Wright emphasized this direction both within and without his houses stems also from the generalized environment for which his houses were intended. "We of the Middle West are living on the prairie. The prairie has a beauty of its own and we should . . . accentuate this natural beauty, its quiet level," he wrote in the first installment of "In the Cause of Architecture." The strength of Wright's purpose transforms the Richardsonian device and makes it his own. Not all Wright houses were built on the wide open spaces of the Midwest. The Robie House in southside Chicago, most famous house of this period, is on a corner urban lot (as is the Meyer May House in Grand Rapids, Michigan, 1908). The unexecuted Metzger House of 1902 for Sault Ste Marie, Michigan, was an expanded version of the *Ladies' Home Journal* design intended to be perched on an elevated site (as was the executed Gilmore House in Madison, Wisconsin). And the midland prairie cannot be extended eastward to western New York state, where Wright built some important houses early in the century, or westward to Montecito, California, where he erected the Stewart House in 1909. But in Wright's usage the prairie was as much concept as actual topography, as much a locus of the mind as a characteristic of the land. He sought to celebrate poetically the broad expansiveness of the vast Midwest, much as Sullivan had sought to emphasize poetically the essence of tallness in buildings such as the Guaranty in Buffalo (Figure 14.5). In his vertically articulated urban block Sullivan had transformed the Philadelphia midcentury commercial facade; in his horizontally extended houses Wright transformed the Richardsonian layered look.

It was characteristic of Wright, then, to see the whole of the inland plain conventionalized in the spreading horizontals of the prairie house exterior or the continuous expanses of its girded interiors, and to see his ornamental details as conventionalized native plantlife. He was heir to an ideal unity of architecture and nature that sprang in this country from Jeffersonian ideals and marked the works of the erstwhile teams of [Andrew Jackson] Downing and [Alexander Jackson] Davis, and [Frederick Law] Olmsted and Richardson. In a sense he merged Richardson's geological analogy in works like the Ames Gate Lodge with the tradition of conventionalization learned at Sullivan's drafting board and with the potentials of the new technology to achieve what he called an "Organic" architecture—an architecture, as he said, "of" the land, not "on" it. The result was the celebration of place (even if that place was a poetic concept rather than a physical location) that is the prairie house, a domestic architectural form that evolved out of the past to become truly his own. It was here that he put his personal stamp upon an entire building type.

The myriad conservative strands that Wright wove into his own personal architecture are perhaps best illustrated and summed up in the crowning achievement in domestic

14.5 Adler and Sullivan, Guaranty (Prudential) Building, Buffalo, New York, 1894–96

14.6 Frank Lloyd Wright, Taliesin, Spring Green, Wisconsin, 1911 and after

design from the early period in his career. This work was his own in every sense of the word, for it was the country retreat he erected for himself on family lands just south of the Wisconsin River near Spring Green in 1911 (rebuilt 1914 to 1915 after the original had been destroyed by arson and rebuilt again after another fire on a more expansive scale from 1925 onward). Taliesin (Figure 14.6), as Wright called his house-studio-farm of wood, plaster, and stone, hangs on the brow of a ledge above the valley, its multiple hip [roof]s echoing the surrounding hills, its golds, browns, yellows, and reds echoing the seasonal colors of the landscape, its interiors enriched by Wright's collection of Oriental objets d'art. In a sense this was the most conservative work of his career, for it recapitulated the development of American rural domestic design from Jefferson's Monticello onward [see Figure 4.11], including the environmental concerns of Downing and Davis and Olmsted, the formal discipline and geological analogy of Richardson, and the conventionalization of nature in the works of Sullivan and his sources. At the same time, it was a house only Wright's "peculiar genius," as the *Architectural Record* labeled it in 1911, could have conceived.

Wright had already provided the ancestral lands near Spring Green with his Hillside Home School of 1901, a conventionalized outcropping of rockfaced limestone ashlar in which Richardson's Ames Monument merged with his Woodland Station and was transformed by Wright's maturing sense of geometry, space, and proportion. Now he returned to a hillside nearer the Wisconsin River to add his own habitation. At Taliesin, Wright was to carry on the ideal of integrated private life, professionalism, and play that had marked his own earlier Oak Park arrangement and Richardson's establishment before him. In Brookline and at Taliesin, the workrooms were strung out like a tail attached to the domestic quarters. But Wright's was the more integrated and the more mature ensemble. Certainly here was a domestic type Melville would have understood; certainly this was the house prescribed by Emerson, whom Wright was quoting at least as early as 1900 (although he typically fails to mention the writer among his consultants in the *Autobiography*). In "Self-Reliance" the essayist assured his readers that "if the American artist will study with hope and love the precise thing to be done by him, considering the climate, the soil, the length of day, the wants of the people, the habit and form of government, he will create a house in which these will find themselves fitted, and taste and sentiment will be satisfied too." Taliesin to a greater extent than any other of Wright's works to 1915 embodied conceptions of family, society politics, environment, history, and conventionalized nature, as well as "taste and sentiment."

Taliesin expressed that ideal of agrarian democracy, a combination of culture and agriculture, that Wright probably derived from Jefferson, a source of ideas he recognizes with the same ambiguity he applied to Richardson. If Wright did not learn of the statesman's works from his writings (although there are passages in his own publications from these years that suggest Wright knew something of Jefferson's social politics), then he did from Jefferson's own home at Monticello. The two-story living room with half-octagonal balcony of the cruciform Isabel Roberts House suggests that Wright knew the identical spatial conformation (with very different details) in the hall at cruciform Monticello. Like Jefferson's perpetual "putting up, and pulling down" at Monticello, Wright was continuously altering and expanding Taliesin out of necessity or desire. Like Monticello, Taliesin is not merely rural, it is anti-urban. Like Monticello, the house at Taliesin was conceptually one-storied, with its wings wrapped around its hillside site just below the summit. Like Monticello, the interior of Taliesin joined its surroundings through tall openings leading onto terraces overlooking the rolling terrain. Like Monticello, Taliesin is not a mere building but an entire environment in which man, architecture, and nature form a harmonious whole. There is at Taliesin Wright's own summing-up of the role of man in nature that stems ultimately from the age of romanticism.

Jefferson was, of course, bound at Monticello by the universal chains of dogmatic Palladian classicism, although he struggled mightily against them, and to a certain degree he achieved within the system an elasticity corresponding to his vision of place. Wright was heir to the picturesque tradition of Downing and Davis, in which classical forms gave way to irregular, asymmetrical, and natural elements. This can be seen, for example, in the correspondences of architecture and place found in the hearth-centered, cruciform plan with asymmetrical utility wing and unbalanced medieval pile of the "Lake or River Villa for a Picturesque Site" in Downing's *Architecture of Country Houses*, or in Davis's neo-Gothic Lyndhurst at Tarrytown, New York (1838–65). Taliesin connects with Monticello through intervening works such as Richardson's Bigelow and Paine houses, and Davis's Lyndhurst.

If Jefferson had been tied to the classical tradition, Downing and Davis in their turn were equally committed to the picturesque Gothic and other revived medieval styles in their books and buildings. As we have seen, Richardson drew upon the achievements of

The penetration of Wright's ideas into American architecture constitutes what we casually consider to be his influence. Influence, however, normally entails three basic processes: imitation, transformation, and parallelism. Imitation implies some attempt to copy, usually relying on the external appearances of objects. Transformation suggests an effort to move beyond making copies to altering either appearance or the meanings underlying forms. Parallelism occurs when objects that appear similar have independent origins. Although the processes of influence can be conscious, most often they are unconscious and open to misinterpretation.

These three modes of influence played out through Wright's work not only in his homeland but also around the globe. In some ways his work is so well known in the United States that familiarity blinds us to a deeper insight into his impact on American life; the effects are so broad that they have simply been ignored. Wright's role in American architecture is so large that decades of study may be required to fully grasp its complexity. Moreover, the impact of his apprentices and students who went on to set up their own practices remains incompletely explored. [. . .]

Historians and critics have traditionally pointed to Wright's impact in Germany around 1910 as a key factor in the evolution of the Modern Movement. The canonical view used to be that Wright's famous publications of 1910–1911, printed in Berlin by the Wasmuth Veflag, had an immediate and dramatic influence on German architects and the rest of the European avant-garde. Every standard architectural history credits these publications—the *Ausgeführte Bauten und Entwürfe von Frank Lloyd Wright*, a two-folio monograph of Wright's buildings and designs; and the similarly titled *Frank Lloyd Wright: Ausgeführte Bauten*, a small picture book of executed work—with this seminal role, particularly vis-à-vis Walter Gropius and Ludwig Mies van der Rohe.[3] Kuno Francke, a professor at Harvard, is said to have been the impetus for these publications, and their impact was supposedly reinforced by an exhibition of Wright's work held in Berlin.

These standard views nicely demonstrate the complexities of influence. Our notion of Wright's influence in Germany came about by one historian repeating the accounts of another without bothering to check if they had any factual basis. Indeed, archival and documentary research has shown them to be a series of myths.[4] The widespread impact of the Wasmuth publications, particularly the folios, is dubious in light of their limited distribution in Europe; they were a vanity printing, paid for by Wright, with only 100 copies of the folios and 3,900 copies of an inferior edition of the picture book (or *Sonderheft*, as Wright called it then) reserved for a European audience, while Wright retained another 900 and 5,100 copies respectively for his American audience. Moreover, Kuno Francke was not the key player in the Wasmuth affair; Wright's connection appears to have been Bruno Möhring, the eminent architect, city planner, and Wasmuth editor who had visited Wright's office in 1904 but missed Wright. Nor is there any evidence of an exhibition open to the general public; Möhring simply lectured on Wright's work and showed a small selection of drawings one evening in February 1910 to an architectural club in Berlin. Decades later Mies and Gropius would recall an "exhibition," but this lecture is the only documented showing of Wright's work in Germany at that time.

The realities of the Wasmuth affair do not contradict the view that Wright's work began to be disseminated in Europe after 1910. Otto Wagner showed a copy of the folio monograph to his students in Vienna in 1911 and proclaimed Wright a paragon worthy of study. Although Le Corbusier would deny that he knew of Wright at the time, he had obtained a copy of the *Sonderheft* for his mentor Auguste Perret during World War I. Others who saw the publications, including the young Austrians Rudolph Schindler and Richard Neutra, would work for Wright in the late 1910s and 1920s. To understand the influence of the publications on these and other figures, however, we need to look more closely at how the images were transmitted, assimilated, and finally interpreted (or misinterpreted) in terms of both intellectual response and built works. Rather than looking closely, many historians have tended to rely on simple visual analogies that reduce the phenomenon of making architecture to a crude transitivity: if A looks like B, then B has influenced A.

Europeans learned about Wright by other means as well, and these also set the stage for his influence. One unexpected source is the avant-garde Czech journal *Volné Smery*, published in Prague, whose editors included Jan Kotera, a former student of Wagner's and a young leader of the Czech modern movement. In 1900, the journal featured an article on architecture in America by a member of the avant-garde Mánes Group who had traveled in the United States; he reported that Louis Sullivan was the emerging modernist, and although he did not mention Wright, the article included two images of his studio in Oak Park.[5] Reproduced from the *Architectural Review* (Boston), these may be the first images of Wright's work to appear anywhere in Europe. In 1904 the noted Viennese critic Max Dvorák referred to *Volné Smery's* illustrations of Wright's work, also pointing out that American architecture had been exhibited at the Prague Modern Gallery.[6]

Far more significant than this early reference was the dissemination of Wright's ideas through Dutch architects in the 1910s. Hendrik Petrus Berlage was Wright's first and most important early champion. A major pioneer of the Dutch modern movement, Berlage visited America in 1911 and saw several of Wright's buildings but missed meeting the architect. Returning to Europe, he gave three lectures in Zurich on American architecture in which Wright's Larkin Company Administration Building and the Darwin Martin House, both in Buffalo, figured prominently. The lectures, which immediately appeared in Dutch and in German-language Swiss publications, stimulated the interest of young Europeans, establishing a critically important "Dutch Connection" between Wright and Holland and sensitizing Swiss architects and engineers to Wright's ideas.[7] Several young Dutch architects even studied Berlage's copy of Wright's Wasmuth folios; chief among them was Jan Wils, who learned presentation techniques by copying the folio's rendered trees and perspectives.[8]

While the Dutch initiated the critical discourse about Wright in the 1910s, his work and ideas were ignored in Germany until the 1920s, when they would play an important role in German debates about modernism. In the years leading up to these debates a series of young European architects sought Wright out, and several came to work with him at Taliesin, in Wisconsin. The European invasion of Wright's office began with the arrival of the Czech Antonin Raymond, who went to work for Wright in 1916. He had studied at the Technical College of Prague, where Kotera held a position similar to that of Otto

Wagner in Vienna, training a generation of modern architects. Although Kotera had seen buildings by Wright in 1904, when he came to America for the St. Louis World's Fair, Raymond appears to have learned of Wright's work only after arriving in the United States. In 1919 he went with Wright to work on the Imperial Hotel in Tokyo and then remained in Japan to establish his own office in 1920.[9]

The Austrian Rudolph Schindler worked for Wright from 1918 through 1921.[10] In December 1919, while in Japan, Wright sent Schindler to California to oversee his practice there and to work on the Barnsdall House. After Schindler's departure from Wright's domestic office, his Austrian friend Richard Neutra arrived. Neutra had met Schindler in 1912 and knew of Wright's work through the Wasmuth folios, which he saw in Vienna. In 1923 Werner M. Moser, a member of a famous family of Swiss architects, came to work for Wright at Taliesin; upon his return to Switzerland five years later he became a founding member of the Congrès Internationaux d'Architecture Moderne (CIAM).

At times Wright's Wisconsin atelier took on the air of an extended family of international architects and their spouses: in July 1924 Wright entertained Richard and Dione Neutra, Werner and Sylva Moser, and Kameki Tsuchiura and his wife, Nobu, from Japan.[11] This soirée preceded the Neutras' move to Taliesin that October and the subsequent arrival of Erich Mendelsohn, for whom Neutra had worked in 1921–22.[12]

Despite the prior arrival of all these young Europeans, Wright welcomed Mendelsohn as "the first European to come and seek him out and truly find him." Indeed, Mendelsohn, who had learned of Wright from Neutra, was the first famous German architect to meet the master.[13] Mendelsohn had recently completed his Einstein Tower in Potsdam (1917–21), and his office was one of the most successful in Berlin.

Mendelsohn became Wright's most distinguished architectural connection to Europe in the mid-1920s. Their meeting reawakened interest about Wright in Germany and made Wright more aware of European developments. Mendelsohn published an early appraisal of Wright in which he described the intimate angularity and abstraction of Wright's work as a synthesis of expressionist tendencies.[14] Subsequent articles stimulated a new round of publications and drew additional visitors.[15] In another reawakening of German interest in Wright, Wasmuth reissued a reduced edition of Wright's folio monograph in 1924, apparently without his permission. The original Wasmuth folios of 1910–11 were out of date and out of print. Meanwhile, two books in preparation, one by the Dutch architect and editor Hendricus Theodorus Wijdeveld and the other by the German architect and writer Heinrich de Fries, promised a more current treatment.

Wright played the authors against each other as a means of disseminating his work, and he used their interest in his architecture to get his designs published in Europe, often long before they appeared in the United States. (Indeed, several were never published there in his lifetime.) As a result, European modernists saw a new version of Wright's modernism, while Americans relied on memories from the Prairie period, if anything. Wijdeveld's major Dutch publication came out in 1925 as *The Life-Work of the American Architect Frank Lloyd Wright*. It consisted of most of the articles that had appeared in seven consecutive special issues of the journal *Wendingen*, which Wijdeveld edited. The book, which became known by the journal's title, marked a high point of interest in Wright; he later said it was his favorite publication of his work.[16]

Wright admired *Wendingen* despite the mildly critical contribution to the volume by J. J. P. Oud, a leading exponent of the New Objectivity—the hyperrational wing of the Modern Movement—who saw Wright's influence in Europe as "a less happy one." For all its "exotic peculiarities," Oud wrote, the simplicity of motifs, expression of structure, and integration with its site made Wright's work immediately convincing—to the extent that it had become too influential on the modern developments in Europe. Architects seduced by Wright's work were emulating form—in this case Wright's—over function. Wright's influence was consequently weakening the role of Cubism, which had developed parallel with his work but in complete independence of him.[17] Oud had defined the central problem of Wright's influence on Europe: images of his architecture commingled with distinct European developments, blurring the differences between them. Wright ignored this assessment, as did historians who subsequently replicated the myth of Wright's influence in Europe without alluding to its problematic nature.

Oud also identified another problem: Wright had never absolutely rejected the past, as the most ardent European modernists did. Speaking of both Wright and the Italian futurist Sant'Elia he noted, "In architecture the old form element was never annihilated, and the emerging products of modern design were always a change of image and an abstraction rather than the creation of shapes."[18] Oud was entirely correct in perceiving Wright's obsession with abstraction, which Wright termed "conventionalization," with the "old form element" emanating from nature and the primary forms of architecture, particularly those still to be found in the non-Western cultures of Japan and the Maya. He saw no need to invent new shapes when nature and "pure" cultures uncontaminated by European values contained the raw material for an infinite variety of expressions.

By the mid-1920s the Dutch painter Theo van Doesburg, a protagonist of neo-plasticism, identified Wright exclusively with modern developments in the United States. His opinions summarized those of many critics. On the one hand he consistently appreciated Wright's innovations from the turn of the century, noting that among leading European architects Wright provided a "constructive conscience," that he helped create a new architecture based on contemporary materials, and that he was one of the first to use reinforced concrete appropriately.[19] On the other hand, his influence on German architects resulted in an "imitation of the outer effect" that was fatal to innovation. Furthermore, summing up Wright's recent work, van Doesburg saw Wright as completely ignorant of new developments in the plastic arts in central Europe and as having returned to "rustic, decorative building."[20] He observed that by 1927 Wright's influence, so unmistakable ten years earlier, had not been seen for a long time; its complete absence at the Werkbund housing exhibition in Stuttgart was strong proof of its eclipse.[21] But in fact Wright may have wanted to show the Germans his approach to low-cost housing on their own soil. That same year he designed five flat concrete roofs, presumably for houses to be built in Frankfurt am Main; we know little else about the project.[22] Nevertheless, by 1929, when familiarity with Wright's work of the 1910s and 1920s had grown in Europe, van Doesburg caustically stated that Wright "has fallen into the most barbaric decorativism (Midway Restaurant, Chicago; Maison Millard, Pasadena, California etc. etc.) and archaism, with no significance whatsoever for the elementaristic architecture of our time."[23]

Van Doesburg had pinioned Wright's weakness from the European perspective, condemning the persistent use of ornament. Ironically, the "archaism" that had fostered Wright's "barbaric decorativism" was stimulated by Wright's travels to Europe in 1909–10, when he encountered the primitivist forms of the late Secession in Vienna.[24] This contact confirmed his interest in archetypal forms and launched new explorations in his ornament. While Wright continued to integrate ornament into his experiments in construction, the major currents of the Modern Movement in Europe saw ornament as absolute decadence; the castigations heaped on Wright had long been leveled at the Viennese, as if ornament and construction were antithetical.

In Germany, meanwhile, Heinrich de Fries's *Frank Lloyd Wright: Aus dem Lebenswerke eines Architekten* (From the life work of an architect) came out in 1926, the first new German book on Wright in sixteen years. In it de Fries attempted to show that Wright's opening of interior spaces made him modern. He also assessed Wright's recent work, seeing in a speculative development for Lake Tahoe a "unity of landscape and water, of solid and moveable building, of air, earth, sun, plants, people and flowers" brought to poetic heights. He defended this design and the grandiose project for Doheny Ranch, in Los Angeles, against accusations that they were fantasies, asserting that visionary schemes were a proper domain of all artists.[25]

At the same time de Fries pointed out what many critics considered a limitation of Wright's work: his designs were essentially for an elite class, to which Wright himself apparently belonged. This observation reflects the intense social consciousness that was part of the European debate on modernism. Ultimately, however, de Fries judged Wright to be not only a socially conscious architect, who, like the European modernists, was concerned with problems of minimum human requirements, but also an architect of nature, whose preoccupation with space, plants, and water led to a higher spiritual goal. One of the reviews of de Fries's *Aus dem Lebenswerke* highlighted some of these issues. Another review appeared in the *Frankfurter Zeitung* in December 1926, proof that the debate about Wright had expanded from the architectural press to the daily newspapers. Wright kept a copy of that review in one of his scrapbooks; whether he was aware of its content is not known. Written by Grete Dexel, the wife of the art critic Walter Dexel, it reflected the social consciousness of European modernists. Dexel declared that Wright's open letter in *Wendingen*, "To My European Co-Workers," said little, that de Fries was overenthusiastic, that the Tahoe and Doherty projects catered to the wealthy elite, and that Wright was aligned with class interests that made his work strongly antisocial. "We all know that Frank Lloyd Wright has decisively influenced the European building of today. Some of his country houses (villas) and ground plans are found in every book on new architecture and shown to us in slides in every pertinent lecture. Nevertheless, Wright's work is also not by a long shot understood yet by the better informed."[26]

It is not surprising that Europeans questioned Wright's commitment to a social program during the 1920s. When they saw illustrations of his project for the hotel and resort San Marcos-in-the-Desert, they assumed Wright was designing exclusively for a leisure class. Their critiques demonstrate how European modernists understood and misunderstood Wright's architecture. Misunderstood were Wright's continuing efforts —even in projects for the wealthy elite, like the Barnsdall House and Doheny Ranch—to find solutions to economical middle-class housing. De Fries published examples of the Textile Block houses, including the Barnsdall House, but overlooked the system's potential uses in mass housing. He also failed to grasp the extent to which Wright, an artist arguing for democratic principles in society, was a misfit in the middle-class mainstream of America. Finally, it was difficult for Europeans to realize that the provision of delight in architecture was in fact part of Wright's social program. On the other hand, they could well understand Wright's vision of social transformation as not merely the expressed coordination of technology (the machine and the materials of construction) and society but as a spiritual transformation. Wright's ideas about the future recalled the manifestoes of the avant-garde and the Bauhaus before 1922 in particular; he called for a renovation of the soul, not merely of the building trades.

Another view of Wright came from Adolf Behne, a German art historian and commentator on the early Modern Movement. In a study written in 1923 and published in 1926 as *Der moderne Zweckbau*, Behne drew on Wright's essays and designs that appeared in the *Architectural Record* of 1908 and on contemporary perceptions of Wright. He noted that Wright had made two particularly important contributions: a free plan of balanced spaces emanating from functional considerations of comfort, quiet, and clarity; and an emphasis on horizontality, which made houses appear a part of the streets on which they were situated. Beyond Berlage, Otto Wagner, and also Alfred Messel (whom Behne cited with reservation), Wright provided the first real breakthrough toward a *sachlich*, or objective, plan. Behne also noted the architects whom he perceived as influenced by Wright: in Germany, Peter Behrens, Gropius, Mendelsohn, and Mies van der Rohe; in Holland, Oud, Wils, Robert van 't Hoff, and W. Greve; and in Switzerland, Le Corbusier. The influences affected the designs of elevations more than the floor plans, Behne remarked, because Wright's floor plans had only recently become understood.[27]

At the same time, like most commentators, Behne saw in Wright what he wanted to see: flat roofs and no ornament. But Wright mixed the use of flat roofs and pitched roofs, and ornament remained essential to all his designs. Behne also read into Wright's plans, with their asymmetrical organization, a fluidity of lifestyle not borne out by the actual fixity of Wright's interiors, particularly in regard to his built-in furniture.[28] Perhaps most telling was Behne's inclusion of the skyscraper design for the *San Francisco Call*, redrawn from Wright's original. A trilingual French, German, and English caption gives the project a date of 1920 and identifies it in French as a project for a house in the form of a tower but in German as a design for a skyscraper. In fact the project for the newspaper's building dates from 1913 and was one of Wright's most Secessionist designs, belonging to the early experimental phase of his work following his return from Europe.[29] Since the Secessionist idiom would have been anathema to Behne, he re-visioned the project as more objective and of a later date.

The critical debates about Wright in Germany and Holland moved into a broad European forum in 1931 with the first major retrospective of his work. Whereas the purported exhibition of Wright's work in Germany in 1910 was actually a rather small event lasting only an evening, the 1931 show provided an important reference point for his German audience and for architects and critics in other countries, although it had originated in the United States. The exhibition opened in 1930 at the Wisconsin State

Historical Library in Madison, only a few miles from Wright's home at Taliesin. There it demonstrated Wright's accomplishments to his fellow citizens, many of whom had disapproved of the unorthodox architect. The exhibition then went to New York, Milwaukee, and Eugene, Oregon, before traveling to Europe, where it appeared in several countries and under variations of the title "Frank Lloyd Wright, Architect," from May to October 1931.

The first European venue of Wright's 1931 international exhibition was the Stedelijk Museum in Amsterdam. Wijdeveld, the publisher of Wright's works in the journal *Wendingen* and collator of his *Life-Work* monograph, organized the exhibition, arranging all the details, from designing a striking poster to installing his daughter, Ruscha, as the ticket taker. This devotion arose from the immense bond Wijdeveld felt with Wright, whom he saw as a kindred spirit capable of bringing a new social consciousness to the world through architecture. Wijdeveld documented the critical reactions to the exhibition, in Holland and subsequent European venues, by making a beautiful scrapbook for Wright.[30]

After Amsterdam the exhibition headed for the Prussian Academy of Fine Arts in Berlin. In contrast to Wright's first visit to Berlin in the fall of 1909, when he arrived virtually unknown in Germany, the exhibition marked a triumphant return, with Wright's architecture receiving both public recognition and critical notice. In January 1932 the Prussian Academy of Arts honored Wright in absentia by naming him an Outstanding Member.[31] The critical reactions placed Wright more squarely in the discourse about modernism in Germany than at any other time in his career. The big debates centered on whether Wright was too much of a romantic and an individualist to allow him a central role in a modernism that privileged rationality and collective action. Ornament, long identified by the avant-garde as decadent, was still considered a sign of reactionary architecture. Yet it was the soul of Wright's architecture, embodying his design concepts at every level of detail, from a floor tile to the plans, sections, and elevations of his buildings. Struggling with where to fit Wright into the Modern Movement, some writers saw his work as expressionist. One journalist called him "the American Poelzig," comparing him to the leading expressionist architect in Germany, Hans Poelzig.[32] While attacked by modernist critics, Wright was also defended by his proponents, including Erich Mendelsohn.

The exhibition moved on to Frankfurt, Stuttgart, Antwerp, and Brussels before returning to the United States. From this point forward Wright's work occupied an international stage, but his problematic role vis-à-vis European modernists was only underscored by the reluctant inclusion of his work in "Modern Architecture: International Exhibition," the Museum of Modern Art's famous introduction to America of the International Style.[33] Nevertheless, architects from around the world continued to seek out Wright. The German Ernst Neufert made the journey to Taliesin in 1936, followed by Mies van der Rohe in 1937; Wright felt a special empathy for the latter's work until late in their relationship.[34] Walter Gropius was less fortunate; though he admired Wright's early work, Wright received him rudely after he moved to America.[35]

Postwar Germany saw Wright's work suspended between two positions, one increasingly propping up rationalistic ideals, the other embracing an organic aesthetic.

Both positions were part of a complex situation and often in conflict with each other. Apart from the pioneering work of Heidi Kief-Niederwöhrmeier, who considers Wright's influence in Germany up to the early 1980s within the context of architectural pluralism, postwar study of Wright's work has been limited.[36] As Nina Nedeljkov, one of the few Wright scholars in Germany, has pointed out, Wright's ideas were often not part of any critical dialogue, and his writings and books in translation were generally unavailable.[37] Consequently, German scholars still apply the perceptual framework of the 1920s and 1930s, with little updating or revision, in their views of Wright.

Other German-speaking countries have their own histories in regard to Wright. Wright's impact in Switzerland presents a situation almost as complex as the one in Germany. The obvious starting point is Berlage's introduction of Wright to the Swiss in 1912. However, it was Werner Moser, a graduate of the Eidgenössische Technische Hochschule (ETH) in Zurich and assistant to Wright in the mid-1920s, who most actively propagated Wright's ideas in that country from 1926, when he returned to Switzerland, through the 1960s. Moser's own architecture displays Wright's idiom, as seen in his competition entry for a primary school with gymnasium and parish house in Rapperswil-Jona (1954), whose plan consists of a pair of pinwheels of squares. Kief-Niederwöhrmeier has suggested that images of Wright's work found their way into the work of other Swiss architects, including Otto R. Salvisberg, Alfred Roth, Tita Carloni, Franco Ponti, Ernest E. Ansderegg, Peppo Brivio, André M. Studer, Peter Steiger, and Justus Dahinden.[38] But other developments in the evolution of the Modern Movement often overshadowed Wright's architecture. Detailed study will be needed to sort out his influence—whether imitation, transformation, or parallel development—in the work of Swiss architects and to determine the vehicles by which it was transmitted.

In Austria and the successor states of the former Austro-Hungarian Empire Wright's influence is more limited. Schindler and Neutra remained in the United States after their contact with Wright and did not return to live in Austria. Wright did meet Josef Hoffmann, cofounder of the Wiener Werkstätte and a leading figure in the Vienna Secession, when Wright returned from his trip to Russia in 1937.[39] And Wright's work emerged, if obliquely, in the studio of the German Peter Behrens, who, in the lineage of Otto Wagner's successors, taught the master class at the Academy of Fine Arts in Vienna. Wright's Wasmuth folios appear to have been required reading in the Behrens class in the mid-1920s for future modernists like Ernst Plischke; these folios may well have been the same ones Wagner had shown to his students some fifteen years earlier.[40]

Wright's work apparently made an impact on the emerging generation of Czech modernists working in the early 1920s. In discussing Wright's impact, Adolf Behne cited, in addition to other European architects, almost the whole range of *sachlich* modernists among Czech architects: Vít Obrtel, Jaromír Krejcar, Oldrich Tyl, Frantisek Cerny, Jan Vísek, Jaroslav Fragner, and Bedrich Feuerstein.[41] Precisely how they were influenced by Wright requires more careful scrutiny than Behne provided. So many currents intersected their work that such assertions require caution. Nevertheless, the quick appearance in 1931 of a translation of Wright's lecture "The City of the Future," which had been part of his Princeton series on modern architecture that same year, attests to Czech interest in Wright's work.[42] On the whole, however, after the dissolution of the Empire, Austria,

Hungary, Czechoslovakia, and the countries that would become Yugoslavia were engaged in an immense struggle for both survival and identity. In the midst of this political and economic turmoil, the Modern Movement was undergoing dramatic changes. Our historical understanding of these developments, and Wright's role in them, if any, has barely begun. [. . .]

Notes

1 See, for example, Elizabeth Gordon, "One Man's House," *House Beautiful* 88 (December 1946): 186–96, 235, on Wright's home, Taliesin West, in Scottsdale, Arizona. Professional journals, devoted entire issues to Wright's work, for example: *Architectural Forum* 68 (January 1938); ibid. 88 (January 1948); ibid. 94 (January 1951); *Architectural Record* 23 (March 1908); as did more popular publications: *House Beautiful* 98 (November 1955); ibid. 101 (October 1959). Many articles appeared in popular magazines as well, for example: "Frank Lloyd Wright," *Town and Country* 92 (July 1937): 56, 85; "Lots Are Circular in This 50-House Group," *House and Garden* 49 (February 1951): 52–55, 100, 111; "Journey to Taliesin West," *Look* 16 (January 1, 1952): 28–31; "A New House by Frank Lloyd Wright Opens Up a New Way of Life on the Old Site," *House and Home* 4 (November 1953): 122–27; "Our Strongest Influence to Enrichment," *House Beautiful* 99 (January 1957): 40–47,105–6; Edgar Kaufmann Jr., "The Tradition of Ornament in Modern Architecture," ibid., 76–77.

2 Bruce Brooks Pfeiffer and David Brooks, eds., *Frank Lloyd Wright: The Masterworks* (New York: Rizzoli, 1993), 8. Seventy-five of Wright's 484 executed buildings have been demolished.

3 See Anthony Alofsin, *Frank Lloyd Wright: The Lost Years, 1910–1922* (Chicago: University of Chicago Press, 1993). For the traditional view, see Henry-Russell Hitchcock, "American Influence Abroad," in Edgar Kaufmann Jr., ed., *The Rise of an American Architecture* (New York: Praeger, in association with the Metropolitan Museum of Art, 1970), 34–38. Although this view has been outmoded by new research, Hitchcock's general treatment of American architectural influence abroad sets the wider context for the issues discussed here in the following essays.

4 See Alofsin, *Lost Years*, 29–78, for an account of Wright's travels to Europe, his dealings with the Wasmuth Verlag, and how both played into creating a previously unrecognized phase in his work.

5 "Architektura v Americe: z dopisu," *Volné Smery* 4 (1900): 177–80. C. Donald Cook kindly drew my attention to this publication in 1988. Collateral evidence indicates that the author was Milos Jiránek. A painter, graphic artist, critic, and author, Jiránek (1875–1911) wrote for *Volné Smery* as of 1899 and would write subsequently on impressionism, Rodin, and French modern art. See *Nová encyklopedie ceského vytvarného umení* (Prague: Academia Praha, 1995): 324. My thanks to Christopher Long for uncovering Jiránek as the author of the review.

6 Alceste [Max Dvorák], "Kunst aus der Welt, XVIII: Nachlese von Wiener Ausstellungen," reprinted in Roman Prahl and Lenka Bydzovská, *Freie Richtungen: Die Zeitschrift der Prager Secession und Moderne* (Prague: Torst, 1993), 150. Not only is Wright's early recognition by Dvorák surprising, but the reference to American architecture exhibited in Prague remains an intriguing topic for further study.

7 The Dutch publications were *Architectura* 12 (March 23, 1912): 91–94; ibid. 13 (March 30, 1912): 93–94, 98, 100; ibid. 14 (April 6, 1912): 106, ill. 107. The German-language version was H. R. Berlage, "Neuere amerikanische Architektur," *Schweizerische Bauzeitung* 60 (September 14, 21, 28, 1912): 148–50, 165–67, 178; also issued as an offprint.

8 See Thomas A. P. van Leeuwen, "The Method of Ariadne: Tracing the Lines of Influence between Some American Sources and Their Dutch Recipients," in *Bouwen in Nederland: Leids kunsthistorisch jaarboek*, vol. 3, 1984 (Delft: DUP, 1985), 239–64. My thanks to Dr. Herman van Bergeijk for drawing my attention to van Leeuwen's essay.

9   See Antonin Raymond, *An Autobiography* (Rutland, Vt.: Charles E. Tuttle, 1973), 46–53, 65–77.

10   See August Sarnitz, *R. M. Schindler, Architect, 1887–1953* (New York: Rizzoli, 1988), 16–17.

11   Robert L. Sweeney, "Frank Lloyd Wright Chronology, 1922–1932," in David G. De Long, *Frank Lloyd Wright: Designs for an American Landscape* (New York: Harry N. Abrams, in association with the Canadian Centre for Architecture, Library of Congress, and Frank Lloyd Wright Foundation, 1996), 190.

12   Neutra contacted Wright in 1921, arrived in America in 1923, and met Wright at the funeral of Louis Sullivan in April 1924. The Neutras would remain at Taliesin until early February 1925.

13   *Erich Mendelsohn: Letters of an Architect*, ed. Oskar Beyer (London: Abelard-Schumann, 1967), 73, 71. Neither Kuno Francke, who was living in the United States, nor Bruno Möhring or the Dutch architect H. R. Berlage, who both traveled to the States and saw Wright's buildings, had been able to meet Wright. On his travels in October 1924, Mendelsohn visited the Larkin Building, then proceeded to Ann Arbor, Michigan, on the twenty-eighth to see Emil Lorch, Eliel Saarinen, and Karl Lonberg-Holm. After meeting Wright in Spring Green, Mendelsohn went to Oak Park and saw the Coonley House, in Riverside, with Barry Byrne, Wright's former apprentice, and the Midway Gardens in Chicago. Mendelsohn's letters indicate that he and Wright liked each other (*Mendelsohn Letters*, 16–18).

14   For Mendelsohn's text, see Hendricus Theodorus Wijdeveld, ed., *The Life-Work of the American Architect Frank Lloyd Wright* (Santpoort, Neth.: C. A. Mees, 1925), 96–100. This book was reprinted as *The Work of Frank Lloyd Wright: The Life Work of the American Architect Frank Lloyd Wright—The Wendingen Edition* (New York: Horizon Press, 1965; Bramball House, [1965]); cited hereafter as *Wendingen*.

15   See Mendelsohn's tribute, "Frank Lloyd Wright," *Wasmuth's Monatshefte* 10, no. 6 (1926): 244–46, which was attacked by Leo Adler in the next issue of the journal, no. 7 (1926): 308–9. For further discussion, see Erich Mendelsohn, "Das Schiff," *Architectura* (Santpoort) 29 (April 18, 1925): 145–46; idem, "Frank Lloyd Wright," *Architectura* (Santpoort) 29 (April 25, 1925): 153–57. Both articles were reprinted from the *Berliner Tageblatt*, for which Mendelsohn was a correspondent as well as the architect of the newspaper's building.
     Debate about the pros and cons of Wright's work continued. Citing the organicism of nature and unified living as the goal of housing, Adolf Rading included illustrations of Wright's Coonley House and Taliesin II, rebuilt after the fire of 1914, in his essay "Die Typenbildung und ihre städtebaulichen Folgerungen," in *Probleme des Bauens*, ed. Fritz Block (Potsdam: Müller & Kiepenheuer, 1928), 80. These illustrations were previously published in Heinrich de Fries, *Frank Lloyd Wright: Aus dem Lebenswerke eines Architekten* (Berlin: Ernst Pollak, 1926).
     Werner Hegemann furthered the debate about the appropriateness of Wright's architecture as a German model and challenged Mendelsohn's accusation of Le Corbusier as merely "literary" in approach by saying the epithet applied to Wright as well; see Hegemann, "Bemerkungen, Baumeister, I, Frank Lloyd Wright," in *Die Weltbühne* 25, no. 26 (June 25, 1929): 982 (my thanks to Christiane Crasemann Collins for calling my attention to this essay). Mendelsohn responded with "Frank Lloyd Wright und seine historische Beudeutung," *Das Neue Berlin* 4 (September 1929): 180–81.

16   For Wright's appreciation of the book, see Olgivanna Lloyd Wright's introduction to *Wendingen*, reprinted, n.p.

17   J. J. P. Oud, "The Influence of Frank Lloyd Wright on the Architecture of Europe," in *Wendingen*, 87, 88.

18   J. J. P. Oud, in *De Stijl* 2, no. 10 (1919), quoted by Theo van Doesburg in *On European Architecture: Complete Essays from "Het Bouwbedriff," 1924–1931* (Basel: Birkhäuser, 1990), 79.

19   Van Doesburg, *On European Architecture*, 62, 63. Van Doesburg's comments appear in a series of perceptive and provocative essays that he wrote from 1924 to 1931 for the Dutch periodical *Het Bouwbedriff*. Founded in October 1924, the periodical was intended for a broad spectrum of individuals and companies involved in the construction industry.

20 Ibid., 68, 15.

21 Ibid., 158. Van Doesburg extends Wright's lack of influence to American architects generally: "America's influence on the new architecture in Europe did not reach beyond the material-technical aspect, and even there only to a slight degree; composition-wise, America could not teach us anything. The reverse is the case." The Stuttgart Werkbund exhibition to which van Doesburg referred surveyed and epitomized the various strands of international modern architecture at a crucial point in the evolution of the Modern Movement.

22 Sweeney, "Chronology," 197.

23 Van Doesburg, *On European Architecture*, 263.

24 See Alofsin, *Lost Years*, 29–260, for Wright's contact with the Secession as the catalyst for the primitivist phase of his work.

25 De Fries, *Aus dem Lebenswerke*, 34.

26 Grete Dexel, *Frankfurter Zeitung*, December 12, 1926, reprinted in Walter Dexel, *Der Bauhausstil—Ein Mythos: Texte 1921–1965* (Starnberg, Ger.: Joseph Keller, 1976), 91–92, 175.

27 Adolf Behne, *The Modern Functional Building*, trans. Michael Robinson, with an introduction by Rosemarie Haag Bletter (Santa Monica, Calif.: Getty Research Institute for the History of Art and the Humanities, 1996), 98–100.

28 See Bletter's perceptive remarks on Behne's interpretation of Wright in ibid., 37, 41.

29 See Alofsin, "The *Call* Building: Frank Lloyd Wright's Skyscraper for San Francisco," in *Das Bauwerk und die Stadt/The Building and the Town: Essays for Eduard F. Sekler*, ed. Wolfgang Böhm (Vienna: Böhlau, 1994), 17–27.

30 The scrapbook is in the collection of the Frank Lloyd Wright Archives, Frank Lloyd Wright Foundation, Scottsdale, Arizona (hereafter referred to as FLWA).

31 The award was signed on January 29, 1932 by Max Liebermann, the academy's president (FLWA).

32 Robert Scholz, "Der Poelzig Amerikas," Wijdeveld Scrapbook, FLWA.

33 The exhibition catalog was by Alfred Barr, Henry-Russell Hitchcock Jr., and Philip Johnson, *Modern Architects* (New York: Museum of Modern Art, 1932). For a view behind the scenes and Wright's positioning as an elder statesman of the Modern Movement, see Terence Riley, "The Landscapes of Frank Lloyd Wright," in *Frank Lloyd Wright, Architect*, ed. Terence Riley (New York: Museum of Modern Art, 1994), 96–108. The slight to Wright was partly corrected when the Museum of Modern Art held an exhibition exclusively on Wright in 1940, his largest to that date. It received mixed critical response.

34 Franz Schulze, *Mies van der Rohe: A Critical Biography* (Chicago: University of Chicago Press, 1985), 210–11, 236–38.

35 For a brief discussion on Wright and Gropius, see my review of *The Architecture of Frank Lloyd Wright* by Neil Levine, *Harvard Design Magazine*, summer 1997: 76–77.

36 Heidi Kief-Niederwöhrmeier, *Frank Lloyd Wright und Europa: Architekturelemente, Naturverhältnis, Publikationen, Einflüsse* (Stuttgart: Karl Krämer, 1983). This work appeared in an earlier edition (1978) as Heidemarie Kief, *Der Einfluß Frank Lloyd Wrights auf die mitteleuropäische Einzelhausarchitektur*. For the division of German critics into warring camps on the subject of Wright in the 1930s (de Fries vs. Gropius, Hegemann vs. Rading, Mendelsohn vs. Adler), see pp. 165–68; for Ernst Neufert's visit to Wright in 1936, see p. 171.

37 My thanks to Nina Nedeljkov for her insights and her participation in our symposium, on April 27, 1994, during which she pointed out that German-language publications on Wright were limited to Werner Moser's *Frank Lloyd Wright: Sechzigjahre lebendige Architektur/Sixty Years of Living Architecture* (1952) and translations of Vincent Scully Jr., *Frank Lloyd Wright* (1960); Peter Blake, *The Master Builders: Le Corbusier, Mies van der Rohe, Frank Lloyd Wright* (1960); and Bruno Zevi, *Frank Lloyd Wright* (1980; French and German editions). The appearance of the English-German-French edition of Bruce Brooks Pfeiffer's *Frank Lloyd Wright*, ed. Peter Gössel and Gabriele Leuthäuser (Cologne: Benedikt Taschen Verlag, 1991), has rectified this situation to some degree.

38   Kief-Niederwöhrmeier, *Wright und Europa*, 323–39.

39   Eduard F. Sekler, *Josef Hoffmann: The Architectural Work* (Princeton: Princeton University Press, 1985), 236. I have supplied the year of Wright's visit to Russia.

40   Ernst A. Plischke, *Ein Leben mit Architektur* (Vienna: Löcker, 1989), 114. A recent graduate of Behrens's master class, Plischke began his career in New York City. When the *New York Times* announced that Wright would be visiting the city in the late 1920s, Plischke and a friend invited the architect to a luncheon, where, according to Plischke, he appeared modest, warm, and friendly.

41   Behne, *Modern Functional Building*, 99.

42   Wright's lectures were published as *Modern Architecture: Being the Kahn Lectures for 1930* (Princeton: Princeton University Press, for the Department of Art and Archaeology of Princeton University, 1931). The Czech translation appeared as "O mestu budoucnosti," *Styl* 16, no. 6 (1931): 93–95, 98.

Chapter 16

Margaret Kentgens-Craig

The search for modernity
America, the International Style, and the Bauhaus

Europe's loss of political and economic power at the end of World War I coupled with an increase in American power lent the New World a strength and independence it had not known before. The United States' new national self-confidence showed in its activities in the cultural sphere. The first museum of modern American art was opened at New York University in 1927; the development of "precisionism" meant a new, genuinely American form of modernity in painting. Even before, American artists had sought liberation from the long dominance of Europe and of France in particular, and countermovements developed. Thus, the members of the Society of American Sculptors, founded as a response to the National Sculptors' Society, unequivocally advocated "Americanism" in their work. In 1923, the League of American Artists published a statement formulated in terms borrowed freely from military rhetoric: "The time has arrived when the American Artist is the equal, if not the superior, of the foreign artist. . . . America is marching on to an artistic renaissance which will carry the nation to a great cultured height."[1]

An awareness of an indigenous cultural identity reverberated in contemporary literature, literary criticism, and historical and sociological studies as well.[2] In the field of architecture, a redoubled search for a contemporary "American" form of expression began despite uncertainty about that architecture's primary constituents. Whether "modern" building was only a question of new technologies or whether it implied a fundamentally different aesthetic vocabulary was a central point of contention. Inextricable from these issues was the debate surrounding the definition of a national identity. As early as 1928, George Edgell, then dean of the School of Architecture at Harvard University, declared the development of an "American architecture" to be a goal of foremost importance.[3] Two years later, Hugh Ferriss pleaded for an "American architecture" in which the "American spirit" and "American ideals" would find expression.[4] In the area of building technologies, this goal had long since been achieved; its aesthetic expression was still found wanting. Nonetheless, the question of just what this contemporary American architecture should look like was difficult to answer as long as the question of the nation's identity remained open. In 1920, the magazine *Freeman* asked directly what America's soul could be. It was a significant question at a time when the country was rallying around the flag in the aftermath of victory and, for a short time, was willing to overlook the extreme ethnic and cultural differences among its groups and regions.[5]

THE CHICAGO TRIBUNE COMPETITION, 1922

The American architectural establishment believed that it could answer easily the questions of identity raised by critically and intellectually oriented journals. This conviction became evident in the call for a new national formal language, which peaked in the Chicago Tribune competition of 1922. Leading architecture journals were filled with calls for architects whose designs would reflect "the sound, strong, kindly and aspiring idealism which lies at the core of the American people."[6] Convinced that the architects able to meet this challenge would be American, the jury selected preliminary competition winners from the 145 American entries already received, even before the deadline for receipt of foreign entries. In the end, the 37 German and other European entries, which included designs by Ludwig Hilberseimer, Max Taut, and Walter Gropius and Adolf Meyer, claimed only a single prize (Figure 16.1), a fact that indicates the egocentric attitude of America in the early 1920s.

America's new, progressive position in the world was held to be best reflected in skyscraper architecture, as in Randolph Sexton's words: "The skyscraper, an American institution, planned to meet modern American requirements and serve modern American purposes, built of materials of modern manufacture in methods peculiarly American, has finally been made to express Americanism in its design."[7] At the same time, George Edgell described contemporary American architecture as a collection of Georgian, French, colonial, and other period-style buildings which, he contended, could all be considered modern as long as they were built "today" in a manner amenable to the "needs and functions of today," regardless of the conservative or mediocre way in which some did so.[8] The apparent contradiction between Edgell's and Sexton's positions seems more understandable if one considers that Sexton's survey ignored aesthetic issues. At that time, a building that bespoke a progressive spirit in its use of materials and its functionality did not have to be "modern" in phenotype in order to be perceived as modern.[9] It was the field of aesthetics, of how "modern" architecture should look, that saw the most virulent controversies, in turn further complicated by the problems of the discussion's terminology. The concept "modern" was defined differently according to the conditions of building. In American usage, it was often synonymous with "recently built." "Modernity" usually described a work of art or architecture which, in its content, dealt with new and contemporary issues, whereas "modernism" referred to the use of new formal means. "Modern" was, however, also used as a synonym for "technologically innovative" or simply "contemporary" and thus was used to describe extremely disparate contemporaneous developments. In the course of time, the concept was to undergo further cultural transformations.

In the eyes of more than a few, the aesthetic of classical modernism of the 1920s contradicted the traditional academic ideal of "beauty," conceived as the natural, true, and good. The consequences of this discrepancy are witnessed by the historicizing shells and false fronts that transformed highly technical buildings into Gothic cathedrals and Greek temples.[10] These also bear witness to the dominance of an aesthetic oriented toward historical precedent among American architects trained at the Ecole des Beaux-Arts,[11] and

16.1 Eliel Saarinen, in association with Wallace and Grenman, second place entry to the Chicago Tribune Tower competition, 1922

16.2 John Mead Howells and Raymond Hood, winning entry to the Chicago Tribune Tower competition, 1922

16.3 Walter Gropius
and Adolf Meyer, entry
to the Chicago Tribune
Tower competition,
1922

the emotionality with which American architects dealt with high-rise architecture at that time. The demand for "beauty" was also framed by the industrial design movement in the late 1920s, a demand made in architecture on the grounds that higher artistic standards had to be found—but also in the hope that "attractive" products would increase sales. All those tendencies became apparent in the Chicago Tribune competition of 1922. Articles published in conjunction with the competition offer a full palette of acknowledged ways to combine "high buildings and beauty."[12] The first prize conferred upon John Mead Howells and Raymond Hood perfectly embodied the dominant aesthetic ideal (Figure 16.2). The uncompromisingly modernist European entries, such as the one by Walter Gropius and Adolf Meyer, were almost entirely ignored by reviews in professional publications (Figure 16.3).[13] Those entries had ignored the fact that, as the Neues Bauen in Europe turned decisively away from ornament and historicizing motifs, American skyscrapers were destined "to be the lyrical castles of Big Business, . . . endlessly distant from the simple and honest principles of the Modern Movement in Europe."[14] It took three more decades for the skyscraper to emerge as a unity of modern construction, modern function, and modern aesthetics.

It would be an oversimplification to contend that the unadulterated expression of technology in architecture was seen in America as barbaric. Unlike the situation in Europe, where World War I had more severely shaken the belief in technological progress and had led to the regulatory integration of technology in a humanistic context, American society seemed less compelled to confront such issues. Critics such as Lewis Mumford, who remained deeply skeptical of the machine and feared that its incorporation into architecture would bring the dehumanization of Western civilization, were exceptions. In general, the sense that technology could represent a threat remained limited to the fields of industry and economics. The loss of ornamental and stylistic cladding, as Walter Gropius and Adolf Meyer proposed in their design for the Chicago Tribune tower, would be perceived rather as a loss of value. It would mean withdrawing all expressive means from a still-young historical tradition that yearned for a finer and more sophisticated cultural and intellectual life; it would have contradicted the conventional image of beauty that big business had propagated in order to realize its goals. On the other hand, American architecture could not retreat complacently to this position. The economic, political, social, and technological changes had not only produced a climate of national reaffirmation but also effected a sense of insecurity about the cultural means to deal with new demands. In this sense, the inherited concept of beauty current in America represented one of the primary barriers to the initial acceptance of the new, abstract aesthetic, which stemmed from the Bauhaus's and other avant-garde movements' search for an elemental and universally valid formal language. The dilemma that faced American architects in the 1920s is reflected in Shepard Vogelsang's 1929 musings: "Contemporary life moves so rapidly and is subject to such varied influences that a creation of a formal vocabulary constituting a style is practically impossible."[15]

In the Chicago Tribune competition, European and American solutions to an architectural problem characteristic of the 1920s clashed for the first time. The participation of Walter Gropius and Adolf Meyer also represents the first time that Bauhaus architects sought to secure a commission on American soil. It was too early for success; the European modernists' designs lacked insight into important developments in America and their implications for contemporaneous and future American architecture. As such, they failed to do justice to that architecture's tradition. Nonetheless, the significance of Gropius's participation should not be underestimated. In the context of a large-scale competition of great national importance, the founder of the Bauhaus helped to prepare the basis for an increasingly attentive reception of his theories and work. Approximately three years after the Chicago Tribune competition, "German skyscraper design" was featured in the *AIA Journal*.[16] The article includes illustrations from the periodical *Deutsche Bauhütte*, for example a "Design for a Skyscraper by Professor Kreis." More than ten years later, when architectural journals began to accompany articles on Gropius with the famous photograph that showed him standing in front of his Chicago Tribune competition entry, it was a reference to this strategic moment.

COMING TO TERMS WITH THE NEW AESTHETIC

If one of the effects of World War I was a strong desire to define a particularly American culture, the war nonetheless brought with it a greater degree of openness toward Europe. After 1919, more than ever before and irrevocably, the nation found itself entangled in a web of international political and economic relationships. In these years, also, a series of movements in art, design, and finally architecture arose that contributed to a receptiveness to the ideas of the Bauhaus. In the spring of 1923, almost a year after its founding in Chicago, the Association of Arts and Industries sponsored an exhibition in the Carson Pirie Scott department store on the art of advertising. The exhibition reflected the organization's efforts to improve the quality of design in industry, a supraregional goal that demonstrates affinities to the German Werkbund's intentions. Early in 1929, the Association mounted "The Modern American Decorative and Industrial Art Exposition," another event promoting ties between art and industrial production.

Meanwhile, however, a heated and controversial discussion on modernism was raging through the American art, design, and architecture scene. In 1927 Henry Russell Hitchcock wrote his first article on modern architecture in the new Harvard journal *Hound and Horn*. Shortly thereafter, the larger American architecture journals *Architectural Forum* and *Architectural Record* began to deal with the Neues Bauen. A wealth of articles on "modern" issues began to appear, with titles like "Modern Architecture," "The Modern House," "Modern Art," "Modern Store Alteration," "Modern Furniture and Decoration," "Modern Design," "Modern Spirit," and "Modern Materials." *Architectural Record*, the most widely circulated and most innovative journal at that time, named A. Lawrence Kocher managing editor in 1927.[17] Under the direction of Kocher and editor-in-chief Michael A. Mikkelsen, the journal appeared the following year with a new and larger format, an improved index, and a modernized image, all for practical as well as philosophical reasons: the board of editors was aware that American architecture was ready for change and hoped to support change with the design and content of their publication.[18] Two other influential architecture journals, *Architectural Forum* and

American Architect, also began modernizing their layout and content in early 1928, though less wholeheartedly than *Architectural Record*.

The new orientation of the magazines was evident in the publication, by *Record* in 1927 and by *Forum* in 1930, of Frank Lloyd Wright's five-part survey of contemporary American architecture.[19] The figure of Wright, whose popularity was then at a low point, was a reminder to the journals and their readership of an indigenous modernist tradition. The second volume of *Architectural Forum* in 1930 reflected this tendency in its choice of topics: it included articles on "Modern Railway Passenger Terminals," "Modernists and Traditionalists," and "Modern Designers Influenced by Modern Materials." A twelve-part series in *Pencil Points*, beginning in May 1932, dealt with the "Philosophy of Contemporary Design" and included essays by leading American architects.

At the end of 1930, George Howe, Buckminster Fuller, Philip Johnson, and Matthew Nowicki founded the journal *Shelter*.[20] It became a forum for the views of the members of the Philadelphia T-Square Club, which, thanks largely to the impetus and activities of George Howe, would contribute significantly to a rapprochement with modernism during the following years.

The effect of single events on the discussion surrounding this change of heart can no longer be accurately measured; but the statements made by George C. Nimmons, a leading Chicago commercial and industrial architect, to a reporter at the 1927 AIA conference indicate the extensive influence exerted by professional publications, especially upon clients: "The demand on the part of the press for a new style of architecture, as they call it ... has been very strong, and the effect of that has not been so much on the architect, because he knows the causes which produce loose styles of architecture, as upon the client. The client now demands a departure from the old line of work. He wants something new."[21] The feeling that change was imminent caused concern among the AIA's more conservative members. They sensed a threat to architecture posed by the alienating complications and confusion that characterized life in the 1920s, a threat that would mean a succession of ever-changing forms and a loss of clarity. In light of the transitory values of the twenties, these were not unfounded concerns. Perhaps they also express skepticism about the avant-garde's claim to the timeless and universal validity of its elemental forms. Derived through processes of intensification and simplification, these forms were intended precisely to counter the complexity of the life around them. On the other hand, it was impossible to ignore the demands of certain clients or to disregard the knowledge that architecture, like other genres of art, was subject to the changes of the times and compelled to redefine its standpoint. Still, many architects hoped that the new would be expressed with moderation, as in the streamlined forms of Bertram Goodhue, Paul Philippe Cret, Ralph Walker, Ely Jacques Kahn, and Raymond Hood.[22]

The fundamental if cautious willingness on the part of American architects in the early thirties to open themselves to the new European aesthetic was reflected in a comment in *Pencil Points* in 1931:

> Finally, our conclusions as to the advent of modernism in America: from the conservatism which still seems to be in control in America, from the degree to which purely speculative solution is avoided, and from the marked acceptance with which meritorious design is

received and advanced, we may safely welcome the modernist. More and more power, we may well wish, to those whose skill brings fresh solutions to our ever-widening problems and opportunities, that they may interpret the living spirit of architecture. Whether our future be of gigantic forces of commerce and industry, corporate machines beyond the sensibilities of the individual, and whether such shall ever deny the individual's longing for beauty, we cannot say, but it is my impression that so long as the glory of Roman structure remains known to our architects, and so long as the monuments of the Middle Ages afford an emotional background for the romantic imagination, beauty in architecture will be repossessed in each successive century in a new manner and with refreshed power.

The architect shall no longer work in the spirit of history but in the knowledge of its substance and by the zeal of creative research shall a new beauty come, crystalline, clean and with power to lift high the imagination.[23]

The attributes "purity" and "crystalline" lent the concept of beauty new dimensions. "Fresh," "sincere," and "attractive" were other adjectives that appeared in the course of this discussion. By the early thirties, America had clearly begun to move toward modernism; but its precise direction remained at first uncertain.

CRITIQUE OF CONTEMPORARY ARCHITECTURE

Critical awareness of the discrepancy between the ambitions and the actual condition of American architecture at the end of the twenties was largely based on the memory of the early modernist tradition in the United States, including the skyscraper idiom of the Chicago school and the prairie style of Frank Lloyd Wright.[24] The architects who had given life to the Chicago school and thus established their reputations, including Louis Sullivan, Dankmar Adler, William Le Baron Jenney, Daniel Burnham, William Holabird, Kevin Roche, and John Wellborn Root, were still active in the first decades of the twentieth century or had at least found fitting heirs to their legacies. This second generation of architects in the Chicago school shifted the emphasis of their activity from the commercial to the public sector and to the building of single-family houses.[25]

Sullivan's Carson Pirie Scott building is an exception to this development. By the end of World War I, the Chicago school's prime was over. The subsequent generation did unquestionably include innovative architects whose thoughts and intentions had some commonalities with those of the European avant-garde's protagonists. Nonetheless, they seem to have been unconcerned with establishing a movement to assert their influence beyond their immediate environs. Carl Condit explains this decline as a result of decreased interest on the part of commercial clients in realizing a heroic, bold, and emancipated architecture.[26] This agenda was revitalized by the country's gains in political and economic power subsequent to the war; nonetheless, American architecture remained unable to regenerate its vitality within the strong tradition of the original Chicago school, nor could it provide convincing answers to new demands. Whether the call for revitalization, voiced repeatedly during these years, corresponded to an actual need or only to a particular group's subjective perception is irrelevant in considering its consequences. In any case, what economists might call a "latent demand" resulted in a mental inventory of all solutions proposed in the country, along with an unmistakably critical reflection on the present and future of American architecture and the search for new directions.

PROFESSIONAL PRACTICE

This activity was the concern of a limited circle of critical and analytical professionals.[27] They found little to recommend. Alfred Barr, Jr., spoke of a "chaos of architectural styles";[28] in his 1927 article "The Decline of Architecture," Henry-Russell Hitchcock condemned the situation:

> Standing then, as we do, beyond the downslope of the nineteenth century and the apparent gap of the war, and disregarding our architecture, we are led to demand whether the time of its discard is at hand or whether, after the superficially historical wastes of the last century, it may be reintegrated or has already been reintegrated as a sound organ in an aging body. For if what passes today for architecture is but a blonde wig and gold teeth; no ghost rather, but a soulless imitation of its former body, it were better such illusions of second childhood were at once dispensed with and the possibility of a future without architecture frankly faced.[29]

Like Hitchcock, James Monroe Hewlett saw enslavement to tradition, paired with an attempt to be modern, as one reason for the stagnation. The architect was inevitably caught in a dilemma: on the one hand, experimentation and innovation were desired; on the other, the lack of tangible alternatives hindered new concepts from taking hold: "The great majority of the artists of the country today are neither extreme modernists nor are they old fogies. They desire to be modern in thought and performance but they do not wish to throw over the traditions of the past until they are sure that they have found something better to substitute for them."[30] If Hitchcock placed his hope for change in the nation's own reservoir of creative and talented architects,[31] others nonetheless concluded that the United States did not have the energy to overcome the deficit of new ideas simply through its own efforts. The one exception of that time, Frank Lloyd Wright, was no longer considered capable of successfully revitalizing a broad-based professional field.[32]

The critics blamed the state of affairs on practicing architects' general lack of ability, dominant interest in superficial appearance,[33] and lack of an intellectual foundation. The conditions under which they worked were also the subject of complaint:[34] the client's demand that a project be individualized and the concomitant isolation and subjectivity in its conceptualization;[35] the introduction of nationalistic motifs in postwar art and architecture and the misuse of the arts as a political and commercial instrument; the low standard of craftsmanship; the neglect of aesthetic values resulting from an obsession with technical perfection;[36] the unwillingness to depart from traditional concepts of art; and indecision in evaluating other directions.[37] It is also plausible that a general sense of uncertainty in the early thirties among Americans, especially urbanites, confronted with the loss of traditional values and of authority, made it difficult for new ideas and directions to flourish.

EDUCATION

Architecture schools and their protégés offered little promise of a way out of this stagnation. The nineteenth century's admiration for French culture continued to hold sway over architectural education well into the first decades of the twentieth century. Teachers, who were by no means compelled to be practicing or reputed architects, in many cases remained faithful to the conservative doctrine and traditional styles of the Ecole des Beaux-Arts.[38] The Massachusetts Institute of Technology had decided in 1865 to model its curriculum on the Ecole des Beaux-Arts; as late as 1921, the yearbook of the School of Architecture at Harvard University still included only classical designs. Even then, two years after the founding of the Bauhaus, there was no sign in the yearbook—aside from the attention paid to issues of construction—of any concerns comparable to those of the contemporary European avant-garde.[39] The goal of the education process was graphic facility, and the exercise most often assigned to students was accordingly the design of a monument. The designs were in turn evaluated by the instructors on the basis of "good taste."[40] Morris Lapidus described his education at Columbia University at the end of the twenties as follows:

> My background from Columbia University School of Architecture was completely classical. As I was completing my architectural studies in 1927, when I graduated, we had at Columbia a kind of insulated academic background—so much that none of the instructors or professors would even talk about the International Style, the Bauhaus and what was going on in Europe. That was 1923–1927. Of course, the International Style was well along by then, but Columbia University was quite reactionary, conservative. They just did not talk about it. It was only in one lecture that we were told about it; and I remember that lecture so well. We were almost taken in, as if we were going to be told some dirty stories. "We'll tell you about it, but forget it," and then we learned all about Gropius, Le Corbusier, Mies van der Rohe and some of the De Stijl group in Holland.[41]

Columbia University was one of the most important schools of architecture in the country; it was also no exception in its refusal to acknowledge modern architecture. The American architect Anthony Lord, who for a time worked with Marcel Breuer, tells of similar experiences at Yale University.[42] Furthermore, the educational experience provided at these schools seems not to have inspired many students to extend their studies beyond the minimum acceptable degree. Kocher points out that, according to a study of 424 students who graduated between 1915 and 1930 from eight architecture schools, only 15—less than 4 percent—chose to continue their studies on a postgraduate level. By comparison, some 32 percent of medical students during that period sought higher and more specialized degrees.[43]

As the thirties began, the discrepancy between traditional education and the new demands of the profession continued to grow. The influence of the Ecole des Beaux-Arts had declined noticeably. Nonetheless, there seemed to be no new fertile ground for creative activity. A mood of stagnation asserted itself, a feeling that "something had to be done."[44] These words, spoken by George Danforth in retrospect, confirm the opinions voiced in discussions published by *Architectural Forum* and *Architectural Record*. At the center of the discussions was the problem's origin and its possible solutions.[45] Kenneth Stowell, the editor of *Architectural Forum* in 1931, formulated the demand for a qualitatively higher and more contemporary education as follows:

> The coordination of efforts calls for a man of deep social consciousness, great breadth of vision, extensive technical knowledge, executive ability and unquestioned integrity. The education of such men is the responsibility of the architectural school. . . . The schools are still engaged largely in training designers or draftsmen rather than fitting men for leadership in the industry.[46]

Stowell's call for social conscience, visionary perspective, and technical competence in response to the challenges of industrial society recalls fundamental Bauhaus principles. Nonetheless, this affinity remains unspoken. Only in the mid-thirties was the Bauhaus first mentioned in these discussions as a model for the kind of architectural education that could satisfy the demands of American society. This does not mean that the Bauhaus's ideas were welcomed in academic circles. Here, as among architectural societies and practitioners, they met with opposition, perhaps in part because they were seen as an attack on the established curricula, methods, and aims of academia. [. . .]

THE INTERNATIONAL STYLE AND THE BAUHAUS

In the exhibition "Modern Architecture: International Exhibition" at the Museum of Modern Art [New York, 1932] and the accompanying publications, only Le Corbusier and J. J. P. Oud were represented as extensively as [Bauhaus architects] Gropius and Mies. The prominent position granted to the Europeans led to accusations that [curators Henry-Russell] Hitchcock and [Philip] Johnson had intended to force a foreign style of building onto the United States. [. . .]

This event was to determine for many years the course of the reception of these two German architects [Gropius and Mies] and, synonymously, of Bauhaus architecture. The exhibition fostered an image of a homogeneous architecture at the Bauhaus and an understanding of classical modernism as a unified movement. The elimination of the different characteristics of each individual avant-garde tendency facilitated the postulation of their equality within the modern movement, as Peter Eisenman has convincingly argued.[47] Especially on the east coast, which, unlike California, had not developed its own genuine American version of modernism, the Bauhaus soon became synonymous with the International Style simply on the strength of the "Modern Architecture" exhibition and the book *The International Style*.[48] This parity is not tenable, even when applied to aesthetic qualities. The Bauhaus architects certainly absorbed achievements made by other avant-garde movements,[49] just as their impact on the rest of the international movement known as the Neues Bauen is indisputable. Nonetheless, the Bauhaus was only one of the pillars of European modernism. Its institutionalization, efficiently productive workshops, highly visible faculty, efficient self-promotion machinery,[50] and iconic building in

Dessau,[51] helped to propel the Bauhaus particularly far in comparison to [the Dutch] De Stijl and [the French] L'Esprit Nouveau.

If the effect was not immediate, this was only because the reception of the "Modern Architecture" show was initially cautious and, at least among architecture critics, descriptive and detail-oriented. These kinds of reviews may not have been intended by the curators or even by the authors, but they were implicit in the strategy and purpose of the show. Hitchcock and Johnson had analyzed the individual and national manifestations of the modern movement not on the basis of their specificity but primarily with an eye to the commonalities in their formal language, use of materials, and construction methods. The intention was to prove that modernism was a universal phenomenon.[52] Accordingly, Alfred Barr, Jr., wrote in the foreword to *The International Style*: "I believe that there exists today a modern style as original, as consistent, as logical and as widely distributed as any in the past. The authors have called it the International Style. . . . [This new style] exists throughout the world, is unified and inclusive, not fragmentary and contradictory."[53] It was on this basis that they formulated a "unified architectural language . . . an index of formal and architectural usages"[54] consisting of three primary characteristics: emphasis on volume rather than mass, regularity instead of axial symmetry, and the use of distinguished materials and surfaces, technical perfection, and proper proportions instead of applied ornament.[55] These were to become the principles of a new "post-functionalist" style that Barr, Hitchcock, and Johnson dubbed "the International Style."[56] Nonetheless, Hitchcock had already used the term in *Modern Architecture* based upon Gropius's first Bauhaus book, *Internationale Architektur* [1925]. The growing international and transcultural thinking among avant-garde architects at the end of the twenties resounded in other [. . .] books and exhibitions, notably in Ludwig Hilberseimer's book *Internationale Neue Baukunst* and in the "International Plan and Model Exhibition" organized in connection with the Weissenhof-Siedlung exposition [Frankfurt, 1927]. The semantics of the adjective "international" were also politically loaded in the twenties, due to its adoption by the Bolshevik and socialist movements.

Hitchcock, Barr, and Johnson credited their brainchild with being the only true style of the twentieth century, comparable to the great styles of the past. The authors' position bespeaks their rejection of historicism and eclecticism, a stance that was characteristic for the Neues Bauen in the twenties and for the Bauhaus. Instead, "the foundation provided by the nineteenth century's development of forces of production, new materials, construction techniques, and technologies, expressed in iron and glass or reinforced concrete building, was to underpin the future development of architecture."[57]

"Modern Architecture: International Exhibition" exposed the schism between the American reception and Europe's reception of its avant-gardes. The Bauhaus architects saw their work as timelessly valid, as the long-sought and finally discovered formal vocabulary that marked the last phase of architecture. The formulation of an "International Style" thus ran counter to the Bauhaus's perception of itself. The school's architects in particular had always resisted any commitment to stylistic criteria. In their eyes, the new forms did not represent any absolute values but were instead the architectural expression of social aims; these forms represented no more than suggestions of ways in which collective life could be organized.[58] Gropius did not understand the

Bauhaus's architecture as a mere system of forms, materials, and construction methods but as a result of long-lived principles and accomplishments. He countered the idea of a "Bauhaus style" as follows:

> Only too often have our true intentions been misunderstood, as they still are today. The Bauhaus movement has been seen as an attempt to create a "style"; and so every building and object that is unornamented and unindebted to any historical style is perceived as an example of this imaginary "Bauhaus style." This approach is diametrically opposed to what we strive toward. The aim of the Bauhaus does not comprise the propagation of some style or other, some system or dogma, but rather the hope that a vital influence can be brought to bear on design. A "Bauhaus style" would mean regression to an uncreative, stagnated academicism, to that which the founding of the Bauhaus was meant to resist. Our efforts aim to find a new approach that allows the development of a creative consciousness and thus, finally, a new attitude toward life. As far as I know, the Bauhaus was the first institution in the world that risked introducing this principle into a concrete pedagogic program. The concept of this program derived from an analysis of the relationships within our industrial age and its fundamental currents.[59]

Mies van der Rohe also resisted the determinacy of a formal stylistic categorization. In a 1927 letter to Dr. Riezler, then editor of the German Werkbund magazine *Die Form*, he wrote: "Is form really an aim? Is it not instead a product of the design process? Is it not the process which is essential? Does not a small shift in the process's conditions produce an entirely different result? Another form? I would therefore wish that we march on without a flag."[60] Nonetheless, the Bauhaus itself was only a temporal manifestation, a style, according to Gottfried Semper's definition: "Style is the revelation of the fundamental idea raised to the level of artistic significance; it includes all the internal and external coefficients which act to modify that idea in its manifestation as a work of art."[61] The usual American definition of style deviates from Semper's to mean in general the sum of a building's essential formal characteristics. As defined in a standard reference work published by the Historic American Buildings Survey Organization, style is "a definite type of architecture, distinguished by special characteristics of structure and ornament."[62] According to this criterion, which corresponds to Hitchcock and Johnson's, style is an essentially phenotypic quality. The fact that the reception of the International Style degenerated into a one-dimensional image of abstract, cubic volumes made of steel, concrete, and planes of glass with smooth white walls and a flat roof, horizontal strip windows, and large terraces cannot be pinned on Hitchcock and Johnson. In fact, that image shares just as much with such descriptions as Walter Gropius's criteria in *The New Architecture and the Bauhaus*.[63]

The Bauhaus ironically proved more amenable than other movements to formulating the International Style. This is clear even in the movement's name, which seems to have been inspired by the first Bauhaus book, Walter Gropius's *Internationale Architektur*. The works by Gropius shown in the exhibition date exclusively from the Dessau period. By securing a privileged place among the architects presented for Mies van der Rohe, the curators and authors paid homage to the Bauhaus director then in office.

The influence of the two architects goes beyond what is superficially apparent. Hitchcock, Barr, and Johnson's definition of the Style relies considerably on the views developed by Gustav Adolf Platz five years earlier in his standard reference work *Die Baukunst der neuesten Zeit*, in which he described the characteristics of Gropius's and Mies van der Rohe's avant-garde works. This book, which was in such great demand that a second edition was already issued by Propyläen Press in 1930, suggested the internationalism of the new architecture most convincingly, although Platz did not use the term "international architecture." The idea was further promoted in a book by Frederick Kiesler titled *Contemporary Art Applied to the Store and Its Display*. Including a number of illustrations of works of contemporary art, architecture, and design, the text entertained the idea of the internationality of the new modern architecture in Europe, two years before Hitchcock and Johnson formulated their definition of the "International Style."[64]

The conflation of individual works of the avant-garde within the context of a common movement was not a new idea, either. Five years before *The International Style*, Platz had built a similar argument. Philip Johnson knew *Die Baukunst der neuesten Zeit*, perhaps through *Architectural Record*. In a 1928 issue of that magazine, Pauline Fullerton, then the head librarian in the Department of Art and Architecture at the New York Public Library, had included the book in her recommended reading list: "A discussion of the new movement in architecture, followed by more than four hundred illustrations of various types of buildings, predominantly German. There is a brief dictionary of architects and their works, and . . . an index of text and plates."[65] Johnson, who could read the book in the original German and was thus not limited to its extensive photographic documentation, cited it favorably in a 1931 review, published in the *New Republic*, of Cheney's book *New World Architecture*: "Judged merely as a picture book, 'The New World Architecture' falls short of the standard set by the second edition of Platz's 'Baukunst der Neuesten Zeit.'"[66] While he used the book as a source of information and an architectural travel guide when he visited Europe in 1930,[67] it probably served as an eye-opener for the avant-garde's works as well. Thus, an architectural criticism of the Bauhaus was incorporated directly into the formulation, presentation, and reception of the International Style via *Die Baukunst der neuesten Zeit*. A glance at Platz's bibliography reveals his sources, including:

> Walter Gropius and Karl Nierendorf, eds., *Bauhaus, Staatliches, in Weimar, 1919–1923*; Walter Gropius, *Internationale Architektur and Neue Arbeiten der Bauhaus-Werkstätten*; Mies van der Rohe, "Industrielles Bauen"; and Publications by the "Ring" group in the journal *Bauwelt*.[68]

A comparison of the table of contents in *The International Style* with that of Platz's book reveals a series of common criteria for describing the new style. Some of the topics covered by the authors of *The International Style* were:

- The influence of early American modernism on the Neues Bauen;[69]
- The growth of the new aesthetic from the bond between art and technology, excluding rigid functionalism;[70]

- Horizontality, dissolution of the building's massing, and rejection of ornament as fundamental principles, and the attribution of aesthetic power to composition and materials;[71]
- Paradigmatic character of the Dessau Bauhaus building with regard to these principles;[72]
- The pioneering position of Mies van der Rohe, Gropius, and Oud in the movement.[73]

Platz and others had already envisioned the new buildings' rise to the status of a style.[74] In *Baukunst der neuesten Zeit*, he had written: "A new architecture is arising . . . We are at the beginning of a development process . . . that will precipitate a new style." Even the equivalence implied between the "new style" and historic styles, such as Gothic, and the belief that this new style would lead away from the "chaos" of historicism, already appear in Platz's work. In addition to its explicit references to Gropius and Mies, Platz's book refers indirectly to the philosophical positions and mode of production of both these architects. Listing the common characteristics of the "new architecture," the author cites the conception of architecture as "an expression of the era" and "the era's will," both ideas that Mies propounded at that time. He also cites the consideration of economically disempowered portions of the population in the new planning and "the metaphysical roots [of the new architecture] . . . in a new recognition of the dignity of man as the only true basis of nobility."[75] In the latter two passages, the social motivation and democratic conviction that in part motivated the founding of the Bauhaus are revealed. It is mainly in this regard that *The International Style* clearly distanced itself from *Baukunst der neuesten Zeit*.

Notes

1   Statement of the League of American Artists, New York, 1923, quoted in Milton W. Brown, *American Painting: From the Armory Show to the Depression* (1955) (Princeton, 1972 revised ed.), 82.
2   Robert Stern, "Relevance of the Decade," *Journal of the Society of Architectural Historians* 24 (March 1965): 8.
3   George H. Edgell, *The American Architecture of To-day* (New York, 1928), 4.
4   Hugh Ferriss, "Power of America," *Pencil Points* 13 (June 1942): 61
5   E. A. M., "Toward Internationalism in Art," *The Freeman* 2 (September 22, 1920): 43.
6   Louis H. Sullivan, "The Chicago Tribune Competition," *Architectural Record* 53 (February 1923): 156. Also see Irving K. Pond, "High Buildings and Beauty," *Architectural Forum* 38 (April 1923): 182.
7   Randolph W. Sexton, *American Commercial Buildings of Today* (New York, 1928), 2. The author cites Bertram Goodhue's monumental state capitol building in Lincoln, Nebraska, as an example of an "ultramodern" building. It is a work whose Gothic verticality, exterior decoration, and emphatic massing contain extremely historicizing elements but whose individual components—for example, its punctured windows without decorative embrasures—indicate new architectural ideas.
8   Edgell, *The American Architecture of To-day*, 4ff.
9   Dwight J. Baum, "This Modernism," *Pencil Points* 13 (September 1932): 598.
10   Leo Friedlander, "The New Architecture and the Master Sculptor," *Architectural Forum* 46 (January 1927): 5.

11   Martha and Sheldon Cheney, *Art and the Machine* (New York, 1936), 7. On the commercial motivation of the movement, see Calkins, "Beauty, the New Business Tool," *Atlantic Monthly* 140 (1927): 145–156.

12   The title of Irving K. Pond's extensive feature in *Architectural Forum*. Cf. fn. 6.

13   See the articles on the Chicago Tribune competition in *American Architect* (December 1922): 545–547; (January 1923): 23–25; *Architectural Record* (February 1923): 151–157; and *Architectural Forum* (February 1923): 41–44; (April 1923): 179–182, 378ff.; (September 1924): 100; (January 1927): 7.

14   See Messler, *The Art Deco Skyscraper in New York*, 2nd ed. (New York, 1986), 1.

15   Shepard Vogelsang, "Copying versus Creating" *Architectural Forum* 50 (January 1929): 97.

16   Irving K. Pond, "From Foreign Shores," *American Institute of Architects Journal* 12 (November 1925): 405.

17   See "Professor Kocher Joins the Architectural Record Staff," *Architectural Record* 62 (August 1927): 167. Lawrence A. Kocher had been director of the Department of Architecture at the University of Virginia, where he had succeeded Joseph Hudnut in 1926.

18   See Michael A. Mikkelsen, "A Word about a New Format," *Architectural Record* 63 (January 1928): 1f.

19   Frank Lloyd Wright, "In the Cause of Architecture," *Architectural Record* 62 (August 1927): 163–166; (October 1927): 318–324; "Modern Architecture: Frank Lloyd Wright and Hugh Ferriss Discuss Modern Architecture," *Architectural Forum* 53 (November 1930): 535–538.

20   Author's interview with Philip Johnson, September 21, 1992. The journal initially appeared under the title *T-Square*.

21   George C. Nimmons, "Interview at the AIA Convention, 1927," *Inland Architect* 131 (1927): 701.

22   Stern, "Relevance of the Decade," 9.

23   William W. Watkin, "The Advent of the New Manner in America," *Pencil Points* 12 (July 1931): 530.

24   See Richard B. McCommons, "Architecture Education in America," in *Guide to Architecture Schools in North America* (Washington, DC, 1982), viii.

25   Author's interview with George E. Danforth, April 26, 1992.

26   Carl W. Condit, *The Chicago School of Architecture* (Chicago and London, 1964), 182.

27   See Hans M. Wingler, *Bauhaus in Amerika* (Berlin, 1972), 5. In the early 1980s, Tom Wolfe denounced the Eurocentricity of this circle as a selfish enterprise intended to recreate the chicness and excitement that they had experienced in Europe by transplanting modernism to the United States. Tom Wolfe, *From Bauhaus to Our House* (New York, 1981), 41.

28   Alfred H. Barr, Jr., foreword to Henry-Russell Hitchcock and Philip C. Johnson, *The International Style* (New York, 1932), 12. Even in retrospect, Barr's evaluation stands; as late as 1986, Howard Dearstyne speaks of the "bankruptcy of American architecture during the 1920's." Howard Dearstyne, *Inside the Bauhaus* (New York, 1986), 23.

29   Henry-Russell Hitchcock, "The Decline of Architecture," *Hound and Horn* 1 (September 1927): 29ff.

30   James M. Hewlett, "Modernism and the Architect," *American Institute of Architects Journal* 16 (September 1928): 340.

31   Henry-Russell Hitchcock, "Four Harvard Architects," *Hound and Horn* 2 (September 1928): esp. 47.

32   Ibid., 41.

33   See Charles W. Killam, "Modern Design as Influenced by Modern Materials," *Architectural Forum* 53 (July 1930): 40.

34   See Stephan Richebourg, "Some Thoughts on Modern Architecture," *American Institute of Architects Journal* 10 (May 1922): 143.

35   Henry S. Churchill sees one reason for the tendency to conformity and convention, especially among the clients of commercial buildings, in the fear that any deviation from the predictable

would have a negative effect on rentals. "The New Architecture," *The Nation* 117 (November 1923): 553.

36   Hitchcock, "The Decline of Architecture," 30ff.

37   Barr, foreword to Hitchcock and Johnson, *The International Style*, 12.

38   Sigfried Giedion, *Space, Time and Architecture* (1941), 5th ed. (Cambridge, 1967), 501, 504.

39   See Reginald R. Isaacs, *Walter Gropius*, 2 vols. (Berlin 1983, 1984), 2: 839.

40   McCommons, "Architecture Education in North America," viii.

41   Morris Lapidus interviewed in John W. Cook and Heinrich Klotz, *Conversations with Architects* (New York, 1973), 149.

42   Author's interview with Anthony Lord, March 22, 1990.

43   Lawrence A. Kocher, "Keeping the Architect Educated," *Architectural Record* 67 (January 1930): 45.

44   Author's interview with George E. Danforth, April 26, 1992.

45   Herbert Croly, "A Modern Problem in Architectural Education," *Architectural Record* (May 1928): 469f.

46   Kenneth K. Stowell, "Leadership and Education," *Architectural Forum* 54 (April 1931): 439.

47   Peter Eisenman, introduction to Philip Johnson, *Writings* (New York, 1979), 11–12.

48   The architect Harwell Hamilton Harris noticed subsequent to his move from California to North Carolina that the name "Bauhaus" was used interchangeably with "modern architecture" on the east coast: "Bauhaus was in the East synonymous to modern architecture. Modern was what we would call the Bauhaus, not the mixture we had in California." Interview with Harwell Hamilton Harris, February 26, 1990. See Edgar Kaufmann, Jr., *Introduction to Modern Design*, 3rd ed. (New York, 1969), 15. In the fifties, this indiscriminate perception began to influence the popular reception, as is evident in the weekly architecture column of the *New York Times*. See Wolfe, *From Bauhaus to Our House*, 71; Eric Stange, "MIT has Designs on Bauhaus," *Boston Herald* (October 10, 1986).

49   Kaufmann, *Introduction to Modern Design*, 15ff.

50   Walter Dexel *et al.* use the word "propaganda" in *Der "Bauhausstil"—ein Mythos* (Starnberg, 1976), 17. See also Julius Posener, *From Schinkel to the Bauhaus*, Architectural Assn. Paper no. 5 (London, 1972), 48.

51   William H. Jordy called the building "a demonstration of the full range of visual possibilities" and "a compendium of the architectural elements" of the Style. Jordy, *American Buildings and Their Architects*, Vol. 5, *The Impact of European Modernism in the Mid-Twentieth Century* (New York, 1972), 5: 134.

52   Christoph Hackelsberger, *Die aufgeschobene Moderne* (Munich and Berlin, 1985), 14. William H. Jordy concludes that the concept of "modernism" as defined by Hitchcock and Johnson was appropriated by historians but that the architects and critics who at the time were concerned with the "Style" did not use the term. Jordy, *American Buildings and Their Architects*, 5: 118. Vincent Scully notes that most protagonists of the new architecture would have found the designation "tasteless." Scully, "Henry-Russell Hitchcock and the New Tradition," 10.

53   Barr, introduction to Hitchcock and Johnson, *The International Style*, in Helen Searing, ed., *In Search of Modern Architecture: A Tribute to Henry-Russell Hitchcock* (New York, 1982), 11, 19.

54   José A. Dols, *Moderne Architektur* (Hamburg, 1978), 62.

55   Hitchcock and Johnson, *The International Style*, 13. The exhibition catalogue mentioned a fourth principle: flexibility.

56   Hitchcock and Johnson credit Alfred Barr with coining the phrase "the International Style." See Jordy, *American Buildings and Their Architects*, 5: 434, and Peter Eisenman, introduction to Johnson, *Writings*, note 10.

57   Behr, "Das Bauhausgebäude in seiner Bedeutung für die Entwicklung der neueren Architektur," *Wissenschaftliche Zeitschrift der Hochschule für Architektur und Bauwesen Weimar* 23, no. 5/6 (1976): 464.

58 Manfredo Tafuri, *Architecture and Utopia* (Cambridge, 1976), 77.

59 Walter Gropius, *Architektur. Wege zu einer optischen Kultur* (Frankfurt and Hamburg, 1956), 16f. These thoughts are reflected earlier in Gropius' *The New Architecture and the Bauhaus* (London, 1935), 61f.

60 Ludwig Mies van der Rohe, letter to Dr. Riezier, undated, Mies van der Rohe Archive, private files of Dirk Lohan, Chicago.

61 Gottfried Semper, quoted in Wingler, *Das Bauhaus, 1919–1933*, 24.

62 John C. Poppeliers, S. Allen Chambers, and Nancy B. Schwartz, *What Style Is It?, A Guide to American Architecture* (Washington, DC, 1983), 10.

63 Gropius, *The New Architecture and the Bauhaus*, 20ff.

64 Dieter Bogner, "Architecture as Biotechnique," in Matthias Boeckl, ed., *Visionäre und Vertriebene, Österreichische Spuren in der modernen amerikanischen Architektur* (Berlin, 1995), 147.

65 Pauline Fullerton, "List of New Books on Architecture and the Allied Arts," *Architectural Record* 64 (July 1928): 85. In the thirties and forties, bibliographies of the most important books on modern architecture included Platz's work.

66 Philip Johnson, "Modernism in Architecture," *The New Republic* 66 (March 18, 1931): 134.

67 According to Franz Schulze, *Mies van der Rohe: A Critical Biography* (Chicago, 1985). Also see Terence Riley, *The International Style* (New York, 1992), 202.

68 Platz does not include footnotes. Thus, the reader has to recover his use of the literature mentioned in the bibliography.

69 Gustav Adolf Platz on Frank Lloyd Wright: "it is not surprising that this great artist had a strong influence on German architects. . . . Many currents tying us to America emanate from Wright's rural houses and sober industrial buildings but most of all from his skyscrapers" (*Die Baukunst der neuesten Zeit* [Berlin, 1927], 67). Compare to Hitchcock and Johnson: "But it was in America that the promise of a new style appeared first and, up to the war, advanced most rapidly [particularly with Wright's continuation of the Chicago school]" (*The International Style*, 25).

70 Platz, quoting Peter Behrens's maxim in his text: "We do not want a technology that follows its own course in isolation but rather a technology that is sensitive to the *Kunstwollen* of the era." Behrens also warns of the "dangers of functional architecture" (*Die Baukunst der neuesten Zeit*, 66). Compare Hitchcock and Johnson: "The new conception that building is science and not art, developed as an exaggeration of the idea of functionalism" (*The International Style*, 35).

71 Platz, *Die Baukunst der neuesten Zeit*, 65, 75. Compare Hitchcock and Johnson, *The International Style*, 13.

72 Platz calls the building "a convincing symptom of the pendulum swing" toward the new architecture. Hitchcock and Johnson: "The Bauhaus is something more than a mere development from the technical triumph of the Alfeld factory," in reference to a previous description of the Fagus factory as the prototype of the style.

73 Platz does not mention Le Corbusier because his book is limited to German and Dutch architecture; *Die Baukunst der neuesten Zeit*, 64ff. Compare Hitchcock and Johnson, *The International Style*, 28, 31, 33.

74 Also see the writing of Walter Curt Behrendt from the twenties.

75 Platz, *Die Baukunst der neuesten Zeit*, 17–20, 76–78, 90. The bibliography includes Ludwig Mies van der Rohe (91).

Part 5 |

Shifting scenes: modernism and postmodernism

After World War II, the pre-war trickle of International Style modern architecture in the US burst into the mainstream. Corporations built gleaming new minimalist factories and office towers; modernists designed airports, schools, hospitals, hotels, churches, museums, concert halls, and government buildings. Yet, in the domestic sphere—however enthusiastically they embraced modern technology and convenience, and the cost savings brought on by mass production and distribution—most Americans continued to favor more traditional design approaches. It was, for the most part, the unconventional client who obtained for him or herself an unconventional house.

Two such unconventional clients are at the center of Alice T. Friedman's comparative essay. Drawing on reception aesthetics, feminist theory, and queer studies, Friedman presents a cultural and social history of Mies van der Rohe's house for Edith Farnsworth and Philip Johnson's own Glass House. Friedman probes the often-fraught realm of architect-client relations and the persistence in American architecture of traditional notions of family, gender, morality, and domesticity. On this last score her article provides an especially productive comparison with Gwendolyn Wright's earlier piece on nineteenth-century cottage design.

In another sort of comparative study, Joan Ockman considers the design choices made by more conventional post-war clients. The "symbiotic social relationship" between the public-masculine-productive-modern sphere of downtown (as represented by Skidmore, Owings, and Merrill's Lever House) and the private-feminine-consumptive-traditional one of suburbia (as in the case of Levittown) were, in fact, two sides of the same capitalist coin. They differed mainly in the image they projected—and this in a time and a place when image was becoming a paramount social and economic concern. Ockman ends by arguing that with the basis of modern architecture shifting in this period from one of social idealism to image—"architecture as a system of arbitrary signs . . . design [used for] purposes of 'corporate identity' and 'marketing strategy'"—we observe the transition from modernity to postmodernity.

While modernist-style housing might not have been the first choice of most Americans, in post-war public housing projects such as St Louis' Pruitt-Igoe, it became the reality for thousands of the poorest and most powerless members of society. By the time Pruitt-Igoe was demolished in the 1970s, it had become a symbol for the presumptive failure and demise of modern architecture, a key marker of postmodernity's emergence. Yet, as Katharine G. Bristol shows in her look at Pruitt-Igoe's critical reception, contrary to popular belief, the project's failure was a matter less of architectural design and more of flawed economic and political policies. The postmodern account of Pruitt-Igoe, says Bristol, reinforced earlier modernist beliefs in architecture's ability to cause or cure behavioral problems. The real power of architects, she reminds us, is in most cases far more limited, subject to numerous mitigating factors; meanwhile by placing too much emphasis on design, critics and historians have deflected attention from more pressing issues, such as race and class discrimination.

Neil Levine offers another perspective on the transition from modernity to post-modernity. Unlike Bristol, however, he keeps his focus on the architect. Levine looks at Robert Venturi's early experiments in representation and contextualization—his surprising and seminal embrace of historicism after decades of modernist aversion to historical quotation. Levine's essay provides a detailed and contained discussion of American architectural theory and design in the 1960s, one that eschews the more wide-ranging social historical approaches of the others in this section. He ends, however, by claiming that Venturi's ultimate achievement "was in the public realm, signaling a revitalization of cultural memory and a desire for urban reform."

Cultural memory and its construction are core issues in Mary McLeod's piece on the Vietnam Veterans Memorial (VVM) in Washington, DC. Hers is the one essay in this section that does not refer to domestic architecture, yet, like the other authors, she is also interested in the reworking and dismantling of conventions. If monumentality and memorialization posed profound ideological and aesthetic problems for modernists, they presented different but no less serious problems for postmodernists. How, for example, could one create a permanent, public monument that accommodated diverse subjectivities and allowed for what was now recognized as the mutability of meaning? In recounting the competition and controversy surrounding the VVM—formally a sort of "anti-monument" (black, abstract, underground, non-heroic, ideologically indeterminate), making it, perhaps, the quintessential postmodern monument—McLeod, like Bristol, reminds us of the larger processes of design in a public forum, and of the many, necessary compromises that mediate the architect's singular vision. In this case, however, the resulting structure was one of tremendous suggestive power and sustained popular appeal—lending support to the argument that just as history's determination is too important to be left to an elite few, so too is public architecture.

Further reading

Alofsin, A., *The Struggle for Modernism: Architecture, Landscape Architecture, and City Planning at Harvard*, New York: W. W. Norton and Co., 2002.

Bruegmann, R. (ed.), *Modernism at Mid-Century: The Architecture of the United States Air Force Academy*, Chicago, IL: University of Chicago Press, 1994.

Chase, J., "The Role of Consumerism in American Architecture," *Journal of Architectural Education* 44: 4 (1991): 211–224.

Ghirardo, D., "The Deceit of Postmodern Architecture," in Gary Shapiro (ed.), *After the Future: Postmodern Times and Places*, Albany, NY: State University of New York Press, 1990.

Ghirardo, D., *Architecture After Modernism*, London: Thames and Hudson, 1996.

Goldhagen, S. W. and R. Legault (eds), *Anxious Modernisms: Experimentation in Postwar Architectural Culture*, Montreal and Cambridge, MA: Canadian Centre for Architecture and MIT Press, 2000.

Harris, S. and D. Berke (eds), *Architecture of the Everyday*, New York: Princeton Architectural Press, 1997.

Hine, T., *Populuxe*, New York: Alfred A. Knopf, 1987.

Jordy, W. H., *American Buildings and Their Architects, Vol. 5, The Impact of European Modernism in the Mid-Twentieth Century*, New York: Oxford University Press, 1972.

Kelley, B. M., *Expanding the American Dream: Building and Rebuilding Levittown*, Albany, NY: State University of New York Press, 1993.

Marder, T., *The Critical Edge: Controversy in Recent American Architecture*, New Brunswick, NJ and Cambridge, MA: Jane Voorhees Zimmerli Art Museum and MIT Press, 1985.

McLeod, M., "Architecture and Politics in the Reagan Era: From Postmodernism to Deconstruction," *Assemblage* 8 (1989): 22–59.

Sanders, J. (ed.), *Stud: Architectures of Masculinity*, New York: Princeton Architectural Press, 1996.

Schwarzer, M., "Modern Architectural Ideology in Cold War America," in Martha Pollak (ed.), *The Education of the Architect*, Cambridge, MA: MIT Press, 1997.

Tzonis, A., L. Lefaivre, and R. Diamond, *Architecture in North America Since 1960*, Boston, MA: Bulfinch Press, 1995.

Chapter 17

Alice T. Friedman

People who live in glass houses

Edith Farnsworth, Ludwig Mies van der Rohe,
and Philip Johnson

The Farnsworth House (1945–51, Figure 17.1), in Plano, Illinois, by Ludwig Mies van der Rohe (1886–1969) is one of a handful of modern buildings that always seem extraordinary [. . .]. Perched in the middle of a grassy meadow on the bank of the Fox River, some fifty miles west of Chicago, the Farnsworth House appears to be the perfect embodiment of Mies's dictum "Less is more." Even from a distance one is struck by the elegance and simplicity of its form. Eight slender columns of white-painted steel support a transparent glass box; two horizontal planes—crisp, parallel bands of steel hovering above the ground—represent the floor and the roof. Though barely making physical contact with its site, the house seems securely anchored in the green sea that surrounds it; there is a toughness and immutability to the structure, which contrast with the thinness and apparent insubstantiality of the forms. With its low terrace and ladderlike suspended staircases, the house appears to be a life raft or a tent platform, a place of refuge from the turbulence of nature. This image (and experience) of insularity is reinforced by the fact that the interior of the house is almost totally sealed off from the outside world: the only openings in the glass "skin" are a door on one short side of the rectangle, which serves as the entrance, and two small windows set low on the opposite wall.

A thin but seemingly impermeable membrane of glass thus forms the boundary between inside and outside on all four sides of the box; grass, trees, and river are visible through the "walls," yet they seem distant and abstracted, like elements in a landscape painting. This is not simply because the views from the house are framed by the rectilinear structure, but because objects and landscape beyond the glass appear recessed and diminished, as though the surface of the wall were a picture plane and the objects behind it were imaginary, not real. When one looks at things inside the house, however, this equation is reversed: there is an immediacy that is inescapable—one's awareness of the material world is heightened. In part this is due to the fact that the interior is simply one large room (the entire platform measures 77×28 feet), subdivided by a freestanding wooden core, which encloses two bathrooms, a fireplace, and a galley kitchen. This block at the center and a lower bank of cupboards at the far end of the house screen and subdivide the space to some degree, but the living areas remain essentially open and unbounded. Within this interior environment, sights and sounds are magnified, people and objects move closer and seem more tangible and tactile.

17.1 Ludwig Mies van der Rohe, Farnsworth House, Plano, Illinois, 1945–51

Mies's architecture thus calls attention not only to itself but also to the physical and aesthetic experience of the occupant. It is important to note that the experience is not always positive. As Mies's grandson, the architect Dirk Lohan, explained:

> [The house] owes its stature as one of the highlights of modern architecture to its spiritual rather than its functional values. The concept, a country retreat from the big city, has been elevated to such a spiritual abstraction that it demands complete acceptance of its inner logic from the occupant. So unconventional is the house that every move and every activity in it assume an aesthetic quality which challenges behavior patterns formed in different surroundings.[1]

The "occupant" in this case was Edith Farnsworth (1903–1977), an unmarried doctor who lived and worked in Chicago. In her mid-forties and financially secure, Farnsworth had begun to think about the advantages of owning a small weekend house in the country some months, or even years, before she met the German architect Ludwig Mies van der Rohe, in 1945. Through Mies, who had emigrated to the United States in the late 1930s and was already well known among American architects and critics for the unrelenting discipline and formality of his work, Farnsworth later came to view her project as an important statement about modern architecture, but at the outset her concerns were those of a typical client: what she was looking for was "a really fine [design] solution for an inexpensive weekend retreat for a single person of my tastes and pre-occupations," as she later recalled in her memoirs.[2] She assumed that whatever else happened in the process of working with an architect, her new house would be a place in which she could relax and find some relief from the strain of her life as a doctor. There is no evidence to suggest that she sought to have her behavior challenged by the "inner logic" of Mies's unyielding architectural vision; on the contrary, she seems to have had a clear idea about how she wanted to live and she expected the architect to respect her views.

Farnsworth's assumptions about her role and rights in the architect-client relationship proved to be unfounded; she soon discovered that what Mies wanted, and what he thought he had found in her, was a patron who would put her budget and her needs aside in favor of his own goals and dreams as an architect. By 1945 Mies and his followers (including Philip Johnson, an architect himself and head of the Department of Architecture at The Museum of Modern Art in New York) were acutely aware of the fact that what he needed most was a wealthy patron and a job. The lack of opportunities for building in wartime Germany, combined with the strict minimalism of his formal language, had ensured that Mies had few clients and even fewer realized buildings over the last fifteen years. He had built a handful of well-known works in Europe, including the German Pavilion at the Barcelona World's Fair in 1929 and the Tugendhat House in Brno, Czechoslovakia, in 1930, but the majority of his designs remained on paper. This was especially true of his houses: although he had come up with some radically new ideas for living spaces and produced some extraordinary drawings, nothing much had come of them in either Germany or the U.S.[3] Mies's reputation was impressive and his work was admired in elite and academic circles, but he needed exposure—he needed to build. Dr. Edith Farnsworth seemed to be the answer to his prayers.

The first part of this chapter looks at the history of the Farnsworth House and at the process through which it came to be designed and constructed. [. . .] Throughout the long process of design development we can identify and analyze multiple ways in which attitudes about gender and sexuality influenced the project; we can also look at how these and other factors contributed to the house's uncertain reception by the American public in the early 1950s. Nevertheless, it is very important at the outset to be clear about what this approach to the house does, and does *not*, tell us. Neither Farnsworth's conflict with the architect nor the unprecedented design of the Farnsworth House was simply the result of her being a woman. Many works of architecture, built for a variety of clients and purposes, have similar histories: there are often persistent and unresolved questions about power, professional status, money, and, ultimately, about who is in control of the project. Architects and clients frequently struggle, both publicly and privately, to enlist support for their points of view, using all the personal and professional artillery available to them. Moreover, gender values—assumptions about how men and women should behave in their daily lives often play a role in architectural design, particularly in domestic architecture, since these values shape both the explicit and the implicit requirements of a building's program. There is no guarantee that architect and client will agree on these matters, especially in cases where unconventional ways of living are being planned for. Architecture is a process of negotiation.

What is unusual in this case, however, [. . .] is that questions of gender and sexuality were explicitly focused on by the participants, and that they came to assume an unusually prominent and complex role in the design process as it was discussed and described at the time. Edith Farnsworth may have been a successful doctor, but the fact that she was also a single woman made her more dependent on the architect both personally and professionally.[4] Ambiguities about their roles, not simply as architect and client but also as man and woman, blurred the boundaries of their relationship, which was especially problematized by the attitudes and prejudices of 1950s America. This opened the way for deep-rooted conflicts between them, which were played out in questions about authority, money, and control of the project.

Although this situation clearly tainted the undertaking for both of them, it is possible that these factors, especially Mies's assumptions about his own power and his willingness to disregard the client's wishes, actually set the stage for the greatness of the design by freeing Mies to pursue his vision of the weekend house as a work of "pure" architecture, a building almost completely devoid of a program. Whatever way we look at it—whether we are dismayed by Mies's desire to exploit the situation or by Farnsworth's tardy realization that she was not the all-powerful client she expected to be—it is clear that gender and sexuality played an unusually prominent role in shaping this extraordinary house.

The second half of the chapter focuses on Philip Johnson's Glass House/Guest House complex (1949), in New Canaan, Connecticut, a weekend retreat in the country, north of New York City. Johnson (b. 1906) played a significant part in creating a reputation for Mies van der Rohe in the United States: not only had Johnson prominently featured Mies's buildings in the influential International Style exhibition of 1932 at The Museum of Modern Art, but he had also been Mies's first American client, having commissioned the architect to remodel his own New York apartment in 1930.[5] As an influential curator and critic, Johnson had a hand in shaping American ideas about contemporary design, publicizing and promoting work by European architects who conformed to a hard-edged, elegant, modern style. His own Glass House in New Canaan emulated Mies's Farnsworth House and served as a commentary on it. Although the Glass House was finished a year before Mies's project was completed, it was universally viewed as having been derived from it; a model of the Farnsworth House was shown at The Museum of Modern Art in 1947 as part of an exhibition of Mies's work that Johnson curated, and his Glass House incorporated many of its most innovative features. Johnson reinforced this patrilineal connection by describing his debt to Mies in a widely read article published in the *Architectural Review* in 1950.

Nevertheless, close examination of the two projects reveals the profound differences between them. Despite Johnson's debt to Mies, his Glass House is in many ways less rigid than the Farnsworth House, more picturesque in its siting, more decorative in its details, and more open to the landscape around it. Moreover, paired with the windowless brick Guest House (which stands opposite the Glass House but is often overlooked in discussions of the project), the Glass House calls attention to the complexity of the domestic program, especially to issues of sexuality and privacy, raising questions about how a glass-walled, modern building can be a usable home and not simply an architectural object in an ideal landscape. The dialogue between the Farnsworth House and the Glass House is especially resonant because of the way in which Johnson framed his architectural argument, quoting Mies directly and incorporating elements of vernacular architecture and popular culture in subtle yet significant ways.

morphology of an organism or disease. Having found a site by the Fox River some fifty miles west of the city, she began leafing through books and bulletins on modern architecture that she discovered on the "shelves of bookstores and the coffee tables of [her] friends." She marveled that she:

> had been so slow to take an interest in architectural forms and purposes. The interest once found, the erection of even a small house in an out-of-the-way spot began to seem an action calling for a certain sense of responsibility. As in every other situation, there must be a really fine solution for an inexpensive weekend retreat for a single person of my tastes and pre-occupations and, conversely, it would be unbearably stupid to "put up" some contractor's cottage which could only ruin the site and remain as a token of empirical mediocrity.[14]

Two key themes circulate throughout Farnsworth's narrative: uncertainty about the contradiction between family life and singleness, and concern with cultural values, particularly the choice between taste and "mediocrity." These issues would resurface throughout the project, structuring Farnsworth's experience as she was to represent it in interviews and in her writings, and shaping critical reaction in the professional and the popular press. Because they also loomed large on the broader American scene, fueled by the growth of suburban consumer culture and contact with European art and architecture, the Farnsworth House would become an emotional *cause célèbre* invested with meaning that went far beyond matters of architectural design. Although the principal players in this drama—Ludwig Mies van der Rohe, Edith Farnsworth, and the weekend house in Plano, Illinois—were in every respect atypical of the categories they were supposed to represent, they became the focus of an intense debate, hashed out in newspapers and magazines, about American domesticity, sexuality, and the politics of modern architecture.

Long before she met Mies, Farnsworth had revealed an interest in the arts and an affinity for European culture. Born in 1903, she attended classes in English literature and composition at the University of Chicago in the early 1920s, but she focused her attention on the violin and traveled to Rome for further study.[15] In 1927 Farnsworth returned to America, although she made numerous trips to Europe until the outbreak of the war. She took her medical degree at Northwestern University in 1939 and built a successful practice in Chicago. Her interest in architecture came relatively late, given her broad travel experience, but once awakened, it developed quickly. Returning from that first evening with Mies at the home of her friends, Farnsworth consulted her books and found illustrations of the Barcelona Pavilion and Tugendhat House. Her perception of his work was astute: "I searched the sundry texts which lay about the apartment, and saw in them an architect whose austerity had kept him from popularity and whose manner was determined by his insight."[16] Although these texts (which probably included some of the publications of The Museum of Modern Art) said very little about the work aside from commenting on the unusually luxurious materials, Farnsworth recognized in Mies's most important European projects both his minimalism and his single-mindedness in exploring the discipline of architectural design. Farnsworth, like everyone else, seems to have been unclear about what his "insight" may have been—the characteristically laconic Mies said little about it—but she was intrigued by what she read and heard. She was also pleased with Mies's enthusiasm for her project.

The visit to the site in Plano, which Mies agreed was beautiful, was the first of many "Sunday excursions" they would take over the course of the next two years; sometimes the two were accompanied by "the boys" from Mies's office or by others. Mies and Farnsworth also began to socialize together in the city, and she frequently stopped by the office and even cooked dinners for the young associates in the practice. For Farnsworth the office became "a club-room, a sanctuary and a kibbutz."[17]

Although it was widely assumed that the two were romantically involved, there is nothing in Farnsworth's memoirs to support that contention. Throughout her life she developed strong attachments to the powerful men she admired—to her teachers and supervisors at the hospital, to Mies himself, and, late in her life, to the poet Eugenio Montale, whose work she translated—but her closest relationships seem to have been with women.[18] Nevertheless, it is clear that for Farnsworth, a headstrong, proud, and rather snobbish person, the friendship with Mies represented a profound emotional and intellectual connection. She immersed herself in Mies's world, struggling through the writings of philosophers who were important to him. She read the work of the Catholic theologian Romano Guardini in order, as she put it, to "lend [her] self to the concept of liturgy," a subject of concern to Mies as it affected architecture. In her enthusiasm, she recalled, she would read "anything which might enrich [her] own awareness, presumably by showing [her] how Mies had been enriched."[19]

Thus Farnsworth became a "disciple," and when, in 1947, the model of her house was exhibited at The Museum of Modern Art, she felt proud of the project and of her role in it: "It was the pivotal point of the exhibit, and I was happy as I boarded the train back to Chicago, reflecting that our project might well become the prototype of new and important elements of American architecture."[20] Although she was no doubt unaware of it, Farnsworth had by this point made a critical transition from client to patron in the minds of her architect and his supporters, unconsciously blurring the boundaries between her own self-interest in the house and her enthusiasm for the larger intellectual and artistic implications of the project. At the same time that Farnsworth was allowing an unusually long time to elapse in the design development phase and was taking part in the emotional life of the office, she was permitting financial, programmatic, and scheduling questions to slide—a dangerous condition in any architectural project but one that was particularly grievous for a client of Mies, for whom theoretical and formal considerations always came before practical ones. Moreover, Farnsworth seemed to have trusted what she saw in presentations like the model for her house—which was at best a sketch of the overall form and not only showed the glass walls as opaque, but gave no indication at all of how the interior would be configured—and never insisted on an explanation of the details. Her failure to understand fully how the plans and models might translate into built form and space would come back to haunt her.

The house as built, with its open plan, glass walls, and freestanding partitions, was as pure an exercise in architectural minimalism as Mies could have hoped for; he would later cite the fact that it was intended for a single person as a significant opportunity because programmatic demands intruded so little on his thinking.[21] As Fritz Neumeyer has shown, Mies's work was shaped by philosophical principles, in particular a search for architectural order and truth based on a rational approach to design. His goal was to develop a language of form that reflected universal, rather than particular, aspects of human activity and concern.[22] Principles of design and form, rather than programmatic or even typological concerns, always came first. Thus, while Farnsworth may have been, for Mies, an entertaining companion and a committed partisan, as a client she represented a means to an architectural end. Just as the Barcelona Pavilion, designed for no other function than to provide the king and queen of Spain with a place in which to sign a guestbook, receive visitors, and drink champagne, was the perfect vehicle for Mies's thinking in 1929, so the Farnsworth House was to be a pure expression of architectural ideas developed in his later career.

In his inaugural speech as director of the Department of Architecture at Armour Institute on November 20, 1938, Mies made his views on architecture clear in his typically terse, aphoristic manner:

> The long path from material through purpose to creative work had only a single goal: to create order out of the godforsaken confusion of our time. But we want an order that gives to each thing its proper place, and we want to give each thing what is suitable to its nature. We would do this so perfectly that the world of our creations will blossom from within. More we do not want; more we cannot do. Nothing can unlock the aim and meaning of our work better than the profound words of St. Augustine: "Beauty is the radiance of truth."[23]

Beauty was produced by analyzing and recapitulating the structure of the natural order. At the riverbank site in Plano, the immediacy of nature would permit an unprecedented closeness with the work of architecture. Mies was quite clear about this. Farnsworth recalled that on one occasion, as the two of them stood by the Fox River on one of their Sunday visits, she asked what sort of materials he was thinking of using for her house. He replied that he would not approach the problem in that way:

> I would think that here where everything is beautiful, and privacy is no issue, it would be a pity to erect an opaque wall between the outside and the inside. So I think we should build the house of steel and glass; in that way we'll let the outside in. If we were building in the city or in the suburbs, on the other hand, I would make it opaque from outside and bring in the light through a garden-courtyard in the middle.[24]

This statement, with its emphasis on the view of natural beauty from inside the house, reveals an approach that was new to Mies and peculiar to his work in America. As in the project for the Resor House (1938), in Jackson Hole, Wyoming, which Mies represented with a photomontage showing a view of the Rocky Mountains through the living room windows, Mies's thinking for the Farnsworth House rested on a concept of uninhabited open landscape; the issue of privacy, and the possibility of being seen from outside, were not considered as problems. In European projects of the late 1920s and 1930s, by contrast, Mies explored the relationship between the glass curtain wall and the courtyard plan, most significantly in the Nolde House (1929), the house at the Berlin Building Exposition (1931), the Gericke House (1932), and the Hubbe House (1935).[25] Mies's approach to the Hubbe House is particularly revealing since it was to be occupied by a single woman. His concern for the client's privacy in the Hubbe House offers a striking contrast with his attitude toward the Farnsworth project: "Although living alone in the house [the client] wanted to cultivate a relaxed social life and hospitality. This also is reflected by the interior arrangement. Here also, the required privacy combined with the freedom of open room forms."[26]

The Farnsworth House represented a radical departure from this view of the domestic environment. Concerns about privacy, or about sexuality and social life, were repressed; for Mies, the house was a place for contemplation, an ordered space free of distractions. Speaking to an interviewer in 1959, he said that he felt the house had been misunderstood: "I was in the house from morning to evening. I did not know how colourful nature really was. But you have to be careful inside to use neutral colours, because you have the colours outside. These absolutely change and I would say it is beautiful."[27] In conversation with Christian Norberg-Schulz in 1958 Mies extended his argument further:

> Nature, too, shall have its own life. We must beware not to disrupt it with the color of our houses and interior fittings. Yet we should attempt to bring nature, houses and human beings together into a higher unity. If you view nature through the glass walls of the Farnsworth House, it gains a more profound significance than if viewed from outside. This way more is said about nature—it becomes a part of the larger whole.[28]

By the late 1940s Mies believed in his architecture's ability not only to transcend nature but also to provide a framework for interpretation, a screen through which to look and understand. If Edith Farnsworth agreed in principle—or hoped she did, in the early days—it is clear that for her a great deal was lost in the translation from the model to the house in which she was supposed to live.

Relations between Mies and Farnsworth had begun to cool by the time construction was started in the summer of 1949: the two socialized together less, and Edith spent less time at the office. The reasons for this change remain unclear, but the situation deteriorated further as problems with the building became evident. When Farnsworth moved in, in December 1950, the roof leaked badly and the heating produced a film that collected on the inside of the windows. A local plumber, seeing that the systems were all gathered together in one inaccessible stack, suggested the house be named "My Mies-conception." The electrician advised that the wiring be completely redone. Nevertheless, according to Mies's office notes, the two were "still on good terms in February 1951."[29]

The final rupture was precipitated by disagreements over money.[30] With costs mounting to almost twice the original estimate of $40,000 (already a high figure considering that a house in a suburban development such as Levittown could be bought in 1950 for less than one quarter of that price) and under pressure from family and friends, Farnsworth began to voice some of her concerns about the unconventional design and construction methods used in her house. Mies reportedly told her "to stick to her nephritis."[31] To add insult to injury, he also seems to have decided at this point to charge a fee for his services, something that Farnsworth claimed had never been discussed; this demand was especially galling as Farnsworth had acted as his physician without fee.[32]

Having spent nearly $74,000, Farnsworth refused to pay any more bills or to take delivery of the furniture, designed by Mies, that he had intended to place in the house. By the spring of 1951 she and Mies had stopped speaking altogether. Fearing that Mies never really wanted "a friend and a collaborator . . . but a dupe and a victim," Farnsworth wrote a letter dated March 1, 1951, in which she informed him that she was turning the matter over to her lawyer. In July, Mies sued for the outstanding balance of $3,673.09. He also claimed he was owed fees of $15,000 and $12,000 for architect's and supervisory services. Farnsworth filed a counterclaim in October 1951, which accused him of fraud, alleging that he had falsely represented himself as "a skilled, proficient and experienced architect" and demanding the return of $33,872.10, the amount she had paid to date above the original estimate.[33] After a trial that dragged on until June 1953, Mies was awarded $14,000; Farnsworth's lawyers appealed, and the matter was finally settled out of court on May 11, 1956, with Farnsworth paying a far smaller sum.

The most important battle, however, was not fought in the courtroom, but in the press. Once the case was brought to the attention of the public, the architect and his costly building were treated with incredulity and derision. Farnsworth too was ridiculed. To her horror, crowds of people came on weekends to look at the house "reputed to be the only one of its kind" but in reality "a one-room, one-story structure with flat roof and glass and steel outer walls."[34] She wrote that she found it "hard to bear the insolence and boorishness of those who invaded the solitude of [her] shore and [her] home . . . flowers brought in to heal the scars of the building were crushed by those boots beneath the noses pressed against the glass."[35]

Disdainful of the public yet furious at Mies, Farnsworth made statements in the press that fueled curiosity and provided antimodernist journalists with the ammunition they needed. In an article by Elizabeth Gordon entitled "The Threat to the Next America," published in *House Beautiful* in April 1953, the author used Farnsworth's case as a starting point for a far-reaching denunciation of modernism:

> I have talked to a highly intelligent, now disillusioned woman who spent more than $70,000 building a 1-room house that is nothing but a glass cage on stilts. . . . There is a well-established movement in modern architecture, decorating and furnishings which is promoting the mystical idea that "less is more" . . . they are promoting unlivability, stripped-down emptiness, lack of storage space and therefore lack of possessions.[36]

Gordon pointed to "a self-chosen elite who are trying to tell us what we should like and how we should live." For her, such architectural totalitarianism and the denial of American consumerism paved the way for fascism; the threat was especially menacing because the architect in question was German:

> For if we can be sold on accepting dictators in matters of taste and how our homes are to be ordered, our minds are certainly well prepared to accept dictators in other departments of life. The undermining of people's confidence is the beginning of the end . . .
>
> So, you see, this well-developed movement has social implications because it affects the heart of our society the home. Beyond the nonsense of trying to make us want to give up

our technical aids and conveniences for what is supposed to be a better and more serene life, there is a social threat of regimentation and total control. [. . .]

The following month another author, Joseph A. Barry, weighed in in the same magazine with his "Report on the American Battle Between Good and Bad Modern Houses." Again Farnsworth played the role of outraged antimodernist. Citing the many rave reviews of the house in such journals as *Architectural Forum* and *House and Garden*, Barry asked, "How about Dr. Farnsworth herself on the subject of her house?":

> "Do I feel implacable calm?" she repeated. "The truth is that in this house with its four walls of glass I feel like a prowling animal, always on the alert. I am always restless. Even in the evening. I feel like a sentinel on guard day and night. I can rarely stretch out and relax . . .
>
> "What else? I don't keep a garbage can under my sink. Do you know why? Because you can see the whole 'kitchen' from the road on the way in here and the can would spoil the appearance of the whole house. So I hide it in the closet farther down from the sink. Mies talks about 'free space': but his space is very fixed. I can't even put a clothes hanger in my house without considering how it affects everything from the outside. Any arrangement of furniture becomes a major problem, because the house is transparent, like an X-ray."[37]

While it is unlikely that these concerns were as grievous as Farnsworth made them sound in the thick of combat with Mies—she did, after all, remain in the house for twenty years—they nonetheless contain critical indices for the meaning of the building in its time and place. Concerns over family, gender, and the control of appearances, particularly in the domestic environment, loom large. Much of what was said against the house and modern architecture generally focuses on its departure from the traditions of the American home, and the vulnerability of its occupant to the prying eyes of others. Farnsworth complained more than once, in her memoirs and to the press, about the problem of being looked at by people both inside and outside her home. In an interview published by *Newsweek* she complained that Mies had wanted to build the interior partitions 5 feet high "for reasons of art and proportion" but that she had objected: "I'm six feet tall," she said, "and I wanted to be able to change my clothes without my head looking like it was wandering over the top of the partition without a body."[38]

The way the house foregrounded Farnsworth's single life and her middle-aged woman's body struck at the heart of American anxiety. As Lynn Spigel has shown, the popularity of television in the U.S. in the 1950s stemmed in part from American preoccupations with privacy, consumerism, and family life. Through its ability to provide a close-up look at other people's lives and homes, television filled a need to know and compare that was fueled by the ever-present lure of the marketplace through advertising. Moreover, television, like the picture window itself, blurred the distinction between public and private realms and problematized the very act of looking, particularly at women.[39] In this cultural climate Farnsworth's insecurities found a wide and attentive audience. [. . .]

Gendered language pervades Farnsworth's own expression of her doubts about the workability of the house. She complained that it had two bathrooms, including one for guests, but no enclosed bedroom. In addition, guests were expected to sleep on the sofa or on a mattress on the floor. While Mies may have seen this arrangement as liberating, for Farnsworth, the real-life occupant of the house, it was embarrassing. She complained that she and her guests would "inhabit a sort of three-dimensional sketch, I in my 'sleeping space' and he in his—unless sheer discomfort and depression should drive us together."[40] In a house for a single woman, such an arrangement in fact represents a repressed (or negated) rather than a freed sexuality, just as the doubling of the bathrooms suggests a desire to modestly hide the female body and its functions. Despite pronouncements about freedom, Mies let it be known that the provision of a "guest bathroom" at the Farnsworth House was meant to keep visitors from "seeing Edith's nightgown on the back of the bath-room door."[41] Ultimately, this piece of women's clothing, this emblem of femaleness, sexuality, and the body, had to be hidden away precisely because it served as a reminder of the very things that Mies (and mainstream culture generally) wanted to deny.

The choice of furnishings also caused friction between architect and client, as it had in other modern projects (notably Le Corbusier's Villa Stein-de Monzie), and here again the conflict raised broader issues concerning domesticity and gender. Mies's theories about interior design are summarized by the poster for the Werkbund exhibition, *The Dwelling*, held in Stuttgart in 1927: in response to the question "How to live?" (Wie wohnen?), a large red "x" has been drawn across an image of a Victorian interior. As a number of writers have suggested, this approach cut to the heart of consumer culture and seriously undermined the means by which bourgeois women constructed identity and memory in the late nineteenth and early twentieth centuries.[42] As a single woman, and as a member of the American upper class, Farnsworth took the threat to the heirlooms and personal mementos in her home very seriously, and she had strong feelings about what her house would say about her. She "could never consent to Mies's furnishing ideas," she wrote in her memoirs. Apparently Mies had planned to put pink suede Barcelona chairs in her house; these, she claimed, would not only be too heavy but would "make the house look like a Helena Rubenstein studio."[43] Besides, she commented, "There is already the local rumor that it's a tuberculosis sanitorium."[44] As snapshots taken in the 1950s show, her own ideas about furnishing the house favored heirloom antique chairs in the dining room and Fu dogs on the terrace, which to her mind suggested continuity and American tradition. [. . .]

It is well worth asking, by way of conclusion, how Farnsworth could possibly have been as offended and shocked by her house as she professed to be, given her frequent visits to Mies's studio and close association with the project over the five or six years of design development. Having seen the model and the plans, Farnsworth ought to have known better. She could see that the house was going to have glass walls, so why was she so surprised when they finally appeared? The obviousness of the question pushes us to look further for answers, for, of course, the essence of Mies's design, and of Farnsworth's objections to it, ultimately lie less with the exterior walls than with the severity of the interior. The latter is something Farnsworth could have known little about from the model, and even if she knew the drawings well, she would hardly have recognized—as, indeed, very few critics have—how the subtleties of interior planning and furnishing profoundly alter the experience of the house. Mies's rigid axial planning, evident in the rectilinear arrangement of the freestanding core and minimalist furniture, is what gives the house its discipline and creates the effect of a domestic theater—in which Farnsworth became an isolated object of scrutiny, a moving figure in a landscape of immovable forms. Unlike Johnson's Glass House, which features clusters of large and small objects throughout the interior and doorways on all four walls, the interior of the Farnsworth House is unrelenting in its ordered geometry—and this was something Farnsworth discovered only through living in the house over time.

In the end Farnsworth gave up the struggle, but she fought a good fight. She spent twenty years in her glass house, furnishing it with her family heirlooms, working to make it a home; in spite of her complaints, she was no doubt aware of the fact that the house was widely recognized as one of the masterpieces of modern architecture, not only in the United States but in the world. She battled Mies in court and in the press, and she managed to win support for her position. Yet having sold the house (to a Mies enthusiast who filled it with furniture designed by the architect) and moved to Italy in the early 1970s, she looked back on the whole experience with bitterness. She had been for too long the focus of other people's curiosity, too long a nonconformist. Now she wanted nothing more than to become invisible: "I would prefer to move as the women do in the Old Quarter of Tripoli, muffled in unbleached homespun so that only a hole is left for them to look out of." Best of all, she said, the world outside would "not even know where the hole was."[45]

PHILIP JOHNSON'S GLASS HOUSE/GUEST HOUSE AS "GAY SPACE"

In a 1993 interview Philip Johnson (then age eighty-seven) was asked to respond to the suggestion that there were some people who had interpreted his Glass House, in New Canaan, Connecticut (Figure 17.2), as "a form of exhibitionism." He replied:

> Yes, needless to say a great number of them have said that. In fact, they went so far as publishing in a magazine, "People that live in glass houses should ball in the basement." But I don't have a basement, so I don't ball in the basement. But much more important than exhibitionism is the interface of architecture and the desire for all kinds of sexual experiments. Whether you want to close yourself in is Freudian in one way, but exposing yourself is Freudian in another way.
>
> As a good Puritan Unitarian, it did not come to mind, but there are other ways of having it come to mind. I mean the idea of a glass house, where somebody just might be looking—naturally, you don't want them to be looking. But what about it? That little edge of danger in being caught. . . .[46]

Although this statement was made more than forty years after the Glass House was completed, it serves as an appropriate starting point for a comparison between Johnson's house in New Canaan and Mies's Farnsworth House, the building that was its acknowledged source and inspiration. Johnson's provocative comments immediately highlight the differences between his and Farnsworth's experiences as occupants of their houses, raising

17.2 Philip Johnson, Glass House, New Canaan, Connecticut, 1949. Note brick Guest House in left foreground (Ezra Stoller © Esto. All rights reserved)

a wide range of questions about how each of the houses responds to issues of gender, household structure, and the roles of the architect and client. Surprisingly, given the enormous fame of both buildings and the volume of critical writing that has been produced—including a 1993 anthology of texts entitled *Philip Johnson: The Glass House*, edited by David Whitney and Jeffrey Kipnis—very little has been said about how each of the two houses confronts and interprets questions of sexuality or about how each represents and accommodates domesticity. Yet it is precisely the way in which each house responds to these concerns that gives it its particular character as a work of domestic architecture.

Perhaps the repression of these questions in the critical and historical literature is not so surprising after all. Farnsworth was a single woman; Philip Johnson is gay. The fact was well known to his friends and, indeed, to the broad circle of colleagues and critics he knew through The Museum of Modern Art, the New York art scene, and the East Coast architecture schools.[47] But, true to the taboos of the time, Johnson's gayness was never openly acknowledged, let alone publicly discussed in connection with his life and work. When he came out in a number of published magazine interviews in the early 1990s, his frankness in disclosing his sexual orientation was considered newsworthy because he was, and is, a powerful public figure and because an admission of this sort is so rare among men or women of his class and status (of whatever age) and still considered compromising.[48] The subject simply wasn't discussed. The notion that sexual orientation might be relevant to Johnson's work—even to a design as intimate as that of his own home—was completely suppressed. Moreover, for most architecture critics, this suppression hardly presented a problem, given the formalist preoccupations that continue to dominate the field. Johnson's New Canaan project, like Mies's house for Edith Farnsworth, was about architectural design. That was all.

In a 1950 article in the *Architectural Review*, Johnson himself established the direction for critical appraisal of his house by offering up, in his most polished art historical manner, a systematic listing of the sources in the history of architecture and design from which he had drawn. He presented a list of twenty-two points, each accompanied by an illustration, which ostensibly provided a guide to the design process and thus to the house's meaning as a work of architecture. The *Review*'s editor added introductory comments that express his gratitude for this process of demystification: "Since the work is proclaimed by the architect as frankly derivative, in this publication of it and the adjacent guest building, Mr. Johnson has taken the unusual and, it should be granted, praiseworthy expedient of revealing the sources of his inspiration. These are presented in consecutive order and precede the illustrations of the two houses."[49] Johnson dutifully ran through the first ten points, which included such exalted and obscure examples as Le Corbusier's Farm Village plan of 1933, Mies's site plan for the Illinois Institute of Technology, the plan and perspective of the Acropolis from Choisy's *L'Histoire de l'art grec* (to illustrate the oblique approach), the front and rear facades of Schinkel's casino near Potsdam (to illustrate siting), Ledoux's design for a spherical guardhouse at Maupertuis (an example of "absolute" form), and Malevich's *Suprematist Element: Circle—1913*, which, Johnson noted, is "obviously the inspiration for the plan of the Glass House."

A photograph of the model of the Farnsworth House from the 1947 Museum of Modern Art exhibition of Mies's work is presented as point number 8. Here Johnson included the following caption:

> The idea of a glass house comes from Mies van der Rohe. Mies has mentioned to me as early as 1945 how easy it would be to build a house entirely of large sheets of glass. I was skeptical at the time, and it was not until I had seen the sketches of the Farnsworth House that I started the three-year work of designing my glass house. My debt is therefore clear, in spite of obvious differences in composition and relation to the ground.[50]

The remaining points present the plans and views of the two houses, with commentary about Johnson's design and Mies's influence on his work.

Despite the apparent usefulness of Johnson's art historical self-analysis, confidence in and gratitude for his so-called revelations seems entirely misplaced. Far from the "praiseworthy expedient" the *Review* editor welcomed, Johnson's description of his sources brings to mind another image: that of the wily fox leading a pack of hounds farther and farther off his scent—and ultimately popping up behind them, laughing with glee at their inability to catch him. Philip Johnson as designer, client, *and* critic all rolled into one? Johnson providing a checklist of sources and monuments with which his work could be decoded? The very notion suggests an element of parody (and self-parody), which published discussions of the Glass House and its sources have entirely missed.

Johnson's quick wit, erudition, and acerbic humor are by now quite legendary; in lectures, panel discussions, and interviews, he is always ready with the *bon mot* that will disconcert friends and foes alike—to the delight of his audiences. Honed by a lifetime of social and institutional maneuvering, his skills as a critic and conversationalist stem from the same fundamental talents that underlie his success as an architect: a gift for understanding and responding to the particular anxieties and preoccupations of a given audience at a specific time, and the quickness to keep one step ahead of them. These are not merely the facile charms of the polished, high-society socialite nor even the blandishments of the successful New York architect; on the contrary, Johnson deploys his wit defensively, and his parodic charm has the effect of disarming, and dazzling, those around him. Such "camp" devices and mannerisms—elegance, distance, outrageousness, trenchant humor, cunning, charm, parody, and above all a certain imperviousness to hurt—though largely unfamiliar to mainstream observers, are the stock in trade of the gay male culture in which he has moved throughout his life. Like other gay men, no matter what class they belonged to, Johnson had to learn to "pass" by wearing a mask in public, and he mastered the art of playing a role, assuming whatever protective coloration was appropriate for the context in which he found himself. He also had to confront the homophobia of straight friends and colleagues, as well as his own self-doubt in an era before gay liberation. One suspects that his camp humor and deftly wielded one-liners were useful weapons in the battle.[51] With consummate skill Johnson brought this bittersweet sensibility to the world of architecture and architectural criticism. Nowhere is this more evident than in his discussion of the Glass House/Guest House complex, where the sophisticated formalist genealogy presented in the *Architectural Review* serves as a mask that conceals as much about the architect's identity as the transparent walls of the house reveal. This is not to say that one or the other was Johnson's "true" self; on the contrary, what the New Canaan project makes clear are the multiplicity of personae Johnson and his gay contemporaries could assume and the overarching sense of humor that colored the entire process.

Johnson's use of irony and self-parody have not gone unnoticed, but this practice has been interpreted (in the few instances where anyone has taken the trouble to analyze it) as an indication of some deeper psychological conflict rather than as a strategy for dealing with homophobia. For example, in his 1978 introduction to *Philip Johnson: Writings*, Peter Eisenman focused on "the metaphor of glass" to analyze Johnson's elusive manner:

> Johnson is at his most opaque when he is speaking of himself—the historian speaking of the architect, the critic reviewing his own book, the architect presenting his house. It is Johnson as a surrogate for Johnson.
>
> One finds the often repeated cadence, particularly in his presentations to university audiences, of Johnson taking off on Johnson, of Johnson being flippant at his own expense. His words, seemingly casually chosen, are diabolical mirrors. Not only do they mask his intentions, they also strip and fracture his audience. They beam yet another multiple inversion. Words and audience: first, belief; second, irony and disbelief. So far this is obvious. It is the third mirror that is crucial. It penetrates beneath his own facade. It is his own attempt to make himself believe what he is saying—to suspend his own disbelief. For in this final turn, words attempt to cover the fragility of Johnson's own uncertainty about himself and his own art. Whether he can deceive us or not, he can never wholly deceive himself. He alone lives locked within the reality of his works—they reveal to him what his words attempt to hide.[52]

This metaphor serves as a foundation for Eisenman's analysis of the Glass House and of the architect himself. "Johnson is at his most transparent—the lucid ideologue", wrote Eisenman, "when speaking of his own house." Oddly enough, he then went on to praise Johnson's *Architectural Review* piece as "modest, straightforward and telling," calling it "the first instance in which Johnson talks seriously, without his usually self-deprecating irony." What follows comes as a surprise. In a passage that has become a much-quoted milestone in the critical response to the house, Eisenman suggested a personal rather than an architectural reading of the imagery of the Glass House. He began by quoting the caption for Johnson's illustration number 17, which showed the "Glass Unit at Night": "The cylinder, made of the same brick as the platform from which it springs, forming the main *motif* of the house was not derived from Mies, but rather from a burnt wooden village I saw once where nothing was left but foundations and chimneys of brick."[53] For Eisenman, this is a reference to Johnson's deep, psychological conflict over his well-known involvement with fascism during World War II: "How are we to interpret such a metaphor? Who builds a house as a metaphoric ruin? Why the burnt-out village as a symbol of one's own house? But further, that Johnson should reveal the source of his imagery seems the most telling of all: the Glass House is Johnson's own monument to the horrors of war. It is at once a ruin and also an ideal model of a more perfect society."[54] Thus Eisenman concluded that the house was an expression of Johnson's "personal atonement and rebirth as an individual."

The burnt-out village, the house as ruin, drained of gay content and severed from the company of its companion Guest House, Johnson's artistic metaphor at the Glass House seems to point to wartime tragedies. Johnson, with the memory of his pro-Nazi activities kept always in the foreground by critics and historians, seems content to accept this view, at least in public.[55] Yet if we restore Johnson's gay identity to the historical picture, and once again open up a space for gay culture within the heterosexist world of architecture, a completely different set of meanings emerges.

New Canaan in the late 1940s wasn't wartime Poland but suburban America, and the most obvious war there was a bitterly fought struggle over who was, and who was not, a "normal" American, a member of a family, living life in the "right" way. Just as Edith Farnsworth confronted these issues, so did Philip Johnson. Americans were increasingly suspicious about the lives of single men and women, and it is clear from popular books and magazine articles about social behavior and family life that the pressure to conform to accepted norms was enormous.[56] Additionally, because of widely publicized negative attention by the federal government and by psychologists, attitudes toward homosexuality had become more fixed and narrow-minded. Efforts to ferret out "sexual perverts" in the U.S. government and in the armed forces (Johnson himself had briefly served as a private in the army, but his superiors seem to have been far more nervous about his right-wing politics than about his homosexuality) put gay men and lesbians at a new disadvantage by creating a climate of anxiety about sexuality, conformity, and loyalty—even among those not directly involved with the military.[57] According to George Chauncey, antigay sentiment—which had been gaining force since the early years of the century, particularly among middle-class men—was closely tied to a "growing concern that the gender arrangements of their culture were in crisis."[58] Changes in the structure of work and family life, the increasing visibility and power of women, and ambiguity about the definition of masculinity in an increasingly "feminized" society all contributed to a marked and growing antipathy toward gay people, which peaked in the 1950s; markers of nonconformity—such as effeminate behavior for men, masculine behavior for women, or anything about the ways in which people lived that looked unconventional—were subject to scrutiny.[59] Questions about surveillance and privacy, and heightened attention to codes of meaning in social behavior and in the material world of American postwar consumer culture helped produce a new awareness of the importance of being, and appearing, "normal."

Gay men and lesbians coped with this repressive situation in a multiplicity of ways. They developed a rich "underground" culture of their own, with a separate system of language, dress, and behavior, which mainstream American society knew little about. For gay men in particular, camp behavior, attitudes, and objects—with a heavy emphasis on irony, exaggeration, artifice, and of course humor—provided a way to live a separate and safe existence within heterosexual culture and afforded much-needed distance and protection from hostility.[60] Moreover, camp was not only theatrical in itself but cast doubt on the whole weighty, self-sustaining system of gender roles, social norms, and conventional appearances. As Jack Babuscio put it in an essay entitled "Camp and Gay Sensibility":

> To appreciate camp in things or persons is to perceive the notion of life-as-theater, being versus role playing, reality and appearance. If "role" is defined as the appropriate behavior associated with a given position in society then gays do not conform to socially expected ways of behaving as men and women. Camp, by focusing on the outward appearances of role, implies that roles and, in particular, sex roles, are superficial—a matter of style. Indeed, life itself is role and theater, appearance and personification.[61]

Johnson's Glass House must be understood within the context of this sophisticated manipulation of culture and language. The house appeared to be a fishbowl in which his life was put on display for all to see, but it actually raised more questions than it answered, focusing attention on the very theatricality of its own form and of the life that was lived within its transparent glass walls. Rather than actually enabling outsiders to satisfy their curiosity about what went on inside (as the Farnsworth House did), the Glass House screened, distorted, and overtly denied visual access through the landscaping of the hilly site and by a series of architectural devices, especially the long, tree-lined driveway that leads to the house from the main road and entrance gate. This handling contributed to the irony of transparency and to a more acute representation of the double-sided nature of domestic life, particularly for gay men who were compelled to hide their private lives from outsiders.

Paired with the solid block of the Guest House, which faces it, the Glass House becomes more meaningful. Linked by a paved pathway, which forms a diagonal axis between the two rectangles, the open and closed spaces of the two houses become an essay on the overt and hidden sides of domestic life. The Guest House appears to be a windowless bunker, a defensible space of intimacy as well as a "closet" containing the unseen apparel of a gay man's life. Like the nondescript gay bars of the period, it turns its back on its surroundings, "passing" behind its blank walls in a way that is diametrically opposed to the celebratory transparency of the Glass House.

For Johnson, who unlike Farnsworth had a sophisticated grasp of architectural language, there was no question that each element in the design had a carefully constructed meaning. Thus, the cylindrical brick chimney at the core of the Glass House makes an obvious and clearly ironic reference to the architecture of the traditional American family home and to the sentimentalized view of domesticity that had gained widespread currency since the late nineteenth century. Rather than invoke the image of wartime Poland, this freestanding chimney seems to refer to the tragedies of the domestic battlefield inhabited by the American family of the late 1940s, and to Johnson's outsider's view of that way of life. The fact that the house was a comfortable weekend retreat where Johnson entertained gay friends from New York at elegant cocktail parties and dinners only served to reinforce this sense of remove.[62] Moreover, with his deep understanding of the work of Frank Lloyd Wright—in a 1949 article entitled "The Frontiersman," Johnson called him "the greatest living architect"—Johnson produced a highly pictorial, American commentary on family and tradition, hearth and shelter that is about as far from Mies's world (and Wright's) as one can imagine.[63] While some people accused Johnson of "exhibitionism" because they felt that what they were seeing through the glass walls of the house was private life, it is quite clear that their inquiring looks were met instead with a theatrical parody of the very concepts of privacy and normalcy.

Further, by pairing the Glass House with the virtually windowless Guest House (described by Arthur Drexler in an early review of the house—in an unconsciously apt phrase—as the "neighboring block of closet-like rooms"[64]), Johnson acknowledged not only his own need for privacy but also the impossibility of the Glass House's serving as a family home. The brick Guest House represented an unequivocal drawing of the curtain and an emphatic rejection of all those prying eyes that had suddenly become so ubiquitous in American society.

HOUSE-BODY/HOME-BODY

From here it is a long way back to the Farnsworth House. Even the most cursory glance at the plans of the two glass-walled houses immediately reveals how different they really are. The Farnsworth House, a glass box on stilts, is suspended above the ground, cut off from its surroundings and yet completely permeable to the gaze of outsiders. The service core has the effect of constricting and focusing the life of the occupant. The fireplace, kitchen, and bathrooms become signs for the most basic functions within the home, but there are no "signposts" for social spaces, beyond the furniture groupings, to guide movement from one moment or activity to the next. The house thus reads more like a diagram of life-sustaining bodily activities than as a social or relational environment. [. . .]

Johnson's approach, on the other hand, is metaphoric, discursive, and picturesque. Changing views of the architectural "events" that form the domestic landscape—the cylindrical chimney/bathroom, the bedroom storage partition, the kitchen bar, the luxurious, white living room rug with its grouping of chairs, chaise longue, and table—encourage movement through the space. The surfaces are covered with carefully chosen objects of the sort that Mies would never have tolerated, such as flowers, an ashtray, and a small table sculpture by Johnson's friend Mary Callery; these items also function as episodes in an unfolding story. The low parapet, a sort of wainscot or chair rail of steel that encircles the house, not only establishes a human scale but serves as a reminder of the traditional New England vernacular. Doors on each of the four sides of the house help define interior "rooms" by providing access to outdoor spaces and changing vistas. As Kenneth Frampton noted in a 1978 article, "The Glass House Revisited," where Mies is "always tectonic, Johnson is invariably scenographic."[65] Compared to Mies's unrelenting discipline, the Glass House is almost frivolous. In effect, the architecture begins to form a narrative on the subject of domesticity as interpreted by Johnson: elegant, precise, social, hospitable.

Johnson's Glass House was meant to be part of a complex of buildings that offered a choice of environments to Johnson and his many visitors. Unlike the Farnsworth House, in which the experience of seeing and concerns about domestic privacy were never resolved, Johnson's Glass House/Guest House accommodates both. Frampton described this double function:

> The conceptual conflict between the belvedere and the court house was to be finally resolved by treating the whole bluff as a court house on a mini-acropolis, in which the trees surrounding the house serve as the perceptual limits of the domain. These limits are unambiguously established at night by floodlit trees, while during the day the domain is determined by the extent of the manicured lawn, the tapis vert upon which the open and closed boxes are nothing but revealed chambers within a much larger conceptual but "invisible" domain of domesticity.[66]

Each of the "chambers" in Johnson's domain served a different aspect of his life: the Glass House represented the public side of that life, the Guest House the hidden, private side.[67] Just as the processional route through the entire complex is carefully choreographed, so too are the interiors of both the Glass House and Guest House. The Guest House was originally quite simple, with two identical bedrooms flanking a sitting room; with its 1953 remodeling as a luxurious and seductive pleasure palace, an exotic room within a room defined by tall, spindly arches and pink Fortuny fabric wall-coverings, it became a virtual celebration of queenly camp, about as close as any modern architect could come to Las Vegas-style, floor-show drag (Figure 17.3). Johnson himself pointed to John Soane as a source of his use of stepped arches and indirect lighting, but it seems evident that what is being suggested here has more to do with a camp reading of popular culture than with historical precedent.[68] That this decorative, arcuated mode within Johnson's oeuvre is sometimes referred to as "ballerina classicism" only serves to confirm the point. Unlike Mies, Johnson recognized that, for Americans at least, Architecture with a capital "A" would never triumph over individualism, nor would it have absolute authority to dictate the rhythms and choices of daily life.

Johnson was clear about the fact that his New Canaan complex was a highly personal essay about domesticity and architecture and not a realistic solution to the

17.3 Philip Johnson, Guest House, bedroom, New Canaan, Connecticut, 1953 (Ezra Stoller © Esto. All rights reserved)

problem of the modern American family home. Speaking of his Wiley House, also in New Canaan (1953), a glass box set atop a low, stone base, Johnson commented that it was:

> one more attempt to reconcile the (perhaps) irreconcilable. Modern architectural purity and the requirements of living American families. Why can't people learn to live in the window-less spheres of Ledoux or the pure glass prisms of Mies van der Rohe? No, they need a place for Junior to practice the piano while Mother plays bridge with her neighbors. . . . The Wiley House "solution" of putting private functions below . . . gives the architect great freedom. The client can design downstairs as he pleases. . . . The architect can design the pavilion above.[69]

While Johnson's Glass House was, in a sense, both a negation of and a memorial to the middle-class family home in which "Mother" and "Junior" go about their daily rounds, the Guest House was a celebration of the messy "private functions" of the domestic realm. By exaggerating the feminine, the sensual, the secret, and the decorative sides of architecture in the Guest House, Johnson not only created a foil to the International Style Glass House but also offered a further parody of the rigid sex roles so beloved by middle-class America. The Guest House, as remodeled in 1953, smacked of exactly the sort of vulgar, ultrafeminine salon decor that Farnsworth referred to when she made her comment about how Mies's pink Barcelona chairs reminded her of a Helena Rubenstein studio. Johnson and his gay friends recognized the Guest House as a camp stage set, remodeled, according to Johnson, because he "wanted to play."[70] While the architect in him may have designed the glass pavilion, it was the client (indeed, the gay client) who recognized and accommodated the program in the brick bunker.

Ultimately this is what distinguishes Johnson's New Canaan complex from Mies's Farnsworth House: the profound understanding of the fact that while the architect of a house can remain fully clothed at all times, the client must ultimately strip naked if the house is to become a home. Thanks to Johnson's gay sensibility, he also recognized that how, where, and when we dress and undress is as critical to architecture as the form of the buildings we inhabit. This knowledge may not make the house a better work of architecture as Mies or other professionals understood it, but it certainly made for a more successful project from the client's point of view. The Glass House/Guest House complex thus serves not only as a self-portrait of the architect and as a statement about the successes and failures of architecture, but also as a home for the client who had to live there—and happily continues to do so to this day.

Notes

1   Dirk Lohan, *Mies van der Rohe: Farnsworth House, Plano, Illinois, 1945–50* (Tokyo: Global Architecture, 1976), 4.
2   Edith Farnsworth, "Memoirs," unpublished ms. in three notebooks, Farnsworth Collection, Newberry Library, Chicago, ch. 11, unpag.
3   For an overview of Mies's career, see Franz Schulze, *Mies van der Rohe: A Critical Biography* (Chicago: University of Chicago Press, 1985), esp. chs. 4–6.
4   Farnsworth recalled, for example, that Mies "never showed [her] the trivial courtesies or the greater ones." He never called a taxi for an "unescorted female visitor" but left her to "scurry through the dark streets however she saw fit." Farnsworth, "Memoirs," ch. 11.
5   Terence Riley, *The International Style: Exhibition 15 and the Museum of Modern Art* (New York: Rizzoli, 1992), 21–23.
6   Farnsworth, "Memoirs," ch. 3.
7   Ibid., ch. 11.
8   The suggestion in Schulze, *Mies*, 252, that Farnsworth chose Mies from a list of architects supplied by The Museum of Modern Art is based on the transcript of a June 1, 1973, interview with Myron Goldsmith, the project architect for the Farnsworth House, but it is contradicted by Farnsworth's own recollections.
9   Farnsworth, "Memoirs," ch. 11.
10 Gwendolyn Wright, *Building the Dream: A Social History of Housing in America* (Cambridge, Mass.: MIT Press, 1981), ch. 13.
11 Clifford E. Clark, Jr., *The American Family Home, 1800–1960* (Chapel Hill: University of North Carolina Press, 1986), ch. 7.
12 Gerald Gurin *et al.*, *Americans View Their Mental Health* (New York: Basic Books, 1960), esp. 117. The survey also found that single women were happier but worried more than single men, and that they "experienced an approaching nervous breakdown less often than other women"; 233–35. See also Wini Breines, *Young, White and Miserable: Growing up Female in the Fifties* (Boston: Beacon Press, 1992); Elaine Tyler May, *Homeward Bound: American Families in the Cold War Era* (New York: Basic Books, 1988); and Rochelle Gatlin, *American Women Since 1945* (Jackson: University Press of Mississippi, 1987). Farnsworth's nephew, Fairbank Carpenter, remembers her "regaling the family with tales" at holiday dinners: "She was a spellbinding story teller and totally wrapped up in her own experiences. No one minded her

selfishness as she was so entertaining." (Fairbank Carpenter, letter to Alice Friedman, October 22, 1991).

13 See Wini Breines, "Alone in the 1950s: Anne Parsons and the Feminine Mystique," *Theory and Society* 15 (1986): 805–43.

14 Farnsworth, "Memoirs," ch. 11.

15 Ibid., ch. 3.

16 Ibid.

17 Edward A. Duckett and Joseph Y. Fujikawa, *Impressions of Mies: An Interview on Mies van der Rohe* (Chicago: [no publisher], 1988), 26. See also Farnsworth, "Memoirs," ch. 12.

18 See Eugenio Montale, *Provisional Conclusions*, trans. Edith Farnsworth (Chicago: H. Regnery Co., 1970). Farnsworth's early friendships with women are described in "Memoirs," ch. 4.

19 Farnsworth, "Memoirs," ch. 11.

20 Ibid.

21 "Interview with Ludwig Mies van der Rohe," *The Listener* (October 15, 1959): 620–22 (transcript of BBC interview, Ludwig Mies van der Rohe file, Library of Congress, Washington, D.C.).

22 Fritz Neumeyer, *The Artless Word: Mies van der Rohe on the Building Art*, trans. Mark Jarzombek (Cambridge, Mass.: MIT Press, 1991), esp. part 5.

23 Ibid., 317.

24 Farnsworth, "Memoirs," ch. 11.

25 See Wolf Tegethoff, *Mies van der Rohe: The Villas and Country Houses*, trans. Russell M. Stockman (Cambridge, Mass.: MIT Press, 1985), 99–104, 110–19, 121–22 (projects 12, 14, 15, 17).

26 Ludwig Mies van der Rohe, "Haus. H., Magdeburg," *Die Schildgenossen* 14, no. 6 (1935): 514–15; reprinted in English in Neumeyer, *Artless Word*, 314.

27 "Interview with Ludwig Mies van der Rohe," *The Listener*, 621.

28 Christian Norberg-Schulz, "A Talk with Mies van der Rohe," *Baukunst und Werkform* 11, no. 11 (1958): 615–18; reprinted in Neumeyer, *Artless Word*, 338–39 (the quotation is on p. 339).

29 Farnsworth folders 11, 28, Mies van der Rohe Archive, The Museum of Modern Art, New York (hereinafter referred to as Mies Archive). See also Farnsworth, "Memoirs," ch. 13.

30 The story is told in detail in Schulze, *Mies*, 252–59.

31 Farnsworth, "Memoirs," ch. 13. For costs of Levitt houses, see Kenneth T. Jackson, *Crabgrass Frontier. The Suburbanization of the United States* (New York: Oxford University Press, 1985), 234–38.

32 "Defendant's Brief," December 1952, Farnsworth folder 31, Mies Archive.

33 For Mies's office notes on the house, assembled in preparation for the trial, see Farnsworth folder 31, Mies Archive. Myron Goldsmith recalled that Mies only decided to charge a fee at the suggestion of his business manager. The case was heard in the Kendall County Circuit Court in Yorkville, Ill.; the information about the suits comes from a court summary of the proceedings. The matter is discussed in Farnsworth, "Memoirs," ch. 13.

34 "Charges Famed Architect with Fraud, Deceit," *Chicago Daily Tribune* (October 30, 1951), Farnsworth clipping file, Mies Archive.

35 Farnsworth, "Memoirs," ch. 13.

36 Elizabeth Gordon, "The Threat to the Next America," *House Beautiful* 95 (April 1953): 250.

37 Joseph A. Barry, "Report on the American Battle Between Good and Bad Modern Houses," *House Beautiful* 95 (May 1953): 270.

38 "Glass House Stones," *Newsweek* (June 8, 1953): 90.

39 Lynn Spigel, *Make Room for TV: Television and the Family Ideal in Postwar America* (Chicago: University of Chicago Press, 1992), esp. chs. 3, 4.

40 Farnsworth, "Memoirs," ch. 12.

41 As reported by Myron Goldsmith in conversation with Alice Friedman, April 1988.

42 See Paulette Singley, "Living in a Glass Prism: The Female Figure in Mies van der Rohe's Domestic Architecture," *Critical Matrix* 6, no. 2 (1992): 47–76. See also Miriam Gusevich,

"Decoration and Decorum: Adolf Loos's Critique of Kitsch," *New German Critique* 43 (Winter 1988): 97–123, and Remy G. Saisselin, *The Bourgeois and the Bibelot* (New Brunswick, N.J.: Rutgers University Press, 1988).

43 Farnsworth, "Memoirs," ch. 13.

44 Ibid.

45 Farnsworth, "Memoirs," ch. 14.

46 Hilary Lewis and John O'Connor, *Philip Johnson: The Architect in His Own Words* (New York: Rizzoli, 1994), 49.

47 For Johnson's biography, see Franz Schulze, *Philip Johnson: Life and Work* (New York: Knopf, 1994).

48 See Kurt Andersen, "Philip the Great," *Vanity Fair* (June 1993): 130–38, 151–57; earlier articles contain indirect references to Johnson's homosexuality in their titles, such as John Brodie, "Master Philip and the Boys," *Spy* (May 1991): 50–58, and Denise Scott Brown, "High Boy: The Making of an Eclectic," *The Saturday Review* (March 17, 1979): 54–58.

49 *Architectural Review* 108 (September 1950): 152–59; reprinted in *Philip Johnson: Writings*, foreword by Vincent Scully, introduction by Peter Eisenman, commentary by Robert A. M. Stern (New York: Oxford University Press, 1979), 212–25, and in David Whitney and Jeffrey Kipnis, eds., *Philip Johnson: The Glass House* (New York: Pantheon, 1993), 9.

50 Whitney and Kipnis, *Philip Johnson: The Glass House*, 11.

51 For Johnson's early struggles with homophobia, see Schulze, *Johnson*, 35–36.

52 Scully *et al.*, *Philip Johnson: Writings*, 20.

53 Ibid., 22–23.

54 Ibid., 23.

55 See, for example, Johnson's statement in a 1993 interview: "I regret having said that. Because the burned-out village was in World War II, and I was on the wrong side. So we don't talk about that anymore. My enemies do, of course. That's a part of my life I'd rather forget." Lewis and O'Connor, *Philip Johnson: The Architect in His Own Words*, 31.

56 Cf. fn. 12.

57 See John D'Emilio, *Sexual Politics, Sexual Communities. The Making of a Homosexual Minority in the United States, 1940–1970* (Chicago: University of Chicago Press, 1983), 40–49; for Johnson's military service, see Schulze, *Johnson*, 160–68.

58 George Chauncey, *Gay New York: Gender, Urban Culture and the Making of the Gay Male World, 1890–1940* (New York: Basic Books, 1994), 111.

59 Ibid., esp. 111–27.

60 For a full discussion of camp, see David Bergman, ed., *Camp Grounds: Style and Homosexuality* (Amherst: University of Massachusetts Press, 1993). See also Chauncey, *Gay New York*, esp. 286–91.

61 Jack Babuscio, "Camp and Gay Sensibility," in Bergman, *Camp Grounds*, 19–38. See also Judith Butler, *Gender Trouble: Feminism and the Subversion of Identity* (New York: Routledge, 1990).

62 Schulze, *Johnson*, 217.

63 Philip Johnson, "The Frontiersman," *Architectural Review* 106 (August 1949): 105–10; reprinted in Scully *et al.*, *Philip Johnson: Writings*, 188.

64 Arthur Drexler, "Architecture Opaque and Transparent," *Interiors and Industrial Design* 109 (October 1949): 90–101; reprinted in Whitney and Kipnis, *Philip Johnson: The Glass House*, 3–7 (the quotation is on p. 6).

65 Kenneth Frampton, "The Glass House Revisited," *Catalogue* 9 (September–October 1978), 38–59; reprinted in Whitney and Kipnis, *Philip Johnson: The Glass House*, 92–105; the quotation appears on p. 94.

66 Frampton, "The Glass House Revisited," quoted in Whitney and Kipnis, *Philip Johnson: The Glass House*, 99.

67 As time went on, Johnson added other places to the complex: he designed the Pavilion on the lake (1962), intended as a "playhouse," complete with the thin "Syrian" arches employed in the

Guest House but constructed at a reduced scale; the Painting Gallery (1965); the Sculpture Gallery (1970); the Library/Study, the "Gehry Ghost House," and the Lincoln Kirstein Tower (all completed in 1985); and he acquired two older houses at the edges of the property. See Schulze, *Johnson*, 254–55, 287–93, 386, 391.

68   Ibid., 237–38.

69   Ibid., 214.

70   Lewis and O'Connor, *Philip Johnson: The Architect in His Own Words*, 36.

Chapter 18

Joan Ockman

Mirror images

Technology, consumption, and the representation of gender
in American architecture since World War II

Two well-known images might be said to define American architecture in the first decades
after World War II. One is Lever House, an early icon of International Style modernism,
public face of American corporate capitalism (Figure 18.1). The other is Levittown,
embodiment of suburban single-family domesticity, a vision of private life socially traditional and aesthetically conservative (Figure 18.2). How is this apparent schism in the built
representation of postwar America to be explained? Why was a modernist aesthetic
acceptable in the public realm but not in the private one? What is the relationship between
this—literally and figuratively—high and low architecture? In what follows I shall attempt
to answer these questions by postulating the existence of a kind of unstated "bargain" or
social arrangement facilitated by basic assumptions about gender roles. From this analysis
I shall then consider some significant shifts that have taken place more recently in the
context of postmodernism.

It is necessary to begin by redescribing these two emblematic images in terms of the
dominant ideologies they represented. The International Style as developed in the corporate and administrative framework of postwar America explicitly embodied the values of
technocracy—the ethos of rationalism, bureaucracy, and technoscientific progress on
which both big business and government were predicated. The exposed high-rise structural frame infilled with the repetitive modulations of an abstract curtain wall reflected the
expansionist ambitions and laconic demeanor of American capitalism in an age of cold-
war geopolitics.

Ironically, this "strong silent type" came to represent the "new monumentality" that
Sigfried Giedion had called for during the war years, although not, to be sure, in the civic
sense he had envisioned. Its cold, hard, unornamental, technical image supplied the
American government with what it wanted out of its professional elites during the cold-
war period. This was, as historian Godfrey Hodgson has put it, "a maximum of technical
ingenuity with a minimum of dissent."[1]

Having its major origin in the interwar modern movement in Europe, the postwar
International Style was an outcome of the doctrine codified by Henry-Russell Hitchcock
and Philip Johnson in their 1932 show at the Museum of Modern Art and of the teachings
disseminated by the European emigrés who began at this time to head America's most prestigious schools of architecture. But American postwar modernism also had an indigenous
source in the formidable imagery of native American technology: in engineering achievements like the Ford plant at River Rouge, the TVA dam, and, most recently, the arsenal of

18.1 Skidmore, Owings & Merrill, Lever House, New York, New York, 1952

military production that had brought the United States and its allies to triumph in the war. As a recent exhibition at the National Building Museum in Washington illustrated,[2] the ascendancy of the postwar International Style coincided with the emergence of the American military-industrial complex. American architectural firms, led by offices like Skidmore, Owings & Merrill, designers of Lever House, reproduced these values in their own technically sophisticated and increasingly bureaucratic professional structures. SOM, still a moderate-sized firm at the beginning of the 1940s, got its major breakthrough during the war when it received a $60 million commission from the U.S. government to design a new town for fifty thousand people at Site X of the Manhattan Project, a location near Knoxville, Tennessee, where the atomic bomb was secretly being developed.

It is apparent that the imagery of technological power, highly rationalized and disciplined production, and wealth projected by this postwar architecture was a product of the male-dominated hierarchy whose expression it was and whose values were at stake in it. Geared to optimizing the labor of a new class of capitalist worker whom sociologists

18.2 *Bernard Levey and Family*, Levittown, New York, 1950

would dub "organization man," it reflected a major shift in social orientation. In the earlier phase of modern architecture, the urbanized factory worker had been the protagonist of culture, at least symbolically, and factories and social housing were the inspirational programs. In postwar America, corporate headquarters, embassy buildings, and detached single-family houses became architecture's defining instances, and the man in the gray flannel suit commuting to a wife and children in the suburbs its prototypical occupant. Nor is this characterization belied by the fact that behind the office tower's glass facade, the corporation's CEO furnished his penthouse suite in the style of Louis XIV or the executive dining room like an Edwardian gentleman's club; below, the middle managers, secretaries, and staff worked and lunched in "office landscapes" programmed for maximum functional efficiency. Indeed, the implementation of modernism as the prestige style of corporate capitalism was not a matter of a significant change in taste, as Russell Lynes pointed out in 1949 in his book *The Tastemakers*.[3] Rather, it was a symbolic display of power. The American philosopher George Santayana had observed four decades earlier: "The American Will inhabits the skyscraper; the American Intellect inhabits the colonial mansion. The one is the sphere of the American man; the other, at least predominantly, of the American woman. The one is all aggressive enterprise; the other is all genteel tradition."[4]

In the postwar period this split between the work world and domestic life characterized not only the upper class. For the burgeoning middle class, too, the domestic abode became, if not the place for the ritual enactment of gentility, at least the antithesis to the workaday routine and the repository of bourgeois comfort. The "male" culture of production found its complement in the "female" culture of consumption.

The postwar house thus reflected the other dominant ideology of the postwar period, that of *consumerism*. By the second quarter of this century, mass consumption had become central to the development of American capitalism. Even during the years of World War II, when consumer goods were greatly restricted because of war production needs, the public's appetite for postwar plenitude was whetted by the media and by government-sanctioned advertising (Figure 18.3). Above all, it was feared that the economy, having reached peak productivity during the years of emerging mobilization, would slide back into a depression if conversion from a military to a domestic economy did not occur rapidly. Postwar planners now spoke of "mobilizing for abundance." Crucial to the viability of the economy's domestic sector was the low- and middle-cost housing market. During the war years, job-hungry architects and an eager building industry indulged in wildly optimistic predictions about the postwar housing market. Nor did their optimism prove unfounded. In the unprecedented boom that followed the war, the suburban dream house became a form of compensation for the privations and sacrifices endured during the years of war and economic stagnation, a realization of the material prosperity to which Americans considered themselves at long last entitled. As the postwar office building became a machine for streamlined white-collar production, so the private house became a machine especially for white middle-class consumption.

18.3 Advertisement for United States Steel (from *Architectural Forum*, July 1943)

It was a machine, however, that dissembled its mechanistic nature. If the American public momentarily became intrigued during the war years with Bucky Fuller's Dymaxion Dwelling Machine—whose advantages Fuller had been proselytizing for more than a decade with the question, "Madam, do you know how much your house weighs?"—the sheen of a lightweight metal domicile quickly wore off in comparison with the more rooted-looking Cape Coddage offered by a canny developer like William J. Levitt.

> Home, in the American dream, is a quaint little white cottage, shyly nestled in a grove of old elms or maples, bathed in the perfume of lilacs, and equipped with at least one vine-covered wall. Its steep gabled roof, covered with rough, charmingly weathered shingles, shows a slight sag in the ridge. The eaves come down so low that one can almost touch them. Tiny dormers on one side poke themselves through the old roof and let in light through tiny-paned windows to the upstairs bedrooms. In front of the house there is invariably a picket fence, with day lilies poking their heads between the white palings. Let into the fence, at the end of a flagstone walk bordered with alyssum and verbena, is a swinging gate, where husband and wife embrace tenderly as he dashes for the 8:11 and the workaday world.[5]

This was the nostalgic idyll that George Nelson and Henry Wright set out to dispel in their book of 1945, *Tomorrow's House*, but nothing that they or other modernist proselytizers had to offer seemed able to replace it. Levittown was a margarine substitute, but an appealing one for the thousands of returning GIs and their wives. The fact that like the Dymaxion its Taylorized construction process contradicted its traditionalist image was not a fatal defect for buyers who were, in no small measure, purchasing a life-style, a dream. Moreover, the Levitt was hardly lacking in up-to-dateness; it came equipped with one or more of the latest conveniences, from Bendix washing machines to "built-in" television sets. The idea of the built-in derived from modernist spatial concepts, but Levitt was quick to realize its economic benefit: it qualified equipment to be paid on the mortgage. The buyer was also given, in the later Levitt developments, some limited choice as to plan type, elevation details, and finishes. The marketing strategy of "standardized diversity" catered at least minimally to the deep American desire for individualism.[6] William Levitt appears to have understood the compromise that a large segment of the American public wanted as Fuller and other architects promoting a more radical image of the low-cost house did not. This is not to suggest that Levitt was a populist. He was a businessman. Acknowledging himself that the renderings in his sales brochures could appear deceptive—they portrayed Levittown houses set on spacious, private lawns surrounded by lush foliage—he quipped, "The masses are asses."[7]

But the postwar campaign to redomesticate women after their brief taste of equal employment opportunity in the wartime work force was abetted not only by the tangible amenities of the new suburban dream house but also by its essentialism. Women, voluntarily making room in the job market for the returning veterans, were induced or seduced to return to home and child-rearing through intensive propaganda by government, businessmen, psychologists, religious leaders, and others on behalf of "family values." As one feminist historian has commented, "'Rosie the Riveter' was . . . transformed with dizzying speed from a wartime heroine to a neurotic, castrating victim of penis envy."[8] The mythological imagery of the house as a nest and haven presided over by a nurturing mother figure was fundamental in reestablishing the traditional division of labor in the American family. The new tract divisions served in a literal way to enforce the gulf of space and time between private life and work world. Women's separation increased along the lengthening network of highways; homemaking became increasingly distanced from the making of history.[9]

Nor, to most women at the time, did it seem a bad bargain. After the traumatic dislocations of the war, stability and nest building came as a welcome relief for many. So did economic prosperity, which meant that the domestic abode, for all its cozy image, did not need to have humble aspirations. It could be added to, or if rendered obsolete by the family's changing needs and status, shed for a new and larger home. Planned obsolescence became an important economic strategy after the war; an approach similar to that used for selling automobiles had its application to mass-market housing. Meanwhile, the cornucopia of new domestic goods churned out by a retooled economy was aggressively marketed to the new generation of housewives, the appointed "managers of consumption," as Margaret Mead described them in 1948.[10] While their husbands strove to move upward in the corporate hierarchy, the "wives of management"[11] attended to the parallel task of keeping up with the neighboring Joneses. Wartime savings fueled a postwar spending spree, heavily abetted by advertising. Having from its inception targeted "Mrs. Consumer" as the prime object of its sales pitch, American advertising increased sixfold between 1920 and 1950 and then doubled again between 1951 and 1960.[12] Women who had remained on the home front during the war, encouraged in a time of rationing to be "generals in their own kitchens," now were assured that the newest gadgetry would free them from domestic "drudgery"—an oft-repeated Dickensian word. The myth of the happy housewife—the flawed logic that a streamlined kitchen was sufficient to liberate a woman from a patriarchal society's oppression—was parodied by British Pop artist Eduardo Paolozzi in a 1948 collage entitled *It's a Psychological Fact Pleasure Helps Your Disposition*.

Moreover, now that technology had presumably released women from the burdens of old-fashioned housework, questions remained of how they should spend their new leisure time. In an ironic turn, the fundamental capitalist axiom "time is money" was reformulated for a consumer society. Certainly as far as the advertising industry was concerned, leisure time was time available for consumption, for shopping. In his widely read book *The House and the Art of Its Design*, the architect Robert Woods Kennedy acknowledged, "Our general desire is for women to consume beautifully."[13] During the 1950s the beautiful consumers would play their part. At the beginning of the decade *Fortune* magazine forecast that they would incite $10 billion in spending on home construction and $12 billion on home furnishings.[14] It was Betty Friedan who explosively deconstructed this system ten years later, in 1963, in *The Feminine Mystique*. Stopping short of alleging a conscious conspiracy aimed at women, she wrote, "The perpetuity of housewifery, the growth of the feminine mystique, makes sense (and dollars) when one realizes that women are the chief customers of American business. Somehow, somewhere, someone must have figured out that women will buy more things if they are kept in the underused, nameless-yearning, energy-to-get-rid-of state of being housewives."[15]

It would seem, in short, that the prevailing dichotomy between Lever House and Levittown amounted to a highly efficient, eminently practical, and symbiotic social arrangement. In a society that sought simultaneously to promote maximum productivity and maximum consumption, the public and private spheres had separate but complementary roles to play. Architecture served to reproduce and reinforce this gendered social division, providing an efficacious image for each.

In actuality, of course, the two forms of representation were mirror images of a single system, two sides of the capitalist coin. Both Lever House and Levittown were predicated on highly rationalized and optimized production processes; both were geared to a postwar mass society. Where they differed was in the image they projected, in the one case of elite modernist aesthetics, in the other of midcult taste. Despite his antipathy for the latter, Theodor Adorno acknowledged the fundamental identity of these two antagonistic forms of the contemporary world: "Both [modernism and mass culture] bear the stigmata of capitalism, both contain elements of change. . . . They are torn halves of an integral to freedom to which, however, they do not add up."[16]

Meanwhile, the image of architectural modernism, too, was becoming precisely that—an image. In the context of postwar America, of the cold war and McCarthyism, the social idealism that had animated the vanguard architecture of the 1920s began to appear naive or hollow. The postwar glass-grid skyscraper seemed duplicitous in its reference, its elegant, abstract transparency alluding to the utopian vision of a radiant, egalitarian, dynamically open society, while embodying the reality of panoptic, hierarchical bureaucracy. In an influential article published in 1951 entitled "Origins and Trends in Modern Architecture," the architect Matthew Nowicki characterized American architecture at this date as preoccupied more with structure and form than with function. Instead of following function, suggested Nowicki, form now followed form; moreover, he noted, the new architectural formalism was tending toward the "decoration of structure" (this almost twenty years before Denise Scott Brown and Robert Venturi would coin the concept of the decorated shed). Certainly the buildings produced in these years by young architects like Philip Johnson, Edward Durrell Stone, Minoru Yamasaki, and Paul Rudolph, and even older masters like Gropius and Le Corbusier, not to mention Frank Lloyd Wright, were undermining modernist orthodoxy with eclectic and personal inputs. Nowicki probably had in mind Ludwig Mies van der Rohe's famous details at Illinois Institute of Technology and the Lake Shore Drive apartments, where Mies used steel mullions more for expressive purposes than strictly structural ones, in writing, "The symbolic meaning of a support has also been rediscovered, and a steel column is used frankly as a symbol of structure even when it is not part of the structure itself."[17]

And precisely in this revelation of architecture as a system of arbitrary signs, in the dissociation between image and reality, in the use of design for purposes of "corporate identity" and "marketing strategy," in the recognition that modern architecture was simply another historical style—in all this, the transition from modernity to postmodernity took place. With this, I'd like to extend my argument about the relation between technology, consumption, and gender conceptions to the present period, although my comments here can only be very preliminary.

We have said that the postwar International Style was a symbolic representation of the virility of American technology. Starting in World War II, however, a subtle change began to occur, even if culture was to take a number of years to register it. With the emergence of a so-called postindustrial economy, technological power began to be associated with something besides industrial hardware and large-scale, discrete mechanical objects—besides the rockets, bridges, munitions factories, not to mention grain elevators, airplanes, ocean liners, and plumbing fixtures that had defined modernity earlier. Advanced technology now also came to mean cybernetic processes, software systems, miniaturized electronics, artificial intelligence, telecommunications, and other sophisticated instrumentalities eluding physical form. *The imagination of power* inevitably began to take inspiration from the new logic of global networks, integrated circuits, microchips, smart weapons, virtual fields.[18] The penetration of these often invisible technologies into the unconscious—especially through the impact of advertising and the media on everyday life—served to unleash potent new images and desires. Alison and Peter Smithson wrote in 1956:

> Gropius wrote a book on grain silos,
> Le Corbusier one on aeroplanes,
> And Charlotte Perriand brought a new object to the office
> every morning;
> But today we collect ads.[19]

Architecture would remain no less bound than before to rehearse the technocratic background from which it sprang, but the repository from which it would draw its symbolic content would necessarily change with the new modes of production and reception.

At the same time, consumerism would also undergo a change. If gender stereotypes had previously served to reproduce the binary relations of production and consumption—consumption being marked as female and therefore socially less valuable—then increasingly, after World War II, these relations ceased to be so clear-cut. As Robert Bocock has written,

> The modern period was marked by [a] gender division between mothering and consumption, on the one hand, and production and making war on the other. The post-modern has been, by comparison, a period of peace in Western Europe, North America and Japan. This has allowed a change in gender roles for men. No longer required in large numbers as fighters, men, especially younger men, have become consumers too since the 1950s.[20]

Men, too, now construct their identities in terms of what they consume, from sports and cars to movies, food, and clothing. The sociopolitical emergence of gays within capitalist culture, with their frank patterns of consumption, has further challenged the traditional dichotomy that marks consumption as feminine and production as masculine, just as the new politics of childbearing, child rearing, and healthcare have expanded the concept of production to include women's biological reproduction and the whole hitherto excluded economy of the home. At the same time, the increasing participation of women in every echelon of the conventional work force, the shift of the workplace not only from city to suburbs but into the home itself, and the accelerating computerization of both work and everyday life have effectively blurred the lines between production and consumption, public and private realms, undoing the simple bargain between technocracy and consumerism that obtained in the postwar decades. The old dichotomy between home and history has been superseded by public/private relationships deeply inflected by the new commercially and technologically mediated conditions of contemporary life. As German film theorists Oskar Negt and Alexander Kluge have suggested in their book *The Public Sphere and Experience*, our concept of the public realm has to be rethought today across a broadly inclusive and interconnected horizon of social relations.[21] Going beyond traditional liberal civic models, such a reconceptualization of public space would extend to privately owned spaces of commerce and consumption (including, for example, shopping malls), as well as to those less physical and more ephemeral sites where public opinion and consciousness are formed—television and the movies, the print media, the computer internet.

But if the intrusion of commerce and sophisticated technology into every crevice of daily life can hardly be considered cause for comfort, it is also the case that the built representations of postmodern society are no longer charged so heavily with dichotomous gender stereotypes. Both the "softening" of technology and the universalizing of the consumer have obliged architecture to seek new forms of representation. In this context, the initial phase of postmodernist architecture, characterized by the decorative facade treatments of corporate buildings like Johnson's AT&T and civic ones like Michael Graves's Portland, may be described as "cross-dressing"—scandalous with respect to the "strong silent" typology, but symptomatic of the mixing up of technocratic and consumerist values and gender stereotypes in today's society. A current obsession on the part of many architects with using glass on the facade—no longer as a repetitive infill within a clearly articulated and primary structural frame, but as a screening element veiling the structure, or, as Diana Agrest has suggested in an article entitled "Architecture of Mirror/ Mirror of Architecture," a reflective element dissolving materiality into paradox and disarticulating the conventional relationships between architectural language and image, surface and depth[22]—offers a further ambiguation of the postwar imagistic clarities.

The ideologies of technocracy and consumerism that we have inherited from the period after World War II are no less entrenched in contemporary architecture than they were at the moment when Lever House and Levittown were conceived. The design and practice of architecture continue to be bound up with the representation of power and the marketing of pleasure. I believe, however, that these twin imperatives are now less reinforced by, and reinforcing of, undesirable gender stereotypes. From a feminist perspective, this is something positive.

Notes

1   Godfrey Hodgson, "The Ideology of the Liberal Consensus," in William H. Chafe and Harvard Sitkoff, eds., *A History of Our Time: Readings on Postwar America* (New York: Oxford University Press, 1991), 133.

2   *World War II and the American Dream: How Wartime Building Changed a Nation*, with catalogue edited by Donald Albrecht (Cambridge, Mass.: MIT Press, 1995). See also Elizabeth Mock, ed., *Built in U.S.A.—1932–1944* (New York: Museum of Modern Art, 1944).

3   Russell Lynes, *The Tastemakers* (New York: Harper & Brothers, 1949), 305–9.

4   George Santayana, *Winds of Doctrine: Studies in Contemporary Opinion* (London: J. M. Dent, 1913), 188.

5   George Nelson and Henry Wright, *Tomorrow's House: How to Plan Your Post-War Home Now* (New York: Simon and Schuster, 1945), 4.

6   Stewart Ewen, *All Consuming Images: The Politics of Style in Contemporary Culture* (New York: Basic Books, 1988), 229. The unilevel ranch, almost equally popular at this date, especially in the West, represented a less nostalgic image of modern living; it appealed more for its easy life-style, however, than its aesthetic pretensions.

7   John Liell, "Levittown: A Study in Community Development" (Ph.D. diss., Yale University, 1952), III; cited in Ewen, 227.

8   Karen Anderson, *Wartime Women: Sex Roles, Family Relations, and the Status of Women During World War II* (Westport, Conn.: Greenwood Press, 1981), 176. See also Maureen Honey, *Creating Rosie the Riveter: Class, Gender, and Propaganda During World War II* (Amherst: University of Massachusetts Press, 1984).

9   See Dorothy Dinnerstein, *The Mermaid and the Minotaur: Sexual Arrangements and Human Malaise* (New York: Harper & Row, 1976).

10   Margaret Mead, "The American Family as an Anthropologist Sees It," *American Journal of Sociology* 53 (1948), 454; cited in Robert H. Bremner and Gary W. Reichard, eds., *Reshaping America: Society and Institutions 1945–1960* (Columbus: Ohio State University Press, 1982), 4. It may, of course, be questioned to what extent women actually controlled the purse strings, especially where large purchases were concerned.

11   "The Wives of Management" is the title of a well-known article by William H. Whyte Jr., first published in *Fortune* 44 (October 1951), 68–88, 204–6. Whyte satirically sets out the rules according to which corporate wives should behave.

12   Mary P. Ryan, *Womanhood in America from Colonial Times to the Present* (New York: New Viewpoints, 1975), 260; Douglas T. Miller and Marion Nowak, *The Fifties: The Way We Really Were* (Garden City: Doubleday, 1975), 117.

13   Robert Woods Kennedy, *The House and the Art of Its Design* (New York: Reinhold, 1953), 40.

14   Cited in Ryan, 301.

15   Betty Friedan, *The Feminine Mystique* (1963) (Harmondsworth: Penguin, 1983), 181.

16   Letter from Adorno to Walter Benjamin (1936), cited in Thomas Crow, "Modernism and Mass Culture in the Visual Arts," in Francis Frascina, ed., *Pollock and After: The Critical Debate* (New York: Harper & Row, 1985), 263.

17   Matthew Nowicki, "Origins and Trends in Modern Architecture," *Magazine of Art*, November 1951; republished in Joan Ockman, ed., *Architecture Culture 1943–1968: A Documentary Anthology* (New York: Rizzoli, 1993), 156.

18   On technology as symbolic form in architecture, a classic essay is Alan Colquhoun's "Symbolic and Literal Aspects of Technology" (1962), republished in Colquhoun, *Essays in Architectural Criticism: Modern Architecture and Historical Change* (Cambridge, Mass.: MIT Press, 1981), 26–30.

19   Alison and Peter Smithson, "But Today We Collect Ads," *Ark* 18 (November 1956), republished in David Robbins, ed., *The Independent Group: Postwar Britain and the Aesthetics of Plenty* (Cambridge, Mass.: MIT Press, 1990), 185.

20   Robert Bocock, *Consumption* (London: Routledge, 1993), 96.

21   See Oskar Negt and Alexander Kluge, *The Public Sphere and Experience* (1972), trans. Peter Labanyi, Jamie Daniel, and Assenka Oksiloff (Minneapolis: University of Minnesota Press, 1993).

22   Diana Agrest, "Architecture of Mirror/Mirror of Architecture," in Agrest, *Architecture from Without: Theoretical Framings for a Critical Practice* (New York: Princeton Architectural Press, 1991), 138–55.

Chapter 19

Katharine G. Bristol

The Pruitt-Igoe myth

Few architectural images are more powerful than the spectacle of the Pruitt-Igoe public housing project crashing to the ground (Figure 19.1). Since the trial demolition of three of its buildings in 1972, Pruitt-Igoe has attained an iconic significance by virtue of its continuous use and reuse as a symbol within a series of debates in architecture. In these discussions there is virtual unanimity that the project's demise demonstrated an *architectural* failure. When Charles Jencks announced in 1977 that the demolition of Pruitt-Igoe represented the death of modern architecture, he invoked an interpretation of the project that has today gained widespread acceptance. Anyone remotely familiar with the recent history of American architecture automatically associates Pruitt-Igoe with the failure of High Modernism, and with the inadequacy of efforts to provide livable environments for the poor.

This version of the Pruitt-Igoe story is a myth. At the core of the myth is the idea that architectural design was responsible for the demise of Pruitt-Igoe. In the first section of this essay I debunk the myth by offering a brief history of Pruitt-Igoe from the perspective of its place within a larger history of urban redevelopment and housing policy. This history engages the profoundly embedded economic and political conditions that shaped the construction and management of Pruitt-Igoe. I then consider how the Pruitt-Igoe myth came to be created and disseminated, both by the national press and by architects and architecture critics, and how each successive retelling of the Pruitt-Igoe story has added new dimensions to the myth. I want to focus particular attention on one of the most important aspects of the myth: the alleged connection between the project's failure and the end of modern architecture. In the final section I argue for an interpretation of the Pruitt-Igoe myth as mystification. By placing the responsibility for the failure of public housing on designers, the myth shifts attention from the institutional or structural sources of public housing problems. Simultaneously it legitimates the architecture profession by implying that deeply embedded social problems are caused, and therefore solved, by architectural design.

THE PRUITT-IGOE STORY: PUBLIC HOUSING AND URBAN DEVELOPMENT

Pruitt-Igoe was created under the United States Housing Act of 1949, which made funds directly available to cities for slum clearance, urban redevelopment, and public housing.

19.1 Demolition of the Pruitt-Igoe, 1972

Like many other cities in the postwar era, St. Louis was experiencing a massive shift of its predominantly white middle-class population towards the suburbs. At the same time, central city slums were expanding as poor households moved into units abandoned by those leaving the city.[1] Located in a ring immediately surrounding the central business district, these slums were racially segregated. Blacks occupied the area immediately north of downtown, while whites tended to live to the south. The black ghetto expanded particularly fast with the postwar influx of poor black population from the South. As the growing slums crept closer to the central business district, city officials and the local business community feared the accompanying decline in property values would threaten the economic health of downtown real estate. They responded by developing a comprehensive plan to redevelop the zone immediately surrounding the downtown business core.[2]

Using the urban redevelopment provisions of the 1949 Housing Act, St. Louis' Land Clearance and Redevelopment Authority planned to acquire and clear extensive tracts within the slums and to sell them at reduced cost to private developers. These redevelopment projects were slated to accommodate mainly middle-income housing and commercial development in an effort to lure the middle class back to the central city. At the same time, the St. Louis Housing Authority would clear land for the construction of public housing. These projects were intended to provide large numbers of low-rent units to the poor in order to stem ghetto expansion, and also to accommodate households displaced by redevelopment and other slum clearance projects.[3]

Pruitt-Igoe was one of these public housing projects. Located on a 57-acre site on the north side black ghetto, it was one of several tracts that had been targeted for slum clearance under the postwar redevelopment plan. In 1950 St. Louis received a federal commitment for 5800 public housing units, about half of which were allocated by the St. Louis Housing Authority to Pruitt-Igoe. The 2700-unit project would house 15,000

19.2 Leinweber, Yamasaki & Hellmuth, Pruitt-Igoe public housing project, St. Louis, Missouri, 1950–54

tenants at densities higher than the original slum dwellings. The high density resulted from housing and redevelopment officials' expectations that these projects would eventually come to house not only those displaced by slum clearance for Pruitt-Igoe, but also by demolition for redevelopment projects and for future public housing.

In 1950 the St. Louis Housing Authority commissioned the firm of Leinweber, Yamasaki & Hellmuth to design Pruitt-Igoe. The architects' task was constrained by the size and location of the site, the number of units, and the project density, all of which had been predetermined by the St. Louis Housing Authority. Their first design proposals called for a mixture of high-rise, mid-rise, and walk-up structures. Though this arrangement was acceptable to the local authority, it exceeded the federal government's maximum allowable cost per unit. At this point a field officer of the federal Public Housing Administration (P.H.A.) intervened and insisted on a scheme using 33 identical eleven-story elevator buildings (Figure 19.2).[4] These design changes took place in the context of a strict economy and efficiency drive within the P.H.A. Political opposition to the public housing program was particularly intense in the conservative political climate of the early 1950s. In addition, the outbreak of the Korean war had created inflation and materials shortages, and the P.H.A. found itself in the position of having to justify public housing expenditures to an unsympathetic Congress.[5]

Despite the intense pressure for economical design, the architects devoted a great deal of attention to improving livability in the high-rise units. One of their strategies was to use two popular new design features: skip-stop elevators and glazed internal galleries. These were intended to create "individual neighborhoods" within each building. The galleries, located on every third floor, were conceived as "vertical hallways." Skip-stop elevators transported residents to the gallery level, from which they would walk to their apartments. Laundry and storage rooms also opened off the galleries. When Pruitt-Igoe was published in the *Architectural Forum* and *Architectural Record*,[6] it was these specific design features that received the most attention. The *Architectural Record* praised the skip-stop elevators and galleries as innovative compensations for the shortcomings of the high-rise housing form:

> Since all of these are, under federal legislation, combined low-rent housing and slum-clearance projects, located near the heart of the city, a high-rise, high-density solution was inescapable, and the problem was how to plan a high-rise project on a huge scale, and still provide, to the greatest extent possible under present legislation, communities with individual scale and character which would avoid the "project" atmosphere so often criticized.[7]

Even after the architects had switched to an all high-rise scheme, they faced continued pressure from the Public Housing Administration to keep costs to a bare minimum. In a 1975 study of the St. Louis Housing Authority's expenditures on Pruitt-Igoe, political scientist Eugene Meehan analyzed the extent to which these budget constraints affected the final design. In addition to the elimination of amenities, such as children's play areas, landscaping, and ground-floor bathrooms, the cost cutting targeted points of contact between the tenants and the living units. "The quality of the hardware was so poor that doorknobs and locks were broken on initial use. . . . Windowpanes were blown from inadequate frames by wind pressure. In the kitchens, cabinets were made of the thinnest plywood possible."[8]

Pruitt-Igoe was completed in 1954. Though originally conceived as two segregated sections (Pruitt for blacks and Igoe for whites), a Supreme Court decision handed down that same year forced desegregation. Attempts at integration failed, however, and Pruitt-Igoe was an exclusively black project virtually from inception. Overall Pruitt-Igoe's first tenants appeared pleased with their new housing. Despite the relatively cheap construction quality, the units still represented a much higher level of amenity than the dilapidated units they had vacated or been forced to leave.

By 1958, however, conditions had begun to deteriorate. One of the first signals was a steadily declining occupancy rate. As Roger Montgomery has persuasively argued, St. Louis' housing officials failed to anticipate changing postwar demographic trends that dramatically affected the inner-city housing market and threatened the viability of public housing projects.[9] Pruitt-Igoe was conceived at a time when the demand for low-income housing units in the inner city had never been higher, due to widespread dislocation caused by slum clearance, urban renewal, and the federal highway program. However, by the time the project opened in 1954, this demand had tapered off. Slow overall metropolitan population growth and the overproduction of inexpensive suburban dwellings helped open up the previously tight inner-city rental market to blacks. Many chose to live in

This interpretation of the demise of Pruitt-Igoe received strong reinforcement when it appeared in Oscar Newman's *Defensible Space* in the same year as the trial demolition. This seminal text of the then emerging discipline of environment and behavior argued that there was a direct relationship between physical environments and human behavior. According to Newman, the widespread vandalism and violence at Pruitt-Igoe resulted from the presence of excessive "indefensible" public space.[18] Corridors were too long and not visible from the apartments. The residents did not feel that these spaces "belonged" to them and so made no effort to maintain or police them. The entryways, located in large, unprotected open plazas, did not allow tenants any control over who entered the buildings. Newman further argued that by designing public housing in such a way as to provide an appropriate amount of private, semiprivate, and public space, architects could reduce violence and vandalism in the environment.

With all the attention being paid to the project's design in the early 1970s, a strong associative link was forged between architectural flaws and Pruitt-Igoe's deterioration. In 1965 James Bailey had taken care to point out that two of the major causes of the deterioration of Pruitt-Igoe were chronically inadequate maintenance and the increasing poverty of tenants. By 1972 these crucial elements of the story had been all but forgotten in the rush to condemn the architecture. It is the privileging of these design problems over the much more deeply embedded economic and social ones that constitutes the core of the Pruitt-Igoe myth.

The myth ignores the connection between Pruitt-Igoe's problems and the fiscal crisis of the St. Louis Housing Authority, or what Eugene Meehan has called the "programmed failure" of American public housing.[19] Political and social ambivalence to public housing had resulted in a token housing program burdened by impossible fiscal management constraints. The federal Public Housing Administration also impeded public housing efforts by insisting on unrealistically low construction costs. The myth also omits the subordination of public housing to postwar urban redevelopment programs. Federal dollars helped cities clear unsightly slums and assisted private interests in developing valuable inner city land. Public housing projects were confined to the unwanted sites in the heart of the slums, and developed at high densities to accommodate those displaced by the wholesale clearance of poor neighborhoods.

The myth also ignores the connection between social indifference to the poverty of inner city blacks and the decline of Pruitt-Igoe. In 1970 sociologist Lee Rainwater wrote *Behind Ghetto Walls*, based on the findings of a massive participant observer study conducted during the mid-1960s at Pruitt-Igoe.[20] Rainwater argued that the violence and vandalism that occurred at the project were an understandable response by its residents to poverty and racial discrimination. In his view architectural design was neither the cause nor the cure for these problems. Improved housing conditions and other efforts directed at changing the behavior of the poor were, in his opinion, useless if not accompanied by efforts to raise their income level.

This evidence directly contradicts the Pruitt-Igoe myth by demonstrating the significance of the political and economic sources of Pruitt-Igoe's decline. In addition, it reveals that the type of argument proposed in *Defensible Space* is a subtle form of blaming the victim. The idea of defensible space is based on the assumption that certain "populations" unavoidably bring with them behavioral problems that have to be designed against. This kind of argument does not question why public housing projects tend to be plagued by violent crime in the first place. It naturalizes the presence of crime among low-income populations rather than seeing it as a product of institutionalized economic and racial oppression.

PRUITT-IGOE AND THE END OF MODERNISM

Despite the extensive evidence of multiple social and economic causes of Pruitt-Igoe's deterioration, the Pruitt-Igoe myth has also become a truism of the environment and behavior literature. For example, John Pipkin's *Urban Social Space*, a standard social-factors textbook, uses Pruitt-Igoe as an example of indefensible space and of the lack of fit between high-rise buildings and lower class social structure. "In social terms, public housing has been a failure. Social structures have disintegrated in the desolate high-rise settings. . . . Many projects are ripe for demolition. One of the most notorious . . . was Pruitt-Igoe. When built, it won an architectural prize, but . . . it epitomized the ills of public housing."[21]

This passage is notable because it illustrates one particular example of how the Pruitt-Igoe myth has grown by incorporating misinformation. Though it is commonly accorded the epithet "award-winning," Pruitt-Igoe never won any kind of architectural prize. An earlier St. Louis housing project by the same team of architects, the John Cochran Garden Apartments, did win two architectural awards. At some point this prize seems to have been incorrectly attributed to Pruitt-Igoe. This strange memory lapse on the part of architects in their discussions of Pruitt-Igoe is extremely significant. Beginning in the mid-1970s, Pruitt-Igoe began increasingly to be used as an illustration of the argument that the International Style was responsible for the failure of Pruitt-Igoe. The fictitious prize is essential to this dimension of the myth, because it paints Pruitt-Igoe as the iconic modernist monument.

The association of Pruitt-Igoe's demise with the perceived failures of the Modern movement had begun as early as 1972. In the aftermath of the project's demolition, several writers suggested that insensitivity to residents' needs was typical of modern architecture. The *Architect's Journal* called the demolition of Pruitt-Igoe "the modern movement's most grandiloquent failure."[22] With the critique of Modernism emerging in the 1970s, it was not surprising that a number of critics and theorists, who can be loosely termed Postmodern, began to use the project in their writing to represent the Modern movement.

The first important appearance of Pruitt-Igoe in a critique of Modernism came in 1976 when Colin Rowe and Fred Koetter used the photograph of the demolition in their introduction to *Collage City*. This section of the book was devoted to a demonstration of the premise that the Modern movement's architectural and social revolution had backfired. Instead of furthering the development of a new society, "the city of modern architecture, both as psychological construct and as physical model, had been rendered tragically ridiculous . . . the city of Ludwig Hibersheimer and Le Corbusier, the city celebrated by CIAM and advertised by the Athens Charter, the former city of deliverance is everyday found increasingly inadequate."[23] Though Rowe and Koetter do not refer to Pruitt-Igoe specifically, the implication of the photograph's inclusion is clear. Pruitt-Igoe is used as an example of this "city of modern architecture" whose revolution failed. It presents Pruitt-Igoe as a product of the ideas of Hibersheimer, Le Corbusier, and CIAM [Congrès Internationaux d'Architecture Moderne, founded in La Sarraz, Switzerland, in 1928] and implicates the inadequacy of their ideas in the demolition of the project.

Only one year after the publication of *Collage City*, Charles Jencks further advanced this interpretation in *The Language of Post Modern Architecture*. In the introduction to his discussion of Postmodernism, Jencks asserted that the demolition of Pruitt-Igoe represents the death of modern architecture. Like Rowe and Koetter, he associated Pruitt-Igoe with the rationalist principles of CIAM, and particularly with the urban design principles of Le Corbusier. According to Jencks, even though the project was designed with the intention of instilling good behavior in the tenants, it was incapable of accommodating their social needs:

> Pruitt-Igoe was constructed according to the most progressive ideas of CIAM . . . and it won an award from the American Institute of Architects when it was designed in 1951. It consisted of elegant slab blocks fourteen storeys high, with rational "streets in the air" (which were safe from cars, but, as it turned out, not safe from crime); "sun, space and greenery", which Le Corbusier called the "three essential joys of urbanism" (instead of conventional streets, gardens and semi-private space, which he banished). It had a separation of pedestrian and vehicular traffic, the provision of play space, and local amenities such as laundries, crèches and gossip centers—all rational substitutes for traditional patterns.[24]

These uses of the Pruitt-Igoe symbol added significantly to the Pruitt-Igoe myth. Like the defensible space argument popularized by Oscar Newman, these accounts failed to locate Pruitt-Igoe in its historical context and thereby ignored evidence that economic crisis and racial discrimination played the largest role in the project's demise. Now, they added a set of ideas about the architects' intentions in designing the project. Both accounts presented the project as the canonical modernist monument (Jencks in particular perpetuating the mistaken idea that it was an award-winning design). They described the project as Modernist not only in formal terms, but in political and social terms as well, as reflecting an agenda for social engineering.

These uses of Pruitt-Igoe misrepresented the designers' intentions and the extent to which the architects controlled the project's design. As the summary of Pruitt-Igoe's history demonstrates, much of the project's design was determined by the St. Louis Housing Authority and the federal Public Housing Administration. The architects had no control over the project's isolated location, its excessive densities, the elimination of amenities, or the use of high-rise elevator buildings. Their task was limited to providing the form of the individual buildings and incorporating as much amenity as possible, given the restricted budget.

In carrying out this task, the architects did follow the formal conventions of modern architecture. Pruitt-Igoe was one of Leinweber, Yamasaki & Hellmuth's first major commissions, so it is certain that they wished to make an impression on their architectural peers. The glazed galleries combined with skip-stop elevators, the extensive open spaces between the slabs, and the minimalist surface treatment certainly reflected the prevailing interest in Modernism as elaborated by CIAM. However, the use of these formal conventions does not demonstrate that the architects had particular intentions for social reform. In fact, in published statements Minoru Yamasaki expressed doubt that the high-rise form would have a beneficial effect on public housing tenants.

These statements appeared in a series of articles in the *Journal of Housing* in which Yamasaki engaged in a debate with the progressive housing reformer Catherine Bauer.[25] Yamasaki defended high-rise design, not on its architectural merits, but as the best possible response to what he perceived as the social imperative of slum clearance and the economic necessity for urban redevelopment. Given the high cost of urban land occupied by slum housing, he argued, it is most economically efficient to acquire small parcels and build at high densities. Yet despite its economic advantages, Yamasaki was skeptical of the value of the high-rise as a form for mass housing: "the low building with low density is unquestionably more satisfactory than multi-story living. . . . If I had no economic or social limitations, I'd solve all my problems with one-story buildings."[26] He defended high-rise design as the only way to respond to external economic and policy conditions.

In her defense of low-rise housing, Catherine Bauer suggested that the policy of clearing slums and then rehousing low-income populations in high-density central city projects is not necessarily the result of economic imperatives but a conscious choice on the part of policy-makers. High-density inner city projects are the result of making public housing subordinate to urban redevelopment schemes: If business interests and city officials were willing to locate projects on the urban periphery then the high-density, high-rise projects would be unnecessary. Bauer criticized Yamasaki less for his architectural views than for his politics; he was too willing to give in to prevailing profit-motivated redevelopment and housing policy.

In his statements in this debate, Yamasaki hardly fits the image of the radical social reformer depicted by the Pruitt-Igoe myth. His firm did indeed adopt particular design features in order to conform to the latest trends and was insensitive to the potential effects of those features. The architects also incorrectly assumed that the galleries would help promote community interaction in what was bound to be a harsh environment. Yet before making any of these decisions, they had agreed to work within the framework of the large-scale, high-rise, high-density project mandated by urban redevelopment practices. Rather than social reformers destroying the public housing program with their megalomaniac designs, the architects were essentially passive in their acceptance of the dominant practices of their society.

Despite its dubious authenticity or historical accuracy, the Pruitt-Igoe myth had achieved the status of architectural dogma by the late 1970s. The idea that Pruitt-Igoe's failure resulted from the insensitivity of orthodox modernist design found a receptive audience and became an illustration for many Postmodern and anti-Modern texts. Peter Blake, in *Form Follows Fiasco: Why Modern Architecture Hasn't Worked* echoed the assertion that Pruitt-Igoe followed "Ville-Radieuse" design ideas. As a result, he argued, there was "no way this depressing project could be made humanly habitable" and communities of high-rises are inherently doomed.[27] It also became a convenient symbol for Tom Wolfe to include in his attack on the importing of German-inspired 1930s architecture to the United States after World War II.[28] In *From Bauhaus to Our House* Wolfe repeated the by now generally accepted fiction that the project was an award winner, and then added a fabrication of his own, asserting that in 1971 a general meeting was held at which the residents called for blowing up the buildings.[29]

THE PRUITT-IGOE MYTH AS MYSTIFICATION

Why is the Pruitt-Igoe myth so powerful? There is clearly ample evidence that architectural design was but one, and probably the least important, of several factors in the demise of the project. Why then has the architecture community been so insistent that the failure of Pruitt-Igoe was its own fault?

At one level, the myth can be understood simply as a weapon in an ongoing conflict between different factions within the architecture profession. The two most central critiques of the design of Pruitt-Igoe have come from successor movements to High Modernism: Postmodernism, and environment and behavior. For proponents of these new approaches, such as Oscar Newman or Charles Jencks, Pruitt-Igoe provides a convenient embodiment of all the alleged failings of Modernism. However, though these successors are critical of the modernist approach to the design of public housing, they do not question the fundamental notion that it is at the level of *design* that public housing succeeds or fails. They attribute the problems of public housing to architectural failure, and propose as a solution a new approach to design. They do not in any significant way acknowledge the political-economic and social context for the failure of Pruitt-Igoe. This is because the myth is more than simply the result of debate within architectural culture: It serves at a much more profound level the interests of the architecture profession as a whole.

As we have seen in tracing the rise of the Pruitt-Igoe myth, the architects' version has consistently insisted on the primary significance of the project's overall design in its demise. This interpretation denies the existence of larger problems endemic to St. Louis' public housing program. By attributing more causal power to architecture than to flawed policies, crises in the local economy, or to class oppression and racism, the myth conceals the existence of contextual factors structuring the architects' decisions and fabricates a central role for architecture in the success or failure of public housing. It places the architect in the position of authority over providing low-income housing for the poor.

This presentation of the architect as the figure of authority in the history of Pruitt-Igoe is reinforced by linking the project's failure to the defects of High Modernism. The claim that Pruitt-Igoe failed because it was based on an agenda for social reform, derived from the ideas of Le Corbusier and the CIAM, not only presupposes that physical design is central to the success or failure of public housing, but also that the design was implemented to carry out the architects' social agenda. What this obscures is the architects' passivity in the face of a much larger agenda that has its roots not in radical social reform, but in the political economy of post-World War II St. Louis and in practices of racial segregation. Pruitt-Igoe was shaped by the strategies of ghetto containment and inner city revitalization—strategies that did not emanate from the architects, but rather from the system in which they practice. The Pruitt-Igoe myth therefore not only inflates the power of the architect to effect social change, but it masks the extent to which the profession is implicated, inextricably, in structures and practices that it is powerless to change.

Simultaneously with its function of promoting the power of the architect, the myth serves to disguise the actual purpose and implication of public housing by diverting the debate to the question of design. By continuing to promote architectural solutions to what are fundamentally problems of class and race, the myth conceals the complete inadequacy of contemporary public housing policy. It has quite usefully shifted the blame from the sources of housing policy and placed it on the design professions. By furthering this misconception, the myth disguises the causes of the failure of public housing, and also ensures the continued participation of the architecture profession in token and palliative efforts to address the problem of poverty in America. The myth is a mystification that benefits everyone involved, except those to whom public housing programs are supposedly directed.

Notes

1 St. Louis City Plan Commission, *Comprehensive City Plan* (St. Louis, 1947), pp. 27–34; James Neal Primm, *Lion of the Valley* (Boulder, CO: Pruett, 1981), pp. 472–473.
2 "Progress or Decay? St. Louis Must Choose: The Sordid Housing Story," *St. Louis Post-Dispatch*, March 3, 1950, Part Four in a Series.
3 For the role played by the public housing program in St. Louis redevelopment plans, see Roger Montgomery, "Pruitt-Igoe: Policy Failure or Societal Symptom," in Barry Checkoway and Carl V. Patton, eds., *The Metropolitan Midwest: Policy Problems and Prospects for Change* (Urbana: University of Illinois Press, 1985), pp. 230–239; and Kate Bristol and Roger Montgomery, "The Ghost of Pruitt-Igoe" (paper delivered at the Annual Meeting of the Association of Collegiate Schools of Planning, Buffalo, NY, October 28, 1988). On the relationship of public housing to urban renewal more generally, see Mark Weiss, "The Origins and Legacy of Urban Renewal," in P. Clavell, J. Forester, and W. Goldsmith, eds., *Urban and Regional Planning in an Age of Austerity* (New York: Pergamon Press, 1980); Richard O. Davies, *Housing Reform During the Truman Administration* (Columbia: University of Missouri Press, 1966); and Arnold Hirsch, *Making the Second Ghetto: Race and Housing in Chicago, 1940–1966* (Cambridge: Cambridge University Press, 1983).
4 Eugene Meehan, *The Quality of Federal Policymaking: Programmed Failure in Public Housing* (Columbia: University of Missouri Press, 1979), p. 71; James Bailey, "The Case History of a Failure," *Architectural Forum* 123 (December 1965): 23.
5 U.S. Public Housing Administration, *Annual Report* (Washington, D.C., 1951); Davies, *Housing Reform*, pp. 126–132.
6 "Slum Surgery in St. Louis," *Architectural Forum* 94 (April 1951): 128–136; "Four Vast Housing Projects for St. Louis: Hellmuth, Obata and Kassabaum, Inc.," *Architectural Record* 120 (August 1956): 182–189.
7 "Four Vast Housing Projects for St. Louis," 185.
8 Meehan, *Quality*, p. 71.
9 Montgomery, "Pruitt-Igoe," pp. 235–239.
10 Meehan, *Quality*, pp. 60–63, 65–67, 74–83.
11 In 1965 the U.S. Public Housing Administration (P.H.A.) was incorporated into the newly created Department of Housing and Urban Development (H.U.D.).
12 "What's Wrong with High-Rise?," *St. Louis Post-Dispatch* (November 14, 1960).
13 Bailey, "Case History," 22–23.

14   "St. Louis Blues," *Architectural Forum* 136 (May 1972): 18; *Architect's Journal* (July 26, 1972); Wilbur Thompson, "Problems that Sprout in the Shadow of No Growth," *AIA Journal* 60 (December 1973); "The Experiment That Failed," *Architecture Plus* (October 1973).

15   "The Tragedy of Pruitt-Igoe," *Time* (December 27, 1971): 38; Jerome Curry, "Collapse of a Failure," *The National Observer* (May 20, 1972): 24; Andrew B. Wilson, "Demolition Marks Ultimate Failure of Pruitt-Igoe Project," *Washington Post* (August 27, 1973): 3.

16   "The Experiment That Failed," 18.

17   Wilson, "Demolition," 3.

18   Oscar Newman, *Defensible Space* (New York: Macmillan, 1972), pp. 56–58, 66, 77, 83, 99, 101–108, 188, 207.

19   Meehan, *Quality*, pp. 83–87, 194–198.

20   Lee Rainwater, *Behind Ghetto Walls; Black Families in a Federal Slum* (Chicago: Aldine Publishing, 1970), pp. 9, 403.

21   Mark LaGory and John Pipkin, *Urban Social Space* (Belmont, CA: Wadsworth, 1981), p. 263.

22   *Architect's Journal* (July 26, 1972): 180.

23   Colin Rowe and Fred Koetter, *Collage City* (Cambridge, MA: MIT Press, 1976), pp. 4, 6.

24   Charles Jencks, *The Language of Post-Modern Architecture* (New York: Rizzoli, 1977), pp. 9–10.

25   Minoru Yamasaki, "High Buildings for Public Housing?" *Journal of Housing* 9 (1952): 226; Catherine Bauer, "Low Buildings? Catherine Bauer Questions Mr. Yamasaki's Arguments," *Journal of Housing* 9 (1952): 227.

26   Yamasaki, "High Buildings," 226.

27   Peter Blake, *Form Follows Fiasco: Why Modern Architecture Hasn't Worked* (Boston: Atlantic Monthly Press, 1977), pp. 80–81.

28   Tom Wolfe, *From Bauhaus to Our House* (New York: Simon and Schuster, 1981), pp. 73–74.

29   Actually in the late seventies a local community redevelopment group that included former Pruitt-Igoe residents made a proposal to buy and renovate four of the buildings, but were turned down by H.U.D. Mary Comerio, "Pruitt-Igoe and Other Stories," *Journal of Architectural Education* 34 (Summer, 1981): 26–31.

Chapter 20

Neil Levine

Robert Venturi and "the return of historicism"

Among the many reasons why Robert Venturi can be considered one of the most influential architects of the last quarter of the twentieth century, perhaps first and foremost is his understanding of the role history must play in the restoration of a representational dimension to modern architecture. To discuss his work exclusively in terms of the appropriation of elements of pop culture and vernacular traditions seems to me to miss, or even purposely to conceal, that much more important point. Long before *Learning from Las Vegas* (1972) [...] came the first manifesto of what Nikolaus Pevsner was already bemoaning as "the return of historicism," Venturi's *Complexity and Contradiction in Architecture* (1966).[1] And even before that came Guild House, with its radical and prophetic use of the historical precedent of classical composition and detailing for what was, in effect, "merely" another example of economic modern housing.

Guild House, the apartment building in Philadelphia that was constructed between 1960 and 1966, was the first major design of Venturi's to be built and can appropriately be taken as the point of reference for this essay (Figure 20.1). Its predominant segmental arch, ultimately deriving from Roman sources, became a leitmotif of his architecture as well as the basis for pastiche after pastiche by countless other designers over the next quarter century. The subsequent Vanna Venturi House (built 1963–64), Trubek House (1970–71), and Wu Hall (1980–83) must all be seen in terms of the representational meaning Guild House gave to historical allusion as well as the specific contextual purpose that building first articulated for the revival of traditional forms and ideas of design.

The idea of historical precedent, which directed Venturi's very earliest projects, became the touchstone of his discussion of architectural theory in *Complexity and Contradiction in Architecture*, written after Guild House was designed and published [as] the building was [being] completed. In his preface to the book, Venturi quoted T. S. Eliot to explain how tradition, meaning "the historical sense"—"a conscious sense of the past"—guided his own work,[2] and the hundreds of small photographs included in the margins of the text were meant to illustrate how, in Venturi's mind, an architect must draw on historical precedent in order to represent an architectural thought. That sense of historical precedent was shown to be as broad and as eclectically based as one might imagine, with images on a single page (Figure 20.2), for instance, drawn from Gothic France, Baroque England, Mannerist Italy, Rococo Bavaria, Romantic-Classical London, ancient Rome, twentieth-century modernity as well as, and this is what is so important, twentieth-century historicism, the last represented by the photograph at the upper left of

20.1 Venturi and Rausch, with Cope and Lippincott, Guild House, Philadelphia, Pennsylvania, 1960–66

Brasini's Forestry Building at the E. U. R. site outside Rome. And, in the even later *Learning from Las Vegas*, Venturi's main theoretical contribution was an essay on architectural symbolism that differentiated traditional "representational art" from modern "abstract expressionism" according to the values of "Historical and Other Precedents" that might lead back "Towards an Old Architecture."[3] Here again, the expression and "symbolic meaning" to be associated with nineteenth-century stylistic revivals was put forth, still fairly radically for the time, as the all-important link in the chain of tradition that connected the twentieth century to the past.

Although Venturi may have been unique among architects in the wide range of his references to the past, as well as his positive valuation of the "eclecticism" over which the "purism" of the so-called Modern Movement had triumphed, he was hardly alone in the late 1950s and early 1960s in his desire to return architecture to some semblance of historical form. Indeed, at the very same time Guild House was going up, Venturi's former mentor Louis Kahn was completing the designs for the Meeting House and Living Quarters of the Salk Institute at La Jolla [California], which were to be faced with panels of Roman, travertine arches. Already by 1961, when Pevsner launched his attack on Neo-Historicism, describing it as "the belief in the power of history to such a degree as to choke original action and replace it by action which is inspired by period precedent,"[4] there was a plethora of examples of such buildings to point to, by Philip Johnson, Eero Saarinen, and Louis Kahn in the United States, or Franco Albini and Ignazio Gardella in Italy. The late work of both Wright and Le Corbusier was affected by such ideas, as were even some

20.2 Page 68 from Robert Venturi, *Complexity and Contradiction in Architecture*, New York: Museum of Modern Art, 1966 (digital image © The Museum of Modern Art/Licensed by SCALA/Art Resource, NY)

of the projects by Gropius's Architects' Collaborative. Everyone seemed to be aware of the need to reach beyond the Modernist dogma of pure functional expression.

The result, however, was by no means a single monolithic approach. Historical precedent could be revived for purely decorative purposes, resulting in the ubiquitous, screen-like curtain walls of [Minoru] Yamasaki, [Edward Durrell] Stone, and others. It could become a new, almost abstract Formalism, as numerous critics characterized Philip Johnson's designs of the time.[5] It could be used on a mostly ad hoc, purely contextual basis, as was so often the case in Italy. It could serve as a way of adjusting Modernist strategies to the desire for a "new monumentality."[6] By reading the present into the past, it could become a way of justifying a historicist basis for Modernist ahistoricism, just as it could also serve, by contrast, as the basis for a reinvestigation of the primitive roots of architectural forms and typologies.

From a theoretical point of view, two very distinct and divergent streams of thought developed, the one represented by the critic/architect Colin Rowe, and the other by the art historian Vincent Scully. Rowe's position, articulated in a number of pithy articles in the London-based *Architectural Review*, beginning in the late forties, was a revisionist view of history in which he maintained, contrary to popular belief, that history had in fact never been denied by the Modern Movement; it was just a bit "deconstructed." The Modernist architecture of the 1920s that had always prided itself on its freedom from the classical past was thus explained as a new form of classicism itself. In his "Mathematics of the Ideal Villa," published in 1947, Rowe argued with great effectiveness that Le Corbusier's private houses, such as the Villa Savoie or Villa Stein at Garches, followed the same essential principles of organization as Palladio's Villa Rotonda, and thus deserved to be considered as modern variants of the same classical ideal.[7] Through this logic, the classical was disembodied of its traditional forms and associations. No direct historical references were any longer necessary since Modernism had arrived at the "thing in itself." And, even more to the point, since the very idea of classicism was abstracted from its historical context and forms, the notion of abstraction was given a kind of historical validity.

The purist logic in fact derived from Le Corbusier himself who, in his polemical writings of the twenties, had insisted on how the "regulating lines" of his proportioning system were essentially the same as those used in classical buildings of the past.[8] Photographs of Michelangelo's High Renaissance Campidoglio or Gabriel's mid-eighteenth-century Petit Trianon at Versailles were reproduced in *Vers une architecture* with superimposed right triangles in order to clarify the analogy with his own designs. But, that is not all these comparisons make evident, for Le Corbusier obviously meant to differentiate as much as to equate. In the case of Gabriel's garden pavilion, those black lines read not so much as overlapping triangles but as great Xs crossing out the columns and pediments and cornices of the classical building as if to suggest that they are not only frivolous and unnecessary, but also wrong—or, at least, would be so in the twentieth century. Indeed, the final message of *Vers une architecture* was that the only way to rival the past was to disencumber the present of its burden:

> Architecture finds itself confronted with new laws. Construction has undergone innovations so great that the old "styles," which still obsess us, can no longer clothe it . . . [T]he "styles"

no longer exist, they are outside our ken; if they still trouble us, it is as parasites. If we set ourselves against the past, we are forced to the conclusion that the old architectural code, with its mass of rules and regulations evolved during four thousand years, is no longer of any interest; it no longer concerns us: all the values have been revised; there has been revolution in the conception of what Architecture is.[9]

The point on which Modernist theory and its revisionist version both agreed was the supposed bankruptcy of nineteenth-century eclecticism. Here is where the chain of history had been broken and the "styles" proved themselves to be a "lie,"[10] a stage set on which the eclectic architects of the nineteenth century played out their wildest fantasies and wish fulfillments in a dream turned nightmare. Alienated from the continuum of history by an interregnum of nearly two centuries, the very conception of history became in Rowe's theory a complete abstraction. This strangely compelling historical amnesia of revisionist Modernism continued into the sixties and seventies ultimately to determine the battle lines drawn between what came to be called the "Whites"—the Modernist purists [e.g., Richard Meier, Peter Eisenman]—and the "Greys"—those who evolved a more inclusive and more reasoned understanding of history and our connection to it through the lesson of Scully's thought and its intimate relation to the architecture of both Venturi and Kahn [e.g., Charles Moore, Robert Stern].[11]

In his book on *The Shingle Style*, written as a doctoral dissertation for Yale University in the late 1940s and published in 1955, Scully, like Rowe, addressed the problem of modern classicism. But instead of reading out most of the recent past, Scully tried to show the continuity of the classical tradition by bringing it up to date, across the nineteenth century and well into the twentieth, with the work of McKim, Mead and White and Frank Lloyd Wright.[12] He pictured history not as an alien world to which one only has access through a highly intellectualized process of analogy and abstraction, but rather as a world that has informed our own, through the local character and vernacular quality of the architecture in which we grew up. Scully himself showed how Venturi's architecture early on expressed this direct and organic connection to history, most particularly in the house he designed for his mother in 1961.[13] This, Scully related to Frank Lloyd Wright's own house in Oak Park [Illinois] of 1889, and then on back to Bruce Price's Shingle Style cottages in Tuxedo Park [New York] of a few years before. In all of them, the representational elements of the classical tradition were shown to have been used in such a way as to condense the image of shelter into a traditionally recognizable form. Stylistic references to Palladio or Serlio were not direct but filtered through more than three centuries of continuous experience, and thus continually transformed by the changing local conditions and materials.

Throughout his scholarly and critical writings of the fifties and sixties, ranging over subjects as diverse as Greek architecture, Michelangelo, Louis Kahn, and Frank Lloyd Wright, Scully presented the relation between the modern experience and the historical past as sympathetic rather than adversarial. Kahn, he liked to point out, was "trained in the Beaux-Arts to regard the buildings of the past as friends rather than as enemies."[14] This attitude toward the past, which Venturi clearly shared with Scully and Kahn, was no longer simply traditionalism. By then, it took a wholly new, less dogmatic view of modern architecture to see how to reintegrate the present with the past. During the high moment of Modernism in the first half of this century, most of the forms and organizational patterns of traditional architecture had in fact been jettisoned in the hope of arriving at something unforeseen, a new architecture that would be specifically appropriate to the machine age. Wright called his Larkin Building of 1903–6 the "Great Protestant" and described its interlocking, nearly abstract cubic forms as "negating" all historical reference.[15] In Le Corbusier's Villa Savoie, that abstract idea of pure forms in space was taken to a logical conclusion, and the modern notion of an architecture totally responsive to its own internal factors of material, program, and space was given its "classic" (not classical) statement. The open plan, free-flowing space, clear rectilinear form, and reinforced concrete structure all offered an image of architecture totally unhooked from the past and, indeed, from everything around it. This *was* the ideal of Modernism, "the thing in itself."

Naturally, as the free plan, the free facade, the idea of *pilotis*, and what Colin Rowe liked to call "peripheric composition"[16] came to be synonymous with modernity, the single most regressive form that might be revived from a premodern condition was the arch, or its extension as a dome or vault. Of all those elements banished from the canon of modern design, the arch was one of the first that had to go. It spoke of the weight of tradition, of massive structural systems of masonry, of hierarchy and symmetry, of closure and formal classical order. It also spoke of connectedness to everything around it, and to everything that preceded it in time and space. Where Scully would see in the arches of Kahn or Venturi a "gesture" full of rich human possibilities, Rowe described such "episodic blisters" as "sclerotic" and "regressive" in terms of the machine aesthetic.[17]

As a gauge of the general movement back to historical precedent in the post-war period, it is significant then that both Le Corbusier and Wright began to use arches and vaults in various projects, although in very different ways—Wright tending to emphasize more and more the representational character of the motif and Le Corbusier tending to stress its purely structural possibilities at the expense of any historical associations. In the 1940s, Le Corbusier designed a number of buildings, such as the Roq and Rob housing community on the Mediterranean coast of France, using a system of segmental, Catalan vaults, inspired by local traditions of masonry construction, and building on some of his experiments of the previous two decades. By contrast, Wright used the arch in a much more explicitly historicizing way, to express the connection with local history, in a project for a house in El Paso, Texas, of 1942, that was to have been built in adobe.

This difference between the structural expression of Le Corbusier's return to the arch and Wright's more representational use became clearer in the later forties and fifties. In his Maisons Jaoul, built in the wealthy Neuilly suburb of Paris in the mid-fifties, Le Corbusier stressed the archaizing, primitive nature of the sheltering vault and, as in the Roq and Rob project, merely indicated the arch on the exterior as an extrusion of the vault. It is almost as if, though drawn to the arch, Le Corbusier had to rationalize its use in a contemporary situation by denying its imagistic content. In the vaulted structures of his most important and monumental buildings of the period, such as the High Court at Chandigarh, or the Chapel of Notre-Dame-du-Haut at Ronchamp, both of the early 1950s, Le Corbusier went so far as to subvert the traditional meaning of the arched shape. At Chandigarh, the continuous vault of the roof is strictly contained within a rectilinear

20.3 Frank Lloyd Wright, Marin County Civic Center, San Rafael, California, 1957–70

framework that defines the expressive charge of the building, thus relegating the vault to a purely structural condition. In the chapel at Ronchamp, the normally soaring vault of a church is turned upside down to create a sense of implosion and cause the space to be felt not as something contained but rather as something pushing down and out.

In his 1948 design for the Morris Store, in San Francisco, Wright, on the other hand, accepted the traditional function of the arch as an expression of entrance and used its continuous form to urbanistic purpose, helping to link his building to the others along the narrow, downtown street. In the Marin County Civic Center (Figure 20.3) of ten years later, his last major building, Wright went even further in treating the arched shape as a purely symbolic cutout, with no structural reason other than that of representation. Making direct reference to a Republican Roman aqueduct such as the Pont du Gard, near Nîmes, Wright accepted the precedent of historical form as a means of conveying the image of civic purpose in public works.

Following the example of such "form-givers" as Le Corbusier and Wright, as well as the cryptoclassical designs of engineers like [Pier Luigi] Nervi, [Robert] Maillart, and [Felix] Candela, architects throughout the world in the 1950s picked up on this use of the arch for both structural and representational purposes. For [Eero] Saarinen in his Chapel at MIT, it helped create the image of a stripped-down, late antique baptistry, stranded in a land of technology; for Oscar Niemeyer in his Presidential Palace at Brasilia, it gave a certain expression of pomp to an otherwise emaciated Chandigarh. The abstracted, inverted arcade is used as a screen and could thus be rationalized, in functional terms, as a decorative *brise-soleil*, or sun-break, in Corbusian terminology.

Of all the architects who experimented with the arch in the 1950s, Louis Kahn undoubtedly came closest to providing a serious rationale for its reincorporation in modern architecture as an element of structural clarity as well as a form of rich, symbolic significance. Between 1959 and 1961, Kahn designed both the U.S. Consulate in Luanda, Angola, and the Meeting House and Staff Living Quarters for the Salk Institute for Biological Studies in La Jolla, in which he used the flat, cutout shape of the arch in a new and powerful way. In both projects, the large-scale Roman arch with its light slot below creates, in a structurally integral way, the facade of the building while at the same time detaching itself from the structure to function as a light-diffusing screen, again a Corbusian *brise-soleil* in effect. In Luanda, the flat, arched screens are set up along the flanks of the consulate under the overhanging roof "umbrella," protecting the interior from the glare of the sun just as the roof would keep out the rain.

The form of an arch piercing the plane of the wall to provide a soft, mysterious sense of light had other poetic connotations for Kahn, however, which depended on certain historical associations with Roman vaulted construction that were inspired by the melancholic nature of ruins. Kahn described these designs of his as resulting from the idea of "wrapping ruins around buildings."[18] In the Salk Meeting House, in particular, one can read Kahn's design as a kind of recycling of the past in which rooms of circular and square plan have been reconstructed and inserted within an existing Roman fabric of curving and straight arched planes. At this poetic level of interpretation, then, the notion of using the ruin as a model for retrieving history allows the modern architect rationally to reinvest his work with the past without having to accept all of it fully. The ruin represents only part of what once existed: it exhibits what remains of the past once time and the forces of nature have done their work to reduce the complete body of the building to a mere skeleton.

Kahn's historicism still reveals a profound allegiance to Modernist thought in its prohibition against decoration or ornament, that is to say, in its proscription of what can be thought of as extraneous to the structural order of the building. One can therefore read Kahn's notion of the ruin as a poetic justification for the idea of getting back to basics, an idea which was at the heart of the modern theory of structural rationalism so eloquently propounded in the later nineteenth century by [Eugène-Emmanuel] Viollet-le-Duc. As Viollet explained in his comparative analysis of Greek, Roman, and Gothic architecture, the trabeated, decorative treatment of Roman buildings was entirely extraneous to the underlying structural order of arches and vaults.[19] In order to assess such works at their true value, the architect had to try to imagine these great engineering marvels stripped of all ornament. Drawings such as the *Analysis of Roman Baths* he produced for the history course at the Ecole Spéciale d'Architecture in the 1860s illustrate the stages in the actual process of construction (Figure 20.4). Reading from left to right, we can see how the underlying brick skeleton of arches and vaults was "masked" by the added layer of historic decoration. Viollet's modern, X-ray vision, however, allows us to "see through" the mistakes of history, for with hindsight we can also read the drawing backwards, from right to left, deconstructing the building so to speak, in order to arrive at a more elemental and truthful level of information. The underlying brick and concrete structure of the building is what makes the building "what it wants to be," in Louis Kahn's terms, whereas

20.4 Eugène-Emmanuel Viollet-le-Duc, *Analysis of Roman Baths*, mid-1860s

the overlay of columns and entablatures is merely a rhetorical gesture, an unnecessary and, in the end, dissimulating device denying an expression of internal truth and authenticity.

When, in the 1960s, beginning with his work at Dhaka, Kahn was able to put this historical theory of design into practice, the result was an architecture of elemental power and integrity. In the library at Phillips Exeter Academy (Figure 20.5), Kahn once again made load-bearing brick walls of Roman arched construction serve as an outer casing for the enormous concrete void at the center. Here, in effect, was a historical precedent of the most "regressive" sort used to fulfill the archetypally modern idea of the building standing alone as an object, a thing in itself, internally consistent, and entirely self-contained. History, in the process, was somehow denuded, for something was obviously left out. Buildings like the Exeter Library almost immediately looked, if not literally like ruins, then like something existing in a state of arrested development, in a process of becoming that is not yet complete. Kahn's library is like looking at the Viollet drawing of a Roman bath with a blinder over your right eye. There is a reference to the past, but to a past that will never be allowed to come into its own. Exeter Library has four faces but no facade; a central hall without a dedicated purpose; an enclosed portico with nothing to connect to.

20.5 Louis Kahn, Library, Phillips Exeter Academy, Exeter, New Hampshire, 1965–72

It is against the idealism and hermeticism of Kahn's fully mature work[20] that Venturi's significance can best be appreciated, for it seems to me that one of the most important things Venturi did was to take off the blinders and look at the full historical picture, from the left all the way to the right. Thus he began to put back into that picture the signifying elements of representation that allow architecture to function as part of a larger social and urban form of discourse. In the house he built for his mother in 1963–64, just outside Philadelphia, the decorative features are explicitly applied to read as if appliqued (Figure 20.6). Unlike the Exeter Library, where the integral and self-contained nature of the structural order is all-important, in the Vanna Venturi House, the parts of the building, as they relate to external factors, pull away from the whole, denying its internal consistency and thus distinguishing themselves in purely representational terms. In this process of returning to the idea of making a *facade* that would be a singular thing, different from any other part of the building and thus necessarily marked by certain features normally associated with the passage from the public realm into a more private one, Venturi soon came to the realization that he was transgressing a fundamental principle of Modernism. Instead of considering the building in isolation and designing it uniquely from the inside out, Venturi had reversed the process to take both sides into account. "Designing from the outside in," he later explained in *Complexity and Contradiction in Architecture,*

> as well as the inside out, creates the necessary tensions, which help make architecture. Since the inside is different from the outside, the wall—the point of change—becomes an

20.6 Venturi and Rausch, Vanna Venturi House, Chestnut Hill, Philadelphia, Pennsylvania, designed 1959–63, built 1963–64

architectural event. Architecture occurs at the meeting of interior and exterior forces of use and space. These interior and environmental forces are both general and particular, generic and circumstantial. Architecture as the wall between the inside and the outside becomes the partial record of this resolution and its drama.[21]

"And by recognizing the difference between the inside and the outside," Venturi concluded, "architecture opens the door once again to an urbanistic point of view."[22]

The Vanna Venturi House presents to the path that leads in from the street a traditional facade in order to create a sense of continuity with the suburban environment. The gable and arch over the central entrance are indications of shelter and invitations readily understood from a distance. The difference between Venturi's conception of how a house should relate to its context and Kahn's view of the same problem is quite striking when we compare the Vanna Venturi House to the abstract, almost completely inward-looking design of Kahn's nearly contemporary Fisher House of 1960, located in the nearby suburb of Hatboro, or his Esherick House of 1959–61, located just down the street from Venturi's mother's house. But it is perhaps only in the even earlier Guild House, designed for a truly urban situation, that one can begin to see not only how far Venturi diverged from Kahn but also how much the factor of historical representation had to do with his search for a more contextual architecture.

Guild House is located on a main thoroughfare of Philadelphia, not quite a boulevard but still a significant street. The rear of the brick-clad structure is almost completely undistinguished and looks like a fairly straightforward piece of pragmatic, functional design. As it turns the corner, however, a very slight, though evident change occurs at the next-to-top-floor level of windows. The more the building opens up to the street, however, the more the white line of bricks, which is at first a bit difficult to understand, becomes clearly legible as a historical sign indicating a stringcourse. It is just a trace, but still something extra, added on. The apartment house then narrows in from its broad rear through a series of breaks and chamfers that finally telescope the building into a central pavilion that meets the line of the street. Here, the white stringcourse near the cornice stops; but at the street level, where the building meets the ground, a nearly two-story plane of white brick brings the historical imagery down to ground level onto the support of a freestanding, axially placed, black column.

The entrance pavilion, with its overriding arched shape, magnifies the historical reference and brings the entire building into focus at the plane of the street. In contrast to Kahn's Exeter Library, where the generalized reference to Roman construction is diffused in equal parts throughout the building, and therefore diluted nearly beyond recognition, the specific historical references in Guild House are concentrated at the point where the building comes into direct contact with the street. The rhythm and progression from abstract functional form to explicit historical allusion are so subtle, yet so marked, that one cannot help but realize that Venturi was making a very simple yet profound point in this, his first major building.

The arch and the arcade have traditionally been associated in urban terms with the idea of making a street. As Venturi surely learned during the time he spent in Italy, an arcade might be used to connect disparate buildings along the street while, at the same time, through the device of a triumphal motif, an axis of approach to a major public monument might be marked with suitable fanfare. Although it is obvious in his design of Guild House that Venturi understood the significance of the arch as an element that can both define a street-line and indicate a point of entry into a more private space, more important than the specific determination of elements is the very fact that it was only at the street-line, the point where the building comes into direct contact with the public frame of reference, that Venturi concentrated the historical devices he used. It was as if he was saying that, when a building takes its place in the public realm, it must begin to use a language of conventional reference and meaning in order to articulate its relation to the preexisting conditions; and, in doing that, it necessarily becomes part of history.

Indeed, one can see the stripping away of historical reference from the body of modern architecture as concomitant with the withdrawal of modern buildings from any determinative connection with the surrounding environment. The evolution of Wright's planning, for instance, from his houses of the 1890s to the mature Prairie Style, as illustrated in his Ward Willits House of 1901–2 [see Figure 14.3], shows how he arrived at a modern, integral sense of interpenetrating space by centering his design on the intersection of axes out of which the peripheric composition develops. The pinwheel action around the central fireplace determines the flow of space, which can be read as expanding infinitely outward. In Le Corbusier's seminal city planning projects of the 1920s, the cruciform shapes of the prismatic glass towers likewise symbolize the growth of an architectural idea out of its own internal factors of program and construction, without any need to refer to external factors such as context or history. His iconic image of the Dom-ino system of reinforced concrete construction, drawn in 1914, makes the elemental purity of this idea absolutely transparent. A totally rational structural grid, answering to its own laws, is set up, in isolation, as the basis for a completely indeterminate system of free planning, eventually to be encased by a free facade. The world is treated as a *tabula rasa* upon which the architect can start from scratch. Structure, program, and materials become the purely internal factors that govern design.

The ultimate outcome of this Modernist idea, that each specialized medium should acknowledge only those factors that are peculiar to itself and not shared by any other, reached a high point of development in the Brutalist architecture of the late 1950s and early 1960s. The *withdrawal* of Kevin Roche's Richard C. Lee High School in New Haven, or Moshe Safdie's Habitat for the Montreal Expo, for instance, could be rationalized as the result of a totally logical system of planning, programming, or construction technique, but the result of such thinking was catatonic, and catastrophic for the urban environment. In trying to heal these wounds, it soon became clear that piazzas would not help, for they almost immediately become moats, further separating the building from its urban context. The fact may just well be that, despite all the talk of *pilotis* and *brise-soleils* as constituting a new formal vocabulary to replace that of the past, modern architecture never was able to develop a coherent language for articulating the relation between the building and its site as a form of public discourse. Isolated, autonomous, and self-centered, modern architecture seemed to offer no system of detailing, of relating part to part, that might serve as a way of informing and connecting that which is new with that which already exists. This, I think, is what Venturi understood before everyone else—and this is the ultimate lesson of Guild House.

In Guild House, as is perhaps even more true of the house he did for his mother, Venturi historicized Kahn's philosophy of "form" and "design."[23] Kahn's abstract geometric order was given an explicit historical image, while the circumstantial impact of function was shaped to meet the contingencies of location and use.[24] In this interaction of forces coming from without and within, the idea of the facade reemerged in architecture with all its traditional significance of distinction and pronouncement. This willingness on the part of Venturi to let the building share some part of its meaning with the context around it, and preceding it, owed its origins to his belief in the continuity of history as a tradition which, in T. S. Eliot's sense, never could be broken for it was always being remade. In accepting nineteenth-century architecture, and not just its engineering, as part of the modern condition, Venturi was able to begin thinking about reinvesting form with the values of what he would call "explicit 'denotative' symbolism."[25]

In Guild House, as even more in Venturi's later buildings such as Wu Hall at Princeton, we are presented with an architecture that perhaps more than any other of our time attempts to accommodate itself to preexisting conditions. For that reason, it seems, it has come to rely more and more on explicit historical details and references. And so Venturi's architecture ultimately raises a fundamental question of our times: Is it not inevitable that modern architecture must return to the use of historical form in order to relate to what is around it? In Wu Hall, the keystones, the heraldic pattern over the entrance, the gentle Tudor-Gothic bay windows, as well as the stone balls at the base of the steps all seem naturally to define a set of paths through the Princeton campus that no previous modern building was able to do. How much do the historical references have to do with this? Perhaps more than we think. But then, how literal do such allusions have to be?

Whereas Venturi was quite alone in 1960 in his understanding of historicism as a means toward representation, that is obviously not the case today. The range of references now extends from the most intensely literal and reconstructive classicism of an Allan Greenberg or a Leon Krier through the more contextually based choices of a James Stirling to the large-scale, prefabricated images of a [Ricardo] Bofill to the simplified abstractions of an Aldo Rossi. All, however, are involved in one way or another with using the past to make an architecture of accommodation and association. While it is clearly too sweeping a statement to say that Venturi alone was responsible for this present state of affairs, I think it can safely be said that it was his early work, such as the Guild House, that made us aware that the "return of historicism" was as far from a loss of originality as it was from a strategy for justifying the inadequacies of the most recent past. Nor could it remain at the level of an abstraction; for as a means to representation, its ultimate purpose was in the realm of public discourse, signaling a revitalization of cultural memory and a desire for urban reform. And whatever ironies were once felt necessary by Venturi to maintain that position in a situation of "alarming" loss of faith in the present, as Pevsner felt the case to be in 1961,[26] are surely no more the case a quarter of a century later. The unself-conscious directness with which Venturi has dedicated his architecture, most recently at Princeton and now in London, to a supple and easy-going continuity with the past makes it abundantly clear how beliefs have changed, so that perhaps even the quotation marks may already be unnecessary when referring to history.

Notes

1   See Nikolaus Pevsner, "The Return of Historicism," originally published in the *Journal of the Royal Institute of British Architects*, 3rd ser., vol. 68, 1961; reprinted in N. Pevsner, *Studies in Art, Architecture and Design*, vol. 2: *Victorian and After* (London: Thames and Hudson, 1968), pp. 242–59.

2   Robert Venturi, *Complexity and Contradiction in Architecture*, with an introduction by Vincent Scully, Museum of Modern Art Papers on Architecture, no. 1 (New York: Museum of Modern Art, in association with the Graham Foundation for Advanced Studies in the Fine Arts, 1966), pp. 18–19.

3   Robert Venturi, Denise Scott Brown, and Steven Izenour, *Learning from Las Vegas* (Cambridge, Mass.: MIT Press, 1972), pp. 72–73.

4   Pevsner, *Studies in Art, Architecture and Design*, p. 243.

5   Cf. Jürgen Joedicke, *Architecture Since 1945: Sources and Directions* (New York: Frederick A. Praeger Publishers, 1969), pp. 139 ff.

6   The phrase, a new monumentality, was first used in this sense by Sigfried Giedion in "The Need for a New Monumentality," in *New Architecture and City Planning*, ed. Paul Zucker (New York: Philosophical Library, 1944), pp. 549–68.

7   Reprinted in Colin Rowe, *The Mathematics of the Ideal Villa and Other Essays* (Cambridge, Mass.: MIT Press, 1976), pp. 1–27.

8   Le Corbusier, *Towards a New Architecture*, trans. Frederick Etchells (orig. pub. 1923; ppb. ed., New York: Holt, Rinehart, and Winston, n.d.), pp. 63–79.

9   Ibid., pp. 266–68.

10 Ibid., p. 27.

11 See Robert A. M. Stern, "Stomping at the Savoye," *Architectural Forum* 138 (May 1973): 46–48.

12 Vincent J. Scully, Jr., *The Shingle Style: Architectural Theory and Design from Richardson to the Origins of Wright* (New Haven, Conn.: Yale University Press, 1955), pp. 113 ff.

13 See, e.g., his introduction to Venturi, *Complexity and Contradiction*, p. 13; and his *The Shingle Style Today, or the Historian's Revenge* (New York: George Braziller, 1974), esp. pp. 26–32.

14   V. Scully, *Louis I. Kahn* (New York: George Braziller, 1962), p. 11.

15   Frank Lloyd Wright, *An Autobiography*, rev. and enl. ed. (New York: Horizon Press, 1977), pp. 174–76.

16   Rowe, *Mathematics of the Ideal Villa*, pp. 128 ff. ("Neo-'Classicism' and Modern Architecture I," orig. pub. 1973).

17   Ibid., pp. 150, 154, 156 ("Neo-'Classicism' and Modern Architecture II," orig. pub. 1973).

18   "Kahn," an interview in *Perspecta* 7 (1961): 9.

19   See, e.g., Eugène-Emmanuel Viollet-le-Duc, *Discourses on Architecture*, vol. 1, orig. pub. 1863; trans. Henry Van Brunt (Boston: James R. Osgood and Company, 1975).

20   Such an interpretation of Kahn's later work, like so much else in this essay, derives from Vincent Scully's lectures, and writings of the period, as well as numerous discussions with him on the subject of Kahn and Venturi.

21   Venturi, *Complexity and Contradiction*, pp. 88–89.

22   Ibid., p. 89.

23   For the clearest statement of Kahn's philosophy, see his "Form and Design," originally recorded for the Voice of America *Forum Lectures*, 1960; reprinted in Scully, *Kahn*, pp. 114–21.

24   For Venturi's translation of Kahn's design method, see his discussion of the house for his mother in *Complexity and Contradiction*, pp. 117–21.

25   Venturi, *Learning from Las Vegas*, p. 72.

26   Pevsner, *Studies in Art, Architecture and Design*, p. 243.

Chapter 21

Mary McLeod

The battle for the monument
The Vietnam Veterans Memorial

> The notion of a modern monument is a contradiction in terms; if it is a monument, it is not modern, and if it is modern, it cannot be a monument.
>
> (Lewis Mumford, *The Culture of Cities*, 1938)

For much of this century, modern architects condemned monumentality as an antiquated relic of a previous era. They saw monumentality not only as antithetical to the basic functional and social premises of the new architecture, but also as perpetuating the very social hierarchies that they sought to overthrow. One of their primary goals was the obliteration of the fundamental division between the everyday and the monumental; as Alfred Roth later explained, this division was counter to the "basic idea of the equal dignity and form-worthiness of all architectural tasks and the oneness of all means of aesthetic expression."[1] Modern architects believed that if a new public architecture was to emerge, it should develop from the new public functions—libraries, gymnasiums, hospitals—rather than from the symbolic programs of earlier regimes—royal squares, triumphal arches, city gates. Of course, strong aesthetic allegiances underlay this moral stance. In the minds of the modern pioneers, monumental architecture meant classicism, and with it, the triumph of the academy.

After World War II, however, modern architects began to reassess strict function-alist dogma. Although practitioners of the new architecture, most notably Le Corbusier, had never excluded symbolism and references to tradition in their built work, few modern public buildings of any stature had been successfully realized. Faced with the massive reconstruction programs after the war, architects were forced to confront questions of public scale and space. These themes were explored in 1948 at a conference, sponsored by the *Architectural Review*, in which Henry-Russell Hitchcock, Walter Gropius, and Sigfried Giedion among others tackled the issue of "a new monumentality." Hitchcock's general definition, adopted by most of the contributors, reasserted some of the traditional attributes of monuments without directly evoking classicism: durability, solidity, dignity, large size, and fundamental emotional impact.[2] Three years earlier, Philip Johnson had written an essay specifically addressing the problem of war memorials, in which he forcefully rejected the modernist solution of "living memorials." Citing man's need for concrete symbols, he claimed that functional objects like bridges, libraries, and play-grounds never stimulated the same emotional and spiritual response as "useless" memorials. He proposed two archaic models: the mound and the megalith.[3]

For the most part, however, the question of an architectural language for monuments remained open. Both the modern movement and, more generally, the pluralism of modern society had precluded traditional architectural solutions; by 1945 few American architects could accept the classical model of the recently constructed Jefferson Memorial (Washington, D.C., 1937–43) as a standard for the future. Given this lack of clear precedents, competitions became an obvious vehicle to stimulate new solutions. In the early years of the United States, architecture competitions had played a similar role, as a democratic means of creating new types of public monuments. More recent results have been mixed. The winning entry of the Jefferson National Expansion competition for St. Louis, one of the first competitions after World War II, was greeted with widespread popular acclaim.[4] Eero Saarinen's solution, the well-known St. Louis arch, answered popular needs for familiar imagery and representation while meeting critics' demands for pure lines and minimal form. The noncontroversial nature of the program probably aided in its acceptance. At the other extreme was the Franklin Delano Roosevelt Memorial competition of 1961, in which Pedersen and Tilney's winning entry was rejected immediately by the public and dubbed "instant Stonehenge."[5] Besides the aesthetic issues involved and the ambivalent feelings about Franklin Delano Roosevelt himself, the primary focus of controversy was the long-standing question of a "living" versus a "useless" memorial.

The Vietnam Veterans Memorial competition in 1981 definitively concluded this debate. Throughout the competition process, almost no one questioned the appropriateness of having a memorial, and almost no one has done so since its realization. By all accounts, the memorial succeeds as a "modern monument." Today it is the most popular monument in the nation's capital, visited by about five million people each year (Figure 21.1). No structure built since World War II has had a greater impact on public attitudes in the United States. Its construction instigated a kind of national catharsis, dissolving the bitter disputes that divided the nation. The renewed interest in veterans' causes, the numerous publications about the war, and the recent plethora of Vietnam movies, in short the current ubiquity of Vietnam is in part a product of the memorial. Its

21.1 Maya Lin, Vietnam Veterans Memorial, Washington, D.C., 1981

success has, in fact, spurred the construction of numerous other memorials.[6] Few architects or critics now speak of monuments as symbols of stasis, hierarchy, or dictatorship.

But if the Vietnam memorial resolved Mumford's proclaimed contradiction between modernity and monumentality, the competition itself generated an intense controversy about the nature of public art and revealed how conflicted the interpretations of monumentality and public art remain in contemporary society. Initially seen as the most democratic means to achieve a memorial design, the competition process itself was later blamed for the winning design's purported failure to achieve public consensus. Its critics raised a series of questions that could not be ignored: Why were there no veterans on the jury? Why wasn't a flag required? Why did the program emphasize contemplation and reflection over celebration? And what finally did the victor—a Chinese-American "girl," a "gook," they said—know of war and patriotism? At the heart of this conflict were such long-standing issues as abstract versus representational art, professional authority versus participation, and artists' rights versus popular opinion.

THE COMPETITION

The Vietnam Veterans Memorial (VVM) began as the idea of a young army veteran from rural Maryland—Jan Scruggs. Like so many former veterans, he was deeply disturbed by the nation's apathy and disdain for those who had fought in the Vietnam war; but unlike many of his colleagues, he believed that a memorial would make a major difference. He proposed his idea at a local meeting of Vietnam Veterans in the spring of 1979, where Robert Doubek, a lawyer and former Air Force officer, offered his assistance. The two quickly formed a corporation, the Vietnam Veterans Memorial Fund, and taking a half-salary cut in pay, Doubek became the Fund's first full-time staff officer. He later directed the design competition and managed the memorial's construction. Other important participants included John Wheeler, a Washington lawyer and West Point graduate; Bob Frank, a certified public accountant; and Sandie Fauriol, a professional fund-raiser.[7]

Although none of the Fund officers were directly involved in the visual arts, they had several important ideas about the nature of the memorial. First, they sought a prominent site for the memorial, one that would be seen by all Washington tourists. Arlington, the location of the national cemetery, was too far removed. With the consultation of a prominent landscape firm, EDAW, the group eventually selected Constitution Gardens, the northern section of the mall between the Washington Monument and the Lincoln Memorial. Jack Wheeler, the chairman of the board, suggested a landscape solution, similar to the park memorializing Vietnam veterans that he had campaigned for at West Point. This was compatible with the interests of the National Park Service, whose officials had stated in meetings that they would not approve anything that disrupted the character of the mall. Hence, vertical structures were ruled out, and flags were considered unnecessary given the numerous flags surrounding the nearby Washington Monument. From the start, Scruggs envisioned that the names of those who had died serving in Vietnam would be listed on the memorial. The Fund officers all agreed that the memorial should be reconciliatory and apolitical, but it was also clear that the group would not arrive at an aesthetic consensus.

Robert Doubek proposed that the VVM Fund hold a competition, and after considering whether to limit participants, the group decided on an open competition as the most democratic and the most practical means to obtain a design, given their own inexperience and lack of expertise. The Fund also recognized the publicity value of a national competition, and with it, the potential for raising funds. In May 1980, the group hired the Washington architect Paul Spreiregen, a leading authority on architecture competitions, as their professional adviser.[8] Meanwhile Senator Charles Mathias of Maryland had introduced legislation to grant public land for the memorial. Congress approved the bill unanimously, and President Carter signed it into law July 1, 1980. As is usual in these matters, the legislation stipulated that the design be approved by the National Capital Planning Commission (NCPC), the Commission of Fine Arts (CIA), and the Secretary of the Interior.

Fund-raising was a more difficult matter. The VVM Fund elected a direct mail campaign to gain as broad a popular base as possible for a heretofore unknown cause. Money slowly began to come in—mostly small contributions from private citizens. In late April 1980, an appeal to his readers by syndicated columnist James J. Kilpatrick resulted in $60,000. The group also received $5,000 for a preliminary site study from the National Endowment for the Arts (NEA), which had earlier supported the idea of a VVM competition.[9] Another boost, and the donation most significant to the later controversy, was $160,000 from Texas billionaire H. Ross Perot to cover the costs of the competition.[10] The eventual goal was set at $7 million, which represented the estimated total costs of the project.[11]

Through the summer of 1980, the Fund worked closely with Spreiregen to develop the rules, criteria, and documents for the design competition. The program itself stated the officers' interests: that the memorial be "contemplative and reflective," be harmonious with its site, display the names of the 57,692 dead and missing,[12] and take no political position on the war. The brochure presentation especially emphasized the site. Included were photos of Constitution Gardens in both winter and summer and a history of the planning of the Mall. All Americans eighteen and over were eligible to enter. Drawings were limited to two 30- by 40-inch boards, and printed "rub-off" lettering was specifically prohibited in the hope that amateurs would not be deterred.[13]

The jury that the Fund agreed upon, however, was eminently professional, exclusively male, and gray-haired (all had been students or teachers at Ivy League schools and their average age was sixty-five). Spreiregen stressed that professional status would help attract first-class competitors and minimize professional controversy. This was considered particularly important, given the role of the Commission of Fine Arts and the looming ghost of the FDR Memorial competition. The eight-person jury that he proposed consisted of two architects, Pietro Belluschi (probably the most experienced juror in the United States) and Harry Weese; two landscape architects, Garrett Eckbo and Hideo Sasaki; three sculptors, Richard Hunt, Constantino Nivola, and James Rosati; and one critic, Grady Clay, editor of *Landscape Architecture* magazine.[14] The Fund debated about including a veteran on the jury, but at the urging of Spreiregen and Doubek, this was eventually ruled out. Issues of tokenism, potential deference to a veteran by other jury members, and ability to interpret drawings were the objections. Each member of the jury, however, was interviewed at length by the veterans' group to ensure confidence in his selection.[15]

The period between announcing the competition and judging the entries went smoothly. As in most competitions, participants were permitted to send queries. More than five hundred questions were submitted, and although some touched such sensitive issues as the political tone of the monument and popular participation in its design, the answers appeared (if the lack of public dissension can serve as a measure) to satisfy the competitors.[16] The Fund itself publicized the competition well, and it gained considerable coverage from both the architectural and the general press. Numerous architecture schools gave the project as a design exercise, including Yale, Columbia, and the University of Virginia. The eventual winning entry was, in fact, a project for a class in funerary architecture at Yale.

In terms of the number of entrants, the competition was a resounding success. More than 5,000 competition guideline booklets were requested and sent out, nearly 2,600 teams registered to participate (3,800 individuals in all), and 1,421 entries were mailed in by the March 31, 1981 deadline, making the competition the largest ever held in the United States and Europe.[17] The range of participants was broad: ages spanned from eighteen to at least sixty-six, all fifty states were represented, and the group included a wide mixture of professionals and amateurs. Less than 50 percent were registered architects, and approximately 25 percent were complete amateurs.[18] Two groups notable in their absence were well-known corporate architecture firms and recognized members of an architecture avant-garde. Such firms as Skidmore, Owings & Merrill (SOM); I.M. Pei and Partners; and Caudill, Rowlett, Scott (CRS); and such individual architects as Peter Eisenman, Michael Graves, Charles Moore, and Robert Venturi were all missing from the ranks. The same was true for well-known artists.[19] And although there might have been highly talented designers among the entrants, none was world-famous. The very openness of the competition may have discouraged established professionals, but just as likely a deterrent was the fear of placing a hard-earned architectural or artistic reputation at stake in such a potentially charged context. Interdisciplinary teams were another type of competitor that was only marginally represented. The VVM Fund had, in fact, envisioned many more of these entrants; at an earlier stage, when considering a limited competition for architects, one of its criteria of selection was that the winner be able to work effectively with a sculptor who was to be chosen later.[20]

The variety of designs submitted was immense: abstract, minimal forms and highly representational ones; freely configured, organic plans and rigorous, geometric ones; landscape solutions and traditional pavilions; earthworks and soaring obelisks. Some were of stone and metal; others used glass, plastic, neon, holographs, and even sound. This diversity contrasted sharply with the submissions to other Washington competitions, especially the ill-fated FDR Memorial competition, which was dominated by brutalist designs of the 1960s. The broad spectrum of participation and the range of architectural and sculptural styles current during the early 1980s contributed to the variety of approaches.

The most significant formal division between the projects, and one that would prove critical later, was that between abstract and representational designs. The vast majority of the projects were abstract in character; ordinarily, they involved some combination of architecture and landscape elements. In most schemes the structure displaying the names—walls, posts, or Stonehenge slabs—constituted the primary built feature. A surprisingly large percentage was circular in configuration, whether for vague symbolic reasons—a symbol of harmony, reconciliation—or for lack of imagination; in either event, a circular plan was easier to reconcile with Constitution Gardens' network of curving paths than an orthogonal one. Variants included water elements, steps, berms, and vistas to the Washington and Lincoln memorials. However in general, the abstract projects were highly repetitive and evoked few images beyond that of the names themselves, with the notable exception of the amphitheater schemes. Here, the audience of the dead confronted, sometimes wistfully, sometimes brutally, those remaining on stage. Students and young architects produced most of these designs.

In contrast, most of the figurative projects were by amateurs. The imagery varied enormously, but fell into certain broad categories: traditional symbols of patriotism (flags, stars, eagles); more pointed comments on the war (the helicopter, army boots, a map of Vietnam, a giant steel helmet riddled with bullet holes); symbols of peace and rebirth (a dove, a phoenix, guns at rest, a field of wheat); and finally, symbols of grief (eternal flames, a pool of tears, cypress trees, and a fallen sequoia). Of course, there were also a fair number of soldiers, a few heroic, though most of them were either "buddy sculptures"—one GI helping another—or more surprising, a GI helping an Asian child. In the majority of these, the war imagery was realistic and army garb was depicted in painstaking detail.

In other projects, the symbolism became even more literal—in the form of verbal inscriptions. As part of their designs, veterans usually included declarations honoring those who served and frequently accompanied their submissions with long descriptions explicating their projects. These projects suggest a struggle to find a communicative vehicle. Aside from their lack of graphic skills, the amateurs seemed less willing than the professional designers to settle for a certain mood (as in the landscape projects) or a traditional symbol of monument (as in some of the postmodern projects) to convey their objectives. Only some of the younger architecture students, infatuated with narrative trends, came up with proposals that matched the verbosity of the amateurs' entries.

Paradoxically, style appeared to have little correlation with the project's communicative power or effectiveness in meeting the veterans' program. The competition was held at a time when postmodernism reigned in the schools, and a large percentage of the student projects was either classical or Italian rationalist in style.[21] The competition, in fact, might be viewed as an ideal testing ground for postmodernism's appropriateness as a style for public monuments and for its capacity to communicate values, which were two of its advocates' primary objectives in countering the muteness and abstraction of modernism. But the postmodern designs seemed no more capable of realizing the tone of reconciliation and contemplation that the veterans sought than the leftover brutalist structures or the minimal sculptures of the 1960s. For all their figurative detail, few of the classicizing works managed to transcend either a clichéd patriotism or a decorative prettiness, the latter recalling garden pavilions rather than war monuments. Heavily indebted to Aldo Rossi's design for the Modena Cemetery, the rationalist projects frequently resembled cemeteries more than memorials. In both instances, what appeared to be expressed first was style, or architectural allegiance, rather than any interpretation of the memorial program itself.

If the entries conveyed no broad consensus about the nature of a war memorial, they also suggested little questioning along the lines of the earlier "living memorial" debate. When competitors challenged traditional interpretations of monumentality, their challenge stemmed more from the memorial's subject—the Vietnam War—than from the appropriateness of monumentality itself. Almost no one added a "useful" purpose to the memorial; any questioning of the program revealed itself in formal and conceptional ways: a simple grass bed; an elegant white marble path whose engraved names would disappear with use, leaving little trace once Vietnam had faded from public memory. If this last project had a disturbing underpinning—trampling on the dead—few projects were overtly cynical or dismissive. Again the sincerity of the program, with its open declaration of the war's ambiguity, mitigated against overtly propagandistic condemnations of the war. This same aspect also explains the paucity of overtly heroic designs—such as the Iwo Jima memorial or the Arc de Triomphe.

Although the program had a strong impact on the emotional tone of the solutions, few projects approached Maya Lin's first-place scheme in solving its specific contextual and psychological requirements: that the memorial be integrated in the landscape and be contemplative in nature. Lin's project also accomplished this with a minimum of means, making most of the other entries look overwrought or ostentatious. It is in essence a landscape sculpture: a polished black granite retaining wall, 400 feet long, bent at its center point in an open V formation.[22] The earth is carved out on the south side of the wall, forming a small open-sided valley. Only a few inches high at its end points, the wall itself gradually descends to a depth of ten feet at the vertex. One arm of the V points to the Lincoln Memorial, the other to the Washington Monument. Instead of being listed alphabetically or by division as is usual in war memorials, the 57,939 names are inscribed chronologically, in the order that each died or became missing. The list begins at the vertex on the eastern flank, then when it reaches the end of the wall, continues again at the beginning of the western flank, ending at the vertex where it began, suggesting that an era had completed its cycle. Lin's accompanying statement eloquently expressed her intentions.

> These names, seemingly infinite in number, convey the sense of overwhelming numbers, while unifying those individuals into a whole. For this memorial is meant not as a monument to the individual, but rather as a memorial to the men and women who died during the war as a whole. . . . Brought to a sharp awareness of such loss, it is up to each individual to resolve or come to terms with this loss. For death is in the end a personal and private matter and the area contained within this memorial is a quiet place, meant for personal reflection and private reckoning.[23]

What appealed to the jury? The project's "strength" and "deceptive simplicity," its "superbly harmonious" relation with its site, its response to the existing monuments, and its rejection of clichés and conventional symbolism. One member commented that "in a heterogeneous society symbols don't work; they arrest thought rather than expanding it."

Yet, the jurors clearly felt that the design was more than a purely formal statement. Their report concluded: "This is very much a memorial of our own times, one that could not have been achieved in another time and place. The designer has created an eloquent place where the simple meeting of earth, sky and remembered names contain messages for all who will know this place."[24]

Retrospectively, the criteria for selecting the second and third-place winners do not seem so clear. The second-place project, designed by Marvin Krosinsky, Victor Ochakovsky, and David Fisher—this was juror Clay's initial favorite—featured a looming, crushed bronze sculpture, supported on gray granite walls.[25] The third-place project, designed by a team including the original consulting landscape architect Joseph Brown and sculptor Frederick Hart, consisted of a semicircular wall, terminated at each end with realistic cast soldiers. Both projects were oriented toward the Washington Monument. The stylistic differences, however, could not have been greater. As Spreiregen notes, the placed projects in a large competition are not necessarily second or third best, but are often those designs that permit debate or that are most representative of certain approaches. He sees the third-place winner in this competition as reminiscent of World War I memorials; the second-place, of World War II memorials; and the first-place, as undoubtedly belonging to the present generation.[26] The awards for honorable mention followed this pattern of representing a variety of approaches: a circle of trees, a sculpture garden with stepping stones, a series of convex bronze obelisks, a pool with memorial trees, a field of soldiers, a flag with stars of pleached trees and stripes of granite, a curvilinear white retaining wall. If any biases of the jury emerged clearly, they were the rejection of representational imagery, a concern for context, and an endorsement of landscape solutions.[27] The latter two preferences reflected those of the veterans and the aesthetic thrust of many competition entries; the former, however, was to prove critical to the subsequent controversy.

Whatever private reservations individuals may have had, the Fund warmly endorsed the jury's unanimous choice. Veterans, jurors, competitors, and the public together agreed that the competition had worked: it was democratic, it generated publicity, and it resulted in a highly original project that met the Fund's criteria. Clay, the head of the jury, declared it the best-run competition he had encountered. Spreiregen requested all participants to give their reactions to the competition process; there were few complaints.[28]

Yet, the classic problems of selecting a design through a competition quickly surfaced. First, there was the issue of rapport between the patron and client. Lin and the veterans could not have been more radically different. Young and sheltered, she knew nothing of war or suffering; nor was she interested in learning more about Vietnam or the soldiers. For their part, the veterans were put off by her youth, her hippy appearance, and her inability to perceive that the monument was theirs, not hers.[29] Another issue concerned the question of professional control, a problem compounded by the fact that the winner was not a registered architect. Lin rejected the first contract that the VVM Fund offered her, which made her little more than a public relations agent. In the second contract she was assured an advisory role in the design's elaboration. Tensions also developed immediately over the choice of a project architect.[30] Eventually, the Fund and Lin settled on the Washington firm of Cooper-Lecky as the architect of record. Cesar Pelli, the dean of Yale

University's School of Architecture, had recommended the partners Kent Cooper and William Lecky to Lin as having enough experience to realize her project effectively but not such large design egos that they would alter her idea. That advice proved sound.[31]

Artistic control, however, remained a contentious issue. The competition process allowed no dialogue between patron and designer. To what extent was the winning scheme only a winning idea, which the patron had the right to elaborate or change? To what extent were alterations a violation of the jury's choice and the competition process itself? One early conflict concerned the addition of an inscription. Lin believed any additional text would rob the names of their emotional power. The veterans insisted that an inscription was necessary in order for the memorial to honor all men who fought in Vietnam, not just those who died. In time, Lin agreed to a prologue and epilogue that would complete the booklike cycle of the chronological listing. The final wording, a group effort, respected the quiet tone of the memorial itself.[32] Although these issues might have arisen in any design process, here they were only the beginning of a much deeper struggle.

Initial critical reaction to the memorial's design was almost universally positive. The *New York Times* cited its "extreme dignity and restraint"; the *Cleveland Plain Dealer* "its understated brilliance"; and Wolf Von Eckhart of the *Washington Post* said, "It seemed too much to expect that a worthy memorial could emerge from the mess that was Vietnam. But it did."[33] Professional journals were equally enthusiastic,[34] and veterans' groups quickly endorsed the project and began campaigning for contributions. One of the most positive statements of support came from the American Gold Star Mothers, whose official paper reprinted a *New York Times* editorial stating that "ideas about heroism, or art, for that matter are no longer what they were before Vietnam."[35] The only major public attacks came from the *New Republic* and the *Chicago Tribune*; the latter's architecture critic, Paul Gapp, called Lin's design "inane . . . an erosion control project."[36]

The public hearings held by the Commission of Fine Arts and the National Capital Planning Commission during the summer of 1981 went smoothly; little testimony was presented against the design, and it received enthusiastic approval from both organizations. It appeared that the VVM Fund had avoided the pitfalls of the FDR competition, and that the organization was well on its way to realizing a dedication ceremony on Veterans Day 1982.

THE CONTROVERSY

In the fall of 1981, however, the public perception of the memorial changed abruptly. The critical event was a routine meeting of the Commission of Fine Arts on October 13 that was scheduled to review granite samples. In contrast to earlier meetings, the room was filled with journalists and TV cameramen. Tom Carhart, a twice-wounded Vietnam veteran and former volunteer of the VVM Fund,[37] appealed to the commission to reconsider its approval of Lin's design. Echoing a recent article in the *National Review*, he claimed that the memorial was an antiwar statement, more appropriate as a "statement of the political war of the country" than as a monument honoring veterans.

He considered this an inevitable result of having no veterans on the jury. He particularly objected to the black walls, calling the memorial "a shameful, degrading ditch, a black gash of sorrow and degradation." His final criticism was directed at the chronological listing of names. They were a "random scattering . . . such that neither brother nor father nor lover nor friend could ever be found."[38]

The commission confirmed its earlier approval of Lin's design, but the controversy had only begun. Two members of the Fund's sponsoring committee, H. Ross Perot and the novelist James Webb, also opposed the design, and both had considerable clout—Perot had money and Webb had friends on Capitol Hill.[39] (Webb was then serving as the Minority Counsel to the House Veterans Affairs Committee.) The two campaigned energetically to block the design, and others soon joined forces with them. The group included conservative congressmen and their staffs, key assistants to interior Secretary James Watt,[40] and Milton Copulos, a veteran and staff member of the right-wing Heritage Foundation.

The primary objections to Lin's design had been voiced by veteran Carhart: that it was black, that it was underground, and that all the names were listed (and in chronological order). Other complaints that surfaced were the lack of a flag and the neutral tone of the proposed inscription. A few objected to the wall's V formation as representing a peace symbol. All this added up to the fact that the memorial did not honor veterans enough—that it was about dying, grief, and shame rather than glory and respect. It was "a black spot in the nation's history," a "mass grave." As Webb stated at a press conference, "It is . . . a place not for celebration, but to go and be depressed."[41] The critics claimed that the project failed to meet its congressional mandate to honor all veterans; it paid homage to the dead alone. The memorial's emphasis on the individual made this especially disturbing. "The mode of listing the names makes them individual deaths, not deaths in a cause: they might as well have been traffic accidents."[42] [. . .]

What few acknowledged was that it would be nearly impossible to design a heroic or celebratory monument and respect the "philosophy" outlined in the program statement itself. Specific design directives further worked against traditional monumentality: the request that it be "contemplative and reflective," that it "should be harmonious with its site," and that it must include the 58,000 names of the dead and missing. It is hard to imagine how any monument with such a listing would not generate feelings of sadness and loss, rather than of celebration. Only in a few monuments of World War I, where extreme loss for a questionable cause was also an issue, is there a similar emphasis on individual tragedy rather than collective heroic death—the most notable being Sir Edwin Lutyens' memorial at Thiepval, which Lin cites as an important influence.[43]

The conflict over the Vietnam memorial has been characterized by some as an artistic battle and by others as a political battle. In fact it was both, as the lines between the two were not always clear. One of the first artistic issues that emerged was populism. Why were there no veterans on the jury? Why weren't popular expectations taken into account? Opponents complained that the competition results could only be a product of an elitist group that had no understanding of veterans' needs, much less those of the public. Henry Hyde, the Republican representative from Illinois, stated that "memorials may be too important to leave to artists and architects." Sybil Stockdale, the wife of the famous POW [John Stockdale], was even more emphatic: "Let's put art where it belongs. In the art museums."[44]

This disregard for public taste was the major theme of an article by Tom Wolfe, written on the eve of a major meeting of the Commission of Fine Arts to discuss alterations to Lin's design. With his usual caustic hyperbole, Wolfe claimed that the design was a product of the "Mullahs of Modernism," who were attempting to impose their elitist values in the manner of a "Savonarola," or even "a Red Guard-style cultural revolution." Their goal was to overturn bourgeois taste and to implement "the arcane principles of modernism . . . whether the poor beasts like it or not." Wolfe compared Lin's design to Carl Andre's *Stone Field* and Richard Serra's *Tilted Arc*, artworks that "baffled or ignored" the public. In his view, the art jury reflected the same sector of society that "didn't go" to Vietnam: the managerial and merchant classes, epitomized by Harvard, the home of the Mullahs. He characterized the veterans, on the other hand, as belonging to two classes represented by Carhart and Scruggs: the professional military and the "proles."[45] What Wolfe did not acknowledge is that opposition to the winning scheme was almost exclusively led by military academy graduates—Carhart, Webb, and Perot. The "proles" of the VVM Fund supported Lin's design.[46]

Although the complaints about popular participation and the exclusion of veterans from the jury were numerous, few critics went along entirely with Wolfe's indictment of modernism.[47] However much they admired the Iwo Jima memorial, they did not seek a representational sculpture as the solution to their complaints. Carhart, in an article published in the *Washington Post* immediately after he testified to the Commission of Fine Arts, argued that making the memorial white, raising it above ground, and placing a flag at its apex would change it from a degrading monument to one properly honoring those who served.[48] Webb took the same stance. What was being disputed primarily was meaning, not style. The *National Review* made this position explicitly clear: "Our objection to this Orwellian glop does not issue from any philistine objection to new conceptions in art. It is based upon the clear political message of this design."[49]

Almost all of the critics saw Lin's design as a left-wing, antiwar statement. In fact, few of them complained that the meaning was obscure at all. Phyllis Schlafly called the wall a "tribute to Jane Fonda,"[50] a phrase that became frequently quoted and was used even as the closing line of Wolfe's own indictment. Many commentators now interpreted the controversy as being "due to the nature of the war itself."[51] Those who praised the memorial were antiwar; those who condemned it, prowar. But like the issue of abstraction versus representation, this division again only partially explains the controversy. Although almost everybody opposed to the monument was a former supporter of the war and a declared conservative, many advocates of the design were also politically conservative. One of the most passionate defenders of Lin's work was the syndicated columnist James J. Kilpatrick, who had been pro-Vietnam. The memorial design was also praised by William Buckley and General William C. Westmoreland, the latter calling the black polished granite "handsome" and the monument a reflection of "dignity and good taste."[52]

Another crucial issue in this skirmish was the emotionally charged problem of representing what it is to be a soldier and to sacrifice one's life for one's country. Could the concept of honor be expressed through quiet contemplation, reflection, and solitude?

Or did it demand grandeur, celebration, and an acknowledgment of heroism?[53] At times it seemed as if questions of manhood and masculinity were at the root of these differences. Wolfe's article referred to the veterans as "young men who passed Vietnam's horrifying tests of manly honor," who "felt that they were part of a special, even elite, brotherhood."[54] Webb's critique of Lin's design was full of similar machismo. The focus of the attack had shifted quite clearly to the idea of monumentality itself.

> Watching then the white phallus that is the Washington Monument piercing the air like a bayonet, you feel uplifted. You are supposed to feel uplifted. This was the intention of the designers. That is the political message. And then when you peer off into the woods at this black slash of earth to your left, this sad, dreary mass tomb, nihilistically commemorating death, you are hit with that message also. That is the debate. That is the tragedy of this memorial for those who served.[55]

That Lin herself was a woman—and a small and young woman at that—did not help.[56] Even complimentary remarks, such as those given at an awards ceremony of the American Institute of Architects (AIA), took on traditional gender overtones: "she spoke softly where others were wont to shout."[57] Of course, none of this was new to discussions of war memorials. General Winfield Scott's mare on Scott Circle in Washington, D.C. was retroactively transformed into a stallion.

Ultimately, the various objections—artistic, political, emotional—can be understood as revolving around a notion of history. Webb in particular was acutely conscious of this. As he later explained, the memorial would occupy "a permanence in the national mindset, with an even greater power than history itself." History could be reevaluated with new facts and different interpretations. But a piece of art remained "as a testimony to a particular moment in history . . . we are under a solemn obligation to get that moment down as correctly as possible."[58] However sincere these remarks, a new form of national amnesia characterized the opposition's motivation and strength.[59] Like President Reagan confronting the Nazi dead at Bitburg, the nation seemed swept with a desire to forget the pain of an earlier era; in fact, as Garry Wills has argued, Reagan's own popularity represented in part a yearning for old values, for clear heroes, for an earlier epoch—simpler and more innocent.[60] In an essay written during the memorial controversy, the novelist Tim O'Brien, a Vietnam veteran, eloquently described the nation's inability to confront the complexities of Vietnam.

> It would seem that time and distance erode memory. . . . For many of us, years later, Vietnam is seen with a certain tempered nostalgia. A half-remembered adventure. We feel, many of us, proud of having "been there," forgetting the terror, straining out the bad stuff. . . . We have forgotten, or lost the energy to recall, the terribly complex and ambiguous issues of the Vietnam War. . . . We're all adjusted. The whole country. . . . I wish we were more troubled.[61]

In the two months following Carhart's testimony the controversy escalated.[62] Perot financed a Gallup poll of 567 former Vietnam POWs to determine their opinions of the design; predictably, they turned out to be highly critical.[63] Webb and Carhart began exploring the possibilities of a lawsuit against the Fund, on the basis that the memorial's listing of names was an invasion of privacy.[64] And in late December 1981, conservative Congressman Henry Hyde launched what he called his "Christmas offensive." He rallied twenty-seven Republican colleagues to sign a letter to President Reagan requesting that Secretary Watt block the memorial. The letter alluded to Lin's design as "the Black Hole of Calcutta" and demanded the appointment of a new jury, one "less intent on perpetuating national humiliation no matter how artistically expressed."[65] Meanwhile rumors were circulating that four or five jurors were antiwar activists and that one of them, Garrett Eckbo, was a member of the American Communist Party.[66]

The Fund officers were still firmly committed to Lin's design and fought back vigorously. Black, they explained, was a color of dignity and respect: both the Iwo Jima and the Seabees' memorials were black. The obtuse angle of the memorial's walls could not possibly be a "peace sign": no one could spread his or her fingers that wide. An inscription honoring all of those who fought would be part of the memorial, despite claims to the contrary. And the design was not a left-wing statement; indeed it had been highly praised by all sides of the political spectrum. To counter the rumors of Communist affiliation, the VVM Fund issued a fact sheet entitled "The Truth About the Vietnam Veterans Memorial," which declared that "allegations that they [the jurors] were influenced or controlled by communists or that they were attempting to make an anti-war or un-American statement are pure bunk."[67] While the statement adroitly skirted the issue of former communist affiliation—Eckbo had taught at the California Labor School in the 1940s—it explained that all of the jurors had been interviewed at length by the veterans to determine if they were sympathetic to the veterans' design criteria and that four of the jurors had been veterans of other wars. Many rallied to the Fund's support, and contributions continued to pour in.[68] In late December, the Veterans of Foreign Wars donated $180,000 and the American Legion had nearly attained its goal of one million dollars. But the opposition had close connections to the Reagan administration. In January 1982, Secretary Watt stated that he would block the memorial unless the Fund accommodated the opponents. The Fund asked Senator John Warner, an earlier supporter of the project, to set up a "compromise meeting" between the two groups.

At this point the debate moved behind closed doors. What was to have been a small meeting turned into a gathering of about a hundred people crowded into a Senate hearing room. Fund representatives were outnumbered by at least five to one. Perot arrived with a group of about ten people. Earlier he had sent an aide to Washington to organize the opposition. Lin was not informed of the gathering. The critics wanted their proposed changes: a white memorial, above ground, with a flag. Scruggs and the Fund agreed to the flag but made no headway in defending Lin's design. General George Price, one of America's highest ranking black officers, finally silenced the opposition's demands for white: "Black is not a color of shame. . . . Color meant nothing on the battlefields of Korea and Vietnam. . . . Color should mean nothing now."[69] After still more hours of highly charged debate, General Michael S. Davidson, who led the 1970 Cambodian invasion, found the solution: a stronger inscription and the addition of a statue and a flag. The Fund accepted these additions, and in exchange, the opponents agreed "to cease their political effort to block approval of the design and to allow the planned March 1 groundbreaking to occur on schedule."[70] In early March, the Commission on Fine Arts, the National Capital Planning Commission, and Secretary Watt approved these additions in principle. Lin was adamantly opposed to the changes but agreed to be silent until construction was far enough along that Watt could not reverse his stand.

The dissident factions now focused their energy on the location of the sculpture and the flag. A second meeting of the "compromise" committee was scheduled for March 11 to discuss designs for the sculpture. Again, the VVM Fund was vastly outnumbered by opponents. The gathering voted to put the flag on top of the memorial, at the vertex, and the sculpture on the ground below, in front of the V. But the decision was not final. Placement still had to be approved by Watt, the Commission of Fine Arts, and the National Capital Planning Commission.

The manner in which the sculpture was selected contrasted sharply with the earlier competition process. The VVM Fund hired no consultants; there was no question of a second competition. Instead, the Fund appointed a selection committee consisting of two opponents to Lin's wall—James Webb and Milton Copulos—and two supporters—Bill Jayne and Art Mosely. All were veterans; none had training in the visual arts. The group reviewed the winning entries and chose the highest-placed representational sculptor— Frederick Hart. Hart quickly presented a maquette of three soldiers (one black, one Hispanic, and one white) which won the committee's enthusiastic endorsement. Hart was to receive $330,000 for the piece, plus one-half of the profits resulting from the sale of souvenir miniatures (in comparison to Lin's $20,000 prize money and consultant's fee of $15 per hour).[71]

Publicly, the officers of the VVM Fund supported the additions completely.[72] They were anxious to have the memorial dedicated by Veterans Day at almost any cost, and the compromise, which all the official veterans groups enthusiastically endorsed, seemed to make that goal possible. But then fierce opposition to the plan was voiced by Maya Lin and the architecture community. Lin compared Hart's additions to "drawing mustaches on other portraits."[73] She argued that the sculpture was aesthetically incompatible with her design and symbolically unnecessary; the wall itself represented the living and the dead. The additions turned the wall into little more than a backdrop for the sculpture and a pedestal for the flag. Nor could she accept Secretary Watt's mandate to compromise. If need be, the Fund should wait to dedicate the wall; it was not a "McMonument." The AIA, professional adviser Paul Spreiregen, and jury members Harry Weese and Grady Clay all supported her objections on the grounds of preventing artistic interference and of maintaining the integrity of the jury process. Cooper-Lecky, the architects of record, did not actively oppose the compromise whether out of political considerations (they had numerous government contracts) or out of loyalty to the Fund.[74]

Meanwhile, the Fund itself continued to receive pressure from the earlier opponents, who feared that their selection for the sculpture's site would not be respected. Perot talked of auditing the group's books; another Texan, John Baines, hired Roy Cohn, a former aide to Joseph McCarthy, to begin financial investigations.[75] Perot released the results of his POW poll, and Carhart continued his editorial crusade.[76] The critical show-down took place at the October 1982 meeting of the Commission of Fine Arts, and the final decision was made by Washington's arbiter of taste, Carter Brown: the statue and the flag would be included, but at a considerable distance from the wall. The veterans could have their national salute on Veterans' Day, November 11, 1982, and the statue would be added later.

Although the monument's fate had been decided, opposition among veterans continued. Efforts were made to introduce new legislation in Congress to overrule the Commission of Fine Arts' decision on the sculpture's location;[77] only the adroit talents of Senator Mathias kept a bill from getting to the floor. Opponents of the final compromise kept pressing their allegations of financial improprieties until a Government Accounting Office (GAO) audit was completed in 1984. Webb remained angry to the end, exchanging bitter letters with Scruggs through 1984.[78]

THE MEMORIAL

When the memorial was at last dedicated on November 11, 1982, public opposition dissolved. Veterans, former antiwar demonstrators, grieving parents, tourists—all stood in front of the memorial, paying respect to those who had served in Vietnam. The experience was and continues to be overwhelming. Far from being the cold, baffling object that Wolfe described, it is one of intense emotion, perhaps the most cathartic memorial in the nation's history. For two years it stood alone, unadorned by the "compromise" sculpture.

But is it a monument? As critics quickly grasped, the wall inverts most conventions of monumentality. It is horizontal, not vertical; cut into the earth, not elevated on a pedestal above; it is black, not white; and it can barely be seen from a city street.[79] Unique among American national war monuments, it lists every death. But if the wall represents a radical interpretation of conventions, it maintains others—indeed, those that Hitchcock deemed essential to monumentality in 1948: scale, presence, a sense of permanence.[80] Its very break from tradition, in fact, contributes to its singularity and power; and unlike figurative imagery, the meaning of which fades with changing conventions, the names will remain a constant sign of the memorial's purpose. Furthermore, the wall captures the balance between symbolic suggestion and openness to interpretation typical of the most powerful of traditional monuments. Its color, its material, its location, the names—all make it unquestionably a place to reflect on those who served in Vietnam. But whether black means grief, shame, respect, or dignity, whether its path emphasizes descent into the earth or ascent toward existing monuments, whether the inscription of the names evokes individual deaths or collective loss, and whether the memorial is primarily for the dead or for the living who confront the wall—all are left to each individual to decide.[81]

One component of its monumentality is new: participation (Figure 21.2). Many traditional monuments, such as the Washington Monument or the Arc de Triomphe in Paris, are urban landmarks, whose primary impact is from afar. In comparison, the wall must be approached closely to be seen and experienced. Imbedded in the rock, the names gain a materiality in themselves, inviting viewers to touch them, to make rubbings—now so much a part of the ritual of the wall that vendors sell "gold rubbing kits." As Lin envisioned, the polished black surface creates reflections—each visitor sees himself or

21.2 Maya Lin, Vietnam Veterans Memorial

herself along with the names of the dead. That the wall is visible on one side only intensifies this sense of confrontation and absorption. But the strongest element of engagement results from the chronological listing of the names. Finding a name requires time and often assistance; volunteers share grief with the visitors and discuss the wall's meaning with them. The chronological listing is especially poignant for surviving soldiers, who, once they discover a name, then recognize others who died in the same battle. For the veterans, the wall can also re-create a sense of war's peculiar time, as they realize that the lines on a panel can represent the consequences of an entire year or just one horrible day (as do those marking the Tet offensive). Many visitors leave flowers, flags, letters, and even articles of clothing that had been worn by dead soldiers. These gifts and the rubbings allow the memory inspired by the monument to live far beyond its confines.[82] This involvement answers many of the criticisms posed by modernists against traditional memorials. But unlike the "living memorial," the only "useful" function of the wall is its symbolic role.

Related to this sense of participation is a new personal or private dimension to the memorial, which challenges traditional notions of monumentality in yet another way. The park setting, the path's descent into the earth, the granite's mirror effect, and the linear character of the wall permitting each individual a singular focus—all contribute to a sense of private reflection. Unlike the Lincoln Memorial or the Washington Monument, the wall contains no point toward which all gaze. This emphasis on the individual does not deny collective dimensions. The vistas to other monuments and reflections of them in the wall serve as constant reminders that private contemplation remains in a public arena, with public consequences.

In the local Vietnam memorials that have followed, this balance has frequently been lost because of an attempt to monumentalize the private dimension; at these other memorials the public content becomes the personal experience. Instead of the constant flow of letters brought to the Washington memorial, a few sample letters are permanently etched in glass in New York City, and in Sacramento, California, a memorial sculpture will show a soldier reading a letter from back home. Once again, we see an effort to rewrite history; with the overlay of sentiment the war itself becomes less of an issue.[83]

What finally is the political meaning of the wall? Is it elitist, a left-wing statement, or antiwar, as some of its critics have charged? The charges of elitism are the easiest to dismiss. Long before Hart's statue, the memorial soon became "The Wall," and even "Our Wall," to thousands of veterans. The number of visitors quickly surpassed those to both the Lincoln Memorial and the Washington Monument. Nor does its message seem particularly left-wing; its symbols are not specific enough for such readings. The feelings that it evokes—grief, respect, quiet reflection—transcend labels, and its audience crosses political boundaries. But two qualities of the memorial do suggest ideological criticism. The wall is egalitarian: no ranks, no branches of the service, no individual heroes are designated in the sea of names. And it asks questions. It forces visitors to wonder whether Lincoln's statue of contemplation at one end and Washington's monument of soaring aspiration at the other relate in any way to the deaths in the middle?

In one respect, the wall is an antiwar statement. It is impossible to look at the sea of names and not feel the immensity of the loss and the pain.[84] Any cause would seem difficult to justify in the face of such sacrifice, but especially one so controversial. Paradoxically, this message was not Lin's, but the veterans'. The program made death the overwhelming fact. What the memorial's opponents never appeared to understand was how few Vietnam veterans sought glory or heroic imagery; most simply wanted acknowledgment. Although the names call attention to the dead, they also call attention to the enormous suffering of all involved. Many veterans did not want to rewrite history; they only wanted to be included as part of it.

Have the additions of the flag in 1983 and the statue in 1984 substantially altered the experience of the memorial? Art critics opposed to the sculpture predicted that it would turn the memorial into a monumental battle between two artistic styles and two attitudes toward memorializing the war—the wall, "a tribute to Jane Fonda"; and the sculpture, "an homage to John Wayne."[85] In contrast, Hart and his supporters believed that the sculpture would complement and comment upon the wall, serving as a kind of Greek chorus to Lin's tragedy. In fact, it does neither. First, the imagery of the statue is hardly heroic. Although the three young soldiers are handsome, strong, and rugged in their combat fatigues, fulfilling American stereotypes of masculinity and duty, they also look dazed. The sculpture conveys no moment of triumph (such as the flag striking ground in Iwo Jima) or even a sense of purpose beyond a vague feeling of camaraderie and mutual support. The mood is not celebratory; whatever formal and psychological reassurances the statue provides, it is not a prowar monument.[86] Second, the statue is small and somewhat removed. It does not stand in battle or dialogue with the wall but exists simply as a separate, smaller memorial, to be passed en route. Sightseers generally stop at the sculpture briefly, photograph it, sometimes comment upon the realism of the army garb, and then move on. Few stay longer than five minutes.[87]

The flag has resulted in even less involvement. It acts merely as a reflexive sign of certainty and security, for it is too familiar and ubiquitous an icon to demand contemplation or even attention. Ironically, given the controversy surrounding the flag's initial omission, the wall itself is almost always adorned with small flags. (There were 147 when I visited one day in July 1987.)

The question remains whether the wall would have been a more effective monument without these "infringements"? In an insightful essay written eighty-five years ago, the German aesthetician Alois Riegl argued that monuments should be considered in terms of both artistic value and historical value.[88] Riegl was attempting to establish criteria for preservation, but his two standards have relevance to our understanding of present-day intentions in creating monuments. To what extent is a monument a work of art to be appreciated for its emotional and formal power apart from its historical circumstance? To what extent is its value dependent on its historical role and its embodiment as a visual artifact of that role?

From almost any artistic perspective, the three elements of the Vietnam Veterans Memorial are not formally compatible. Nor would many claim any independent artistic value for Hart's sculpture; it is a competent but highly predictable piece of social realism.[89] Lin's design, however, is also subject to formal criticism. Although the wall is well-detailed and effectively scaled, other elements, such as the path (with its awkward conjuncture of granite boulders and slabs) and the directory booths lack invention and formal refinement. Even the siting, which has been universally praised, does little to alter our perception of space; the symmetrical design, the exact orientation to existing monuments embody none of the formal risks of a sculpture by Richard Serra or Michael Heizer. Such formalist analyses of public monuments, of course, risk trivialization. Few monuments succeed in purely visual terms; their meanings cannot be separated from their purposes and contexts.

In the case of the Vietnam Veterans Memorial this seems especially true. Its artistic and historical value are completely intertwined. Right now, the historical function takes first priority, and it will probably continue to do so for at least another generation. However incompatible artistically, the flag and the sculpture are now a part of that historical understanding. They recall with the wall the conflicting visions of the war and the difficulties in coming to a consensus about representing the past. As pluralism diminishes the possibility of shared public symbols, a pluralist monument may be one of the few recourses to public dialogue. The Latin word *monere* does not mean merely "to remember," but also "to admonish," "warn," "advise," and "instruct."[90] This tripartite monument, like some fragmented acropolis, accomplishes these diverse tasks. Nevertheless, it is not the uneasy partnership among such seemingly incompatible elements that is the VVM's most remarkable feature, but the existence of the wall itself. In a period when amnesia substitutes for history, when President Reagan himself represented a yearning to forget, that this fragmented understanding should be realized at all is a rare public acknowledgment of historical complexity.

These issues are much larger than the competition process. But it is also clear that many of them would never have surfaced without it, much less have been embodied in the final memorial. By staging a competition, the veterans gained a major role in shaping the tone and the character of the memorial; indeed, they wrote the program, probably the single most powerful determinant of the process. It is doubtful that the veterans would have defined their own objectives so clearly had they simply commissioned a designer. Nor would a well-known architect or sculptor have necessarily permitted the veterans' criteria to subsume his or her own style or attitudes. Although the competition may have limited the dialogue between designer and client, it prohibited an artist from unduly influencing the program itself. The competition also opened up the range of competitors and possible solutions. It was vulnerable to criticism where it failed to meet a popular constituency—for instance, in the composition of the jury—but in the face of criticism it gave credibility to the results. Lin's design would never have been selected as the memorial without the competition; it would not have generated so much controversy had the jury been different; but it would not have survived the criticism had the competition itself not been widely viewed as being democratically and professionally run. Finally, the competition contributed both in its process and subsequent controversy to the memorial's importance; it encouraged discussion about that which was buried—ambivalent attitudes toward the representation of war, honor, and monumentality. In short, it contributed to making the memorial *public*.

Notes

All archival documents are from the manuscript division of the Library of Congress unless otherwise noted.

1   Quoted in Gregor Paulsson, *et al.*, "In Search of a New Monumentality," symposium, *Architectural Review* (September 1948): 121. Although this statement was made in 1948, it represents the attitudes of many modernists before the war.
2   Gregor Paulsson, *et al.*, 117–28.
3   Philip C. Johnson, "War Memorials: What Aesthetic Price Glory?" *Art News* 44 (September 1945): 8–10, 24–25. For discussion of the postwar debate about "living memorials," see Bernard Barber, "Place, Symbol, and Utilitarian Function in War Memorials," *Social Forces* 28 (October 1949): 64–68. One of the most thoughtful defenses of the "living memorial" is Joseph Hudnut's essay "The Monument Does Not Remember," *Atlantic Monthly* (September 1945). Arguments for artistic and symbolic memorials include Margaret Cresson "Memorials Symbolic of the Spirit of Man," *New York Times Magazine* (July 22, 1945); and Lincoln Rothschild, "What 'Lives' in a War Memorial?" *Saturday Review of Literature* (June 22, 1945). An insightful discussion of these themes in relation to the Vietnam Veterans Memorial can be found in Catherine M. Howett, "The Vietnam Veterans Memorial: Public Art and Politics," *Landscape* 28, no. 2 (1985): 1–9.
4   Like all major structures, the arch was criticized, however, by a few critics, who considered its abstract form "fascist." These individuals were disturbed by its resemblance to Adalberto Libera's arch (1938) for Mussolini's proposed E'42 exhibition in Rome.
5   Quoted in Thomas H. Creighton, *The Architecture of Monuments: The Franklin Delano Roosevelt Memorial Competition* (New York: Reinhold, 1962), p. 6. [. . .]
6   See "143 Vietnam Memorials, Vast and Small, Rising Around the Nation," *New York Times* (November 9, 1986). [. . .]
7   [. . .] For accounts of the VVM Fund and the realization of the memorial, see Robert W. Doubek, "The Story of the Vietnam Veterans Memorial," *Retired Officer* (November 1983): 17–24; Jan

C. Scruggs and Joel L. Swerdlow, *To Heal a Nation: The Vietnam Veterans Memorial* (New York: Harper and Row, 1985). [...]

8 The National Endowment for the Arts (NEA) recommended the VVM hire a professional adviser. The group had contacts with NEA in February 1980 about the possibility of an open competition, and the government agency, which voiced enthusiasm about the project, was influential in the VVM Fund's decision to proceed with an open as opposed to limited competition. [...]

9 Livingston L. Biddle to Robert Doubek, September 8, 1980. NEA later awarded the VVM Fund $15,000 toward costs of the design competition. See Doubek to Biddle, August 28, 1981. [...]

10 Earlier in January 1981, Perot had contributed $10,000 to the Fund; this was its second major contribution. Although Perot's donation of $160,000 in April 1982 was widely publicized, at that moment the Fund already had $800,000 invested. Memorandum on the history of Perot's involvement with the VVM Fund, n.d. (chronology stops December 1981), p. 1; Robert Doubek, comments on author's manuscript, March 14, 1987.

11 The initial goal was $2.5 million. Eventually, the VVM Fund raised approximately $10 million. Over 650,000 people gave ten dollars or less. Scruggs and Swerdlow, p. 96.

12 These were the official totals for US military killed and missing in Vietnam when the VVM was being planned. The death figure now exceeds 58,000; names have been added to the wall each year.

13 VVM Fund, "The Vietnam Veterans Memorial Design Competition" (brochure sent to prospective competitors), November 24, 1980; VVM Fund, "Design Program: The Vietnam Veterans Memorial Design Competition" (program brochure sent to registered competitors), December 31, 1980.

14 Spreiregen and the VVM Fund initially hoped to include a "generalist" and invited James Michener, Eric Sevareid, René Dubos, Walter Cronkite, Robert Penn Warren, Edith Hamilton, Herman Wouk, and S. Dillon Ripley to be jury members. All declined. The magazine editor, Grady Clay, as the one nonpractitioner, was eventually seen as fulfilling the "generalist" role. See correspondence between the VVM Fund and potential jurors (October–November 1980) in the Library of Congress archives.

15 In hindsight, both Doubek and Spreiregen believe the omission of a veteran was correct; Scruggs, however, thinks it was probably a mistake. Doubek, interview with author, July 7, 1987; Spreiregen, interview with author, July 30, 1987; Scruggs, interview with author, July 7, 1987.

16 The questions and answers were consolidated in one document and mailed to each entrant. [...] See "Questions and Answers: The Vietnam Veterans Memorial Design Competition," p. 15; also quoted in Grady Clay, "The Art of Choice," *Discovery*, bound in *Harvard Magazine* (July–August 1985): 56E–56F.

17 [...] VVM Fund, "Design Competitions: A Historical Perspective," news release, pp. 1–2. For statistics on the competitors, see "Questions and Answers," p. 16. No detailed profile of the competitors has been made to date.

18 Grady Clay, the head of the jury, also estimates that about 25 percent of the entrants were complete amateurs, or presented amateurlike drawings. Clay, telephone interview with author, August 19, 1987. Paul Spreiregen, however, estimates that 80 percent of the participants were amateurs. The discrepancy in estimates can probably be explained by the large number of architecture students and recent graduates who entered the competition. This group may account for as much as 60 percent of the entrants. Spreiregen, interview with author, July 30, 1987.

19 There were no submissions from well-known artists, such as Donald Judd, Richard Serra, Dan Flavin, or even from younger artists, such as Mary Miss, Jackie Windsor, or Elyn Zimmerman (though the latter complained in a letter to Scruggs, May 9, 1981, that Maya Lin's project was highly derivative of one of her projects). [...]

20 Art Mosley, memorandum to Doubek, February 6, 1989, pp. 2–4.

21 Italian rationalism is the name ordinarily used to describe the work of such architects as Aldo Rossi, Giorgio Grassi, and Franco Purini. In contrast to the designs of early American postmodernists, their architecture tends to be abstract, with the emphasis on morphological type

and compositional organization rather than on figurative reference. The Italian movement shares with its American counterpart, however, a distrust of functional determinism and a desire for historical continuity. In much contemporary criticism, both tendencies are called postmodern.

22 Aesthetically, the project's strongest affinities are with contemporary earthworks. Although Lin's knowledge of modern sculpture was limited at this point, she expressed admiration of Richard Serra's work. In the built project the angle of the wall is 125 degrees, and its length is 493 feet. The arms of the wall were extended to reduce the slope of descent for wheel-chaired veterans. The names could also be more readily accommodated.

23 Maya Ying Lin, "Statement of Winning Designer." This statement, which was released by the VVM Fund, originally appeared on Lin's design panels.

24 Pietro Belluschi, Grady Clay, Garrett Eckbo, Richard H. Hunt, Constantino Nivola, James Rosati, Hideo Sasaki, Harry M. Weese, "Report of the Vietnam Veterans Memorial Design Competition." One of the jurors, Belluschi, subsequently explained that he thought Maya Lin's innocence and lack of involvement with the political issues surrounding Vietnam contributed to the design's meaning: "Her design rises above [politics]. It was very naive . . . more what a child will do than what a sophisticated artist would present. It was above the banal. It has the sort of purity of an idea that shines." Quoted in Phil McCombs, "Maya Lin and the Great Wall of China," *Washington Post* (January 3, 1982). For further discussion of the juror's reaction, see Clay, "The Art of Choice," 56; and Howett, 5–6. I am also grateful to Grady Clay for giving me a copy of his manuscript "The Vietnam Veterans Memorial: Winners and Losers," 1983.

25 Clay, telephone interview with author, August 19, 1987.

26 Spreiregen, interview with author, July 30, 1987.

27 These biases resulted in few amateurs or veterans receiving citations from the jury. [. . .] As a Chinese-American, only 21 years old, and a beginning architecture student, Lin embodied the democratic spirit of the competition that the veterans envisioned (although as Doubek admitted, the fact that the winner was a young Asian woman was also a bit unnerving for some members of the VVM Fund).

28 These letters are in the AIA archives in Washington, D.C. A number of participants complained about the jury's choice, but many called the competition "the best" they had seen. [. . .]

29 Scruggs, Doubek, and Lin, interviews with author, July and August 1987. Today Lin readily admits that "she was difficult," just as the officers of the Fund now seem to have a greater understanding of her desire to maintain the design's integrity. See also, Scruggs and Swerdlow, pp. 76–79.

30 The veterans, who had grown to respect Spreiregen, had proposed him as the project architect. Lin, while recognizing his skills in administering the competition, feared his lack of construction experience. Another concern involved the question of professional conflict, which the AIA raised privately with Spreiregen. He quickly withdrew from consideration and has stated subsequently to Lin that she was correct to seek another architect.

31 Some incidents arose about professional recognition. The Henry Bacon Medal, which the AIA awarded to the memorial in 1984, for instance, listed in bold type "Cooper-Lecky" as project architects above "Maya Lin, designer."

32 The final inscription was: "[prologue] In honor of the men and women of the armed forces of the United States who served in the Vietnam War. The names of those who gave their lives and of those who remain missing are inscribed in the order they were taken from us. [epilogue] Our nation honors the courage, sacrifice, and devotion to duty and country of its Vietnam veterans. This memorial was built with private contributions from the American people. November 11, 1982."

33 Wolf Von Eckhart, "Of Heart and Mind: The Serene Grace of the Vietnam Memorial," *Washington Post* (May 16, 1981).

34 Among the positive reviews in architecture magazines were "Vietnam Veterans Memorial Design Competition," *Architectural Record* 169 (June 1981): 47; and Allen Freeman, "An Extraordinary Competition," *AIA Journal* 70 (August 1981): 47–53.

35   Scruggs and Swerdlow, p. 72.

36   Paul Gapp, "Proposed Memorial to Vietnam War Inane," *Chicago Tribune* (June 28, 1981). For a discussion of critical reaction to the monument and the subsequent controversy, see Nicholas J. Capasso, "Vietnam Veterans Memorial," in Tod A. Marder, ed., *The Critical Edge: Controversy in Recent American Architecture*, exhibition catalogue, The Jane Voorhees Zimmerli Art Museum, Rutgers, The State University of New Jersey (Cambridge, Mass.: MIT Press, 1985).

37   An early volunteer for the VVM Fund, Carhart had helped arrange a $45,000 bank loan that financed the first direct-mail fund-raiser.

38   Tom Carhart, "Statement to the US Fine Arts Commission," October 13, 1981. [...]

39   [...] For an account of Webb's role in the controversy over the memorial, see Christopher Buckley, "The Wall," *Esquire* (September 1985): 61–73. [...]

40   Watt's conservative posture was succinctly captured in his public declaration that there were two kinds of US citizens—"liberals and Americans." Quoted in Scruggs and Swerdlow, p. 81.

41   James Webb, "Remarks, Press Conferences," November 4, 1982, p. 1.

42   "Stop that Monument," *National Review* (September 8, 1981): 1064.

43   Lutyens' Memorial to the Missing of Somme (1927–30) includes the names of the 73,357 men who died in the Somme offensive during World War I. For the influence of Lutyens' memorial on Lin, see Scruggs and Swerdlow, p. 77, and McCombs.

44   Quoted in Elizabeth Hess, "A Tale of Two Memorials," *Art in America* (April 1983): 121; quoted in Scruggs and Swerdlow, p. 106. [...]

45   Tom Wolfe, "The Battle of the Vietnam Memorial: How the Mullahs of Modernism Caused a Stir," *Washington Post* (October 13, 1982).

46   Although Scruggs, Doubek, and numerous volunteers in the VVM Fund can readily be classified as "proles," there were also many military academy graduates who played major roles in the VVM Fund. Among these were Jack Wheeler, Art Mosley and Dick Radez, all West Point graduates, and John Woods, from the Citadel.

47   Several members of the VVM Fund did seem to have an initial sympathy for representational art. [...] Scruggs admits that when the jury first announced the results he was impressed with Brown and Hart's third place entry and thought that Lin's scheme resembled "a big bat. A weird-looking thing that could have been from Mars." See Scruggs and Swerdlow, pp. 49–50, 64.

48   Tom Carhart, "A Better Way to Honor Viet Vets," *Washington Post* (November 15, 1981).

49   "Stop That Monument," 1064.

50   Phyllis Schlafly, "Viet Memorial Opens Old Wounds," *Buffalo Evening News* (January 15, 1982).

51   Benjamin Forgey, "Model of Simplicity: Another Look at the Vietnam Memorial," *Washington Post* (November 14, 1981).

52   Jan C. Scruggs, "In Defense of the Vietnam Veterans Memorial," *Wall Street Journal* (January 14, 1982).

53   Arthur Danto makes a similar distinction between the meanings of "monument" and "memorial" in his insightful analysis of the Vietnam Veterans Memorial. He writes: "We erect monuments so that we shall always remember, and build memorials so that we shall never forget. . . . Very few nations erect monuments to their defeats, but many set up memorials to the defeated dead. Monuments make heroes and triumphs, victories and conquests, perpetually present and part of life. The memorial is a special precinct, extruded from life, a segregated enclave where we honor the dead. With monuments we honor ourselves." [...] See Arthur Danto, "The Vietnam Veterans Memorial," in *The State of the Art* (New York: Prentice Hall, 1987). Another provocative discussion of monumentality can be found in William H. Gass's essay "Monumentality/Mentality," *Oppositions*, no. 25 (Fall 1982): 126–44.

54   Wolfe also claimed with regard to Lin's memorial that the antiwar movement had transformed "the shame of the fearful into the guilt of the courageous." Wolfe, "The Battle of the Vietnam Memorial."

55   James Webb, "Remarks," November 4, 1982, p. 3. [. . .]

56   Typical of the tone of some of the critics' remarks is Don Lassen's statement in *Static Line* (October 1982), a newspaper for paratroopers: "Mind you, now, this designer is a 22 year old girl who now says that the additions of the flagpole and the statue ruin her original concept." Quoted in Hon. Larry McDonald, "That Vietnam Memorial—The Sad Facts," *Congressional Record* (February 15, 1983): E-472.

57   Quoted in Forgey, "Model of Simplicity." [. . .]

58   Webb, "Remarks," November 4, 1982, p. 1. This statement was quoted in "Viet Vets Push Additions to Memorial," *Washington Times* (November 5, 1982).

59   Scruggs and Swerdlow, p. 94. [. . .]

60   Garry Wills, *Reagan's America: Innocents at Home* (New York: Doubleday, 1987).

61   Quoted in Scruggs and Swerdlow, pp. 94–95.

62   Carhart and Webb gained access to the op-ed pages. See Tom Carhart, "Insulting Vietnam Vets," *New York Times* (October 24, 1981); James Webb, "Reassessing the Vietnam Veterans Memorial," *Wall Street Journal* (December 18, 1981). The opponents held a press conference December 7, 1981, which was widely publicized in syndicated articles throughout the country. UPI, "Veterans Fault Vietnam War Memorial Plans," *Washington Post* (December 8, 1981).

63   Of the 265 respondents, 67 percent said that they disliked Lin's design, 33 percent approved of it, 70 percent thought the color of the memorial should be white instead of black, 96 percent felt a flag should be added in a prominent location, and 82 percent wanted the monument above ground. The poll results were not released to the public until October 11, 1982, two days before a meeting of the Commission of Fine Arts to decide on the flag and sculpture additions. Although Perot called the design a "slap in the face" of those who served, he said that he would withdraw his objections if a poll showed veterans supported the monument. Associated Press, "Most Ex-POWs Polled Dislike Vietnam War Memorial Design," *Washington Post* (October 12, 1982). Perot has continuously maintained that his objections were based on his sense of veterans' reactions and not his own personal aversion. When asked if he saw the controversy as a battle about political (pro- or anti-Vietnam) or artistic (popular versus elitist) attitudes, he answered promptly the latter. Telephone interview with the author, July 24, 1987.

64   RWD [Doubek], memorandum recording telephone conversation with Robert Spanogle of the American Legion, November 3, 1982.

65   Henry Hyde, letter to Ronald Reagan and James Watt, January 1982.

66   Patrick Buchanan raised the Communist allegation in his article, "An Insulting Memorial," *Chicago Tribune* (December 26, 1981). Garret Eckbo denies that he was ever a Communist Party member. Eckbo, telephone conversation with author, March 15, 1988.

67   VVM Fund, "The Truth about the Vietnam Veterans Memorial," pp. 5–6.

68   *Time* magazine honored Lin's design as one of the five best architectural designs of 1981, calling it a "brilliantly simple solution." *Time* (January 4, 1982).

69   Scruggs and Swerdlow, p. 100.

70   "Statement of the Vietnam Veterans Memorial Fund Regarding Compromise Agreement," December 14, 1982, p. 1.

71   Hart and the VVM Fund share the copyright on the statue. [. . .]

72   Scruggs stated: "We really fought for Maya's design, but we're happy with the compromise. The way it's done does not detract from the design. It makes it 100 percent better, much more beautiful." Isabel Wilkerson, "Art War Erupts Over Vietnam Veterans Memorial," *Washington Post* (July 8, 1982). [. . .]

73   Rick Horowitz, "Maya Lin's Angry Objections," *Washington Post* (July 7, 1982); and Maya Lin, interview with author, August 18, 1987.

74   Robert Doubek insists Cooper-Lecky's motivation was completely honorable. Doubek, telephone conversation with author, March 16, 1988. [. . .]

75   [. . . Jan Scruggs], memorandum on telephone conversation with J.W. about Roy Cohn, March 7, 1983; [Jan Scruggs], memorandum on telephone conversation with Cyrus Vance about Roy

Cohn, July 6, 1983; Gerald W. Thomas, record of telephone conversation with Bill Stensland about Roy Cohn, January 31, 1984.

76   Tom Carhart, "Veteran's Memorial Should Not be Mournful," letter to the editor, *Washington Times* (October 6, 1982).

77   Milt Copulos sponsored a poll of individuals visiting the memorial at the National Salute on November 11, 1982. Ninety-four percent of the veterans wanted a flag "prominently displayed as an integral part of the memorial." Fifty-four percent said that their impression of the wall design was "strongly unfavorable." Copulos and other opponents tried to use this poll (which the VVM Fund called "unscientific") to overrule the initial ruling of the Commission of Fine Arts on the flag's placement. See Milt Copulos, "Background to Betrayal: Viet Vets Want Their Memorial Back," *Soldier of Fortune* (May 1983): 18–21, 85–88. [. . .]

78   The culmination of these allegations was a broadcast on Washington television by Pulitzer Prize winner and former Vietnam marine Carlton Sherwood. Sherwood resigned his job in broadcasting after the VVM Fund argued that his accusations were false. For Webb's reactions and his defense of Sherwood, see especially Webb's 20-page account of the controversy, which he submitted to Scruggs, instead of granting an interview to Scruggs's co-author, Joel Swerdlow. This manuscript was sent with a letter, dated January 17, 1984.

79   These inversions of traditional monumentality have been interpreted as "the expression of a female sensibility" (Hess, 126). While such a reading risks suggestions of female "essentialism" and Freudian clichés (buried, dark, recessive, etc.), it does indicate how the monument avoids stereotypical images of masculinity, whether resulting from figurative imagery or formal devices associated with "masculine assertiveness."

80   Cf. fn. 2.

81   The two most complete analyses of the memorial's meaning are William Hubbard, "A Meaning for Monuments," *Public Interest* 74 (Winter 1984): 17–30; and Charles L. Griswold, "The Vietnam Veterans Memorial and the Washington Mall: Philosophical Thoughts on Political Iconography," *Critical Inquiry* 12, no. 4 (Summer 1986): 688–719. [. . .]

82   These mementoes are collected regularly by the National Park Service and stored at the Museum and Archaeological Regional Storage Facility. [. . .]

83   [See] Michael Clark, "Remembering Vietnam," in Richard Berg and John Carlos Rowe, eds., "American Representations of Vietnam," *Cultural Critique*, no. 3 (Spring 1986): 46–78.

84   One of the most eloquent summaries of the wall's meaning appeared in a "letter to the editor" in the *Washington Post* (November 17, 1982) by Robert J. Brugger, a former captain in the Marines. Brugger writes: "Monuments are useful because they help to place ourselves on the historical landscape and somehow thank the dead. But they may also hinder our view of what has gone before. As symbols that simplify, they have the power to distort as well as to inspire. Perhaps memorial architect Maya Lin's call to memory will prove an exception—offering a chastened conception of war, inviting us to remember the actual tragedy of this war of doubtful ends and horrendous means. Maybe its message of muted bravado will sink in, and all of us, like the men and women matured by the Vietnam experience, will stand the better for it."

85   See Hess, 126.

86   Although the tone is hardly that which Webb initially sought, he is delighted with the sculpture and a replica sat on his desk while he was serving as Secretary of the Navy. *Parade Magazine*, in *Washington Post* (November 29, 1987). Ironically, the wall's critics never seem bothered by Hart's open acknowledgment of having participated in anti-Vietnam demonstrations.

87   Almost no one touches the sculpture or grieves there; it is at the wall where contemplation and participation primarily occur. If the soldiers are gazing toward the wall, they are only echoing the experience of the visitor. Once one approaches the wall, the soldiers disappear completely, for one's back is to them. For a scholarly and more sympathetic critique of Hart's statue, see Karal Ann Marling and Robert Silberman, "The Statue Near the Wall: The Vietnam Veterans Memorial and the Art of Remembering," *Smithsonian Studies in American Art 1*, no. I (Spring 1987): 5–28. [. . .]

88 Alois Riegl, "The Modern Cult of Monuments: Its Character and Its Origin," trans. Kurt W. Forster and Diane Ghirardo, *Oppositions*, no. 25 (Fall 1982): 20–51. [. . .]

89 Paul Spreiregen was tempted to ask Carter Brown, the director of the National Gallery, if he would have permitted Hart's statue to stand in front of the gallery's East Wing. Spreiregen, interview with the author, July 30 1987.

90 Griswold, p. 691.

Part 6 |

The city in question

The three essays in this final section represent the tremendous expansion in recent years of urban spatial and historical studies. More pointedly, they exemplify widespread concern during the 1990s over the shifting character and quality of American urban life—particularly around issues of public space.

In his introduction to an influential (and justly pessimistic) book of essays on "the end of public space" in "the new American city," architect and critic Michael Sorkin points to a group of themes occupying center stage in 1990s-vintage urban studies. He writes of the rise of rapid transportation and electronic communications and their effect in breaking down the connective tissues and stable geographical relations of the city as traditionally conceived. He expresses alarm over the new obsession with security and surveillance, the subsequent rise in "new modes of segregation," and the blandly simu-lated, themed nature of so much contemporary architectural and urban design. His remarks are politically and humanistically charged—and arguably rather nostalgic—grounded in concern over the loss of intimacy and real democratic potential that the new American city inscribes.

In an equally impassioned and polemical essay—a version of which appeared in Sorkin's book—the Marxist social historian Mike Davis provides a socio-spatial critique of downtown Los Angeles as it was redeveloped beginning in the 1980s. Davis describes this environment as a battlefield for renewed class struggle, one where the battle is all but over. He finds that real public space in Los Angeles is nearly gone, genuine democracy is in a state of shambles, security and privatization are on the rise, and the poor and under-privileged are on the run through "sadistically" designed street environments. In what seemed at the time something of a tonic to the hero worship he more regularly received, Davis cast architect Frank Gehry in the sinister role of paranoiac-aggressive *auteur*—a designer whose "work clarifies the underlying relations of repression, surveillance and exclusion" that characterize Los Angeles's new spatial realities.

The final essay in this collection, by journalist Marc Spiegler, discusses the increas-ingly peculiar and troubled relationship between a major international airport—in this case Chicago's O'Hare—and the city it purportedly serves. In fact, O'Hare and other airports like it, have become virtually independent, self-contained "communities." Like scores of shopping malls, office parks, and highway strips across the US, O'Hare provides the focal point for an "edge city." Sprawling and placeless, drawing life and business away from downtown, based on convenience rather than culture or community, O'Hare is a

"town" with a church but no parish. We see here one final view of the ongoing reconceptualization and reconfiguration of the American city, in the emergence of the new,
generic landscape.

Further reading

Blakely, E. J. and M. G. Snyder, *Fortress America: Gated Communities in the United States*,
    Washington, DC: Brookings Institution Press, 1997.
Deutsche, R., *Evictions: Art and Spatial Politics*, Cambridge, MA: MIT Press, 1996.
Findlay, J. M., *Magic Lands: Western Cityscapes and American Culture After 1940*, Berkeley, CA:
    University of California Press, 1992.
Fogelson, R. M., *Downtown: Its Rise and Fall, 1880–1950*, New Haven, CT: Yale University Press,
    2001.
Garreau, J., *Edge City: Life on the New Frontier*, New York: Doubleday, 1991.
Hayden, D., *The Power of Place: Urban Landscapes as Public History*, Cambridge, MA: MIT Press,
    1995.
Hise, G., *Magnetic Los Angeles: Planning the Twentieth-Century Metropolis*, Baltimore, MD: The
    Johns Hopkins University Press, 1997.
Judd, D. R. and S. S. Fainstein (eds), *The Tourist City*, New Haven, CT: Yale University Press, 1999.
Legates, R. T. and F. Stout (eds), *The City Reader*, 3rd edn, London: Routledge, 2003.
Light, A. and J. M. Smith (eds), *Philosophy and Geography II: The Production of Public Space*,
    Lanham, MD: Rowman and Littlefield Publishers, 1998.
Lofland, L. H., *The Public Realm: Exploring the City's Quintessential Social Territory*, New York:
    Aldine de Gruyter, 1998.
Mitchell, D., "The End of Public Space? People's Park, Definitions of the Public, and Democracy,"
    Annals of the Association of American Geographers 85: 1 (1995): 108–133.
Pascucci, E., "This City Belongs to That Girl," *ANY* 12 (1995): 50–59.
Rothman, H. K., *Neon Metropolis: How Las Vegas Started the Twenty-First Century*, New York:
    Routledge, 2002.
Sennett, R., *The Fall of Public Man*, New York: Alfred A. Knopf, 1977.
Whyte, W. H., *The Social Life of Small Urban Spaces*, Washington, DC: Conservation Foundation,
    1980.

Chapter 22

Michael Sorkin

Introduction
Variations on a theme park

With the precise prescience of a true Master of the Universe, Walter Wriston recently declared that "the 800 telephone number and the piece of plastic have made time and space obsolete." Wriston ought to know. As former CEO of the suggestively named Citicorp, he's a true Baron Haussmann for the electronic age, plowing the boulevards of capital through the pliant matrix of the global economy.

This comparison isn't meant to be flip: Wriston's remark begs fundamental questions about urbanity. Computers, credit cards, phones, faxes, and other instruments of instant artificial adjacency are rapidly eviscerating historic politics of propinquity, the very cement of the city. Indeed, recent years have seen the emergence of a wholly new kind of city, a city without a place attached to it.

This ageographical city is particularly advanced in the United States. It's visible in clumps of skyscrapers rising from well-wired fields next to the Interstate; in huge shopping malls, anchored by their national-chain department stores, and surrounded by swarms of cars; in hermetically sealed atrium hotels cloned from coast to coast; in uniform "historic" gentrifications and festive markets; in the disaggregated sprawl of endless new suburbs without cities; and in the antenna bristle of a hundred million rooftops from Secaucus to Simi Valley, in the clouds of satellite dishes pointed at the same geosynchronous blip, all sucking Arsenio and the A-Team out of the ether.

In fact, the structure of this city is a lot like television. TV's main event is the cut, the elision between broadcast bits, the seamless slide from soap opera to docudrama to a word from our sponsor. The "design" of television is all about erasing differences among these bits, about asserting equal value for all the elements in the net, so that any of the infinite combinations that the broadcast day produces can make "sense." The new city likewise eradicates genuine particularity in favor of a continuous urban field, a conceptual grid of boundless reach. It's a process of erasure much noted. In the 1950s and 1960s, the alarm was sounded over "urban sprawl" and "Megalopolis," the spread of an uninterrupted zone of urbanization along the American Northeast coast, a city become region. More recently, attention has focused on the explosion of so-called "suburban cities" on the fringes of existing metropolises. In this vast, virtually undifferentiated territory—stretching from Fairfax County, Virginia, to Orange County, California—homes, offices, factories, and shopping malls float in a culturing medium, a "non-place urban realm" that provides the bare functions of a city, while doing away with the vital, not quite disciplined formal and social mix that gives cities life (Figure 22.1).

22.1 Suburban sprawl, Las Vegas, Nevada, 1999

The city described in this book, though, is not simply a phenomenon of extent. Its growth no longer merely physical—a matter of egregious densities or metastasizing reach—the new city also occupies a vast, unseen, conceptual space. This invisible Cyburbia—so aptly evoked by Wriston—takes form as necessary, sprouting like sudden mushrooms at capital's promiscuous nodes. What's missing in this city is not a matter of any particular building or place; it's the spaces in between, the connections that make sense of forms.

The history of cities is embedded in the ways their elements are juxtaposed, the structures of art and regulation that govern urban amalgamation. Questions both of what goes with what and what yields to what are at the basis of urban form-making. Traditional cities have adjudicated such questions via relations to central places. Whether agora, castle, piazza, or downtown, the idea of a city of centers stands, at a minimum, for the idea of a spatial city, a city in which order is a function of proximity. This physical city has historically mapped social relations with a profound clarity, imprinting in its shapes and places vast information about status and order. Whether "the other side of the tracks" in a small town, the New England commons, or the bar-graph of real estate values visible in the Manhattan skyline, social order has long been legible in urban form. In the new, recombinant city, however, the legibility of these orders has been dramatically manipulated, often completely obscured. Here, anything seems to go with anything—hierarchies are both reinforced and concealed, at once fixed and despatialized. Value is still a function of location, but the invisible hand has learned a new geometry. As phone and modem render the street irrelevant, other dimensions become preeminent. Main Street is now the space between airports, the fiber-optic cables linking the fax machines of the multinational corporations' far-flung offices, an invisible worldwide skein of economic relations. Liberated from its centers and its edges by advances in communication and mobility and by a new world order bent on a single citizenship of consumption, the new city threatens an unimagined sameness even as it multiplies the illusory choices of the TV system.

Three salient characteristics mark this city. The first is the dissipation of all stable relations to local physical and cultural geography, the loosening of ties to any specific space. Globalized capital, electronic means of production, and uniform mass culture abhor the intimate, undisciplined differentiation of traditional cities. The new city replaces the anomaly and delight of such places with a universal particular, a generic urbanism inflected only by appliqué. Here, locality is efficiently acknowledged by the inclusion of the croque-monsieur at the McDonald's on the Boul' Miche or the Cajun Martini at the airport lounge in New Orleans (and you're welcome to keep the glass). This "place" is fully ageographic: it can be inserted equally in an open field or in the heart of town; the inward-looking atrium hotel is as apt to the featureless greensward as it is to teeming unreclaimed downtowns. With its components reduced to a repetitive minimum, space is departicularized. Obsessed with the point of production and the point of sale, the new city is little more than a swarm of urban bits jettisoning a physical view of the whole, sacrificing the idea of the city as the site of community and human connection.

A second characteristic of this new city is its obsession with "security," with rising levels of manipulation and surveillance over its citizenry and with a proliferation of new modes of segregation. The methods are both technological and physical. The former consist of invasive policing technologies—domesticated versions of the "electronic battlefield"—and a growing multitude of daily connections to the computer grid, ranging from encounters with the automated teller to the full-blown regulatory environment of the electronic workplace. The physical means are equally varied: parallel, middle-class suburban cities growing on the fringes of old centers abandoned to the poor; enclaved communities for the rich; gentrification; the globe-girdling cocoon that envelops the business traveler as he or she encounters the same airport, hotel, and office building from Denver to Dubai; the lacework of overhead and underground circulation systems imposed in Minneapolis or Edmonton to permit shoppers and office workers to circulate in climate-regulated security through threatening urban territory. This impulse to a new urban segregation seems ubiquitous: throughout America, city planning has largely ceased its historic role as the

22.2 Bergman, Walls & Youngblood, Paris Hotel and Casino, Las Vegas, Nevada, 1999

integrator of communities in favor of managing selective development and enforcing distinction.

Finally, this new realm is a city of simulations, television city, the city as theme park. This is nowhere more visible than in its architecture, in buildings that rely for their authority on images drawn from history, from a spuriously appropriated past that substitutes for a more exigent and examined present (Figure 22.2). In most American cities, the "historic" has become the only complicit official urban value. The result is that the preservation of the physical remnants of the historical city has superseded attention to the human ecologies that produced and inhabit them. Today, the profession of urban design is almost wholly preoccupied with reproduction, with the creation of urbane disguises. Whether in its master incarnation at the ersatz Main Street of Disneyland, in the phony historic festivity of a Rouse marketplace, or the gentrified architecture of the "reborn" Lower East Side, this elaborate apparatus is at pains to assert its ties to the kind of city life it is in the process of obliterating.

Here is urban renewal with a sinister twist, an architecture of deception which, in its happy-face familiarity, constantly distances itself from the most fundamental realities. The architecture of this city is almost purely semiotic, playing the game of grafted signification, theme-park building. Whether it represents generic historicity or generic modernity, such design is based in the same calculus as advertising, the idea of pure imageability, oblivious to the real needs and traditions of those who inhabit it. Welcome to Cyburbia.

This book [*Variations on a Theme Park*] is not an attempt to theorize this new city but to describe it. The sites discussed are representative; they do not simply typify the course of American urbanism but are likely to be models for urban development throughout the world. The frame of reference is thus limited: it is not about Soweto, the South Bronx, or Dhaka. Nor is it directly about Urbino, Paris, or Savannah, those pleasant centers of traditional urbanity. And yet it is. The danger in this new city is in its antithesis: in Victor Hugo's famous phrase, "This will destroy that." The new city has the power simply not only to bypass the traditional scenes of urbanity but to co-opt them, to relegate them to mere intersections on a global grid for which time and space are indeed obsolete.

"City air makes people free," goes a medieval maxim. The cautionary essays collected here describe an ill wind blowing through our cities, an atmosphere that has the potential to irretrievably alter the character of cities as the preeminent sites of democracy and pleasure. The familiar spaces of traditional cities, the streets and squares, courtyards and parks, are our great scenes of the civic, visible and accessible, our binding agents. By describing the alternative, this book pleads for a return to a more authentic urbanity, a city based on physical proximity and free movement and a sense that the city is our best expression of a desire for collectivity. As spatiality ebbs, so does intimacy. The privatized city of bits is a lie, simulating its connections, obliterating the power of its citizens either to act alone or to act together.

This is the meaning of the theme park, the place that embodies it all, the ageographia, the surveillance and control, the simulations without end. The theme park presents its happy regulated vision of pleasure—all those artfully hoodwinking forms—as a substitute for the democratic public realm, and it does so appealingly by stripping troubled urbanity of its sting, of the presence of the poor, of crime, of dirt, of work. In the "public" spaces of the theme park or the shopping mall, speech itself is restricted: there are no demonstrations in Disneyland. The effort to reclaim the city is the struggle of democracy itself.

23.1 "The privatization of the architectural public realm," Los Angeles, California, 1999

person" is in itself a harrowing index of the devaluation of public spaces. To reduce contact with untouchables, urban redevelopment has converted once vital pedestrian streets into traffic sewers and transformed public parks into temporary receptacles for the homeless and wretched. The American city, as many critics have recognized, is being systematically turned inside out—or, rather, outside in. The valorized spaces of the new megastructures and super-malls are concentrated in the center, street frontage is denuded, public activity is sorted into strictly functional compartments, and circulation is internalized in corridors under the gaze of private police (Figure 23.1).[2]

The privatization of the architectural public realm, moreover, is shadowed by parallel restructurings of electronic space, as heavily policed, pay-access "information orders," elite data-bases and subscription cable services appropriate parts of the invisible agora. Both processes, of course, mirror the deregulation of the economy and the recession of non-market entitlements. The decline of urban liberalism has been accompanied by the death of what might be called the "Olmstedian vision" of public space. Frederick Law Olmsted, it will be recalled, was North America's Haussmann, as well as the Father of Central Park. In the wake of Manhattan's "Commune" of 1863, the great Draft Riot, he conceived public landscapes and parks as social safety-valves, *mixing* classes and ethnicities in common (bourgeois) recreations and enjoyments. As Manfredo Tafuri has shown in his well-known study of Rockefeller Center, the same principle animated the construction of the canonical urban spaces of the La Guardia-Roosevelt era.[3]

This reformist vision of public space—as the emollient of class struggle, if not the bedrock of the American *polis*—is now as obsolete as Keynesian nostrums of full employment. In regard to the "mixing" of classes, contemporary urban America is more like Victorian England than Walt Whitman's or La Guardia's New York. In Los Angeles, once-upon-a-time a demi-paradise of free beaches, luxurious parks, and "cruising strips," genuinely democratic space is all but extinct. The Oz-like archipelago of Westside pleasure domes—a continuum of tony malls, arts centers and gourmet strips—is reciprocally dependent upon the social imprisonment of the third-world service proletariat who live in increasingly repressive ghettoes and barrios. In a city of several million yearning immigrants, public amenities are radically shrinking, parks are becoming derelict and beaches more segregated, libraries and playgrounds are closing, youth congregations of ordinary kinds are banned, and the streets are becoming more desolate and dangerous.

Unsurprisingly, as in other American cities, municipal policy has taken its lead from the security offensive and the middle-class demand for increased spatial and social insulation. De facto disinvestment in traditional public space and recreation has supported the shift of fiscal resources to corporate-defined redevelopment priorities. A pliant city government—in this case ironically professing to represent a bi-racial coalition of liberal whites and Blacks—has collaborated in the massive privatization of public space and the subsidization of new, racist enclaves (benignly described as "urban villages"). Yet most current, giddy discussions of the "postmodern" scene in Los Angeles neglect entirely these overbearing aspects of counter-urbanization and counter-insurgency. A triumphal gloss—"urban renaissance," "city of the future," and so on—is laid over the brutalization of inner-city neighborhoods and the increasing South Africanization of its spatial relations. Even as the walls have come down in Eastern Europe, they are being erected all over Los Angeles.

The observations that follow take as their thesis the existence of this new class war (sometimes a continuation of the race war of the 1960s) at the level of the built environment. Although this is not a comprehensive account, which would require a thorough analysis of economic and political dynamics, these images and instances are meant to convince the reader that urban form is indeed following a repressive function in the political furrows of the Reagan-Bush era. Los Angeles, in its usual prefigurative mode, offers an especially disquieting catalogue of the emergent liaisons between architecture and the American police state.

THE FORBIDDEN CITY

The first militarist of space in Los Angeles was General Otis of the *Times*. Declaring himself at war with labor, he infused his surroundings with an unrelentingly bellicose air:

> He called his home in Los Angeles the Bivouac. Another house was known as the Outpost. The *Times* was known as the Fortress. The staff of the paper was the Phalanx. The *Times* building itself was more fortress than newspaper plant, there were turrets, battlements, sentry boxes. Inside he stored fifty rifles.[4]

A great, menacing bronze eagle was the *Times*'s crown; a small, functional cannon was installed on the hood of Otis's touring car to intimidate onlookers. Not surprisingly, this overwrought display of aggression produced a response in kind. On October 1, 1910 the heavily fortified *Times* headquarters—citadel of the open shop on the West Coast—was destroyed in a catastrophic explosion blamed on union saboteurs.

Eighty years later, the spirit of General Otis has returned to subtly pervade Los Angeles's new "postmodern" Downtown: the emerging Pacific Rim financial complex which cascades, in rows of skyscrapers, from Bunker Hill southward along the Figueroa corridor. Redeveloped with public tax increments under the aegis of the powerful and largely unaccountable Community Redevelopment Agency, the Downtown project is one of the largest postwar urban designs in North America. Site assemblage and clearing on a vast scale, with little mobilized opposition, have resurrected land values, upon which big developers and off-shore capital (increasingly Japanese) have planted a series of billion-dollar, block-square megastructures: Crocker Center, the Bonaventure Hotel and Shopping Mall, the World Trade Center, the Broadway Plaza, Arco Center, CitiCorp Plaza, California Plaza, and so on. With historical landscapes erased, with megastructures and superblocks as primary components, and with an increasingly dense and self-contained circulation system, the new financial district is best conceived as a single, demonically self-referential hyperstructure, a Miesian skyscape raised to dementia.

Like similar megalomaniac complexes, tethered to fragmented and desolated Downtowns (for instance, the Renaissance Center in Detroit, the Peachtree and Omni Centers in Atlanta, and so on), Bunker Hill and the Figueroa corridor have provoked a storm of liberal objections against their abuse of scale and composition, their denigration of street landscape, and their confiscation of so much of the vital life activity of the center, now sequestered within subterranean concourses or privatized malls. Sam Hall Kaplan, the crusty urban critic of the *Times*, has been indefatigable in denouncing the anti-pedestrian bias of the new corporate citadel, with its fascist obliteration of street frontage. In his view the superimposition of "hermetically sealed fortresses" and air-dropped "pieces of suburbia" has "dammed the rivers of life" Downtown.[5]

Yet Kaplan's vigorous defense of pedestrian democracy remains grounded in hackneyed liberal complaints about "bland design" and "elitist planning practices." Like most architectural critics, he rails against the oversights of urban design without recognizing the dimension of foresight, of explicit repressive intention, which has its roots in Los Angeles's ancient history of class and race warfare. Indeed, when Downtown's new "Gold Coast" is viewed en bloc from the standpoint of its interactions with other social areas and landscapes in the central city, the "fortress effect" emerges, not as an inadvertent failure of design, but as deliberate socio-spatial strategy.

The goals of this strategy may be summarized as a double repression: to raze all association with Downtown's past and to prevent any articulation with the non-Anglo urbanity of its future. Everywhere on the perimeter of redevelopment this strategy takes the form of a brutal architectural edge or glacis that defines the new Downtown as a citadel vis-à-vis the rest of the central city. Los Angeles is unusual amongst major urban renewal centers in preserving, however negligently, most of its circa 1900–30 Beaux Arts commercial core. At immense public cost, the corporate headquarters and financial district was shifted from the old Broadway-Spring corridor six blocks west to the greenfield site created by destroying the Bunker Hill residential neighborhood. To emphasize the "security" of the new Downtown, virtually all the traditional pedestrian links to the old center, including the famous Angels' Flight funicular railroad, were removed.

The logic of this entire operation is revealing. In other cities developers might have attempted to articulate the new skyscape and the old, exploiting the latter's extraordinary inventory of theaters and historic buildings to create a gentrified history—a gaslight district, Faneuil Market or Ghirardelli Square—as a support to middle-class residential colonization. But Los Angeles's redevelopers viewed property values in the old Broadway core as irreversibly eroded by the area's very centrality to public transport, and especially by its heavy use by Black and Mexican poor. In the wake of the Watts Rebellion, and the perceived Black threat to crucial nodes of white power (spelled out in lurid detail in the McCone Commission Report), resegregated spatial security became the paramount concern.[6] The Los Angeles Police Department abetted the flight of business from Broadway to the fortified redoubts of Bunker Hill by spreading scare literature typifying Black teenagers as dangerous gang members.[7]

As a result, redevelopment massively reproduced spatial apartheid. The moat of the Harbor Freeway and the regraded palisades of Bunker Hill cut off the new financial core from the poor immigrant neighborhoods that surround it on every side. Along the base of California Plaza, Hill Street became a local Berlin Wall separating the publicly subsidized luxury of Bunker Hill from the lifeworld of Broadway, now reclaimed by Latino immigrants as their primary shopping and entertainment street. Because politically connected speculators are now redeveloping the northern end of the Broadway corridor (sometimes known as "Bunker Hill East"), the CRA is promising to restore pedestrian linkages to the Hill in the 1990s, including the Angels' Flight incline railroad. This, of course, only dramatizes the current bias against accessibility—that is to say, against *any* spatial interaction between old and new, poor and rich, except in the framework of gentrification or recolonization.[8] Although a few white-collars venture into the Grand Central Market—a popular emporium of tropical produce and fresh foods—Latino shoppers or Saturday strollers never circulate in the Gucci precincts above Hill Street. The occasional appearance of a destitute street nomad in Broadway Plaza or in front of the Museum of Contemporary Art sets off a quiet panic; video cameras turn on their mounts and security guards adjust their belts.

Photographs of the old Downtown in its prime show mixed crowds of Anglo, Black and Latino pedestrians of different ages and classes. The contemporary Downtown "renaissance" is designed to make such heterogeneity virtually impossible. It is intended not just to "kill the street" as Kaplan fears, but to "kill the crowd," to eliminate that democratic admixture on the pavements and in the parks that Olmsted believed was America's antidote to European class polarizations. The Downtown hyperstructure like some Buckminster Fuller post-Holocaust fantasy—is programmed to ensure a seamless continuum of middle-class work, consumption and recreation, without unwonted exposure to Downtown's working-class street environments.[9] Indeed the totalitarian semiotics of ramparts and battlements, reflective glass and elevated pedways, rebukes any affinity or sympathy between different architectural or human orders. As in Otis's fortress *Times* building, this is the archisemiotics of class war.

Lest this seem too extreme, consider *Urban Land* magazine's recent description of the profit-driven formula that across the United States has linked together clustered development, social homogeneity, and a secure "Downtown image":

HOW TO OVERCOME FEAR OF CRIME IN DOWNTOWNS

Create a Dense, Compact, Multifunctional Core Area. A downtown can be designed and developed to make visitors feel that it—or a significant portion of it—is attractive and the type of place that "respectable people" like themselves tend to frequent. . . . A core downtown area that is compact, densely developed and multifunctional will concentrate people, giving them more activities. . . . The activities offered in this core area will determine what "type" of people will be strolling its sidewalks; locating offices and housing for middle- and upper-income residents in or near the core area can assure a high percentage of "respectable," law-abiding pedestrians. Such an attractive redeveloped core area would also be large enough to affect the downtown's overall image.[10]

SADISTIC STREET ENVIRONMENTS

This conscious "hardening" of the city surface against the poor is especially brazen in the Manichaean treatment of Downtown microcosms. In his famous study of the "social life of small urban spaces," William Whyte makes the point that the quality of any urban environment can be measured, first of all, by whether there are convenient, comfortable places for pedestrians to sit.[11] This maxim has been warmly taken to heart by designers of the high-corporate precincts of Bunker Hill and the emerging "urban village" of South Park. As part of the city's policy of subsidizing white-collar residential colonization in Downtown, it has spent, or plans to spend, tens of millions of dollars of diverted tax revenue on enticing, "soft" environments in these areas. Planners envision an opulent complex of squares, fountains, world-class public art, exotic shubbery, and avant-garde street furniture along a Hope Street pedestrian corridor. In the propaganda of official boosters, nothing is taken as a better index of Downtown's "livability" than the idyll of office workers and upscale tourists lounging or napping in the terraced gardens of California Plaza, the "Spanish Steps" or Grand Hope Park.

In stark contrast, a few blocks away, the city is engaged in a merciless struggle to make public facilities and spaces as "unlivable" as possible for the homeless and the poor. The persistence of thousands of street people on the fringes of Bunker Hill and the Civic Center sours the image of designer Downtown living and betrays the laboriously constructed illusion of a Downtown "renaissance." City Hall then retaliates with its own variant of low-intensity warfare.[12]

Although city leaders periodically essay schemes for removing indigents *en masse*—deporting them to a poor farm on the edge of the desert, confining them in camps in the mountains, or, memorably, interning them on a derelict ferry at the Harbor—such "final solutions" have been blocked by council members fearful of the displacement of the home-less into their districts. Instead the city, self-consciously adopting the idiom of urban cold war, promotes the "containment" (official term) of the homeless in Skid Row along Fifth Street east of the Broadway, systematically transforming the neighborhood into an outdoor poorhouse. But this containment strategy breeds its own vicious circle of contradiction. By condensing the mass of the desperate and helpless together in such a small space, and denying adequate housing, official policy has transformed Skid Row into probably the most dangerous ten square blocks in the world—ruled by a grisly succes-sion of "Slashers," "Night Stalkers" and more ordinary predators.[13] Every night on Skid Row is Friday the 13th, and, unsurprisingly, many of the homeless seek to escape the "Nickle" during the night at all costs, searching safer niches in other parts of Downtown. The city in turn tightens the noose with increased police harassment and ingenious design deterrents.

One of the most common, but mind-numbing, of these deterrents is the Rapid Transit District's new barrel-shaped bus bench that offers a minimal surface for uncom-fortable sitting, while making sleeping utterly impossible. Such "bumproof" benches are being widely introduced on the periphery of Skid Row. Another invention, worthy of the Grand Guignol, is the aggressive deployment of outdoor sprinklers. Several years ago the city opened a "Skid Row Park" along lower Fifth Street, on a corner of Hell. To ensure that the park was not used for sleeping—that is to say, to guarantee that it was mainly utilized for drug dealing and prostitution—the city installed an elaborate overhead sprink-ler system programmed to drench unsuspecting sleepers at random times during the night. The system was immediately copied by some local businessmen in order to drive the home-less away from adjacent public sidewalks. Meanwhile restaurants and markets have responded to the homeless by building ornate enclosures to protect their refuse. Although no one in Los Angeles has yet proposed adding cyanide to the garbage, as happened in Phoenix a few years back, one popular seafood restaurant has spent $12,000 to built the ultimate bag-lady-proof trash cage: made of three-quarter-inch steel rod with alloy locks and vicious outturned spikes to safeguard priceless moldering fishheads and stale french fries.

Public toilets, however, are the real Eastern Front of the Downtown war on the poor. Los Angeles, as a matter of deliberate policy, has fewer available public lavatories than any major North American city. On the advice of the LAPD (who actually sit on the design board of at least one major Downtown redevelopment project),[14] the Community Redevelopment Agency bulldozed the remaining public toilet in Skid Row. Agency planners then agonized for months over whether to include a "free-standing public toilet" in their design for South Park. As CRA Chairman Jim Wood later admitted, the decision not to include the toilet was a "policy decision and not a design decision." The CRA Downtown prefers the solution of "quasi-public restrooms"—meaning toilets in restaur-ants, art galleries and office buildings—which can be made available to tourists and office workers while being denied to vagrants and other unsuitables.[15] The toiletless no-man's-land east of Hill Street in Downtown is also barren of outside water sources for drinking or washing. A common and troubling sight these days are the homeless men—many of them young Salvadorean refugees—washing in and even drinking from the sewer effluent which flows down the concrete channel of the Los Angeles River on the eastern edge of Downtown.

Where the itineraries of Downtown powerbrokers unavoidably intersect with the habitats of the homeless or the working poor, as in the previously mentioned zone of gentrification along the northern Broadway corridor, extraordinary design precautions are being taken to ensure the physical separation of the different humanities. For instance, the CRA brought in the Los Angeles Police to design "24-hour, state-of-the-art security" for the two new parking structures that serve the *Los Angeles Times* and Ronald Reagan State Office buildings. In contrast to the mean streets outside, the parking structures contain beautifully landscaped lawns or "microparks," and in one case, a food court and a historical exhibit. Moreover, both structures are designed as "confidence-building" circulation systems—miniature paradigms of privatization—which allow white-collar workers to walk from car to office, or from car to boutique, with minimum exposure to the public street. The Broadway Spring Center, in particular, which links the Ronald Reagan Building to the proposed "Grand Central Square" at Third and Broadway, has been warmly praised by architectural critics for adding greenery and art (a banal bas relief) to parking. It also adds a huge dose of menace—armed guards, locked gates, and security cameras—to scare away the homeless and poor.

The cold war on the streets of Downtown is ever escalating. The police, lobbied by Downtown merchants and developers, have broken up every attempt by the homeless and their allies to create safe havens or self-organized encampments. "Justiceville," founded by homeless activist Ted Hayes, was roughly dispersed; when its inhabitants attempted to find refuge at Venice Beach, they were arrested at the behest of the local councilperson (a renowned environmentalist) and sent back to the inferno of Skid Row.

The city's own brief experiment with legalized camping—a grudging response to a series of exposure deaths in the cold winter of 1987[16]—was ended abruptly after only four months to make way for construction of a transit repair yard. Current policy seems to involve a perverse play upon Zola's famous irony about the "equal rights" of the rich and the poor to sleep out rough. As the head of the city planning commission explained the official line to incredulous reporters, it is not against the law to sleep on the street per se, "only to erect any sort of protective shelter." To enforce this prescription against "cardboard condos," the LAPD periodically sweep the Nickle, confiscating shelters and other possessions, and arresting resisters. Such cynical repression has turned the majority of the homeless into urban bedouins. They are visible all over Downtown, pushing a few pathetic possessions in purloined shopping carts, always fugitive and in motion, pressed between the official policy of containment and the increasing sadism of Downtown streets.[17]

FRANK GEHRY AS DIRTY HARRY

If the contemporary search for bourgeois security can be read in the design of bus benches and mega-structures, it is also visible at the level of *auteur*. No recent architect has so ingeniously elaborated the urban security function or so brazenly embraced the resulting *frisson* as Los Angeles's Pritzker Prize laureate, Frank Gehry. As we saw earlier, he has become one of the principal "imagineers" (in the Disney sense) of the neo-boosterism of the 1990s. He is particularly adept as a crossover, not merely between architecture and modern art, but also between older, vaguely radical and contemporary, basically cynical styles. Thus his portfolio is at once a principled repudiation of postmodernism and one of its cleverest sublimations; a nostalgic evocation of revolutionary constructivism and a mercenary celebration of bourgeois-decadent minimalism. These amphibian shifts and paradoxical nuances in Gehry's work sustain a booming cottage industry of Gehry-interpretation, mostly effused with hyperbolic admiration.

Yet [...] Gehry's strongest suit may simply be his straightforward exploitation of rough urban environments, and his blatant incorporation of their harshest edges and detritus as powerful representational elements in his work. Affectionately described by colleagues as an "old socialist" or "street-fighter with a heart," much of his most interesting work is utterly unromantic and anti-idealist.[18] Unlike his popular front mentors of the 1940s, Gehry makes little pretense at architectural reformism or "design for democracy." He boasts of trying "to make the best with the reality of things." With sometimes chilling luminosity, his work clarifies the underlying relations of repression, surveillance and exclusion that characterize the fragmented, paranoid spatiality towards which Los Angeles seems to aspire.

A very early example of Gehry's new urban realism was his 1964 solution of the problem of how to insert high property values and sumptuary spaces into decaying neighborhoods. His Danziger Studio in Hollywood (Figure 23.2) is the pioneer instance of what has become an entire species of Los Angeles "stealth houses," dissimulating their luxurious qualities with proletarian or gangster façades. The street frontage of the Danziger—on Melrose in the bad old days before its current gourmet-gulch renaissance—was simply a massive gray wall, treated with a rough finish to ensure that it would collect dust from passing traffic and weather into a simulacrum of nearby porn studios and garages. Gehry was explicit in his search for a design that was "introverted and fortress-like" with the silent aura of a "dumb box."[19]

"Dumb boxes" and screen walls form an entire cycle of Gehry's work, ranging from his American School of Dance (1968) to his Gemini G.E.I. (1979), both in Hollywood. His most seminal design, however, was his walled town center for Cochiti Lake, New Mexico (1973): here ice-blue ramparts of awesome severity enclose an entire community (a plan replicated on a smaller scale in the 1976 Jung Institute in Los Angeles). In each of these instances, melodrama is generated by the antithesis between the fortified exteriors, set against "unappealing neighborhoods" or deserts, and the opulent interiors, open to the sky by clerestories and lightwells. Gehry's walled compounds and cities, in other words, offer powerful metaphors for the retreat from the street and the introversion of space that characterized the design backlash against the urban insurrections of the 1960s.

This problematic was renewed in 1984 in his design of the Loyola Law School located on the western edge of Downtown Los Angeles in the largest Central American barrio in the United States. The inner-city situation of the Loyola campus confronted Gehry with an explicit choice between the risks of creating a genuine public space, extending into the community, or choosing the security of a defensible enclave, as in his

23.2 Frank Gehry, Danziger Studio and House, Hollywood, California, 1964–65

previous work. The radical, or simply idealist, architect might have gambled on opening the campus to the adjacent community, giving it some substantive stake in the design. Instead, as an admiring critic explained, Gehry chose a fundamentally neo-conservative design that was:

> open, but not *too open*. The South Instructional Hall and the chapel show solid backs to Olympic Boulevard, and with the anonymous street sides of the Burns Building, form a gateway that is neither forbidding nor overly welcoming. It is simply there, like everything else in the neighborhood.[20]

(This description considerably understates the forbidding qualities of the campus's formidable steel stake fencing, concrete bloc ziggurat, and stark frontage walls.)

But if the Danziger Studio camouflages itself, and the Cochiti Lake and Loyola designs bunch frontage in stern glares, Gehry's baroquely fortified Frances Howard Goldwyn Regional Branch Library in Hollywood (1984) positively taunts potential trespassers "to make my day." This is undoubtedly the most menacing library ever built, a bizarre hybrid (on the outside) of dry-docked dreadnought and Gunga Din fort. With its fifteen-foot security walls of stucco-covered concrete block, its anti-graffiti barricades covered in ceramic tile, its sunken entrance protected by ten-foot steel stacks, and its stylized sentry boxes perched precariously on each side, the Goldwyn Library (influenced by Gehry's 1980 high-security design for the US Chancellery in Damascus) projects the same kind of macho exaggeration as Dirty Harry's 44 Magnum.

Predictably, some of Gehry's intoxicated admirers have swooned over this Beirutized structure as "generous" and "inviting," "the old-fashioned kind of library," and so on. They absurdly miss the point.[21] The previous Hollywood Regional Branch Library had been destroyed by arson, and the Samuel Goldwyn Foundation, which endows this collection of filmland memorabilia, was fixated on physical security. Gehry accepted a commission to design a structure that was inherently "vandalproof." The curiosity, of course, is his rejection of the low-profile, high-tech security systems that most architects subtly integrate in their blueprints. He chose instead a high-profile, low-tech approach that maximally foregrounds the security functions as motifs of the design. There is no dissimulation of function by form; quite the opposite, Gehry lets it all hang out. How playful or mordantly witty you may find the resulting effect depends on your existential position. The Goldwyn Library relentlessly interpellates a demonic Other (arsonist, graffitist, invader) whom it reflects back on surrounding streets and street people. It coldly saturates its immediate environment, which is seedy but not particularly hostile, with its own arrogant paranoia.

Yet paranoia could be a misnomer, for the adjacent streets are a battleground. Several years ago the *Los Angeles Times* broke the sordid story about how the entertainment conglomerates and a few large landowners, monopolizing land ownership in this part of Hollywood, had managed to capture control of the redevelopment process. Their plan, still the object of controversy, is to use eminent domain and public tax increments to clear the poor (increasingly refugees from Central America) from the streets of Hollywood and reap the huge windfalls from "upgrading" the region into a glitzy theme-park for international tourism.[22] Within this strategy, the Goldwyn Library—like Gehry's earlier walled compounds—is a kind of architectural fire-base, a beachhead for gentrification. Its soaring, light-filled interiors surrounded by bellicose barricades speak volumes about how public architecture in America is literally being turned inside out, in the service of "security" and profit. [. . .]

Notes

1   See National Committee on the Causes and Prevention of Violence, *To Establish Justice, To Ensure Domestic Tranquility—Final Report* (Washington, D.C., 1969).

2   "The problems of inversion and introversion in development patterns, and ambiguity in the character of public space created within them, are not unique to new shopping center developments. It is commonplace that the modern city as a whole exhibits a tendency to break down into specialized, single-use precincts—the university campus, the industrial estate, the leisure complex, the housing scheme . . . each governed by internal, esoteric rules of development and implemented by specialist agencies whose terms of reference guarantee that they are familiar with other similar developments across the country, but know almost nothing of the dissimilar precincts which abut their own." Barry Maitland, *Shopping Malls: Planning and Design* (London, 1985), p. 109.

3   Cf. Geoffrey Blodgett, "Frederick Law Olmsted: Landscape Architecture as Conservative Reform," *Journal of American History* 62: 4 (March 1976); and Manfredo Tafuri, "The Disenchanted Mountain: The Skyscraper and the City," in Giorgio Ciucci, *et al.*, *The American City* (Cambridge, Mass., 1979).

4   David Halberstam, *The Powers That Be* (New York, 1979), p. 102.

5   *Los Angeles Times* (November 4, 1978): X–13. See also Sam Hall Kaplan, *L.A. Follies: A Critical Look at Growth, Politics and Architecture* (Santa Monica, 1989).

6   Governor's Commission on the Los Angeles Riots. *Violence in the City—An End or Beginning?* (Los Angeles, 1965).

7   In the early 1970s the police circularized members of the Central City Association about an "imminent gang invasion." They urged businessmen "to report to the police the presence of any groups of young Blacks in the area. These are young people between the ages of twelve and eighteen, both boys and girls. One gang wears earrings and the other wears hats. When encountered in groups of more than two they are very dangerous and armed." *Los Angeles Times* (December 24, 1972): I–7.

8   Gentrification in this case is "Reaganization." In a complex deal aimed at making the north end of the Broadway corridor an upscaled "bridge" linking Bunker Hill, the Civic Center and Little Tokyo, the CRA has spent more than $20 million inducing the State to build the "Ronald Reagan Office Building" a block away from the corner of Third and Broadway, while simultaneously bribing the Union Rescue Mission $6 million to move its homeless clientele out of the neighborhood. The 3,000 civil servants from the Reagan Building are intended as shock troops to gentrify the strategic corner of Third and Broadway, where developer Ira Yellin has received further millions in subsidies from the CRA to transform the three historic structures he owns (the Bradbury Building, Million Dollar Theater and Grand Central Market) into "Grand Central Square." The "Broadway-Spring Center"—discussed in the text—provides "security in circulation" between the Reagan Building and the Square.

9   In reflecting on the problem of the increasing social distance between the white middle classes and the Black poor, Oscar Newman, the renown theorist of "defensible space," argues for the federally ordered dispersion of the poor in the suburban residential landscape. He insists, however, that "bringing the poor and the black into the fold" (*sic*) must be conducted "on a tightly controlled quota basis" that is non-threatening to the middle class and ensures their continuing social dominance. *Community of Interest* (Garden City, NJ, 1981), pp. 19–25. Such "tightly controlled quotas," of course, are precisely the strategy favored by redevelopment agencies like Los Angeles's as they have been forced to include a small portion of low or very-low income housing in their projected "urban villages." It seems inconceivable to Newman, or to these agencies, that the urban working class is capable of sustaining their own decent neighborhoods or having any voice in the definition of public interest. That is why the working poor are always the "problem," the "blight" in redevelopment, while the gilded middle classes always represent "revitalization."

10 N. David Milder, "Crime and Downtown Revitalization," in *Urban Land* (September 1987): 18.

11 William Whyte, *The Social Life of Small Spaces* (New York, 1985).

12 The descriptions that follow draw heavily on the extraordinary photographs of Diego Cardoso who has spent years documenting Downtown's various street scenes and human habitats.

13 Since crack began to replace cheap wine on Skid Row in the mid 1980s, the homicide rate has jumped to almost 1 per week. A recent backpage *Times* story—"Well, That's Skid Row" (November 15, 1989)—claimed that the homeless have become so "inured to street violence" that "the brutal slayings of two people within two blocks of each other the night before drew far less attention than the taping of an episode of the television show, 'Beauty and the Beast.'" The article noted, however, the homeless have resorted to a "buddy system" whereby one sleeps and the other acts as "spotter" to warn of potential assailants.

14 For example, the LAPD sits on the Design Advisory Board of "Miracle on Broadway," the publicly funded body attempting to initiate the gentrification of part of the Downtown historic core. *Downtown News* (January 2, 1989).

15 Interviews with Skid Row residents; see also Tom Chorneau, "Quandary Over a Park Restroom," *Downtown News* (August 25, 1986): 1, 4. In other Southern California communities the

very hygiene of the poor is being criminalized. New ordinances specifically directed against the homeless outlaw washing oneself in public "above the elbow."

16   See "Cold Snap's Toll at 5 as Its Iciest Night Arrives," *Los Angeles Times* (December 29, 1988).

17   See my "*Chinatown*, Part Two? The Internationalization of Downtown Los Angeles," *New Left Review* (July–August 1987). It is also important to note that, despite the crack epidemic on Skid Row (which has attracted a much younger population of homeless men), there is no drug treatment center or rehabilitation program in the area. Indeed within the city as a whole narcotic therapy funding is being cut while police and prison budgets are soaring.

18   "Old socialist" quote from architect and "Gehry Kid" Michael Rotundi of Morphosis; Gehry himself boasts: "I get my inspiration from the streets. I'm more of a street fighter than a Roman scholar." Quoted in Adele Freedman, *Progressive Architecture* (October 1986): 99.

19   The best catalogue of Gehry's work is Peter Arnell and Ted Bickford, eds, *Frank Gehry: Buildings and Projects* (New York, 1985). Also cf. Institute of Contemporary Art, *Frank O. Gehry, An Exhibition of Recent Projects* (Boston, 1982); and University of Southern California, *Frank Gehry: Selected Works* (Los Angeles, 1982).

20   Mildred Friedman, ed., *The Architecture of Frank Gehry* (New York, 1986), p. 175.

21   Pilar Viladas, "Illuminated Manuscripts," *Progressive Architecture* (October 1986): 76, 84.

22   See David Ferrell's articles in the *Los Angeles Times* (August 31 and October 16, 1987). In a letter to the *Times* (September 16, 1987) the former Los Angeles Director of Planning, Calvin Hamilton, corroborated that the Hollywood Chamber of Commerce "dominated and aggressively manipulated for their own purposes the decision process. In most areas of planning concern, in my opinion, they were only interested in maximizing their own profit, not in doing a comprehensive, balanced plan for the improvement and long-term benefit of all the people in Hollywood."

Chapter 24

Marc Spiegler

Planes of existence
Chicago and O'Hare International Airport

Palm Sunday, Chicago. The congregation at the O'Hare Airport interfaith Chapel spans a wide spectrum of race, age, and attire. Their only unifying link: palm fronds held tightly in their hands. In a town built upon the successive backs of the Irish, Poles, and Mexicans, Catholic services are a big draw, especially among those marooned by duty at the airport. A few sleek suits grace the room, but the dominant motif is the uniform—cop, stewardess, fast-food server, pilot. Twenty minutes into Mass, a man wearing the outfit of a United Airlines baggage handler steps forward to read from the Bible.

Despite the serenity of the 35-minute service, O'Hare permeates the experience. Under the flock's seats, carry-on luggage items are neatly stowed. But in the chapel's aisles, jammed together like junks in Hong Kong's harbor, larger suitcases wait patiently for their owners to dash them onto imminently departing flights. When my eyes drift right I see American Airlines' silvery planes skimming from the runway. To my left, cars cycle through the airport's concrete arteries, pumping in and out with O'Hare's lifeblood, the 69 million passengers a year that help make it the busiest airport on Earth. After communion, the priest directs our attention to a fund-raising pamphlet. I swing its flaps outward and fixate on a single phrase: "Serving God's People on the Move."

In 1946, Chicago's political leaders decreed that a second airport, O'Hare (Figure 24.1), would be built on land that then sat just beyond the city's northwestern extremities. The landing ground had been the Douglas Aircraft company's Orchard Field, and the site's sparsely settled surroundings fit the name. But in the half-century since, the area has exploded.

"O'Hare changed from a sleepy little community with tract homes and farms into a mushrooming edge city," says Lori Stone of the Greater O'Hare Association of Commerce and Industry. "It created what has become the largest contiguous series of industrial parks in North America; without the airport, this would still basically be farmland." Some companies came for easy access to air shipping. Others were lured by the massive infrastructure of roads and highways erected around the airport. A third wave followed, drawn by the convenience of so many small manufacturers close together. As Stone explains, "They liked the idea of being only a mile or two from their suppliers or clients."

Nestled between Chicago and the airport lies the village of Rosemont, a singularly striking example of O'Hare's economic magnetism. For tax purposes, an umbilical cord of road connects O'Hare to the rest of municipal Chicago, a mile-plus strip of freeway only 185 feet wide that runs straight through Rosemont. Though the current hotel-building spree has not yet reached completion, the village already boasts a better than

24.1 O'Hare International Airport, Chicago, Illinois, 2003

one-to-one ratio between hotel rooms and village residents. Despite its population of fewer than 4,000, its ever-active meeting halls make it the sixth most popular major convention site in the country. With per-capita real estate values running more than five times higher than those in Chicago, Donald Stephens, the village's rabidly pro-development mayor, wields a $93 million budget. The key to Stephens' power? In the fine tradition of Chicago aldermen, he spreads the wealth, doling out "home improvement" grants that function as de facto property-tax refunds.

But forget for a moment the edge city that sprawled out from the airport epicenter. In and of itself, O'Hare has nearly become a self-contained community, with many elements of an urban core. For a period, the airport even had a homeless problem. But Mayor Richard M. Daley took a hard line on such matters, so O'Hare's Chicago Police Department unit locks up any vagrant who refuses to either take aid or take off. Citizens with fatter wallets, though, could live in relative contentment within the airport's 7,700 acres. Lodging? The Hyatt is a 10-minute stroll from most of the airport. Health club? Right underneath the Hyatt, open all night to guests. Bars? In every terminal. Playground? See Kids on the Fly, the Chicago Children's Museum satellite site in Terminal 2. Architecture? Walk through Perkins & Will's International Terminal, gaze up at I.M. Pei's hexagonal control tower, take the 744-foot-long, neon-lit, aura-hallucinogenic ride into Helmut Jahn's United Terminal. Meetings? Convention space abounds. Worship? There are services for every faith, from Muslim to Jewish to Christian fundamentalist.

Visitors to O'Hare regularly live exactly this way, contained within the airport complex. Sure, for kicks they might stray past the airport's boundary and take in a show at the Rosemont Horizon, Chicagoland's largest sports and entertainment venue. But many never feel a need to shell out $30 for the cab ride into the city, or ride the noisy elevated train toward the Loop. That ride could hardly be simpler. Chicago's mass-transit system makes the trip a breeze. You hop one train, which runs 24 hours a day and skirts traffic to arrive 40 minutes later in the North Loop. Nonetheless, if the current trend of large corporations dropping anchor near the airport continues, fewer visitors will descend into Chicago's maw every year. Already, towering office parks line the Kennedy Expressway's approach to O'Hare, like so many gravestones for the distant downtown. In a very real sense, the airport has served as the nucleus for a second city, built on economics rather than ethnicity, on convenience more than culture.

O'Hare is no anomaly. Nationwide, air travel has ignited similar evolutions. Denver International Airport, the only major American airport built in the last two decades, lies almost 40 miles from the city whose name it bears (Figure 24.2). The rural-road shortcuts that limos speed down on their way to and from Denver would fit nicely in any western back country. Gleaming white in the open space around it, DIA seems a mirage. As new airports were being planned and built in the Forties and Fifties, some futurists suggested plopping down airline hubs even farther from visible cities. Built on cheap land in the middle of nowhere, the airports would have existed independent of any civic affiliation, with limitless possibilities for expansion. The idea itself nose-dived, but its conceptual underpinning—that airports are on a par with cities—grows stronger every day.

I have visited Atlanta several times, seen its lush greenness spread below me. And yet I have never breathed Atlanta's air, at least not without an air circulator having first digested it for me. Same thing with Nashville and Houston—or was it Dallas? I can't remember, and that's the point. (Can you imagine that someone from even a half-century ago could have forgotten which Texan metropolis they had visited?)

For me—and tens of thousands of other travelers—Atlanta, Capital of the New South, remains five terminals strung together by a people mover. Its only distinguishing feature: the prominence of the words "Magnolia" and "Peachtree" in store monikers. Houston (Dallas?) seems even more generic to me, a paranoia-inducing spot filled with the fatigued and the sweaty. Then again, I've only been there on too-long early morning layovers from Los Angeles, when much of the airport lies shuttered, and shambling janitors try to erase the passage of 10,000 gummy shoes.

Clearly, airports make a city's crucial first—and sometimes only—impression on travelers (Figure 24.3). Yet reflecting the locale has never been the overwhelming mission of airport designers. Instead, they focus on creating a sense of safety for fliers about to entrust their lives to laws of physics that only a small portion of them understand. To make us feel safe, airport designs stress modernity, the brushed steel, gleaming floors, and flickering monitors enabling a few hours' suspension of disbelief. Even the chapel at O'Hare shines with polished metal and frosted glass, its aesthetic conveying "hospital" more than "house of worship." Local color comes second, shoehorned in once the greater mission seems fulfilled. Thus, airports have become the visual echo of the uninflected anchorwoman's tones that bring us news nationwide—little differentiates San Diego from

24.2 Denver International Airport, Denver, Colorado, 2003

New York, Tallahassee from Toledo. True, Denver's airport roof sprouts a tent-like canopy that rises in peaks, putatively mirroring the Rockies lying 80 miles westward. Yet a similar structure rises from Riyadh's airport in Saudi Arabia's desert.

In airports, sense of place often seems an ephemeral concept. At O'Hare, Midwest Gourmet sells local specialties from a small niche. Yet, America To Go, a larger store a hundred paces away, offers myriad American goods—Hopi kachina dolls from Arizona, Maker's Mark barbecue sauce from Kentucky, turquoise jewelry, New England maple syrup, California license plates, and so on. (The only local item: Lava Lamps from the Chicago company that invented the hip-again Sixties icon.) Atlanta, of course, has Magnolia and Peachtree everything, while Columbia, South Carolina's new airport décor features a sanitized version of the traditional Southern main street, complete with electrified versions of ornate gas lamps.

Those indoor "streetlights" scream irony, for the absence of a main drag, town square, or any such site of human interaction defines the pseudo cities around airports. Geared to rapidly dispersing passengers toward distant points, airports abhor the amassing of bodies in a single space; the classic "terminal city" design involves a series of interconnected terminals strung around a roadway, which itself encloses a series of parking lots.

From those lots to the ticketing booths to the runways, airports thrive on transience. Naturally, then, the communities they seed spread outward in patterns determined by the availability of cheap land and expressway on-ramps; they do not form around a shared

24.3 O'Hare International Airport, 2003

set of values, social mores, or religious beliefs. It's no accident that J.G. Ballard set much of his 1973 novel *Crash* on the roads surrounding a London airport. In a zone without a core, no moral center could impinge on the fetishization of twisted steel, dashboard-molded bruises, and emotionless sex.

But airports have not always been conceived as inherently peripheral to cities. In the Twenties, when aviation for the masses seemed unimaginable, Le Corbusier suggested building them at the pinnacle of towering high rises, sited dead-center in the metropolis. Luckily, level heads prevailed and planners deliberately placed airports far from city cores, hoping to spare residents their noise—and the constant risk of having their homes flattened by errant landings. But cities wanted to reap the bounty of freight and travel taxes, so airports tend to lie within the city limits, however nominally. Although several of O'Hare's runways cross the county line, none of its businesses do. The airport was to be a mere appendage, funneling cash and customers to the city's centralized downtown economy.

But over time those downtowns became less important. Connected by phone and fax to customers, Chicago businesses need not maintain a presence in the Loop. Not surprisingly, many have decamped for suburban locations, drawn by cheap land, welcoming ordinances, and distance from the inner city's congestion and crime.

Having grown up in the ethnic enclave of Albany Park on Chicago's Northwest Side, Lori Stone realizes how little the "city" around O'Hare resembles what Chicago was.

Traditional cities, built in a pre-automobile age, organized their cores around civic functions, economic engines, and cultural centers. But now each sphere of human activity occupies its own space. "O'Hare is the economic center," she confirms, "but from a commercial standpoint it would be Woodfield." Neither a town nor a village, "Woodfield" is the town of Schaumburg's Woodfield Mall, a colossal structure in a league with Minnesota's Mall of America, the country's most famous mega-mall. If Woodfield is the commercial core, then perhaps Rosemont, with its auditorium and musical stage, would be considered the "entertainment downtown." This concept of functional rather than geographic downtowns, of course, hinges on cars. "We're automobile people," explains Stone. "We don't need a walkable central area."

In any case, humans represent an increasingly less important factor in the aviation economy. As air freighters replaced trains and trucks in the shifting of goods from manufacturer to market, whole industries sprang up around such conveyance. Drive the winding 10-mile perimeter of O'Hare and you'll see endless arrays of cargo buildings, windowless warehouses fronting private access roads. Outward from the perimeter lies a tangle of hotels and cheap banquet halls, convention centers and office parks. Another ring outward, the neighboring residential areas remain at arm's length from the airport, their boundaries delimited by railroad tracks or highways. Sure, planes thunder overhead, but the residents stay because there's work here and they have escaped the city for a safe place. In fact, the one place many of these car people won't drive lies just 20 minutes down the expressway: Downtown Chicago.

Could airports play the modern Oedipus, killing off their city sires? Certainly, telecommuting and the shifting of service industries toward cheaper overseas labor will further sap power from the city's economic engine. You need only drive through Detroit or Los Angeles to see where many downtowns are headed: oblivion. In Chicago, the term "reverse commuting" has been rendered obsolete—so many urbanites head toward suburban jobs that grinding traffic crushes souls going both directions. The problem will only get worse; Lori Stone says suburban employers have tapped out the local labor pool and started to recruit heavily among city dwellers. For the most part, they work the entry-level and service jobs that don't entice the O'Hare-area locals.

In the short term, the airport zones seem destined to grow in power, their roles looming larger for both local and global markets as economies of scale make air travel and freight shipping even cheaper. But the fact that central cities are struggling both economically and socially does not necessarily mean that airports will ultimately supplant them. Despite its difference from the traditional city core, the O'Hare "city" cannot entirely elude the problem natural to any economic boom. Land prices nearby have risen, especially in some of the boomtowns near the airport, such as Schaumburg. Congestion clogs its surrounding expressways at rush hour, and the crazy-quilt patchwork of roads spirals outsiders and some locals into wild goose chases. Though several major companies have moved their headquarters within a five-mile radius of the airport, there are still plenty of vacancy signs at the office parks.

Already in Chicagoland the most powerful growth lies farther out than O'Hare, in cities such as Arlington Heights and Naperville. Lori Stone warns that developers have seen projects around the airport threatened by farther-flung communities' more modern industrial and office parks. And the phenomenon of intense business traveling that drives the "community" around O'Hare cannot be considered permanent; video conferencing grows more common daily. Even Chicago's convention business juggernaut has showed signs of weakness lately; Las Vegas has outstripped the city in the number of annual attendees. Orlando has mounted a well-funded and successful promotional effort to lure conventioneers to its new meeting halls—and their families to Disney World.

Other airports will also compete with O'Hare. And it's not just hub cities like Atlanta that will draw business away. Though its placement has ignited fights among Illinois power brokers—and put off any actual construction—the creation of a third major airport near Chicago seems a fait accompli. Hemmed in by the residential development it spawned, O'Hare cannot keep expanding, and as Chicago's metropolitan area continues to sprawl, some of the newer suburbs lie almost two hours away from the airport. Meeting those peoples' needs, major passenger flight recently began departing for the first time out of Gary, Indiana, just across the state line.

If the airport business falters—due to technological advances or economic recession—what would happen around O'Hare? A pessimist might suggest that the community that has arisen would evaporate. After all, the defining characteristic of such areas is the way in which economic strength has been disconnected from actual residents. If the money goes, there's nothing to keep people around. Cities that survive downturns draw on deeper roots than airports can ever sink—few people feel passion for the endless parking lots and office parks surrounding travel complexes. Real communities are built around repeated human interactions: Go into the bakery once and it's a business transaction; go there daily and it becomes a ritual, a bonding with the baker. Much like troubled Washington, D.C., the "city" based around an airport suffers from the handicap of a largely transient population. For all their accouterments, these are not communities in the traditional sense, in the same way that hotels are not neighborhoods. Economic interest is a fickle faith. The airport church has no parish.

Can the airport-centered "cities" replace the original downtown? Not quite, but they have turbo-charged their dissolution. In time, these zones may come to seem like transition stages, the last gasp of concentrated economic power. Inevitably, it seems, these airport epicenters will sprawl outward and suffer from many of the same problems as older cities. Likewise, the original cities may come to resemble the airport zones, with economics rather than ethnicity serving as the tie that binds. When O'Hare was built in the Fifties, Chicagoans saw it as a modern-day equivalent to the stockyards that had fueled the city's Civil War-era growth into a true metropolis. But no one guessed how much economic muscle the airport would develop. It's ironic, but the burgeoning airport zone and the degenerating downtown might eventually merge into a nebulous sprawl, transforming Chicago into a sort of heartland Los Angeles.

Index

Pages containing illustrations are indicated in bold.

International style 307–8; "living memorials" 380, 386; Wiley House 337
joined-frame structures 40, **41**
Joseph Jordan Farmstead, Virginia **82**
Joseph R. Walker House, Salt Lake City **160**
Journal of the American Society of Architectural Historians, The 10

Kahn, Louis 366, 369, 375, 377; arches 372; Exeter Library 373, **374**, 376; historicism 372–3; Salk Institute 366, 372; U. S. Consulate, Luanda 372
Kane, John 137
Kaplan, Sam Hall 416
Kassabaum, George 357
Kellum, John, Stewart's store **207**, 219
Kemble, Frances Anne 107
Kennedy, Robert Woods 347
Kentgens-Craig, Margaret 248, 294–312
Kentucky, plantations 100
Kief-Niederwöhrmeier, Heidi 289
Kiesler, Frederick 308
King House, Suffolk, Virginia **83**
Kinney, Leila 261
kinship, Native-American dwellings 45
Kiowa dwellings 43
kitchens, rural cottages 144
Kocher, A. Lawrence 300, 304
Koetter, Fred 359–60
Kostof, Spiro 1
Kotera, Jan 283–4
Krimmel, John Lewis, *Quilting Frolic* **145**
Kubler, George 10–11, 51, 57, 68, 71 n. 25

Ladies' Home Journal, prairie house design 267, **268**, 276
Ladies' Mile, New York 207, 221, 223
Lafever, Minard 5
Lake Tahoe development 286
Lancaster Co. Courthouse, Virginia **79**
Land Ordinance (1785) 36
landscapes: office 344; planters' 95–104; slaves' 95, 104, **105**, 106–9
Langewiesche, Wolfgang 25
Language of Post Modern Architecture, The (Jencks) 360
Lapidus, Morris 304
Larkin Building, Buffalo 370
Larmon and McCormick office blocks, Chicago 190, 194
Las Trampas, New Mexico 68
Las Vegas **408**; Paris Hotel and Casino **410**

Latrobe, Benjamin Henry 93, 112–13, 117–19, **120**, **123**, 124–7, 133, 238; architectural drawings 125; assistants 124–5; Baltimore Cathedral 119, **120**, 121; Bank of Pennsylvania 121, 122, 137; Capitol building 119, 122–3, 124; Fairmount Waterworks 122, **123**; finances 125, 126; New Orleans commission 124; Sedgeley 121, 122; supervision of work 121, 122, 124, 125; Virginia State Penitentiary 121, 122
Leach, William 218, 221–2
League of American Artists 294
Learning from Las Vegas (Venturi) 366
Le Corbusier 241, 283, 287, 305, 348, 359–60, 366, 368–9, 376, 380, 430; arches/vaults 370–1; Maisons Jaoul 370; Villa Savoie 368, 370
Lee, Thomas, Stratford Hall 98
L'Enfant, Pierre 117, 238
Lenox Library, New York 229
Lenthall, John 124
Letarouilly, Paul Marie 233
Lever House, New York 342, **343**, 348
Levine, Neil 314, 365–79
Levitt, William J. 346
Levittown, New York 342, **344**, 346, 348
Lienweber, Yamasaki, and Hellmuth *see* Pruitt-Igoe project; Yamasaki, Minoru
Life-Work of the American Architect Frank Lloyd Wright, The (Wijdeveld) 284
light courts, Chicago skyscrapers 190–3
Lin, Maya, Vietnam Veterans Memorial **381**, 386, 387–8, 389–94, **395**, 396
Lincoln capitol building, Nebraska 309 n. 7
lintels, Hispanic churches 67
"living memorials" 380, 386
lobbies, Chicago skyscrapers 186, **188**, 189
locks, Hispanic churches 67
log cabins 151
Lohan, Dirk 317
London, England, Greek Revival style 133
Lord, Anthony 304
Los Angeles 405; destruction of public space 413, **414**, 415–18; homeless/poor 418–20, 424 n. 13; Loyola Law School 421–2; security 412, 417–18, 420, 421–3; social segregation 416–18, 424 n. 8; *see also* Hollywood
Los Angeles Times 415–16, 423
Louisiana: plantation houses 102–3; plantations **99**, 100, 101, 104, 107–8; *see also* New Orleans